Historical Dictionary of U.S.–Latin American Relations

Historical Dictionary of U.S.–Latin American Relations

David W. Dent

Greenwood Press
Westport, Connecticut · London

Library of Congress Cataloging-in-Publication Data

Dent, David W.

Historical dictionary of U.S.–Latin American relations / David W. Dent.

p. cm.

Includes bibliographical references and index.

ISBN 0–313–32196–5 (alk. paper)

1. Latin America—Foreign relations—United States—Encyclopedias. 2. United States—Foreign relations—Latin America—Encyclopedias. 3. Latin America—Foreign relations—Decision making—Encyclopedias. 4. United States—Foreign relations—Decision making—Encyclopedias. 5. Presidents—America—History—Encyclopedias. 6. Politicians—America—History—Encyclopedias. I. Title.

F1418.F457 2005

327.7308'09'03—dc22 2005007698

British Library Cataloguing in Publication Data is available.

Library of Congress Catalog Card Number: 2005007698
ISBN 0–313–32196–5

First published in 2005

Greenwood Press, 88 Post Road West, Westport, CT 06881
An imprint of Greenwood Publishing Group, Inc.
www.greenwood.com

Printed in the United States of America

The paper used in this book complies with the Permanent Paper Standard issued by the National Information Standards Organization (Z39.48–1984)

10 9 8 7 6 5 4 3 2 1

Latin America doesn't matter. Long as we've been in it, people don't give one damn about Latin America, Don.

—President Richard Nixon advising Donald Rumsfeld in 1971 about how knowledge of countries and world regions might further his career. Quoted in James Mann, *Rise of the Vulcans: Bush's War Cabinet* (New York: Penguin Books, 2004: 16).

Contents

Preface

The *Historical Dictionary of U.S.–Latin American Relations* is designed to serve as a reference tool for anyone seeking a better understanding of the long history of U.S. policy toward Latin America, but will be particularly useful to students and non-specialist readers with an interest in Latin America or U.S. foreign relations. The book contains over 260 entries—terms, Washington policymakers, U.S. presidents, Latin American politicians, policies, doctrines, films, covert operations, treaties, and major events—that help define the history of U.S.–Latin American relations beginning in the early years of the nineteenth century. Each entry includes "suggested reading" with a wide range of bibliographic sources to explore the topic in greater detail. To make this volume a truly user-friendly reference tool, each entry contains cross-references in bold type and "see also" links to other relevant entries that dovetail with that entry. The dictionary also includes a timeline of U.S.–Latin American relations, a select bibliography of additional information sources, and a separate listing of relevant online resources. An extensive subject index also provides more detailed access to information contained within the entries.

The relationship between the United States and Latin America is based on the fact that the United States is infinitely more powerful than any single Latin American nation. This asymmetry in power has influenced the relationship in numerous ways that are examined in this book. Historically, the United States has never considered Latin America very important as a world region, and there has been a tendency to take Latin America for granted and give it attention only when a crisis—usually defined as an extra-hemispheric threat—forces the United States to focus attention on the region. This lack of attention to Latin America has resulted in a myriad of problems that are still apparent in U.S.–Latin American relations.

At the root of many of these policy dilemmas in dealing with Latin America are historic and persistent negative attitudes that reflect myths, stereotypes, and poor information. The pervasive belief in the inherent weaknesses of the Latin American people often determines the way in which the United States decides to protect its interests—political, economic, and security—in the region, from the logic of the Monroe Doctrine and Manifest Destiny, to the opposition to revolutionary governments, democracy promotion, and the advancement of human rights. In a strange twist of interests and priorities, U.S. presidents, and others in charge of Latin American policy—most of whom have not lived in Latin America and know little about the region—often devise Latin American policies to satisfy domestic political interests rather than regional concerns in the Americas. Some Latin Americanists claim that at least 90 percent of U.S.–Latin American policy is derived from domestic policy considerations.

The major goals of American foreign policy have expanded since the end of the Cold War in 1989, but much of what the United States is trying to do in the twenty-first century to fight terrorism is a part of the history of U.S.–Latin American relations. Regime change, covert operations, military intervention and occupation, torture and human rights abuse scandals, pre-emptive war and unilateralism, support for friendly dictators, cultural imperialism and government propaganda, and the domino theory have been clearly part of the dark side of U.S.–Latin American relations since the last century. All these themes embedded in American foreign policy are be no means unique to the Middle East. The *Historical Dictionary of U.S.–Latin American Relations* examines these themes along with others that reflect enlightened and productive policies toward the region. There are numerous Latin American political leaders included in this book, along with policies they developed to defend their interests and concerns. The past has many lessons to offer from the U.S.–Latin American relationship, and these are also explored in this book.

The majority of this book was written during the first term of President George W. Bush (2001–2005) and attempts were made to include information of value for readers to judge the impact of the events of September 11, 2001, on Latin America and the conduct of U.S.–Latin American relations between the end of the post–Cold War era and the start of the new war on global terrorism. The dramatic growth in anti-Americanism in Latin America and the loss of faith in economic and democratic reforms in the region does not augur well for a healthy and productive inter-American relationship in the short run; however, the growing importance of Latin America to the United States in the long run suggests that Washington's neglect of the region is likely to haunt U.S. policymakers when another crisis occurs and a Latin American country or leader is again defined as a threat and subject of national debate.

Acknowledgments

I want to thank Larman C. Wilson and Michael Kryzanek for their guidance and recommendations for this project. Professor Wilson read some of my early entries and made valuable suggestions; he was also generous at the end of the project by reading the whole manuscript for clarity and accuracy. I owe him a debt of gratitude for his careful editorial work and advice. Tom Mullen of Dalton State College provided me with a wealth of current material from a wide range of media outlets that I found useful for many of the entries in this book. Charles F. Andrain, former professor (now retired and living in San Diego, California), was generous with his hospitality in Palo Alto while I gathered material in the Stanford University Library. I also received invaluable assistance from staff members of the Hispanic Division at the Library of Congress in Washington, D.C. Each of the above individuals made it possible for me to write and finish this interesting and valuable project. In a project of this magnitude, it goes without saying that the interpretation offered in the materials used and the way in which the entries were crafted rests solely with the author. For those who care about the Western Hemisphere, I hope this single volume contributes to a better understanding and greater appreciation for the inter-American relationship in the new century.

Introduction

The relationship between the United States and Latin America over the past two centuries has been characterized by periods of intense conflict, bilateral and multilateral cooperation, and anger and mistrust often created by the way hemispheric issues are handled by Washington policymakers. From the early part of the nineteenth century, foreign policy decision makers have had to face the difficult question of protecting U.S. national security while addressing idealistic aspirations for stability, self-determination, and liberty in Latin America. During the first century, the United States focused attention on keeping Europe out of the Western Hemisphere while expanding westward and acquiring territory at the expense of Spain and post-independence Mexico. The desire for empire and hegemony characterized the second century, from the war with Spain over the status of Cuba in 1898 to the creation of the North American Free Trade Agreement (NAFTA) in the 1990s. At the start of the twenty-first century, the global war on terrorism propelled inter-American relations to their lowest point since the 1920s as the George W. Bush administration shifted American foreign policy to security interests in the Persian Gulf region and criticized many Latin American states for not joining the "Coalition of the Willing" in Iraq and for creating domestic turmoil and economic chaos through their own mismanagement.

At the root of the U.S.–Latin American relationship is the way the United States has chosen to exercise its commanding power—whether economic, military, or political—over its weaker neighbors to the south. The clear disparities in power have contributed to a set of prevailing beliefs in Washington that justifies prescribing solutions for Latin America's economic and political dilemmas, from reforming the region's economies to promoting democracy, thwarting revolutions, and dealing with dictatorships. Regardless of the pattern of interaction, U.S. policy has always placed a heavy emphasis on protecting the economic, security, and political interests of the United States. In his detailed study of the history of U.S. policy toward Latin America, Lars Schoultz (1998: xv) finds that "A belief in Latin American inferiority is the essential core of United States policy toward Latin America because it determines the precise steps the United States takes to protect its interests in the region." In any case, relations between the United States and the countries of Latin America have often oscillated between inter-American cooperation and solidarity and intense conflict when interests diverge and priorities vary. The basic choices that define the relationship stem from domestic political trends and the nature of the international environment.

Although the nature of the U.S.–Latin American relationship has seen change, there has also been a remarkable amount of continuity and predictability in inter-American relations. Those on the receiving end of the relationship—the Latin Americans themselves—have often struggled to resist U.S. influence/intervention in the name of sovereignty, self-determination, and national pride. U.S. policies having to do with economic assistance, trade, and investment have been welcome, although there have been negative reactions when economic policies have turned out to benefit the United States far more than the Latin American nations. Wartime alliances prior to the Iraq war in 2003 were not difficult to achieve, with the exception of Argentina during World War II, and proved to be beneficial to both the United States and Latin America.

The creation of the inter-American system beginning in 1889 demonstrated the need for institutional mechanisms to deal with hemispheric issues of mutual concern throughout the Americas. The inter-American conferences that ensued proved to be far more beneficial to the United States than to Latin America. Until the creation of the Organization of American States (OAS) in 1948, the United States provided the leadership, controlled the agenda, and made sure that the outcome of these meetings favored the wishes of Washington. Despite the addition of Canada and the Caribbean states to the OAS, the United States still plays a major role in hemispheric affairs through the organization. The Good Neighbor Policy that emerged in the 1920s recognized the legitimacy of Latin American distrust and anger after three decades of intervention, including some instances of prolonged U.S. military occupation, and gradually created agreement for a pledge of nonintervention that was enshrined in the Charter of the Organization of American States. The main themes in the inter-American relationship center on intervention, hegemony and imperial designs, aid to dictatorships, aid, trade and investment, democracy promotion, human rights, Pan-Americanism, ideological and cultural views of the United States and Latin America, and the perennial problems of defining and gauging threats in the region. These historical patterns and political themes form the heart of the relationship between the United States and Latin America.

EARLY ARCHITECTS OF U.S.–LATIN AMERICAN RELATIONS

In the late eighteenth and early nineteenth centuries, the leaders of the new United States of America were more concerned with Europe, particularly the power and authority of Britain, France, and Spain. Europe was given priority by the early architects of American foreign policy because each of these foreign powers possessed territory and maintained economic and political interests in the Americas. Many in the United States feared that Britain might try to regain its lost colonial possessions and held to the prevailing view that close ties with our neighbors to the south were not important to the future development of the United States. Until the first three decades of the nineteenth century, the Latin American colonies were securely under Spanish rule. There was little need to devote diplomatic attention to the region south of the United States because Latin Americans were seen as different in religion, language, and colonial experience. Until the Latin American colonies declared their independence from Spain between 1810 and 1824, the United States devoted most of its attention to boundary disputes and the expansion of territory. Nevertheless, the early architects of American foreign policy came to realize that the United States and Latin America shared an interest in removing Europe from the Western Hemisphere. This commonality of interests posed a number of questions for Washington. How should the United States relate to the revolutionary movements in Latin America? What would be the best way for the United States to protect its own borders—by expanding its empire unilaterally or by creating some sort of collective security agreement to keep Europe out of the Americas?

These and related questions confronted the early architects of U.S.–Latin American relations. The most important figures who set the stage for future relations with Latin America were Thomas Jefferson, John Quincy Adams, James Monroe, and Henry Clay. James Madison was another figure who supported the Latin American wars of independence, but more for economic reasons than security reasons. Thomas Jefferson was one of the early advocates of expansionism and free commerce. He succeeded in gaining territory from Spain and France and was one of the first to support the substance of the "No Transfer" doctrine of keeping independent lands from falling into the hands of Britain or France. Jefferson abhorred war, but realized he would need military power to ensure security and satisfy his expansionist ambitions. Jefferson believed diplomatic recognition should not be based on approval of a country's government, regardless of how it came to power. What was important to Jefferson was that the new government respect its international obligations, not how the government was established in the first place. This classic position lasted until the 1910s, when President Woodrow Wilson introduced the principle that to acquire U.S. recognition a government must have been established through constitutional procedures.

John Quincy Adams was clearly the most influential figure in defining the early imperialist phase of U.S.–Latin American relations. As one of the grand strategists of the nineteenth century, Adams believed in hegemony, unilateralism, and preemption. Adams was a key player because of his ideas about Hispanic culture and the policies he helped apply to Latin America between 1817 and 1829. John Quincy Adams acquired his information about Latin America from his early travels in Spain and from the many reports he read from U.S. agents who traveled to Latin America and returned with negative stereotypes of people of Hispanic culture.

Adams believed that Latin Americans did not possess the skills and education required to establish democracies and became convinced that only partial independence was suitable for Latin America. Adams shaped the early Latin American policy of the United States by influencing Latin American independence movements, relations with Spain, early expansionism (Florida), and the creation of the Monroe Doctrine. After serving as president (1825–1829), Adams was elected to Congress where he opposed the annexation of Texas and the Mexican-American War based largely on his negative views of Mexicans.

James Monroe is known for his address to the U.S. Congress in 1823 in which he articulated what later became known as the Monroe Doctrine. Although his doctrine emphasized European relations and how the United States would deal with the monarchies of the time, his message eventually became associated with U.S. policy toward Latin America. As president (1817–1925), Monroe faced numerous problems associated with the dramatic changes taking place in Latin America—the struggle to gain independence from Spain, the problem of continual European encroachment in the Americas, and how to maintain U.S. security. Monroe's view of Latin Americans differed little from the negative views of John Quincy Adams and other Washington policymakers. The Monroe Doctrine was crafted by Adams, but reflected Monroe's belief that Latin Americans were either unable or unwilling to defend themselves against European powers. The founding fathers of Latin American policy wanted Cuba and Puerto Rico as an integral part of the United States, and considered both natural appendages of U.S. territory, but they worried about the impact of Cuba's large black slave population on slavery in America and the possibility of another Haiti where black slaves established an independent black republic in 1804.

Henry Clay supported Spanish-American movements for independence, expressed Pan-American ideals of cooperation and hemispheric harmony, approved the Monroe Doctrine, and preached the importance of representative democracy for the newly independent Latin American states. Clay's early enthusiasm for Latin American independence and unity changed after he read negative reports from the region while serving as President Adams' secretary of state between 1825 and 1829. He saw no reason to devote much attention to a region that exhibited cultural traits of inferiority, incompetence, and ineptitude for self-government. Nevertheless, as one of the early architects of U.S.–Latin American policy, Henry Clay recognized the connection between events in Latin America and domestic politics in the United States. Since Clay's time in Washington, almost every important theme in U.S.–Latin American relations can be explained in terms of domestic politics in the United States.

The early architects of U.S. policy toward Latin America operated with surprising unanimity in dealing with the region, from its independence struggles to the periods that followed the enunciation of the Monroe Doctrine. Although they had little contact with Latin America and lacked the language skills to communicate effectively with the post-independence leaders of the time, all agreed with the importance of national expansion, Latin American independence from Europe, the essential differences between Anglo-Saxons and Hispanics in terms of temperament and culture, and the idealistic notion that the Western Hemisphere was different and better than the Old World of Europe with its traditions and monarchies. Throughout the nineteenth century, U.S. presidents employed the strategies developed by Adams, Monroe, and Clay to annex territory, intervene militarily, and justify wars in the name of preventing European powers from taking territory. The pre-emptive interventions carried out by Theodore Roosevelt, William H. Taft, and Woodrow Wilson in the early twentieth century were based on the elusive quest for security at the expense of Latin American sovereignty and independence.

EVOLUTION OF U.S. POLICY TOWARD LATIN AMERICA

Over the past two centuries, U.S. policy toward Latin America has passed through a number of distinct phases, each marked by key events and policies aimed at protecting U.S. interests. In the initial phase, the early architects of U.S. policy focused on how best to respond to Latin American independence movements without provoking the wrath of Europe. This was followed by a long period marked by the Monroe Doctrine, Manifest Destiny, and the thirst for annexation of territory that once belonged to Spain. U.S. expansionism was marked by President James K. Polk's war with Mexico, and the determined agents of Manifest Destiny called filibusters, who attempted to acquire Cuba, Mexico, and Nicaragua for the slave-owning South. The U.S. Civil War in the 1860s led to a long period of neglect before the United States began to flex its imperial muscles in the 1890s. Although the Pan American Movement also began around 1890, it was quickly overshadowed by the interventionist period that began with Secretary of State Richard Olney's note on the hegemony of the United States in Latin America. Between 1895 and 1930, the United States engaged in protective imperialism to drive Europe out of the Western Hemisphere and establish undisputed U.S. hegemony over Latin America, particularly Mexico, Central America, and the Caribbean. This three-decade period saw three U.S. presidents—Theodore Roosevelt, William H. Taft, and Woodrow Wilson—put teeth in the Monroe Doctrine to help solidify U.S. influence over the Americas. The United States was no longer the smug protector of the status quo in the Caribbean region, a role it played throughout most of the nineteenth century. By 1900, the United States was ready to assume the role of a full-fledged imperial power. This period in U.S.–Latin American relations was marked by the Spanish-Cuban-American War, the creation of protectorates such as the Platt Amendment in Cuba, the Roosevelt Corollary to the Monroe Doctrine, Dollar Diplomacy, Big Stick diplomacy, and the League of Nations. It was a period in which Gunboat Diplomacy allowed the United States to seize Panama from Colombia, build the Panama Canal, and provide the necessary security for U.S. financial investment in Latin America to flourish under U.S. protection. It is interesting that the United States did not intervene in South America, at least not to the degree that occurred in Central America and the Caribbean.

After more than three decades of military intervention and occupation, a new era began in the 1920s with the intention of assuaging Latin American resentment by proclaiming the Good Neighbor Policy. The Clark Memorandum repudiated the Roosevelt Corollary to the Monroe Doctrine and other interpretations and Presidents Herbert Hoover and Franklin D. Roosevelt pledged to not intervene in Latin America's internal affairs, abrogated the protectorates, and searched for ways to rid Latin America of its Yankeephobia. Unfortunately, the Good Neighbor Policy was undermined by the installation of "friendly dictators," who protected U.S. interests in the region without having to resort to U.S. military intervention and occupation.

The Cold War era lasted from the late 1940s until the collapse of the Soviet Union in 1991. The efforts to confront outside threats to the hemisphere through collective security marked this period with the creation of the United Nations and the Organization of American States, each with charters that included strong language prohibiting intervention in the affairs of other member states. It was also a period in which Communist threats were greatly exaggerated, leading to a return of U.S. intervention. The Good Neighbor Policy was abandoned, and the United States found that it now had to respond to a growing number of Latin American revolutions. The U.S. response to revolutionary change in Latin America, beginning in Guatemala in 1954, resulted in many blunders and scandals that undermined the U.S.–Latin American relationship. Fidel Castro's success in overthrowing the Cuban tyrant, Fulgencio Batista, in 1959 led to President John F. Kennedy's Alliance for Progress; however, the failure to topple Castro at the Bay of Pigs in 1961 led to an escalation of counter-insurgency warfare training and a policy of "no second Cubas" to keep future Castros from threatening U.S. interests. Some of the veterans of the Bay of Pigs invasion returned to play a part in the death of Che Guevara in the 1960s, the Watergate burglary in the 1970s, and the Iran-Contra scandal in the 1980s. U.S. policy became more strategic, ideological, and issue-based during the Cold War, and this contributed to the often misguided assessments of security threats that contributed to the overthrow of Salvador Allende in Chile and the Contra war against the Sandinistas in Nicaragua in the 1980s. The policy shifts described above also overlapped with intermittent efforts to deal with human rights, democracy, drugs, immigration, and trade matters.

The post–Cold War relationship between the United States and Latin America lasted through three presidential terms (one for George H.W. Bush and two for Bill Clinton) with more emphasis on domestic issues and economic concerns than the security threat framework that dominated the Cold War era. Through hemispheric summitry and improved communications, the U.S.–Latin American relationship experienced a convergence of economic policies and democratic political systems. The Bush and Clinton presidencies established the North American Free Trade Agreement (NAFTA), linking the economies of Mexico, Canada, and the United States, but after ten years there were serious concerns about the overall success of trade policies that lowered tariffs, urged privatization and a downsized government, and promoted the removal of subsidies for core commodities. By 2000, there was a growing disillusionment with both democracy and free trade, although few wanted to return to the era when military-authoritarian governments ruled and death squads dominated the political landscape.

The events of September 11, 2001, marked the beginning of a new relationship between the United States and Latin America that was defined by the global war on terrorism. As the United States shifted its foreign policy interests to a region of the world that was found to be behind the attacks on New York and Washington, Latin America, with the exception of Colombia and its drug war, seemed to move off the radar screen as a region of security concern. As a result, during President George W. Bush's first term (2001–2005), the United States paid little attention to Latin America. The doctrine of regime change in the Middle East and pre-emptive war did not go over well in Latin America because it reminded many of previous U.S. policies in Latin America that applied the same doctrines and rhetoric to advance American interests south of the border. From the U.S. perspective, the global war on terrorism is rooted in the principles of the Bush Doctrine—pre-emptive war, unilateralism, and American hegemony—that have deep roots in the U.S.–Latin American relationship. It seems clear that American presidents, beginning with James Monroe and John Quincy Adams, more often than not believed that enlarging security would need to come from territorial expansion, regional hegemony, and democratization. This elusive quest for security and democratic principles would inevitably require military action by the United States, with allies if possible, without them if necessary.

Guide to Related Topics

Ambassadors and Envoys

Ambassadors
Ball, George Wildman (1909–1994)
Barrett, John (1866–1938)
Beaulac, Willard Leon (1899–1990)
Berle, Adolf A., Jr. (1895–1971)
Bidlack, Benjamin Alden (1804–1849)
Bonsal, Philip Wilson (1903–1995)
Braden, Spruille (1894–1978)
Bryan, William Jennings (1860–1925)
Bunker, Ellsworth (1894–1984)
Cabot, John Moors (1901–1981)
Daniels, Josephus (1862–1948)
Eisenhower, Milton S. (1899–1985)
Frelinghuysen, Frederick Theodore (1817–1885)
Gordon, [Abraham] Lincoln (1913–)
Hay, John Milton (1838–1905)
Kirkpatrick, Jeane Jordan (1926–)
Lodge, Henry Cabot, Sr. (1850–1924)
Morrow, Dwight Whitney (1873–1931)
Negroponte, John Dimitri (1939–)
Olney, Richard (1835–1917)
Peurifoy, John Emil (1907–1955)
Poinsett, Joel Roberts (1779–1851)
Reich, Otto Juan (1945–)
Rockefeller, Nelson Aldrich (1908–1979)
Slidell, John (1793–1871)
Smith, Earl E.T. (1903–1991)
Trist, Nicholas Philip (1800–1874)
Walters, Vernon A. (1917–2002)

Concepts, Beliefs, and Theories

Anti-Americanism
Backyard Metaphor
Banana Republic
Blowback
Death Squads (Escuadrones de Muerte)
Dependency Theory
Domino Theory
Friendly Dictators
Hegemony
Imperialism
Manifest Destiny
Race and Racism
Recognition and Non-Recognition
Regime Change
Terrorism
Threat Perception/Assessment
Yankee *Fidelistas*

Covert Operations and Military Plans

Agee, Philip (1935–)
Bay of Pigs (1961)
Bernays, Edward L. (1891–1995)
Bissell, Richard (1909–1994)
Blowback
Boland Amendments
Central Intelligence Agency (CIA)
Church Committee Report
Cold War
Contras
Covert Operations
Dulles, Allen Welsh (1893–1969)
Helms, Richard McGarrah (1913–2002)
Iran-Contra Scandal
Missing (1982)
Noriega, Manuel Antonio (1940–)
North, Oliver Lawrence (1943–)
Operation Blast Furnace
Operation Condor
Operation Just Cause
Operation Mongoose
Operation Northwoods
Operation Urgent Fury (1983)
Ostend Manifesto (1854)

Dictators and Dictatorships

Banana Republic
Banana Wars
Beals, Carleton (1893–1979)
Betancourt, Rómulo (1908–1981)
Blowback
Caribbean Legion
Carter, James (Jimmy) Earl (1924–)
Cold War
Death Squads (Escuadrones de Muerte)
Dictatorships
Friendly Dictators
Good Neighbor Policy
Gordon, [Abraham] Lincoln (1913–)
Lansky, Meyer (1902–1983)
Noriega, Manuel Antonio (1940–)
Operation Just Cause
Pérez Jiménez, Marcos (1914–2001)
Pinochet Ugarte, Augusto (1915–)

Recognition and Non-Recognition
Regime Change
Somoza Debayle, Anastasio "Tachito" (1925–1980)
State of Siege (1973)
Tobar Doctrine
Trujillo Molina, Rafael Leónidas (1891–1961)

Diplomacy and Summitry

Berle, Adolf A., Jr. (1895–1971)
Bidlack, Benjamin Alden (1804–1849)
Big Stick Diplomacy
Braden, Spruille (1894–1978)
Buchanan, James (1791–1868)
Bunau-Varilla, Philippe (1859–1940)
Bunker, Ellsworth (1894–1984)
Cabot, John Moors (1901–1981)
Calvo Clause
Carter, James (Jimmy) Earl (1924–)
Contadora Group
Cuban Missile Crisis (1962)
Cultural Imperialism
Dollar Diplomacy
Earth Summit, Rio de Janeiro (1992)
Economic Sanctions
Estrada Doctrine (1930)
Hay, John Milton (1838–1905)
Human Rights
Miranda, Carmen (1909–1955)
Organization of American States (OAS)
Panama Canal Treaties
Pan-Americanism
Smith, Earl E.T. (1903–1991)
Summit of the Americas
Trist, Nicholas Philip (1800–1874)
Walters, Vernon A. (1917–2002)

Doctrines

Bush, George W. (1946–)
Doctrines
Drago Doctrine
Estrada Doctrine (1930)
Johnson Doctrine
Kennan, George Frost (1904–2005)
Lodge Corollary (1912)
Mann Doctrine
Monroe Doctrine (1823)
Polk, James Knox (1795–1849)
Reagan Doctrine
Roosevelt Corollary to the Monroe Doctrine
Tobar Doctrine

Economic and Military Assistance

Agency for International Development (AID)
Alliance for Progress
American Institute for Free Labor Development (AIFLD)
Andean Initiative
Arms Trade
Bogotá Conference (1948)
Brady Plan (1989)

Father Roy: Inside the School of Assassins (1997)

Plan Colombia

Private Military Contractors

September 11, 2001

Entreprenuers, Economic Policies, and Development Strategies

Alliance for Progress

Andean Initiative

Brady Plan (1989)

Bunau-Varilla, Philippe (1859–1940)

Caribbean Basin Initiative (CBI)

Carnegie, Andrew (1835–1919)

Chicago Boys

Dependency Theory

Dollar Diplomacy

Earth Summit, Rio de Janeiro (1992)

Economic Sanctions

Enterprise for the Americas Initiative (EAI)

Free Trade Area of the Americas (FTAA)

Grace, William Russell (1832–1904)

Inter-American Development Bank (IADB)

Knox, Philander Chase (1853–1921)

Lansky, Meyer (1902–1983)

Mas Canosa, Jorge L. (1939–1997)

North American Free Trade Agreement (NAFTA)

Operation Pan America

Plan Colombia

Rockefeller, Nelson Aldrich (1908–1979)

United Fruit Company

Vanderbilt, Cornelius (1794–1877)

Washington Consensus

Zemurray, Samuel (1877–1961)

Globalization

Brady Plan (1989)

Bush, George W. (1946–)

Chicago Boys

Clinton, William Jefferson (1946–)

Earth Summit, Rio de Janeiro (1992)

Free Trade Area of the Americas (FTAA)

North American Free Trade Agreement (NAFTA)

Terrorism

Washington Consensus

Ideological Perspectives and Mentalities

Anti-Americanism

Anti-Imperialism

Backyard Metaphor

Banana Republic

Beals, Carleton (1893–1979)

Bemis, Samuel Flagg (1892–1973)

Braden, Spruille (1894–1978)

Butler, Smedley Darlington (1881–1940)

Carnegie, Andrew (1835–1919)

Castro Ruz, Fidel (1926–)

Clay, Henry (1777–1852)

Cold War

Cultural Imperialism
Dependency Theory
Dictatorships
Doctrines
Domino Theory
Elián González Incident
Father Roy: Inside the School of Assassins (1997)
Friendly Dictators
German Threat
Hegemony
Human Rights
Imperialism
Johnson Doctrine
Kirkpatrick, Jeane Jordan (1926–)
Manifest Destiny
Martí y Pérez, José Julián (1853–1895)
Media
Missing (1982)
Monroe Doctrine (1823)
Operation Condor
Pan-Americanism
Partisanship and Policy
Political Cartoons
Propaganda
Public Opinion
Race and Racism
Rockefeller, Nelson Aldrich (1908–1979)
Roosevelt, Theodore (1858–1919)
Roosevelt Corollary to the Monroe Doctrine
State of Siege (1973)
Terrorism
Walker, William (1824–1860)
Washington Consensus
Washington Policymakers
Wilsonianism
Yankee *Fidelistas*

Inter-American System

Blaine, James Gillespie (1830–1893)
Bogotá Conference (1948)
Carnegie, Andrew (1835–1919)
Chapultepec Conference (1945)
Clark Memorandum
Democracy and Democracy Promotion
Dictatorships
Drug Trafficking
Human Rights
Inter-American Treaty of Reciprocal Assistance (1947)
Organization of American States (OAS)
Pan American Union
Truman, Harry S. (1884–1972)

Intervention

Banana Republic
Banana Wars
Bay of Pigs (1961)
Beals, Carleton (1893–1979)
Bernays, Edward L. (1891–1995)
Big Stick Diplomacy
Butler, Smedley Darlington (1881–1940)
Calvo Clause
Caribbean Legion
Chapultepec Conference (1945)

Clark Memorandum
Cold War
Contadora Group
Contras
Covert Operations
Cultural Imperialism
Drago Doctrine
Economic Sanctions
Filibusters/Filibustering
Good Neighbor Policy
Gordon, [Abraham] Lincoln (1913–)
Grenada Invasion (1983)
Guatemala, U.S. invasion of (1954)
Gunboat Diplomacy
Hegemony
Imperialism
Intervention and Non-Intervention
Iran-Contra Scandal
Manifest Destiny
Missing (1982)
Noriega, Manuel Antonio (1940–)
Operation Condor
Operation Just Cause
Operation Northwoods
Operation Urgent Fury (1983)
Organization of American States (OAS)
Platt Amendment (1902)
Recognition and Non-Recognition
Roosevelt Corollary to the Monroe Doctrine
State of Siege (1973)
Walker, William (1824–1860)

Latin American Presidents and Policymakers

Allende Gossens, Salvador (1908–1973)
Ambassadors
Arbenz Guzmán, Jacobo (1913–1971)
Arévalo Bermejo, Juan José (1904–1990)
Arias Sánchez, Oscar (1940–)
Aristide, Jean-Bertrand (1953–)
Balaguer Ricardo, Joaquín (1907–2002)
Batista, Fulgencio (1901–1973)
Betancourt, Rómulo (1908–1981)
Bolívar, Simón (1783–1830)
Calvo Clause
Castro Ruz, Fidel (1926–)
Chicago Boys
Cold War
Drago Doctrine
Martí y Pérez, José Julián (1853–1895)
Pérez Jiménez, Marcos (1914–2001)
Perón, Juan Domingo (1895–1974)
Pinochet Ugarte, Augusto (1915–)
Somoza Debayle, Anastasio "Tachito" (1925–1980)
Trujillo Molina, Rafael Leónidas (1891–1961)

Organizations (Universal and Inter-American), Groups, and Agencies

Alpha 66
American Institute for Free Labor Development (AIFLD)
Carter Center
Central Intelligence Agency (CIA)
Inter-American Development Bank (IADB)
International Court of Justice (ICJ)
International Criminal Court (ICC)
International Law
League of Nations
National Endowment for Democracy (NED)
National Security Council (NSC)
Operation Condor
Organization of American States (OAS)
Pan American Union
School of the Americas (SOA)
Southern Command
United Nations (UN)

Policies and Strategies

Alliance for Progress
Andean Initiative
Anti-Imperialism
Arms Trade
Assassination
Backyard Metaphor
Banana Wars
Bay of Pigs (1961)
Berle, Adolf A., Jr. (1895–1971)
Bernays, Edward L. (1891–1995)
Big Stick Diplomacy
Blowback
Boland Amendments
Bryan, William Jennings (1860–1925)
Bush, George W. (1946–)
Calvo Clause
Caribbean Basin Initiative (CBI)
Carter, James (Jimmy) Earl (1924–)
Casey, William Joseph (1913–1987)
Central Intelligence Agency (CIA)
Chicago Boys
Church Committee Report
Clark Memorandum
Clay, Henry (1777–1852)
Contadora Group
Contras
Covert Operations
Cuban Missile Crisis (1962)
Cultural Imperialism
Death Squads (Escuadrones de Muerte)
Democracy and Democracy Promotion
Dependency Theory
Dollar Diplomacy
Domino Theory
Drug Trafficking
Economic Sanctions
Elián González Incident
Enterprise for the Americas Initiative (EAI)
Free Trade Area of the Americas (FTAA)
Friendly Dictators
German Threat
Good Neighbor Policy
Guerrilla Warfare

Policy-Making Process

September 11, 2001
Southern Command
State Department
Think Tanks
Threat Perception/Assessment
Washington Policymakers

Propaganda

Anti-Americanism
Bernays, Edward L. (1891–1995)
Bunau-Varilla, Philippe (1859–1940)
Central Intelligence Agency (CIA)
Cultural Imperialism
Democracy and Democracy Promotion
Domino Theory
German Threat
Miranda, Carmen (1909–1955)
North, Oliver Lawrence (1943–)
Propaganda
Public Opinion
Radio Martí
Reich, Otto Juan (1945–)
Rockefeller, Nelson Aldrich (1908–1979)
Terrorism
Threat Perception/Assessment

Revolutions and Revolutionaries

Anti-Imperialism
Arbenz Guzmán, Jacobo (1913–1971)
Beals, Carleton (1893–1979)
Betancourt, Rómulo (1908–1981)
Castro Ruz, Fidel (1926–)
Contras
Estrada Doctrine (1930)
Friendly Dictators
Guantánamo Bay
Guatemala, U.S. invasion of (1954)
Guerrilla Warfare
Guevara, Ernesto "Che" (1928–1967)
Iran-Contra Scandal
Martí y Pérez, José Julián (1853–1895)
Matthews, Herbert (1900–1977)
Media
Revolutions
Sandinistas
Sandino, Augusto César (1895–1934)
Scandals and Blunders
State of Siege (1973)
Szulc, Tadeusz Witold (1926–2001)
Terrorism
Tobar Doctrine
United Fruit Company
Villa, Francisco "Pancho" (1878–1923)
Yankee *Fidelistas*

Scholars of Foreign Policy

Ball, George Wildman (1909–1994)
Beals, Carleton (1893–1979)
Bemis, Samuel Flagg (1892–1973)
Herring, Hubert Clinton (1889–1967)
Kennan, George Frost (1904–2005)
Kissinger, Henry Alfred (1923–)
Lowenthal, Abraham F. (1941–)
Mahan, Alfred Thayer (1840–1914)
Pastor, Robert A. (1947–)
Valenzuela, Arturo (1944–)
Wiarda, Howard J. (1939–)

Terrorism and 9/11

Alpha 66
Anti-Americanism
Bush, George W. (1946–)
Fox Quesada, Vicente (1942–)
Imperialism
International Criminal Court (ICC)
Kerry, John F. (1943–)
Plan Colombia
Private Military Contractors
September 11, 2001
Terrorism

Think Tanks and Interest Groups

American Enterprise Institute (AEI)
Americas Watch
Council of the Americas (COA)
Council on Hemispheric Affairs (COHA)
Cuba Lobby
Elián González Incident
Heritage Foundation
Inter-American Dialogue (IAD)
Latin American Working Group (LAWG)
Lowenthal, Abraham F. (1941–)
Mas Canosa, Jorge L. (1939–1997)
Think Tanks
Washington Office on Latin America (WOLA)
Wiarda, Howard J. (1939–)

Treaties, Agreements, and Laws

Adams-Onís Treaty (1819)
Bidlack-Mallarino Treaty (1846)
Boland Amendments
Bryan-Chamorro Treaty (1916)
Bucareli Agreements (1923)
Clayton-Bulwer Treaty (1850)
Drug Trafficking
Guadalupe Hidalgo, Treaty of (1848)
Guantánamo Bay
Hay-Bunau-Varilla Treaty (1903)
Helms-Burton Law (1996)
Hickenlooper Amendment (1962)
Inter-American Treaty of Reciprocal Assistance (1947)
International Court of Justice (ICJ)
International Criminal Court (ICC)

International Law
League of Nations
Organization of American States (OAS)
Ostend Manifesto (1854)
Panama Canal Treaties
Platt Amendment (1902)
Teller Amendment or Resolution (1898)
Thomson-Urrutia Treaty (1921)
Tlatelolco, Treaty of (1968)
United Nations (UN)

U.S. Presidents and Policymakers

Abrams, Elliott (1948–)
Adams, John Quincy (1767–1848)
Agee, Philip (1935–)
Ambassadors
Backyard Metaphor
Ball, George Wildman (1909–1994)
Barrett, John (1866–1938)
Beaulac, Willard Leon (1899–1990)
Berle, Adolf A., Jr. (1895–1971)
Bidlack, Benjamin Alden (1804–1849)
Bissell, Richard (1909–1994)
Blaine, James Gillespie (1830–1893)
Bonsal, Philip Wilson (1903–1995)
Braden, Spruille (1894–1978)
Bryan, William Jennings (1860–1925)
Buchanan, James (1791–1868)
Bunker, Ellsworth (1894–1984)
Bush, George Herbert Walker (1924–)
Bush, George W. (1946–)
Butler, Smedley Darlington (1881–1940)
Cabot, John Moors (1901–1981)
Carter, James (Jimmy) Earl (1924–)
Casey, William Joseph (1913–1987)
Clark Memorandum
Clay, Henry (1777–1852)
Cleveland, Stephen Grover (1837–1908)
Clinton, William Jefferson (1946–)
Daniels, Josephus (1862–1948)
Doctrines
Dulles, Allen Welsh (1893–1969)
Dulles, John Foster (1888–1959)
Eisenhower, Dwight David (1890–1969)
Eisenhower, Milton S. (1899–1985)
Ford, Gerald R. (1913–)
Frelinghuysen, Frederick Theodore (1817–1885)
Garfield, James A. (1831–1881)
Gordon, [Abraham] Lincoln (1913–)
Harding, Warren (1865–1923)
Hay, John Milton (1838–1905)
Hayes, Rutherford B. (1822–1893)
Helms, Jesse Alexander, Jr. (1921–)
Helms, Richard McGarrah (1913–2002)
Hoover, Herbert (1874–1964)
Hull, Cordell (1871–1955)
Johnson, Lyndon Baines (1908–1973)
Kennan, George Frost (1904–2005)
Kennedy, John Fitzgerald (1917–1963)
Kerry, John F. (1943–)
Kirkpatrick, Jeane Jordon (1926–)
Kissinger, Henry Alfred (1923–)
Knox, Philander Chase (1853–1921)
Lodge, Henry Cabot, Sr. (1850–1924)
Mahan, Alfred Thayer (1840–1914)
Mann, Thomas Clifton (1912–)
McKinley, William (1843–1901)
Monroe, James (1758–1831)
Morrow, Dwight Whitney (1873–1931)

Negroponte, John Dimitri (1939–)
Nixon, Richard Milhous (1913–1994)
North, Oliver Lawrence (1943–)
Olney, Richard (1835–1917)
Pastor, Robert A. (1947–)
Peurifoy, John Emil (1907–1955)
Pierce, Franklin (1804–1869)
Poinsett, Joel Roberts (1779–1851)
Polk, James Knox (1795–1849)
Reagan, Ronald W. (1911–2004)
Reich, Otto Juan (1945–)
Rockefeller, Nelson Aldrich (1908–1979)
Roosevelt, Franklin Delano (1882–1945)
Roosevelt, Theodore (1858–1919)
Root, Elihu (1845–1937)
Slidell, John (1793–1871)
Smith, Earl E.T. (1903–1991)
Taft, William Howard (1857–1930)
Taylor, Zachary (1784–1850)
Trist, Nicholas Philip (1800–1874)
Truman, Harry S. (1884–1972)
Walters, Vernon A. (1917–2002)
Washington Policymakers
Wilson, Thomas Woodrow (1856–1924)

Wars and Major Conflicts

Banana Wars
Bay of Pigs (1961)
Butler, Smedley Darlington (1881–1940)
Chapultepec Conference (1945)
Cold War
Contras
Drug Trafficking
Elián González Incident
Falklands/Malvinas War (1982)
Filibusters/Filibustering
German Threat
Guerrilla Warfare
Iran-Contra Scandal
Media
Mexican-American War (1846–1848)
Plan Colombia
Polk, James Knox (1795–1849)
September 11, 2001
Soccer War (1969)
Spanish-Cuban-American War (1898)
Terrorism
Threat Perception/Assessment
Walker, William (1824–1860)
World War I
World War II
Zimmermann Telegram (1917)

Timeline of U.S.–Latin American Relations

1794–1804	Revolution against France in Saint-Domingue (Haiti)
1804	Haitian independence from France is achieved
1816	Argentina declares independence from Spain
1819	Signing of Adams-Onís Treaty in which the United States acquires Florida from Spain
1822	U.S. diplomatic relations established with Argentina, Colombia
1823	Monroe Doctrine declared in annual message to Congress by U.S. President James Monroe
1824	United States recognizes Brazil's independence from Portugal
1826	Panama Conference is organized by Simón Bolívar
1831	U.S. naval vessels clash with Argentina over Falklands/Malvinas Islands
1832	United States establishes diplomatic relations with Chile
1833	British forces seize Falkland Islands (Islas Malvinas)
1836	Texas wins independence from Mexico
1844	Dominican Republic gains independence from Haiti
1846–1848	Mexican-American War; "All-of-Mexico" movement demands that U.S. President James Polk seize all of Mexico

1848	Signing of Treaty of Guadalupe-Hidalgo, which ends Mexican-American War and gives California, New Mexico, and parts of other southwestern states to the United States
1848–1851	Narciso López organizes three unsuccessful filibustering expeditions from the United States to liberate Cuba from Spanish control
1850	Anglo-British Clayton-Bulwer Treaty is signed regarding future construction of any Central American canal linking the Atlantic and Pacific Oceans
1853	Gadsden Purchase allows the United States to acquire Mexican territory that will become the southern part of Arizona
1854	U.S. ministers to Spain, Britain, and France agree to the Ostend Manifesto recommending that the United States purchase Cuba from Spain
1855–1857	William Walker filibustering expeditions in Mexico and Nicaragua
1860	Walker captured and executed in Honduras
1864–1870	Triple Alliance War: Argentina, Brazil, and Uruguay against Paraguay
1868	Calvo Doctrine enunciated
1870	U.S. President Ulysses S. Grant seeks approval of a treaty that would annex the Dominican Republic to the United States
1871	W.R. Grace & Co. is founded in New York
1873	*Virginius* affair in Cuba
1876–1911	Porfirio Díaz rules Mexico, a period known as *Porfiriato*
1879–1884	War of the Pacific: Chile and Bolivia against Peru
1887–1889	Venezuela boundary dispute between Venezuela and Great Britain
1889–1890	First International Conference of American States begins the inter-American phase of the Pan American Movement in Washington, D.C.
1891	*Baltimore* Incident inflames U.S.–Chilean relations
1895	Olney Corollary to the Monroe Doctrine is enunciated by U.S. Secretary of State Richard Olney
1895–1898	Second Cuban war of independence
1898	Spanish-Cuban-American War: Battleship *Maine* explodes in Havana harbor; United States declares war on Spain

1898–1902	Treaty of Paris allows for the U.S. military occupation of Cuba
1899	Anti-Imperialist League is founded; organization is opposed to U.S. colonial expansion after the Spanish-Cuban-American War of 1898
1899	Treaty of Paris: Spain loses Cuba and Puerto Rico to the United States; United Fruit Company is formed
1900	Puerto Rico becomes territory of the United States
1901	U.S. Congress passes the Platt Amendment placing severe restrictions on Cuban sovereignty
1902	Drago Doctrine enunciated
1902	Platt Amendment is attached to Cuban constitution
1902	Republic of Cuba is established
1902	Cuban Reciprocity Treaty lowers tariffs on goods traded between the United States and Cuba
1903	Panama is separated from Colombia by the United States
1904	Roosevelt Corollary to the Monroe Doctrine proclaimed by U.S. President Theodore Roosevelt
1906–1909	Second U.S. intervention in Cuba after rebellions that follow Estrada Palma's re-election in 1906
1907	Central American Court of Justice is established (lasts until 1918)
1909–1913	Dollar Diplomacy aims at enlarging U.S. diplomatic influence and strategic advantages through the promotion of U.S. commercial expansion
1910	Bureau of American Republics becomes Pan American Union
1911–1920	Mexican Revolution creates decade of civil war and political instability in Mexico
1912	U.S. forces intervene in Cuba to protect U.S. citizens' properties in eastern Cuba
1912–1925	U.S. Marines occupy Nicaragua
1914–1918	Chile, Argentina, Paraguay, Colombia, Venezuela, and Mexico remain neutral during World War I
1914	Bryan-Chamorro Treaty gives the United States assorted rights and territorial concessions in Nicaragua (ratified by the United States in 1916)
1914	Thomson-Urrutia Treaty is signed (ratified by the United States in 1922)

1914	Panama Canal opens
1915–1934	U.S. Marines occupy Haiti
1916	U.S. military intervention in and occupation of the Dominican Republic begins (ends in 1924)
1916	U.S. Punitive Expedition against Mexican revolutionary Francisco "Pancho" Villa
1917	U.S. troops intervene in Cuba to restore order
1920	Covenant of League of Nations approved and League established, but the United States never joins
1923	Bucareli Agreement, a compromise accord between the United States and Mexico over title to subsoil minerals
1926–1933	U.S. Marines reoccupy Nicaragua in an effort to capture Sandino
1927	Dwight Morrow appointed U.S. ambassador to Mexico
1930	Clark Memorandum is published; Memorandum repudiates Roosevelt Corollary to the Monroe Doctrine after years of Latin American resentment over U.S. interventionism in the Caribbean and Central America
1930	Hawley-Smoot Tariff Act reduces Cuban share of U.S. market
1932–1935	Chaco War between Bolivia and Paraguay
1933	President Franklin D. Roosevelt proclaims the Good Neighbor Policy
1933	Josephus Daniels appointed U.S. ambassador to Mexico
1933	Fulgencio Batista begins his rise to power in Cuba
1934	United States abrogates Platt Amendment in Cuba
1936	Buenos Aires Conference provides for Pan-American consultation in the event of any menace to peace and a protocol denouncing intervention
1937–1956	Anastasio Somoza García is dictator of Nicaragua
1939, September 1	World War II begins in Europe (ends in May 1945)
1941–1945	U.S. government carries out massive deportation of Germans (4,058), Japanese (2,264), and Italians (288) from Latin America to the United States for internment based on a false perception of a Nazi takeover of the Western Hemisphere by a "fifth column"; deportation program violates the letter and spirit of the Good Neighbor Policy
1942–1964	Bracero program provides opportunities for Mexican workers to meet manpower needs in the United States

1943	Samuel F. Bemis publishes *The Latin American Policy of the United States*
1943	American Enterprise Institute founded in Washington, D.C.
1944, July	International Monetary Fund established
1945, February–March	Inter-American Conference on the Problems of War and Peace meets in Mexico City
1945–1946	Adolf Berle, Jr., becomes U.S. ambassador to Brazil
1946	U.S. Army School of the Americas founded in Panama
1946–1955	Juan D. Perón is president of Argentina
1947	U.S. President Harry S. Truman visits Brazil to sign Rio Treaty
1947	Cold War begins (ends in 1989)
1947	Caribbean Legion formed to rid Latin America of dictators
1948	Economic Commission for Latin America is established
1948	Inter-American Treaty of Reciprocal Assistance (Rio Treaty) goes into effect
1948	Organization of American States (OAS) is created in Bogotá, Colombia
1950	George F. Kennan, a U.S. State Department official, tours Latin America and returns to write "Latin America as a Problem in United States Foreign Policy," a secret report that endorses U.S. support for repressive political regimes as the only way to fight communism
1951	Organization of Central American States established (in effect in 1955)
1952	In his first trip to the United States, Che Guevara travels to Miami, where he witnesses white racism against blacks
1952	Bolivian Revolution
1952	Colombia signs military pact with the United States
1953	Chile signs defense pact with the United States
1953	Milton Eisenhower travels to Latin America as special representative of his brother (President Dwight Eisenhower) to assess the state of U.S.–Latin American relations
1954	U.S. initiates covert intervention in Guatemala to remove President Arbenz
1954	Ecuador seizes U.S. tuna boats in coastal waters
1954	U.S. President Dwight Eisenhower puts forth the domino theory to justify further American military involvement in Vietnam

1957–1971	François "Papa Doc" Duvalier is dictator of Haiti
1957	*New York Times* reporter Herbert Matthews interviews Fidel Castro in Sierra Maestra mountains, contradicting Fulgencio Batista's claim that Castro's revolutionary cadre had been eliminated
1958	Vice-President Richard M. Nixon's tour of Latin America is met by angry mobs and anti-American sentiment
1959, January 1	Fidel Castro replaces Cuban dictator Batista and launches the Cuban Revolution
1959, April	Castro meets with Vice-President Nixon in Washington, D.C.
1959	Inter-American Development Bank established
1960	Organization of Petroleum Exporting Countries (OPEC) is established
1961	U.S. President Eisenhower severs diplomatic relations with Cuba
1961	U.S. President John F. Kennedy announces Alliance for Progress
1961	Agency for International Development (AID) is established
1961, April	U.S. sponsors unsuccessful invasion of Cuba at the Bay of Pigs
1961, April	*New York Times* correspondent Tad Szulc discovers and publishes information detailing U.S. preparation for Bay of Pigs invasion
1961	Rafael L. Trujillo is assassinated in Dominican Republic
1961, August	Alliance for Progress is approved at Inter-American meeting in Uruguay
1962	Center for Strategic and International Studies (CSIS) founded
1962, January	Cuban participation in OAS suspended because of Communist government
1962, October	Cuban Missile Crisis
1964–1985	Generals rule Brazil with considerable U.S. support
1964	Flag Riots in Panama inflame U.S.–Panamanian relations
1964	Che Guevara addresses the UN General Assembly in New York, attacking colonialism, American interventionism, and supports wars of liberation taking place in the Third World
1965	Project X, a U.S. Army intelligence program, is developed to train Latin American officers in techniques of torture and interrogation

1965, April	U.S. military intervenes in the Dominican Republic to prevent a "second Cuba"
1966–1983	Military rule in Argentina
1967	Che Guevara captured in Bolivia and executed with help of U.S. military
1967	Treaty of Tlatelolco signed (in effect in 1968)
1967–1979	Anastasio "Tachito" Somoza Debayle is dictator of Nicaragua
1968–1981	Colonel Omar Torrijos is dictator of Panama
1968, April	Organization for the Prohibition of Nuclear Weapons in Latin America is established
1969, July	Soccer (Fútbol) War between El Salvador and Honduras is initiated
1970–1971	Tuna Wars continue between Ecuador and the United States
1970–1973	Salvador Allende is president of Chile
1971–1986	Jean Claude "Baby Doc" Duvalier is dictator of Haiti
1973	CIA-backed coup topples democratically elected Chilean president Salvador Allende
1973–1975	Church Committee investigates the intelligence community, issuing a damning report that reveals assassination plots and illegal covert operations
1973–1989	General Augusto Pinochet is dictator of Chile
1974	Grenada becomes independent
1975	Philip Agee publishes *Inside the Company*, an anti-CIA memoir that forces the CIA to cease or alter a number of its operations
1975	Operation Condor formed among South American military regimes to share intelligence and coordinate cross-border operations against opponents of their authoritarian governments
1976	Letelier/Moffitt assassinations in Washington, D.C., are a result of state-sponsored terrorism based in Pinochet's Chile
1976	Cole Blasier publishes *The Hovering Giant: U.S. Response to Revolutionary Change in Latin America*, a bestseller with analysis and lessons for understanding U.S.–Latin American relations
1976–1982	Dirty War era dominates Latin American military dictatorships
1977	U.S. President Jimmy Carter declares that the United States will stop supporting repressive dictatorships in Latin America;

	Cuba and the United States establish diplomatic interest sections in each other's capitals
1977	Panama Canal Treaties signed at OAS headquarters (in effect in 1978)
1979, July	Sandinista National Liberation Army deposes Anastasio ("Tachito") Somoza in Nicaragua
1979–1992	El Salvador Civil War
1980	*Mariel* boat lift brings over 125,000 Cubans to the United States
1981	Cuban American National Foundation (CANF) is founded
1981	Cancún Summit addresses international economic issues
1981	U.S. President Ronald Reagan endorses covert support for Nicaraguan Contras
1981	El Salvador White Paper issued on arms buildup by insurgents in El Salvador
1981	Reagan administration flouts neutrality laws by allowing Nicaraguan exiles to engage in military training in Florida; Contra war begins
1980–1990	United States increases funding of anti-drug programs in Colombia
1981, July	Organization of Eastern Caribbean States is established
1982	In a speech to the British Parliament, U.S. President Reagan announces his commitment to the promotion of democracy abroad
1982	Falklands/Malvinas War between Argentina and Great Britain
1982	Caribbean Basin Initiative (CBI) aims at the development of stable, free-market democracies in the Caribbean and Central America to provide safeguards against Communist insurgencies
1982–1985	Boland Amendments restrict U.S. aid to Nicaraguan Contras
1983–1989	General Manuel Antonio Noriega is de facto military ruler of Panama
1983	Contadora Group is formed to settle Central American conflict
1983	U.S. military invades Grenada; Argentina returns to civilian rule
1984	U.S. President Reagan's Caribbean Basin Initiative (CBI) goes into effect
1984	Nicaraguan harbors are mined by the CIA in violation of international law and without notifying Congress as stipulated by law

1984	Nicaragua brings case against the United States before the International Court of Justice (ICJ) (Court rules against the United States in November)
1985	U.S. President Reagan informs a news conference that the aim of the Contra war is to impel the Sandinistas to cry "uncle"
1985	United States inaugurates Radio Martí to broadcast programs to Cuba
1986	Iran-Contra scandal reveals high-level deceit, White House involvement, and violations of international law
1986	Jean Claude Duvalier is overthrown in Haiti
1986	Operation Blast Furnace brings 160 U.S. troops to Bolivia
1988	Chilean dictator Augusto Pinochet is defeated in plebiscite
1989, October	U.S. Senator Jesse Helms skewers Bush administration for bungling coup against Panamanian dictator General Noreiga
1989, December	U.S. military invades Panama to capture General Noriega
1990	Canada becomes member of the OAS
1990	U.S. President George H.W. Bush announces Enterprise for the Americas Initiative (EAI)
1990	Sandinistas defeated in controversial election in Nicaragua
1991	First free democratic elections in Haiti; Jean-Bertrand Aristide elected president
1991	Cold War ends with collapse of Soviet Union
1991	U.S. President George H.W. Bush announces Andean Initiative to fight drug wars
1991	OAS approves Santiago Resolution on Representative Democracy
1991	Peace accord signed to end civil war in El Salvador
1992	U.S. President George H.W. Bush attends Earth Summit in Rio de Janeiro; Torricelli Bill enacted to increase trade sanctions against Cuba
1993	Monroe Doctrine ceases to have any meaning after Soviet troops depart from Cuba
1994	North American Free Trade Agreement (NAFTA) approved in the United States
1994	U.S. military units land in Haiti; deposed President Aristide returns one month later
1994	First Presidential Summit of the Americas meets in Miami

1995	United States and Cuba reach agreement to control illegal immigration to the United States
1995	President Aristide disbands the Haitian army and replaces it with a civilian police force
1996	World Trade Organization (WTO) is established
1996	U.S. President Bill Clinton signs Helms-Burton legislation designed to punish Castro's Cuba after Cuban air force shoots down two Miami-based exile group planes
1996	Guatemalan government and leftist guerrillas sign peace accord ending thirty-five years of conflict and violence
1997	U.S. Southern Command moves to Miami after being in Panama for decades
1998	U.S. President Clinton, on a visit to Chile, declares that "the day of the dictators is over"
1998	General Augusto Pinochet is arrested in London on charges of committing crimes against humanity while dictator of Chile
1998	U.S. military reports that Colombian rebels are winning the war against Colombian government
1998	Second Summit of the Americas meets in Santiago, Chile
1999, November	Elián González incident causes further tensions in U.S.–Cuban relations
2000	General Pinochet is released from custody in London and returns to Chile to find over 150 criminal complaints against him
2000, July	Mexico's dominant party suffers first loss in over seventy years; President Vicente Fox assumes presidency on December 1
2001–2003	U.S. President George W. Bush faces difficulty in getting his nominees (mostly hawkish conservatives) for top Latin American post approved by the U.S. Senate
2001	Third Summit of the Americas meets in Quebec City in April 2001
2001	U.S. President George W. Bush travels to Latin America to push trade and better relations with the United States
2001, September 11	Terrorists (mostly from Saudi Arabia) associated with Osama bin Laden's Al-Qaeda organization attack the United States with hijacked jet airliners
2001	U.S. military base at Guantánamo Bay, Cuba, becomes expanded detention center for suspected Middle East terrorists labeled "enemy combatants"

2002	Vernon Walters, former CIA official and translator for Vice-President Richard Nixon during his good-will tour of Latin America in 1958, dies
2002, May	Former U.S. President Jimmy Carter visits Cuba and calls for an end to the U.S. trade embargo of the island and more freedom for Cubans
2002	Venezuelan president Hugo Chávez proposes the creation of an alliance of leftist governments—Venezuela, Cuba, and Brazil—called the "Axis of Good" to oppose the Bush administration's push for the Free Trade Area of the Americas (FTAA)
2002, November	U.S. President George W. Bush signs a secret order allowing U.S. Special Forces to hunt down and wipe out Colombian rebel groups as part of U.S. war against terrorism; Henry Kissinger is named to head commission to investigate the causes of the September 11, 2001, terrorist attacks on the United States (resigns one month later, before commission is formed)
2002	Controversial film, *Trials of Henry Kissinger,* appears in movie theaters across the country, stirring up more controversy over President Nixon's former national security adviser and his involvement in Chile
2002	U.S. and Chile sign a NAFTA-like free trade agreement
2002–2003	Triple Frontier—where Argentina, Brazil, and Paraguay meet—targeted by Bush administration as center of South American Islamists and terrorists
2003	U.S. signs free-trade agreement with five Central American nations
2003	Americans become kidnap victims in Colombia
2003	War with Iraq stirs resentment in Latin America over Washington's process of recruiting governments to join the "coalition of the willing"
2003	U.S. relations with Cuba worsen over Bush administration support of dissidents on the island, fears of more hostility stemming from the war with Iraq, and Castro's crackdown on opposition groups
2003	U.S. Secretary of State Colin Powell tells a reporter that the U.S. role in the overthrow of Salvador Allende on September 11, 1973, "is not a part of our country's history that we are proud of"
2003	U.S. House and Senate challenge President George W. Bush's policy by voting to ease curbs on travel to Cuba

2003, December	Bush administration signs Central American Free Trade Agreement (CAFTA) with Guatemala, Honduras, El Salvador, and Nicaragua
2004, January	Haiti celebrates two centuries of independence, but events are marked by pro- and anti-government demonstrations, violence, and dozens of deaths
2004, January	Brazilians begin documenting arriving Americans in response to new U.S. anti-terror regulations requiring citizens from Brazil, and other nations, to be fingerprinted and photographed when entering the United States
2004, January	U.S. President George W. Bush proposes ambitious reform of the U.S. immigration laws, including a new initiative that would include a guest-worker program for immigrants seeking low-skilled, low-wage jobs, and legal status
2004, January	Special Summit of the Americas takes place in Monterrey, Mexico, to discuss economic growth, social development, and democratic governance and prepare the way for the 2005 summit in Argentina
2004, February	Armed rebels in Haiti seize control of Gonaives, adding continuing pressure on President Aristide to resign two years before the end of his term
2004, March	Bush administration encourages rebel forces in Haiti and assists with the removal of President Jean-Bertrand Aristide from power; Bush orders U.S. Marines to secure the island after Aristide's departure
2004, May	U.S. President George W. Bush accepts recommendations from his "Commission for Assistance to a Free Cuba" that initiate new, harsh travel and remittance regulations for those wishing to travel to Cuba
2004, June	Former U.S. President Ronald Reagan, known for his aggressive anti-Communist foreign policy in Latin America, dies after more than a decade of suffering from Alzheimer's disease
2004, August	Hugo Chávez survives recall vote on terminating his presidential term despite massive U.S. assistance to the anti-Chávez opposition; former U.S. President Jimmy Carter declares the voting fair and free of fraud
2004, November	U.S. President George W. Bush gains a second term by beating his Democratic opponent John F. Kerry by a margin of 51 percent to 48 percent; the contest is remarkable for its inattention to U.S.–Latin American relations
2004, December	Augusto Pinochet declared fit to stand trial and indicted for alleged human rights crimes

2005, March	Head of SOUTHCOM warns of growing threat from China as the Asian nation increases its military presence in Latin America
2005, April	John D. Negroponte, former U.S. Ambassador to Honduras, becomes first director of national intelligence
2005, April	Venezuelan President Hugo Chávez raises tensions with Washington by terminating a thirty-five-year military cooperation agreement with the United States and deporting U.S. military instructors
2005, November	Fourth Summit of the Americas meets in Mar del Plata, Argentina

A

Abrams, Elliott (1948–) Controversial political appointee in the 1980s who played a major role in U.S.–Latin American relations as assistant secretary of state for inter-American affairs. Until the late 1970s, Abrams was a liberal Democrat on many issues but became disenchanted with the left because of student protests at Harvard and elsewhere. While working on Capitol Hill, he was influenced by two Democratic senators with strong anti-Communist views: Henry Jackson of Washington and Daniel Patrick Moynihan of New York. His criticism of liberal cultural attitudes comes from his family ties to the neo-conservative movement. Abrams' mother-in-law is Midge Decter, and his stepfather is Norman Podhoretz, both leading members of the neo-conservative movement. Born in New York City in 1948, Abrams earned a B.A. from Harvard in 1969, an M.S. from the London School of Economics in 1970, and a law degree from Harvard in 1973. He practiced law in New York before working for the federal government. While some admire Abrams' intellect and management skills, his knowledge of Latin America is limited. His true passion was not to understand Latin America, but to further his intense political ambitions as player and advocate among **Washington policymakers**. His new passion is to convince American Jews to join hands with evangelical Christians in rallying support for Israel. He was a strong advocate for going to war against Iraq in 2003, arguing that Saddam Hussein posed a serious threat to the security of the United States and Israel.

Elliott Abrams was appointed assistant secretary of state for international organization affairs in 1981, followed by four years as assistant secretary of state for **human rights** and humanitarian affairs (1981–1985). Abrams gained much of his knowledge about Latin America while working on human rights matters at the

State Department. During President Ronald **Reagan**'s second term, Abrams was appointed to the post of assistant secretary of state for inter-American affairs (1985–1989). He was the most prominent witness to appear before Congress (although not always the most reliable, as it turned out) to testify before committees with jurisdiction over the Western Hemisphere. While in charge of the State Department's human rights office during the first Reagan administration, Abrams was a forceful advocate of Reagan's policy of avoiding public criticism of human rights violations by anti-Communist governments in Latin America. While in his top Latin American post, Abrams spent most of his time denouncing the **Sandinistas** in Nicaragua and aiding the **Contras**, a Nicaraguan exile group waging war against the Sandinistas. He was in constant battle with those who opposed the **Reagan Doctrine** in Central America, whether on Capitol Hill, inside the foreign policy bureaucracy, or in the news **media**. He was a master of counter-point and deception, challenging those who disagreed with Reagan's Central American policy by attacking their alleged left-liberal bias. Elliott Abrams was also a fervent believer in the **Monroe Doctrine**. In a speech before the James Monroe Freedom Award Dinner at the State Department on April 28, 1987, Elliott Abrams praised the Monroe Doctrine as a living symbol of America's determination to oppose foreign powers—in this case the Soviet Union—that seek to impose their "despotism and colonialist impulses" on Latin America.

In October 1986, he told Congress in sworn testimony that he was unaware of secret U.S. government efforts to supply the Contras, but in late 1991 Abrams pleaded guilty to two misdemeanor counts of failing to give "full and complete testimony" to Congress; however, he was pardoned for his deceptive deeds by President **George H.W. Bush** in December 1992 after the president lost his bid for re-election. On the charges that he misled Congress during the **Iran-Contra scandal**, Abrams defended himself by saying he was only following administration policy at the time and was a victim of abuses by a special prosecutor.

Abrams was a fierce supporter of the Nicaraguan Contras during the Reagan administration, despite Congress' ban on military aid to the anti-Sandinista rebels. Abrams believed strongly in the Contras as a solution to the Nicaraguan problem and lied to Congress about his involvement in fund-raising for the rebels and the counter-revolution. His false testimony to Congress undermined his credibility on Capitol Hill where many called for his resignation. As a policymaker, Elliott Abrams was unsuccessful in removing the Sandinistas from Nicaragua and a failure at ousting General Manuel Antonio **Noriega** from power in Panama through economic sanctions and diplomatic pressure. During the **Clinton** years, he wrote his own version of the Iran-Contra affair while working in several conservative **think tanks** in Washington.

After **George W. Bush** assumed the presidency in 2001, Abrams was appointed to head the **National Security Council**'s office for democracy, human rights, and international operations, but without direct responsibility for Latin American affairs. In December 2002, he was appointed to lead the National Security Council's office for Near East and North African affairs where his responsibilities were to oversee Arab-Israeli relations and efforts to promote peace in the region. By 2003, the Bush administration had appointed four key figures from Iran-Contra to diplomatic and security-related posts in Washington: Elliott Abrams, John D. **Negroponte** (ambassador to the United Nations), John M. Poindexter (Director of the Information Awareness Office at the Pentagon), and Otto J. **Reich** (special envoy for Western Hemisphere Affairs in the White House). Bush's appointments did not inspire a great deal of confidence among those who felt the Iran-Contra "retreads" would be of little help in the war against terrorists. *See also* Terrorism; Washington Policymakers.

Suggested Reading

Elliott Abrams, ed., *The Influence of Faith: Religious Groups and U.S. Foreign Policy* (Lanham, MD: Rowman and Littlefield, 2001); Abrams, ed., *Close Calls: Intervention, Terrorism, Missile Defense, and 'Just War' Today* (Washington, DC: Ethics and Public and Policy Institute, 1998); Abrams, *Security and Sacrifice: Isolation, Intervention, and American Foreign Policy* (Indianapolis: Hudson Institute, 1995); Abrams, *Undue Process: A Story of How Political Differences Are Turned into Crimes* (New York: The Free Press, 1993); Abrams, "The Spirit Behind the Monroe Doctrine," *Current Policy* 949 (Washington, DC: Department of State, 1987); Abrams, *U.S. Interests and Resource Needs in Latin America and the Caribbean* (Washington, DC: U.S. Department of State, Bureau of Public Affairs, 1987); Abrams, *Development of U.S. Nicaragua Policy* (Washington, DC: U.S. Department of State, Bureau of Public Affairs, 1987); Abrams, *Drug Wars: The New Alliance Against Traffickers and Terrorists* (Washington, DC: U.S. Department of State, Bureau of Public Affairs, 1986); Eric Alterman, "Elliott Abrams: The Teflon Assistant Secretary," *The Washington Monthly*, Vol. 19, No. 4 (May 1988); Cynthia J. Arnson, *Crossroads: Congress, the Reagan Administration, and Central America, 1976–1993* (University Park: Pennsylvania State University Press, 1993); Thomas Carothers, *In the Name of Democracy: U.S. Policy Toward Latin America in the Reagan Years* (Berkeley: University of California Press, 1991); Lloyd Grove, "Elliott Abrams: The Contras' Patron," *The Washington Post National Weekly Edition* (February 2, 1987); George P. Shultz, *Turmoil and Triumph: My Years as Secretary of State* (New York: Maxwell Macmillan International, 1993); Steven R. Weisman, "Abrams Back in Capital Fray At Center of Mideast Battle," *New York Times* (December 7, 2002).

Adams, John Quincy (1767–1848) John Quincy Adams played a key role in defining the early imperialist phase of U.S.–Latin American relations, both through his ideas about Hispanic culture and through the policies he helped apply to the region. As secretary of state from 1817 to 1825 and president from 1825 to 1829, Adams was arguably the most influential U.S. foreign policy official of the time. As a young man, John Quincy Adams learned from his father—John Adams—and from Thomas Jefferson to view Latin Americans as an inferior species, incapable of progress and self-rule, and of providing the necessary security for the United States. Adams' knowledge about Latin America also stemmed from reports he read from U.S. agents who traveled to Latin America and returned to write critically of the people as lazy, superstitious, and depraved, hardly a prescription for self-government, economic progress, and protection from foreign intruders. On the basis of these negative stereotypes, and the cultural divide that separated the Anglo and Hispanic American characters, Adams concluded that the United States should have as little as possible to do with Latin Americans. The core beliefs of Adams and others about the political and cultural inferiority of Latin Americans have changed little over time.

Born in Braintree (now Quincy), Massachusetts, to John and Abigail Adams, John Quincy was the first son of a celebrated politician and his renowned wife whose upbringing and education uniquely shaped his diplomatic and political career. At only eleven years of age, John Quincy Adams accompanied his father to Europe where an unpleasant experience in Spain clearly influenced his negative attitude toward Latin America. In a trip across Spain, he wrote in his diary that the Spanish were "lazy, dirty, nasty, superstitious, and ignorant." He was influenced by his father, who believed the people of Latin America did not possess the skills and knowledge to establish democracies. His friendship with Thomas Jefferson, another towering figure with contacts in Latin America, convinced him that only partial independence was suitable for Latin America. On the basis of his travels and friendships with high-ranking diplomats and politicians, John Quincy Adams played a major role in the early Latin American policy of the United States, influencing Latin American independence movements, relations with Spain, territorial expansion, and the creation of the **Monroe Doctrine**.

Adams received his education in Europe and at Harvard. He began practicing law in 1790 and in 1794 began a succession of diplomatic posts in Europe and Russia that would pave the way to his eight-year tenure as secretary of state during the presidency of James **Monroe** (1817–1825). John Quincy Adams played a key role in the U.S. acquisition of Florida through the **Adams-Onís Treaty** (1819) and the language of the Monroe Doctrine (1823). After serving one term as president (1825–1829), Adams stayed in Washington as a member of Congress. He was a strong opponent of the annexation of Texas and of the **Mexican-American War**, based in part on his negative views of Mexicans. Historian Samuel F. **Bemis** considers him the most significant diplomatic figure in the United States before the Civil War. Adams remained in Congress until his death in 1848. *See also* Clay, Henry; Race and Racism.

Suggested Reading

Samuel Flagg Bemis, *John Quincy Adams and the Foundations of American Foreign Policy* (New York: Alfred A. Knopf, 1949); James E. Lewis, Jr., *John Quincy Adams: Policymaker for the Union* (Wilmington, DE: SR Books, 2001); Dexter Perkins, *Hands Off: A History of the Monroe Doctrine* (Boston: Little Brown, 1941); Perkins, *The Monroe Doctrine, 1823–1826* (Cambridge, MA: Harvard University Press, 1927); Robert Vincent Remini, *John Quincy Adams* (New York: Times Books, 2002); Lars Schoultz, *Beneath the United States: A History of U.S. Policy Toward Latin America* (Cambridge, MA: Harvard University Press, 1998); William Earl Weeks, *John Quincy Adams and American Global Empire* (Lexington: University of Kentucky Press, 1992).

Adams-Onís Treaty (1819) Also known as the Transcontinental Treaty, it helped resolve several territorial disputes between the United States and Spain after the

U.S. acquisition of the Louisiana territory from France in 1803. Earlier efforts by Presidents Thomas Jefferson and James Madison to solve these issues were complicated by the U.S. annexation of West Florida, the invasion of East Florida, and the growing number of revolts by Latin American revolutionaries against Spanish colonial rule. The negotiations between John Quincy **Adams** and Spanish minister to the United States, Luis de Onís, resulted in a treaty that settled U.S. control over Florida and identified the boundary between the United States and Spanish territory from the mouth of the Sabine River northwestward to the 42nd parallel on the Pacific Coast. Historian Samuel Flagg **Bemis** (1971: 37) calls the treaty "the greatest diplomatic victory ever won by an American Secretary of State" because it canceled all claims of either party against the other, established the treaty line that included the Mississippi River, and provided for the acquisition of Florida and a new frontier line. Its importance, according to Bemis (1971: 38), was that: "It was the first recognition by a European colonial power of an undisputed right of the United States to territory clear through to the Pacific Coast." Although Adams was prepared to include Texas in the treaty, he settled for less under direction from President James **Monroe**. The exclusion of Texas caused problems for subsequent administrations, but Spain's willingness to abandon its claims to the Pacific Northwest provided diplomatic leverage for the United States in later negotiations with Britain over the Oregon Territory. *See also* Manifest Destiny; Mexican-American War (1846–1848).

Suggested Reading

Samuel Flagg Bemis, *The Latin American Policy of the United States: An Historical Interpretation* (New York: W.W. Norton, 1967, 1971); Philip Coolidge Brooks, *Diplomacy and the Borderlands: The Adams-Onís Treaty of 1819* (Berkeley: University of California Press, 1939); William Earl Weeks, *John Quincy Adams: American Global Empire* (Lexington: University of Kentucky Press, 1992).

AEI. *See* America Enterprise Institute

Agee, Philip (1935–) Renegade U.S. **Central Intelligence Agency (CIA)** officer who resigned from the CIA in 1968 after serving in Ecuador, Uruguay, and Mexico to become active in publicly criticizing the agency. He was the first ideological defector from the agency. Philip Agee's covert action assignments soon disillusioned him with the way U.S.–Latin American policy was conducted during the 1960s and led him to publish a book detailing his experiences with the agency. In an interview with *Playboy* magazine in 1975, Agee explained that "I finally understood, after 12 years with the agency, how much suffering it was causing, that millions of people all over the world had been killed or at least had their lives destroyed by the CIA and the institutions it supports. I just couldn't sit by and do nothing." He was disturbed by President Lyndon **Johnson**'s invasion of the Dominican Republic in 1965, the negative consequences of American capitalism, and Washington's indifference to injustice at home and abroad. Agee claims he resigned because he rejected capitalism and resented having to be an intelligence agent in support of such a system and its holy war against communism. After leaving the CIA, Agee began a topsy-turvy career of exposing the agents and covert activities of the CIA, particularly in Latin America and the Caribbean.

The CIA recruited Agee through his college placement bureau at the University of Notre Dame in Indiana. During a time of economic recession in the United States, he was attracted by the recruiter's pitch of interesting work, good pay, foreign travel, and opportunity for rapid advancement, although he declined the offer until it appeared that he might be drafted. He soon changed his mind and began a CIA training program that allowed him to serve his compulsory military service as part of the U.S. Air Force. After two years of cover in the Air Force, he returned to Washington in 1959 where he began training as a CIA officer at both Langley and Camp Peary, both in northern Virginia. After training to set up and operate a network of spies and other agency operatives, Agee headed for his first overseas assignment in Ecuador. However, it was in Uruguay (1964–1966) that he began having a change of heart about the CIA. Realizing that some of the people he fingered were being tortured by the police, Agee came to believe that covert actions conducted by the CIA were misguided and unethical, and he decided to take action by resigning and campaigning for their discontinuation through critical public exposure. His first exposé was *Inside the Company: A CIA Diary* (1975), a lengthy book published in Britain to avoid possible U.S. government censorship. It was later published in the United States. It provided a detailed account of clandestine activities, including the names of agency employees, which soon forced the CIA to cancel or alter a number of its covert operations abroad. Philip Agee's strategy of public criticism of U.S. intelligence activities—holding press conferences, authoring articles and books, and editing *Counterspy*, a magazine that identified and exposed U.S. intelligence officers—generated both admirers and critics beginning in the 1970s.

Philip Agee also found himself confronting the U.S. government over attempts to revoke his passport on national security grounds. Secretary of State Cyrus Vance revoked Agee's U.S. passport in 1979, and Agee challenged the constitutionality of the decision on grounds that he was entitled to his own beliefs and associations. Nevertheless, Agee lost in a Supreme Court decision in 1981 in which the **State Department** argued that under the 1926 Passport Act, the U.S. government had the right to revoke the passport of an American citizen who is considered a threat to the nation's security. Many believe that Agee's blowing the whistle on CIA dirty tricks was behind the 1982 passage of the Intelligence Identities Protection Act, a draconian law that carries a fine of up to $50,000 and imprisonment of up to ten years for government officials and non-officials who knowingly disclose the identity of a CIA agent or officer. Vice-President **George H.W. Bush** was particularly incensed with Agee's work and went so far as to call him "a traitor to our country" at a celebration marking the fiftieth anniversary of the CIA. The Agee case surfaced again in 2003 when members of the **George W. Bush** administration were alleged to have been behind the news leak that the wife of retired U.S. diplomat Joseph Wilson, a critic of Bush's war in Iraq who debunked the White

House claim that Saddam Hussein was rebuilding his nuclear program—was a CIA operative dealing with weapons of mass destruction.

Agee has been a thorn in the side of the United States for more than three decades, continuing to criticize the intelligence **scandals and blunders** associated with the "immoral" ways in which the United States goes about the task of gathering intelligence abroad for the purpose of national security. Although Agee is somewhat of a loner in his crusade against the CIA, there have been other intelligence officers who have resigned in protest and written critical books on U.S. policy and covert action programs aimed at radicals and other regime opponents in Latin America and other parts of the world. In any case, it is largely through Agee's critical work that we know how the CIA operates in Latin America. In Agee's *Covert Action Information Bulletin* (*CAIB*), he devotes a considerable amount of space to exposing the names and locations of undercover CIA officers, the methods used to shape U.S. foreign policy abroad and public opinion at home, and training manuals used to train spies and agents in Latin America. In the August-September 1980 issue of *CAIB*, the editors published "Principles of Deep Cover" by C.D. Edbrook, a basic text in CIA training of agents involved in deep cover operations, including the mechanics of getting "unwelcome officers covertly into other countries" through official government jobs (diplomatic missions, consulates, and other official representations in the field). Philip Agee is currently the director of an online travel service designed to promote tourism in Cuba. *See also* Anti-Americanism; Cold War; Covert Operations.

Suggested Reading

Philip Agee, *On the Run* (Secaucus, NJ: Lyle Stuart, 1987); Agee, *Inside the Company: A CIA Diary* (New York: Stonehill, 1975); *Covert Action Information Bulletin*, No. 10 (August-September 1980); *Haig v. Agee* (U.S. Supreme Court) 453 U.S. 280 (1981); *Playboy Interview with Philip Agee* (August 1975); Warner Poelchan, ed., *White Paper Whitewash: Interviews with Philip Agee on the CIA and El Salvador* (New York: Deep Cover Books, 1981).

Agency for International Development (AID) The U.S. Agency for International Development (USAID) was founded in 1961 to signal the importance of providing development assistance to Third World countries based on the belief that U.S. foreign economic aid would ensure the political security and cooperation of strategically important allies during the **Cold War**. Commonly referred to as AID, it has primary responsibility for U.S. foreign economic aid programs in the form of loans, grants, and technical assistance for the poorer countries of the world. As a semi-autonomous agency within the **State Department**, its rationale was a blend of humanitarian assistance and fear of communism, particularly after the success of Fidel **Castro**'s revolution in Cuba. Although the amount of U.S. economic assistance was small, as measured by per capita gross national product, aid was given to promote economic development in Latin America. There is also the belief that aid was based on the moral principle that wealthy governments have an obligation to assist poor countries in need of economic assistance. In the beginning, most of the initial funds were used to launch the **Alliance for Progress** in Latin America under President John F. **Kennedy**. Those who endorsed and implemented Kennedy's Third World aid programs believed that long-term economic assistance would help lead to self-sustaining economic growth, democratization, friendship toward the United States, and more resistant to the appeals of both right-wing **dictatorships** and Communist regimes. Some saw Kennedy's emphasis on economic assistance as a belated Marshall Plan for Latin America, sparked by the threat to security interests as seen in the Cuban-Soviet alliance. President Kennedy had difficulty drumming up support for such an ambitious program, with many in Congress skeptical about spending such huge sums without more discernible links to specific foreign policy objectives.

There are three major categories of aid administered by AID: Economic Support Funds, Development Assistance, and Food for Peace. Economic assistance also goes to support the Peace Corps, the Inter-American Foundation (IAF), antinarcotics efforts, and funding for multilateral institutions such as the World Bank and the **United Nations**. Economic Support Funds (ESF) are the largest portion of the U.S. economic assistance abroad, aimed mainly at politically important countries with developmental/security problems. The majority of ESF resources are allocated to Israel and Egypt, aimed at advancing U.S. security and domestic political objectives. Although ESFs are not supposed to be used for military purposes abroad, they frequently end up as military assistance due to loopholes and the flexibility of unrestricted grants that allow an aid recipient to boost military spending. Development Assistance (DA) provides grants to support specific social and economic development programs—health, population, education, agriculture, and rural development—although this category is the most susceptible to budgetary cuts by Congress. AID also administers food aid, mostly in the form of sending grain surpluses to food-deficient countries.

AID missions are active in most of the Latin American countries receiving bilateral economic aid from the United States. The most significant programs of assistance include agriculture, health care, education, and various technical projects. During the **Clinton** administration, AID changed it mission to respond to shrinking budgets and new development challenges after the Cold War. The new areas of concern include trade, investment and employment; democracy promotion; encouraging sustainable development; and providing humanitarian assistance. AID has developed responsibility for addressing the spread of HIV/AIDS and reducing threats to the environment.

Suggested Reading

Doug Bandow, "Economic and Military Aid," in Peter J. Schraeder, ed., *Intervention in the 1990s: U.S. Foreign Policy in the Third World* (Boulder, CO: Lynne Rienner, 1989); Graham Hancock, *Lords of Poverty: The Power, Prestige, and Corruption of the International Aid Business* (New York: Atlantic Monthly Press, 1989); Steven W. Hook, *National Interest and Foreign Aid* (Boulder, CO: Lynne Rienner, 1995); Paula Hoy, *Players and Issues in International Aid*

(West Hartford, CT: Kumarian Press, 1998); Michael O'Hanlon and Carol Graham, *A Half Penny on the Federal Dollar: The Future of Development Aid* (Washington, DC: Brookings Institution Press, 1997); Robert Zimmerman, *Dollars, Diplomacy and Dependency: Dilemmas of U.S. Economic Aid* (Boulder, CO: Lynne Rienner, 1993).

AID. *See* Agency for International Development

AIFLD. *See* American Institute for Free Labor Development

Allende Gossens, Salvador (1908–1973) Salvador Allende was president of Chile from 1970 until his overthrow and death in a bloody military coup in 1973. His political platform and Marxist ideology raised the ire of the **Nixon** administration at a time when it was being criticized for its conduct of the war in Vietnam. Allende's term in office was cut short by a U.S.–backed coup that ushered in seventeen years of military **dictatorship** under General Augusto **Pinochet**. The question of U.S. involvement in the coup and the subsequent support of the Chilean military led to the publication of hundreds of books on the subject, a feature-length film (***Missing***), and a congressional investigation that led to efforts to limit CIA covert action programs, and the elevation of human rights to a central feature of American foreign policy. The 1998 arrest of General Pinochet on charges of torture and murder, and the court cases against Nixon's national security adviser, Henry **Kissinger**, have led to the release of previously classified documents about the U.S. role in undermining Chile's democracy, the death of several Americans caught up in the coup, and what lessons exist for those who seek major social and economic change in Latin America. Through the Chile Project at the National Security Archive in Washington, D.C., more and more documents now reveal what were at one time either outright denials or murky speculation, namely, the participation and encouragement of the United States in the destabilization and coup that brought the Allende administration to a close. With a pending law suit against the U.S. government for its role in the death of Chilean democracy, those with close ties to Henry Kissinger continue to deny what they call "the legend" that the United States instigated the coup against Allende and then helped General Pinochet consolidate his power with aid and covert support. When a student queried Secretary of State Colin Powell in April 2003 about the role of the United States in the 1973 military coup in Chile, he admitted that "It is not a part of American history that we're proud of." This unwelcome comment was challenged by Kissinger's supporters and the **State Department** was forced to issue a counter statement asserting that the U.S. government "did not instigate the coup that ended Allende's government in 1973."

Salvador Allende was born in Valparaíso to an upper-middle-class family of lawyers and doctors. He received a public school education and graduated from the University of Chile with a medical degree in 1932. He was a founding member of the Socialist Party of Chile in 1933 and served in Congress from 1937 until 1970, first as a member of the Chamber of Deputies (1937–1945) and then as a senator

(1945–1970). Allende ran unsuccessfully for president of Chile three times (1952, 1958, 1964) before he was elected by a narrow plurality in 1970. With the success of the Cuban Revolution in 1959, the United States became concerned about an Allende presidency, and the **Johnson** administration funded a CIA-funded covert operation to defeat Allende's Socialist-Communist ticket in 1964. Between his loss in 1964 and his narrow victory in 1970, the ruling Christian Democratic Party began to lose legitimacy and growing polarization between the left and right undermined the nature of electoral politics. In November 1970, Salvador Allende, candidate of the Popular Unity Coalition, was elected president of Chile by the National Congress since none of the major presidential contenders received a majority of the popular vote. After a fiercely contested, three-way race, Allende's share of the popular vote was only 36.5 percent, a 1.2 percent plurality that raised the possibility of international intrigue to prevent Allende from ascending to the presidency.

Salvador Allende was the first candidate running on a Marxist platform to be elected president of a non-Communist country in a democratic election. As in the 1964 presidential election, the United States opposed an Allende regime in Chile. The Nixon administration viewed the Chilean president as a controversial "Communist" and "revolutionary" who threatened hemispheric security. Henry Kissinger, President Nixon's national security adviser, predicted that Allende's "peaceful road" to socialism—income redistribution, economic nationalization, and agrarian reform—would "soon be inciting anti-American policies, attacking hemispheric solidarity, making common cause with Cuba, and sooner or later establishing close relations with the Soviet Union" (Kissinger, 1979: 654). Over the next several decades, with the declassification of official documents from the period, the depth and determination of the effort to destroy Allende became a well-known and controversial part of the **Cold War** history of U.S.–Latin American relations.

The Nixon administration and many of its corporate supporters refused to accept the legitimacy of a democratically elected Chilean Marxist attempting to move his country rapidly toward socialism. Although Nixon failed to prevent Allende from taking power, he succeeded in destabilizing Chile through covert activity, economic warfare, and media propaganda. In terms of threat perception, Nixon and Kissinger believed that Allende would undermine U.S. national security by establishing a second Communist state in the Americas. Kissinger worried about a **domino theory** in South America because of Chile's close proximity to Argentina, Bolivia, and Peru, all plagued by radical Socialist movements. To prevent the emergence of a government hostile to the interests of the United States, President Nixon decided to maximize economic pressure on Allende by opposing World Bank, **Inter-American Development Bank (IADB)**, or other financial assistance to Chile. In addition, more than $8 million was spent on a wide variety of covert measures to support Allende's political opposition—ultra-rightist groups in the Chilean military and conservative media outlets—and anti-Allende plotting. One of the CIA's most extensive **propaganda** campaigns was waged against Allende from the years before his election in 1970 until his overthrow and death in 1973. The CIA spent millions of dollars to produce a stream of anti-Allende news reports, editorials, and broadcasts throughout Latin America. Some of these false or distorted stories were picked up by U.S. newspapers and used by the Nixon administration to justify its condemnation of Chile. As a result, domestic polarization and turmoil intensified in Chile between 1971 and 1973, contributing to social protests and a stalemate within Allende's coalition government.

With the backing and encouragement of the United States, the military struck with force on September 11, 1973; Allende committed suicide during the coup, and General Augusto Pinochet took command of the military government. Despite brutal killings (including two Americans), torture, and imprisonment of opposition figures, Pinochet's takeover was applauded by members of the Nixon administration. As Schmitz (1999: 295) points out, "Nixon, Kissinger, and Gerald Ford all believed that supporting Pinochet was necessary to protect American interests, provide order, and combat communism." Despite the application of "realist theory" to Chile, the Nixon administration's policy of destabilization and open hostility toward Allende's "revolution in liberty" served to undermine the credibility of the United States in its support for **democracy** in Latin America.

The "success" of the Chilean coup led to allegations of U.S. complicity and responsibility for the destruction of democracy and "**blowback**" for the conduct of American foreign policy. In the year following the coup, security leaks detailing the CIA's involvement in Chile lead to a major investigation by the Senate Select Committee on Intelligence Activities that would recommend tighter controls over covert action. Liberal Democrats in the Senate slashed aid to Pinochet and in June 1976 the **Kennedy** Amendment banned all U.S. military aid to Chile pending congressional certification of improvement in human rights. Several months later, agents of Chile's secret police (*Dirección de Inteligencia, DINA*)—in a coordinated effort by the dictatorship as part of **Operation Condor**—blew up the car of Orlando Letelier (Allende's former ambassador to the United States) on Embassy Row in the heart of Washington, D.C., killing Letelier and his American assistant, Ronni Moffit. An act of state-sponsored **terrorism**, the death of Letelier clearly illustrated the reach of the Chilean dictatorship and the extremes to which the regime would go to silence its opponents. The United States was able to trace the Letelier car bombers to Pinochet's Chile and sought an investigation into the matter. At first, the Chilean junta offered little assistance in the investigation; however, after the **Carter** administration imposed military and economic sanctions against Chile, Pinochet extradited a U.S. citizen (Michael Townley) who had organized the attack. After a trial, Townley and several Cuban Americans involved in the bombing were sent to prison.

After Chile's return to civilian rule in 1990, Allende's corpse was exhumed and given a state funeral to honor him as president of a democratic Chile. Despite the release of thousands of documents pertaining to the U.S. role in the downfall of Chile, controversy remains about the motivations, level of involvement, and support for the military government that ruled for seventeen years after Allende's death. *See also* Chicago Boys; Central Intelligence Agency (CIA); Covert Operations; Democracy and Democracy Promotion; International Criminal Court (ICC); September 11, 2001.

Suggested Reading

Pilar Aguilera and Ricardo Fredes, eds., *Chile: The Other September 11* (New York: Ocean Press, 2003); James D. Cockcroft, *Latin America: History, Politics, and U.S. Policy*, 2nd ed. (Chicago: Nelson-Hall, 1996); James Cockcroft and Jane Carolina Canning, eds., *Salvador Allende Reader: Chile's Voice of Democracy* (New York: Ocean Press, 2003); Pamela Constable and Arturo Valenzuela, *A Nation of Enemies: Chile Under Pinochet* (New York: W.W. Norton, 1991); Nathaniel Davis, *The Last Two Years of Salvador Allende* (Ithaca, NY: Cornell University Press, 1985); Mark Falcoff, *Modern Chile, 1970–1989: A Critical History* (New Brunswick, NJ: Transaction Books, 1989); Henry Kissinger, *The White House Years* (Boston: Little, Brown, 1979); Peter Kornbluh, *The Pinochet File: A Declassified Dossier on Atrocity and Accountability* (New York: The New Press, 2003); Róbinson Rojas, *The Murder of Allende and the End of the Chilean Way to Socialism* (New York: Harper and Row, 1976); David F. Schmitz, *Thank God They're on Our Side: The United States and Right-Wing Dictatorships, 1921–1965* (Chapel Hill: University of North Carolina Press, 1999); Paul Sigmund, *The Overthrow of Allende and the Politics of Chile, 1964–1976* (Pittsburgh: University of Pittsburgh Press, 1977); William F. Slater, *Chile and the United States: Empires in Conflict* (Athens: University of Georgia Press, 1990).

Alliance for Progress Ambitious U.S. policy for Latin America launched by President John F. **Kennedy** to deal with the poverty, social ills, and political instability in the wake of the Cuban Revolution. While campaigning for the presidency in 1960, Kennedy promised that, if elected, he would engage in a common effort throughout the hemisphere to "strengthen the forces of democracy" and expand job training and educational opportunities throughout the Americas. After **World War II** and years of neglect, the Alliance for Progress signaled a new commitment to do something to improve the living conditions of people living in Latin America or run the risk of Communist subversion and radical revolutions like the one that had just taken place on the island of Cuba. At his inauguration speech on January 20, 1961, President Kennedy proposed a new foreign policy for Latin America based on a vision in which he said, "If a free society cannot help the many that are poor, it cannot save the few that are rich." At the core of Kennedy's rhetoric was the belief that a social-economic approach would foster political stability—primarily a democratically oriented middle class—and a climate hospitable to U.S. values and interests. While he pledged a "new alliance for progress" for "our sister republics south of the border," he also warned "we shall join with them to oppose aggression or subversion anywhere in the Americas." On taking office, Kennedy appointed Adolf A. **Berle**, Jr., to head a task force on Latin America to recommend strategies for accomplishing these lofty goals. In his Alliance for Progress speech on March 13, 1961, Kennedy proposed a ten-point, ten-year program and asked Congress to approve $500 million to support the new initiative. In August 1961 twenty member states of the Western Hemisphere met at Punta del

Este, Uruguay, to sign the Alliance for Progress Charter and the Declaration of Punta del Este. To achieve the goals set forth in the charter, the ten-year program called for a $20 billion aid package to Latin America. Some Alliance planners estimated that $100 billion would ultimately be required to succeed and would require approximately $80 billion to be generated within Latin America itself. In exchange for the massive funding promises from the U.S. government, Latin America was expected to carry out needed changes, including tax reform, economic integration, agrarian reform, encouragement of private financing of development projects, better monetary and fiscal policies, improvement in health and education, and the building of democratic institutions. Funds for the Alliance were to be channeled through appropriations to the World Bank, **Inter-American Development Bank (IADB)**, and U.S. government agencies such as the Export-Import Bank and the Agency for International Development (AID). Determined to win the **Cold War**, President Kennedy saw Latin America as a region where he could build anti-Communist societies to defeat the Soviet Union. According to historian Stephen G. Rabe, "The Kennedy administration designed the Alliance for Progress to prevent the spread of communism" (Rabe, 1999: 32).

The Alliance for Progress was hailed as the most bold and innovative Latin American policy since the **Good Neighbor Policy**. The U.S. commitment to such a progressive, redistributive agenda in Latin America was unprecedented. With such a bold and concerted political commitment, it is not surprising that the alliance generated opposition and criticism, both for what it achieved and what it failed to accomplish. Critics of the Alliance for Progress say it failed, claiming that it brought neither progress nor alliance, was overly ambitious in its developmental assumptions, and fostered the climate that led to the emergence of harsh military **dictatorships** that swept across Latin America in the 1960s and 1970s. In economic terms, the alliance produced an unimpressive average annual growth rate of about 2 percent and unemployment rose during the 1960s. Social goals—life expectancy, reducing infant mortality, and eliminating adult illiteracy—improved slightly, but nowhere near what the alliance planners had counted on. When security concerns emerged in discussion of American foreign policy, counter-insurgency doctrine replaced slow-paced goals of the Alliance for Progress. Land reform failed due in large part to the ability of Latin American elites to block policies that threatened their economic and political power. Expanding population growth rates undermined many of the advances in both the economic and social areas. The alliance failed in its political goals to promote **democracy** throughout the hemisphere: six democratically elected governments were toppled by military coups during the Kennedy years.

Defenders of the alliance pointed to important achievements in the areas of national planning and state building, prevention of "second Cubas," and the inculcation of the importance of collective responsibility for regional development. The alliance also improved U.S. foreign policy toward the region after decades of either ignoring Latin America or supporting right-wing dictatorships that feared a revolt of the masses in favor of democratic rule. The Alliance for Progress put new life in the **Organization of American States (OAS)** by giving it new administrative, supervisory, and coordinating functions. Long-time supporters of the alliance claim that the emphasis on summitry and economic integration issues in the 1990s were made possible by what was created under the Alliance for Progress decades earlier. The fact that the alliance drew inspiration from the Marshall Plan marked a change in attitude and commitment to development programs for Latin America and signaled a serious departure from the failed policies of the past. For many of the defenders of the Alliance for Progress, the fact that it did not achieve many of its lofty goals does not mean that it failed and judging the success or failure of the program means a much longer span of measurement than the few years that were spent under Kennedy and **Johnson** to lessen the appeal of revolutionary Communist movements. The alliance was terminated by the U.S. Congress in 1973 after it concluded that the policy's main objectives had not been achieved. Latin America may be better off today—more stable, peaceful, democratic and prosperous—than it was in 1960; however, it is inaccurate to attribute these gains to the Alliance for Progress, even though it is often difficult to disentangle Latin America's checkered development path from the contributions made by alliance and its policy planners and executioners. *See also* Castro Ruz, Fidel; Imperialism; Revolutions.

Suggested Reading

Elliott Abrams, *The Alliance for Progress and Today's Development Policy* (Washington, DC: U.S. Department of State, Bureau of Public Affairs, 1986); Victor Alba, *Alliance Without Allies: The Mythology of Progress in Latin America* (New York: Praeger, 1965); Chamber of Commerce of the United States, *The Alliance for Progress: A Hemispheric Response to a Global Threat* (Washington, DC: Chamber of Commerce of the United States, 1965); John C. Dreier, *The Alliance for Progress: Problems and Perspectives* (Baltimore, MD: Johns Hopkins University Press, 1962); Michael D. Gambone, *Capturing the Revolution: The United States, Central America, and Nicaragua, 1961–1972* (Westport, CT: Praeger, 2001); Lincoln Gordon, *A New Deal for Latin America: The Alliance for Progress* (Cambridge, MA: Harvard University Press, 1963); Simon Gabriel Hanson, *Dollar Diplomacy Modern Style: Chapters in the Failure of the Alliance for Progress* (Washington, DC: Inter-American Affairs Press, 1970); Michael E. Latham, *Modernization as Ideology: American Social Science and "Nation Building" in the Kennedy Era* (Chapel Hill: University of North Carolina Press, 2000); Jerome L. Levinson and Juan de Onís, *The Alliance that Lost its Way: A Critical Report on the Alliance for Progess* (Chicago: Quadrangle Books, 1970); Edwin M. Martin, *Communist Subversion in the Western Hemisphere* (Washington, DC: U.S. Government Printing Office, 1963); Herbert K. May, *Problems and Prospects for the Alliance for Progress: A Critical Examination* (New York: Praeger, 1968); Peter R. Nehemkis, *Latin America: Myth and Reality* (New York: Knopf, 1964); Warren Nystrom and Nathan A. Haverstock, *The Alliance for Progress, Key to Latin America's Development* (Princeton, NJ: Van Nostrand, 1966); Robert A. Packenham, *Liberal America and the Third World: Political Development Ideas in Foreign Aid and Social Science* (Princeton, NJ: Princeton University Press, 1973); Kimber Charles Pearce, *Rostow, Kennedy, and the Rhetoric of Foreign Aid* (East Lansing: Michigan State University Press, 2001); Harvey S. Perloff, *Alliance for Progess: A So-*

cial Invention in the Making (Baltimore, MD: Johns Hopkins University Press, 1969); Stephen G. Rabe, *The Most Dangerous Area in the World: John F. Kennedy Confronts Communist Revolution in Latin America* (Chapel Hill: University of North Carolina Press, 1999); Robert L. Rhodes, *Imperialism and Underdevelopment: A Reader* (New York: Monthly Review Press, 1971); William D. Rogers, *The Twilight Struggle: The Alliance for Progess and the Politics of Development in Latin America* (New York: Random House, 1967); L. Ronald Scheman, ed., *The Alliance for Progress: Retrospective* (New York: Praeger, 1988).

Alpha 66 Anti-**Castro** terrorist organization created after the failure of the **Bay of Pigs** invasion to continue commando-type attacks on Cuba and maintain the will to defeat Fidel Castro and the Cuban Revolution. Members of the group consider themselves "freedom fighters" determined to liberate Cuba from communism. Alpha 66 was created in Puerto Rico in late 1961, but its office is in Miami, Florida. Its name stems from the 66 men who founded the group and use of the first letter in the Greek alphabet to symbolize the beginning of the battle to fight communism in Cuba. Some of the members fought against the Fulgencio **Batista dictatorship** in the 1950s. Andrés Nazario Sargén was one of the founders and has been in charge of training camps and military operations in South Florida. To fight the Castro regime, the group uses commando raids, guerrilla warfare, sabotage, strategically planted bombs, and the destruction of factories, cane fields, tobacco houses, and tourist facilities. Alpha 66 claims to have cells and training camps inside Cuba as well as in the United States. Once Castro is overthrown, Alpha 66 claims it will take some of the credit, transform itself into a national political party, and work with the new government to "insure a triumphant democratic revolution."

The Cuban community abroad battled over the most effective method to deal with the homeland. From the late 1980s to the early 1990s, the Cuban exile community was divided into two currents of opinion—one pro-dialogue, the other anti-dialogue. Alpha 66 was one of many anti-dialogue forces that favored military action instead of economic pressure and political isolation. After the creation of the 2506 Brigade and the failure to topple Castro at the Bay of Pigs in 1961, the United States shifted its policy to economic and political isolation. This produced a backlash by those who argued for a hardline approach, and there emerged numerous small terrorist organizations opposed to any dialogue with Fidel Castro. In addition to Alpha 66, Omega 7, Cuban Power, others relied on terrorist actions, both in the United States and in Cuba. In 1980, the Federal Bureau of Investigation (FBI) named Omega 7 as the most dangerous terrorist organization in the United States. Between 1973 and 1980, over 115 bombings of targets related to U.S.–Cuba policy were reported and attributed to a variety of emigre groups in the United States. Cuban terrorists working closely with the Augusto **Pinochet** dictatorship in Chile were found responsible for the deaths of Orlando Letelier and Ronnie Moffitt in Washington, D.C., in 1976. While the FBI managed to find the source of many of these bombings and other acts of **terrorism**, prosecution appeared to be either sluggish or non-existent. *See also* Operation Condor.

Suggested Reading

María de los Angeles Torres, *In the Land of Mirrors: Cuban Exile Politics in the United States* (Ann Arbor: University of Michigan Press, 2001); Jeff Stein, "Inside Omega 7," *Village Voice* (March 10, 1980).

Ambassadors Ambassadors are diplomatic officials of the highest rank assigned to represent a foreign government in a host country. In the United States, ambassadors are appointed by the president and require Senate confirmation before assuming their posts abroad. As the official chief of mission in a host country, the ambassador is responsible for representing the interests of the United States, conducting negotiations under instructions from the **State Department** or president, sending messages to and from the host government, and providing the White House with political, economic, foreign policy information, and advice. Recommendations from U.S. ambassadors are often taken seriously in Washington, given that persons sent to important postings, whether they are career Foreign Service officers or political appointees, are often distinguished individuals themselves and eminently capable of expressing their opinions. Diplomats are often at the center of how governments communicate and conduct inter-American relations. According to Roorda (1998: 235), "the ranking diplomat in each foreign country *is* the state; he embodies it and speaks for it." Diplomacy in Latin America is more often the result of actions and attitudes of diplomats than the constitutional authority granted to the Department of State or other government agencies. Ambassadors and other diplomats enjoy immunity from harm and even arrest, although the host government can expel them from the country even though embassies possess some of the characteristics of the ambassador's own country and territory. It is also common for an ambassador to be recalled by his or her government to express displeasure with the host government. When the ambassador is withdrawn, the embassy is then headed by a chargé d'affaires.

The power of U.S. ambassadors in Latin America has been both significant and at times the source of resentment among host governments. In January 1961, Fidel **Castro** referred to the U.S. embassy in Havana as "a nest of spies" and demanded that the embassy staff be reduced to eleven, the same number of Cubans in Washington. After receiving word from the embassy staff in Havana that a break in diplomatic relations was in order, President **Dwight Eisenhower** severed diplomatic relations, a move that accelerated the **Bay of Pigs** invasion. The U.S. government has often used the tool of diplomatic **recognition and non-recognition** to assign or deny legitimacy to regimes and leaders in Latin America.

Modern ambassadors can trace their roots to the Congress of Vienna in 1815 following the Napoleonic Wars that set common rules regarding the appointment of ambassadors and standards of diplomatic protocol. By establishing rules of procedure, nations were now able to concentrate on functional issues of importance instead of debating such things as privileges and diplomatic standing. The great European powers exchanged ambassadors, persons accredited to their sovereign or to another royal court, while lesser powers, including the United States, sent and received ministers or envoys of lesser rank. The United States did not raise diplomatic relations to the ambassadorial level with any Latin American states until it exchanged ambassadors with Mexico in 1898, followed by Brazil in 1913, and Argentina and Chile in 1914. Those who made up the diplomatic corps and represented the United States in Latin America invariably came from the upper ranks of American society; their upper-class backgrounds and Ivy League educations provided the bond that gave them a common purpose and uniformity of outlook that dominated American diplomacy throughout most of the twentieth century. By the late 1970s, however, the pin-striped plenipotentiaries who made up the U.S. Foreign Service began to represent a wider segment of American life, thus offering a better representation of the heterogeneity of American society. This trend toward a more "democratic" diplomatic corps has also eroded the common frame of reference among U.S. ambassadors and their missions than was the case before. Most U.S. embassies in Latin America are large with staffs numbering in the hundreds and who are recently working in buildings designed to prevent terrorists attacks should they occur. Diplomatic activity often goes hand-in-hand with intelligence gathering where **Central Intelligence Agency (CIA)** agents operate under cover as embassy personnel.

Recent studies of the composition of U.S. ambassadors in Latin America indicate that career status—often referred to as "career" and "non-career," or political appointees—is an important variable in distinguishing types of diplomats and their behavior and outlook toward Latin America. Career ambassadors are professionals trained specifically for the Foreign Service; non-career ambassadors are appointed by the president, often individuals who are wealthy contributors to the president's political party, former members of Congress or state governors, military officers, or leaders from academia or the arts. One noted study found that 59 percent of ambassadors in Latin America between 1913 and 1992 were career Foreign Service officers, while 41 percent were non-professional political appointees of the president, usually ideological soul mates and large campaign contributors. For example, President Ronald **Reagan** appointed movie star John Gavin to be U.S. ambassador to Mexico in the 1980s, and President Bill **Clinton** appointed Thomas Dodd, Georgetown history professor, and brother of Senator Christopher Dodd, to be U.S. ambassador to Uruguay and Costa Rica during the 1990s. The same study found that U.S. ambassadors in Latin America between 1913 and 1992 were almost exclusively male with less than 1 percent female during an eighty-year period. The same study found that approximately two-thirds of U.S. ambassadors engaged in interventionist policies in their host countries during this period, but this type of behavior was not distinguished by either career or non-career status. This is somewhat bewildering given the fact that diplomatic training tends to emphasize behavior that avoids interfering with the sovereignty of other states. Ambassadors who are not trusted by the White House and the CIA are sometimes excluded from secret planning against foreign governments. For example, Edward Korry, U.S. ambassador to Chile from 1967 to 1971, was kept in the dark by the

Nixon administration's plans about a military coup to prevent Salvador **Allende** from being elected in 1970. Although Korry was a fervent anti-Communist, engaged in hard-ball diplomatic tactics against Salvador Allende, he was later found to have nothing to do with the coup-plotting and most certainly would have warned the White House to stay out if he had known of the secret, misguided efforts.

Despite the fact that the United States agreed to the **international law** principles of non-interference and non-intervention signed at the Montevideo Conference on the Rights and Duties of States in 1933, and the support of the strongly non-interventionist Charter of the **Organization of American States (OAS)** in 1948, the historical record is replete with ambassadors who have been accused of arrogant and belligerent meddling in the domestic affairs of Latin American countries where they are stationed. Sumner **Welles** was sent to Cuba in 1933 to change regimes considered harmful to American interests. During his brief stay on the island Welles used his ambassadorial influence by toppling two Cuban presidents and replacing them with two others considered more compatible with the wishes of Washington. Spruille **Braden**, like Welles a career diplomat, was briefly U.S. ambassador to Argentina in 1945 where he tried to prevent the democratic election of Juan **Perón** due to his association with fascists and support for the pro-German position until the end of **World War II**. Adolf A. **Berle**, Jr., U.S. ambassador to Brazil, criticized the **dictatorship** of Getulio Vargas in a speech to Brazilian journalists in 1945. The Brazilian military demanded and received Vargas' resignation a year later. John E. **Peurifoy,** Jr., was instrumental in the overthrow of Jacobo **Arbenz** in 1953–1954, a stance he pursued even before arriving in Guatemala. U.S. Ambassador Lawrence Pezzullo's 1979 intervention against Nicaragua's dictator Anastasio "Tachito" **Somoza** Debayle was a successful attempt to end what had become a corrupt and disastrous family dynasty. The historical record of U.S. ambassadors in Latin America would suggest that they are rarely neutral observers in their roles since many have intervened to remove governments—elected and unelected, authoritarian and democratic—and are often aided by domestic groups in Latin American countries that have urged the United States to intervene.

U.S. ambassadors are key actors in setting the style and determining the success of the United States in its relationship with Latin America. There are several reasons why ambassadors remain important, despite the fact that instant communications and rapid air transportation often reduce the importance of the individual ambassador. First, they support the prevailing view of Latin America as part of the U.S. sphere of influence, different from other world regions and part of a united Western Hemisphere. Second, despite advances in travel, communication, diplomatic summits, and the growing importance of intergovernmental organizations like the **United Nations (UN)** and the OAS, ambassadors "in country" still possess enormous autonomy and power in determining the binational relationship, particularly in the smaller Latin American countries. As representatives of the president of the United States, ambassadors arrive at their posts in Latin America prepared to improve relations or resolve an outstanding controversy. Third, U.S. ambassadors—with privileges legally reinforced by the 1961 Vienna Convention on Consular and Diplomatic Relations—often come to understand their host country better than their superiors in the State Department and the White House. Fourth, U.S. ambassadors—particularly those who are allowed to remain in their post for a considerable period of time—are important agents in defining the substance and style of U.S.–Latin American relations. Unfortunately, there are far too few ambassadors who make the effort to relate their experiences in Latin America, often reluctant to criticize the president who appointed them, or fellow members of the diplomatic "fraternity." Diplomatic historians who engage in multi-archival research offer more insights into the policy-making process and U.S.–Latin American relations. *See also* Castro Ruz, Fidel; Cold War; Gordon, [Abraham] Lincoln; Negroponte, John Dimitri; Reich, Otto Juan; Washington Policymakers.

Suggested Reading

G.R. Berridge, *Diplomacy: Theory and Practice* (London: Prentice-Hall, 1995); Jack R. Binns, *The United States in Honduras, 1980–1981: An Ambassador's Memoir* (Jefferson, NC: McFarland and Co., 2000); Edward S. Mihalkanin and Warren Keith Neisler, "The Role of the U.S. Ambassador," in David W. Dent, ed., *U.S.–Latin American Policymaking: A Reference Handbook* (Westport, CT: Greenwood Press, 1995); C. Neale Ronning and Albert P. Vannucci, eds., *Ambassadors in Foreign Policy: The Influence of Individuals on U.S.–Latin American Policy* (New York: Praeger, 1987); Eric Paul Roorda, *The Dictator Next Door: The Good Neighbor Policy and the Trujillo Regime in the Dominican Republic, 1930–1945* (Durham, NC: Duke University Press, 1998); Wayne S. Smith, *The Closest of Enemies: A Personal and Diplomatic Account of U.S.–Cuban Relations Since 1957* (New York: W.W. Norton, 1987); Charles Morrow Wilson, *Ambassadors in White: The Story of American Tropical Medicine* (New York: Henry Holt, 1942).

American Enterprise Institute (AEI) Moderately conservative **think tank** based in Washington, D.C., that emerged in the 1980s as a vociferous champion of President Ronald **Reagan**'s Central American policy. AEI was founded in 1943 as a businessman's lobbying organization with an emphasis on the free-market ideas of Friedrich von Hayek and Gottfried Harberler. At first called the American Enterprise Association, it served as a counter to the more liberal Brookings Institution in its efforts to influence domestic economic, social, and political issues. In contrast to Brookings, it supported most **Dwight Eisenhower** proposals and opposed Democratic Party initiatives of Presidents **Kennedy** and **Johnson**. Gradually over the course of the 1950s and 1960s it emerged as a full-scale think tank with a foreign policy arm to go along with its economic and social policy divisions. Most of its foreign policy analysts were strong advocates of going to war against Saddam Hussein in 2002–2003.

The election of Ronald Reagan in 1980 opened the door for AEI's staff of resident scholars and fellows to apply their expertise to national security, arms control, **international law**, and geopolitical issues. During the 1980s AEI had two senior scholars (Howard J. **Wiarda** and Mark Falcoff), several military and student interns, research assistants, a secretary, and several visiting adjunct scholars.

In addition, AEI had a number of other well-known scholars—Jeane **Kirkpatrick**, Michael Novak, Ben Wattenberg, and Howard Penniman—who also conducted research and wrote on Latin American policy issues during this period. Backed by an array of policy briefs—books, periodicals, and scholarly papers—AEI became a champion of Reagan's defense buildup and the controversial policy of supporting anti-Communist resistance movements worldwide.

Although AEI was usually thought of as a conservative think tank during the Reagan era, its policy positions on Latin America were more ideologically complex. For example, Mark Falcoff provided a consistently conservative point of view in his writing, but Howard Wiarda saw himself as a centrist and pragmatist dedicated to educating the Reagan administration and the many "instant experts" on Latin America who surfaced at the time of the importance of moving Central American policy back to the mainstream. Wiarda claims that his more centrist views on U.S.–Latin American relations was the main reason he was appointed lead consultant to the National Bipartisan Commission on Central America in the early 1980s. After AEI experienced unprecedented financial troubles in the mid-1980s, Falcoff assumed a significantly diminished role, and Howard Wiarda severed his ties with the institute altogether and returned to academia. The most notable member of AEI during the Reagan era was Jeane D. Kirkpatrick, a former Democrat who gained fame for her criticism of President Jimmy **Carter**'s **human rights** policy and her article "Dictatorships and Double Standards." One of the major sources of AEI influence over U.S.–Latin American policy involved luncheon and dinner meetings where key policymakers from the congressional and executive branches could mingle with scholars, journalists, or just about anyone doing something of interest in U.S.–Latin American relations. During the 1980s it was not unusual for **National Security Council (NSC)** personnel such as Lt. Colonel Oliver **North**, ambassadors and journalists headed for Latin America, Executive Office personnel, and Pentagon planners to show up at AEI's events to mingle over food, drinks, and informal conversation. There is ample evidence that AEI's contributions to the **Kissinger Commission** had a considerable influence in pulling Reagan's Latin American policy back to the center from the more ideological viewpoints contained in the first report of the Santa Fe Committee several years earlier. As a center-right policy-oriented think tank, the American Enterprise Institute serves as a key source of private power in the formulation and execution of U.S.–Latin American policy. It received $7 million in foundation funds between 1992 and 1994, second on the list of conservative foundation think tanks.

Foreign policy analysts are divided by policy topics and regions. U.S. foreign policy analysts in 2003 included Georgetown University Professor Jeane J. Kirkpatrick, neo-conservative scholars Danielle Pletka, Richard Perle, David Frum, and former member of Congress from Georgia, Newt Gingrich. Most of their current analysis is directed at such subjects as the use of force abroad, anti-terrorism, and strategies for advancing political and economic freedom worldwide. Mark Falcoff is the lone scholar focusing on Latin America at AEI; in 2003 he published *Cuba the Morning After*, which addressed the implications for U.S. policy toward the island in a post-**Castro** Cuba. *See also* Washington Policymakers.

Suggested Reading

Donald E. Abelson, *Do Think Tanks Matter? Assessing the Impact of Public Policy Institutes* (Montreal: McGill-Queen's University Press, 2002); Abelson, *American Think Tanks and Their Role in U.S. Foreign Policy* (New York: St. Martin's Press, 1995); Paul Dickson, *Think Tanks* (New York: Atheneum, 1971); Edwin J. Feulner, *Ideas, Think Tanks, and Governments* (Washington, DC: Heritage Foundation, 1985); Daniel Guttman, *The Shadow Government: The Government's Multi-Billion-Dollar Giveaway of its Decision-Making Power to Private Management Consultants, "Experts," and Think Tanks* (New York: Pantheon Books, 1976); James G. McGann and R. Kent Weaver, eds., *Think Tanks and Civil Societies: Catalysts for Ideas and Action* (New Brunswick, NJ: Transaction Publishers, 2000); David M. Ricci, *The Transformation of American Politics: The New Washington and the Rise of Think Tanks* (New Haven: Yale University Press, 1993); James Allen Smith, *The Idea Brokers: Think Tanks and the Rise of the New Policy Elite* (New York: The Free Press, 1991); Donald M. Snow, *Puzzle Palaces and Foggy Bottom: U.S. Foreign and Defense Policy-Making in the 1990s* (New York: St. Martin's Press, 1994); Laurence C. Soley, *The News Shapers: The Sources Who Explain the News* (New York: Praeger, 1992); Jean Stefancic, *No Mercy: How Conservative Think Tanks and Foundations Changed America's Social Agenda* (Philadelphia: Temple University Press, 1996); Diane Stone, *Capturing the Political Imagination: Think Tanks and the Policy Process* (Portland, OR: Frank Cass, 1996); Howard J. Wiarda, "Think Tanks," in David W. Dent, ed., *U.S.–Latin American Policymaking: A Reference Handbook* (Westport, CT: Greenwood Press, 1995).

American Institute for Free Labor Development (AIFLD) Founded in 1962, AIFLD is one of four international affairs institutes of the AFL-CIO. It was created to serve as the organizational vehicle for U.S. labor's participation in the U.S. foreign aid program in Latin America and to encourage non-Communist trade unions throughout the region. It often worked in conjunction with the **Central Intelligence Agency (CIA)** during the **Cold War**. AIFLD's principal operating departments—Education, **Human Rights**, and Social Projects—during the Cold War tried to strengthen democratic-left unions in Latin America so that they would be more effective in promoting democracy, equitable economic growth, and social justice. Beginning with President John F. **Kennedy**'s **Alliance for Progress**, AIFLD was often criticized by those on the left who maintained that its primary labor-organizing activities were part of U.S. security efforts to reverse Communist and **Castro**-backed penetration of unions. However, AIFLD always maintained at the time that it was unabashedly against **dictatorships** of both the left and right, and pro-**democracy** in its ideological orientation. AIFLD was funded by the **Agency for International Development (AID)**, the **National Endowment for Democracy (NED)**, and the AFL-CIO, with 93 percent coming from AID. Since the end of the Cold War, it has become more involved in the creation of regional trade pact negotiations, with particular emphasis on seeing that workers' rights are protected and enforced and multinational codes of conduct are included in such agreements as the **North American Free Trade Agreement (NAFTA)**, the Central American Common Market (CACM), and others. In their reports to the AFL-CIO, AIFLD has assisted in providing petitions to the Office of U.S. Trade Representative to ensure that trade benefits under the U.S. Generalized System of Preferences (GSP) are only available to those countries that have taken serious efforts to enforce internationally recognized worker rights. The GSP petition has been a successful tool in combating labor problems in Panama, El Salvador, Guatemala, and the Dominican Republic. During Cuba's "Special Period," AIFLD intensified its efforts to create democratic trade unions and improve human rights while working through the AFL-CIO Cuba Committee, whose ultimate goal is regime change on the island. Despite its Cold War notoriety, some scholars claim AIFLD has transformed itself into a more progressive body devoted to a more flexible and pro-democratic agenda: "from covertly interventionist it has become openly participatory in the political life of nations to the south" (Buchanan, 1991: 179). *See also* Democracy and Democracy Promotion; National Endowment for Democracy (NED).

Suggested Reading

Tom Barry and Deb Preusch, *AIFLD in Central America: Agents as Organizers* (Albuquerque, NM: The Resource Center, 1990); Paul G. Buchanan, "The Impact of U.S. Labor," in Abraham F. Lowenthal, ed., *Exporting Democracy: The United States and Latin America. Themes and Issues* (Baltimore, MD: Johns Hopkins University Press, 1991); Michael J. Sussman, *AIFLD, U.S. Trojan Horse: In Latin America and the Caribbean: A Joint Venture of the AFL-CIO, Dept. of State, U.S. Corporations, and the CIA* (Washington, DC: EPICA, 1983); Al Weinrub and William Bollinger, *The AFL-CIO in Central America: A Look at the American Institute for Free Labor Development (AIFLD)*, (Oakland, CA: Labor Network on Central America, 1987).

Americas Watch One of the major **human rights** interest groups that were founded between 1974 and 1981 when military-authoritarian governments in Latin America were engaged in massive human rights violations. As part of the human rights lobby in Washington, Americas Watch played an active role in the debate over the conflict in Central America during the 1980s. By monitoring human rights legislation, foreign assistance programs, and democratization efforts in the region, Americas Watch and other interest groups devoted most of their energy to influencing Congress and not the Executive branch of government. However, most of these groups have had only a marginal impact on changing the direction of U.S. policy toward Latin America due to the fact that they often promote unpopular causes, espouse a leftist political ideology, do not have a wide regional base, rarely make campaign contributions, and lack a large membership base with which to build coalitions. As a human rights interest group, Americas Watch devotes most of its time to research and publications on human rights abuse and protection, peaceful settlement of disputes, and general critiques of U.S.–Latin American relations. *See also* Democracy and Democracy Promotion.

Suggested Reading

Americas Watch, *With Friends Like These: The Americas Watch Report on Human Rights and U.S. Policy in Latin America* (New York: Pantheon, 1985); *The Reagan Administration's Human Rights Policy in 1983* (New York: Americas Watch, Helsinki Watch, and Lawyer's Committee for International Human Rights, 1984); Lars Schoultz, *Human Rights and United States Policy Toward Latin America* (Princeton, NJ: Princeton University Press, 1981).

Andean Initiative Inaugurated with great fanfare in 1990 by the **George H.W. Bush** administration, the Andean Initiative (also called the Andean Strategy) was a five-year, multifaceted, $2.2 billion program to reduce the flow of illicit narcotics, primarily cocaine, into the United States from Latin America. Responding to public and congressional pressure to broaden the U.S. military's support role, the Andean Initiative sought among other things to involve the military forces of Colombia, Peru, and Bolivia more deeply in anti-narcotics efforts. Over $400 million in military assistance was allotted to Andean Initiative countries between 1988 and 1992, and large amounts of excess defense stocks were ferried to Andean anti-drug forces.

Prior to the announcement of his Andean Initiative, President Bush (1989–1993) declared a "war" on drugs in 1989, stating that drugs not only afflicted America's health, but national security as well. His rhetorical strategy was to link Latin America's drug war to U.S. national security. In his first year in office, Bush demonstrated a willingness to utilize and expand the role of the military—both the United States and Latin American armed forces—in a purported war on drugs. In September 1989, President Bush unveiled his highly publicized Andean Initiative. The plan militarized the war on drugs in Latin America by supplying $65 million in emergency military aid to Colombia and $261 million in anti-drug assistance programs for Bolivia, Colombia, and Peru. To the dismay of Andean political leaders who had appealed to the United States for economic development assistance, crop substitution, and debt relief to ease domestic dependence on the enormous hard currency generated by narcotics, almost all of the aid package was designated for military and police activities. These included expanded counter-insurgency on the part of Colombia's and Peru's armed forces, newly created elite police units, excess stocks of U.S. conventional weapons shipped to Andean anti-drug forces, and training by U.S. military advisers in intelligence gathering and forward fire-basing. Given the past involvement of Latin American armed forces in politics, this militarization of the war on drugs threatened the stability of these fragile democracies. Moreover, Andean leaders resisted cooperating too closely with the United States for fear of appearing as dependent puppets of Washington. Finally, Latin American leaders virulently disagreed with the U.S. emphasis on supply-side measures aimed at interdiction and suppression programs, rather than focusing on demand-side solutions, such as treatment, education, and prevention programs in the United States.

United States and Latin American differences over drug policy threw the Andean Strategy into disarray almost from the beginning. The U.S. military had widespread doubts regarding the effectiveness of military involvement in interdiction and enforcement, and the lack of clarity surrounding the mission given to American armed forces that a "war" on drugs must result in a vaguely defined "total victory." By 1991, the Andean Strategy had lost much of its momentum and direction and by the time the initiative neared the end of its five-year mandate in 1994 the program was in financial and political trouble. The end of the **Cold War** resulted in falling levels of U.S. foreign aid, which in turn reduced spending on the Andean Strategy after members of Congress became disillusioned with the lack of will and commitment to fighting the drug wars by Latin American leaders. For example, only $35 million was ultimately allocated by Congress in 1994 out of an original $204 million requested. *See also* Drug Trafficking; Noriega, Manuel Antonio; Plan Colombia; Threat Perception/Assessment.

Suggested Reading

Charles T. Call, "The U.S. Military," in David W. Dent, ed., *U.S.–Latin American Policymaking: A Reference Handbook* (Westport, CT: Greenwood Press, 1995); Scott B. MacDonald, *Dancing on a Volcano: The Latin American Drug Trade* (New York: Praeger, 1988); Peter H. Smith, ed., *Drug Policy in the Americas* (Boulder, CO: Westview Press, 1992); United Nations Office for Drug Control and Crime Prevention, *World Drug Report 2000* (Oxford, UK: Oxford University Press, 2000).

Anti-Americanism Negative attitudes toward the United States have been a constant in U.S.–Latin American relations since the early nineteenth century. Even some of the more assertive and positive efforts—**Good Neighbor Policy**, **Alliance for Progress**, **democracy** promotion, and dictator removal initiatives—have been met with resentment by some people in Latin America. Because of the ebb and flow of U.S. policy toward Latin America, a love-hate relationship has developed and continues to the present day. Anti-Americanism is not rooted in jealousy of U.S. institutions or values, but how the United States has treated Latin America, particularly when its **hegemony** in the region has been challenged. Much of Latin America's national identity is rooted in negative views of the United States that stem from diplomatic blundering and ignorance, arrogance, **racism**, military **intervention**, and economic dependency and exploitation. A burst of anti-Americanism followed the U.S.–led war with Iraq in 2003, raising doubts and suspicions of U.S. motives in Latin America. Some argue that the basis of the current negative views in Latin America is more anti–**George W. Bush** than anti-American. Some U.S. presidents, for example, John F. **Kennedy**, Jimmy **Carter**, and Bill **Clinton**, are remembered fondly for how they dealt with Latin America.

Anti-Americanism following the war to remove Saddam Hussein is tied to several aspects of the U.S.–Latin American relationship, including: (1) three American invasions—Grenada, Panama, and Haiti—in the past twenty years; (2) indifference to Latin America's current economic crisis and other issues such as the ongoing civil war in Colombia, the long strike in Venezuela against Hugo Chávez, and the forced eradication of coca in Bolivia and Peru; (3) the failure of free markets and globalization; (4) Bush's appointment of hard-line Cubans and retreads from the policy scandals during the **Reagan** era; (5) the refusal to believe President Bush when he says the war against Iraq was to remove a brutal dictator and build a viable democracy; (6) the hypocrisy of telling the Latin American military to forget about doing anything about internal subversion and **terrorism** in the 1970s and 1980s on **human rights** grounds while the United States pursues a no-holds-barred war on terrorism around the world; (7) the decades-long economic and political hostility toward Fidel **Castro**'s Cuba; and (8) the negative effects of U.S. anti-drug efforts, which have destroyed a major source of revenue among poor and indigenous communities. Anti-drug policy anger in Bolivia in 2003 forced President Gonzálo Sánchez de Losada from office in a bloody confrontation between protesters and the democratic government. One of the women leaders of the opposition summed up the feelings of resentment by saying "the money from the United States is in the name of eradication, but it comes to us as bullets, machine guns, tear gas and deaths" (Lindsay, 2003: 2A).

While anti-American sentiments are strongest among those on the left and a deep tradition exists for blaming the United States when things are not going well in Latin America, **blowback** from previous policies in Latin America and President Bush's determination to use vast amounts of U.S. military power even at the cost of international cooperation is very alarming to millions of Latin Americans. Indeed, the fallout from interventionist policies often makes it more difficult for the United States to achieve a broad range of policy objectives in Latin America, including forward progress on immigration reform, the creation of a **Free Trade Area of the Americas (FTAA)**, and the normalization of relations with Castro's Cuba.

Anti-Americanism, or anti-Yankeeism, followed in the wake of Latin America's independence in the early part of the nineteenth century. Widespread anti-American sentiment developed when Latin Americans realized that Washington had little interest in establishing democratic systems and viable economies and preferred the use of force to deal with Latin America's political and security problems. What has evolved over the past one hundred years is a love-hate relationship that fluctuates on the basis of how Latin Americans are treated by Washington. After the **Clark Memorandum** was published in 1930 and the **Franklin D. Roosevelt** administration made serious efforts to become a "good neighbor," the U.S.–Latin American relationship improved. The creation of the **Organization of American States (OAS)** after **World War II** and the adoption of the Rio Treaty in 1948 helped to establish a more cooperative working relationship. The emphasis on **Cold War** ideology, beginning in the 1950s produced a rebirth of anti-Americanism, particularly the support for "**friendly dictators**," covert action to overthrow democratically elected governments, the failure to include Latin America in plans for government-sponsored economic recovery after World War II (until after Castro's revolution in 1959), and the increasing role of multinational corporations in the Latin American economies. President **Dwight Eisenhower**'s decision to remove Fidel Castro was based in part on his anti-American speeches that were having serious adverse affects on U.S.–Latin American relations and the obvious propaganda advantages for international Communist movements. *See also* Cultural Imperialism; Imperialism; Intervention and Non-Intervention; Media; Public Opinion; Propaganda; Scandals and Blunders.

Suggested Reading

Alison Brysk, "Beyond Hegemony: U.S.–Latin American Relations in a 'New World Order'?" *Latin American Research Review* 27, No. 3 (1992); Richard Crockett, *America Embattled: September 11, Anti-Americanism, and the Global Order* (New York: Routledge, 2003); Oscar Handlin, *The Distortion of America*, 2nd ed. (New Brunswick, NJ: Transaction Publishers, 1996); Stephen Haseler, *Anti-Americanism: Steps on a Dangerous Path* (London: Institute for Defense and Strategic Studies, 1986); Paul Hollander, *Anti-Americanism: Critiques at Home and Abroad, 1965–1990* (New York: Oxford University Press, 1992); Reed Lindsay, "In Bolivia, U.S. is the Bad Guy," *Baltimore Sun* (November 23, 2003); Daniel C. Maguire, *The New Subversives: Anti-Americanism of the Religious Right* (New York: Continuum, 1982); Larry Rohter, "The Faraway War Set Latin America on Edge," *New York Times* (April 20, 2003); Ernest E. Rossi and Jack C. Plano, *Latin America: A Political Dictionary* (Santa Barbara, CA: ABC-CLIO, 1992); Alvin Z. Rubinstein and Donald E. Smith, *Anti-Americanism in the Third World: Implications for U.S. Foreign Policy* (New York: Praeger, 1985); Ziauddin Sadar and Merryl Wyn Davies, *Why do People Hate America?* (Cambridge: Icon, 2002); Peter Scowen, *Rogue Nation: The American the Rest of the World Knows* (Toronto: McClelland and Stewart, 2003); Thomas Perry Thornton, ed., *Anti-Americanism: Origins and Context* (Newbury Park, CA: Sage Publications, 1988).

Anti-Imperialism An argument against overseas expansion and **hegemony** that developed into a broad-based movement in the United States during the 1890s. Many anti-imperialists believed that the acquisition of a colonial empire violated the U.S. Constitution and negated the American belief in self-government. For those who opposed and distrusted a foreign policy based on territorial annexation, intervention, and occupation, **imperialism** presented significant dangers to the fabric and well-being of American society. The voices of anti-imperialism ranged from novelist Mark Twain, labor leader Samuel Gompers, industrialist Andrew **Carnegie**, and social reformer Jane Addams. One of the most noteworthy anti-imperialists of the nineteenth century was Carl Schurz, a German immigrant who opposed slavery and attempts to assimilate people who lived in the tropics. He considered these tropical populations to be alien, turbulent, and backward and therefore unfit to be citizens of the United States. His anti-imperialism contained ideological and ethnic-geographic bases, but he also argued that national security would be jeopardized by acquiring, and defending, major overseas possessions. Nineteenth-century anti-imperialists opposed the **Spanish-Cuban-American War**, annexation of the Dominican Republic, and the rising jingoism associated with the new **Manifest Destiny** of the time. Anti-imperialists were deeply divided over the notion of the white man's burden as a justification for expansion; some saw it as a rhetorical prop to justify conquest while others refused to see either the duty or the possibility of uplifting the "lower races."

Carl Schurz and other anti-imperialists were well organized and began late in 1898 to form "Anti-Imperialist Leagues" in major Eastern cities in the United States. The following year the new movement moved westward across the nation, and soon the assorted local chapters were consolidated into a single American Anti-Imperialist League. The disciples who made up the league varied in their ideology and concerns over the growing imperialist nature of American foreign policy. On the far left were socialists such as Morrison I. Swift who argued that the purpose of imperialism was to benefit the plutocracy. He attacked **Theodore Roosevelt**'s belief that the United States needed wars to keep it healthy. Andrew Carnegie was far less radical than Swift and supported the movement with his immense wealth. William Jennings **Bryan** fought against imperialism and tried to convert William Randolph Hearst to anti-imperialism after the Spanish-Cuban–American War. Between 1897 and 1900 the anti-imperialists fought against the annexation of Hawaii, the ratification of the peace treaty with Cuba, and the re-election of William **McKinley**. They lost every battle since their critique of imperial expansion did not seem to resonate with the frenzy of U.S. overseas expansion in the 1890s. The fact that the Spanish-Cuban–American War was seen as necessary on humanitarian grounds and brought a quick victory helped to set the stage for further imperialist adventures in the Caribbean basin, the predominant region of interest to the United States. The movement faded from the national scene after the defeat of William Jennings Bryan in 1900, Roosevelt's reluctance to acquire more colonial possessions, and the death of many leaders of the anti-imperialist movement.

The spark for many twentieth-century revolutions in Latin America was U.S. imperialism in the form of economic and political hegemony. In Cuba, for example, Fidel **Castro**'s revolution was based on removing sixty years of informal control over the island. Che **Guevara** was convinced that imperialism was the enemy and guerrilla warfare the remedy for Latin America's developmental problems. Many of those who believed in the "dependency" theory of Latin American development argued that U.S. imperialism played a major role in impoverishing the region. The more recent manifestations of U.S. imperialism in Latin America can be attributed to the war on **terrorism**, the drug war, the privatization of American foreign policy, and the policy prescriptions tied to the **Washington Consensus**. *See also* Anti-Americanism; Dependency Theory; Race and Racism.

Suggested Reading

Robert L. Beisner, *Twelve Against Empire: The Anti-Imperialists, 1898–1900* (New York: McGraw-Hill, 1968); Philip S. Foner and Richard C. Winchester, eds., *The Anti-Imperialist Reader: A Documentary History of Anti-Imperialism in the United States* (New York: Holmes and Meier, 1984); David Healy, *U.S. Expansionism: The Imperialist Urge in the 1890s* (Madison: University of Wisconsin Press, 1970); Walter LaFeber, *The New Empire: An Interpretation of American Expansion, 1860–1898* (Ithaca, NY: Cornell University Press, 1963); Gerald E. Markowitz, ed., *Anti-Imperialism, 1895–1901* (New York: Garland, 1976); Frank A. Ninkovich,

The United States and Imperialism (Malden, MA: Blackwell, 2001); Thomas G. Paterson, ed., *American Imperialism and Anti-Imperialism* (New York: Crowell, 1973); Richard V. Salisbury, *Anti-Imperialism and International Competition in Central America, 1920–1929* (Wilmington, DE: SR Books, 1989); E. Berkeley Tompkins, *Anti-Imperialism in the United States: The Great Debate, 1890–1920* (Philadelphia: University of Pennsylvania Press, 1970); William Appelman Williams, ed., *From Colony to Empire: Essays in the History of American Foreign Relations* (New York: John Wiley, 1972).

Arbenz Guzmán, Jacobo (1913–1971) Military figure and populist-nationalist president of Guatemala (1951–1954) whose economic policies and leftist ideology contributed to his overthrow by the **United Fruit Company**, the U.S. press, pro-counsel ambassadors, and anti-Communist zealots in the White House who feared the Soviets were in the process of creating a beachhead for international communism on America's doorstep. Using highly sophisticated **propaganda**, public fears of Communist advances in the hemisphere, and psychological warfare, the United States succeeded in the overthrow of the democratically elected Arbenz in June 1954. The covert campaign against Arbenz was directed by **Central Intelligence Agency (CIA)** men—**Allen Dulles**, Richard **Bissell**, Colonel J.C. King, E. Howard Hunt, and David Phillips—who believed, contrary to government intelligence estimates, that there was a link between Guatemalan Communists and Moscow. No link has ever been established between Jacobo Arbenz and a Soviet bid for influence in the Western Hemisphere. The success of the Guatemalan intervention set the stage for further use of covert action to bring about regime change in other parts of Latin America, including Cuba, British Guiana, Brazil, and Chile. The successful overthrow of President Jacobo Arbenz in 1954 was a serious blow to **Franklin D. Roosevelt**'s **Good Neighbor Policy** and marked the end of the Guatemalan populist and reformist revolution begun under Juan José **Arévalo** ten years earlier. Its future impact on the rest of Latin America and the United States was profound: it contributed to the radicalization of Che **Guevara** who was in Guatemala City during the whole affair; President John F. **Kennedy**'s **Alliance for Progress**, a program of development designed to counter Communist advances in the hemisphere; the **Bay of Pigs** invasion, a similar plan to covertly topple Cuba's Fidel **Castro**; and it inspired over thirty years of military-dominated governments in Guatemala that violated **human rights** and contributed to hundreds of thousands of civilian deaths. In toppling Arbenz, President **Dwight Eisenhower** believed he had found the solution to eliminating hostile regimes, preserving the appearance of non-intervention, and not being bound by **international law**: using secrecy, deception, and covert intervention. The cost of getting rid of Arbenz was enormous, both for the people of Guatemala and American foreign policy.

Jacobo Arbenz was born in Quezaltenango to a Swiss father and a Guatemalan mother. He received his military training at the Escuela Politécnica, graduated in 1935, and in 1939 married María Cristina Vilanova, the daughter of a wealthy Salvadoran planter. His wife was alleged to have Communist sympathies and a fierce determination to address the needs of Guatemala's underclass with the help of her husband's political power. Arbenz participated in the 1944 uprising that toppled the conservative **dictatorship** of President Jorge Ubico, but opposed his successor and went into exile for a short while before returning to help elect Juan José Arévalo to power through the ballot box. He was named minister of defense by President Arévalo, but spent most of his time expanding his power base with the intention of becoming president himself in the 1950 elections. He won with a large majority, backed by a coalition of the military, peasants, students, and workers.

Once in power, Arbenz moved further to the left by promoting land reform, courting the Communist Party, and defying the United States and United Fruit. As he amplified his revolutionary program, Arbenz weakened his ties to the Guatemalan military, betrayed the hopes of the **Truman** administration, and moved closer to the leaders of the fledgling Communist Party and leftist labor organizations. Although he was interested in Communist ideas and welcomed the political support he received from the left, Arbenz was essentially a Guatemalan nationalist whose goal was to expand his power base through benefits to the workers and peasants. As he deepened the revolution's social reforms—higher taxes on the wealthy, social welfare programs, land reform, and better conditions for the average worker—he confronted growing opposition from the conservative opposition, the United Fruit Company, members of Congress, and high officials within the **State Department**.

The specter of a Communist state in Central America raised fears inside the Eisenhower administration that Guatemala might become a Soviet "beachhead" in the Americas. Although Arbenz threatened the economic interests of the United Fruit Company, allowed a few Communists in his government, and had attempted to purchase light arms from Czechoslovakia, Guatemala was not a Communist state in 1954. With the help of the public relations wizard of the United Fruit Company, Edward **Bernays**, the Eisenhower administration came to believe that Arbenz was either a Communist or under Communist domination. In 1953 the United States set out to destabilize Arbenz's government through **economic sanctions**, diplomatic pressure in the **Organization of American States (OAS)**, and **Central Intelligence Agency (CIA)** anti-Arbenz propaganda and plans to mount a counter-revolution with the help of a rightist army faction led by Col. Carlos Castillo Armas. In June 1954, the CIA-supported National Liberation Army, led by Castillo Armas, invaded Guatemala from neighboring Honduras. The armed forces refused to defend the government, and Arbenz was forced to resign and go into exile, living in Cuba, Uruguay, France, Switzerland, and Mexico, where he died in 1971. Once Arbenz resigned, U.S. Ambassador John **Puerifoy** organized the regime transition that brought Castillo Armas to the presidency a week later. The successful overthrow of President Arbenz induced a sense of euphoria in Washington concerning the ease with which the regime collapsed, and it led to repetition of mistakes in dealing with future revolutionaries in Latin America. To celebrate the removal of Arbenz, President Eisenhower had a grand celebration in the White House for the CIA agents who carried out the deed. He shook their hands and gave special thanks to Allen Dulles, director of the CIA: "Thanks, Allen, and thanks to all of you. You've averted a Soviet beachhead in our hemisphere" (Rabe, 1988: 61). After the installation of Col. Carlos Castillo Armas, the United States lost interest in promoting **democracy** in Guatemala and a long, bloody period of repression ensued. His **assassination** in 1956 ushered in decades of political violence and authoritarianism for millions of Guatemalans. *See also* Ambassadors; Braden, Spruille; Cold War; Dulles, John Foster; Friendly Dictators; Revolutions; Threat Perception/Assessment.

Suggested Reading

Thomas P. Anderson, *Politics in Central America* (New York: Praeger, 1983); John A. Booth and Thomas W. Walker, *Understanding Central America* (Boulder, CO: Westview Press, 1989); Nick Cullather, *Secret History: The CIA Classified Account of its Operations in Guatemala, 1952–1954* (Stanford, CA: Stanford University Press, 1999); Piero Gleijeses, *Shattered Hope: The Guatemalan Revolution and the United States, 1944–1954* (Princeton, NJ: Princeton University Press, 1991); Stephen Kinzer, "Revisiting Cold War Coups and Finding Them Costly," *New York Times* (November 30, 2003); Stephen G. Rabe, *Eisenhower and Latin America: The Foreign Policy of Anticommunism* (Chapel Hill: University of North Carolina Press, 1988); Stephen Schlesinger and Stephen Kinzer, *Bitter Fruit: The Untold Story of the American Coup in Guatemala* (Garden City, NY: Doubleday and Co., 1982); Gaddis Smith, *The Last Years of the Monroe Doctrine: 1945–1993* (New York: Hill and Wang, 1994); Ralph Lee Woodward, Jr., *Central America: A Nation Divided*, 2nd ed. (New York: Oxford University Press, 1985).

Arévalo Bermejo, Juan José (1904–1990) Intellectual, educator, and elected president of Guatemala (1945–1951) during a period of transition from the **dictatorship** of Jorge Ubico to the beginnings of a democratic revolution. After the 1944 downfall of Ubico led by an opposition composed of disgruntled military officers and civilians (mostly doctors, lawyers, teachers, and students) who demanded national elections and democracy, Arévalo was elected by a landslide in December 1944. After taking office in 1945, he set out to institutionalize democratic structures and make the existing capitalist system more responsive to the downtrodden masses. During his six years in office, Arévalo opened up the political system by respecting freedom of speech and press and allowing political parties to form and compete for office. Labor unions were encouraged and given favorable treatment by the government, and the large Indian population received numerous benefits from the new government. Although they were not interpreted as such, Arévalo's reforms were modeled after **Franklin D. Roosevelt**'s New Deal. Arévalo's domestic reforms would ultimately lead to a conflict with the **United Fruit Company (UFC)**, a wealthy and politically powerful landowner in Guatemala. Many of his supporters believed that UFC—controlled by U.S. stockholders and the beneficiary of lucrative contracts with prior dictators—exploited Guatemala for the benefit of foreigners.

As Arévalo's left-of-center policies gained support among the workers and dispossessed, the Guatemalan elite and middle class became concerned about the nature of the new society that was being put in place. Although President Arévalo was opposed to Communism, his critics labeled him and his supporters "Communists" and conspired to bring about his downfall. The United States, confused about the nationalist character of Arévalo's politics, felt that the disparity of wealth and land ownership in Guatemala made the country ripe for Communist expansion in the hemisphere. During his tenure in office, Dr. Arévalo proved to be a shrewd juggler of political forces, survived more than a dozen plots against his regime, but managed in the end to serve his full six-term term.

Juan José Arévalo was born of middle-class parents in Taxisco in Santa Rosa province. He followed in his mother's profession by training as a teacher. After graduating from the Central Normal School for Boys, Arévalo worked for two years in the Ministry of Education in Guatemala City before traveling to Europe and eventually settling in Argentina in 1934 because of authoritarian rule in Guatemala. It was in Argentina that Arévalo acquired his doctorate in philosophy from the University of La Plata, became a popular professor, and lived the next fourteen years in voluntary exile during the remainder of the Ubico dictatorship (1931–1944). What disgusted Guatemalan intellectuals like Arévalo was the persistence of "a corrupt cadre of caudillos who were more interested in personal aggrandizement than in national development" (Dosal, 1993: 230). For Guatemala the Ubico dictatorship represented a long line of right-wing despotisms that ruled the country by exploiting the huge Indian population.

The leaders of the October 1944 revolution that ousted Ubico and brought Dr. Arévalo to power comprised a broad sector of Guatemala's nascent, educated middle class, including teachers, business and professional leaders, and university students. *Arevalistas* (followers of Juan José Arévalo) advocated four broad types of change: agrarian reform, social welfare for labor, better education for the masses, and the consolidation of political democracy. Many had watched the revolutionary events in Mexico unfold under President Lázaro Cárdenas (1934–1940) who expropriated American oil interests, strengthened organized labor, and carried out major land reform on behalf of large numbers of *campesinos* (peasants). Despite the success of these reforms in Mexico, Guatemala's entrenched oligarchy perceived the proposed reforms as a threat to their power and way of life.

Juan José Arévalo was an ideal choice to lead the vanguard of change in Guatemala. He was not a military man nor a landed aristocrat, but rather an educator who had risen from the middle sectors and at the time of revolt was teaching at the University of Tucumán in Argentina. Although his long exile had left him with few ties to Guatemala. The absence from his homeland had left him untainted by the negative effects of *Ubiquismo*. His appearance and style—40 years of age, six-feet tall, and a muscular 200 pounds—added vigor and passion to the revolutionary movement on behalf of urban workers and rural Indians. He won the election easily in December 1944, winning over 85 percent of the votes cast by the literate, male electorate.

The political ideas that guided Arévalo's presidency were referred to as "spiritual socialism" and centered on progressive, center-left plans to improve the lot of Guatemala's underclass. His noble effort at reform suffered from the lack of governmental expertise and the slow pace of reforms to improve the lives of the masses. Unable to satisfy the heightened demands unleashed by the October revolution, "spiritual socialism" lost much of its appeal and momentum by 1950. During his first year in office corruption and opportunism overtook his government, and conservative opponents of social and economic reform grew increasingly intransigent and violent. President Arévalo normalized relations with the Soviet Union in April 1945, a move that facilitated the growth and influence of the Guatemalan Communist Party. In 1947 he enacted a new Labor Code, modeled after the Wagner Act in the United States, that would reduce management's control over labor, a change that worried the United Fruit Company. While most of these progressive measures were only partly carried out, many felt that for the first time democratic ideas had some meaning in Guatemala. In charge of a fragile coalition opposed to the alliance of large landowners, rightist military, conservative clergy, and foreign companies, President Arévalo faced more than two dozen abortive coup attempts during his first four years in office. Yet, for all of his political difficulties and lack of governing experience, he proved to be a shrewd political juggler who survived the constant plotting and intrigue against him, and completed his full six-year term.

After a peaceful transfer of power to his democratically elected successor, Colonel Jacobo Arbenz Guzmán, Arévalo left Guatemala as a roving ambassador with few duties and a large expense account. He turned to writing and produced *The Shark and the Sardines* (1956), a polemical critique of the role of the United States in Latin America that made Washington fearful of the possible spread of his ideas to other parts of Latin America. His ideas influenced the more radical reforms pushed by President Arbenz and ultimately contributed to the CIA-engineered counter-revolution that toppled Arbenz in June 1954. While in Mexico in 1962, Arévalo declared that he would run for president again in 1963, a decision that prompted the "preventive" coup against President Ydígoras Fuentes. The military cancelled the elections, a move that put an end to the return to power of civilians like Arévalo and led to a succession of military governments for the next several decades. He then returned to exile, living abroad during the turbulent 1960s and 1970s when authoritarian governments prevailed. In the early 1980s he returned to Guatemala City to witness the nation's slow and painful transition to democracy after almost thirty years of civil war and dictatorship. Juan José Arévalo died in Guatemala on October 7, 1990, forty-five years after the October revolution that ousted Ubico. *See also* Anti-Americanism; Arbenz Guzmán, Jacobo; Guatemala, U.S. Invasion of (1954); Revolutions.

Suggested Reading

Juan José Arévalo, *The Shark and the Sardines*, trans. June Cobb and Raúl Osegueda (New York: Lyle Stuart, 1961); Arévalo, *Anti-Kommunism in Latin America: An X-ray of the Process Leading to New Colonialism*, trans. Carleton Beals (New York: Lyle Stuart, 1963); Paul J. Dosal, *Doing Business with the Dictators: A Political History of United Fruit in Guatemala, 1899–1944* (Wilmington, DE: SR Books, 1993); Georges A. Fauriol and Eva Loser, *Guatemala's Political*

Puzzle (New Brunswick, NJ: Transaction Books, 1988); Piero Gleijeses, *Shattered Hope: The Guatemalan Revolution and the United States, 1944–1954* (Princeton, NJ: Princeton University Press, 1991); Richard H. Immerman, *The CIA in Guatemala: The Foreign Policy of Intervention* (Austin: University of Texas Press, 1982); Stephen Schlesinger and Stephen Kinzer, *Bitter Fruit: The Untold Story of the American Coup in Guatemala* (Garden City, NY: Doubleday and Co., 1982); Ronald M. Schneider, *Communism in Guatemala, 1944–1954* (New York: Praeger, 1958); Robert H. Trudeau, *Guatemalan Politics: The Popular Struggle for Democracy* (Boulder, CO: Lynne Rienner, 1993); Ralph Lee Woodward, Jr., *Central America: A Nation Divided*, 2nd ed. (New York: Oxford University Press, 1985).

Arias Sánchez, Oscar (1940–) Intellectual, diplomat, and president of Costa Rica (1986–1990) who clashed with the **Reagan** administration over ways to promote peace in Central America. A serious student, Arias attended Boston University, the University of Essex in England, and the London School of Economics before earning a law degree in Costa Rica, the youngest president to achieve the position. Running as a peace candidate of the National Liberation Party, Arias promised to keep Costa Rica out of Nicaragua's war with Washington. After he won the general election against the old guard, Arias pledged that "Costa will not be converted into a dormitory for the contras," arguing that aid for the **Contras** (Reagan's so-called "freedom fighters") would be better spent promoting economic development. Arias soon found himself the target of top officials in the Reagan administration, from the president on down—President Reagan, Vice-President **George H.W. Bush**, National Security Adviser Frank Carlucci, Chief of Staff Howard Baker, Deputy Secretary of State John C. Whitehead, Assistant Secretary of State for Inter-American Affairs Elliott **Abrams**, **National Security Council (NSC)** staffer Oliver **North**, **Central Intelligence Agency (CIA)** Director William **Casey**, Ambassador Lewis Tambs, and Reagan's special envoy to Central America Philip Habib. In White House meetings on the Central American crisis, Reagan and his top aides would lecture Arias on the evils of communism and the threat posed by the **Sandinistas**, the need to support the Contras, and the flaws in the Costa Rican's peace efforts. President Arias countered that by betting on war, and opposing efforts to achieve a diplomatic settlement, the United States was becoming isolated and irrelevant as a player in ending the conflict between the Sandinistas and the U.S.–backed Contras. The hardliners in Washington were opposed to any diplomatic accord that did not get rid of the Sandinistas in Nicaragua.

In February 1987 President Arias presented a peace plan that ultimately dismantled the Reagan administration's proposal to keep the Contras alive to drive the Nicaraguan Sandinistas from power. The plan discussed was by the five Central American presidents in Esquipulas, Guatemala, and in August 1987 the agreement was signed, much to the chagrin of the Reagan administration. The plan closely followed Arias' draft and each government pledged itself to democratic pluralism, free elections, and serious efforts to end internal fighting through a cease-fire with its armed opponents, including amnesty for them, and to begin a process of political reconciliation and dialogue. Each country was to refrain from supporting or offering refuge for armed groups and together called upon other governments to do the same. The White House expected the plan to collapse as many were convinced the Sandinistas would never sign the agreement, regardless of whether Esquipulas offered the hope of putting an end to the Contra war. Abrams opposed the provisions set forth in the Esquipulas II agreement, arguing that "Communists win these kind of negotiations" and that President Arias was obstructing Washington's strategy of military pressure on Nicaragua. Pragmatists with the Reagan administration endorsed the plan for peace; hardliners remained hell-bent on pursuing a military solution. Not content to let the peace plan work, the Reagan administration set out to undermine the Arias presidency by withholding economic assistance, complaining about Costa Rican diplomatic activity, and financing Arias' political opponents in the Social Democractic Party, and by top-level **propaganda** aimed at the Sandinistas for non-compliance with the Esquipulas accord. When Oscar Arias received the Nobel Peace Prize in 1987 for his efforts in Central America, Elliott Abrams' assistant, Robert W. Kagan, expressed his contempt for Arias that flowed throughout the Reagan administration: "all of us who thought it was important to get aid for the Contras reacted with disgust, unbridled disgust" (quoted in LeoGrande, *Our Own Backyard: The United States in Central America, 1977–1992*: 528). After his tenure as president, Oscar Arias used his peace prize award to establish a center and peace university in San José, Costa Rica, and lectured frequently on disarmament, demilitarization, and democratization. In 2005, he decided to make another run for the presidency of Costa Rica in 2006. *See also* Iran-Contra Scandal; Reagan Doctrine.

Suggested Reading

Jack Child, *The Central American Peace Process, 1983–1991: Sheathing Swords, Building Confidence* (Boulder, CO: Lynne Rienner, 1992); Guido Fernández, *El desafío de la paz en Centroamérica* (San José: Editorial Costa Rica, 1989); Eldon Kenworthy, *America/Américas: Myth in the Making of U.S. Policy Toward Latin America* (University Park: Pennsylvania State University Press, 1995); William LeoGrande, *Our Own Backyard: The United States in Central America 1977–1992* (Chapel Hill: University of North Carolina Press, 1998); Seth Rolbein, *Nobel Costa Rica: A Timely Report on Our Peaceful Pro-Yankee, Central American Neighbor* (New York: St. Martin's Press, 1989).

Aristide, Jean-Bertrand (1953–) Haitian president (1991, 1994–1995, 2001–2004) and controversial and charismatic Roman Catholic priest who fought against the Duvalier **dictatorship** and military rule during the 1980s and 1990s. Haiti's first democratically elected (and youngest) president in 1990, Jean-Bertrand Aristide presided over the nation's tumultuous democratic transition beginning in the 1990s. Aristide was born on July 15, 1953, in the small village of Port Salut in southwest Haiti. Aristide's family were peasants eking out a living in a region barren of trees, and without paved roads, electricity, or running water. Aristide's father died shortly after his birth, and the family moved to Port-au-Prince in 1958 where Jean-Bertrand started parochial school with the Salesian Brothers. He was an outstanding student, multilingual, and developed a concern for the Haitian poor at an early age. At fourteen Aristide entered the Notre Dame secondary school in Cap Haitien, in preparation for the priesthood. Following graduation from the seminary at the age of twenty-one, Aristide spent a year in the Dominican Republic before returning to Port-au-Prince where he matriculated at the National University and earned a psychology degree in 1979. In 1982, Aristide was ordained to the priesthood and sent to the parish of St. Joseph in the slums of the capital where his outspokenness on behalf of the poor and against the traditional church and elites caught the notice of the Duvalier regime. After only three months in his slum parish, Aristide was sent to Canada for "pastoral reorientation." At the University of Montreal, Aristide earned a master's degree in biblical theology. He spent most of the next six years (1979–1985) in exile in Canada, as well as in Italy and Greece.

When Jean-Bertrand Aristide returned to Haiti in 1985, the struggle to overthrow the longstanding Duvalier dynasty was entering a final, critical phase, one that mirrored much of the country's violent past. Although Haiti achieved its independence from France in 1804, Haitians have experienced little freedom and no **democracy**. What existed in Haiti was a history of notorious dictators, brutal repression, and army intervention in politics that created a praetorian state, creating one of the poorest in the Western Hemisphere. Haiti's authoritarian political system remained unstable despite an American military occupation of Haiti from 1916–1934 that did little for Haitian political and economic underdevelopment. U.S. Marines trained the modern Haitian military, which assumed a major role in politics after American forces departed in 1934, making and unmaking political leaders until François ("Papa Doc") Duvalier came to power with military support in 1957.

Duvalier's dictatorship was very much a personalist regime; Duvalier was the classic "strongman" who totally dominated the political system. While the Haitian army was a mainstay of the regime, it often worked in tandem with a parallel secret police apparatus (the *Tontons Macoutes*) and a network of spies and informers. An estimated 40,000 people were jailed, tortured, or killed during the Duvalier era (1957–1986), with many more thousands forced into exile. The United States ignored Duvalier's blatant human rights violations, supporting the regime for it's virulent anti-communism and proximity to Fidel **Castro**'s Cuba. The one exception during Duvalier's long period of rule was during the **Kennedy** administration when, under the **Alliance for Progress**, the Haitian regime was criticized and efforts were made to train and professionalize his army. In response, Papa Doc expelled the U.S. military mission and the United States retaliated by cutting off economic assistance. The Duvalier dictatorship then turned inward and made some gestures toward Africa to bolster the regime's falling legitimacy. Aid was resumed by President Lyndon B. **Johnson** when it was decided that the United States needed Haiti's support during the invasion of the Dominican Republic.

In return for Haiti's slavish adherence to U.S. anti-Communist policies, the Duvalier dynasty garnered American economic aid, technical and military assistance loans and grants. The end of the long Duvalier dynasty (father "Papa Doc" followed by son "Baby Doc") came after serious food riots in 1985, when the second **Reagan** administration began withdrawing the carte blanche support that had kept Haiti afloat. To bring about the necessary **regime change**, Duvalier, his family, and cronies, were flown to exile in France in February 1986, aboard a U.S. cargo plane.

From the fall of the Duvalier dynasty in 1986 until 1990, Haiti suffered an institutional crisis as four military-dominated regimes came and went and an unrelenting popular struggle for democracy intensified. The Haitian military and the dreaded *Tontons Macoutes* remained in power and fought to preserve the power and privileges they had acquired during the thirty years of the Duvalier dictatorship, what some called "Duvalierism without Duvalier." As the single most important source of resistance to the repressive, corrupt neo-Duvalierist, militarist regime, Aristide quickly became the most important political figure in Haiti between 1986 and 1990. Aristide's humble origins set him apart from Haitian elites; his ability to merge anti-*macoutism*, martyrdom (he had survived three **assassination** attempts) and mysticism lent a messianic quality to his priestly aura. Aristide also severely criticized the United States for its long and blind support of the Duvaliers. Tensions escalated as Aristide's anti-capitalist ideology and liberation theology threatened the Haitian bourgeoisie and the military. Many conservatives in Washington believed that Aristide was both an ideological and strategic threat to the United States. Well before his election, U.S. perceptions of Aristide were shaped by embassy cables to Washington characterizing him as an unsteady, anti-American, left-wing populist, and a mentally disturbed radical. Elliott **Abrams** characterized Aristide as being "democratically elected" but certainly "not a democrat" (Ortmayer and Flinn, 1993: 15). Senator Jesse **Helms**, relying on negative information provided by his aide Deborah De Moss, called Aristide "one of the most brutal people to hold office in this hemisphere in my lifetime," and a "psychopathic killer" who put gasoline-drenched tires around the necks of his opponents and then set them afire.

In the midst of violence, strikes, escalating class warfare, exaggerated fears of an impending Communist dictatorship, and charges of U.S. indifference, Haitian General Raoul Cedras launched a military coup in September 1991 that ousted Aristide, who escaped to Venezuela and eventually to Washington, D.C. While in exile in Washington, he addressed the **Organization of American States (OAS)** about the need to restore democracy in Haiti; the hemispheric body condemned the coup and called for the immediate restoration of Aristide, and, when that failed, backed an economic embargo of the island. Meanwhile, an estimated 5,000 civilians, mainly Aristide supporters, were killed by the military and its allies following the coup. The scale of the military junta's repression, together with the privations created by the economic embargo, contributed a rash of Haitian "boat people" attempting to flee Haiti for the United States.

The **Clinton** administration spent almost two years negotiating the removal of the Haitian military junta and the return of the democratically elected Aristide. Several diplomatic agreements (the Washington Agreement in 1992, the Governor's Island Agreement in 1993) were signed, but Haiti's generals remained intransigent.

As Aristide's exile dragged on, relations between Washington and Aristide cooled rapidly given U.S. antagonism to Aristide's populism, the double standard by which Haitian (economic) and Cuban (political) refugees were treated, and accusations by the Congressional Black Caucus that Clinton's Haitian policy was discriminatory and racist. In March 1994, Randall Robinson of TransAfrica began a hunger strike to change U.S. policy and Aristide charged that America was ignoring a hemispheric "holocaust" (Martin, 1997: 5). After facing a summer of criticism by members of Congress and an assortment of interest groups, President Clinton threatened to invade Haiti in September 1994 unless the junta stepped down on September 16. An eleventh-hour diplomatic initiative by former President Jimmy **Carter** enabled him to negotiate the removal of the military leaders and the return of President Aristide. On September 19, 1994, American troops landed to re-establish order and, without firing a shot and were met with widespread appreciation. Aristide returned to Haiti and resumed the presidency a month later. Under U.S. pressure and the terms of the Governor's Island Agreement, Aristide did not seek a second term as president. After the invasion, Haiti remained mired in poverty and corruption and political infighting continued over the next four years as hundreds of **United Nations (UN)** peace-keeping and U.S. troops remained to assist in the difficult task of nation building.

After submitting to the dictates of his American benefactors and forced to make concessions to his domestic enemies, Aristide won a second term as president on May 26, 2001, in a landslide, winning 91.7 percent of over 2.6 million ballots cast. Aristide's electoral victory did not provide him with any legitimacy in Washington; the administration of **George W. Bush** had already decided on taking office that Aristide had to go. It froze all multilateral development assistance to Haiti and in doing so guaranteed there would be a crisis—balance of payments, rise in inflation, and a collapse of living standards—that would bring down the regime. To the wealthy elite who boycotted the election, however, Jean-Bertrand Aristide remained the symbol of their fear of the politicized poor. Although Jean-Bertrand Aristide did not succeed in his efforts to make Haiti more just and equitable, he did remove the more odious vestiges of Duvalierism such as the praetorian military, the secret police, and the murderous **death squads**. After more than a month of violent demonstrations and over 100 deaths in early 2004, President Aristide was forced from power by rebel forces encouraged by the United States. The way in which Aristide was removed from office and the U.S. role in the sordid affair left a number of unanswered questions about whether the democratically elected president was "forced to resign" and fell victim to a coup since the Bush administration refused to defend the presidential palace before Aristide and his wife left for exile in the Central African Republic. When Aristide arrived at the airport, U.S. officials refused him entry to the airplane until he signed a letter of resignation. President Bush quickly reversed his hands-off policy by sending 2,000 U.S. forces to Haiti to join French and Canadian troops to restore order. After the government of Gerard Latortue was installed in Haiti by the United States, the Caribbean Community (CARICOM) leaders decided to withhold **recognition** of the interim government until the **United Nations (UN)** General Assembly investigated the circumstances surrounding the ouster of President Aristide. Aristide continues to maintain that he was abducted by U.S. agents and therefore remains the constitutionally elected president of Haiti. And the mainstream media in the United States displayed little interest in the plight of President Aristide or in challenging the White House's version of events that led to the removal of the Haitian president. Jean-Bertrand Aristide has not given up on the idea of returning to Haiti, either as president or priest.

Those who make policy toward Latin America seemed imbued with the notion that quick fixes will suffice for a coherent policy. For example, after assisting Aristide to return to power in 1994, the United States and other nations spent millions of dollars setting up a police force along with training in the United States and high salaries to blunt the temptation of accepting bribes. All were required to take an entrance exam. However, the international forces left after two years, and Haiti descended into anarchy and chaos once again. Haiti could not be turned around in two years, given the long-term challenge of dealing with development in one of the poorest countries in Latin America. Ten years later the United States was forced to invade again, this time to assist in the removal of Aristide from power amid growing turmoil and threats from paramilitaries. *See also* Dependency Theory; Threat Perception/Assessment; Washington Policymakers.

Suggested Reading

Jean-Bertrand Aristide, *Eyes of the Heart: Seeking a Path for the Poor in the Age of Globalization* (Monroe, ME: Common Courage Press, 2000); *Haiti: Harvest of Hope* (video) (Hyattsville, MD: Distributed by Haiti Reborn/Quixote Center, 1998); Alex Dupuy, *Haiti in the New World Order: The Limits of the Democratic Revolution* (Boulder: Westview Press, 1997); Robert Fatton, Jr., *Haiti's Predatory Republic: The Unending Transition to Democracy* (Boulder, CO: Lynne Rienner, 2002); Georges A. Fauriol, *The Haitian Challenge: U.S. Policy Considerations* (Washington, DC: Center for Strategic and International Studies, 1993); Fauriol and Andrew S. Faiola, "Prelude to Intervention," in Georges A. Fauriol, ed., *Haitian Frustrations: Dilemmas for U.S. Policy* (Washington, DC: Center for Strategic and International Studies, 1995); Robert Debs Heinl and Nancy Gordon Heinl, *Written in Blood: The Story of the Haitian People, 1492–1995* (Lanham, MD: University Press of America, 1996); Anthony P. Maingot, "Haiti and Aristide: The Legacy of History," *Current History*, Vol. 90 (February 1992); Curtis Martin, *President Clinton's Haiti Dilemma, Pew Case Studies in International Affairs*, Case 375 (Washington, DC: Institute for the Study of Diplomacy, 1997); Louis Ortmayer and Joanna Flinn, *Hamstrung Over Haiti: Returning the Refugees, Pew Case Studies in International Affairs*, Case 355 (Washington, DC: Institute for the Study of Diplomacy, 1993); Roland I. Perusse, *Haitian Democracy Restored, 1991–1995* (Lanham, MD: University Press of America, 1995); Brenda Gayle Plummer, *Haiti and the United States: The Psychological Moment* (Athens: University of Georgia Press, 1992); Bob Shacochis, *The Immaculate Invasion* (New York: Penguin Putnam, 1999).

Arms Trade The sale of arms to Latin American countries has been a mainstay of U.S. Latin American policy since the end of **World War II**. The United States supplies more arms to Latin America than any other major arms supplier. As the arms industry has grown in the United States it has amassed a vast amount of power to lobby the White House and Congress for the opportunity to export weapons to Latin American militaries. The rationale for selling arms to Latin American governments rests on several arguments: (1) to promote security and stability; (2) to create friendly regimes dependent on U.S. supplies and largesse; (3) to allow major arms manufacturers such as Lockheed Martin and McDonnell Douglas to increase market share and protect American jobs against European competitors; (4) to give Latin American governments the resources with which to fight against terrorists, drug traffickers, indigenous movements, and urban and rural guerrillas; (5) the sale of conventional weapons, albeit useful for a wide variety of terrorist activities, does not have the same level of threat as does nuclear proliferation, and by having these weapons, countries are less likely to want nuclear weapons; and (6) exporting arms is extremely profitable, as annual arms sales pump billions of dollars into the U.S. economy. In the year 2005, U.S. arms exports accounted for 60 percent of all registered international arms deliveries.

The arms trade, despite its importance to the United States, is often seen as having a negative effect on Latin America. The arms trade can exacerbate militarism and undermine democratic rule in Latin America. In May 1977, President Jimmy **Carter** issued Presidential Decision Directive 13, which terminated the sale of high-tech weapons to Latin America. However, twenty years later President Bill **Clinton** lifted the ban on a case-by-case basis to appease the arms lobby that worked on behalf of large weapons manufacturers in the United States. Critics of the decision, including many Latin American governments, argued that a resumption of arms sales would undermine the democratic advances and usher in the return of military rule, **human rights** abuses, and further distort the allocation of scarce economic resources.

For decades the United States has used arms transfers as a way of rewarding allies and punishing those who are less sympathetic to American foreign policy motives, particularly the protection of human rights. While the United States has passed laws with the intention of protecting human rights, there is frequently weak enforcement of the legislation. For example, Section 502B of the Foreign Assistance Act states that "no security assistance may be provided to any country the government of which engages in a consistent pattern of gross violations of internationally recognized human rights." In 1999, the U.S. Congress passed the Arms Sales Code of Conduct Act as an amendment to the Foreign Assistance Act. The secretary of state was required by the law to report to Congress whether the countries involved in the transactions were in compliance with the law. Nevertheless, the United States often sells billions of dollars worth of arms to Latin American countries that are in violation of the law as measured by human rights abuses.

After the attacks on the United States on **September 11, 2001**, the **George W. Bush** administration agreed to provide weapons to countries that lined up in support of the United States despite the fact they had been criticized in the past for human rights violations, the lack of **democracy**, and even the support of **terrorism**.

According to the Center for Defense Information in Washington, D.C., between 1990 and 1999 the United States supplied sixteen or eighteen countries where known terrorist groups were operating, and this pattern continued under the George W. Bush administration. The arms sales were carried out through the Foreign Military Sales (FMS) program, or through a variety of Direct Commercial Sales (DCS) programs. With two major terrorist organizations operating in Colombia, both active in the illicit drug trade, the U.S. government sent over $370 million in arms and military assistance. Others worry about an arms race among countries that have mutual disputes and want new weaponry, particularly in Chile, Argentina, and Brazil. The current policy of selling weapons to Latin American governments is often portrayed in terms of protecting jobs in the United States instead of providing for the security and development of poor Latin American countries. Unfortunately, President Clinton's decision to lift the ban on the export of sophisticated arms to Latin America was preceded by heavy lobbying and substantial financial contributions by Lockheed Martin and McDonnell Douglas. Until there is more concern about the consequences of supplying arms to Latin America, it is difficult to imagine improvement in human rights, advances in democracy, and the devotion of more scarce resources to creating a more liveable society. *See also* Economic Sanctions; Partisanship and Policy; *State of Siege*; Terrorism; Threat Perception/Assessment.

Suggested Reading

Jurgen Brauer and J. Paul Dunne, eds., *Arming the South: The Economics of Military Expenditure, Arms Production, and Arms Trade in Developing Countries* (New York: Palgrave, 2002); Patrick Brogan and Albert Zarca, *Deadly Business: Sam Cummings, Interarms, and the Arms Trade* (New York: W.W. Norton, 1983); Gideon Burrows, *No-Nonsense Guide to the Arms Trade* (London: Verso, 2002); Center for Defense Information, *CDI Terrorism Project: A Risky Business: U.S. Arms Exports to Countries Where Terrorism Thrives* (Washington, DC: Center for Defense Information, November 29, 2001); Helen Collinson, *Death on Delivery: The Impact of the Arms Trade on the Third World* (London: Campaign Against Arms Trade, 1989); William W. Keller, *Arm in Arm: The Political Economy of the Global Arms Trade* (New York: Basic Books, 1995); Victor Millan and Michael Morris, *Controlling Latin American Conflicts: Ten Approaches* (Boulder, CO: Westview Press, 1983); David Mussington, *Understanding Contemporary International Arms Transfers* (London: Brassey's, 1994); Rachel Stohl, "The Tangled Web of Illicit Arms Trafficking," *Center for Defense Information Report* (Washington, DC, 2004); John Tirman, *Spoils of War: The Human Cost of America's Arms Trade* (New York: Free Press, 1997); *World At Risk: A Global Issues Sourcebook* (Washington, DC: CQ Press, 2002).

Assassination The use of murder as an instrument of foreign policy is not a common strategy of the United States in dealing with Latin American leaders and governments. For years it was unthinkable that the United States would consider assassination as an instrument of foreign policy since many assumed it would open up American leaders to similar retaliation from enemy regimes, even in times of peace. The **Cold War** hardened the belief that the United States faced such an implacable enemy, whose main goal was world domination, that it had no choice but to resort to more clever ways of dealing with Communist enemies. After the creation of the **Central Intelligence Agency (CIA)** in the late 1940s, and the increased use of covert action, Washington began to support or encourage the use of assassination in Latin America and elsewhere in the Third World. The CIA, at the behest of the White House, considered or planned (or assisted others) at different times the assassination of Jacobo **Arbenz**, leader of Guatemala; Cuban leader Fidel **Castro**, and his brother, Raúl; Dominican dictator Rafael **Trujillo**, Argentine-born leader of the Cuban Revolution, Ernesto Che **Guevara**; François "Papa Doc" Duvalier, leader of Haiti; José Figueres, president of Costa Rica; Francisco Caamaño, Dominican Republic opposition leader; Salvador **Allende**, president of Chile; General Rene Schneider, Commander-in-Chief of the Chilean army; General Omar Torrijos, leader of Panama; General Manuel Antonio **Noriega**, chief of Panama Intelligence; Michael Manley, prime minister of Jamaica; Miguel d'Escoto, foreign minister of Nicaragua; and members of the **Sandinista** National Directorate, Nicaragua. During the Mexican Revolution the United States was involved in efforts to assassinate Francisco I. Madero and Francisco "Pancho" **Villa** (Blum, 2000).

After the American public learned in 1973 that the CIA considered assassination as a tool of foreign policy, then-CIA Director William Colby announced he would put a stop to it. In its report on assassination of foreign leaders in 1975, the Church Committee tried to minimize the previous efforts at assassinating Latin American leaders as "aberrations" that did not represent the values and ideals of the United States. This was followed by President Gerald R. **Ford**'s executive order in 1976 that banned any U.S. government employee from involvement in assassination. Presidents Jimmy **Carter** and Ronald **Reagan** issued similar presidential orders prohibiting assassinations; however, President Reagan cancelled his executive order so that he could more effectively fight terrorism. President **George H.W. Bush** added his own version of the assassination prohibition by allowing "accidental killings" if U.S. forces "were employed against the combatant forces of another nation, a guerrilla force, or a terrorist or other organization whose actions pose a threat to the United States." Presidents Bill **Clinton** and **George W. Bush** do not appear to have issued any official statements confirming or changing U.S. government policy on assassination. During the 1980s U.S. Army and CIA training manuals were discovered to contain instructions for undermining leftist regimes in the region. For example, a manual written for the U.S.–backed **Contra** forces fighting in Honduras and Nicaragua contained instructions on how "to neutralize carefully selected and planned targets considered communists or Cuban-inspired Marxist guerrillas." The World Court found that the United States was in violation of general principles of humanitarian law, and the offensive manuals were revised to reflect different strategies.

The most determined effort to rid a Latin American government of its leader occurred in Cuba when the **Dwight Eisenhower** and **Kennedy** administrations instructed the CIA to conduct a series of attempts on Fidel Castro's life. Castro claims that the CIA plotted to kill him at least two dozen times between 1959 and 1965, including the hiring of a Las Vegas mobster to kill Castro with a high-powered rifle. Following the assassination of President Kennedy in 1963, a number of conspiracy theories emerged claiming that Kennedy's death was an act of revenge by Fidel Castro for the plots against him or by angry anti-Castro Cubans who felt betrayed after the blunder at the **Bay of Pigs** in 1961. The U.S. government was also involved in the plot to find and kill Pablo Escobar, head of the Medellín (Colombia) drug cartel.

The altered mood of the nation in the wake of the Watergate Affair compelled the Church Committee to make its report public, concluding that "assassination is an abhorrent practice that must never again be undertaken in times of peace by the U.S. government" and that acts of assassination should be prohibited by law. The Church Committee also worried about the subversion of democratic accountability after finding out that some in the Kennedy administration resorted to "plausible deniability" when discussing plans to assassinate a foreign leader. In spelling out the danger of avoiding the truth with discussing the elimination of foreign leaders, the 1975 Senate report on assassination plots stated, "Failing to call dirty business by its rightful name may have increased the risk of dirty business being done." The current war on terrorism seems to have contributed to the general feeling that the ban on assassination should not apply to military actions directed at rogue states and terrorist organizations.

Assassination became an issue during the Reagan administration when a psychological operations manual was discovered that was being used by the U.S.–supported Contras against the leftist government of Nicaragua. Critics of Reagan's Central American policy claimed that the manual violated the executive order banning assassination; the president claimed that the document was not an official CIA publication and therefore not in violation of the law. The U.S. war on **terrorism** and related international conflicts have contributed to the belief that **regime change**, pre-emptive war, and pro-active responses to security threats at home and abroad may require that the ban on assassination be rescinded or overridden. Shortly after the **September 11, 2001**, attacks President George W. Bush authorized the CIA to conduct a covert war against Osama bin Laden's Al-Qaeda terrorist network, including the authority to assassinate, capture, and interrogate terrorist suspects. In a January 2004 speech criticizing the Bush administration for having a plan for Cuba after the demise of Fidel Castro, Cuba's president accused President George W. Bush of plotting with Miami exiles to assassinate him, a charge U.S. officials deny. The use of assassination remains a subject of debate at the highest level of the U.S. government, largely because of the moral, practical, and legal consequences that confront **Washington policymakers** and the American public. *See also* Alpha 66; Bissell, Richard; Church Committee Report; Lansky, Meyer; Operation Mongoose; Terrorism.

Suggested Reading

William Blum, *Rogue State: A Guide to the World's Only Superpower* (Monroe, ME: Common Courage Press, 2000); "Castro Says Bush Aims to Kill Him," *Seattle Times* (January 31, 2004); Paul Elliott, *Assassin! The Bloody History of Political Murder* (London: Blandford, 1999); Alex

Gibney, *The Trials of Henry Kissinger* (video) (New York: First Run/Icarus Films, 2002); Miles Hudson, *Assassination* (Stroud, UK: Sutton, 2000); Gail Pellette, *Justice and the Generals* (video) (New York: Gail Pellette Productions, 2002); Walter Pincus, "CIA had hit list of 58 Guatemalans in the 1950s," *Washington Post* (May 24, 1997: A4); Ward Thomas, *The Ethics of Destruction: Norms and Force in International Relations* (Ithaca, NY: Cornell University Press, 2001); U.S. Senate, *Alleged Assassination Plots against Foreign Leaders* (Washington, DC: U.S. Government Printing Office, 1975).

B

Backyard Metaphor One of the ways Latin America as a geographic region has been characterized by the United States, often suggesting proprietary rights and obligations, subordination to Washington, and an unspoken bias in diplomatic discourse. The term "yard" (front or back) has been evoked frequently by U.S. policymakers to refer to Central America or the Caribbean when there is a paramount need to justify the protection or promotion of a vital interest in the region. As a fear-based rhetorical strategy, it often contains the subliminal message that only the president and his top advisers can deal personally with the alleged threat lurking at America's "doorstep," convincing the otherwise apathetic public that cares or knows little about Latin America that it must rely on the wisdom of the White House to deal with threats inside the Western Hemisphere. While it sometimes competes with "good neighbor" as a way of characterizing Latin America, the "yard" metaphor is rarely questioned by a public audience willing to believe that Washington possesses the right to act as the "natural protector" when it asserts that it is facing threats by Communists, terrorists, evil-doers, and other malcontents close to the United States. In reality, Latin America is not in the "yard" (front or back) of the United States, although it could be more accurately portrayed as part of a hemispheric neighborhood, willing to act collectively to address whatever interests are being threatened. The ability of the Executive Branch to manipulate symbols and metaphors is of tremendous importance in selling a controversial foreign policy. As Kenworthy (1995: 49) points out:

> There is no mystery to how one sells a foreign policy in an era of advertising: evoke the fears and fantasies present in the audience one

> hopes to persuade (e.g., fear of communism) and then transfer those emotions to new signifiers about which the audience knows little and perhaps cares less (e.g., **Sandinistas**). If the audience cared, there would be less need to sell; if it knew, there would be less scope for advertising.

Although President Ronald **Reagan**'s speeches often contained "backyard" metaphors designed to convince the American people, and Congress, to support his "freedom fighters" in Central America, it is used far less because of its negative connotations. Mexico's **United Nations (UN)** ambassador, Adolfo Aguilar Zinser, was pressured in 2003 to resign his post after criticizing the United States for wanting a "relationship of convenience and subordination" with Mexico. Reflecting widely held views in Mexico, he also stated that the United States "sees us as a backyard." In response, Secretary of State Colin Powell rejected Zinser's remarks, stating that, "We never, ever, in any way treat Mexico as some backyard or as a second-class nation." Zinser's critical remark came at a time when many unresolved issues—the legal status of millions of Mexican migrants in the United States, the war on terrorism, trade, energy, and border security—have chilled relations and complicated the center-right government of President Vicente **Fox**. Current political discourse in U.S.–Latin American relations is more likely to rely on terms such as "free trade," "freedom," "freedom fighters," "hemispheric unity," and "democracy-building" to sell foreign policy initiatives in the age of terrorism. During the 2004 presidential campaign John F. **Kerry** called for a new Community of the Americas, a "partnership with Latin America built on mutual respect, dialogue and cooperation, where neighbors look after neighbors and strive toward common goals." President **George W. Bush**'s rhetoric has relied more on trade agreements and generalized notions of "freedom" than past presidents when speaking about U.S.–Latin American relations. *See also* Good Neighbor Policy; Media; Monroe Doctrine (1823); Roosevelt, Franklin Delano; Terrorism; Threat Perception/Assessment; Washington Policymakers.

Suggested Reading

Eldon Kenworthy, *America/Américas: Myth in the Making of U.S. Policy Toward Latin America* (University Park: Pennsylvania State University Press, 1995); Tim Weiner, "Mexico Dismisses Its U.N. Envoy for Critical Remark About U.S.," *New York Times* (November 19, 2003).

Balaguer Ricardo, Joaquín (1907–2002) Dominican poet and anti-Communist politician who played a key role in the politics of the Dominican Republic, both during the **Trujillo** era (1930–1961) and afterward. During the Trujillo era he served as the dictator's presidential secretary, ambassador, education minister, vice-president, and president. He developed a power base that would help him dominate post-Trujillo Dominican politics; according to many of his critics, his style of leadership and policies resembled *Trujilloismo* without Trujillo. Joaquín Balaguer was president when Trujillo was assassinated in 1961. He was forced into exile after Trujillo was killed, living in the United States from late 1962 to 1966, but it did not take him long to return to power.

Joaquín Balaguer was born to a wealthy family in Villa Bosono and educated at private schools in the Dominican Republic. He went on to achieve law degrees in Santo Domingo and Paris before becoming involved in Dominican politics in 1930. As a member of the Patriotic Citizens Council, he helped overthrow President Horacio Vásquez and in doing so was attracted to Rafael L. Trujillo. Their personal friendship and political teamwork would last for the next thirty-one years as Trujillo ruled the Dominican Republic with an iron fist. He published several scholarly books on Trujillo's regime before Trujillo's demise as well as after to explain the period of chaos and revolt between Trujillo's death and the revolution of 1965.

After the United States invaded in 1965, Balaguer dominated the chaotic and brutal politics of the Dominican Republic through fraud and electoral manipulation. During the brief period of foreign intervention a short-lived interim government assumed power on August 31, 1965, and governed until elections were scheduled for 1966. According to Gilderhus (2000: 193), "The winner, Dr. Joaquín Balaguer, a politician with Trujillista antecedents, served two consecutive terms, represented elite interests under a democratic facade, and became a fixture in Dominican politics for the next twenty-five years." It was an acceptable outcome for the United States since Juan Bosch was prevented from taking office, another Fidel **Castro** was thwarted, and the chances of a Communist takeover looked extremely remote. Balaguer won five elections between 1966 and 1990, assisted by the backing he received from the Dominican military and the United States. During his first three terms as president Balaguer benefitted from massive amounts of U.S. aid and generous revenues from high sugar prices. With the support of Washington and flush accounts, President Balaguer defeated left-wing guerrilla groups while at the same time coopting opposition groups through the dispensation of patronage.

However, the fraudulent nature of the 1978 presidential election, and the **Carter** administration's emphasis on honest elections, led to public censure by the United States and the **Organization of American States (OAS)**. Balaguer was not reelected in 1978, but after two opposition party victories he returned to power in 1986 and then was re-elected in 1990 and 1994. His last electoral victory was again marred by fraud, leading to an agreement that he would serve only two years of a four-year term and would be prohibited from running again after his two-year term was up in 1996. His final exit from Dominican politics in 1996 marked the end of a long, corrupt, and brutal period of rule, one that had many of the earmarks of the Trujillo era. Blind and in declining health, Joaquín Balaguer died in Santo Domingo at the age of ninety-five. His legacy of authoritarian politics and economic dependency on the United States continues to plague the Dominican Republic. *See also* Assassination; Dependency Theory; Friendly Dictators; Kennedy, John F.

Suggested Reading

G. Pope Atkins and Larman C. Wilson, *The Dominican Republic and the United States: From Imperialism to Transnationalism* (Athens: University of Georgia Press, 1998); David W. Dent, *The Legacy of the Monroe Doctrine: A Reference Guide to U.S. Involvement in Latin America and the Caribbean* (Westport, CT: Greenwood Press, 1999); Mark T. Gilderhus, *The Second Century: U.S.–Latin American Relations Since 1889* (Wilmington, DE: SR Books, 2000); William O. Walker, III, "Mixing the Sweet with the Sour: Kennedy, Johnson, and Latin America," in Diane B. Kunz, ed., *The Diplomacy of the Crucial Decade: American Foreign Relations During the 1960s* (New York: Columbia University Press, 1994).

Baker Plan. *See* Brady Plan (1989)

Ball, George Wildman (1909–1994) George Ball was U.S. undersecretary of state (1961–1966) in the **Kennedy** and **Johnson** administrations. Although he rose no higher than this number two post in the **State Department**, Ball was an influential, and often dissenting, force in American foreign policy in the 1960s. George Ball was a key figure during the **Cuban Missile Crisis** in 1962. He was also a leading exponent of aid to underdeveloped nations. In a career that spanned a half-century, Ball was distinguished as few others in the post–**World War II** American foreign policy establishment by the breadth of his experience in government, politics, and international law. George Ball was a lawyer, author, economist, investment banker, diplomat, and adviser to presidents.

Born in Iowa, Ball eventually became one of the most articulate and leading internationalists of his generation. When he was eleven years old, Ball's family moved to Evanston, Illinois, where he later enrolled at Northwestern University, majored in English, graduated in 1930, and earned his law degree in 1933. Eager to be a part of the New Deal, Ball went to Washington and worked in the Farm Credit Bureau and the Treasury Department. Returning to Chicago in 1935, he joined a tax law firm. In 1942, Ball joined the office of Lend-Lease Administration. Moving to London, Ball was appointed director of the U.S. Strategic Bombing Survey by President **Franklin Delano Roosevelt** in 1944. Following World War II, Ball returned to private practice, focused increasingly on international law and represented foreign clients from his Washington law firm of Cleary, Gottlieb, Steen and Ball. From 1945 to 1961, George W. Ball cultivated important international connections and political friends. Ball's close association with his old Chicago law partner, Adlai E. Stevenson, put him in touch with John F. Kennedy, who appointed Ball undersecretary of state for economic affairs in January 1961.

In November 1961, Ball replaced Chester Bowles as undersecretary of state. During the October 1962 Cuban Missile Crisis, Ball was a member of President Kennedy's inner circle of advisers (the so-called ExCom) and coordinated consultations with European allies following the decision to blockade Cuba. Following Kennedy's **assassination** in 1963, Ball managed the transition to the Johnson administration and became a key troubleshooter for President Johnson, notably during the 1965 U.S. invasion of the Dominican Republic, when he traveled to Santo Domingo to ease tensions and halt the fighting.

Although regarded as a member of the foreign policy establishment, Ball often took positions pitting him at odds with prevailing orthodoxy. Most notable was Ball's early (1961), forceful, continuous opposition to America's deepening involvement in Vietnam; a singular view across the upper echelons of the Kennedy and Johnson administrations. Finding himself more and more at odds with the Johnson administration's Vietnam policy, Ball quietly resigned from the State Department in 1966. A taciturn midwesterner who remained personally loyal to Lyndon Johnson, Ball's principled and sustained opposition to the war only became widely known with the publication of the Pentagon Papers in 1971. Ball spent 1967 traveling extensively in the Far East and Europe in connection with his investment banking activities as a partner in Lehman Brothers. On April 24, 1968, Ball was appointed U.S. ambassador to the **United Nations (UN)** by President Johnson to succeed Arthur Goldberg, but left that post the following September to join Senator Hubert Humphrey's doomed presidential campaign as "principal foreign policy adviser." After 1968, George Ball became one of the strongest critics of President Richard **Nixon**'s Vietnam policy, détente, and the "shuttle diplomacy" of Henry **Kissinger**.

George Ball returned to government service in 1976 and played a major role in drafting the foreign policy plank of the Democratic Party platform and was considered a front-runner for the post of secretary of state that ultimately went to a younger Cyrus Vance. Still, Ball continued to advise the **Carter** administration as a special counsel to the president and was appointed to President Carter's **National Security Council (NSC)** to help formulate America's response to the fall of the Shah of Iran. In 1978, Ball also helped the Carter administration negotiate the **Panama Canal Treaties** with General Omar Torrijos that eventually abrogated the 1903 treaty and set the termination date of U.S. control over the canal for December 31, 1999. Ball also helped mount the bipartisan effort for Senate ratification of the Canal Treaties.

George Ball was a forceful speaker whose style, in writing too, struck an academic tone with literary finesse. Ball was the author of five books, *The Discipline of Power* (1968), *Diplomacy for a Crowded World* (1976), *The Past Has Another Pattern: Memoirs* (1982), *Error and Betrayal in Lebanon* (1983), and *The Passionate Attachment*, a history of American-Israeli relations, written with his son, Douglas, in 1992. At his death, Ball was working on a book about America at the end of the twentieth century. He was eighty-four years old and lived in Princeton, New Jersey. *See also* Cold War; World War II.

Suggested Reading

George W. Ball, *The Past Has Another Pattern: Memoirs* (New York: W.W. Norton and Co., 1982); Ball, *Diplomacy for a Crowded World: An American Foreign Policy* (Boston: Little, Brown, and Co., 1976); David Halberstam, *The Best and the Brightest* (New York: Random

House, 1969); Steven Hook and John Spanier, *American Foreign Policy Since World War II* (Washington, DC: CQ Press, 2000).

Banana Republic William Sydney Porter, a popular fiction writer and embezzler, coined the term "banana republic" after spending several months in Central America at the turn of the century. Under the pseudonym O. Henry, Porter wrote *Cabbages and Kings* (1904), a fictional account of his adventures in Coralio, Anchuria (most likely Tegucigalpa, Honduras), where he spent most of his time. In describing the nature of Honduran politics, Porter used "banana republic" to convey the corruption, inept public administration, and the absurdity of the Anchurian political game. With bananas the major export, the Caribbean coast of Central America became increasingly dependent on U.S.–based banana companies and the North American market. The two main competitors for the banana trade, and land concessions, at this time were the **United Fruit Company** and Cuyamel Fruit Company. To obtain favorable concessions from the Honduran government, agents of the banana companies used bribery, intrigue, and manipulation. Once the banana industry developed into large foreign-controlled plantations, capital-starved governments—anxious to develop their countries any way they could—were forced to concede much of their sovereignty and national economic independence to multinational corporations.

Before long, journalists, politicians, and others were using banana republic as a disparaging reference to poor and politically incompetent Central American countries whose economies depended solely on the export of tropical fruits (mainly bananas) and whose governments included poor administrators and corrupt and unstable dictators. Although banana republics were often ripe for revolution, and foreign intervention, the multinational fruit companies liked doing business with the dictators, as long as their concessions and profits were untouched. The policy of the United States in the early decades of the twentieth century was not to challenge this arrangement since it coincided with the growing hegemony of the United States in the area. In fact, there were many cases in which the United States used military intervention and occupation to forestall **revolutions** and protect the interests of the fruit companies in Guatemala, Honduras, and Nicaragua. These actions throughout the twentieth century have often been counter-productive, leaving military authoritarianism, political corruption, and mass poverty in its wake. Although less common than in the past, "banana republic" still appears from time to time when talking about corrupt and incompetent governments around the world, even those that have never produced, or exported, bananas to the United States. After being plagued with global competition, hurricanes, and stagnant demand in the United States, Central America's banana industries have declined dramatically.

The 2000 presidential election crisis in the United States brought forth a wave of ridicule from Latin America, where many people felt vindicated after decades of U.S. contempt for the lack of **democracy** and flawed elections in the region. For the first time the United States was referred to as a "banana republic" because of its archaic and faulty system for counting the Al Gore and **George W. Bush** votes, especially in the state of Florida, in November-December of that year. After years of being criticized for its "sham" elections, the Cuban news media started referring to the United States as the "large banana republic to the north" and urged the winner—whoever he might be—to remove the economic blockade against the island that has poisoned the bilateral relationship for over four decades. The term has become so common as a shibboleth to define inept government that the **media** now use it to describe just about any government that some feel deserves ridicule for its policies. *See also* Banana Wars; Butler, Smedley Darlington; Dictatorships; Friendly Dictators; Guatemala, U.S. Invasion of (1954).

Suggested Reading

Alison Acker, *Honduras: The Making of a Banana Republic* (Boston: South End Press, 1988); David W. Dent, *The Legacy of the Monroe Doctrine: A Reference Guide to U.S. Involvement in Latin America and the Caribbean* (Westport, CT: Greenwood Press, 1999); Paul J. Dosal, *Doing Business with Dictators: A Political History of United Fruit in Guatemala, 1899–1944* (Wilmington, DE: Scholarly Resources, 1993); Dario A. Euraque, *Reinterpreting the Banana Republic: Region and State in Honduras, 1870–1972* (Chapel Hill: University of North Carolina Press, 1997); Lester D. Langley, *The Banana Wars: United States Intervention in the Caribbean, 1898–1934* (Chicago: Dorsey Press, 1988); Lester D. Langley and Thomas Schoonover, *The Banana Men: American Mercenaries and Entrepreneurs in Central America, 1880–1930* (Lexington: University Press of Kentucky, 1995); Ralph Lee Woodward, Jr., *Central America: A Nation Divided*, 2nd ed. (New York: Oxford University Press, 1985).

Banana Wars The numerous U.S. military interventions in the circum-Caribbean region between 1898 and 1934 were referred to as the "banana wars" by the U.S. Marines who fought to create America's empire in the tropics. From the U.S. intervention and occupation of Cuba in 1898 until the failed effort to capture Augusto **Sandino** in Nicaragua, the United States acted as an "international police power" to restore order and uplift backward peoples. The military officers who carried out these interventions were called banana warriors and included such flamboyant figures as Smedley D. **Butler**, William Banks Caperton, John Lejeune, Joseph H. Pendleton, Leonard Wood, and Fred Funston. During this thirty-year period the United States ruled in Cuba, Haiti, the Dominican Republic, Nicaragua, Honduras, and Mexico. America's tropical empire lacked the colonial experience of nineteenth-century colonial powers, relied on the military to carry out its nation-building efforts, and ultimately failed to created the institutions and values conducive to economic modernization, political stability, and democratic rule. The banana wars were not inter-American "wars" as much as they were military interventions in which a relatively small number of U.S. troops—Navy, Army, and Marine Corps—were dispatched to help extend the power of the United States in Central America and the Caribbean. Despite large banana industries in Colombia and Ecuador, there were no banana wars in South America.

The banana wars are still viewed as a disgraceful era among the subject countries, and the legacy of the long occupations is mostly critical of what the banana warriors failed to accomplish. Despite some achievements in the areas of health, education, and communication, the banana warriors failed as rulers of conquered lands. Lester Langley points out that the American military took to its task reluctantly, but assumed they could improve the conditions of people in the tropics by an American form of tutelage. However, as saviors of poor and dark-skinned people, "Their presence, even when it meant a peaceful society and material advancement, stripped Caribbean peoples of their dignity and constituted an unspoken American judgement of Caribbean inferiority" (Langley, 2002: 220). Washington's motives for intervention were many, including strategic and economic considerations; however, some lumped every justification for intervention under the rubric of eliminating "disorder and chaos." In each case of military intervention in civil wars, rebellions, or **revolutions**, presidents exaggerated the threats to U.S. national security to mobilize support from Congress and the American people. Although the **Monroe Doctrine** set the foundation for national security on removing foreign threats, the banana wars demonstrated that a more aggressive foreign policy often required the manipulation of foreign dangers abroad to achieve specific political goals at home. The failed interventionism during the period when the banana wars flourished led to the U.S. propensity to support Latin American dictators who in return promised to maintain order and respect American lives and property. The banana wars helped expand an empire based on military intervention and occupation, war, military government, and enlightened guidance. What the United States failed to realize was that its Caribbean **imperialism** did not take into account the strong desire within the occupied countries to be ultimately in charge of their own destinies. This seeped into the political cultures of these countries and eventually produced a backlash in the form of anti-American revolutionary ferment. *See also* Banana Republic; Intervention and Non-Intervention; Threat Perception/Assessment.

Suggested Reading

Lester D. Langley, *The Banana Wars: United States Intervention in the Caribbean, 1898–1934*, rev. ed. (Wilmington, DE: Scholarly Resources, 2002); Langley, *The Banana Wars: An Inner History of American Empire, 1900–1934* (Lexington: University of Kentucky Press, 1983); Allan R. Millett, *Semper Fidelis: The History of the United States Marine Corps* (New York: Macmillan, 1980); Dana G. Munro, *Intervention and Dollar Diplomacy in the Caribbean: 1900–1921* (Princeton, NJ: Princeton University Press, 1964); Ivan Musicat, *The Banana Wars: A History of U.S. Military Intervention in Latin America from the Spanish American War to the Invasion of Panama* (New York: Macmillan, 1990); Whitney Perkins, *Constraint of Empire: The United States and Caribbean Interventions* (Westport, CT: Greenwood Press, 1981); Emily S. Rosenberg, *Financial Missionaries to the World: The Politics and Culture of Dollar Diplomacy, 1900–1930* (Cambridge, MA: Harvard University Press, 1999); Steve Striffler and Mark Moberg, eds., *Banana Wars: Power, Production, and History in the Americas* (Durham, NC: Duke University Press, 2003).

Barrett, John (1866–1938) Diplomat, journalist and promoter of **Pan-Americanism** who served in Latin America during the progressive era. After changing his party affiliation from Democrat to Republican, Barrett was appointed by President **Theodore Roosevelt** to serve in Argentina (1903), Panama (1904), and Colombia (1905). His work in improving relations between the United States and Colombia after the revolution and separation of Panama helped him become the director-general of the **Pan American Union**, a post he held for thirteen years after his appointment in 1907. He wrote several books on Pan-Americanism after his diplomatic career ended and before his death in 1938. A native of Vermont, Barrett graduated from Dartmouth College in 1889; he retired to his home state and spent his last years there writing and following world affairs. *See also* Organization of American States (OAS).

Suggested Reading

John Dumbrell, *The Making of U.S. Foreign Policy* (New York: Manchester University Press, 1997); Salvatore Prisco, III, *John Barrett, Progressive Era Diplomat* (University: University of Alabama Press, 1973); *New York Times* (October 1, 1938).

Batista, Fulgencio (1901–1973) A military and political leader of Cuba from the 1930s to his overthrow by Fidel **Castro** and his 26th of July Movement on January 1, 1959. He rose to power in 1933 as one of the key members of the Sergeant's Revolt that overthrew President Machado, paving the way for the short-lived 1933 Revolution. Despite having been elected president of Cuba in 1940 for a four-year term, Batista finished his presidential term and spent more time in Florida than in Cuba during the next two administrations. Although he was a candidate in the 1952 presidential election, Batista decided he could not wait for the election and seized power in a bloodless coup that year. Once in power again he proceeded to establish a repressive dictatorship. The national revulsion against the corruption and greed of his government, and the violent counter-measures against opponents drove him into exile. In the early stages of the Cuban Revolution, Batista's followers and supporters, particularly his hated secret police, who engaged in torture and **assassination** prior to 1959, were subject to criminal prosecution. After a brief stay in the Dominican Republic after fleeing Cuba, Batista fled to Portugal and finally Spain, where he lived in comfortable exile until his death in 1973.

Fulgencio Batista was born on January 16, 1901, in Banes, Oriente Province. His father was a railroad laborer, and Batista spent his early years in poverty. He attended a Quaker missionary school in Oriente, but left school to work at a variety of menial jobs before joining the Cuban army at age twenty. The military provided Batista with the opportunity for social and economic mobility. After graduating from the National School of Journalism, Batista was promoted to sergeant and assigned to Camp Columbia in Havana where he came in contact with frustrated and ambitious non-commissioned officers and civilian opponents of the Machado **dictatorship**. In what became known as the Sergeant's Revolt, Batista and a number of younger officers and disenchanted students seized control of the government on September 4, 1933. This was a significant event in Cuban political life as it brought the Cuban military into national political life, energized high school and university students to pursue a **revolution** that would rid the country's constitution of the **Platt Amendment** and the dominant role of the United States in Cuban political life. The 1933 Revolution brought Dr. Ramón Grau San Martín to power with a revolutionary agenda of dramatic political and economic change.

After President Ramón Grau became president of Cuba in September 1933, U.S. Ambassador Sumner **Welles** shifted his support from Grau to Batista, an army chief who he believed represented the best hope for stability, authority, and protection of U.S. economic interests. By denying President Grau the necessary recognition from the United States, Batista became one of the **friendly dictators** who Washington thought saved Cuba from disorder and anarchy. Batista enjoyed American support from 1934 until his dictatorship collapsed in 1958. After his coup in 1952, Batista welcomed organized crime figures from the United States to run Havana's casinos and increased his ties with the United States to help maintain his dictatorship. Meyer **Lansky**—the chief mob boss in Havana—is reported to have deposited more than $3 million in Batista's Swiss bank accounts, and the dictator's total wealth was estimated at somewhere between $100 and $300 million by the time he was driven into exile. Until he became a political embarrassment to the United States in 1958, Batista was viewed as a "strong and vigorous leader" who maintained a tough stance against the Communists and who was a key ally in the **Cold War**. Members of the Eisenhower administration praised Batista for his anticommunism, close ties with the Cuban military, and his reliability as a client of the United States. The new generation of regime opponents, including Fidel Castro, mobilized and tried to kill Batista, but were unsuccessful. Batista's repressive government met **terrorism** with counter-terrorism; thousands were imprisoned for their political beliefs, tortured, and assassinated by the secret police and the military. The strength of Castro's guerrilla army and the weak and unprofessional army of Batista brought an end to the Batista dictatorship on the evening of December 31, 1958. Batista left for the Dominican Republic and later to the Portuguese Madeira Islands where he wrote several books condemning Fidel Castro, the United States, and offering numerous justifications for his failed regime. He spent his last years in Madrid, Spain, before he died on August 6, 1973, at the age of seventy-two. Batista's son moved to Florida; his grandson, Raoul Cantero, became a Florida Supreme Court Justice and a strong supporter of the dissident movement, inside and outside Cuba. *See also* Dictatorships; Eisenhower, Dwight D.; Friendly Dictators.

Suggested Reading

Fulgencio Batista, *The Growth and Decline of the Cuban Republic* (New York: Devin-Adair, 1964); Batista, *Cuba Betrayed* (New York: Random House, 1962); Edmund A. Chester, *A Sergeant Named Batista* (New York: Henry Holt, 1954); Irwin F. Gellman, *Roosevelt and Batista: Good Neighbor Diplomacy in Cuba, 1933–1945* (Albuquerque: University of New Mexico Press, 1973); Thomas M. Leonard, *Castro and the Cuban Revolution* (Westport, CT: Greenwood Press, 1999); Thomas G. Paterson, *Contesting Castro: The United States and the Triumph of the Cuban Revolution* (New York: Oxford University Press, 1994); Harold Sims, "Cuba," in Leslie Bethell and Ian Roxborough, eds., *Latin American Between the Second World War and the Cold War, 1944–1948* (Cambridge: Cambridge University Press, 1992).

Bay of Pigs (1961) A major foreign policy blunder named after the coastal area southeast of Havana where the United States sponsored an invasion of Cuba in 1961 to topple the **Castro** government. Code-named "Operation Zapata," the Bay of Pigs invasion was one of many covert operations carried out by U.S. presidents against the Cuban government and its revolutionary leaders. After taking a "wait-and-see" posture toward Castro's revolution, by early 1960 the **Dwight Eisenhower** administration decided it could no longer remain tolerant of Fidel Castro and his brand of anti-Americanism, pro-communism, and support for **revolutions** that threatened U.S. **hegemony** and investments in Latin America and the Caribbean. Convinced that it would be impossible to get along with Castro because of his political and economic orientations, Eisenhower's Latin American advisers devised a plan that included the organization of a relatively small expeditionary force of Cuban exiles who were recruited in Miami, Florida, and then sent to secret camps in Guatemala and Nicaragua where the **Central Intelligence Agency (CIA)** would supply and train them for an eventual invasion of the island.

At its core, the Bay of Pigs invasion relied on **Cold War** policymakers in Washington who believed that Castro's revolution posed an ideological and security threat to the United States and the rest of Latin America. At first, the debate inside Washington centered on whether Fidel Castro was a Communist and if so, what kind was he? Was he a Soviet agent under Moscow's domination and therefore a proxy Communist government that threatened the historical domination of the United States in Latin America? Fidel Castro decided to visit the United States in April 1959 and spent an afternoon discussing the revolution and its goals with Vice-President Richard **Nixon**. In a memo written after the meeting that took place in the Old Executive Office Building, Nixon concluded that Castro was "incredibly naive about communism" and eventually came to believe that Castro was an authentic Communist. Nixon's memo from that brief encounter would soon become the genesis of the Bay of Pigs invasion two years later.

In March 1960, Eisenhower set in motion plans that would eventually culminate in the disastrous Bay of Pigs invasion on April 17, 1961, one of the major foreign policy blunders during the Cold War. Eisenhower's top aides apparently ignored **public opinion** polls indicating an overwhelming degree of support for Fidel Castro on the island. Nevertheless, with CIA successes in Guatemala (1954) and Iran (1953) in mind, Operation Zapata went forward despite faulty planning inside the White House and erroneous assumptions about Castro and the Cuban Revolution. Political pressures in the United States to "do something" about Castro increased as he confiscated more and more U.S. property and the Soviets appeared to be creating a Russian colony near the U.S. mainland. The politics of hostility that would dominate U.S.–Cuban relations for decades after the revolution grew out of the pattern of domination that the United States exercised over Cuba since the days of the **Spanish-Cuban-American War** of 1898. When the

United States eliminated Cuba's sugar quota, thereby wiping out the large U.S. market, Castro retaliated by nationalizing American-owned industrial and agrarian enterprises, as well as banks and public utility companies.

For many foreign policy bureaucrats in the Eisenhower administration, Castro's presence in Cuba amounted to a grave challenge to the **Monroe Doctrine** and America's security. As Castro's links to the Soviet Union became more firm, **Washington policymakers** began increasingly to refer to the Monroe Doctrine in the press and in Congress as the primary justification for some kind of hostile action against Cuba. For example, in legislative debate on June 30, 1960, Congressman Mendel Rivers (D-SC) lashed out at Cuba by demonizing Fidel Castro, invoking the Monroe Doctrine, and asserting a military formula for revenge:

> We should issue a proclamation telling him [Fidel Castro] what this Nation proposes to do if he keeps on blackmailing and vilifying our President [Eisenhower] and our people and taking property without due process of law. We should assert the Monroe Doctrine. We should threaten Castro with [a military] blockade. We should, if necessary, and if conditions demand it, occupy Cuba. (*Congressional Record*, June 30, 1960, p. 15228)

Shortly thereafter Soviet premier Nikita Khrushchev called a press conference and announced the death of the Monroe Doctrine, putting the United States on notice that it was no longer the sole hegemonic power in the Western Hemisphere. By this time the United States was furious at the Cubans and the Soviets and demands for military **intervention** in Cuba increased.

Meanwhile, Cuba became an issue in the hotly contested 1960 presidential election. John F. **Kennedy** attacked the Eisenhower administration for its failure to remove Castro, to defuse the Cuban threat, and stated publicly that as president he would support the use of armed Cuban forces in exile to overthrow Fidel Castro. Kennedy's position was quite popular at the time, and he agreed to implement the CIA plan to overthrow forcefully Castro three months after he took office. In their televised debate on October 21, 1960, Vice-President Nixon distinguished himself from Kennedy's views for handling Castro by stating that what Senator Kennedy recommends is "the most dangerously irresponsible recommendations that he's made during the course of this campaign." Not knowing that Kennedy, as had the vice-president, had been fully briefed by the CIA on the secret plans for the invasion of Cuba, Nixon (1962: 355) countered Kennedy's interventionist rhetoric with the following: "Now I don't know what Senator Kennedy suggests when he says that we should help those who oppose the Castro regime both in Cuba and without. But I do know this, that if we were to follow that recommendation that we would lose all of our friends in Latin America, we would probably be condemned in the **United Nations (UN)**, and we would not accomplish our objective. I know something else. It would be an open invitation for Mr. Khrushchev to come in, to come into Latin America and to engage us in what would be a civil war and possibly even worse than that." Vice-President Nixon was essentially correct in his rebuttal, but he did not know it at the time, and his rhetoric lost him both the debate and the presidential election.

The Eisenhower-Nixon plan to remove Castro was inherited by Kennedy and continued on course for almost two years as a covert operation. Using the successful removal of President Jacobo **Arbenz** in 1954 as a model, the CIA trained and equipped exile mercenaries to overthrow Castro using an amphibious landing at Playa Girón, a stretch of beach inside the Bay of Pigs where the decisive battle took place. However, the April 17–19 invasion was a disaster for the Kennedy administration, as Castro managed to defeat the invaders in a series of lopsided battles that lasted only seventy-two hours. Most of the 2506 Brigade (the numbers were inflated to portray a much larger invasion force) were taken prisoner and later released after the United States traded $50 million in medicines and equipment for their return. In a spirit of vengeful retaliation, President Kennedy spent the remainder of his presidency trying to remove Castro from power by means of secret assassination attempts, economic sanctions in the form of a trade embargo to undermine the revolution, and pressuring the **Organization of American States (OAS)** for his removal on the basis of his "Marxist-Leninist" government. After the Bay of Pigs invasion Kennedy spoke publicly of some useful lessons to learn from the Cuban debacle, namely, the growing threat of communism in Cuba and in every corner of the globe, including Vietnam and other regions where "free nations" are threatened and exploited.

All of Washington's plans for violent action against Castro were a total failure. The blundering attempts of each successive American president to remove the Cuban leader only solidified his rule and helped provide the Soviet Union with a nearby military (or nuclear) base against the United States, the exact opposite of what the United States had intended. It was clearly a shining example of how not to conduct foreign policy or covert intervention in the hemisphere. To keep America's pledge to the inter-American doctrine of non-intervention in the affairs of neighboring states, Kennedy agreed to go ahead with Operation Zapata, but insisted that U.S. armed forces would not be involved. The failure at the Bay of Pigs damaged the Kennedy administration's legitimacy in Latin America, led directly to the **Cuban Missile Crisis** in 1962, drove Cuba further into the Soviet camp, and trained a bevy of Cuban-American agents to carry out Washington's secret and dirty work abroad. In many ways, the Bay of Pigs failure was a Godsend for Castro; it undermined U.S.–Latin American relations and boosted Castro's political legitimacy as a stalwart foe of Yankee **imperialism**. During a meeting in Montevideo, Uruguay, with Kennedy envoy Richard Goodwin, Che **Guevara** thanked the United States for the Bay of Pigs invasion since it had done wonders for Castro's revolutionary stature throughout the hemisphere. Some of the veterans of the Bay of Pigs invasion formed **terrorist** organizations in the United States and carried out numerous terrorist acts at home and abroad in an effort to weaken or destroy the Cuban Revolution. Many of the key participants in the Bay of Pigs operation were recruited for subsequent secret activities such as Watergate and the **Iran-Contra**

scandal. The Bay of Pigs invasion was a costly covert operation. Of the 1,453 brigade members, 114 were killed and more than 1,000 were captured by Castro's militia and armed forces. The United States lost four members of the Alabama Air National Guard who joined in the invasion, and close to 150 Cubans died defending Cuban territory.

Until the end of the Cold War, most of the sensitive documents pertaining to Operation Zapata were classified secret and kept from public view. However, by the late 1990s the U.S. government was pressured to release a number of documents under the Freedom of Information Act to the National Security Archive in Washington, D.C. In 1998, the CIA produced a 150-page report—a brutally honest self-criticism that exposed the blunders at the Bay of Pigs in 1961—that depicted the secret operation as "ludicrous or tragic or both" and claimed that among the officers chosen to carry out the ill-fated invasion, "very few spoke Spanish or had Latin American background knowledge" to do the job adequately. The "perfect failure" at the Bay of Pigs prompted the military to engineer a series of plans to take charge and do what Kennedy failed to do: rid Cuba of Castro. In a recent book by James Bamford, *Body of Secrets*, he discovered documents from the National Security Agency that the Pentagon had concocted **Operation Northwoods** to provoke a war (and invasion) with Cuba by blaming terrorists' acts in the United States on Fidel Castro. Fortunately, those at the highest levels of the American government refused to sign-off on the operation.

After more than forty years, the Bay of Pigs invasion remains one of the worst foreign policy decisions of the United States and one of the hallmarks of Cuban resistance to Washington's hostility and aggression in Latin America and the Caribbean. Kennedy's failure to remove Castro created a new world in which he felt the need to act more aggressively to show the Soviets he had the guts to be president of the United States, as well as retain the credibility of American commitments around the world. Tourists who visit the Bay of Pigs today will find a large billboard at the entrance that reads: "Playa Girón: First Defeat of Yankee Imperialism in the Western Hemisphere." *See also* Alpha 66; Assassination; Bissell, Richard; Blowback; Covert Operations; Intervention and Non-Intervention; Scandals and Blunders; Szulc, Tadeusz Witold.

Suggested Reading

Richard M. Bissell, *Reflections on a Cold Warrior: From Yalta to the Bay of Pigs* (New Haven: Yale University Press, 1996); James G. Blight and Peter Kornbluh, eds., *Politics of Illusion: The Bay of Pigs Invasion Reexamined* (Boulder, CO: Lynne Rienner, 1999); Fidel Castro, *Playa Girón* (New York: Pathfinder Press, 2001); *Congressional Record*, 86th Congress, 2nd Session (June 30, 1960), vol. 106, Part II, p. 15228; Trumbull Higgins, *The Perfect Failure: Kennedy, Eisenhower and the CIA at the Bay of Pigs* (New York: W.W. Norton, 1987); Robert H. Holden and Eric Zolov, eds., *Latin America and the United States: A Documentary History* (New York: Oxford University Press, 2000); Haynes B. Johnson, *The Bay of Pigs: The Leader's Story of Brigade 2506* (New York: Norton, 1964); Peter Kornbluh, ed., *The Bay of Pigs Declassified: The Secret CIA Report on the Invasion of Cuba* (New York: The New Press, 1998); Richard M. Nixon,

Six Crises (Garden City, NY: Doubleday, 1962); *Operation Zapata: The "Ultrasensitive" Report and Testimony of the Board of Inquiry on the Bay of Pigs* (Frederick, MD: Aletheia Books, 1981); *The Truth About Lies* (video) (Alexandria, VA: PBS Video, 1989); Warren A. Trest and Don Dodd, *Wings of Denial: The Alabama Air National Guard's Covert Role of the Bay of Pigs* (Montgomery, AL: NewSouth Books, 2001); Victor Andres Triay, *Bay of Pigs: An Oral History of Brigade 2506* (Gainesville: University Press of Florida, 2001); Tim Weiner, "CIA Bares Its Bungling in Report on Bay of Pigs Invasion," *New York Times* (February 22, 1998: A6); Peter Wyden, *Bay of Pigs: The Untold Story* (New York: Simon and Schuster, 1979).

Beals, Carleton (1893–1979) Controversial freelance journalist best known for his support of revolutionary and anti-imperialist movements in Latin America from the 1920s to the 1960s. As a leftist journalist, he was one of the first to specialize in Latin American affairs. During his long career, Beals traveled throughout Latin America where he found social inequality, exploitation of the poor by the rich, and an overbearing presence of the United States in Mexico, Cuba, Nicaragua, Guatemala, and Peru. He endorsed the importance of sweeping social change to improve the lives of the impoverished masses and the exploited, by revolution and violence, if necessary. He found himself in the thick of the debate over U.S. imperialism in the 1920s, siding with Nicaragua's Augusto **Sandino**. His articles on Sandino for *The Nation* gained him the reputation as the leading spokesman of anti-imperialism and the enmity of the United States. Throughout his career, Beals claimed the United States was an imperialistic power because of its overbearing **hegemony** in Latin America. Critical of military **intervention**, diplomatic intimidation, protectorates, and economic exploitation, Beals was reviled by international business leaders, the U.S. **State Department**, and many Latin American dictators friendly to the United States.

Carleton Beals visited many Latin American countries during times of turmoil and dramatic change and over time came to realize that American meddling did more harm than good. In *Banana Gold* (1932: 301), Beals wrote that "Nicaragua, under our [United States] paternal tutelage for so many years, had become the most backward and miserable of all Central American Republics." Beals was in Cuba prior to the downfall of Gerardo Machado and wrote *The Crime of Cuba* (1933), which appeared in print only days after the fall of Machado in the summer of 1933. The word "crime" in the title carried a double meaning for Beals, who hoped to publicize the plight of the Cuban people. The first referred to the criminal nature of Cuba's corrupt and despotic governments; the second referred to the unwarranted involvement of the United States in Cuba's internal affairs that Beals saw as the root cause of Cuba's political and economic problems. In *Great Guerrilla Warriors* (1970: 4) he asserted that "The major cause of our century's desperate guerrilla revolts is patently **imperialism** in its various aspects." In much of his writing, Beals sided with the underdog in a Robin Hood defense for those who carried out guerrilla tactics. Through his writings on timely and important issues in Latin America, Beals hoped to publicize the deplorable conditions he saw and arouse sympathy for the unfortunate people in Latin America.

Carleton Beals was born in Medicine Lodge, Kansas, on November 13, 1893, to parents who were staunch leftists active in the Populist party. His father was a lawyer and newspaper publisher in Medicine Lodge. His mother was born in Iowa, attended Oberlin College, and was active in feminist and prohibitionist activities before becoming a schoolteacher. Their political activism and socialist beliefs contributed to Beals' radical views. He received his B.A. from the University of California, Berkeley (1916) and a master's degree in History from Columbia University Teachers College (1917). Upset with the conservative approach to economics in an introductory class, Beals and a few other students went to Paul Blissen, a leftist economist who offered them a special non-credit course in "heretical" economics where they studied Ricardo, Engels, and Marx. One of his heroes at the time was Eugene V. Debs, a socialist labor leader he admired for his oratory and anti-war rhetoric. Both Beals and Debs—strong supporters of the American democratic tradition—rejected the notion that critical dissent is somehow anti-American or unpatriotic. Critics considered Beals' cynicism and misguided sympathies for some governments to be naive and unpatriotic. Through his books and articles, Carleton Beals offered a leftist approach to U.S.–Latin American relations, one that shared much in common with Juan José **Arévalo** and Alonso Aguilar. Conservative observers of U.S.–Latin American relations during the Beals era included Samuel Flagg **Bemis**, Dexter Perkins, Graham Stuart, and James L. Tigner.

After college, Beals headed south to Mexico and Central America where he encountered poverty, **dictatorships**, and American **Big Stick diplomacy**. While he wrote books on many topics, Beals became best known for his works on Latin America. The *New York Times* once referred to Beals as the "dean of correspondents in Latin America" for the depth and range of his on-site reporting. His lifelong interest in American imperialism, dictatorships, and guerrilla uprisings came from his own observations on life in Latin America. As an independent journalist, Beals visited over forty countries, all those in Latin America, where he observed numerous governmental turnovers and **revolutions**, and the heavy hand of the United States in Latin America. He was pleased by the defeat of colonialism and the rise of independent states, but he also said he was displeased with the string of "puppet dictatorships of the United States in Chile, Argentina, Uruguay and Brazil, frightful regimes all of them." In *Pan America* (1940), Beals looked at the dangers of U.S. dependency on critical raw materials such as petroleum, particularly with war clouds looming over Europe.

Over the years Beals discovered that Latin American topics failed to interest the reading public in the United States. Some editors resented his critical assessments of Latin American societies and prevailing U.S. policies. Carleton Beals was impressed with the reformist government of Guatemalan President Juan José Arévalo, a view that put him at odds with U.S. Central American policy and U.S. publishers who were reluctant to publish materials on Guatemala by those who held leftist beliefs. For criticizing the "military dictatorship" of Castillo Armas' government in Guatemala, Vice-President Richard **Nixon** called for a government investigation of Beals as a potential Communist.

The rise of Fidel **Castro** gave Beals the chance to report on another Latin American revolution, one he embraced with considerable enthusiasm and optimism. Castro's popularity in the U.S. **media** produced a surge of interest in Cuba and Latin America that motivated Beals to write more on the island nation in the throes of a revolution. He published nine articles on Cuba in 1959, but his age and the strains of first-hand investigation appear to have prevented him from writing a full-length book about Castro's Cuba. Five months before the disastrous **Bay of Pigs** invasion, Beals reported that the Castro government was increasingly aware of a U.S.–sponsored invasion of the island.

In 1960, Beals joined the Fair Play for Cuba Committee (FPCC), a loose coalition of U.S. leftists—C. Wright Mills, I.F. Stone, and Scott Nearing—sympathetic to the Cuban Revolution. The fact that Lee Harvey Oswald, the assassin of President John F. **Kennedy**, used the FPCC as a front for his activities damaged the legitimacy of the organization and led to right-wing attacks on Beals and other prominent writers who belonged to the organization. Carleton Beals and others were subject to FBI surveillance and newspaper attacks that asserted that the FPCC was a propaganda arm of the Castro regime and that its members were either Communist sympathizers or Communist dupes. He worked for Prensa Latina, a Cuban-based press syndicate whose purpose was to counter the bias in Reuters, UPI, and AP throughout Latin America. Beals would eventually leave the FPCC and Prensa Latina because of his aversion to hard-line Marxism, but he was hounded by the Kennedy administration for his caustic criticism of U.S.–Latin American policy. Beals retired to his farm in Killingworth, Connecticut, where he devoted his time to writing and following news events. Like most leftists, he was critical of Kennedy's **Alliance for Progress** and America's gradual involvement in the folly of Vietnam. However, he was inspired by the civil rights movement and the war protesters of the time.

Throughout his career he published more than 35 books and over 200 articles, although not all concerning Latin America and the Caribbean. His best-selling work, *The Coming Struggle for Latin America* (1938), dealt with the growing fear of totalitarian penetration of the Americas. His critical dissent never reached a wide audience, but his anti-imperialist and pro-revolutionary views served a purpose in challenging the dogmatic conservatism and racist views that influenced the Latin American policy of the United States. Carleton Beals died in 1979, the result of complications from an abdominal operation. After 1970, he was unable to find a publisher for his books, despite his depth of knowledge and decades of first-hand experience in Latin America. *See also* Anti-Imperialism; Friendly Dictators; Imperialism; Media; Somoza Debayle, Anastasio "Tachito"; Yankee *Fidelistas*.

Suggested Reading

Carleton Beals, *Great Guerrilla Warriors* (New York: Prentice-Hall, 1970); Beals, *Latin America: World in Revolution* (New York: Abelard Schuman, 1963); Beals, *What Latin Americans Think of Us* (New York: R.M. McBride, 1945); Beals, *Pan America: A Program for the Western Hemisphere* (Boston: Houghton Mifflin, 1940); Beals, *The Crime of Cuba* (Philadelphia: J.B.

Lippincott, 1933); Beals, *Banana Gold* (Philadelphia: J.B. Lippincott, 1932); Beals, *Con Sandino en Nicaragua* (San José, Costa Rica: Comité Pro-Sandino, 1929); John A. Britton, *Carleton Beals: A Radical Journalist in Latin America* (Albuquerque: University of New Mexico Press, 1987); Lester D. Langley, *The Banana Wars: U.S. Intervention in the Caribbean, 1898–1934* (Wilmington, DE: SR Books, 2002); Neil Macaulay, *The Sandino Affair* (Durham, NC: Duke University Press, 1985).

Beaulac, Willard Leon (1899–1990) Career diplomat and writer who held important ambassadorships in five Latin American countries from 1944 until his retirement from the **State Department** in 1960. Born in Pawtucket, Rhode Island, Beaulac attended Brown University, served in the U.S. Navy during **World War I**, and graduated from Georgetown University in 1921. After graduation, he joined the Foreign Service and served in numerous consular posts until 1933. He served as assistant chief, Division of Latin American Affairs and in several embassy posts in Havana, Cuba, and Madrid, Spain, before beginning his string of ambassadorships beginning in Paraguay in 1944. After three years in Asunción, he was appointed ambassador to Colombia (1947–1951), Cuba (1951–1953), Chile (1953–1956), and Argentina (1956–1960). During his career he worked to implement development programs, foster more democratic societies, create new educational exchange programs, and helped in the creation of the **Organization of American States (OAS)** in 1948. Beaulac went to Argentina soon after the overthrow of **Juan D. Perón** and welcomed Vice-President Richard **Nixon** on his 1958 "good will" visit to Argentina. Shortly before and after his retirement he wrote several books on Latin America, including *Career Ambassador* (1951) and *A Diplomat Looks at Aid to Latin America* (1970), and *The Fractured Continent* (1980). Willard Beaulac died in 1990 at the age of ninety-one. *See also* Ambassadors.

Suggested Reading

Willard L. Beaulac, *The Fractured Continent: Latin America in Close-up* (Stanford, CA: Hoover Institution Press, 1980); Beaulac, *A Diplomat Looks at Aid to Latin America* (Carbondale: Southern Illinois Press, 1970); Beaulac, *Career Ambassador* (New York: Macmillan, 1951).

Bemis, Samuel Flagg (1892–1973) Prize-winning writer and professor of diplomatic history and inter-American relations known for his staunch patriotism and defense of conservative Latin American policies. His writings defended the **Monroe Doctrine**, **Manifest Destiny**, the **Good Neighbor Policy**, protectorates such as the **Platt Amendment**, benevolent or protective **imperialism**, and the legitimacy of force to stop communism in the Western Hemisphere. He argued that the Latin American policy of the United States always contained two elements—national security and idealism—with national security always the most important of the two. He interpreted the imperialism in U.S.–Latin American policy from 1898 to 1930 as "a comparatively mild imperialism" designed to protect, first, the security of the United States and, second, the security of the entire Western Hemisphere. "It was, if you will, an imperialism against imperialism. It did not last long and it was not really bad" (Bemis: 1971: 386). Bemis believed that U.S. motives for interfering in Latin America were based on fostering political and economic stability to prevent European **intervention** in the New World. For those who criticized the United States for its diplomatic blunders, economic imperialism, and arrogance toward the Latin Americans, Bemis would say that U.S. policy has been rooted in a desire to create a better hemisphere, not to control or dictate the fate of the Latin American republics.

Bemis was born in Worcester, Massachusetts, received college degrees from Clark University and Harvard where he earned advanced degrees in history. From 1917 when he began his teaching career at Colorado College, he taught at Whitman College, George Washington University, Harvard, and Yale. He spent the last twenty-five years of his distinguished career at Yale University. A proponent of multiarchival research, Bemis wrote many diplomatic histories that were sometimes criticized for their defense of American foreign policy. He admired John Quincy **Adams** and his two-volume biography of Adams won Bemis a second Pulitzer Prize. He established himself as one of the major scholars on the history of U.S.–Latin American relations in *The Latin American Policy of the United States* (1943), a widely used textbook on the subject until the 1960s.

Despite his long teaching career at Yale and his prize-winning books on diplomacy and American foreign policy, Samuel F. Bemis had little impact on policymakers in Washington. His robust patriotism and assertive views of U.S. intervention in Latin America made him an outcast in diplomatic and academic circles. Bemis did not try to hide his belief in Anglo-Saxon racial superiority and in much of his writings he supported a foreign policy that emphasized strategic and military interests. Bemis believed that the United States had engaged in "benevolent imperialism" in Latin America and that U.S. intervention would bring lasting positive results to countries that needed the guidance and stewardship of Washington. Bemis did not worry about questions of sovereignty, economic exploitation, and the consequences of supporting **friendly dictators**. There was never any doubt in Bemis' writing of North American superiority and the legitimacy of U.S. **hegemony** in Latin America. According to Berger (1995: 63), "Bemis measured the history of Latin America against a nationalist interpretation of the political and economic progress of the United States. Latin America's failure to achieve the level of civilization of the United States was ultimately traced to racial and meteorological handicaps." Bemis made himself an outcast in academic circles during the **Cold War** by arguing that members of the Communist Party should not be allowed to teach in American universities. Samuel Flagg Bemis died in Bridgeport, Connecticut, on September 26, 1973. *See also* Imperialism; Intervention and Non-Intervention; Scandals and Blunders; Washington Policymakers.

Suggested Reading

Samuel Flagg Bemis, *The Latin American Policy of the United States* (New York: W.W. Norton, 1961, 1971); Bemis, *American Foreign Policy and the Blessings of Liberty and Other Essays* (New Haven: Yale University Press, 1967); Bemis, *A Diplomatic History of the United States*

(New York: Holt, Rinehart and Winston, 1965); Bemis, *The American Secretaries of State and Their Diplomacy* (New York: Cooper Square Publishers, 1963); Bemis, *John Quincy Adams and the Foundations of American Foreign Policy* (New York: Alfred A. Knopf, 1949); Bemis, *The Latin American Policy of the United States: An Historical Interpretation* (New York: Harcourt Brace, 1943); Mark T. Berger, *Under Northern Eyes: Latin American Studies and U.S. Hegemony in the Americas 1898–1990* (Bloomington: Indiana University Press, 1995); Mark T. Gilderhus, "Founding Father: Samuel Flagg Bemis and the Study of U.S.–Latin American Relations," *Diplomatic History*, 21 (winter 1997).

Berle, Adolf A., Jr. (1895–1971) Adolf Berle was a key figure in Latin American affairs from the administration of **Franklin Delano Roosevelt** to that of John F. **Kennedy**. Berle was a Boston native who earned a B.A. and M.A. at Harvard University before graduating from Harvard Law School in 1916. He practiced law until 1917 before serving as an intelligence officer in the U.S. Army in the Caribbean. His legal background helped him become a delegate to the Paris Peace Conference where he negotiated the Treaty of Versailles that ended **World War I**. Prior to joining Roosevelt's campaign for president in 1932, he was a successful corporate lawyer in New York and a teacher at Columbia Law School. During the Roosevelt administration he helped execute the **Good Neighbor Policy**, attended several Pan-American conferences as special representative of the president, and drafted the president's policy on wartime relations with the Latin American states during **World War II**. Disillusioned over the outcome of World War I—communism in Russia, the Great Depression, and the rise of Hitler in Germany—Berle believed in economic appeasement as the best way to protect American interests and promote peace in Europe. In 1945, he was appointed ambassador to Brazil; while in that position he represented the United States at an inter-American conference in Mexico City where he helped draft the Act of **Chapultepec** on matters related to Western Hemisphere security. Until he was recruited by President-elect John F. Kennedy to advise him on the creation of a new Latin American policy, he spent fifteen years away from government service.

Adolf Berle's ties to Roosevelt's Latin American policies, and an original member of the president's Brains Trust, made him a logical candidate to advise the Kennedy administration in the aftermath of the Cuban Revolution in 1959. He chaired Kennedy's Task Force on Latin America and in the final report argued for the urgency of keeping China and the Soviet Union out of Latin America. However, this would require a new American foreign policy toward right-wing **dictatorships**. In his view, the United States needed to place more emphasis on **human rights** and governments that are freely elected by the people. The report recognized the need for social and economic reform, political order and stability, and the availability of new resources from the public and private sectors to provide investment, loans, and technical assistance to Latin America. In a private letter to Kennedy, Berle stated that "Success of the American effort in Latin America requires that at all times its policy be based on clear, consistent, moral democratic principles" (quoted in Schmitz, 1999: 239). The Berle report served as the basis for Kennedy's **Alliance for Progress**, a $20 billion aid program conceived as the answer to Latin America's lack of economic progress and the threat from Fidel **Castro**'s recent revolution in Cuba. It was clearly a **Cold War** document, one that stressed the need for a common approach to the development problems confronting the Western Hemisphere. Berle's report also contained elements of Monroeism, suggesting that "alien forces" might attempt to impose the despotisms of the Old World on the people of the New World.

As one of Kennedy's closest advisers, Berle was one of the top officials who endorsed U.S. backing for the disastrous **Bay of Pigs** invasion in 1961. After assisting Kennedy with his Latin American policies, Berle left public service again and returned to New York where he practiced law and taught until his death in 1971 at the age of seventy-six. Having experienced the devastation and blunders associated with World War I and II, Adolf Berle believed that the Soviet Union was doing what the Germans did in Latin America decades earlier: exploit any weakness in Latin America to gain an advantage over the United States. Adolf Berle's reports from Latin America served to reinforce the containment doctrine, so important to the Cold War policies of the United States in Latin America. *See also* Ambassadors; Scandals and Blunders; Threat Perception/Assessment.

Suggested Reading

Adolf Augustus Berle, *Navigating the Rapids, 1918–1971* (New York: Harcourt Brace Jovanovich, 1973); Berle, *Latin America: Diplomacy and Reality* (New York: Harper and Row, 1962); Berle, *The Cold War in Latin America* (Storrs, CT: University of Connecticut Press, 1961); Berle, *Tides of Crisis: A Primer of Foreign Relations* (London: Macmillan, 1957); Beatrice Bishop Berle, *A Life in Two Worlds: The Autobiography of Beatrice Bishop Berle* (New York: Walker, 1983); Stephen G. Rabe, *The Most Dangerous Area in the World: John F. Kennedy Confronts Communist Revolution in Latin America* (Chapel Hill: University of North Carolina Press, 1999); Jordan A. Schwarz, *Liberal: Adolf A. Berle and the Vision of an American Era* (New York: Free Press, 1987); U.S. Department of State, *Foreign Relations of the United States, 1950, 2: The United Nations, The Western Hemisphere,* "Memorandum by the Counselor of the Department (Kennan) to the Secretary of State," March 29, 1950, pp. 598–624 (Washington, DC: GPO, 1976); Randall B. Woods, *The Roosevelt Foreign-Policy Establishment and the "Good Neighbor": The United States and Argentina, 1941–1945* (Lawrence: Regents Press of Kansas, 1979).

Bernays, Edward L. (1891–1995) Known as the father of public relations, Edward Bernays played a key role in crafting the **propaganda** that would set the stage for the overthrow of the elected government of Jacobo **Arbenz** in Guatemala in 1954. He was a master of spin and helped design the political campaign that convinced the U.S. government that Arbenz was a socialist devil that threatened the United States because of his treatment of the **United Fruit Company**. After Bernay's death in 1995, the Library of Congress made public thousands of documents concerning his role in toppling Guatemala's left-leaning regime in the 1950s. In his book, *The Father of Spin* (1998: 156), Larry Tye claims these written materials "make clear how the United States viewed its Latin American neighbors as ripe for economic exploitation and political manipulation—and how the propaganda war Bernays waged in Guatemala set the pattern for future U.S.–led campaigns in Cuba and, much later, Vietnam." His counter-Communist propaganda was not guess work and improvisation; he believed that the **Cold War** could be fought, and won, with scientific precision.

Samuel **Zemurray**, head of United Fruit, hired Bernays as his public relations counsel in the early 1940s. To boost sales of Central American bananas in the United States, Bernays went to work linking bananas to good health, sports competition, national defense, hemispheric solidarity, and **Pan-Americanism**. His approach was rather simple: what's good for United Fruit is good for the United States. However, Bernays also believed that Americans needed to be educated about Central America and the positive role of the United Fruit Company in places like Guatemala, Honduras, Nicaragua, Costa Rica, and Panama. He advised Zemurray that United Fruit needed to demonstrate that it cared about the region where it was making lots of money. If United Fruit had problems with low worker morale and substandard living conditions, Bernays believed that they could all be solved with sound public relations. United Fruit was not interested in this advice for business reforms, but after nine years it finally reconsidered and began to implement some of Bernays' reforms. The belated reforms were too late to do much about the wealth of the United Fruit Company, by 1950 the number one employer, landowner, and exporter with close ties to the Guatemalan elite and **Washington policymakers**.

Guatemala provided the perfect environment for foreign capitalists with caps on workers' earnings, exemption from internal taxation, duty-free imports of goods, and assistance with maintaining its monopoly on the country's only Atlantic seaport and every mile of railroad. Revolutionary change—democratic or nondemocratic—would not be welcome in Guatemala. Bernays helped sound the Cold War alarms by asserting that Guatemala was in the throes of a revolution and the Communists were taking over close to the United States, threatening to ruin American business interests. With a **media** blitz that included the circulation of fact sheets to major newspapers and magazines, Edward Bernays persuaded writers and editors to discuss the "deplorable pro-Communist conditions" in Guatemala and the potential threats to U.S. economic and security interests. He mastered the technique of getting sympathetic publications to print favorable stories supporting his view of the Guatemalan "reality." He carefully staged visits for American journalists to see United Fruit operations in Guatemala, trips geared to make sure that each visit resulted in writers and editors concurring with United Fruit's position on the nature of the conflict. Bernays was so good at subtle propagandizing on behalf of United Fruit that few questioned the veracity of his claims of Communist influence in Guatemala, although Cold War paranoia and ignorance of Latin America also contributed to the power of his manipulation.

Once the **Eisenhower** administration concluded that President Arbenz was a threat, the United Fruit Company and its chief propagandist played a major role in the CIA-backed coup that put an end to Guatemala's revolutionary government. Edward Bernays not only devised a Cold War formula for "**regime change**" in

Guatemala, he convinced Washington policymakers that the same recipe could be repeated easily in Cuba, Chile, and elsewhere in Latin America. Bernays continued his war against communism in Latin America, first, by ensuring the success of the corrupt and repressive Carlos Castillo Armas, Arbenz's successor, and, then, waging a similar battle against Cuba's Fidel **Castro**. After leaving his job at United Fruit in 1959, Bernays spent time answering his critics who claimed he exaggerated the Communist threat in Guatemala, refusing to believe that some would doubt his "objectivity." A pioneer in public relations, propaganda and **public opinion**, Edward L. Bernays died in 1995. He left a legacy that still haunts Guatemala and U.S.–Guatemalan relations.

Suggested Reading

Edward L. Bernays, *Biography of an Idea: Memoirs of Public Relations Counsel Edward L. Bernays* (New York: Simon and Schuster, 1965); Bernays, *Fighting the Fifth Column in the Americas* (Charlottsville, VA: Institute of Public Affairs, 1939); Piero Gleijeses, *Shattered Hope: The Guatemalan Revolution and the United States, 1944–1954* (Princeton, NJ: Princeton University Press, 1991); Daniel James, *Red Design for the Americas: Guatemalan Prelude* (New York: Day, 1954); Charles David Kepner, *The Banana Empire: A Case Study of Economic Imperialism* (New York: Russell & Russell, 1967); Thomas McCann, *On the Inside: A Story of Intrigue and Adventure, on Wall Street, in Washington, and in the Jungles of Central America* (Boston: Quinlan Press, 1987); Stephen Schlesinger and Stephen Kinzer, *Bitter Fruit: The Story of the American Coup in Guatemala*, expanded ed. (Cambridge, MA: Harvard University Press, 1999); Larry Tye, *The Father of Spin: Edward L. Bernays and the Birth of Public Relations* (New York: Henry Holt, 1998); Richard Weiner, *Dictionary of Media and Communications* (New York: Macmillan, 1996).

Betancourt, Rómulo (1908–1981) Venezuelan democratic reformer who headed the revolutionary junta that ruled from 1945 to 1948, and was elected president from 1959 to 1964. As a young lawyer and veteran of previous efforts to replace **dictatorships** with democratic rule, Betancourt played a major role in Venezuelan politics and U.S.–Latin American relations during the first three decades following **World War II**. His ideas of economic development, **human rights**, anti-communism, and social change were incorporated into **Kennedy**'s **Alliance for Progress** as a model for democratic reform governments throughout the hemisphere. He came to power at the same time as Fidel **Castro**, but instead of immediate revolution Betancourt championed gradual reform and eventually broke relations with Cuba in November 1961, charging Castro with interference in Venezuela's internal affairs. His name was associated with the "Betancourt Doctrine," a policy of not recognizing Latin American dictatorships of any stripe, including governments established by military coup. The Kennedy administration embraced Betancourt for his opposition to Fidel Castro and backed the U.S. effort to expel Cuba from the **Organization of American States (OAS)** in 1962 and the OAS-declared economic blockade in 1964.

Rómulo Betancourt represented the ideal type of leader in Latin America for the

Kennedy administration, and Venezuela became one of the key targets for Alliance for Progress largesse. On a visit to Latin America in February 1961, special assistant to the president Arthur Schlesinger, Jr., reported on the major obstacles to modernization and concluded that the United States needed to promote middle-class revolutions to undermine Castro and the Communists. After his visit he told Kennedy that if the upper classes of Latin America make middle-class **revolutions** impossible, they will make revolutions from below inevitable, meaning that "if they destroy Betancourt, they will guarantee a Castro or **Perón**" (Schmitz, 1999: 242). Betancourt played a crucial role in expanding Venezuela's role in hemispheric affairs and managed to keep the country on a democratic path despite five attempted right-wing coups in 1961 and an **assassination** attempt against him by the Dominican Republic's dictator, General Rafael L. **Trujillo** in 1960. During his administration Betancourt played a leading role in the founding of the Organization of Petroleum Exporting Countries (OPEC), but he refused to nationalize the petroleum industry as many Venezuelan nationalists wished. By backing the Betancourt administration, President Kennedy and his advisers hoped to convince aspiring Latin American leaders that the democratic road to national development was far more likely to succeed than the Castro road. Betancourt died after suffering a stroke on a visit to New York City in 1981. *See also* Democracy and Democracy Promotion.

Suggested Reading

Robert Jackson Alexander, *Venezuela's Voice for Democracy: Conversations and Correspondence with Rómulo Betancourt* (New York: Praeger, 1990); Alexander, *Rómulo Betancourt and the Transformation of Venezuela* (New Brunswick, NJ: Transaction Books, 1982); Rómulo Betancourt, *Venezuela, Oil and Politics* (Boston: Houghton Mifflin, 1979); Betancourt, *Venezuela's Oil* (London: Allen and Unwin, 1978); Betancourt, *The Democratic Revolution in Latin America: Possibilities and Obstacles* (Storrs: University of Connecticut Press, 1965); Judith Ewell, *Indictment of a Dictator: Extradition and Trial of Marcos Pérez Jiménez* (College Station: Texas A&M Press, 1981); Larman C. Wilson and David W. Dent, *Historical Dictionary of Inter-American Organizations* (Lanham, MD: Scarecrow Press, 1998).

Bidlack, Benjamin Alden (1804–1849) Lawyer, politician, and diplomat prior to the U.S. Civil War who played a key role in negotiating a treaty with New Granada (as Colombia was then called) that contained transit rights through the isthmus of Panama in return for guarantees of isthmian neutrality and the protection of New Granada's sovereignty. This was the only treaty during the nineteenth century in which the United States agreed to the protection of sovereignty at the request of that state. The commercial treaty known as the **Bidlack-Mallarino Treaty** (signed in 1846 and ratified in 1848) represented the first diplomatic agreement between the United States and Colombia concerning a future Panama Canal. New Granada guaranteed to the United States and its citizens "the right of way or transit across the Isthmus of Panama upon any modes of communication that now exist, or that hereafter may be constructed." In return, the United States guaranteed the neutrality of the isthmus and the "rights of sovereignty and property" over it (Parks, 1968: 206–207). The binational treaty emerged from Bidlack's concern with British aggression in the Caribbean, French interest in a future canal, and Colombia's fear of European attempts to acquire territory in the isthmus. The treaty was a boon to the United States since it ensured canal privileges denied to other foreign powers.

Suggested Reading

Federico G. Gil, *Latin American–United States Relations* (New York: Harcourt Brace Jovanovich, 1971); E. Taylor Parks, *Colombia and the United States, 1765–1934* (New York: Greenwood Press, 1968).

Bidlack-Mallarino Treaty (1846) Also known as the Treaty of New Grenada, the Bidlack-Mallarino Treaty of 1846 was an agreement between the United States and Colombia (New Grenada) establishing transit rights across Colombia's northern province, the isthmus of Panama, in return for U.S. guarantees of Colombia's sovereignty. In the middle of the nineteenth century, French, British, and U.S. interests began to converge on a series of isthmian crossings as these nations vied to enhance their national power in the region. European forays into the Western Hemisphere went unchecked as the United States had neither the will nor the power to push a dynamic Latin American policy. By 1845, however, the United States and the **Polk** administration had fallen under the intoxicating spell of **Manifest Destiny** as the official dogma and territorial expansion became the official policy of the nation. Thus began a generation of imperialistic muscle flexing. The Polk Corollary broadened the definition of the No-Transfer Resolution to prohibit transfer of territory from an American state to a European state and forbade Mexico to sell California to Britain. The same year the United States annexed Texas and in 1846 began a two-year imperialistic war with Mexico and seizing over one-third of Mexico's territory (New Mexico and California). The United States was now a two-ocean nation, and the isthmus was now increasingly viewed as an essential component of the U.S. transportation system, linking the industrial cities of the East with the rapidly expanding Western towns. With new imperialistic pretensions and responsibilities, and on the eve of the great gold strikes in California, the United States again turned its attention to the strategic importance of the isthmus of Panama, province of Colombia, beginning a forced alliance that would last for the next 150 years.

The new American chargé d'affaires in Bogotá, Benjamin Alden **Bidlack** (1804–1849), had been sent by Washington to Colombia to gather information about interoceanic crossing rights at various sites in Central America and to prevent the government in New Grenada from granting transit privileges to any other extra-hemispheric (European) powers. The British had developed a colony in Central America and by controlling what is today the eastern coast of Honduras, Nicaragua, and Costa Rica, clearly threatened the essence of the **Monroe Doctrine**. Moreover, its colony placed Britain in a potentially strategic position to control travel and trade through the isthmus via plans for British interoceanic routes in Nicaragua and Costa Rica. The United States was also concerned with a French transit company that had commissioned an excellent study of the feasibility of a canal route, a railroad, or both through Panama.

American diplomat, Benjamin Bidlack, went far beyond his limited instructions from Washington to gather information, and, acting entirely on his own, negotiated a treaty with Colombia's foreign minister, Manuel María Mallarino. The key clause was contained in Article XXXV, guaranteeing to the United States exclusive and unrestricted transit rights on the isthmus of Panama "upon any mode of communication that now exists, or that may be, hereafter, constructed." In return, the United States assured the neutrality of, and New Granada's sovereignty over, the isthmus (McCullough, 1977: 32–33). The Bidlack-Mallarino Treaty—the only alliance treaty signed by the United States in the nineteenth century—committed the United States to an interoceanic railroad or canal under U.S. control, routed through Panama, with the right to intervene militarily to protect whatever transit facilities existed.

In Washington news of the Bidlack treaty was met with only passing interest, given the ongoing **Mexican-American War**, the fact that Bidlack had acted unilaterally and without instructions, and the old deep-seated American distrust of "entangling" alliances. Another year and a half would pass until the U.S. Senate ratified the Bidlack-Mallarino Treaty, after Mexico's cession, on June 8, 1848.

The Bidlack-Mallarino Treaty deeply altered politics in Central America and provided for an American presence in Panama far beyond what its signatories intended. The United States gained a strategic interest in Panama, one of the first outside its territory. Moreover, once the United States became the guarantor of free transit and Colombian sovereignty in Panama, U.S. leaders now increasingly viewed actions by the British or French as a threat to American national security. The **intervention** clause was exercised a total of thirteen times between 1848 and 1902, with U.S. troops landing a full half-century before the so-called **Banana Wars** of the early 1900s. The Bidlack-Mallarino Treaty was somewhat nullified by the 1850 **Clayton-Bulwer Treaty** that provided for joint U.S.–British control over any future canal. Yet, in 1902, President **Theodore Roosevelt** dusted off the old Bidlack treaty as sufficient legal precedent to proceed with a canal in Panama. To Roosevelt's way of thinking, the right of way at Panama was already "free and open" to the United States as stated in the treaty of 1846. Consequently, according to Roosevelt, the United States should proceed to construct a canal under American control and "fight Colombia if she objects" (McCullough, 1977: 341). *See also* Intervention and Non-Intervention.

Suggested Reading

Kevin Buckley, *Panama: The Whole Story* (New York: Simon and Schuster, 1991); Michael Conniff, *Panama and the United States: The Forced Alliance* (Athens: University of Georgia Press, 1992); David McCullough, *The Path Between the Seas: The Creation of the Panama Canal, 1870–*

1914 (New York: Simon and Schuster, 1977); E. Taylor Parks, *Colombia and the United States, 1765–1934* (New York: Greenwood Press, 1968); James F. Vivian, "The 'Taking' of the Panama Canal Zone: Myth and Reality," *Diplomatic History*, Vol. 4, No. 1 (winter 1980): 95–100.

Big Stick Diplomacy A descriptive phrase attributed to President **Theodore Roosevelt** (1901–1909) and his power-politics approach to dealing with Latin American nations. A West African proverb, "Speak softly and carry a big stick," captured the Latin American foreign policy of the Roosevelt administration; forceful diplomatic pressures and occasional U.S. troop landings were needed to preserve American strategic interests, especially in the Caribbean. Roosevelt feared that corrupt, incompetent governments in the circum-Caribbean might provoke European **imperialism** in violation of the **Monroe Doctrine**. Roosevelt held that power and the willingness to use it would make European creditors fully understand the Monroe Doctrine. In his annual message to Congress on December 6, 1904, Roosevelt amended the Monroe Doctrine's original, passive meaning into a more active U.S. policy toward Latin America with threatening clarity:

> Chronic wrongdoing, or an impotence which results in a general loosening of the ties of a civilized society, may in America, as elsewhere, finally require intervention by some civilized nation, and in the Western Hemisphere the adherence of the United States to the Monroe Doctrine may force the United States, however, reluctantly . . . to the exercise of an international police power. (Dent, 1999: 139)

To avoid any pretext for European **intervention**, the United States would now assume responsibility for maintaining order in the hemisphere. Caribbean and Latin American countries must in the future match their interests to those of the United States. If not, they would be policed. The "Big Stick" was the combined threatening and patronizing U.S. diplomacy toward small Central American and Caribbean states, backed by chronic American military intervention, along with the creation of financial protectorates and rhetorical justifications regarding democracy.

Big Stick intervention in the Dominican Republic in 1904 and Cuba in 1905 provoked widespread Latin American resentment and hostility toward the United States; it was increasingly viewed as a nation that would not hesitate to meddle in the internal affairs of another country to protect its interests. The **Roosevelt Corollary** paved the way for **gunboat diplomacy**—the use of limited naval force short of full-scale war as a supplement to diplomacy—in dealing with small, unstable Central American and Caribbean states, from 1904 until the **Good Neighbor Policy** of President **Franklin Delano Roosevelt** in 1933. Under Roosevelt's Corollary to the Monroe Doctrine, Big Stick diplomacy meant unilateral U.S. intervention in the hemisphere at its own discretion. It served to personify America's rise to world power, as the United States now claimed a regional hegemony in the name of security. Although his successors diverged in some respects from Roosevelt's raw, power politics in consolidating America's tropical empire, for the circum-

Caribbean nations, the big stick stung no less when dressed in President William Howard **Taft**'s **Dollar Diplomacy** or Wilsonian idealism regarding **democracy and democracy promotion**. *See also* Hegemony; Intervention and Non-Intervention; Wilsonianism.

Suggested Reading

Karl Berman, *Under the Big Stick: Nicaragua and the United States Since 1848* (Boston: South End Press, 1986); David Dent, *The Legacy of the Monroe Doctrine: A Reference Guide to U.S. Involvement in Latin America and the Caribbean* (Westport, CT: Greenwood Press, 1999); David Healy, *Drive to Hegemony: The United States in the Caribbean, 1898–1917* (Madison: University of Wisconsin Press, 1988); Edmund Morris, *Theodore Rex* (New York: Random House, 2001); Frank Nikovich, *The Wilsonian Century: U.S. Foreign Policy Since 1900* (Chicago: University of Chicago Press, 1999); Whitney T. Perkins, *Constraint of Empire: The United States and Caribbean Interventions* (Westport, CT: Greenwood Press, 1981).

Bissell, Richard (1909–1994) Economist and intelligence officer who played a major role in removing unfriendly foreign leaders from power in Latin America and other parts of the Third World. A graduate in economics from Yale University, Richard Bissell combined a career in economic analysis with government agencies involved in various aspects of intelligence service. He joined the Office of Strategic Services (OSS) during **World War II** and helped to organize guerrilla fighters and espionage and sabotage operations in Europe. He worked as an administrator of the Marshall Plan in Germany and later became the director of the Economic Cooperation Administration. After the OSS was abandoned and the **Central Intelligence Agency (CIA)** was created in 1947, Bissell joined the CIA and eventually became the agency's head of Directorate for Plans, a component of the CIA responsible for conducting anti-Communist operations around the world. With his deputy, Richard **Helms**, Bissell carried out policies known as Executive Action, secretive operations designed to remove foreign leaders considered a security threat to the United States. He was instrumental in organizing the **propaganda** and the coup d'ètat that overthrew the Guatemalan government of Jacobo **Arbenz** in 1954. Bissell's list of political leaders targeted for removal increased during the **Cold War** and included Patrice Lumumba (Congo), Rafael **Trujillo** (the Dominican Republic), General Abd-al-Karim Kassem (Iraq), Ngo Dinh Diem (South Vietnam), and his main target after 1959, Fidel **Castro** (Cuba). Bissell and Helms planned and organized the **Bay of Pigs** invasion against Castro in 1961, a covert plan to train a Cuban exile paramilitary force outside of Cuba for guerrilla action against Fidel Castro and the Cuban Revolution.

Richard Bissell was behind a number of schemes to undermine Fidel Castro's popularity with the Cuban people and drive him from power. When some of the more cautious schemes—spraying his television studio with an hallucinogenic drug and contaminating his shoes with Thallium powder to make his beard fall out—were rejected, Bissell turned to **assassination** plots with the help of **Allen W.**

Dulles, director of the CIA, and leading figures in the Mafia, including Johnny Roselli, Sam Giancana, Santos Trafficante, and Meyer **Lansky**. Despite the Mafia anger over Castro's closing of their lucrative casino, hotel, and prostitution activities, and a U.S. government offer of $150,000 to kill Castro, Mafia hit men got cold feet and the plot collapsed. Bissell admitted later that he was not prepared or competent to handle relations with the Mafia, but supported it anyway because he figured they had a good chance of success and from a moral standpoint the ends justified the means. In an interview with Bill Moyers in the 1970s, Bissell admitted it was a mistake to engage with the Mafia in a covert plan because of the possibility of blackmail.

The biggest black mark on Bissell's career was the blunder at the Bay of Pigs in April 1961. President John F. **Kennedy** had serious doubts about the venture, but Bissell and Dulles were convinced the plot would work. Kennedy also had a personal fear that he would suffer politically if he appeared to be "soft on communism" among the American public. President Kennedy admitted the invasion was a mistake, took full responsibility for the failure to topple Castro, but fired Allen W. Dulles and forced Bissell to resign. Richard Helms then took over as Director of Plans and continued covert attacks on the Cuban economy. After leaving the CIA, Bissell was president of the Institute for Defense Analysis between 1962 and 1964; during his final years he held top positions in several private companies. Richard Bissell died in 1994, two years before his autobiography, *Reflections of a Cold Warrior: From Yalta to the Bay of Pigs* (1996), was published. It is clear from his autobiography that Bissell's views on how to conduct foreign policy were influenced by his work with the OSS during World War II and the growing fear that the Soviets and Cubans were behind much of the threats to U.S. security in the same way that Germany and Italy threatened the United States and Western Europe in the 1930s and 1940s. *See also* Blowback; Covert Operations; Guatemala, U.S. Invasion of (1954); Revolutions; Threat Perception/Assessment.

Suggested Reading

Richard Bissell, *Reflections of a Cold Warrior: From Yalta to the Bay of Pigs* (New Haven: Yale University Press, 1996); James G. Blight and Peter Kornbluh, eds., *Politics of Illusion: The Bay of Pigs Invasion Reexamined* (Boulder, CO: Lynne Rienner, 1999).

Blaine, James Gillespie (1830–1893) Republican politician, presidential aspirant, and two-time secretary of state who played a major role in U.S.–Latin American relations from 1881 to 1892. As secretary of state during the brief **Garfield** administration, Blaine tried to mediate the War of the Pacific (1879–1884), without success, emphasized his own brand of **Pan-Americanism**, advocated economic expansion under the guise of the **Monroe Doctrine**, and argued strongly that any future canal across the isthmus should be built in Panama, but only under U.S. control and domination. During the War of the Pacific Blaine sided with Peru against Chile, in part because he was promoting U.S. economic interests in Peru to counter those of Great Britain in Chile. As secretary of state under Benjamin Harrison (1889–1993), Blaine became a prime mover in the first Inter-American Conference held in Washington, D.C., in 1889–1890, a movement designed to establish firmer commercial links with Latin America and lay the groundwork for a genuine Pan-American movement.

James G. Blaine was born in West Brownsville, Pennsylvania, in 1830, graduated from Washington College in Pennsylvania in 1847 and then taught until 1854. After purchasing an interest in the *Kennebec Journal*, he moved to Maine where he worked on its editorial staff. From 1863 to 1881, Blaine served in Congress, first in the House of Representatives (1863–1876) and then in the U.S. Senate (1876–1881). He used his power in Washington to move from domestic politics to foreign policy, a shift that enabled him to carry out his vision of America as a world power based on commercial dominance and national greatness. Blaine carried a general view of Latin Americans as uncivilized—violent, cruel, and incapable of peacefully settling their own disputes—that influenced his Latin American diplomacy.

Blaine was known in diplomatic circles for his heavy-handed policies and imperialistic attitude toward Latin America. Dubbed "Jingo Jim" by the American press, Blaine possessed a strong aversion to European involvement in the Americas. His efforts to further U.S. **hegemony** in the Western Hemisphere reflected vestiges of **Manifest Destiny** and his diplomacy reflected the chauvinistic and militant foreign policy of the United States at the time. Blaine was one of the key figures who helped convert the United States from a regional to a world power by stressing greater U.S. involvement in Latin America to undermine European influence in the region.

The question of the Garfield administration's attitude toward Latin America and the Monroe Doctrine were connected in the action taken by Secretary of State Blaine in the controversy with England over the **Clayton-Bulwer Treaty** and the building of an interoceanic canal. The Clayton-Bulwer Treaty was negotiated in 1850 to avoid conflict with British interests in Central America, including British Honduras and a future canal, and offered joint control between British and United States for any canal in Central America. By 1881, Colombia, fearing the "protection" offered by the United States, had proposed admitting European powers to a share in the guarantee of the isthmus. Blaine's objective was to replace the Clayton-Bulwer Treaty with an agreement allowing the United States sole control of a canal, an arrangement that did not materialize until the Hay-Pauncefote Treaty in 1901.

Blaine's heavy-handed diplomacy in mediating the War of the Pacific brought forth criticism from Chile and other Latin American countries that the United States was meddling in its internal affairs. At the heart of the issue was the fear that victorious Chile would force Peru to cede territory leading to more international tensions and a negative business environment. To promote a solution where Chile would accept a monetary indemnity instead, Blaine warned the Chileans that if they balked at his proposal he would promptly convoke an inter-American congress to pressure Santiago to change its mind on the territorial question. Resentful of Blaine's arrogant and forceful diplomacy, Chile resisted Blaine's proposal, arguing that the United States, after seizing over half of Mexican territory in the **Mexican-American War**, would surely understand the right of military victors to annex land from the vanquished.

It was during his second stint at secretary of state in the administration of Benjamin Harrison that James Blaine made his biggest contribution to inter-American affairs. At the first Inter-American Conference held in Washington, D.C., in 1889–1990, Blaine hosted the delegates from every Latin American republic except the Dominican Republic. He strongly urged the delegates to think in terms of regional cooperation and forging greater hemispheric ties by initiating reciprocal trade agreements and reducing excessively high tariffs. In his opening address he told the delegates he favored relations among American states based on "confidence, respect, and friendship." Blaine's rhetoric soared to levels of common interest and hemispheric ideals rarely heard by Latin Americans. At one point he told the assembled delegates that "We believe that friendship and not force, the spirit of just law and not the violence of the mob, should be the recognized rule of administration between American nations and in American nations." By trying to link the personal with the commercial, Blaine's major goal was to foster U.S. expansion and domination of the Western Hemisphere. It was obvious to the Latin American delegates that Blaine was more interested in the economic well-being of the United States than Pan-Americanism. Although Blaine's Washington conference achieved little beyond establishing a Commercial Bureau of American Republics, the gathering of delegates from the American states served as the genesis of the **Pan American Union** (1910–1948) and eventually the establishment of the **Organization of American States (OAS)** in 1948. Blaine's Pan-American conference was an important step in the formation of an intergovernmental body that viewed the Western Hemisphere as one and sought to address problems in a *multilateral* manner.

The most serious international crisis that Blaine faced was the so-called Baltimore affair with Chile in 1891–1892. The *Baltimore* incident involved a drunken brawl in Valparaíso, Chile, in which two U.S. sailors were killed, seventeen beaten severely, and over thirty incarcerated for provoking the incident. With blame flying in both directions, the incident produced enough anger amongst the participants—President Benjamin Harrison, Chile's foreign minister, the U.S. Navy, and Secretary of State Blaine—that the United States began preparations for war if the dispute was not settled properly. After third-party arbitration, and a telegram from the Chilean foreign minister, the debacle was resolved with the United States satisfied that the language in the telegram constituted an apology, Washington's agreement to recall the offensive U.S. minister Patrick Egan in 1893, and the Chilean payment of $75,000 as an indemnity for the affair. An aging, increasingly ill James Blaine resigned as secretary of state on June 4, 1892, and died the following year of Bright's disease, tuberculosis, and heart failure at the age of sixty-three.

Suggested Reading

Edward P. Crapol, *James G. Blaine: Architect of Empire* (Wilmington, DE: SR Books, 2000); David W. Dent, *The Legacy of the Monroe Doctrine: A Reference Guide to U.S. Involvement in Latin America and the Caribbean* (Westport, CT: Greenwood Press, 1999); David Healy, *James G. Blaine and Latin America* (Columbia: University of Missouri Press, 2001); David Saville Muzzey, *James G. Blaine* (Port Washington, NY: Kennikat Press, 1963); Alice Fest Tyler, *The Foreign Policy of James G. Blaine* (Hamden, CT: Archon Books, 1965).

Blowback The term "blowback" was invented by the **Central Intelligence Agency (CIA)** to refer to the unintended negative consequences of American policies abroad. It is often the result of an overextended empire in which **Washington policymakers** insist that what is good for the United States is good for the rest of the world, whether in dealing with "hot spots" that threaten U.S. interests, or in forcing global economic integration on its own terms. Blowback also involves the failure of American citizens to see the true costs and folly of policies carried out in the name of the people. In a brilliant and iconoclastic attack on American foreign policy since the end of the **Cold War**, Chalmers Johnson argues in *Blowback: The Costs and Consequences of American Empire* that American policies toward **human rights**, weapons proliferation, **terrorism**, rogue states, drug mafias, and the environment are often seen as hypocritical by foreigners who resent what the United States *does* abroad. As Johnson points out, "What the daily press reports as the malign acts of 'terrorists' or 'drug lords' or 'rogue states' or 'illegal arms merchants' often turn out to be blowback from earlier American operations" (Johnson, 2000: 8). In the quest for order and stability in much of Latin America, the United States often aligned its foreign policy with **friendly dictators**, or authoritarians, particularly in Nicaragua, El Salvador, and Cuba. While some Washington policymakers acknowledged that supporting repressive right-wing dictators could lead to blowback in the form of anti-Americanism and damage to U.S. prestige (and values) abroad, these risks were always seen as necessary since the alternatives—leftist governments opposed to the United States—were seen as far worse.

There are many examples of "blowback" in U.S.–Latin American relations. The disastrous **Bay of Pigs** invasion contributed to the **Cuban Missile Crisis** and the massive military buildup in Vietnam received a considerable boost from the massive U.S. **intervention** to "stop communism" in the Dominican Republic in 1965. The **Contra** campaign against the socialist-oriented **Sandinista** government in Nicaragua contributed to an epidemic of cocaine and heroin use in the United States as American agents looked the other way when U.S.–trained military insurgents brought illicit drugs back to the United States for sale in American cities to buy arms and supplies for Reagan's Contras. In 2003, the **George W. Bush** administration decertified Guatemala's anti-drug efforts, citing a lack of progress over the past year. However, Guatemala's organized drug business is controlled by former high-ranking military officials who were once allies with the United States during the Cold War. The problem of terrorism and **drug trafficking** in Latin America continues in part from unintended consequences of blindly supporting right-wing dictators that Washington believed were helping defeat leftist insurgents in Central America.

Blowback from the CIA-backed overthrow of Guatemalan president Jacobo **Arbenz** in 1954 led to the creation of a Marxist guerrilla insurgency in the 1980s that in turn brought about CIA-supported military programs of genocide conducted against hundreds of Mayan villages. In some instances, **covert operations** such as the CIA-backed coup against Chile's President Salvador **Allende** produced little blowback onto the United States itself, but produced lethal consequences for others in Chile and throughout Latin America. The September 11, 1973, coup in Chile was violent and offended many throughout the world. Once Allende's replacement, General Augusto **Pinochet**, was firmly in control of the government, he orchestrated the torture, death, or "disappearance" of over 4,000 people in Chile. Pinochet joined other Latin American dictatorships as an active collaborator in **Operation Condor**, a joint operation to hunt down and murder exiled dissidents in the United States, Spain, Italy, and throughout Latin America. Pinochet's arrest—pending an extradition request by a Spanish judge—by British police in October 1998 was a direct consequence of his U.S.–backed "dirty war" activities. Although the **Clinton** administration arranged to have some documents relating to Chile declassified, it opposed Pinochet's extradition, claiming that Chile should be guaranteed immunity from prosecution for past human rights offenders so that it could continue its forward task of democratization. The major point of "blowback" is that these Cold War legacies make it difficult for the United States to convince the rest of the world that it is serious about the protection of human rights, the drug war, **democracy**-building, and terrorism around the globe. Johnson argues that the United States needs a new analysis of its post–Cold War policies, including those who make American foreign policy. To overcome the complacency and arrogance that characterize American officials who deal with Latin America, Johnson argues that "American policy making needs to be taken away from military planners and military-minded civilians, including those in the White House, who today dominate Washington policymaking toward the area" (Johnson, 2000: 33).

Blowback is not an inevitable byproduct of U.S. foreign policy following the end of the Cold War; but when American foreign policy relies more on bluster, military force, and financial manipulation than on diplomacy, **international law**, and economic aid, serious unintended consequences are more likely to occur. In a prescient observation about the costs of empire, Johnson asserts that "Given its wealth and power, the United States will be a prime recipient in the foreseeable future of all of the more expectable forms of blowback, particularly terrorist attacks against Americans in and out of the armed forces anywhere on earth, including within the United States" (Johnson, 2000: 223). If the twenty-first century continues to generate blowback policies formulated during the second half of the twentieth century in Latin America, then the United States will have failed to adjust to a world that needs less imperial **hegemony**—military force and economic bullying—and more civility and diplomacy. President George W. Bush's policy of neglecting Latin America after **September 11, 2001**, combined with diplomatic mistakes in dealings with Mexico (shelving of the 2001 immigration agreement), Venezuela (supporting the opposition against the democratically elected government), Brazil and Argentina (blaming the victim for their economic woes), and Haiti (assisting in the removal of President **Aristide**) has contributed to a political shift toward populism and growing **anti-Americanism** in Latin America. The blowback from focusing almost exclusively on its enemies (Cuba and the so-called "axis of evil") has served to undermine the growing trend toward hemispheric cooperation reaching back to the **George H.W. Bush** administration in the early 1990s. *See also* Intervention and Non-Intervention; Threat Perception/Assessment.

Suggested Reading

Alexander Cockburn and Jeffrey St. Clair, *Whiteout: The CIA, Drugs and the Press* (London: Verso, 1998); Barbara Conry, "The Futility of U.S. Intervention in Regional Conflicts," *Policy Analysis* (Cato Institute), No. 209 (May 19, 1994); William Greider, *Fortress America: The American Military and the Consequences of Peace* (New York: Public Affairs, 1998); Chalmers Johnson, *Blowback: The Costs and Consequences of American Empire* (New York: Henry Holt, 2000; Stephen Schlesinger and Stephen Kinzer, *Bitter Fruit: The Story of the American Coup in Guatemala*, expanded ed. (Cambridge, MA: Harvard University Press, 1999); Christopher Simpson, *Blowback: America's Recruitment of Nazis and Its Effects on the Cold War* (New York: Macmillan Collier Books, 1988); John Tirman, *Spoils of War: The Human Cost of America's Arms Trade* (New York: Free Press, 1997).

Bogotá Conference (1948) The Ninth International Conference of American States, held in Colombia's capital, March 30–May 2, 1948, issued two major documents formalizing the structure of the heretofore loosely organized inter-American system. First, the Bogotá Conference adopted the Charter of the **Organization of American States (OAS)** (Charter of Bogotá), the basic constitution founding the world's oldest regional intergovernmental organization and successor to the **Pan American Union**. The OAS further cemented hemispheric solidarity during the opening years of the **Cold War** and also sought to foster democratic government and economic cooperation and development. Second, the Bogotá Conference issued the Inter-American Treaty on Pacific Settlement (Pact of Bogotá) that outlined machinery for the compulsory nature of peaceful settlement of disputes and collective security. The Pact, in Articles I and II, stated that member states have recourse at all times to pacific procedures for dispute settlement. This was explicitly stipulated and designed to replace inter-American treaties and conventions concluded during the previous half century. Yet, because of the reservations by many states (including the United States), fearing an erosion of state sovereignty, the Treaty on Pacific Settlement was never ratified.

The Bogotá Conference encountered several difficulties, including finding an acceptable name for the new inter-American system, dealing with disputes with the United States over the question of economic development and mob violence that disrupted the conference for nearly a week. Some state delegations wanted to retain the name originally adopted by the First International Conference of American States (sometimes known as the first Pan-American Conference, or Washington Conference) in 1889–1890; and a Union of the American Republics, that marked the institutional beginning of the inter-American system. Mexico's delegation proposed the name Pan American Union, that had been used to designate the permanent office and secretariat in Washington, D.C. The Argentine delegation was opposed to any such names as "association," "community," or "union," fearing that these terms created the impression that the United States was attempting to build a superstate in the Western Hemisphere.

The most controversial subject at the Bogotá Conference was that of economic development. The controversy boiled down to a dispute between the U.S. delegation's defense of private investment to spur economic growth in Latin America versus the Latin American insistence upon the need to use public capital under strong governmental direction. A subsidiary dispute arose over a proposed provision that any expropriation of private (foreign) investments be accompanied by just compensation.

Although this amendment was accepted ultimately, it resulted in strong reservations by several states, particularly the United States. The numerous controversies over the Economic Agreement at Bogotá suggested how deeply the United States and Latin America disagreed over basic principles and theories of development. Led by Secretary of State George C. Marshall and Commerce Secretary Averell Harriman, the American delegation appeared to lack both an understanding of the basic needs of Latin American countries and any desire to gain one. Thus, Marshall's opening address at Bogotá fell like cold rain on Latin Americans when he stated bluntly, "We must face the facts: My people find themselves faced with the urgent necessity of meeting staggering responsibilities in Western Europe, in Germany and Austria, in Greece and Turkey" (Inman, 1965: 246–247). The Latin American states had hoped for something akin to the European Marshall Plan, but here was the namesake himself forsaking any rescue, as he had the Europeans. The United States turned a deaf ear to Latin American requests to alleviate poverty and promote modernization. As a result, the Economic Agreement failed ratification. Fifty years later, relations between the rich, northern United States and the poor, southern developing Latin American states remain strongly conditioned by the unresolved economic problems of the latter.

Finally, in the midst of the Bogotá Conference, increasing bitterness between Colombia's two traditional parties—the Conservatives and Liberals—led to a rising wave of violence. When the charismatic Liberal leader Jorge Eliécer Gaitán was assassinated in the streets of Bogotá on April 9, 1948, an unprecedented wave of urban lawlessness and destruction, the infamous *bogotazo*, spread from the capital across the country. While the tragedy at Bogotá disrupted conference meetings for more than a week, it sparked the much larger, decade-long *la violencia* (the violence), a civil war that raged across Colombia, taking the lives of an estimated 250,000.

Despite the *bogotazo* (rioting and anarchy in Bogotá), the delegates at the Bogotá Conference wrote a comprehensive charter for the inter-American system that had outgrown the ad hoc bilateral agreements since the Washington Conference of 1889–1890. The conference at Bogotá failed to please everyone, particularly the Latin Americans, who had to settle for the formation of the OAS as a diplomatic forum to organize and pressure the United States for greater economic development. Still, in a charter of 112 articles, the new constitution contained the important principles of the Latin Americans, namely, the sweeping prohibition of **intervention** (except for collective action) enshrined in Articles 15 through 18. The principle of non-intervention is the most important law duty in the charter, and it supercedes and transcends all other duties, including the promotion of representative **democracy** and the protection of **human rights**. *See also* Intervention and Non-Intervention; Perón, Juan Domingo.

Suggested Reading

Samuel Guy Inman, *Inter-American Conferences, 1826–1954: History and Problems* (Washington, DC: University Press of Washington, D.C., 1965); William LeoGrande, *Our Own Backyard: The United States in Central America, 1977–1992* (Chapel Hill: University of North Carolina Press, 1998); L. Ronald Scheman, *The Inter-American Dilemma* (New York: Praeger, 1988); Lars Schoultz, *Beneath the United States: A History of U.S. Policy Toward Latin America* (Cambridge, MA: Harvard University Press, 1998); Peter H. Smith, *Talons of the Eagle: Dynamics of U.S.–Latin American Relations*, 2nd ed. (New York: Oxford University Press, 2000); O. Carlos Stoetzer, *The Organization of American States*, 2nd ed. (New York: Praeger, 1993).

Boland Amendments Congressional legislation designed to restrict aid to the U.S.–backed **Contras** from 1982 to 1985. The restrictive measures were named after the chief congressional sponsor of the legislation, Representative Edward P. Boland (D-MA), then chairman of the House Intelligence Committee. The decision to oppose the leftist **Sandinista** regime in Nicaragua was made during the first year of the **Reagan** administration and involved a program of covert assistance to fledgling anti-Sandinista forces. Both Democratic and Republican members of the House Intelligence Committee expressed doubts about the propriety of the Contras as a fighting force and the danger of war between Honduras and Nicaragua with the United States using Honduras as a platform to defeat the revolutionary government in Nicaragua. Part of the debate centered on Nicaragua's justification for supporting guerrilla groups in El Salvador with arms. At first the committee approved an amendment stating that the United States was justified in undertaking covert actions as long as that was the sole objective of the White House. The nondemocratic elements in the Contra leadership worried liberals in Congress, many of whom also opposed the use of U.S. funds to overthrow a foreign government.

Within a year news reports began to surface that the goal of the Contras was to overthrow the Sandinista government. This prompted Congress in December 1982 to pass the first Boland Amendment, or Boland I, expressly to prohibit the use of U.S. funds for the purpose of overthrowing the government in Managua. The amendment was adopted unanimously by a vote of 411–0 in the House of Representatives. President Reagan opposed the legislation, but its attachment to key legislation he favored prevented him from exercising his veto power. Boland I, prohibiting the Pentagon and the **Central Intelligence Agency (CIA)** from supplying the Contras with military aid for the purpose of overthrowing the Nicaraguan government, lasted until December 1983. As the war worsened, the Reagan administration continued covert support on the grounds that support for the Contras was necessary to prevent Managua from supplying leftist rebels fighting the U.S.–backed regime in El Salvador. Boland II made some concessions to the Reagan administration by agreeing to limited U.S. military assistance to the Contras from December 1983 to September 1984. Further U.S. assistance was complicated by the growing intensity of the war in El Salvador and human rights abuses committed by the Contras against the civilian population. Boland III tried to bar any U.S. agency from providing any support to the Contras and was in effect from October 1984 to December 1985.

The Reagan administration did not feel compelled to follow congressionally mandated restrictions on funding the "freedom fighters" considered so crucial to implementing the **Reagan Doctrine**. While President Reagan tried to mobilize public support for funding the war in El Salvador and continued funding of the Contras with alarmist speeches, covert efforts were made to circumvent the Boland restrictions on funding. Efforts to bypass Congress led to the **Iran-Contra scandal** and the resignation of top officials in the Reagan administration who ran the secret government policy. At this point the debate shifted to whether Congress should supply humanitarian aid or military aid to Reagan's Contras since many believed in the **Cold War** doctrine of defeating communism in Nicaragua. Before Boland III expired in December 1985, Congress voted to provide humanitarian assistance to the Contras and extended this legislation through the end of September 1986. Although Reagan managed to win congressional backing for a resumption of U.S. military aid to the Contras beginning in October 1986, the Iran-Contra scandal broke in November 1986, which undermined the White House effort to remove the Sandinistas from power by force. The objectives of the Reagan administration—targeting regions of opportunity where U.S. support for anti-Marxist guerrillas could succeed in toppling governments supported by the Soviet Union and Cuba—clashed with the ideology of the Sandinistas. By putting enormous pressure on the revolutionary government of Nicaragua, the Reagan administration was able to create the threat that justified the measures used to accomplish its international goals. As Robert **Pastor** (1987: 243) points out, "Each action by the Reagan administration prompted the Sandinistas toward a higher level of vituperation against U.S. imperialism, thus justifying and reinforcing the Reagan administration's strategy." With each government ideologically committed to defeating the other—U.S. **imperialism** versus Nicaraguan Communism—compromise was out of the question and Congress had little impact on preventing President Reagan from circumventing the law to accomplish his objectives. Despite Reagan's many speeches designed to fund the overthrow of the Sandinista government, more than three-quarters of the American public opposed overthrowing the Nicaraguan government and a majority were more fearful of "another Vietnam" quagmire than the spread of Communism in Central America. *See also* Imperialism; Scandals and Blunders.

Suggested Reading

William LeoGrande, *Our Own Backyard: The United States in Central America, 1977–1992* (Chapel Hill: University of North Carolina Press, 1998); Robert A. Pastor, *Condemned to Repetition: The United States and Nicaragua*, rev. ed. (Princeton, NJ: Princeton University Press, 1988).

Bolívar, Simón (1783–1830) Native-born Venezuelan who led the northern South American struggle for independence from Spanish control between 1808 and 1824. Born into the Creole aristocracy, he learned about the ideals of the Enlightenment through private tutors. Known as "the Liberator," Bolívar became disillusioned with the Spanish monarchy, seized the opportunity to drive royalist forces from Venezuela, and commanded the liberation armies that eventually defeated the Spanish. After a series of military victories drove the Spanish out of South American, Bolívar assumed power and was elected president of Gran Colombia (Venezuela, Colombia, and Ecuador) in 1825. Bolívar's political philosophy emphasized the importance of unity, both in creating a new government and for achieving cooperation for security among the new American nations. To achieve his goal of a permanent defensive alliance among Spanish American nations, as a shield against future attacks by European powers, Bolívar initiated the 1826 Pan-American or Panama Congress. His original plan was to exclude non–Spanish-speaking countries—Brazil and the United States—but they were invited to the conference over his objections.

The Panama Conference contained the seeds of future Pan-American conferences, but it failed to achieve the unity Bolívar envisioned, and many of the points on the agenda—guaranteeing territorial integrity, denouncing the slave trade, creating a permanent army and navy supported by members of a federation, and the creation of a South American League—were barely discussed and only New Granada ratified what Bolívar wanted out of the meeting. The United States delayed sending two delegates because of debates over foreign entanglements and both delegates never made it to the conference. The Panama Conference also reflected Bolívar's ambivalence toward the United States: He admired the success and power of the United States and its political institutions, but found the presidential-separation of powers model unsuitable for Latin America. Instead, he believed that the British system of constitutional monarchy was better suited to the prevailing conditions in Latin America where a strong, conservative republic run by an intellectual elite was needed. Although the United States sold arms to the rebels and joined ranks with some, he gave little credit to the United States for the defeat of Spanish forces and imposed high tariffs on U.S. items sold in Gran Colombia. Bolívar distrusted the validity of the **Monroe Doctrine**, arguing that it was motivated by economic self-interest rather than a true concern for the region's security and future economic development. Although the Panama Conference failed, and Bolívar lost interest in creating an American confederation, it did reveal the differing views on several matters held by the United States and Latin America. The gradual use of the Monroe Doctrine as a justification for expansion and control served to weaken Bolívar's dream of hemispheric unity. By the end of the 1820s Bolívar had lost popularity, resorted increasingly to authoritarian tactics, and struggled for control of Gran Colombia with Francisco de Paula Santander. In 1830 he resigned from the presidency and returned to the north coast of Colombia where he died later that year of tuberculosis. *See also* Clay, Henry.

Suggested Reading

David Bushnell, ed., *The Liberator; Simón Bolívar: Man and Image* (New York: Alfred A. Knopf, 1970); David Bushnell and Neill Macaulay, *The Emergence of Latin America in the Nineteenth Century*, 2nd ed. (New York: Oxford University Press, 1994); T. Ray Shurbutt, ed., *United States–Latin American Relations, 1800–1850 The Formative Generations* (Tuscaloosa: University of Alabama Press, 1991).

Bonsal, Philip Wilson (1903–1995) Cold War diplomat and government official who served in numerous diplomatic posts between 1938 and 1962. Philip Bonsal was born in New York City, graduated from Yale in 1924, and then worked for AT&T in Latin America between 1926 and 1937. He entered the diplomatic service in 1938 and over the next ten years served in minor positions in Havana, Washington, Madrid, and The Hague. After **World War II** he worked on European affairs until his three Latin American ambassadorial appointments, beginning in 1955. Bonsal served as U.S. ambassador to Colombia (1955–1957), Bolivia (1957–1959), and Cuba (1959–1960). Bonsal's interventionist activities earned him the wrath of government officials in Colombia and Bolivia where he tried to reduce the growth of Communist influence. His time in Cuba coincided with the early years of hostility between Fidel **Castro**'s revolutionary government and the **Eisenhower** administration. After Fulgencio **Batista** fled from Cuba, the United States extended diplomatic recognition to the new government, but also recalled Earle Smith who had alienated many Cubans for his close ties to the Batista regime. Philip Bonsal replaced Ambassador Smith and expressed a more tolerant attitude toward the Cuban Revolution, looking upon the **regime change** on the island as a sign of progress toward **democracy** and social justice. As the Cuban regime became more hostile to American interests, key figures in the Eisenhower administration grew weary of the Cuban leader and expressed the need for a policy designed to either reform Castro or remove him.

Philip Bonsal had to deal with the seizures of U.S. property in Cuba during Castro's first year in office. At first Ambassador Bonsal tried to work out a diplomatic solution to Cuba's intervention in the management of the Cuban Telephone Company and the effects of the Cuban Agrarian Reform Law of May 17, 1959, on U.S. property interests. Bonsal called for the Cubans to make "prompt, adequate, and effective compensation" and fair treatment of U.S. investors and an exchange of views on the subject. Discussions on compensation seemed to rest on payment in long-term bonds, marketable and payable in dollars; however, as the land reform program went forward and seizures of U.S. property continued, tensions between the United States and Cuba increased. With Ambassador Bonsal acting as negotiator, U.S. policy remained focused on efforts to calm troubled waters and hope for a equitable settlement through negotiation. While the problem of reaching an agreement on compensation dragged on, the Eisenhower administration went ahead with plans to mount a counter-revolutionary attack on the Castro regime along with cuts in the Cuban sugar quota and U.S. recommendations to oil companies to refuse to refine Soviet oil. The rapid deterioration of relations between the United States and Cuba made it almost impossible to remedy the problem of compensation for U.S. financial losses in Cuba, according to some estimates in excess of $1 billion. While the United States agreed to accept long-term bonds for expropriated agrarian claims in Mexico, Ambassador Bonsal continued to insist on compensation through cash payments. Ambassador Bonsal left Cuba before diplomatic relations were severed in January 1961 and the disastrous **Bay of Pigs** invasion four months later. *See also* Ambassadors.

Suggested Reading

Philip W. Bonsal, *Cuba, Castro and the United States* (Pittsburgh: University of Pittsburgh Press, 1971); Wayne S. Smith, *The Closest of Enemies: A Personal and Diplomatic Account of U.S. Cuban Relations Since 1957* (New York: W.W. Norton, 1987); Richard E. Welch, *Response to Revolution: The United States and the Cuban Revolution, 1959–1967* (Chapel Hill: University of North Carolina Press, 1985).

Braden, Spruille (1894–1978) U.S. businessman and abrasive diplomat who played a key role in U.S.–Latin American relations between 1933 and 1954. Born to a family with mining interests in Montana and Chile, Braden became one of many **ambassadors** who combined an interest in business and diplomacy in Latin America. After graduating from Yale University in 1914, Braden spent time cultivating his business ventures in Chile and the United States. His Chilean business activities included investment in copper mines and bond negotiations for Westinghouse Electric with the Chilean national army. In 1933, he accepted an appointment as part of the U.S. delegation to the Seventh Pan American Conference in Montevideo, Uruguay, then stayed on as the U.S. delegate to the Chaco Peace Conference in Buenos Aires from 1935 to 1938. Braden's interest in Latin American diplomacy and his generous campaign contributions brought him the nomination to be U.S. ambassador to Colombia (1939–1942) where he paid close attention to the growing Nazi influences in South America. During the 1940s he served as U.S. ambassador to Cuba (1942–1945), a brief period as ambassador to Argentina (1945), and assistant secretary of state for American republic affairs from 1945 to 1947. Braden distinguished himself as a proconsul, often justifying his interventionist activities on the need to root out fascists and fascist sympathizers. His aggressive and controversial treatment of Latin American leaders and their governments resembled a crusade against fascists and Communists. During his brief tenure as U.S. ambassador to Argentina in 1945, Braden attacked the military government for its fascist tendencies and led a vitriolic campaign to deny Juan **Perón** the presidency. Braden's highly publicized attacks included the fabrication and circulation of the "Blue Book on Argentina," a **State Department** document that denounced Argentina for alleged links to the Nazi's during **World War II.** However, Braden's blatant interference in Argentina's election failed to undermine Perón's candidacy, inflamed **anti-Americanism** in Buenos Aires and elsewhere, and almost guaranteed General Perón's landslide victory in 1946. Ambassador Braden's failure to rid Argentina of Perón, and the negative effects of his interventionism throughout the region, led to his recall by the State Department, now worried about relations with Latin America. Braden next served as assistant secretary of American republic affairs (1945–1947), after which he retired from diplomatic life and returned to private business. After being eased into retirement from the State Department, Braden took up the cause of anti-communism, lecturing on the growing influence of "commies" in Central America, particularly Guatemala. Braden was one of many foreign policy bureaucrats who felt that **regime change** represented a legitimate policy of the U.S. government when dealing with unfriendly Latin American governments.

Spruille Braden's next crusade was to join hands with the **United Fruit Company**, pointing out the dangers of Communist influence on the future of the banana business in Guatemala, then experiencing reformist governments interested in land and labor reform after years of suffering under a right-wing dictatorship. To counter the Communist "virus," Braden advocated **intervention** as a last resort to counter Communist subversion. Braden was fond of right-wing dictators such as Anastasio **Somoza** and Rafael **Trujillo** because they did not "pussyfoot" around with Communists and others critical of their regimes. Whether in Cuba, Guatemala, or Argentina, Braden always defended his actions on grounds of furthering **democracy** and fostering inter-American security. His memoirs, *Diplomats and Demagogues*, was published in 1971; he died in Los Angeles, California in 1978. *See also* Arbenz Guzmán, Jacobo; Bernays, Edward L.; Guatemala, U.S. Invasion of (1954); Intervention and Non-Intervention.

Suggested Reading

Spruille Braden, *Diplomats and Demagogues: The Memoirs of Spruille Braden* (New Rochelle, NY: Arlington House, 1971); Braden, *Private Enterprise in the Development of the Americas* (Washington, DC: U.S. Government Printing Office, 1946); Gary Frank, *Juan Perón vs. Spruille Braden: The Story Behind the Bluebook* (Lanham, MD: University Press of America, 1980);

Irwin F. Gellman, *Roosevelt and Batista: Good Neighbor Diplomacy in Cuba, 1933–45* (Baltimore, MD: Johns Hopkins University Press, 1973); Neale C. Ronning and Albert P. Vannucci, eds., *Ambassadors in Foreign Policy: The Influence of Individuals on U.S.–Latin American Policy* (New York: Praeger, 1987); *New York Times* (January 11, 1978).

Brady Plan (1989) A U.S. proposal for dealing with the Latin American debt crisis, presented by Secretary of the Treasury Nicholas F. Brady in the **George H.W. Bush** administration. The Brady Plan was significant because it represented a shift from protecting U.S. commercial banks toward the interests of Latin American debtor countries. It put more emphasis on Latin America's internal development problems rather than the previous administration's narrow concern on the threat posed by Soviet and Cuban influence in Central America, primarily Nicaragua and El Salvador. It replaced the Baker Plan, named for former Secretary of the Treasury James A. Baker, which recommended rescheduling and not reducing the debts of Latin American governments. The centerpiece of the Baker Plan was structural adjustment, meaning a cluster of policy prescriptions in which governments would have to spend within their means, let markets determine prices, privatize industries that had previously been nationalized, and rescind subsidies and regulations to obtain loans from abroad.

Treasury Secretary Brady's plan for debt reduction was built on market solutions and sound economic reforms. According to Brady's three-year plan, collateral would come from the International Monetary Fund (IMF), the World Bank, the **Inter-American Development Bank (IADB)**, and the Japanese government in exchange for a reduction in bank claims. To qualify for debt reduction assistance, Latin American countries had to encourage domestic savings and foreign investment. However, Brady's Plan occurred at the same time the U.S. aid budget was being shaved, and Washington was faced with large trade deficits and a burgeoning public debt of its own. By emphasizing bank reductions (or write-downs) of debt in exchange for guaranteed payment of the balance, the financial condition of U.S. banks and some Latin American economies improved during the 1990s. While Brady's plan prevented the collapse of large banks and restored confidence in the ailing Latin American economies, the economic growth envisioned for Latin American countries was less successful. In any case, many conservative **Washington policymakers** were pleased that trade liberalization, privatization, deregulation, and fiscal reform were replacing the conventional model based on state-interventionist and populist strategies opposed by the international financial institutions.

Suggested Reading

Walden Bello, *Dark Victory: The United States, Structural Adjustment, and Global Poverty* (Oakland, CA: Institute for Food and Development Policy, 1994); Richard E. Feinberg and Delia M. Boylan, *Modular Multilateralism: North-South Economic Relations in the 1990s* (Washington, DC: Overseas Development Council, 1991); Jeffrey Sachs, "Making the Brady Plan Work," *Foreign Affairs*, Vol. 68 (summer 1989): 87–104.

Bryan, William Jennings (1860–1925) Prominent turn-of-the-century Democrat who served in Congress (1891–1895), ran for president (1896, 1900, 1908), and served as secretary of state (1913–1915) during the first Woodrow **Wilson** administration. He became best known for his views expressed during his three presidential campaigns: improving the plight of American farmers and opposition to U.S. imperialism after the **Spanish-Cuban-American War**. While secretary of state he helped negotiate a series of bilateral treaties designed to prevent international disputes, worked to improve U.S.–Latin American relations by criticizing **imperialism** and urging a more just and fair approach in doing business south of the border. As he spent more time trying to solve Latin American problems, Bryan became more a believer in the "**big stick**" if it could be used to replace dictators with more suitable democratic regimes. He favored neutrality during **World War I**, urging President Wilson to keep U.S. ships and passengers out of the areas of naval conflict. He clashed with Wilson's more belligerent approach and resigned in June 1915, but supported Wilson once war was declared two years later. He spent his final years supporting religious fundamentalism, the prohibition of alcohol, and the **League of Nations**. He joined the prosecution in the "monkey trial" of John T. Scopes, but was ridiculed by Clarence Darrow. Exhausted by his court experience, Bryan died five days after the end of the trail. *See also* Bryan-Chamorro Treaty (1916); Democracy and Democracy Promotion; Hegemony; Imperialism.

Suggested Reading

David D. Anderson, *William Jennings Bryan* (Boston: Twayne, 1981); LeRoy Ashby, *William Jennings Bryan: Champion of Democracy* (Boston: Twayne Publishers, 1987); Kendrick A. Clements, *William Jennings Bryan, Missionary Isolationist* (Knoxville: University of Tennessee Press, 1982); Paul W. Glad, ed., *William Jennings Bryan: A Profile* (New York: Hill and Wang, 1968); Michael J. Hogan, ed., *Rhetoric and Reform in the Progressive Era* (East Lansing: Michigan State University Press, 2003); Edward S. Kaplan, *U.S. Imperialism in Latin America* (Westport, CT: Greenwood Press, 1998).

Bryan-Chamorro Treaty (1916) A post–Panama Canal treaty between the United States and Nicaragua that gave the United States the exclusive right to build a canal across Nicaragua. Its effect was to eliminate the possibility of competition if a rival foreign power decided to build a second canal through Nicaragua, the original site for such an isthmian waterway. The treaty was signed shortly before the opening of the Panama Canal on August 15, 1914, by U.S. Secretary of State William Jennings **Bryan** and Emiliano Chamorro, Nicaragua's representative in Washington. The concern over a competitor canal started during the William Howard **Taft** administration, but it became more important during the **Wilson** administration when it decided to finalize the agreement, adding a provision that authorized U.S. military **intervention**. The granting of protectorate status, modeled after the **Platt Amendment** in Cuba, was agreed to by Nicaragua, but eventually was rejected by the U.S. Senate before it ratified the treaty in 1916. The delay in ratification was also due to the fact that Costa Rica and El Salvador opposed the treaty on the grounds that giving the United States rights to build naval bases at the Gulf of Fonseca and on the Corn Islands would impinge on their territory. The controversy ended after Costa Rica asked the Central American Court to nullify the treaty, and the United States and Nicaragua argued that the court did not have jurisdiction over the treaty, with the eventual collapse of the court itself. The treaty, along with all of its provisions, was abrogated in 1970. The termination of the Bryan-Chamorro Treaty paved the way for the negotiations that led to the establishment of two new treaties between the United States and Panama signed during the administration of Jimmy **Carter**. *See also* Panama Canal Treaties; Wilson, Thomas Woodrow.

Suggested Reading

Wilfrid H. Callcott, *The Caribbean Policy of the United States, 1890–1920* (Baltimore, MD: Johns Hopkins University Press, 1942); Dana G. Munro, *Intervention and Dollar Diplomacy in the Caribbean, 1900–1921* (Princeton, NJ: Princeton University Press, 1964).

Bucareli Agreements (1923) The Mexican Revolution and the growing importance of petroleum in U.S.–Mexican relations eventually led to friction over how Article 27 of the Mexican Constitution would affect the nationalization of subsoil mineral and oil deposits. Between 1917 and 1922, the United States and Mexico wrestled with this issue until the diplomatic impasse was broken by the Bucareli Agreements, named after the site of the conference in Mexico City. The Bucareli Agreements amounted to a gentleman's accord between personal representatives of President Warren G. **Harding** and Mexican President Alvaro Obregón. In attempting to pacify the foreign oil companies concerned about constitutional provisions dealing with the ownership of subsoil mineral rights, the agreements modified the effects of Article 27 by establishing the doctrine of "positive acts." This provided an interpretation whereby Mexico recognized the legitimacy of oil concessions made prior to the 1917 Constitution if the owners had taken positive acts (such as drilling a well) to initiate oil production. The significance of the Bucareli Agreements is that they paved the way for the de jure recognition of the Mexican government by the United States and helped improve the long-term relationship between the two countries. Unfortunately, the Bucareli Agreements did not completely settle the issue of oil rights and U.S. **intervention**, two of the hallmarks of the Mexican Revolution.

Between 1923 and 1927 Mexican–U.S. relations worsened when Mexican political leaders enacted petroleum laws limiting the ownership of oil rights, contending that the Bucareli Agreements were binding only on the Obregón regime. As a result, business interests in the United States mounted a vigorous campaign to intervene in Mexico. Relations improved after President Calvin Coolidge appointed Dwight W. **Morrow**, a Wall Street financier, as ambassador to Mexico in late 1927. It was in large part Morrow's *simpático* style that helped pave the way for the **Good Neighbor Policy** under Presidents Herbert **Hoover** and **Franklin D. Roosevelt**. In need of a friendly Mexico on its southern border prior to **World War II**, the United States and Mexico were able to effect a final settlement of their outstanding differences over claims—agrarian properties and expropriated oil interests—reaching back to the nineteenth century. *See also* Intervention and Non-Intervention; Revolutions.

Suggested Reading

David W. Dent, *The Legacy of the Monroe Doctrine: A Reference Guide to U.S. Involvement in Latin America and the Caribbean* (Westport, CT: Greenwood Press, 1999); Antonio Gómez Robledo, *The Bucareli Agreements and International Law* (Mexico: National University of Mexico Press, 1940); Alan Knight, *U.S.–Mexican Relations, 1910–1940: An Interpretation* (San Diego: Center for U.S.–Mexican Studies, University of California, 1987).

Buchanan, James (1791–1868) U.S. congressman (1821–1831), senator (1834–1845), secretary of state (1845–1849), and fifteenth president of the United States (1857–1861). James Buchanan was born on April 23, 1791, near Mercersburg, Pennsylvania, and graduated from Dickinson College in 1809. After reading law, Buchanan was admitted to the Pennsylvania bar in 1812 and began a successful legal career. Buchanan's noted oratorical flair soon earned him a seat in the Pennsylvania state legislature (1815–1816) before he moved to the U.S. House of Representatives for ten years (1821–1831) and then the U.S. Senate for another decade. With James K. **Polk**'s election as president, Buchanan was named secretary of state.

During the **Mexican-American War** (1846–1848), Buchanan strongly supported the expansionist ideas of the president, instructing his envoy, Nicholas P. **Trist**, and U.S. minister to Mexico John **Slidell**, to "negotiate" with Mexican officials (following the fall of Veracruz and the U.S. military occupation of Mexico City) to sell California and New Mexico, to recognize an enlarged Texas, and to settle outstanding claims by U.S. citizens against Mexico. The Treaty of **Guadalupe Hidalgo**, signed by Trist and his Mexican counterpart, Luis G. Cuevas, on February 2, 1848, formalized Mexico's utter defeat. Peace was even more humiliating for Mexico than the war had been. Under the terms of the treaty, Mexico lost more than one-third of its territory—more than a million square miles—in return for a modest, face-saving payment of approximately $15 million. Via raw military power, the United States seized from Mexico all of California, some of present-day Colorado, and most of what is now New Mexico and Arizona.

Buchanan served as United States minister to Great Britain (1853–1856) during the Franklin **Pierce** administration. In 1854, with the U.S. ministers to France and Spain, Buchanan co-authored the **Ostend Manifesto** that urged the U.S. seizure of Cuba, by force if necessary, in the event that Spain refused to sell the colony to the United States, and to protect American slavery against the threat of abolition in Cuba. Anxious to maintain good relations with Spain, President Pierce promptly disavowed the document and Buchanan's diplomatic embarrassment proved short. Buchanan capitalized on his role in the attempted annexation of the slave island to boost his popularity in the South during the 1856 presidential election.

Historians rate him as one of the more mediocre, and thus obscure, U.S. presidents, particularly in his inability to avoid the coming civil war; juxtaposed to his successor, Abraham Lincoln, Buchanan is also remembered as a bold, unapologetic expansionist, in part for his co-authorship of the Ostend Manifesto. Like his predecessor, Franklin Pierce, Buchanan was committed to **Manifest Destiny** and aggressively continued U.S. efforts to acquire territory. Yet, despite President Buchanan's expertise in diplomacy, his administration achieved limited success in its foreign policy goals toward Latin America. As the sectional strife in the United States intensified and began to overshadow all other events, Buchanan's plans to purchase Cuba from Spain encountered insurmountable resistance from Congress. The Buchanan administration's Cass-Yrissari Treaty with Nicaragua (1857) initially bullied the small republic into almost transforming itself into a U.S. protectorate over the country's isthmian transit route, until Nicaraguan nationalists defied Buchanan and voted against ratification. In 1858, in response to continued civil disorder in Mexico, Buchanan asked Congress for authority to establish a military protectorate over the northern Mexican states of Chihuahua and Sonora, but the Senate refused. In 1859, the president again asked Congress for authority to invade Mexico to guarantee U.S. transit across its isthmus and to protect U.S. lives and property. Fortunately for Mexico, the United States was completely focused on John Brown's stunning raid at Harper's Ferry, Virginia.

It is an irony of history that **Theodore Roosevelt**, one the greatest interventionist American presidents, often cited James Buchanan as the prototype of a weak president. But in his foreign policy toward Latin America (itself often erroneously presumed to be manipulated by southern expansionists intending the spread of slavery), Buchanan carried his own "**big stick**" almost a half-century before Roosevelt. Buchanan's administration marked the beginning of the end of British domination in Central America, when it threatened to abrogate the **Clayton-Bulwer Treaty** (1850), providing for joint Anglo-American construction of a canal through the Central American isthmus. Under Buchanan's pressure the British relinquished control over their colony in the Bay Islands (off the east coast of Honduras) and over the British protectorate of the Miskito kingdom. Buchanan also dispatched a flotilla of nineteen American warships and 2,500 U.S. Marines to remote Paraguay to enforce demands for an indemnity and apology by the Paraguayan dictator Carlos Antonio López. Buchanan's military **intervention** was in response to the so-called Water Witch incident (February 1855), in which Paraguayan soldiers fired on a U.S. steamer, killing the American helmsman.

The American Civil War exploded shortly after Buchanan left office in early 1861. James Buchanan had vowed publicly in 1856 that he would serve only one term, but the utter lack of any requests that he break his pledge was another embarrassment. Buchanan retired to his manorial estate, Wheatland, near Lancaster, Pennsylvania, and died there on June 1, 1868. *See also* Filibusters; Intervention and Non-Intervention.

Suggested Reading

Frederick M. Binder, *James Buchanan and the American Empire* (Selinsgrove, PA: Susquehanna University Press, 1994); Philip Shriver Klein, *President James Buchanan: A Biography* (University Park: University of Pennsylvania Press, 1962); Elbert B. Smith, *The Presidency of James Buchanan* (Lawrence: University of Kansas Press, 1975); John Updike, *Buchanan Dying—A Play* (New York: Alfred A. Knopf, 1974); Robert Wood, *The Voyage of the Water Witch* (Culver City, CA.: Labyrinthos Pub., 1985).

Bunau-Varilla, Philippe (1859–1940) French engineer-businessman who played a key role in convincing the United States after the **Spanish-Cuban-American War** to support independence for Panama and build an interoceanic canal in Panama, not Nicaragua. With pressure building to construct a Panama Canal that would complete what the French had failed to do in the nineteenth century, President **Theodore Roosevelt** began the delicate process of unraveling the political and diplomatic knot that would dramatically alter the relationship between the United States and Latin America. The whole affair would require intense lobbying, **gunboat diplomacy**, aggressive public relations, presidential deception and deceit, and afterward result in scandal involving the Frenchman and high government officials in Washington.

Philippe Bunau-Varilla's interest in Panama stemmed from a speech given at his school (École Polytechnique in Paris) by Ferdinand de Lesseps, builder of the Suez Canal with his sights now on a canal across Panama. After serving as a colonial civil engineer in North Africa, Bunau-Varilla volunteered to apply his skills to Panama, then part of Colombia. By the time de Lesseps' French company had gone bankrupt in 1886, Bunau-Varilla was the company's chief engineer. To extricate himself from the scandals that followed the French failure, Bunau-Varilla set out to restore French pride and recoup French investments (including his) by persuading the United States to shift its plans to build a canal in Nicaragua to Panama. A master salesman, Bunau-Varilla befriended President Theodore Roosevelt and managed to convince the U.S. Congress that Nicaraguan earthquakes might imperil a canal there while lobbying Congress to pass the Spooner Act in 1902 approving the Panama site for the canal. The principal figures in the Panama Canal saga were president Roosevelt, Philippe Bunau-Varilla, French representative of the New Panama Canal Company, John **Hay**, secretary of state, and the Colombian chargé d'affaires in Washington, Tomás Herrán. When Colombia refused to go along with the terms of the Spooner Act, Bunau-Varilla helped finance and organize Panama's revolt, arranged for its independence, and had himself appointed to the position of first minister of the new Republic of Panama. *See also* Panama Canal Treaties.

Suggested Reading

Gustave A. Anguizola, *Philippe Bunau-Varilla, The Man Behind the Panama Canal* (Chicago: Nelson-Hall, 1980); Philippe Bunau-Varilla, *From Panama to Verdun, My Fight For France* (Philadelphia: Dorrance and Co., 1940); Bunau-Varilla, *The Great Adventure of Panama* (Garden City, NY: Doubleday, 1920); Bunau-Varilla, *Panama: The Creation, Destruction, and Resurrection* (London: Constable and Co., 1913); David G. McCullough, *The Path Between the Seas: The Creation of the Panama Canal, 1870–1914* (New York: Simon and Schuster, 1977).

Bunker, Ellsworth (1894–1984) Businessman and diplomat during most of the **Cold War**. Known for his skills as a diplomatic troubleshooter, Bunker played a key role in solving a number of Latin American conflicts, including the riots in Panama in 1964, the Dominican crisis in 1965, and the negotiations that eventually led to two new treaties with Panama that restored full Panamanian sovereignty over the Panama Canal. Ellsworth Bunker was born in Yonkers, New York, where his family was involved in the sugar business. After graduating from Yale University in 1916, Bunker joined his father's National Sugar Refining Company, eventually rising to the top of the company. He began his diplomatic career at fifty-seven, serving as U.S. ambassador to Argentina, Italy, India, South Vietnam, and the **Organization of American States (OAS)**. Bunker believed in the Cold War doctrine of halting Communist aggression, wherever it appeared to threaten U.S. interests, and felt the United States was justified in fighting the Vietnam War, and the illegal incursions into Cambodia and Laos against Communist sanctuaries. His most noteworthy diplomatic achievement involved the three years (1975–1978) of negotiations over the future status of the Panama Canal during the administration of Jimmy **Carter**. The **Panama Canal Treaties** were signed in 1977 and ratified in 1978, transferring control over the canal to Panama effective on December 31, 1999.

His diplomatic work had a significant impact on U.S.–Latin American relations during the 1960s and 1970s. While a consultant for the **State Department**, Bunker negotiated a settlement to the 1964 Panama crisis and the following year, as U.S. ambassador to the Organization of American States, supported U.S. **intervention** in the Dominican Republic in 1965 and helped to negotiate the post-invasion recovery plans there. After serving as U.S. ambassador to South Vietnam (1967–1973), Bunker was called upon to help negotiate a new Panama Canal Treaty with Panamanian President Omar Torrijos. His co-negotiator was Sol Linowitz, a Washington lawyer and Xerox Corporation executive, who argued that the festering Panama problem was one of the most serious in the region. Bunker faced a complex web of concerns in his efforts to negotiate an end to what many called the last vestiges of U.S. **imperialism** in Latin America. At the forefront were questions of sovereignty and the management and security of the canal. After years of interest group lobbying for and against handing over the U.S.–built canal to Panama, Bunker's diplomatic skill contributed to the culmination of two new treaties with the Republic of Panama. President Carter's resolve to change the status of the Canal Zone reflected both his personal interest in Latin America and his desire to show that his administration could have a positive impact on Latin America and U.S.–Latin American relations. Although Carter achieved a narrow victory with the help of experienced diplomats such as Bunker, Linowitz, and others, he lost the respect of conservatives who claimed that the president had given away the Panama Canal, weakened the United States in the eyes of the world, and ultimately helped presidential aspirant Ronald **Reagan** defeat him in the presidential election in 1980. Ellsworth Bunker retired in 1978 and died in Brattleboro, Vermont, in 1984. *See also* Ambassadors.

Suggested Reading

Lee H. Burke, *Ambassador at Large: Diplomat Extraordinary* (The Hague: Nijhoff, 1972); Michael L. Conniff, *Panama and the United States: The Forced Alliance* (Athens: University of Georgia Press, 1992); Martin F. Herz, ed., *The Modern Ambassador: The Challenge and the Search* (Washington, DC: Institute for the Study of Diplomacy, 1983); John Major, *Prize Possession: The United States and the Panama Canal, 1903–1979* (New York: Cambridge University Press, 1993); C. Neale Ronning and Albert P. Vannucci, eds., *Ambassadors in Foreign Policy: The Influence of Individuals on U.S.–Latin American Policy* (New York: Praeger, 1987).

Bush, George Herbert Walker (1924–) U.S. president (1989–1993) who failed to win a second term in office despite his vast experience in foreign policy prior to becoming president. He was ambassador to the **United Nations (UN)**, director of the **Central Intelligence Agency (CIA)**, minister to China, and vice-president for eight years under Ronald **Reagan**. Bush was born in Connecticut to a wealthy and politically powerful Republican family. His father, Prescott S. Bush, was an investment banker and U.S. senator from 1952 to 1963. George H.W. Bush attended private preparatory schools and was about to attend Yale University when **World War II** started, and he enlisted in the Naval Reserve and trained as a pilot. He saw combat against the Japanese in World War II. After the war, he married and enrolled at Yale where he majored in economics. He moved to Texas after graduation, entered the oil industry, became politically active, and began a long career as a moderate Republican. After failing to win the Republican nomination in 1980 and serving eight years as vice-president, Bush made a second bid for the presidency and beat Democrat Michael Dukakis in 1988. At first, Bush's interest in foreign policy worked to his advantage; the challenges that followed the end of the **Cold War** and the collapse of the Soviet Union seemed tailor-made to highlight the skills of the president and his foreign policy team. Later, the salience of domestic issues increased as the American public came to expect a peace dividend after the collapse of Communism and now perceived the world as a less-threatening place.

Although Vice-President Bush became involved in the **Iran-Contra scandal** in the Reagan years, he did not consider Latin America a foreign policy priority. However, he recognized that he could not ignore several issues that concerned the American public in the aftermath of the Cold War: **drug trafficking**, immigration, democratization, and hemispheric trade. To help fight the war on drugs, President Bush worked with Colombian President Virgilio Barco to bring drug traffickers to the United States to stand trial and face imprisonment. After a year of bungled efforts to rid Panama of General Manuel **Noriega**, Bush sent thousands of U.S. troops to Panama to remove the Panamanian dictator and bring him to the United States to stand trial. The fact that Bush made no mention of Communist influence and control in Panama as a justification for **intervention** appeared to signal the end of the Cold War as a major component of U.S.–Latin American policy. The magnitude of the U.S. invasion of Panama, and the ability to test new weaponry and urban combat with female troops provided a prelude to Operation Desert Storm in the Persian Gulf in 1990–1991. The Bush administration sold the Panama invasion to the American public through effective use of secrecy, **media** restrictions, and negative political symbolism demonizing General Noriega so his removal would be interpreted as victory for freedom and **democracy**.

Bush appointed Bernard Aronson to head Latin American policy at the **State Department**, hoping to mollify U.S. involvement in Central America after the turbulent years of his predecessor, Elliott **Abrams**. The Aronson appointment had little to do with his expertise in dealing with Latin America; it demonstrated that domestic politics drives a great deal of U.S.–Latin American policy because President Bush knew that as a Democrat Aronson's appointment would be approved by the Senate and at the same time depoliticize the lingering tensions in Congress over the Reagan-Bush policies in Central America. In June 1990, Present Bush proposed the **Enterprise for the Americas Initiative (EAI)** and later signed the **North American Free Trade Agreement (NAFTA)** with Canada and Mexico. In 1991, he ordered the U.S. Coast Guard and Navy to pick up Haitian refugees on the open seas and return them to Haiti. To capture the vital Cuban American vote in Florida, President Bush signed the Cuban Democracy Act in October 1992, another failed attempt at **regime change** by tightening the screws as Soviet subsidies were being withdrawn from Cuba. Bush's involvement in the Iran-Contra scandal raised questions about the veracity of the claim that he was out of the decision-making "loop," and this contributed to his electoral loss to Bill **Clinton** in the 1992 presidential election. His defeat was also attributed to a lingering recession, a three-way race for the presidency, his refusal to jettison Vice-President Dan Quayle, and a more domestic issue–based campaign by Bill Clinton and Al Gore. In what became known as the Christmas pardons in December 1992, President Bush pardoned six Iran Contra defendants, including Casper Weinberger and Elliott Abrams, before retiring to his estate in Kennebunkport, Maine. Bush's passion for foreign policy helped with a cautious approach to the rapidly changing world order of the times; however, his apparent lack of interest in domestic concerns ultimately contributed to the lack of public support he needed to remain in office.

Bush joined the Carlyle Group in the 1990s, but after **George W. Bush**'s war against Saddam Hussein in 2003, his close ties to such a controversial investment company that once had ties to the bin Laden family of Saudi Arabia led him to resign from the group in 2003. George H.W. Bush will be remembered as a foreign policy president who failed to recognize the saliency of domestic problems and policy during a time when many Americans perceived the world as far less threatening than during the Cold War. His two military operations—the U.S. invasion of Panama to capture General Noriega and Operation Desert Storm to drive Iraqi forces out of Kuwait—were judged to be foreign policy successes as measured by public support for his actions. Overall, Bush's presidency will be remembered for its failure to establish a more assertive rationale for U.S. foreign policy in a world of immense change brought about by the end of the Cold War. However, some scholars of the presidency argue that Bush's incremental style of leadership was plausible for the time and deserves a more positive evaluation of his presidency. Once his son, George W. Bush, became president in 2001, the neo-conservatives who had once worked with the first president Bush sought to remedy what they perceived as a need to exert more power over world affairs by amassing vast amounts of power in the U.S. Department of Defense. *See also* Operation Just Cause; Sandinistas.

Suggested Reading

Ryan J. Barilleaux and Mark J. Rozell, *Power and Prudence: The Presidency of George H.W. Bush* (College Station: Texas A&M University Press, 2004); Meena Bose and Rosanna Perotti, eds., *From Cold War to New World Order: The Foreign Policy of George H.W. Bush* (Westport, CT: Greenwood Press, 2002); Michael Duffy and Dan Goodgame, *Marching in Place: The Status Quo Presidency of George Bush* (New York: Simon and Schuster, 1992); Lewis L. Gould, *The Modern American Presidency* (Lawrence: University of Kansas Press, 2003); William M. LeoGrande, "From Reagan to Bush: The Transition in U.S. Policy Toward Central America," *Journal of Latin American Studies* 22 (1990): 595–621; Murray Waas and Craig Unger, "In the Loop: Bush's Secret Mission," *The New Yorker* 68 (1992): 64–83; Bob Woodward, *The Commanders* (New York: Pocket Star Books, 1991).

Bush, George W. (1946–) Businessman, politician, and president of the United States (2001–) who campaigned for the presidency in 2000 promising a greater commitment to Latin America than during the preceding **Clinton** years. After promising to concentrate on building broader and more constructive relations with Mexico based on the importance of trade, drug smuggling, and immigration, President Bush reversed administration policy after the **September 11, 2001**, terrorist attacks and the war against Saddam Hussein. American foreign policy was quickly retooled to fight the international war on **terrorism** and ensure a safer homeland. The principal concern for Bush's first term in office was to develop ways to prevent a potential international terrorist attack against the United States. From this perspective, Latin America became a region of little interest to Washington because of the absence of Al-Qaeda terrorist cells operating in Latin America. Despite some concerns that funding for international terrorist groups may be transferred or laundered through Latin America, particularly the tri-border region between Brazil, Paraguay, and Argentina, the concept and rhetoric of "terrorism" has been inflated to apply to **drug trafficking**, illegal immigration, money laundering, arms trafficking, and intellectual property violations. For example, the Department of Defense now calls illicit drugs a "weapon of mass destruction." After four years of the Bush presidency, Latin Americans believe the United States has lost interest in the region, with the possible exceptions of Colombia and Cuba, and the United States has been of little help with the region's chronic economic difficulties and growing political tensions. According to an October 2003 Zogby International poll of Latin American opinion leaders, 87 percent expressed a negative rating of George W. Bush. While a majority of Latin Americans still express a positive image of the United States (as measured by the 2003 Zogby poll), the numbers are in decline and suggest a rough road ahead to improve U.S.–Latin American relations. In his January 2002 address to the nation, Bush expressed his hopes for the hemisphere by saying, "The future of this hemisphere depends on the strength of three commitments: democracy, security and market-based development. These commitments are inseparable, and none will be achieved by half-measures. This road is not always easy, but it's the only road to stability and prosperity for all the people . . . who live in this hemisphere." Bush has been unable to chart a new course that would strengthen hemispheric ties by taking advantage of new opportunities in Latin America.

George W. Bush was born in New Haven, Connecticut, but grew up in Midland and Houston, Texas. After graduating with a bachelor's degree from Yale University in 1968, Bush joined the Texas Air National Guard. His service in the guard was spotty, and he was allowed to transfer to an Alabama unit where he was rarely seen for duty. He was allowed to terminate his service obligation early so he could attend the Harvard Business School. Bush used his time in the Air National Guard to avoid a tour of duty in Vietnam, a strategy that was not unusual for male Americans at the time. After graduating with a Master of Business Administration from Harvard, George W. Bush returned to Midland, Texas, where he began a career in the oil business. Although his energy business was not successful, Bush began to see the advantages of political life and began to prepare himself for an elected position in Texas. His work on his father's successful 1988 presidential campaign provided the younger Bush with the necessary financial contacts that allowed him to purchase the Texas Rangers baseball franchise in 1989. He used this position as a springboard to his election as governor of Texas in 1994. He was re-elected in 1998 with 68.6 percent of the vote, but resigned in 2000 to run for president of the United States. Bush lost the popular vote to Al Gore by over 500,000 votes, but serious voting irregularities in the State of Florida sent the decision of who was elected president to the Supreme Court. The recount in Florida was stopped, and Bush was selected president by a margin of 537 votes in Florida, giving him the necessary Electoral College votes to become the 43rd president of the United States.

President Bush has tried to convert American foreign policy from one that sought stability at the expense of democratic values. The dictator-friendly realism of his predecessors—Richard **Nixon**, Ronald **Reagan**, and **George H.W. Bush**—would end and the United States would no longer befriend stable "authoritarian" regimes. While some critics have applauded the president's efforts to make the democratic transformation of the world the cornerstone of American foreign policy, others find that Bush has consistently failed to support pro-**democracy** movements or regimes made up of "autocratic democrats" who opposed Washington's policies around the globe. For those who can see through the lofty rhetoric of democratic expansion, there is more often than not interest in the expansion and retrenchment of American power. In many cases, this new foreign policy has contributed to the rise of **anti-Americanism**. The cases where this has happened in Latin America would include Haiti, Venezuela, Bolivia, and Colombia. In other regions, such as Central Asia, South Asia, China, the Middle East, and Africa, the Bush administration has been content with corrupt and authoritarian regimes to ensure oil production, stop weapons of mass destruction, fight terrorism, promote arms exports, and encourage cooperation with the United States in its search for military bases. While President Bush tries to sound Wilsonian in his call for a global expansion of democracy, his actions have converted the United States into an **imperial** power, one that President Woodrow **Wilson** would have denounced as part of a misguided effort to expand U.S. military power at the expense of useful alliances and multilateral institutions. President Bush won a second term in 2004 by beating Democrat John F. **Kerry** by 3 percent of the popular vote; however, the contest focused mainly on terrorism and the war in Iraq and was almost totally devoid of any mention of how to improve the state of U.S.–Latin American relations. *See also* Hegemony; Propaganda; Regime Change; Wilsonianism.

Suggested Reading

Colin Campbell and Bert A. Rockman, *The George W. Bush Presidency: Appraisals and Prospects* (Washington, DC: Congressional Quarterly Press, 2004); Joshua Kurlantzick, "The Republican Democrat?" *Harper's* (September 2004); Saul Landau, *The Pre-emptive Empire: A Guide to Bush's Kingdom* (Sterling, VA: Pluto Press, 2003).

Bush Doctrine. *See* Doctrines

Butler, Smedley Darlington (1881–1940) Smedley Butler was a chauvinistic and paternalistic U.S. Marine Corps officer whose military career spanned the interventionist era in Central America and the Caribbean from 1898 to 1930. Born in West Chester, Pennsylvania, Butler enlisted in the Marine Corps in 1898 and carried out interventionist policies in the Philippines (1899–1900; 1905–1907), China (1900; 1927–1929), Honduras and Panama (1903–1904), Panama (1909–1914), Nicaragua (1909–1910), Haiti (1915–1918), Mexico (1916), and the Dominican Republic (1916). He also served in **World War I** and was commander of the Marine Base at Quantico, Virginia, from 1920–1924. A Pennsylvania Quaker, Butler took his responsibilities of Central American and Caribbean occupation with reserve and optimism, always convinced he could make things better over a period of benign tutelage.

Like many of his fellow officers, Smedley Butler believed that Caribbean peoples were inferior because of a deeply ingrained conviction that browns, blacks, and mulattoes were immature and incapable of ruling themselves without outside guidance and assistance. As one of the instruments of the **Roosevelt Corollary to the Monroe Doctrine**, Butler's occupation forces confronted opposition groups that were often unruly and difficult to subdue. In Haiti, for example, Butler characterized the *caco* guerrillas as "shaved apes, no intelligence whatsoever, just plain low nigger" (Schmitz, 1999: 26). Although Butler did not grow up in the Reconstruction South, he carried the same racial norms of many of his fellow officers who did and considered their subjects of occupation as child-like, too immature and uncivilized to govern themselves. He told a Senate committee investigating the military occupation of Haiti that, "We were imbued with the fact that we were trustees of a huge estate that belonged to minors. That was my viewpoint" (Plummer, 1992: 95).

The U.S. military occupation of Haiti relied on the creation of a constabulary, an armed police force organized as a military unit, but distinct from the regular army. General Butler headed the Gendarmerie (after 1928 it was called the Garde d'Haïti) and staffed it with Marine officers; however, the **Hoover** administration realized the need to revise U.S. policy toward Latin America and began a phased disengagement and normalization called Haitianization that would allow for the withdrawal of Butler's Marines. The whole idea of a constabulary to solve Haiti's political problems—either in the short or long term—proved futile and counter-productive since it strengthened and guaranteed the survival of some of the worst features of Haitian politics: corruption, **human rights** violations, **dictatorship**, and economic decay.

Smedley Butler was one of the typical military warriors who fought in the **banana wars** in Central America and the Caribbean designed to protect America's tropical empire and carry out U.S. policy. This was a time when the **State Department** was staffed with political appointees with little knowledge or the intuitive skills required to deal with the Caribbean region. Therefore, the U.S. government relied heavily on the military to carry out its policies in the tropics, and this soon typified U.S. foreign policy in the region. The Marine Corps members considered themselves a tough bunch of soldiers who could fearlessly pursue any rebel, bandit, and other purveyors of trouble and instability. Butler's experience in Honduras, Nicaragua, and Haiti reinforced his negative views of the people and culture of the region and the corresponding need to bring respect for law and order, the sanctity of private property, and a government consisting of "responsible" leaders. General Smedley Butler considered it a noble task, one that would bring progress and civilization to backward people living in Central America and the Caribbean.

After retiring in 1931, Major General Smedley Butler condemned the politics of **intervention**, U.S. capitalism, and Caribbean **imperialism**—policies that he strongly supported while an officer in the Marine Corps. As he stated in an anti-war speech to a convention of legionnaires (Langley, 1988: 213):

> I spent 33 years being a high-class muscle man for Big Business, for Wall Street and the bankers. In short, I was a racketeer for capitalism. . . . I helped purify Nicaragua for the international banking house of Brown Brothers in 1909–1912. I helped Mexico and especially Tampico become safe for American oil interests in 1916. I brought light to the Dominican Republic for American sugar interests in 1916. I helped make Haiti and Cuba a decent place for the National City [Bank] boys to collect revenue in. I helped in the rape of half a dozen Central American republics for the benefit of Wall Street.

Some attributed Butler's attack on the pillars of American financial and military power as a reaction to being denied the commandant position of the Marine Corps; others felt that Butler's long and violent interventionist military career bothered him and this contributed to his outburst of criticism of American imperialism. President Hoover was enraged by Butler's anti-American speech, but did not see it as symptomatic of the failures of U.S. policies in Haiti, Cuba, Nicaragua, Honduras, and the Dominican Republic. Gradually, beginning in 1920, the United States began to renounce military intervention to pave the way for the **Good Neighbor Policy**. However, as American military forces withdrew from Central America and the Caribbean, the stalwart banana warriors like General Butler were replaced with "**friendly dictators**" who would often serve as surrogates for the imperial conquerors who were sent to protect American interests for over three decades. For thirty years after the Roosevelt Corollary to the Monroe Doctrine, U.S. intervention took several forms, and was justified in a variety of ways, but the cases of outright military occupation seemed to do the most damage to the Latin American policy of the United States. While in the military, Butler was an outspoken racist, but he was also known for his command efficiency and flamboyant style of leadership; many of his fellow officers noted that his stern and rugged appearance made him a perfect subject for a Marine Corps recruiting poster. Major-General Smedley Butler died in Philadelphia in 1940. *See also* Anti-Americanism; Banana Republic; Imperialism; Intervention and Non-Intervention; Race and Racism.

Suggested Reading

Robert T. Cochran, "Smedley Butler, a Marine for All Seasons," *Smithsonian* 15 (June 1984): 137–156; Lester D. Langley, *The Banana Wars: United States Intervention in the Caribbean, 1898–1934* (Chicago: The Dorsey Press, 1988); Allan R. Millett, *Simper Fidelis: The History of the United States Marine Corps* (New York: Macmillan, 1980); *New York Times* (June 22, 1940); Brenda Gayle Plummer, *Haiti and the United States: The Psychological Moment* (Athens: University of Georgia Press, 1992); Hans Schmidt, *Maverick Marine: General Smedley D. Butler and the Contradictions of American Military History* (Lexington: University of Kentucky Press, 1987); Schmidt, *The United States Occupation of Haiti, 1915–1934* (New Brunswick, NJ: Rutgers University Press, 1971); David F. Schmitz, *Thank God They're on Our Side: The United States and Right-Wing Dictatorships, 1921–1965* (Chapel Hill: University of North Carolina Press, 1999); Lowell Thomas, *Old Gimlet Eye: The Adventures of Smedley D. Butler as Told to Lowell Thomas* (New York: Farrar and Rinehard, 1933).

C

Cabot, John Moors (1901–1981) Conservative U.S. diplomat who specialized in Latin American affairs. Cabot came from a wealthy Massachusetts family, attended Harvard and Oxford universities, and entered the Foreign Service in 1924. He served in diplomatic posts throughout Latin America (Peru, the Dominican Republic, Mexico, Brazil, Guatemala, and Argentina) before and during the **Cold War**. At the start of the Cold War, Cabot believed that the national security of the United States was threatened by international communism emanating from the Soviet Union. President Dwight **Eisenhower** appointed him assistant secretary of state for inter-American affairs in 1953, but he clashed with fiscal conservatives over his proposal for a generous development assistance program, and in 1954 was appointed ambassador to Sweden. He returned to diplomatic posts in Latin America and served in Colombia (1957–1959) and Brazil (1959–1961) before being recalled by President John F. **Kennedy** in 1961 for pro–U.S. speeches and ardent support for U.S. corporations that angered nationalist politicians, students, and military officials in Latin America. Cabot was unable to accept Latin American political leaders who espoused an independent foreign policy and tolerance for Fidel **Castro** and the Cuban Revolution. Cabot retired from the Foreign Service in 1966 and died in 1981 at the age of eighty. *See also* Ambassadors.

Suggested Reading

John Moors Cabot, *First Line of Defense: Forty Years Experiences of a Career Diplomat* (Washington, DC: School of Foreign Service, Georgetown University, 1979); Cabot, *Toward Our Common American Destiny: Speeches and Interviews on Latin American Problems* (Medford, MA: Fletcher School of Law and Diplomacy, 1955); Stephen M. Streeter, "Campaigning Against Latin

American Nationalism: U.S. Ambassador John Moors Cabot in Brazil, 1959–1961," *The Americas* (October 1994).

Calvo Clause The Calvo Clause was crafted by Argentine diplomat and jurist Carlos Calvo in 1868 to advance the concept of sovereign immunity. He argued that a sovereign nation should be immune from external **intervention** in its internal affairs, regardless of whether there is political stability in that nation or a reliable national court system in operation. In the 1860s, European powers appeared to pose the greatest danger to Latin American sovereignty; however, this changed toward the end of the nineteenth century when the United States replaced Europe as the major threat to Calvo's principle of absolute sovereignty. Latin American governments insisted on "Calvo Clauses" when negotiating contracts with foreign companies, prohibiting the latter from appealing beyond the courts of the nations. As the debate over non-intervention increased during the first half of the twentieth century, some Latin American states went so far as to include Calvo's principles in their constitutions. As foreign investment expanded in Latin America, a heightened concern developed over the possibility of foreign intervention to protect these interests. In response to tensions over investment, intervention, expropriation, and sovereignty, the U.S. Congress responded with a number of measures intended to counter the Calvo philosophy to protect U.S. companies against expropriation and other threats to their overseas investments. One such measure, the **Hickenlooper Amendment** of 1962, cut off foreign aid to any country that expropriated or nationalized private U.S. holdings without appropriate compensation or due process. *See also* Drago Doctrine; Intervention and Non-Intervention.

Suggested Reading

Donald Richard Shea, *The Calvo Clause: A Problem in Inter-American and International Law and Diplomacy* (Minneapolis: University of Minnesota Press, 1955); Larman C. Wilson and David W. Dent, *Historical Dictionary of Inter-American Organizations* (Lanham, MD: Scarecrow Press, 1998).

Caribbean Basin Initiative (CBI) The growing unrest in Central America in the 1980s prompted the **Reagan** administration to sponsor an inter-American program to develop stable and free-market democracies in the Caribbean and Central America. The genesis of the proposal came from Jamaican Prime Minister Edward Seaga, a staunch anti-Communist and friend of Ronald Reagan. At a speech delivered at the **Organization of American States (OAS)** on February 24, 1982, Reagan outlined a military and economic aid package to protect the Caribbean basin against Communist **terrorism** and unrest. Although the centerpiece was a free trade provision focused on duty-free exports to the United States for a period of twelve years, economic aid to select pro–U.S. countries, and tax incentives to encourage investment by U.S. firms in the region, the main purpose was to curb political unrest in the region and deflate the perceived threat posed by the Soviet

Union and Cuba. After two years, Congress approved the major provisions of the proposal, but the overall provisions were diluted because of worry about the impact of the legislation on U.S. unemployment and corporate interests. At the outset, twenty exporting countries and territories stood to benefit from the preferential treatment of select goods destined for the U.S. market. The CBI represented another U.S. economic policy with overt economic advantages, but with hidden political objectives designed to punish Soviet and Cuban sponsorship of armed leftist rebels in El Salvador, Guatemala, and Grenada. At first the plan was strongly endorsed by Canada, Mexico, and Venezuela; however, they became critical of the initiative once it became known that its real intent was to isolate and punish the pro-Castro **Sandinista** government in Managua. The CBI was extended after the twelve-year period, and it continues to exist even after the approval and implementation of the **North American Free Trade Agreement (NAFTA)**.

Suggested Reading

Michael J. Kryzanek, *U.S.–Latin American Relations*, 3rd ed. (Westport, CT: Praeger, 1996).

Caribbean Legion A conglomerate of armed exile groups from Cuba, the Dominican Republic, Honduras, El Salvador, and Nicaragua founded by José Figueres of Costa Rica to oppose directly Caribbean and Central American **dictatorships** that seemed to flourish during President **Franklin D. Roosevelt**'s **Good Neighbor Policy**. According to Roorda, "The Good Neighbor Policy demonstrated to a generation of Caribbean dictators that they were free to run their countries however they pleased, so long as they maintained common enemies with the United States: first the fascists, then the communists" (Roorda, 1998: 1). These modern-day filibustering expeditions were active from 1946 to 1950, contained distinct leadership and sponsorship, but lacked the coherent military force that the organization's name implies. The most prominent expeditions targeted Rafael L. **Trujillo**, the brutal dictator of the Dominican Republic, but others participated in the Costa Rican civil war in 1948. Figueres used the Caribbean Legion and support from Guatemalan President Juan José **Arévalo** to coordinate the revolution in Costa Rica that removed Teodoro Picado in 1948. The shadow armies of the Caribbean Legion ceased to exist in 1950 after the **Organization of American States (OAS)** established a series of "principles and standards" designed to restrict the activities of political exiles in their efforts to rid Central America and the Caribbean of right-wing dictatorships. Figueres was instrumental throughout his career in helping the **Central Intelligence Agency (CIA)** fund the non-Communist left in Latin America and the Caribbean; during the 1970s he supported opposition efforts (including the **Sandinistas**) to remove long-time Nicaraguan dictator Anastasio Somoza García. The failure of the Caribbean Legion to root out Latin American dictatorships helped build the case for other forms of political change, including urban and rural guerrilla warfare. *See also* Filibusters/Filibustering; Intervention and Non-Intervention.

Suggested Reading

Charles D. Ameringer, *The Caribbean Legion: Patriots, Politicians, Soldiers of Fortune, 1946–1950* (University Park: Pennsylvania State University Press, 1995); Piero Gleijeses, "Juan José Arévalo and the Caribbean Legion," *Journal of Latin American Studies*, 21 (February 1989): 133–145; Thomas M. Leonard, *The United States and Central America, 1944–1949* (Mobile: University of Alabama Press, 1984); Kyle Longley, *The Sparrow and the Hawk: Costa Rica and the United States during the Rise of José Figueres* (Tuscaloosa: University of Alabama Press, 1997); Stephen G. Rabe, "Inter-American Military Cooperation, 1944–1954," *World Affairs*, 137 (fall 1974): 132–149; Eric Paul Roorda, *The Dictator Next Door: The Good Neighbor Policy and the Trujillo Regime in the Dominican Republic, 1930–1945* (Durham, NC: Duke University Press, 1998).

Carnegie, Andrew (1835–1919) U.S. industrialist, philanthropist, and anti-imperialist who spent an enormous amount of his wealth to promote peace and international harmony. Through numerous educational and research foundations, endowments, and gifts Andrew Carnegie carried out his personal conviction that individuals who acquire great wealth have an obligation to allocate a significant portion to projects that promote the general welfare. Carnegie was born in Scotland, but immigrated with his family to the United States in 1848. During the later half of the nineteenth century, Carnegie built a vast business empire that in 1901 was incorporated into the U.S. Steel Corporation. Among his many philanthropic activities included the Carnegie Endowment for International Peace (1902), Central American Court of Justice (1907), and the **Pan American Union** building in Washington, D.C. (1910). The latter became the headquarters of the **Organization of American States (OAS)** in 1948 and continues to operate as the world's oldest international organization. Carnegie's interest in **Pan-Americanism** was demonstrated when he participated as a delegate to the First International Conference of American States held in Washington, D.C., in 1889–1890 and hosted by Secretary of State James G. **Blaine**. *See also* Anti-Imperialism; Blaine, James G.; Imperialism.

Suggested Reading

Samuel Flagg Bemis, *The Latin American Policy of the United States: An Historical Interpretation* (New York: W.W. Norton, 1967, 1971); Robert H. Holden and Eric Zolov, eds., *Latin America and the United States: A Documentary History* (New York: Oxford University Press, 2000); Lars Schoultz, *Beneath the United States: A History of U.S. Policy Toward Latin America* (Cambridge, MA: Harvard University Press, 1998).

Cartagena Summit. *See* Bush, George Herbert Walker (1924–)

Carter, James (Jimmy) Earl (1924–) Governor of Georgia (1970–1974), president of the United States (1977–1981), and Nobel Peace Prize winner in 2002. While serving as president of the United States, Carter actively pursued a foreign policy based on the protection of **human rights**, peaceful resolution of world conflicts, arms control, halting the spread of nuclear weapons, and the pursuit of democratic reform governments to replace those in Latin America that were dictatorial, military, or non-elected. His presidency coincided with the rise of right-wing military **dictatorships** in Latin America that brought torture, disappearances, massive human rights violations, and the deaths of thousands throughout the Western Hemisphere. Despite criticism from conservative Republicans, Carter made serious efforts to improve relations with Cuba. During his term, he lifted travel prohibitions, negotiated agreements on fishing rights and maritime boundaries, and secured the release of 3,600 Cuban political prisoners. Havana and Washington opened "interest sections" to enhance diplomatic contacts, the first move in this direction since President **Dwight Eisenhower** severed relations in January 1961.

Jimmy Carter was born in Plains, Georgia, and attended public schools there before being accepted to the Naval Academy in 1942. After graduating from Annapolis in 1946, Carter served in the U.S. Navy until the death of his father in 1953. He was trained as an engineer and worked with Admiral Hyman Rickover in the development of the nuclear navy. On the death of his father, Carter returned to Plains to run the family's peanut business and begin a life devoted to public affairs. Between 1963 and 1974, he was a member of the Georgia state senate, and a one-term governor of Georgia (1970–1974). By the time he began his run for the presidency in 1975, Jimmy Carter was recognized as one of a new generation of moderate Southern Democrats who supported civil rights progress in the United States. In his 1975 autobiography, *Why Not the Best?,* Carter pledged that he would restore integrity and idealism to government after the destructive effects of the Vietnam War and President Richard **Nixon**'s Watergate scandal. He defeated Gerald **Ford** in a close general election in 1976 and assumed office after eight years of Republican rule.

By the time Jimmy Carter arrived in Washington in 1977, most of Latin America was a graveyard of democracies, and the U.S. Congress had passed legislation requiring human rights considerations before granting foreign aid. His human rights–based Latin American policy was influenced by the work of the Commission on United States–Latin American Relations, a group of prominent business and academic leaders concerned about improving U.S.–Latin American relations. Published in 1975, the commission's report—*The Americas in a Changing World*—provided a comprehensive critique of U.S.–Latin American policy going back to the Truman administration and a condemnation of the principles contained in the **Monroe Doctrine**. It was highly critical of U.S. support for right-wing dictatorships in Latin America. It recommended that the United States bring military interventions and **covert operations** to a close, work toward normalizing relations with **Castro**'s Cuba, and sign and ratify a new treaty with Panama granting it sovereignty over the Panama Canal. In his efforts to condemn past sins and provide a moral rebirth for American foreign policy, President Carter stated that his administration would stop supporting right-wing dictatorships, emphasize the protection of human rights, and begin a process of treating the Latin American countries in a more mature and less paternalistic way. His human rights campaign hit the hardest in Argentina, Brazil, Chile, and Nicaragua, where authoritarian dictatorships tried to ingratiate themselves with the United States by claiming their forceful anti-communism efforts at home and abroad.

Within a month after of taking office, President Carter cut military aid to Argentina and Uruguay by two-thirds, opposed economic assistance, and pursued a vigorous campaign of public diplomacy that included support for critical resolutions in the **United Nations (UN)** and the **Organization of American States (OAS)**. U.S. diplomats were instructed to apply human rights standards as part of American foreign policy, something previous administrations were loathe to carry out. Military governments resisted Carter's new diplomatic efforts, often with the assistance of expensive public relations firms in Washington, on the grounds that they were involved in a war of survival against subversives and Communists intent on destroying the fabric of the "civilized" world. Once Republican Ronald **Reagan** came into office in 1981, criticism of the Argentine military and its repressive policies ceased and the Reagan administration restored military assistance, even going so far as to solicit Argentine assistance against its anti-Communist efforts in Central American countries like Nicaragua where the **Sandinistas** had recently deposed the anti-Communist dictator Anastasio **Somoza** Debayle.

Carter's controversial human rights policy drew criticism from the right and left in the United States. Liberals argued that Carter was not consistent with how he chose countries to denounce on human rights grounds; conservatives criticized Carter's commitment to furthering human rights while ignoring vital security interests around the globe. Some of the right-wing dictators that were forced out of office with the assistance of the new American emphasis on human rights felt betrayed and resentful after helping with the fight against communism. After being denied exile in the United States, and forced to move to Paraguay, Somoza called President Carter "Fidel Carter" for betraying Nicaragua and its friendly support of Washington's **Cold War** doctrine in Latin America. In an effort to further improve relations with Latin America, the Carter administration in 1979 extended diplomatic **recognition** and economic assistance to the new Sandinista government in Nicaragua.

Carter inherited the diplomatic dilemma of negotiating new treaties with the Republic of Panama over the future of the Panama Canal. After the Flag Riots in Panama in 1964, each American president from Lyndon **Johnson** to Gerald Ford found it necessary to draw up a new treaty that would relinquish U.S. control over the Canal Zone and the operation and protection of the canal. The continuing pressure for recognition of Panamanian sovereignty in the Canal Zone, combined with the stalled treaty negotiations due to the Watergate scandal, delayed inter-American diplomacy until the 1976 presidential election. At that point U.S. control over the Panama Canal became a serious campaign issue due in large part to the candidacy of former California Governor Ronald Reagan. In one of his best applause lines,

Reagan asserted that, "We bought it, we paid for it, it's ours and we're going to keep it."

Once Jimmy Carter became president in 1977, he reversed his position (he had said during the campaign that he was against relinquishing U.S. control over the Panama Canal) and proceeded to negotiate two new treaties with the Panamanian government—one to govern the canal during the transition period, the other to define the new relationship with the United States once Panama assumed control at the end of the twentieth century. Despite the heavy opposition among conservatives in Congress and the American people, the Senate ratified the two treaties in 1978 by only one vote. Panama assumed full sovereignty over its canal on December 31, 1999.

Carter's seemingly ineffective handling of the Iran hostage crisis in 1979–1980 seriously undermined his political legitimacy and contributed to the 1980 presidential election of Ronald Reagan. Reagan's victory over Carter in 1980 was also influenced by the crisis over Cuban immigration to the United States, which was known as the Mariel boatlift. Fidel Castro used comments made by Jimmy Carter as a pretext for sending 125,000 Cubans—including some who were in prisons and mental wards—to the United States. After his defeat in 1980, Jimmy Carter returned to Georgia where he founded the Carter Presidential Center in Atlanta and began another life of activity in public affairs. Since its founding in 1982, the **Carter Center** has worked on a variety of global issues, including conflict resolution, arms control, improving agriculture and health conditions in Third World countries, and the use of international observer teams to monitor elections in Latin America to ensure the fairness of the voting process. He observed the 1989 election in Panama where he condemned the maneuvering of Panamanian dictator General Manuel Antonio **Noriega** to manipulate the results in his favor. Carter's election-monitoring teams were instrumental in the controversial 1990 elections in Nicaragua, where he helped persuade Sandinista leader Daniel Ortega to accept defeat by his opponent Violeta Chamorro. He also helped mediate the standoff between Jean-Bertrand **Aristide** and the Haitian military and the general strike aimed at toppling President Hugo Chávez in Venezuela in 2002–2003. In his May 2002 history-making trip to Cuba, Carter spoke (in Spanish) directly to the Cuban people, a speech that was broadcast live on radio and television, praising Cuba's health and education systems, but also criticizing the Castro regime for stifling free speech and not allowing open, democratic elections. On his arrival, Jimmy Carter said, "We are eager to see first-hand your accomplishments in health, in education and in culture." He also met with several dissident groups and praised the Varela project, a petition drive calling for a referendum on government reforms in Cuba. The anti-Castro **George W. Bush** administration was angered by Carter's trip and went to great lengths to discredit Carter for opposing U.S. policy toward Cuba.

After being nominated seven times for the Nobel Peace Prize, Carter was finally awarded the prize in 2002 for his contributions to a safer and healthier world, particularly the peaceful resolution of world conflicts. At the time he accepted the Nobel Peace Prize in Oslo, Carter used the limelight to urge all nations—and by implication, the George W. Bush administration—to think deeply about the grave consequences of war, which he called a "necessary evil" that should always be a last resort. *See also* Friendly Dictators; Human Rights; Panama Canal Treaties.

Suggested Reading

Ariel C. Armony, *Argentina, the United States, and the Anti-Communist Crusade in Central America, 1977–1984* (Athens: Ohio University Press, 1998); Jimmy Carter, *Keeping Faith: Memoirs of a President* (New York: Bantam, 1982); John Dumbrell, *The Carter Presidency: A Reevaluation* (New York: St. Martin's Press, 1993); Jean A. Garrison, *Games Advisors Play: Foreign Policy in the Nixon and Carter Administrations* (College Station: Texas A&M University Press, 1999); William F. Glover, *The President as Prisoner: A Structural Critique of the Carter and Reagan Years* (Albany: State University of New York Press, 1989); Joshua Muravchik, *The Uncertain Crusade: Jimmy Carter and the Dilemma of Human Rights Policy* (Lanham, MD: Hamilton Press, 1986); Herbert D. Rosenbaum and Alexej Ugrinsky, *Jimmy Carter: Jimmy Carter and Post-Presidential Years* (Westport, CT: Greenwood Press, 1994); Aimee D. Shouse, *Presidents from Nixon Through Carter, 1961–1981: Debating the Issues in Pro and Con Primary Documents* (Westport, CT: Greenwood Press, 2002); David Skidmore, *Reversing Course: Carter's Foreign Policy, Domestic Politics, and the Failure of Reform* (Nashville: Vanderbilt University Press, 1990); Gaddis Smith, *Morality, Reason, and Power: American Diplomacy in the Carter Years* (New York: Hill and Wang, 1986); Donald S. Spencer, *The Carter Implosion: Jimmy Carter and the Amateur Style of Diplomacy* (New York: Praeger, 1988); Robert A. Strong, *Working in the World: Jimmy Carter and the Making of American Foreign Policy* (Baton Rouge: Louisiana State University Press, 2000); Kevin Sullivan, "Carter Begins Historic Cuba Visit," *Washington Post* (May 13, 2002); Kenneth W. Thompson, ed., *The President, the Bureaucracy, and World Regions in Arms Control* (Lanham, MD: University Press of America, 1998); Richard C. Thornton, *The Carter Years: Toward a New Global Order* (New York: Paragon House, 1991); Rod Troesler, *Jimmy Carter as Peacemaker: A Post-Presidential Biography* (Westport, CT: Praeger, 1996).

Carter Center Non-profit organization founded by former President Jimmy **Carter** in 1982 to assist in the eradication of preventable diseases, promote peaceful solutions to world conflicts, protect and monitor free elections, and foster **democracy** at various levels throughout the world. Over the past twenty years, the Carter Center—headquartered in Atlanta, Georgia—has devoted a considerable amount of resources and energy to Latin America, monitoring elections and working to provide peaceful, and democratic solutions, to various conflicts. President Carter takes a personal interest in these diplomatic matters, having played an instrumental role in Nicaragua, Panama, Haiti, Cuba, Venezuela, Jamaica, and Guyana. The Carter Center stepped in to the Venezuelan conflict in 2002 by advocating negotiations between President Hugo Chávez and opposition groups. By working with the **Organization of American States (OAS)** and the **United Nations** Development Program, Carter's team of negotiators helped to quell tensions and resolve the deadly conflict. The Carter Center was also involved in overseeing the 2003 petition drive by opposition groups seeking a recall referendum on President Chávez in 2004.

In May 2002, Jimmy Carter traveled to Cuba to begin a dialogue on freedom and offer new prospects for reconciliation between the United States and Cuba. In a speech at the University of Havana, Carter criticized the Cuban government—the first public criticism of the Cuban government in over forty years—and informed the Cuban people that more than 11,000 of their fellow citizens had signed a petition, exercising their little-known constitutional right to do so. The Carter Center's work on issues of global concern was one of the reasons that Jimmy Carter was awarded the 2002 Nobel Peace Prize. *See also* Democracy and Democracy Promotion; Human Rights.

Suggested Reading

Theodore Runyon, ed., *Theology, Politics and Peace* (Maryknoll, NY: Orbis Books, 1989).

Casey, William Joseph (1913–1987) Lawyer, intelligence official, and conservative politician who was appointed to key economic, banking, and intelligence posts in the **Nixon**, **Ford**, and **Reagan** administrations. William Casey was born in New York City, graduated from Fordham University and received a law degree from St. John's University in 1937. His interest in the world of intelligence began during **World War II** when he served in the Office of Strategic Services (OSS), the precursor to the **Central Intelligence Agency (CIA)**. Casey helped with Ronald Reagan's 1980 presidential campaign and was appointed director of the CIA when the Reagan administration took office in 1981. Casey set out to restore the CIA's covert action capabilities after the Carter administration had weakened the CIA in the wake of intelligence abuses and critical congressional investigations. To achieve this objective, Reagan provided Casey with "cabinet rank," in effect politicizing the CIA as part of the presidential advisory system. With the support of President Reagan, both a staunch anti-Communist and foe of the Soviet Union—Casey began a worldwide effort to provide covert support for a wide range of anti-Communist insurgents, from Nicaragua and Afghanistan to Angola and Cambodia. William Casey made the CIA's national intelligence estimates more responsive to political objectives, increased intelligence funding, and developed more aggressive covert capabilities to counter Soviet-backed regimes in the Third World.

With the support of CIA director William Casey, Oliver **North** ran the **Contra** war against the **Sandinistas** in Nicaragua. The Reagan administration's obsession with Nicaragua contained a rhetorical strategy designed to diminish the legitimacy of the Sandinista leadership in the eyes of the American people. President Reagan called Daniel Ortega "a little dictator in green fatigues" and those who worked for CIA Director William Casey often heard him refer to Nicaragua as a "little piss-ant country" trying to bully the United States with the help of international organizations.

As one of the prime movers of what came to be known as the **Reagan Doctrine**, Casey became involved in more anti-Communist crusades than he could handle and soon came under criticism for the CIA mining of Nicaragua's harbors and being a major player in the **Iran-Contra scandal**. The arming of the Contras against the Sandinistas proved unsuccessful as it embroiled both Casey and Reagan in law-breaking activities that angered Congress and produced the Iran-Contra **covert operation** that could have easily led to impeachment of President Reagan if there was not so much fear in the **media** and Congress of another failed presidency. Casey was diagnosed with a malignant brain tumor shortly before he was to testify before a congressional panel investigating the scandal and died in May 1987. Casey's death left unclear the extent of his involvement in these sordid policies and other matters. There are allegations to this day that Casey secretly arranged for Iranian government officials to postpone release of U.S. hostages then being held in captivity in Tehran to discredit President Jimmy **Carter** and enhance Reagan's chances of winning the presidential election in 1980. Those who are convinced of this deceitful act claim that by releasing the American hostages under Reagan's watch it would increase the chances of purchasing weapons from the United States.

Suggested Reading

Eldon Kenworthy, *America/Américas: Myth in the Making of U.S. Policy Toward Latin America* (University Park: Pennsylvania State University Press, 1995); Mark M. Lowenthal, *U.S. Intelligence: Evolution and Anatomy*, 2nd ed. (Westport, CT: Greenwood Press, 1992).

Castro Ruz, Fidel (1926–) Revolutionary leader of Cuba known for his authoritarian politics, socialist ideology, and ability to stand up to more than ten U.S. presidents determined to destroy his regime. The success of his guerrilla war against the tyrant Fulgencio **Batista** brought him to power at the age of thirty-two and provided him with the legitimacy to shape the first socialist revolution in Latin America that did not succumb to U.S. **imperialism**. Despite the politics of U.S. hostility directed at removing Castro from power, he has managed to survive for over four decades, a remarkable feat in the history of U.S.–Latin American relations. Although much of this hostility grew out of the connection between the Cuban Revolution and the **Cold War**, the collapse of the Soviet Union and the acceptance of Cuba by most nations in the world has not ended Cuba's pariah status as far as Washington is concerned. In fact, U.S.–Cuban relations deteriorated in the 1990s as the United States tried to take advantage of Cuba's weakened condition with the withdrawal of Soviet subsidies. After **September 11, 2001**, Fidel Castro was the first world leader to offer his people's condolences for the tragedy, clearly stated that Cuba was against **terrorism**, and stated emphatically that he would not challenge the United States over its decision to hold "enemy combatants" suspected of being Al-Qaeda agents at the U.S. military base located at **Guantánamo Bay**. Nevertheless, President **George W. Bush** claimed that Castro was a terrorist, his regime sponsored terrorism, and he deserved more punishment for his refusal to buckle to U.S. wishes. Although the Bush administration would like to bring about **regime change** on the island, most foreign policy experts see little chance of a preemptive strike to remove Castro from power after almost fifty years.

Fidel Castro's early life offers clues to his rise to fame as one of the world's paramount revolutionary leaders. Fidel Castro's father—Angel Castro—was born in Galicia, Spain, and came to Cuba as a military conscript to fight against Cubans. He was allowed to remain in Cuba after the **Spanish-Cuban-American War**, built a small farm into a prosperous cattle ranch, and fathered nine children by two wives. After the death of his first wife, he married Lina Ruz González, whose parents were both from the same province as Fidel's father. Some have suggested that Castro is more Spaniard (*puro gallego*) than Cuban because of his family roots. Thanks to the family's wealth Fidel Castro received the best education money could buy in Cuba. Raúl Castro, Fidel's younger brother, is head of Cuba's military and is officially in line to succeed his older brother in the event Fidel is killed or dies of natural causes. His sister Juana lives in Miami where she runs a drugstore and is a frequent attendee of rallies where she condemns her brother's revolutionary politics.

Until his enrollment in the University of Havana Law School, Castro attended Jesuit schools in Santiago and Havana, eventually earning a law degree in 1950. While attending the university Castro received much of his political education. It was not long before Fidel Castro, according to Leonard (1999: 92), "acquired a reputation for personal ambition, forcefulness, and fine oratory, yet he never became a prominent student leader." The university environment contained critics of the Cuban government, violence, and level of activism designed to purge the regime of its corruption, lack of morality, and subservience to the United States. The toughness of campus events did not end at the university; Fidel Castro ventured off to Bogotá, Colombia, to protest against the formation of the **Organization of American States (OAS)** and joined a small expeditionary force in a failed attempt to overthrow the Dominican dictator Rafael **Trujillo** in 1948. Fidel married Mirta Díaz-Balart in late 1948 and the following year a son was born, Fidelito. However, the marriage did not last and ended in divorce after Fidel Castro discovered she had a sinecure with the Batista government. Castro did not remarry although he developed a close friendship with Celia Sánchez Mundulay, an ally in the guerrilla war against Batista in the 1950s.

It is hard to pinpoint both the source and impact of political ideas on the mind of Fidel Castro. His exposure to a wide range of political ideologies suggests that he has incorporated most of them into his revolutionary program for a new Cuba after 1959. In any case, Castroism is based on the ideals of José **Martí**, the charisma of Eduardo "Eddy" Chibás and Colombian liberal leader Jorge Eliécer Gaitán, the anti-capitalism and humanitarianism of Karl Marx, and the frustration of watching **democracy** fail in Cuba for most of the twentieth century. Castro would not have survived for so long without the ability to make adjustments and concessions to keep the revolution alive. The Cuban Revolution would not have survived without Castro's ability to align himself with political adversaries of the United States and change course when the survival of the revolution demanded it. Castro's forty-year alignment with the Soviet Union allowed him to consolidate power and demonstrate independence that was not possible during the sixty years of U.S. domination of the island. The renewed tensions between Cuba and the United States that developed after the election of George W. Bush as president of the United States led to a policy where Venezuela sold Castro oil at cut-rate prices in exchange for sending thousands of Cuba doctors to work in poor communities that lacked such services because Venezuelan doctors refused to work under such deplorable conditions. Although some argue that Fidel's ideology and political program is rooted in Marx and Lenin, others point to José Martí as the inspiration for Fidel's nationalism, anti-imperialism, humanitarianism, and political morality.

Fidel Castro has been in command and provided Cuba with political leadership since the January 1, 1959, overthrow of General Batista. By "exporting" his opponents to the United States, and offering state-supported social welfare programs to Cuba's poorer classes, Castro has gained a wide base of support. The losers, mostly members of the Cuban elite and foreign businessmen, have helped to wage economic and political warfare against Castro in hopes of removing him from power. Yet, Castro remains defiant and continues to resist efforts to rid the island of him and the revolution. He has made adjustments in his travels and long-distant speeches, but still commands the respect of millions of Cubans on the island.

Fidel Castro developed a close relationship with the Argentine physician and revolutionary strategist, Ernesto Che **Guevara**, and accepted some of his advice in shifting Cuba toward an industrial economy and the new "socialist man." When it was discovered that these efforts were not going to work, Fidel and Che began to quarrel over the direction of the Cuban Revolution, both at home and abroad. Che's efforts to export his *foco* model of revolution in Africa and Bolivia failed, eventually leading to his death at the hands of the Bolivian army and the U.S. **Central Intelligence Agency (CIA)** in 1967. Nevertheless, Che's image as a revolutionary icon continues to provide the moral and spiritual foundation for Castro and the Cuban Revolution. He is lionized in a large statue, mausoleum, and museum in Santa Clara, Cuba, and the Cuban government is building a new Center for the Study of Che Guevara in Havana.

Fidel Castro's style of governing has angered those who disagree with his authoritarian policies, state control over many institutions, and restrictions on political freedom. There is a fledgling opposition movement on the island, but members of the dissident movement have been criticized for their close contacts with the U.S. government and exiles in Miami. Castro continues to maintain a tight grip on the affairs of state where opposing the views of official policy can mean arrest and prison sentences. The United States knows this and continues to foster policies to stir up trouble for Castro and his followers. As he approaches eighty years of age, Fidel Castro continues to play a revolutionary role that other Latin American rebels could only dream of. He remains a controversial figure for what he has done on the island and his support for revolutionary governments from Angola to Nicaragua. His ideas of revolutionary socialism, Third World nationalism, sovereignty, and independence continue to resonate in other parts of the world. The animosity directed at the United States in the aftermath of the war against Saddam Hussein in 2003 has furthered Castro's image as the embodiment of anti–United

States sentiment. When Bush announced a rash of hostile policy measures against Cuba in May 2004, Castro mobilized 1.2 million Cubans to spend hours marching in protest against policies designed to bring about "regime change" in Cuba. Posters adorned the countryside where Bush's policies are equated with fascism, and he appears dressed as Adolf Hitler along with a Hitler-like mustache. The latest move to tighten the restrictions on trade, travel, remittances, and communication are only part of an obsession with Fidel Castro and his removal from power. After more than forty-five years of revolution it is clear that Castro's main legacy will be his struggle to rid his country of foreign control and reduce the poverty and illiteracy so common throughout the rest of Latin America. *See also* Assassination; Bay of Pigs; Covert Operations; Hegemony; Imperialism; Recognition and Non-Recognition; Revolutions.

Suggested Reading

Peter G. Bourne, *Fidel: A Biography of Fidel Castro* (New York: Dodd Mead, 1986); Jorge I. Domínguez, *Cuba: Order and Revolution* (Cambridge, MA: Belknap Press of Harvard University Press, 1979); Theodore Draper, *Castroism: Theory and Practice* (New York: Praeger, 1965); Carlos Franqui, *Family Portrait with Fidel* (New York: Random House, 1981); Georgie Anne Geyer, *Guerrilla Prince: The Untold Story of Fidel Castro* (Boston: Little, Brown, 1991); Edward González, *Cuba Under Castro: The Limits of Charisma* (New York: Houghton Mifflin, 1974); Maurice Halperin, *The Rise and Decline of Fidel Castro* (Berkeley: University of California Press, 1972); Sheldon B. Liss, *Fidel!: Castro's Political and Social Thought* (Boulder, CO: Westview Press, 1994); Mario Llerena, *The Unsuspected Revolution: The Birth and Rise of Castroism* (Ithaca, NY: Cornell University Press, 1978); Herbert Matthews, *Fidel Castro* (New York: Simon and Schuster, 1969); Andrés Oppenheimer, *Castro's Final Hour: The Secret Story behind the Coming Downfall of Communist Cuba* (New York: Touchstone, 1992); Robert Quirk, *Fidel Castro* (New York: W.W. Norton, 1993); Wayne Smith, *Closest of Enemies: A Personal and Diplomatic Account of U.S.–Cuban Relations since 1957* (New York: W.W. Norton, 1987); Andrés Suárez, *Cuba: Castroism and Communism* (Cambridge, MA: MIT Press, 1967); Tad Szulc, *Fidel: A Critical Portrait* (New York: William Morrow and Co., 1986); Manuel Urrutia-Lleo, *Fidel Castro & Company, Inc.* (New York: Praeger, 1964).

CBI. *See* Caribbean Basin Initiative

Central Intelligence Agency (CIA) The Central Intelligence Agency is the primary information-gathering component of the presidential advisory system. As such its main focus is on secret intelligence research rather than policymaking per se. The CIA was created by the National Security Act of 1947 and is responsible to the National Security Council and to the president of the United States. It succeeded the **World War II** Office of Strategic Services (OSS) and the post-war National Intelligence Authority. Since its founding in the late 1940s, the CIA has played a major role in destabilization campaigns and regime change in Latin America. Those who have worked for the CIA often refer to it as the Company, the Agency, or the Pickle Factory. The CIA flourished during the **Cold War**, particularly in the areas of intelligence gathering, anti-Communist activities, and the implementation of covert operations. After the end of the Cold War the CIA's importance in Latin American policymaking declined, only to be revived once the **George W. Bush** administration declared war on **terrorism** in 2001. The CIA's power in the conduct of foreign relations derived from the fact that it did not have to disclose its activities, and the director of the CIA was able to spend money and assign personnel without public accounting. CIA covert operations grew with White House concern for countering Communist threats, particularly ones that were considered part of the growing Soviet empire.

In Latin America, the Central Intelligence Agency played a role in the politics of just about every Latin American country after 1950. It engineered the overthrow of Guatemala's leftist leader, Jacobo **Arbenz**, in 1954; the Bay of Pigs invasion to remove Fidel **Castro** in 1961; the forced removal of Cheddi Jagan in Guyana in 1964; the Chilean intervention in 1970–1973; the creation and maintenance of the Nicaraguan **Contras** after the overthrow of Anastasio **Somoza** Debayle in 1979; and the coordinated effort to track down and kill Che **Guevara** in Bolivia in 1967. The use of the CIA by American presidents brought considerable criticism of the agency for its secrecy, disdain for democracy, use of assassination as a tool of foreign policy, and its refusal to operate as part of an open and democratic society. After the end of the Cold War, covert operations declined inside the CIA; however, after the George W. Bush administration called for a global war on terrorism in 2001, CIA covert operations picked up again. CIA directors are appointed by the president of the United States, and many became well known for how they conducted U.S.–Latin American relations. Unfortunately, many of the **scandals and blunders** committed by the United States during the Cold War were closely connected to CIA operations. Directors such as Walter Bidell Smith, **Allen W. Dulles**, **George H.W. Bush**, and William **Casey** were close friends of the president, and many felt that they were always carrying out the foreign policy wishes of the president, with or without his direct authorization.

The director of central intelligence (DCI) is in charge of secret intelligence gathering operations at CIA headquarters in Langley, Virginia. The DCI runs the agency through its five directorates, the most controversial of which is the Directorate of Operations. The CIA's Latin American activities take place within the Western Hemisphere unit, one of six geographic units within the CIA. Within the unit responsible for Western Hemisphere affairs, four specialized staffs deal with Covert Action, Counter-intelligence, Counter-narcotics, and Counter-terrorism. DCI's are reticent to publish their own first-hand accounts of the agency and its role in the policy-making process, the result of a close-knit fraternity of spies and the fear of exposing secrets about methods and sources. Two of the most secretive and powerful heads of the CIA—Richard **Helms** and William Casey—played key roles in Latin American policy during the **Nixon** and **Reagan** years. Richard Helms orchestrated the destablization campaign against Chilean president Salvador **Allende**; William Casey carried out a multitude of covert operations in Latin America in the name of the **Reagan Doctrine**, particularly in El Salvador, Honduras, and

Nicaragua. **Covert operations** have become particularly controversial because of congressional investigations and exposés by former CIA agents such as Philip **Agee**. According to Rossi and Plano (1992: 199), "Wherever leftist governments have come to power or have threatened to win power, the CIA has intervened covertly in both the public and private sectors to destabilize such regimes or destroy their effectiveness." The techniques used by the CIA in Guatemala, Cuba, the Dominican Republic, Chile, Guyana, Grenada, Nicaragua, Panama, and Haiti included assassination of political leaders, training and funding of private armies, fomenting strikes and political chaos, the use of bribery, financial support for friendly groups, the rigging of elections, manipulation of the **media**, and other schemes and maneuvers. With the exception of Fidel Castro's Cuba, the CIA was successful in determining the outcomes in these Latin American cases. As a result of CIA involvement in Latin American political and economic affairs, the U.S. government has come to be identified with anti-progressive and anti-revolutionary movements in Latin America and the Caribbean.

Presidential use of the Central Intelligence Agency for covert operations and the challenges to intelligence gathering by congressional oversight committees contributed to a steep decline in the CIA's resources devoted to covert action in the 1990s. The new instruments of accountability changed the ability of the CIA to operate with little oversight until the war on terrorism generated new funds and a realization that the United States needed to put more resources into human intelligence. After Congress enacted the Hughes-Ryan Act in 1974—a law prohibiting the expenditure of funds for CIA covert operations unless the president issues a "finding" stating the importance of such an operation to the national security of the United States and then reports these facts to Congress in a timely fashion—U.S. presidents faced new restrictions on the conduct of foreign policy. The use of clandestine operations to further U.S. foreign policy in Latin America has no doubt contributed to **anti-American** sentiments and genuine skepticism regarding the benevolent rationales offered in the name of U.S. to Latin American policy.

In response to terrorist attacks of **September 11, 2001**, Congress passed an intelligence reorganization bill in 2004 with a new post of director of national intelligence. President George W. Bush nominated John D. **Negroponte** to be the new intelligence czar with the authority to oversee the collection of fifteen intelligence agencies in Washington, including the CIA. Under the new intelligence reform law, Negroponte is obligated to establish a policy-making process that will produce alternative viewpoints on key intelligence matters and a system for handling complaints from intelligence agents about bias and partisan political influence over their analysis and reports. If this bureaucratic change takes place, it could have a major impact on the role of threat assessment on national security. *See also* Assassination; Bay of Pigs; Blowback; Church Committee Report; Threat Perception/Assessment.

Suggested Reading

Robert Baer, *See No Evil: The True Story of a Ground Soldier in the CIA's Counter-Terrorism Wars* (New York: Crown, 2002); William Blum, *Killing Hope: U.S. Military and CIA Interventions Since World War II* (Monroe, ME: Common Courage Press, 2004); Blum, *Rogue State: A Guide to the World's Only Superpower* (Monroe, ME: Common Courage Press, 2000); William Colby and Peter Forbath, *Honorable Men: My Life in the CIA* (New York: Simon and Schuster, 1978); David W. Dent, ed., *U.S.–Latin American Policymaking: A Reference Handbook* (Westport, CT: Greenwood Press, 1995); I.M. Destler, Leslie H. Gelb, and Anthony Lake, *Our Own Worst Enemy: The Unmaking of American Foreign Policy* (New York: Simon and Schuster, 1984); Lloyd Etheredge, *Can Government's Learn: American Foreign Policy and Central American Revolutions* (New York: Pergamon Press, 1985); Rhodri Jeffreys-Jones, *The CIA and American Democracy* (New Haven: Yale University Press, 1989); Jonathan Kwitney, *Endless Enemies: The Making of an Unfriendly World* (New York: Penguin, 1984); Mark M. Lowenthal, *U.S. Intelligence: Evolution and Anatomy* (New York: Praeger, 1984); Gabriel Marcella, "The Presidential Advisory System," in David W. Dent, ed., *U.S.–Latin American Policymaking: A Reference Handbook* (Westport, CT: Greenwood Press, 1995); Thomas Powers, *The Man Who Kept the Secrets: Richard Helms and the CIA* (New York: Alfred A. Knopf, 1979); John Prados, *Lost Crusader: The Secret Wars of CIA Director William Colby* (New York: Oxford University Press, 2003); Prados, *Presidents' Secret Wars: CIA and Pentagon Covert Operations Since World War II* (New York: William Morrow, 1986); John Ranelagh, *The Agency: The Rise and Decline of the CIA* (New York: Simon and Schuster, 1986); Harry Howe Ransom, *The Intelligence Establishment* (Cambridge, MA: Harvard University Press, 1970); W. Michael Reisman and James Baker, *Regulating Covert Action: Practices, Contexts, and Policies of Covert Coercion Abroad in International and American Law* (New Haven: Yale University Press, 1992); Ernest E. Rossi and Jack C. Plano, *Latin America: A Political Dictionary* (Santa Barbara, CA: ABC-Clio, 1992); Peter Dale Scott, *Drugs, Oil and Water: The United States in Afghanistan, Colombia, and Indochina* (Lanham, MD: Roman and Littlefield, 2003); Allan A. Swenson, *The Complete Idiots' Guide to the CIA* (Indianapolis: Alpha, 2003); Stansfield Turner, *Secrecy and Democracy: The CIA in Transition* (Boston: Houghton Mifflin, 1985); Bob Woodward, *Veil: The Secret Wars of the CIA, 1981–1987* (New York: Simon and Schuster, 1987); Peter Wyden, *Bay of Pigs: The Untold Story* (New York: Touchstone, 1979).

Chapultepec Conference (1945) Inter-American conference that took place in early 1945 at Chapultepec Palace in Mexico City to discuss (1) U.S.–Argentine conflict over Buenos Aires' reluctance to declare war against the Axis powers, (2) post-war U.S. economic assistance for Latin America, and (3) the role of the inter-American system in the emerging **United Nations (UN)**. The conference included representatives from twenty-one American republics (excluding Argentina), including the United States. U.S. diplomats were divided between "universalists" who believed that the prerogatives of the United Nations should supercede those of regional security systems and a group of "regionalists" who advocated regional self-defense for the Western Hemisphere. The Latin Americans, worried about protection against external interference and U.S. intervention, supported a regional system. The outcome of the Chapultepec Conference, the Act of Chapultepec, tried to accommodate both the regionalist and universalist positions by allowing for different approaches toward common goals.

The Chapultepec Conference, known formally as the Inter-American Conference on Problems of War and Peace, agreed that Argentina needed to declare war against Nazi Germany to rejoin the inter-American community, endorsed the Latin American preference for collective self-defense through regional security pacts. The Act of Chapultepec served as the basis for Article 52 of the UN Charter, authorizing regional security arrangements, thus foreshadowing the creation of the Rio Treaty in 1947. By providing for a collective response against aggression from outside or inside the region, it expanded the **Monroe Doctrine** from a unilateral guarantee against intervention into a regional security system, including provisions that would prohibit aggression by one state against another state and the creation of a treaty of reciprocal assistance. Latin America's hope for U.S. aid was dashed when the most they got for their demands for loans and grants was a postponed future conference. The United States extolled the achievements of the Chapultepec Conference, the preservation of the Monroe Doctrine and the inter-American system, and the inherent right of individual and collective self-defense. It is important to point out that the decisions reached at the Chapultepec Conference in 1945 left many problems unsolved, particularly the question of a Marshall Plan for Latin America and the continuation of the **Good Neighbor Policy**'s pledge of non-intervention. *See also* German Threat; Intervention and Non-Intervention; Threat Perception/Assessment.

Suggested Reading

G. Pope Atkins, *Encyclopedia of the Inter-American System* (Westport, CT: Greenwood Press, 1997); Gordon Connell-Smith, *The Inter-American System* (New York: Oxford University Press, 1966); David Green, *The Containment of Latin America: A History of Myths and Realities of the Good Neighbor Policy* (Chicago: Quadrangle Books, 1971); Gaddis Smith, *The Last Years of the Monroe Doctrine, 1945–1993* (New York: Hill and Wang, 1994).

Chicago Boys Young Chilean economists who studied economics at the University of Chicago that had a major impact on the political economy of Chile during the **Pinochet** dictatorship (1973–1989). The University of Chicago and the Catholic University of Chile signed an agreement in 1956 that provided scholarships for talented Chilean students to pursue the study of economics at the University of Chicago. Under the guidance of Nobel Prize winner Milton Friedman, and Arnold Harberger, conservative economists known for their anti-statist and free-market approach, Chile developed a network of young civilian technicians anxious to apply their American-acquired knowledge of economics to their homeland. After the overthrow of President Salvador **Allende**, an advocate of socialism and redistributive economic policies, General Pinochet hired the "Chicago Boys" to aid in the consolidation of authoritarian rule while removing all traces of Allende's socialist economics. The Chicago Boys found the perfect environment to apply their right-wing version of modernization theory. Many became defenders of the Pinochet **dictatorship** because it allowed them to postpone **democracy** while at the same time pursuing their belief in economic freedom and a market-based economy. The reforms carried out by the Chicago Boys pleased officials in Washington (including those in the World Bank and the International Monetary Fund [IMF]) and helped to mute some of the **human rights** violations carried out by the military government. Critics of the Chicago Boys claimed their policies of denationalization and openness to foreign investment contributed to greater economic dependency, social inequality, and **anti-Americanism**.

Suggested Reading

Larman C. Wilson and David W. Dent, *Historical Dictionary of Inter-American Organizations* (Lanham, MD: Scarecrow Press, 1998).

Church Committee Report The Watergate scandal (1972–1974), a decade of covert action in Chile (1963–1973), and the controversy over the Vietnam War generated a concern on Capitol Hill about the **covert operations** of U.S. government intelligence agencies. A Senate resolution established a Select Committee to Study Governmental Operations with Respect to Intelligence Activities to investigate whether prevailing government intelligence operations were "illegal, improper, or unethical." The Select Committee held public hearings and issued several reports on the activities of the **Central Intelligence Agency (CIA)** and the Federal Bureau of Investigation. Chaired by Idaho Senator Frank Church, the Senate Committee became known as the Church Committee. The hearings were dramatic and sensitive since they uncovered CIA **assassination** plots against Latin American leaders such as Fidel **Castro** of Cuba and Rafael **Trujillo** of the Dominican Republic, and the efforts to destabilize the democratically elected government of Chilean socialist Salvador **Allende**. The Church Committee cautioned that the findings in their reports should be viewed in the context of stopping the spread of communism in Latin America, but the practice of assassination as a tool of American foreign policy should be rejected because it is incompatible with American principles, **international law**, and morality. The Church Committee also believed that the American people need to be told of such nefarious activities, no matter how embarrassing to the U.S. government. The Senate Committee argued that because **democracy** depends on a well-informed citizenry, disclosure was necessary for the government to maintain the respect of the people. As a result of the Church Committee's findings, as well as those of a House investigating committee, Presidents Gerald **Ford** and Jimmy **Carter** issued executive orders to improve executive branch control over covert operations. *See also* Democracy and Democracy Promotion.

CIA. *See* Central Intelligence Agency

Clark Memorandum A legal study written by Undersecretary of State J. Reuben Clark in the 1920s to reject the previously claimed right of the United States to intervene based on the **Roosevelt Corollary to the Monroe Doctrine**. The decision to separate the **Monroe Doctrine** from the right of **intervention** was made by Secretary of State Frank B. Kellogg at a time when the unilateralism of U.S.–Latin American policy was harshly criticized, following decades of U.S. military intervention and occupation. Also known as the "Memorandum on the Monroe Doctrine," Clark's study was initiated when there was no apparent security threat from outside the hemisphere to either the United States or the Latin American states. In declaring that the Monroe Doctrine "does not apply to purely inter-American relations," but "states a case of United States *vs.* Europe, not of United States *vs.* Latin America," Clark's interpretation stated that U.S. intervention and occupation of places such as Cuba, Haiti, Nicaragua, and the Dominican Republic are not covered by the original terms of the Monroe Doctrine. After the memorandum was made public in 1930, it signaled to the Latin American states a partial move toward a doctrine of non-intervention, helped make the case for the withdrawal of U.S. military forces in parts of the Caribbean and Central America, and paved the way for President **Franklin D. Roosevelt**'s **Good Neighbor Policy** in 1933. The inter-American treaties that were signed in the 1930s abandoning interference and intervention helped to establish a high level of inter-American cooperation during **World War II** that lasted until the 1954 covert intervention in Guatemala that removed the controversial president, Jacobo **Arbenz**. *See also* Hegemony.

Suggested Reading

J. Reuben Clark, *Memorandum on the Monroe Doctrine* (Washington, DC: U.S. Government Printing Office, 1930); Robert H. Holden and Eric Zolov, eds., *Latin America and the United States: A Documentary History* (New York: Oxford University Press, 2000).

Clay, Henry (1777–1852) Pre–U.S. Civil War political leader who supported Spanish-American movements for independence, **Pan-American** ideals, and closer ties between the United States and Latin America. Born in Virginia, Clay eventually moved to Kentucky where he played an active political role, first as a Jeffersonian Republican, and later as member of the Whig Party. He served in the U.S. Senate and the House of Representatives, was elected speaker of the house on three occasions, and unsuccessfully ran for president in 1824, 1832, and 1844. He was President John Quincy **Adams**' secretary of state between 1825 and 1829. Henry Clay was an early enthusiast for recognition of the newly independent Latin American nations. He supported aid for Spanish-American independence movements, prompt recognition of the new Latin American republics, advocated hemispheric unity, preached the importance of representative **democracy**, and approved the **Monroe Doctrine**. As secretary of state, Clay struggled to improve relations with Latin America by speaking of the mutual advantages of hemispheric unity. He was unsuccessful in sending U.S. delegates to the 1826 Panama Conference organized by Simón **Bolívar** because of congressional opposition.

Henry Clay's ardor changed after he read negative reports from the region while secretary of state in the late 1820s. He concluded that there was little to be gained by devoting much attention to a region that exhibited traits of inferiority, incompetence, and such little capability for self-government. During the 1840s Clay became embroiled over the annexation of Texas, U.S. expansionism, and abolitionism. He was a strong opponent of President James K. **Polk**'s war with Mexico but supported its military prosecution once the conflict began in 1846. Henry Clay was one of the early nineteenth-century politicians who recognized the importance that U.S.–Latin American relations could have on domestic politics in the United States. As Lars Schoultz (1998: 370) argues: "While security concerns ebb and flow, domestic U.S. politics have been central to the explanation of nearly every important issue of U.S.–Latin American relations, beginning in the 1820s, when John Quincy Adams and Henry Clay used the question of recognizing Latin American independence to position themselves for the Presidency." *See also* Manifest Destiny; Mexican-American War (1846–1848); Recognition and Non-Recognition.

Suggested Reading

H.L. Hoskins, "The Hispanic-American Policy of Henry Clay, 1816–1828," *Hispanic American Historical Review*, Vol. 7 (1927); Joseph Byrne Lockey, *Pan Americanism: Its Beginnings* (New York: Macmillan, 1920); Robert V. Remini, *Henry Clay: Statesman for the Union* (New York: W.W. Norton, 1991); Lars Schoultz, *Beneath the United States: A History of U.S. Policy Toward Latin America* (Cambridge, MA: Harvard University Press, 1998).

Clayton-Bulwer Treaty (1850) Treaty between the United States and Great Britain designed to provide joint ownership and control over any future ship canal through the Central American isthmus. After the end of the **Mexican-American War** in 1848 and the discovery of gold in California, the United States became more concerned about securing an overland passageway linking the Atlantic and Pacific oceans. The major challenge for the United States was to prevent Great Britain—the world's greatest industrial and military power with strong financial and commercial interests in Central America—from acquiring exclusive domination of a future canal. The Clayton-Bulwer Treaty—named after U.S. Secretary of State John M. Clayton and Sir Henry Bulwer, the British minister in Washington—was designed to end the rivalry between the United States and Great Britain in Central America. However, the treaty contained features that were unacceptable to many in the United States because it sacrificed far too much American control over a vital region and legitimized international control of any isthmian canal.

The most controversial provisions included (1) joint Anglo-American control, (2) guaranteed neutrality, (3) equal tolls for both states' subjects or citizens and (4) the prohibition of fortifications, or any attempt at colonization or domination in Central America. The most severe criticism of the treaty came from a nationalistic faction of the Democratic Party that argued that by allowing a British presence in Latin America it violated the essential characteristics of the **Monroe Doctrine**. Nevertheless, the treaty represented a diplomatic success because it managed to slow British ambitions in Central America and for the first time elevated the United States to equal status with the world's superpower at the time. Once the treaty was ratified by the U.S. Senate in 1850, it remained in effect until 1901 when it was superceded by the Hay-Pauncefote Treaty, giving the United States the exclusive right to build and control (including fortifications) any future canal. *See also* Bidlack-Mallarino Treaty.

Suggested Reading

John E. Findling, *Close Neighbors, Distant Friends: United States–Central American Relations* (Westport, CT: Greenwood Press, 1987); Mary W. Williams, *Anglo-American Isthmian Diplomacy, 1815–1915* (Washington, DC: American Historical Association, 1916).

Cleveland, Stephen Grover (1837–1908) Lawyer, politician and two-term (although not consecutive) president of the United States (1885–1889; 1893–1897) whose foreign policy emphasized the peaceful settlement of disputes, **anti-imperialism**, and the avoidance of European power politics. Born in Caldwell, New Jersey, he moved to Buffalo, New York, where he practiced law and served as mayor and governor of New York State. Cleveland was the first Democrat in the White House since the Civil War and his first administration was marked by honesty and a fairly narrow view of presidential authority. He opposed protectorates (Nicaragua) and treaties of reciprocity in Central America and the Caribbean. During his second term he faced the Venezuelan boundary dispute with Great Britain over British Guiana and the second war for Cuba's independence from Spain. Cleveland believed the Venezuelan boundary claim was just and used the occasion to remind the British to respect the **Monroe Doctrine** and recognize U.S. **hegemony** in the Western Hemisphere. He called for arbitration that lasted until 1899, with terms favorable to Great Britain. In President Cleveland's mind the boundary dispute also put the Monroe Doctrine, international morality, and U.S. honor and influence throughout Latin America at stake in the quarrel. In dealing with Cuba prior to the **Spanish-Cuban-American War**, President Cleveland at first tried to avoid getting entangled with Spain over its colonial possession, worried that a Spanish defeat would jeopardize $50 million in U.S. investments on the island. Cleveland favored Spanish pacification and autonomy for the Cubans rather than complete independence from Spain. However, after the sinking of the battleship *U.S.S. Maine* in Havana harbor in 1898, Cleveland was unable to resist the clamor for action, convinced that instability in Cuba was spilling over into the United States, damaging U.S. economic interests, and causing U.S. humanitarian concerns about the harsh treatment of Cubans by Spanish authorities. What Cleveland faced would become a chronic problem of U.S.–Latin American relations throughout the twentieth century.

After leaving the White House in 1897, Cleveland retired from politics and settled in Princeton, New Jersey, where he wrote many magazine articles on current issues and aspects of his own presidency. He continued to oppose colonial expansion, joined the Anti-Imperialist League as an honorary vice-president, and served as an actively involved trustee of Princeton University. Grover Cleveland died in Princeton in 1908. *See also* Imperialism; Olney, Richard.

Suggested Reading

Alyn Brodsky, *Grover Cleveland: A Study in Character* (New York: St. Martin's Press, 2000); Henry F. Graff, *Grover Cleveland* (New York: Times Books, 2002); Ernest R. May, *Imperial Democracy: The Emergence of America as a Great Power* (New York: Harper and Row, 1961); Rexford G. Tugwell, *Grover Cleveland* (New York: Macmillan, 1968); Richard E. Welch, *The Presidencies of Grover Cleveland* (Lawrence: University Press of Kansas, 1988).

Clinton, William Jefferson (1946–) Lawyer, politician, and popular two-term Democratic president of the United States (1993–2001) known for his post–**Cold War** doctrine of enlargement, that is, expanding market democracies around the world rather than containing communism. The anti-Communist guideposts that provided the basis for Cold War–Latin American policy disappeared after 1990, and Latin America became a low priority among world regions. Global issues in general, and Latin American issues in particular, were regarded by the Clinton White House as undesirable interruptions of the domestic business that Clinton wanted to pursue. In his acceptance speech at the Democratic Convention in 1992, Clinton said nothing about Latin America and little about foreign affairs. Clinton beat President **George H.W. Bush** because of the economy and his domestic agenda, but he could not avoid dealing with Bush's unfinished agenda for Latin America, which included Haiti, free trade summitry, Cuba, **drug trafficking**, and immigration from the Americas. Clinton secured approval of the **North American Free Trade Agreement (NAFTA)** by the U.S. Congress, restored constitutional government to Haiti, and convened an unprecedented **Summit of the Americas** to create a future **Free Trade Area of the Americas (FTAA)** by 2005. Although Clinton achieved each of these three goals in his first term, completing the Bush agenda, he failed to display much interest in Latin America for the rest of his presidency. After the Republicans won control of Congress in 1994, partisan wrangling increased over free trade, defense spending, foreign aid, treaties with other countries, and the ideology of diplomatic representation. With Republican Jesse **Helms** in charge of the Senate Foreign Relations Committee, President Clinton found his policies in Latin America stalemated by conservative Republicans who opposed his appointments and policies. Clinton's second term was marred by a humiliating personal scandal and the first impeachment trial since that of Andrew Johnson in the 1860s, as well as by a lack of progress on trade negotiations and the lack of progress in democratic rule throughout the hemisphere. The one exception was Mexico, where the 2000 presidential election was judged fair and the winner, Vicente **Fox Quesada** of the opposition PAN, defeated the ruling PRI for the first time in seventy-one years. The growing importance of Florida in presidential elections led Clinton to continue previous hard-line policies toward Cuba based on economic sanctions and international condemnation.

Born in the small Arkansas town of Hope, Bill Clinton's early life suffered from the absence of a father (his biological father, William Jefferson Blythe, was killed in a car accident three months before Clinton was born). His grandmother took care of him for long periods of time while his mother studied nursing in New Orleans. According to Maraniss (1996: 612), he would carry both "the freewheeling optimism of his mother and the stubborn will of his grandmother into later life." After his mother married Roger Clinton, a failed auto dealer and alcoholic, the family moved to Hot Springs, but it was not until the age of fifteen that he took his stepfather's name. As a member of the baby-boom generation, Clinton had to reconcile his desire for education with the military draft and the war in Vietnam. He excelled in his educational endeavors, Georgetown's School of Foreign Service and Yale Law School, but like hundreds of thousands of college students of the era, who obtained college deferments, Clinton did not join the armed services. Between Georgetown University and Yale, Clinton studied in England on a Rhodes Scholarship and developed an interest in foreign affairs.

During the 1992 presidential campaign, members of the George H.W. Bush White House attacked Clinton for his lack of foreign policy experience and claimed that his qualifications for commander in chief were limited and suspect. Once elected, Bill Clinton assembled a diverse policy-making team to shape the future of inter-American relations. In an effort to reconcile the ideological differences between the Carterite advisers (Warren Christopher, Anthony Lake, and Samuel Berger) and neo-conservative **Reagan** Democrats (Richard Shifter and Penn Kemble), Clinton tried to elevate economics in U.S. foreign policy and create a decision-making process that was based on committees, task forces, and loosely defined clusters of friends and advisers. At first this new arrangement often produced vacillation and ambiguity; later, as the Clinton team became more experienced and focused, he scored more successes than failures.

The struggle in the White House over how to establish new rules of engagement in regional battles and territorial disputes resulted in the doctrine of enlargement to replace the Cold War–era doctrine of containment. Since fighting communism was no longer the central goal of American foreign policy, the Clinton foreign policy team decided to spread **democracy** and free markets around the world. If it worked, Latin America would consist of a community of democratic, market-oriented neighbors willing to cooperate with the United States on a broad range of issues, from Fidel **Castro**'s Cuba to **terrorism**, drugs, emigration, and refugees. This new doctrine embraced free trade as a tool of American foreign policy with an emphasis on multilateral peace-keeping efforts and international alliances in which the United States would play a key, but not an imperial role. Despite the merits of seeking a replacement for containment, Clinton faced a Republican opposition that favored unilateral American action and cuts in foreign aid. Over the course of his first term, Clinton made concessions that contributed to his success in dealing with the return of Jean-Bertrand **Aristide** in Haiti and the approval of NAFTA. He was heralded for initiating the Summit of the Americas, which agreed to the goal of a free trade area of the Americas by the year 2005. Although unpopular in the United States, Clinton put together a rescue package for Mexico after the collapse of the Mexican peso in late 1994. The significant achievements of Clinton's first term were not matched by his second, which seemed full of missed opportunities. President Clinton was unable to forge a consensus on defending democracy, failed to negotiate an agreement to limit arms purchases in the Americas, and made little headway toward a multilateral approach to drugs. Without a national security threat of the magnitude of Cold War communism, Clinton found it increasingly difficult to persuade Congress and the American people that their security depended on some form of internationalism. According to Robert **Pastor**, Clinton failed "to grasp the opportunities that were available to build a hemispheric democratic community," and "failed the test of a statesman," but "passed the test of politics." Bill Clinton will be remembered more for his skills as a politician who understood the aspirations and concerns of the American people. After the American public turned their attention to domestic problems, there was little to gain politically for the Clinton administration to give much attention to Latin America. By completing the George H.W. Bush agenda and maintaining a hard line toward Castro's Cuba, Clinton felt he had expended about as much political energy as he could afford in solving Latin America's problems. When **George W. Bush** entered the White House in 2001, there were signs that the new Republican president would devote more attention to Latin America; however, the events of **September 11, 2001**, reversed Bush's interest in the Americas, and Latin America again moved to a low priority in dealing with world regions.

Suggested Reading

Richard E. Feinberg, *Summitry in the Americas: A Progress Report* (Washington, DC: Institute for International Economics, 1997); Abraham F. Lowenthal, "United States–Latin American Relations: To the Summit and Beyond," *Current History* 94, No. 589 (February 1995); David Maraniss, "William J. Clinton," in Henry F. Graff, ed., *The Presidents: A Reference History*, 2nd ed. (New York: Charles Scribner's Sons, 1996); David R. Mares, "Securing Peace in the Americas in the Next Decade," in Jorge I. Domínguez, ed., *The Future of Inter-American Relations* (New York: Routledge, 2000); Robert A. Pastor, *Exiting the Whirlpool: U.S. Foreign Policy toward Latin America and the Caribbean*, 2nd ed. (Boulder, CO: Westview Press, 2001); Robert A. Winslow, ed., *Power and the Presidency* (New York: Public Affairs, 1999); Bob Woodward, *The Agenda: Inside the Clinton White House* (New York: Simon and Schuster, 1994).

COA. *See* Council of the Americas

COHA. *See* Council on Hemispheric Affairs

Cold War The Cold War was a critical period of world history, lasting from shortly after **World War II** to 1991. It was marked by intense ideological, political, and economic hostility between the United States and the Soviet Union and ultimately had a major impact on U.S.–Latin American relations and the inter-American system. Throughout the Cold War there was fear of nuclear war and Communist subversion and espionage; however, no American died in the continental United States that can be attributed to the Cold War. Nevertheless, **Washington policymakers** played on the public's fears of what would happen if the United States did nothing about Communist advances beyond the shores of the United States. For example, during the Vietnam War President Lyndon **Johnson** posed the question of whether it was better to fight the Communists in Saigon rather than in San Diego, the same logic that President **George W. Bush** used throughout his first term by saying that "we are fighting the terrorists in Iraq so we don't have to fight them in our cities."

The Cold War provided the backdrop for numerous forms of U.S. **intervention** in the internal and external affairs of most Latin American and Caribbean countries, including the overthrow of Guatemalan President Jacobo **Arbenz** (1954), the **Bay of Pigs** invasion (1961), the Dominican Republic intervention (1965), the CIA-backed overthrow of Chilean President Salvador **Allende** (1973), the **Contra** war against the **Sandinista** government of Nicaragua (1981–1989), and the **Grenada invasion** (1983). Inside Latin America, the Cold War contributed to the perpetuation of several **dictatorships**, military takeovers, massive **human rights** violations against political opposition forces, and right-wing **dictatorships** that expanded the power of the military and received unfailing support from Washington as long as they espoused anti-Communist views and policies. During the Cold War the United States made a distinction between traditional Latin American military authoritarians (acceptable) and Communist, fascist, or other police state regimes (unacceptable), believing that the former were the best route to **democracy** while the latter were clearly incapable of such a political transition. This logic was articulated in its purest form during the **Reagan** administration by U.S. ambassador to the **United Nations (UN)** Jeane **Kirkpatrick**.

In a classic example of the "lesser of two evils" logic, Washington policymakers believed that, "Dictators who protected Western interests, provided stability, and suppressed communism were a much better bet in such a context and had to be supported until their nations matured politically or, given the logic of the **domino theory**, whole areas would fall to communist forces" (Schmitz, 1999: 181). Military campaigns against political opposition forces in Argentina, Chile, El Salvador, Guatemala, and Uruguay led to the formation of **death squads**, disappearances of purported "enemies" of the government, and the deterioration of democratic principles and practices. Through **Operation Condor** the United States supported much of this type of government activity.

The Cold War served as the catalyst for the political hostility between the United States and Cuba over the pace and direction of the Cuban Revolution. The **Cuban Missile Crisis** of October 1962, a direct result of the botched Bay of Pigs invasion and the growing struggle between President John F. **Kennedy** and Premier Nikita Khrushchev over Cuba, raised the possibility of nuclear war between the superpowers, although this was averted narrowly by compromises between Washington and Moscow on the status of Castro's Cuba. Paradoxically, the United States continues its "Cold War" hostility toward the island despite the collapse and disappearance of the Soviet Union, the termination of huge Soviet subsidies to Castro's government, the termination of support for Castro-backed left-wing guerrillas in Central and South America, the withdrawal of Cuban troops from parts of Africa, and the heavy costs born by American businesses, consumers, and workers. The Cold War generated a heightened concern for security among U.S. policymakers in Washington, which in turn led to the commitment of large amounts of economic and military aid to allies in Latin America and the Caribbean beginning in the early 1950s.

The United States spent $13.4 trillion (in 1997 dollars) to conduct the Cold War between 1948 and 1991, costs that many analysts consider higher than necessary with negative consequences throughout the world. While there was a short period from 1946 to 1950 when **State Department** policy opposed Latin American dictators, as the Cold War deepened the United States returned to older and more favorable attitudes toward dictatorial rule, now viewed as vital to the defense of the free world. Despite repeated platitudes concerning the importance of democracy and free-market strategies of economic development, the prevailing view among Cold War policymakers was that Latin Americans were "backward" and therefore in need of supervision until they were "mature" and "sophisticated" enough to rule themselves properly. Thomas **Mann**, President Johnson's top official for Latin America, expressed the commonly accepted negative view of Latin Americans by asserting "I know my Latinos. They understand only two things—a buck in the pocket and a kick in the ass" (Schmitz, 1999: 181).

A small amount of total Cold War spending was used to counter the Soviet-Cuban "threat" in the Western Hemisphere, but Latin Americans did not benefit from the Cold War, even though they sometimes supported anti-Communist initiatives in exchange for U.S. economic and military largesse. For example, the Soviet-American rivalry exacerbated ideological and political intolerance in the region, often leading to torture, other human rights violations, and hundreds of thousands of civilian deaths, and neglect of serious internal problems such as poverty, corruption, environmental degradation, and severe damage to whatever democratic political culture existed in the region. The Cold War contributed to the current imbalance in U.S. government spending where military spending is almost forty times that of U.S. foreign aid around the world.

The Cold War also served to undermine the legitimacy of the **Organization of American States (OAS)** as a peaceful mechanism for resolving disputes and advancing the economic and social development of Latin America and the Caribbean. During the Cold War, the United States converted the OAS into an anti-Communist alliance against Cuba, the Dominican Republic, and other Latin American countries, by emphasizing the primacy of the OAS (an organization over which it had considerable clout) over the United Nations in dealing with regional disputes. The Cold War with its emphasis on anti-communism affected every aspect of inter-American relations, dictating political and security policy, influencing the distribution of economic assistance and multilateral aid programs, and shaping the agenda of inter-American conferences. Unfortunately, the Cold War undermined the years of good will and trust between Latin America and the United States that was fostered by "good neighbor" policies (and diplomats) from 1925 to 1950. *See also* Friendly Dictators; Intervention and Non-Intervention.

Suggested Reading

Thomas Arms, *Encyclopedia of the Cold War* (New York: Facts on File, 1994); G. Pope Atkins, *Encyclopedia of the Inter-American System* (Westport, CT: Greenwood Press, 1997); Atkins, *Latin America in the International Political System*, 3rd ed. (Boulder, CO: Westview Press, 1995); Victor Bulmer-Thomas and James Dunkerley, eds., *The United States and Latin America: The New Agenda* (London: Institute of Latin American Studies and David Rockefeller Center for Latin American Studies, Harvard University, 1999); Thomas H. Carothers, *The United States and Latin America After the Cold War* (Washington, DC: Latin America Program, The Wilson Center, 1990); Walter M. Daniels, *Latin America in the Cold War* (New York: Wilson, 1952); Jorge I. Domínguez, ed., *International Security and Democracy: Latin America and the Caribbean in the Post–Cold War Era* (Pittsburgh: University of Pittsburgh Press, 1998); Benjamin Frankel, ed., *The Cold War 1945–1991* (Detroit: Gale, 1992); Frederick H. Gareau, *The United Nations and Other International Institutions: A Critical Analysis* (Chicago: Burnham, 2002); George Childs Kohn, *Dictionary of Wars*, rev. ed. (New York: Facts on File, 1999); Michael Parenti, *Trends and Tragedies in American Foreign Policy* (Boston: Little Brown, 1971); F. Parkinson, *Latin America, the Cold War and World Powers, 1945–1973: A Study in Diplomatic History* (Beverly Hills, CA: Sage Publications, 1974); Thomas Parrish, *The Cold War Encyclopedia* (New York: Henry Holt, 1996); Douglas W. Payne, *Latin America: U.S. Policy After the Cold War* (New York: Americas Society, 1991); Stephen G. Rabe, *Eisenhower and Latin America: The Foreign Policy of Anticommunism* (Chapel Hill: University of North Carolina Press, 1988); David F. Schmitz, *Thank God They're on Our Side: The United States and Right-Wing Dictatorships, 1921–1965* (Chapel Hill: University of North Carolina Press, 1999); Kenneth W. Thompson, ed., *The President, the Bureaucracy, and World Regions in Arms Control* (Lanham, MD: University Press of America, 1998); Edward J. Williams, *The Political Themes of Inter-American Relations* (Belmont, CA: Duxbury Press, 1971); Eugene R. Wittkopf and Christopher M. Jones, eds., *The Future of American Foreign Policy*, 3rd ed. (New York: St. Martin's Press, 1999); Bryce Wood, *The Dismantling of the Good Neighbor Policy* (Austin: University of Texas Press, 1985).

Communism. *See* Allende Gossens, Salvador; Castro Ruz, Fidel; Cold War; Covert Operations; Doctrines; Domino Theory; Dulles, Allen Welsh; Eisenhower, Dwight David; Friendly Dictators; Guatemala, U.S. Invasion of (1954); Johnson Doctrine; Threat Perception/Assessment; Truman, Harry S.

Contadora Group The growing fear of U.S. **intervention** in Nicaragua gave rise to a four-nation—Colombia, Mexico, Panama, and Venezuela—meeting in January 1983 on the Panamanian island of Contadora in an effort to forestall U.S. intervention and at the same time find a peaceful solution to the conflict in Central America. Once constituted as the Contadora Group, the presidents of these four countries initiated a series of diplomatic negotiations that resulted in a draft treaty by the leaders of the five Central American nations. Known as the Contadora peace process, it initiated the first phase of the Central American peace process, one that did not include the **Organization of American States (OAS)**. Between 1983 and

1985, the Contadora Group clashed with the **Reagan** administration while it tried to bring an end to war and turmoil in the region through negotiations and numerous peace treaties. U.S.–Latin American relations deteriorated as the United States continued to carry out covert actions against Nicaragua, including the mining of harbors, support for the **Contras**, economic embargoes, and a general defiance of OAS and **United Nations (UN)** resolutions in support of the Contadora peace process. This undermined any hope of ending the conflict, resulting in an impasse by July 1985. Convinced that the rebel forces in Nicaragua, Guatemala, and El Salvador were Soviet-Cuban–oriented Communists, the Reagan administration defined the Central American conflicts as a threat to the security of the United States and appeared convinced that the only solution was a military victory for itself and its allies. The perceived threat from the members of the Contadora Group was that foreign intervention and the escalating conflict would destroy the economies of the region and spread to other parts of Latin America. Numerous efforts were made by the Latin American states to revive the peace process by expanding the number of participant countries and increasing the involvement of the OAS and the UN. The Contadora peace process continued to move through various stages, eventually resulting in a settlement between the contending parties, facilitated in great part by Costa Rican president Oscar **Arias**. The elections of **George H.W. Bush** and Violeta Barrios de Chamorro between 1988 and 1990 and the peace-keeping efforts of the international organizations mentioned previously contributed to the international efforts to bring peace to the region. The joint OAS-UN model that provided the critical ingredients for resolving the conflict in Nicaragua became a key factor in bringing about a settlement in El Salvador and Guatemala. Many argued that the peace-keeping role played by the United Nations was one of the major reasons for establishing the framework for peace in Central America, helped in the process by the blunders committed by the Reagan administration in what became known as the **Iran-Contra scandal**. The peace process that ended the wars in Central America also paid a number of unforeseen dividends, including the belief among many that for the first time they could control their fate and refuse to tolerate such things as government corruption, fraud, and **human rights** violations. Since 1990, the United States has been less willing to have economic assistance squandered or stolen as was the case during the **Cold War** when **friendly dictators** were treated with kid gloves if they did not question American foreign policy and displayed the requisite anti-communism at home. The Contadora process succeeded because it operated in a multilateral format, eventually enlisting the help of numerous South American countries with the flexibility to write and rewrite drafts to further fruitful negotiations against the wishes of Washington. *See also* Scandals and Blunders.

Suggested Reading

Bruce M. Bagley, Roberto Alvarez, and Katherine J. Hagedorn, eds., *Contadora and the Central American Peace Process* (Boulder, CO: Westview Press, 1985); Jack Childs, *The Central American Peace Process, 1983–1991: Sheathing Swords, Building Confidence* (Boulder, CO: Lynne

Rienner, 1992); William Goodfellow, "The Diplomatic Front," in Thomas W. Walker, ed., *Reagan Versus the Sandinistas: The Undeclared War on Nicaragua* (Boulder, CO: Westview, 1987).

Contras Counter-revolutionaries trained and supplied by the **Reagan** administration to fight against the Nicaraguan government during the 1980s. Many of the Contras were former National Guard personnel and political allies of the former dictator, Anastasio **Somoza** Debayle; this played a major role in the inability of Reagan's "freedom fighters" to transform themselves into a legitimate force for change in Nicaragua. In his effort to sell Contra aid in the United States, President Reagan often compared the Contras to the Founding Fathers in the United States. However, Contra leaders resented this excessive rhetoric because the wording opened the insurgents to ridicule by those who argued that Nicaragua was of little real importance to the United States. According to Contra chief, Ernesto Palazio, "If Nicaragua were truly as important to the United States as Mr. Reagan says, then your troops would be down there." The Contra army operated out of neighboring Honduras, but they also were assisted by military operations in El Salvador, Costa Rica, and Panama. The problem for the Contras was funding. At first the U.S. Congress provided the necessary funds for the covert war against Nicaragua. Once it was discovered how the war was being fought and the illegitimacy of the Contra forces, Congress cut off funding. It was at this point that the Reagan administration bypassed the Congress and started a series of secret appeals to foreign governments (mostly conservative authoritarian governments) and wealthy private individuals in the United States. With assistance from the **Central Intelligence Agency (CIA)**, the **National Security Council (NSC)**, and the White House, the Contras managed to engage in hit-and-run attacks on the Sandinista government for several years. However, as the war dragged on with little hope of a military success, serious opposition developed in Congress, the **media**, college campuses, and among the general public.

The illegal war against Nicaragua eventually led to the **Iran-Contra scandal**, a counter-productive initiative that involved the illegal selling of arms, at inflated prices, to Iran (then labeled by the U.S. government as a terrorist state) to finance the counter-revolutionaries trying to defeat the **Sandinistas**. Once the public was aware of the scandal, the Central American presidents mobilized a series of efforts to put an end to the war and bring peace to the region. In his determination to keep the Contras funded and armed, President Reagan gave over twenty major speeches on the necessity of Contra aid. Although the Contra war failed militarily, it inflicted great damage on Nicaragua, destroying sections of the nation's infrastructure and causing 30,000 deaths.

After the Contras were disbanded and the Sandinistas defeated in 1990, the guerrilla movement became a political party (Nicaraguan Resistance), and they made feeble efforts to compete in national elections. In 2003 the Nicaraguan Resistance tried to sue the U.S. government for back pay in the war against Nicaragua's leftist government, claiming they were war veterans and deserved such compensation. The resistance movement changed its mind in late 2003 and dropped plans to take the U.S. government to court if it was able to reach a settlement with the U.S. government first. The return of U.S. **intervention** in Nicaragua during the 1980s reminded many Central Americans of previous periods of armed intervention and occupation, including the nefarious exploits of William **Walker** and his band of filibusters in the 1850s. In Nicaragua, William Walker is often referred to as "the first U.S. Marine" to get involved in the country's internal affairs. *See also* Contadora Group; Filibusters/Filibustering; Scandals and Blunders.

Suggested Reading

Timothy C. Brown, *The Real Contra War: Highlander Peasant Resistance in Nicaragua* (Norman: University of Oklahoma Press, 2001); Roy Gutman, *Banana Diplomacy: The Making of American Foreign Policy in Nicaragua, 1981–1987* (New York: Simon and Schuster, 1988); Rogelio Pardo-Maurer, *The Contras, 1980–1989: A Special Kind of Politics* (New York: Praeger, 1990); Robert A. Pastor, *Condemned to Repetition: The United States and Nicaragua*, rev. ed. (Princeton, NJ: Princeton University Press, 1988); Robert Pear, "Contra Chief Faults Reagan Statements," *New York Times* (October 30, 1988); Gary Prevost and Harry E. Vanden, eds., *The Undermining of the Sandinista Revolution* (New York: St. Martin's Press, 1997); Thomas W. Walker, ed., *Revolution and Counter-Revolution in Nicaragua* (Boulder, CO: Westview Press, 1991).

Council of the Americas (COA) The Council of the Americas is a U.S. business association with offices in New York and Washington, D.C., that serves as a nongovernmental advocacy group for its multinational corporate members. Founded in 1958, COA represents over 250 leading multinational corporations with significant economic and financial interests in Latin America and the Caribbean. The purpose of the Council of the Americas is to provide greater understanding and acceptance of the role of private enterprise as a positive force for the development of the Americas. The council acts as an effective vehicle for communicating viewpoints of its members to **Washington policymakers**, Latin American government officials, and to a diversity of private sector leaders in the Western Hemisphere. The majority of its funding comes from corporate members' dues and its high-level meetings and seminars. At its annual Forum of the Americas, over 500 private sector leaders from throughout the Americas come together to discuss trade and investment issues and U.S. policies in the region. COA was a powerful force in the creation and passage of the **Enterprise for the Americas Initiative (EAI)**, **North American Free Trade Agreement (NAFTA)**, and other hemispheric free trade policies initiated by the White House and Congress. The Council of the Americas was also an important advocate for the new **Panama Canal treaties** initiated by President Jimmy **Carter** in 1977–1978. The political power of the council is based on its liaison role, often offering direct contact with the president (and important ministers) of Latin American countries and their counterparts in the United States. According to Lars Schoultz (1981: 67), "The Council's major strength lies in its ability to link executives of member corporations and foreign policy makers at the highest levels of government." As part of the business lobby in the United States, the Council of the Americas has often worked to decrease the influence of **human rights** interest groups because of fear of a loss of markets and investments. *See also* Inter-American Dialogue (IAD); Think Tanks.

Suggested Reading

David W. Dent, ed., *U.S.–Latin American Policymaking: A Reference Handbook* (Westport, CT: Greenwood Press, 1995); Lars Schoultz, *Human Rights and United States Policy Toward Latin America* (Princeton, NJ: Princeton University Press, 1981).

Council on Foreign Relations. *See* Think Tanks

Council on Hemispheric Affairs (COHA) The Council on Hemispheric Affairs was founded in 1975 by individuals opposed to "traditional" U.S. policy toward Latin America. Although it defines itself as a "nonpartisan . . . research and information organization," COHA's emphasis on challenging Washington's policies toward the region often reflects a leftist ideological orientation. COHA also focuses on U.S.–Canadian relations to reflect a more accurate reflection of its name as an organization devoted to hemispheric relations. COHA gained considerable recognition during the Jimmy **Carter** presidency by exposing the problems facing the region and offering alternatives to failed policies in Latin America. The major figures in the creation of COHA were Dr. Kalman Silvert, Rabbi Morton Rosenthal, William Wipfler, Tom Quigley, and Lawrence Birns. As a tax exempt, not-for-profit organization, COHA is prohibited from lobbying or pursuing a distinct political ideology; however, these legal restrictions are difficult to enforce. Grants from liberal foundations provide the bulk of COHA's budget in addition to contributions from private individuals interested in U.S.–Latin American relations. Although COHA once produced the *Washington Report* and other publications, its main source of income stems from foundations that focus on American foreign policy.

Larry Birns has been the director of COHA since its inception and is quoted often by those who write on U.S.–Latin American relations. He taught courses on Latin American issues in Chile before serving as an official with the **United Nations (UN)** Conference on Trade and Development in Chile during the presidency of Salvador **Allende**. While working in Chile he witnessed the CIA-backed overthrow of the Allende government and this experience contributed to his views on **human rights**, right-wing **dictatorships**, ambassadorships, and democratization. Working with a staff of interns who research issues and write op-ed pieces for U.S. newspapers, Birns has been known to engage in a "take-no-prisoners" approach to policy personnel and overturning policies he judges to be mistaken and counter-productive to U.S. interests and values. COHA took a strong position against the Latin American policies of the Reagan era and was particularly critical of the nefarious activities of Assistant Secretary of State for Inter-American Affairs Elliott **Abrams**. Birn's work has also raised the ire of conservatives in Washington who claim that COHA often exaggerates the abuses of right-wing governments while minimizing the threats to the region from Cuba, Nicaragua, Venezuela, and Mexico. When profiled in the

Washington Times or other conservative publications, COHA is criticized for its liberal bias or its ties to radical leftist organizations in the United States. COHA often works with the **Washington Office on Latin America (WOLA)** and the Fund for New Priorities in America to improve hemispheric relations. COHA used its influence to expose the past abuses of Otto **Reich** and educate members of the Senate to deny him confirmation as assistant secretary of states for inter-American affairs during the first **George W. Bush** administration.

The Council on Hemispheric Affairs focuses on all aspects of U.S.–Latin American relations and believes that it provides an objective and alternative source of information on Latin America from the viewpoints found in the mainstream and conservative organizations that dominate the news about Latin America. By providing information on U.S. policies in the electronic and print media, COHA tries to influence members of Congress, various activists groups concerned with human rights and democracy, and the **media**. COHA's work is carried out by a small professional staff, college interns (undergraduate as well as graduate), and former or retired U.S. government employees who have experience in the region and inside information on the policy-making process. There are also more than ten senior research fellows from the United States and Latin America who write reports and monographs for COHA. During COHA's thirty-year existence, almost 1,000 successful candidates have interned in its Washington office.

The news and analysis provided by COHA includes its biweekly publication, *The Washington Report on the Hemisphere* (WRH) and its irregular "News and Analysis" series of press memoranda. Those who work at COHA write letters to the editor for publication in major national and international media, pen op-ed pieces, and attend professional meetings, congressional hearings, and legislative seminars devoted to U.S.–Latin American relations. COHA's letters-to-the-editor are designed to raise important issues, praise or condemn news stories or opinion pieces, and provide alternative insights and different perspectives on the policy-making process. With its close ties with the Latin American press, COHA often covers material that is ignored by the mainstream press in the United States. While COHA is frequently criticized for its style and political views of its director, it is frequently cited in the *Congressional Record*, *London Observer,* the *New York Times*, and the *Washington Post*, among many others. *See also* Ambassadors; Washington Consensus; Washington Office on Latin America (WOLA); Washington Policymakers.

Suggested Reading

David W. Dent, ed., *U.S.–Latin American Policymaking: A Reference Handbook* (Westport, CT: Greenwood Press, 1995); Steven S. Powell, *Covert Cadre: Inside the Institute for Policy Studies* (Ottawa, IL: Green Hill, 1988); Cynthia Watson, *U.S. National Security Groups: Institutional Profiles* (Westport, CT: Greenwood Press, 1990).

Covert Operations Secret measures designed to promote foreign policy objectives abroad that are often considered an alternative means between diplomacy and war for the betterment of the United States. Since **World War II**, covert operations have been a mainstay of U.S. policy toward Latin America. The term is often used interchangeably with covert action, special operations, and clandestine operations and are mostly carried out by the executive branch of the U.S. government. The following techniques are considered to be part of all covert operations: **propaganda** and psychological warfare, paramilitary operations, and political or economic activities designed to affect a particular Latin American country.

The nation's first covert operations organization was the Office of Strategic Services (OSS), formed during World War II to counter enemy forces and propaganda. After World War II the basic framework for secret intelligence operations was established by the **Truman** administration to undermine the Soviet Union's hold on Eastern Europe and guard against nationalist movements that threatened U.S. interests abroad. At the center of this new function was the **National Security Council (NSC)** that took charge of permanent U.S. covert operations capability with the establishment of the Office of Policy Coordination (OPC), a semi-autonomous organization under the **Central Intelligence Agency (CIA)**. Within a few years the OPC had been fully integrated into the covert operations section of the CIA. Since 1952 the CIA has held primary responsibility for the carrying out of clandestine operations for the president of the United States.

Since the **Dwight Eisenhower** administration, the U.S. government has used covert activities to overthrow leftist governments in Latin America. President Eisenhower used covert action to overthrow President Jacobo **Arbenz** in Guatemala (1954); President John F. **Kennedy** relied on ad hoc advisory groups within the NSC to invade Cuba at the **Bay of Pigs** in 1961, a blunder that discouraged similar U.S. endeavors in Latin America. President Richard **Nixon** revived covert activities by putting his NSC adviser in charge of a select panel known as the 40 Committee. Nixon used the NSC and CIA to carry out secret efforts in Chile, first to prevent socialist Salvador **Allende** from coming to power and then destabilizing the democratically elected government through massive anti-Allende propaganda and clandestine support for the September 11, 1973, military coup that would result in Allende's death. The revelations of CIA abuses in the 1970s led presidents Gerald **Ford** and Jimmy **Carter** to require approval of covert operations at the highest levels of the executive branch and greater congressional oversight. Jimmy Carter generally opposed the use of covert operations until the Soviet invasion of Afghanistan in December 1979. President Ronald **Reagan** revived the Central Intelligence Agency and placed greater emphasis on covert action as part of the effort to provide support for anti-Soviet "freedom fighters" in Afghanistan, Angola, and Nicaragua. The secret operations carried out in the name of the **Reagan Doctrine** broke numerous laws, contributed to the **Iran-Contra scandal**, and underscored the need for the proper approval and supervision of covert activities. Presidents Bill **Clinton** and **George W. Bush** put less emphasis on covert action in the conduct of foreign affairs than their predecessors. Covert operations declined after the **Cold War**; with the U.S. war on **terrorism** and the new doctrine of "pre-emptive war," Washington did not have to worry about the constrictions on overt military invasions, including a possible confrontation with the Soviet Union. The war on terrorism announced by President George W. Bush in 2001 has revived executive branch secrecy in the conduct of foreign affairs, but with less concern for accountability, privacy, and social justice in the name of national security. *See also* Assassination; Threat Perception/Assessment.

Suggested Reading

Mark L. Attanasio, *Failures in Covert Operations—U.S. Involvement in Chile* (Providence, RI: Brown University Press, 1979); John J. Carter, *Covert Operations as a Tool of Presidential Foreign Policy in American History from 1800 to 1920: Foreign Policy in the Shadows* (Lewiston, NY: Edwin Mellen Press, 2000); Frank Dorrel, *CIA Covert Operations and U.S. Interventions Since World War II* (video), (Culver City, CA: Frank Dorrel, 2001); Steven Emerson, *Secret Warriors: Inside the Covert Military Operations of the Reagan Era* (New York: Putnam, 1988); Stephen F. Knott, *Secret and Sanctioned: Covert Operations and the American Presidency* (New York: Oxford University Press, 1996); Jonathan Marshall, et al., *The Iran-Contra Connection: Secret Teams and Covert Operations in the Reagan Era* (Boston: South End Press, 1987); John Prados, *Presidents' Secret Wars: CIA and Pentagon Covert Operations from World War II through the Persian Gulf*, rev. ed. (Chicago: I.R. Dee, 1996); Peter Dale Scott and Jonathan Marshall, *Cocaine Politics: Drugs, Armies, and the CIA in Central America* (Berkeley: University of California Press, 1998).

Cuba. *See* Alpha 66; Assassination; Batista, Fulgencio; Bay of Pigs (1961); Castro Ruz, Fidel; Cuba Lobby; Cuban Missile Crisis (1962); Guantánamo Bay; Guevara, Ernesto "Che"; Helms-Burton Law (1996); Kennedy, John Fitzgerald; Martí y Perez, José Julián; Matthews, Herbert; Operation Mongoose; Platt Amendment (1902); Radio Martí; Spanish-Cuban-American War (1898).

Cuba Lobby The Cuba Lobby is not a single-issue interest group since it consists of organizations and individuals that reflect different perspectives and strategies for dealing with Cuba and its leader, Fidel **Castro**. The pro-embargo component opposes any dialogue with the Cuban regime and feels the embargo is justified; the anti-embargo component argues that the U.S. trade embargo against Cuba is counter-productive and should be ended. The pro-embargo, anti–Fidel Castro component of the Cuba Lobby is made up of mostly Cuban Americans who left the island during the early stages of the Cuban Revolution and have been the driving force in maintaining Washington's hostility toward Castro. More than 80 percent of the early refugees were white and most were well-educated and wealthy before they left Cuba. By 2000, over one million Cubans had migrated to the United States with most residing in south Florida and north New Jersey. The anti-embargo forces are more amorphous, of more recent origin, and have far less clout over U.S.–Latin American policy than the pro-embargo side of the Cuba Lobby. Those who make up the anti-embargo segment of the Cuba Lobby include **think tanks**, business-commercial organizations, intellectual/academic groups, foundations, and members of Congress. The common link of the anti-embargo side of the Cuba Lobby is to remove the trade embargo and travel restrictions currently in place; however, each of the various components has different strategic objectives. Among Latino groups, the Cuba Lobby that opposes Fidel Castro and supports the trade embargo is one of the most powerful interest groups when it comes to Latin American policy.

The Cuba Lobby–Pro-Embargo is a product of bipartisan opposition to Castro's Cuba in Congress and the executive branch of government; the wealth of Cuban Americans and their concentration in key electoral college states; and the political clout of the Cuban-American National Foundation (CANF), particularly under the leadership of Jorge **Mas Canosa** until his death in 1997. Mas Canosa used the CANF to discredit its opponents as Communist sympathizers, using massive propaganda campaigns, and assisted by the relative ineffectiveness of an organized opposition to the anti-Castro Cubans. Jorge Mas Canosa was a veteran of the **Bay of Pigs** invasion who spent his entire life in exile trying to convince **Washington policymakers** to maintain a hard-line policy against the island. During the **Reagan**, **George H.W. Bush**, and **Clinton** administrations he enjoyed ready access to the White House and Congress thanks to personal connections and campaign contributions through CANF's Free Cuba Political Action Committee. While governor of Florida, Jeb Bush served as a key linkage between the Cuban exile community, the Cuban American National Foundation, the White House, and Congress. Over the past twenty years the Cuba Lobby–Pro-Embargo has played a key role in formulating and implementing the following policies toward Cuba and Latin America: **Radio Martí**; covert support for the Nicaraguan **Contras**; TV Martí; Cuban Democracy Act; **Helms-Burton Law**; legal maneuvers to keep six-year-old Elián **González** in the United States against his father's wishes and the ruling of American courts; and the tighter restrictions on travel and trade that the **George W. Bush** administration put into effect in 2004. The Cuba Lobby–Pro-Embargo has also been successful in blocking unacceptable appointments to Latin American policy posts, winning federal financial subsidies and grants, and mounting successful get-out-the-vote drives for Republican candidates for office. It also has close ties with the **Central Intelligence Agency (CIA)**, conservative think tanks, international lending agencies, and right-wing academics at Georgetown University in Washington, D.C. During the Reagan years it worked closely with the **National Endowment for Democracy (NED)**, Oliver **North** and the **National Security Council (NSC)** staff, and key players in the effort to provide secret support for the Contras in Nicaragua. The Cuba Lobby–Pro-Embargo now has four Cuban American members of the House of Representatives—Lincoln Díaz-Balart, Mario Díaz-Balart, Robert Menéndez, and Ileana Ros-Lehtinen—and one member of the Senate, Mel Martínez, the first Cuban American member of the Senate. All the Cuban Americans in Congress belong to the Republican Party with the exception of Robert Menéndez.

The Cuba Lobby–Anti-Embargo is newer than the Cuba Lobby–Pro-Embargo, but it has made significant advances with less funding and political clout. There are basically four components of this segment of the Cuba Lobby: intellectuals and academics, business/commercial groups, think tanks, and foundations. They are not well coordinated and have different strategic objectives, but they have been successful in lobbying Congress on issues related to U.S. policy toward Cuba. In some cases, they have passed legislation aimed at easing the trade embargo only to have it undermined by key Republicans in key congressional committees. The intellectual/academic wing consists of the Science and Human Rights Program of the American Association of the Advancement of Science; the American Association of University Professors; the American Association of World Health; the American Physical Society; the Committee of Concerned Scientists; and the Latin American Studies Association. Their main concern is to change travel policy toward Cuba and expand academic and scientific exchanges. The business/commercial wing of the Cuba Lobby–Anti-Embargo is interested in expanding trade and investment opportunities and consists of the U.S.–Cuba Trade and Economic Council; the National Association of Manufacturers; the United States Chamber of Commerce; the American Business Council on Cuba; and USA Engage. The third component is made up of numerous think tanks and interest groups interested in travel, trade, human rights, academic exchanges, and certain religious activities. It is much more amorphous than the other wings, including the Cuban Committee for Democracy, Cambio Cubano, Center for Cuban Studies, Center for International Policy, **Council on Hemispheric Affairs (COHA)**, **Latin American Working Group (LAWG)**, **Washington Office on Latin America (WOLA)**, and the Cuban Program of the Georgetown University Caribbean Project. The fourth component consists of foundations dedicated to activist agendas, including the Arca Foundation, Ford Foundation, and the John D. and Catherine T. MacArthur Foundation. Each of these components has lobbied to alter U.S. policy toward Cuba.

The death of Jorge Mas Canosa in 1997 and the **Elián González incident** two years later weakened the power of the Cuban American National Foundation and created fractures in the leadership that have not healed. These events seem to have galvanized public perceptions of Cuba in the United States and energized the Cuba Lobby–Anti-Embargo to position themselves for changes in U.S.–Cuban relations. However, the election of George W. Bush came at a critical time for supporters of the economic embargo against Cuba and helped reverse the trend in Congress toward easing travel and trade restrictions. President Bush's political appointees—Otto **Reich**, Roger Noriega, and John Maisto—continued the pro-sanctions approach to Castro's Cuba and have helped to implement further measures aimed at cracking down on travel to Cuba and enforcing Treasury Department penalties for illegal travel to the island. The Cuban American National Foundation has also exerted control over the media, from intimidation of the *Miami Herald* to censoring what appears on American television sets if the content is not sufficiently anti-Castro. After being pressured by Jorge Mas Santos, son of the former leader, and now chairman of the Cuban American National Foundation, in 2003, HBO Productions removed Oliver Stone's documentary, titled *Comandante,* from its May 2003 schedule. CANF's chairman resented the fact that the Stone documentary suffered from the lack of context, dissenting views, and unchallenged distortions of the truth about Cuba and U.S.–Cuban relations. The censorship of *Comandante* reflects the power of CANF to control information about the Cuban reality. The lack of context, dissenting views, and unchallenged distortions that are broadcast daily on Radio Martí don't seem to bother some members of the exile community when it comes to anti-Castro material. *See also* Media.

Suggested Reading

Ann Louise Bardach, *Cuba Confidential* (New York: Random House, 2002); David W. Dent, ed., *U.S.–Latin American Policymaking: A Reference Handbook* (Westport, CT: Greenwood Press, 1995); Joan Didion, *Miami* (New York: Pocket Books, 1987); Gaeton Fonzi, "Jorge Who?" *Esquire* (January 1993); Hernando Calvo Ospina, trans. Stephen Wilkenson and Alasdair Holden, *Bacardi: The Hidden War* (Sterling, VA: Pluto Press, 2002); David Rieff, *The Exile: Cuba in the Heart of Miami* (New York: Simon and Schuster, 1993); María de los Angeles Torres, *In the Land of Mirrors* (Ann Arbor: University of Michigan Press, 1999).

Cuban Liberty and Democratic Solidarity Act of 1996. *See* Helms-Burton Law (1996)

Cuban Missile Crisis (1962) One of the most dangerous confrontations between the United States and the Soviet Union over the Soviet emplacement of nuclear-capable missiles in Cuba in October 1962. The crisis brought the two superpowers closer to nuclear war than at any time since the beginning of the **Cold War** and the way in which the crisis was resolved served as a reminder of the importance of diplomacy in times of crisis. Scholars continue to debate the exact role and motives of the major protagonists—President John F. **Kennedy** and Premier Nikita Khrushchev—but the major tensions brought on by the Kennedy administration in its relations with Cuba are given much of the blame. Khrushchev's motives centered on his belief that the imbalance in superpower nuclear capabilities needed to be addressed, and Cuba needed a defensive deterrent as a warning to Washington about its interventionist policies toward Cuba. According to Thomas G. Paterson (1994: 260), if there had been "no exile expedition, no destructive covert activities, and no economic and diplomatic boycott" of Cuba there would have been no missile crisis. The numerous assassination plots against Castro, the establishment of **Operation Mongoose** in 1961, and the 1962 U.S.–backed expulsion of Cuba from the **Organization of American States (OAS)** also added to the confrontation. Castro's fears of another invasion were not groundless, and he apparently welcomed Soviet missiles as a way to discourage another U.S. invasion of the island. For Nikita Khrushchev, the missiles underscored Soviet deterrence capability in defense of the Cuban Revolution. Once the missiles were discovered by U.S. spy aircraft in October 1962, President Kennedy and his advisers were forced to deal with the Soviet challenge. Unlike the **Bay of Pigs** invasion where the **Central Intelligence Agency (CIA)** dominated high-level decision-making sessions, Kennedy formed the EXCOMM (Executive Committee), a small group of close advisers who had difficulty in assessing the magnitude of the threat and the best response to achieve a speedy withdrawal of the missiles. Since his advisers could not agree on either, and often shifted their positions, after a week of deliberations they offered Kennedy the following options: (1) an all-out air attack on Cuba; (2) a diplomatic approach, using the **United Nations (UN)** to confront Fidel

Castro and Khrushchev privately to withdraw the missiles; (3) offer the Soviets a tradeoff or some deal that would involve the removal of U.S. Jupiter missiles from Turkey for Soviet withdrawal of missiles in Cuba, and maybe something on the U.S. military base on Guantánamo; (4) a surgical air strike to remove the missile sites; (5) or some form of blockade, or limited quarantine, to put a halt to future shipments of Soviet weaponry to Cuba.

Kennedy feared the political fallout if he did nothing and wanted a victory in the confrontation to get even with the Soviets for deceiving him. Ultimately, he chose the public confrontation strategy with the naval "quarantine" or blockade of Cuba, which allowed Khrushchev time to ponder his fate and for Kennedy to employ the least dangerous choice and hope for the best. Although Kennedy's decision ultimately worked, critics argue that confronting Khrushchev privately would have been safer; others concluded that Kennedy's public confrontation and the long wait to find out the results of the quarantine was terribly dangerous and could have easily provoked the Soviet premier into a less rational response.

In any case, the Cuban Missile Crisis was a classic case of "brinksmanship" and the crisis ended without a nuclear holocaust. The Soviets publicly agreed to withdraw all of their missiles from Cuba (but not their military forces) in exchange for a personal guarantee by President Kennedy that he would not intervene militarily in Cuba. All sides claimed one type of victory or another. Kennedy got a boost in the opinion polls and was given high marks for getting the Soviets to remove their threatening missiles from Castro's Cuba. Khrushchev claimed he succeeded in protecting an ally, but was forced from office the following year for not getting more concessions in the final arrangement. Fidel Castro was angry that he was left out of the deliberations, but the "no invasion" pledge from Washington provided a victory of sorts for the Cuban leader. The United States also secretly agreed to remove its medium-range missiles from Turkey, a private concession that was publicly denied by President Kennedy at the time. After Kennedy's humiliation after the Bay of Pigs invasion, his handling of the missile crisis helped improve his image as a statesman and world leader. After writing several books on his role in the Vietnam War and the Cuban Missile Crisis, Robert McNamara expressed the view that "luck" played a major role in the uneasy settlement that was worked out. He also admitted that it is much better to rely on diplomacy because "you can't manage crises," suggesting that trying to ascertain lessons from such military confrontations is foolish.

Despite the controversial aspects of the Cuban Missile Crisis, it remains a significant event in United States relations with Latin America, Cuba, and the Soviet Union. The United States did not consult with other Latin American countries before announcing the U.S. response, although Kennedy called for an immediate meeting of the OAS Organ of Consultation and an emergency session of the **United Nations (UN)** Security Council. After the security threat presentation by the United States, the OAS unanimously passed a resolution calling for the withdrawal from Cuba of all Soviet missiles, prevention of the shipment of weapons to Cuba, and support for Kennedy's "quarantine" strategy. The fact that Fidel Castro remained in power after the missile crisis did not go over well within the Kennedy administration, and many remained convinced that Castro would need to be removed by clandestine means, including sabotage and assassination. The Cuban Missile Crisis became the genesis of the efforts of the governments of Latin America to make the region the world's first nuclear-weapons–free zone. Known as the Treaty of **Tlatelolco**, the framers of the treaty agreed to outlaw the acquisition, testing, manufacture, and use of nuclear weapons in their countries. By 1998, thirty-three Latin American and Caribbean states had signed the treaty and the United States, the Russian Federation, France, the United Kingdom, China, and the Netherlands signed and ratified protocols committing themselves to fully respect its provisions. The peril of nuclear war helped create the 1963 U.S.–Soviet agreement on Limited Nuclear Test Ban Treaty and the Kremlin–White House "hot line" to help communicate and defuse future crises. Some analysts believe the missile crisis contributed to the belief that the United States could achieve a similar victory over communism in Indochina, failing to understand both the nature of the conflict and reasons for crisis over missiles in Cuba. The Soviets emerged from the showdown over missiles with their nuclear inferiority exposed and a determination to catch up with the United States and defend the Cuban Revolution. They maintained large-scale subsidies to Castro's government until the collapse of the Soviet Union in 1991. President Kennedy was under intense pressure from some of his advisers to take pre-emptive military action against the Soviets in Cuba; however, he resisted the rush to action and used the threat of force as a tactical device to achieve a peaceful political solution. There is no certainty that other presidents would have handled the threat from a major adversary with such coolness and skill, particularly if it could be demonstrated that weapons of mass destruction were about to be deployed against the United States. *See also* Assassination; Domino Theory; Threat Perception/Assessment.

Suggested Reading

Graham Allison, *Essense of Decision: Explaining the Cuban Missile Crisis* (Boston: Little Brown, 1971); James G. Blight and Philip Brenner, *Sad and Luminous Days: Cuba's Struggle with the Superpowers after the Missile Crisis* (Lanham, MD: Rowman and Littlefield, 2002); James G. Blight, Bruce J. Allyn, and David A. Welch, *Cuba on the Brink: Castro, the Missile Crisis, and the Soviet Collapse*, rev. and expanded Ed. (Lanham, MD: Rowman and Littlefield, 2002); Laurence Chang and Peter Kornbluh, eds., *The Cuban Missile Crisis, 1962: A National Security Archive Documents Reader* (New York: The New Press, 1992); Tomás Diez Acosta, *October 1962: The "Missile" Crisis as Seen from Cuba* (New York: Pathfinder Press, 2003); Robert Divine, *The Cuban Missile Crisis*, 2nd ed. (New York: M. Weiner, 1988); Max Frankel, *High Noon in the Cold War: Kennedy, Khrushchev, and the Cuban Missile Crisis* (New York: Ballantine Books, 2004); Anatoli Gribkov and William Y. Smith, *Operation Anadyr: U.S. and Soviet Generals Recount the Cuban Missile Crisis* (Chicago: Edition, 1994); Robert F. Kennedy, *Thirteen Days: A Memoir of the Cuban Missile Crisis* (New York: W.W. Norton, 1969); Nikita Khrushchev, *Khrushchev Remembers*, trans. and ed. Strobe Talbott (Boston: Little, Brown, 1970); James Nathan, ed., *The Cuban Missile Crisis Revisited* (New York: St. Martin's Press, 1992);

Thomas G. Paterson, *Contesting Castro: The United States and the Triumph of the Cuban Revolution* (New York: Oxford University Press, 1994); Ronald Pope, ed., *Soviet Views on the Cuban Missile Crisis: Myth and Reality in Foreign Policy Analysis* (Lanham, MD: Scarecrow Press, 1982); Sheldon M. Stern, *Averting "the Final Failure": John F. Kennedy and the Secret Cuban Missile Crisis Meetings* (Stanford, CA: Stanford University Press, 2003).

Cuba–U.S. Relations. *See* Assassination; Bay of Pigs (1961); Bonsal, Philip Wilson; Castro Ruz, Fidel; Cuba Lobby; Cuban Missile Crisis (1962); Economic Sanctions; Guevara, Ernesto Che; Ostend Manifesto (1854); Platt Amendment (1902); Radio Martí; Regime Change; Revolutions; Smith, Earl E.T.; Spanish-Cuban-American War (1898); Threat Perception/Assessment; Yankee *Fidelistas*

Cultural Imperialism Sometimes referred to as cultural transfer, cultural imperialism is a complex subject that attempts to establish a linkage between culture, power, and foreign relations. The process—both private and governmental—of trying to force culture, ideology, goods, religion, and way of life on another country is at the core of cultural diplomacy. U.S. policymakers have used cultural imperialism as an instrument of diplomacy to promote **pan-Americanism**, military cooperation, combat enemy **propaganda**, gain access to raw materials and cheap labor, sell the American way of life abroad, and create good will. President **Franklin D. Roosevelt**'s **Good Neighbor Policy** relied on films, radio programs, sports, and entertainment to improve U.S.–Latin American relations and erase negative stereotypes and popular perceptions of Latin America and the United States. Prior to **World War II**, the **State Department** created the Division for Cultural Relations to use culture as a tool of American diplomacy. To create a sympathetic understanding of the United States in Latin America, in 1940 the Roosevelt administration created the Office of Coordinator of Inter-American Affairs (OCIAA), headed by Nelson **Rockefeller**, to promote pan-Americanism, prevent **revolutions** in the Americas, fight Nazi agents, and expand U.S. trade in Latin America. During the **Cold War** years the United States created the United States Information Agency (USIA) and the Fulbright Exchange program to "sell" American culture abroad. The programs developed by USIA were designed to provide a full and fair picture of American life, culture, and society to provide a psychological counterattack against Soviet propaganda and indoctrination. The growing interest in spreading the American life abroad was not based on the belief in the superiority of American culture as much as it was in the belief that a capitalist culture—free market economics, high living standards, and a consumer society—would help spread democratic values around the world and counter-act political ideologies that many considered alien and reprehensible. According to O'Brien (1999: 53),

> American movies became regular entertainment fare in cities throughout Latin America during the 1920s. The wondrous images bore testimony to the technological wonders and achievements of U.S. society. Film images of enormous factories, the skyscrapers of New York,

> spacious homes, and a plethora of consumer goods sent a graphic message of success through the American way to people across the Western Hemisphere. The films of the period suggested through their plot lines that human ills and unhappiness could be resolved through the ameliorating effects of consumerism.

Critics of cultural imperialism identified several distinct categories to discuss and analyze the relationship between culture and foreign policy: the media, national domination, the global dominance of capitalism, and the critique of modernity. Latin Americans developed a **dependency theory** and emphasized media **imperialism** in the study of U.S.–Latin American relations. The most widely read essay was written by Ariel Dorfman and Armand Mattelart, *How to Read Donald Duck: Imperialist Ideology in the Disney Comic* (1975), a scathing critique of U.S. involvement in Latin American affairs. Written in the aftermath of the CIA-backed overthrow of Salvador **Allende** in Chile, the authors argue that the purpose of U.S. cultural imperialism was to indoctrinate the minds of the Chilean people, using Disney cartoons and other consumer products. The debate over the impact of cultural transfer continues as a component of American foreign policy, particularly when the United States attempts to assert its **hegemony** in other regions of the world and is then faced with negative opinions of what is done in the name of American foreign policy. For example, the international opinion polls that showed negative views of President **George W. Bush** prompted government efforts to counter these trends in the Muslim world through cultural imperialism. Since the 1980s, the United States has relied on **Radio Martí** and TV Martí to spread negative views of the Cuban system and positive views of the United States to foster **regime change** on the island. *See also* Media; Public Opinion.

Suggested Reading

Thomas Bender, ed., *Rethinking American History in a Global Age* (Berkeley: University of California Press, 2002); Ariel Dorfman and Armand Mattelart, *How to Read Donald Duck: Imperialist Ideology in the Disney Comic*, trans. David Kunzle (New York: International General, 1975); Paul Hollender, *Anti-Americanism: Critiques at Home and Abroad, 1965–1990* (New York: Oxford University Press, 1992); Ali Mohammadi, ed., *International Communication and Globalization: A Critical Introduction* (Thousand Oaks, CA: Sage Publications, 1997); Thomas O'Brien, *The Century of U.S. Capitalism in Latin America* (Albuquerque: University of New Mexico Press, 1999); John Tomlinson, *Cultural Imperialism: A Critical Introduction* (Baltimore, MD: Johns Hopkins University Press, 1991).

D

Daniels, Josephus (1862–1948) Journalist, secretary of the Navy, and a key figure in improving U.S.–Latin American relations during the 1930s. A native of North Carolina, Daniels trained to become a lawyer; however, he never practiced law professionally after briefly studying the subject and passing the state bar exam. As an editor and publisher of the *Raleigh News and Observer*, he became a leading voice in the South. He considered himself a progressive Democrat, developed close ties with William Jennings **Bryan**, and in 1912 supported the winning candidacy of Woodrow **Wilson**.

Shortly after Wilson's presidential victory Josephus Daniels was appointed secretary of the Navy, a post he served in from 1913 until 1921. **Franklin D. Roosevelt** was appointed assistant secretary of the Navy and worked with Daniels during most of this period. Daniels was considered an activist Navy chief, implementing numerous reforms that greatly expanded the size, efficiency, and battle capability of the U.S. Navy. He returned to his Raleigh newspaper in 1921 and became active in state and national Democratic politics. After ascending to the presidency in 1933, President Roosevelt appointed Daniels as U.S. ambassador to Mexico, an appointment that bothered many due to the U.S. invasion of Veracruz during his time as secretary of the Navy. It was during his eight years (1933–1941) in Mexico City that Daniels helped to implement Roosevelt's **Good Neighbor Policy**, a time of tense relations between the United States and Mexico. Daniels was a skilled diplomat and was recognized as a key figure in averting a return to U.S. **intervention** when Mexico expropriated American petroleum companies and a land reform program nationalized American agricultural properties. The controversy over Mexican oil expropriation was settled in 1941 with Daniels' skilled diplomacy, a key event that helped solidify Mexican support for the United States during **World War II**. He resigned his ambassadorship in late 1941 and returned to the *News and Observer* in Raleigh where he worked until his death in 1948. It was during the Wilson administration that Daniels became familiar with Latin American turmoil and U.S. interventionism and recognized the deleterious effects of U.S. policies motivated by crusading idealism and the diplomacy of the "Big Stick." Daniels died in Raleigh, North Carolina in 1948. *See also* Ambassadors; Big Stick Diplomacy; Intervention and Non-Intervention.

Suggested Reading

David E. Cronon, *Josephus Daniels in Mexico* (Madison: University of Wisconsin Press, 1960); Josephus Daniels, *Shirt-Sleeve Diplomat* (Chapel Hill: University of North Carolina Press, 1947); Joseph L. Morrison, *Josephus Daniels: The small-d Democrat* (Chapel Hill: University of North Carolina Press, 1966); *New York Times* (January 16, 1948).

Death Squads (Escuadrones de Muerte) Right-wing terrorist gangs linked to the military and/or the oligarchy for the purpose of eliminating opponents of the regime in power. They flourished in Latin America from the 1960s to the 1980s, particularly in Central America, Argentina, Chile, and Brazil. During the dirty war in Argentina (1976–1983) they attacked and killed left-wing guerrilla groups perceived to be a threat to the state, then under military rule. The most active death squad in Argentina was the Argentine Anti-Communist Alliance (AAA). They played an important role in the civil war in El Salvador and Guatemala where they used a variety of techniques, including kidnapping, torture, murder, death lists, and "disappearances." The word *desaparacidos* (disappeared ones) was used to refer to suspected victims of death squads who were taken hostage and then quickly disappeared (never to be seen alive again) as part of dirty war strategy. In the case of Chile under dictator Augusto **Pinochet**, thousands of victims were taken on military plane rides and then thrown to their deaths in the Pacific Ocean.

As paramilitary groups, death squads draw their membership from persons in the secret police or security agencies. Many of the victims of death squad activity were members of peasant leagues, political parties, and labor unions, church leaders, intellectuals, students, and indigenous villagers. With the return of **democracy** in southern South America in the 1980s and early 1990s, death squad activity declined. However, in Colombia and Peru where revolutionary movements remained active, death squads continued to flourish into the twenty-first century. The United States often backed dictators associated with death squad activity at home and abroad, including **Operation Condor**, a secret arrangement by right-wing military **dictatorships** to share intelligence and manpower for the purpose of eliminating opposition figures. In Central America it was common for the United States to avoid allocating intelligence resources to investigate death squads and their activities, often either ignoring them or claiming they were private thugs, distinct from the regular government or the wealthy elite. Some members of the oligarchy, in exile in Miami, provided funds for the death squads. In El Salvador, members of military intelligence were **Central Intelligence Agency (CIA)** informants, receiving $90,000 annually to pass along intelligence on the left, but never on the activities of right-wing death squads. Even after Vice-President **George H.W. Bush** visited El Salvador and demanded that something be done to halt the death squads or military aid would be reduced drastically, the level of compliance was minimal. The secrecy associated with death squad activity provided a cover for right-wing governments and U.S. government officials to disassociate them from the government in power at the time, often claiming that they were common criminals with separate agendas. Some in the **human rights** community have noted the difference in treatment between right-wing authoritarian regimes that engage in disappearances (Argentina, Guatemala, El Salvador) and left-radical regimes that jail opponents of the regime (Cuba and Nicaragua) and hold political prisoners for long periods to enforce conformity in thought and support for the ideals of the regime.

Those who conduct U.S. policy toward Latin America have been reluctant to admit past misdeeds that involve human rights abuses by governments supported by the United States, particularly in Central America. During the **Contra** wars in Central America U.S. **ambassadors** were instructed to do what was necessary to oppose the leftist Sandinista government in Nicaragua. John **Negroponte**, U.S. ambassador to Honduras, when asked at his Senate confirmation hearings to become **United Nations (UN)** ambassador in 2001, denied that he had turned a blind eye to human rights abuses in Honduras to advance President Ronald **Reagan**'s policies in the region. Negroponte both denied that human rights abuses were part of "a deliberate government policy" and that death squads even existed. "To this day," he told the Senate committee, "I do not believe that death squads were operating in Honduras." After his time in Tegucigalpa, Honduras, Negroponte assumed other diplomatic posts, including UN ambassador in 2001 and the first U.S. ambassador to Iraq in 2004. Some foreign policy analysts contend that the United States contributes to **anti-Americanism** in Latin America by insisting that ambassadors with ties to such sordid activities are reappointed with fanfare, often ignoring the negative impact they once had on fostering a democratic culture and enforcing the rule of law. *See also* Terrorism; Threat Perception/Assessment.

Suggested Reading

Martha K. Huggins, ed., *Vigilantism and the State in Modern Latin America: Essays on Extralegal Violence* (New York: Praeger, 1991); William M. LeoGrande, *Our Own Backyard: The United States in Central America, 1977–1992* (Chapel Hill: University of North Carolina Press, 1998); Ernest E. Rossi and Jack C. Plano, *Latin America: A Political Dictionary* (Santa Barbara, CA: ABC-CLIO, 1992); Diana Jean Schemo, "Latin Death Squads and the U.S.: A New Disclosure," *New York Times* (October 23, 2002); William Stanley, *The Protection Racket State: Elite Politics, Military Extortion, and Civil War in El Salvador* (Philadelphia: Temple University Press, 1996); Steven R. Weisman, "Negroponte Is Expected to Be Picked for Iraq Post," *New York Times* (April 14, 2004).

Democracy and Democracy Promotion The United States and Latin America have often been at odds over what constitutes good governance in Latin America.

With a strong authoritarian heritage, democratic rule has never taken root like it has in other parts of the world. During the nineteenth century the United States was content with dictators and put little emphasis on promoting democracy in Latin America as a viable goal in Latin America. According to Schoultz (1998: 367), "For nearly two centuries, three interests have determined the content of U.S. policy toward Latin America: the need to protect U.S. security, the desire to accommodate the demands of U.S. domestic politics, and the drive to promote U.S. economic development." Using character-based explanations of Latin American behavior, senior officials in Washington became convinced that the failure of democracy to establish roots in the region was due to the inferiority and immaturity of Latin Americans themselves. Nevertheless, beginning in the early part of the twentieth century the United States, and Latin Americans themselves, made numerous efforts to establish democratic institutions and practices as a way to foster political stability. If some form of democracy could be "exported" to Latin America, then the region would be much safer for foreign investment. However, when **revolutions** occurred, and Nazi and Communist advances threatened U.S. interests in Latin America, Washington closed ranks with dictators (military and civilian) because of their anti-communism and their willingness to welcome U.S. corporate executives. According to Kryzanek (1996: 207), "One of the major disappointments in our long relationship with Latin America is that we have been unable to successfully 'graft' liberal democratic principles and practices onto the body politic of these nations." Despite these frustrations, there have been concerted efforts after the **Cold War** to devise measures that would help consolidate representative democracy in the Americas.

The **Organization of American States (OAS)**, since its inception in 1948, has been concerned with the theory and practice of democratic governance, one in which popular sovereignty allows individuals to rule through their elected representatives. The Charter of the OAS stressed the importance of having the "effective exercise of representative democracy," but this political principle was often subordinated to that of national sovereignty and non-intervention. During the Cold War the OAS served as more of an "anti-dictator alliance" than a body that would emphasize collective measures to promote democracy. However, with the end of the Cold War the OAS began to put more emphasis on democracy promotion. It created the Unit for the Promotion of Democracy in 1993 and later created a Democratic Charter to encourage democratic consolidation by devising measures that would punish nations that became undemocratic.

Politicians and political scientists in the United States have become enamored with the idea that democracy is important because some claim that democracies do not go to war with each other. In his 1994 State of the Union address, President Bill **Clinton** declared that "democracies do not attack each other," and "are more likely to keep the peace." While there are some exceptions to this rule, there is no doubt that democracy promotion rhetoric has become a major part of the discourse among inter-American organizations and hemispheric leaders.

The fragility of democracy in Latin America is evident in the turmoil that has led to violence and removal of seven elected heads of state between 2000 and 2005. In a widely noted **United Nations (UN)** survey of 19,000 Latin Americans in 18 countries in 2004, a majority said they would choose a dictator over an elected democratic leader if that provided measurable economic benefits. President **George W. Bush**'s war with Iraq is designed to globalize democracy by **regime change** followed by elections and some form of democratic regime in Baghdad. Critics argue that Bush's efforts to build democracy in Iraq are misguided because of his belief that American democracy functions well because Americans believe in the values of tolerance and respect for others and are guided by religious faith, not because of the institutional restraints and constitutional protections on the exercise of power both at home and abroad. While it is true that some Americans believe that their unique virtues—good versus evil—should allow them to act above the law, democracy requires that individuals are constrained by institutions and by law.

War and other forms of intervention seldom create democracy. George Packer cites a pre-Iraq war article in 2003 that "of the 18 regime changes forced by the United States in the 20th century, only 5 resulted in democracy, and in the case of wars fought unilaterally, the number goes down to one—Panama." The Latin American experience would suggest that democracies only take root from within, and in some cases will never emerge regardless of foreign policy rhetoric that assumes there is a seed of democracy inside every society waiting to be released by an outside power protecting its own interests. Bananas can be exported; revolutions and democracies cannot. When authoritarian political systems such as Mexico's operate for over seventy years, and the United States rarely complains about corruption, fraud, violence, and nepotism south of the border, it is difficult to avoid the conclusion that other interests suggested by Schoultz and others are far more important to the United States than the quality of governance in Latin America.

In an effort to refute the notion that democratic states have rarely, if ever, gone to war, some scholars argue that the historical evidence from Latin America suggests that it has been relatively peaceful despite the lack of mature democracies. In fact, there is a distinct possibility that the perpetual peace in the Western Hemisphere may be due to the hegemonic role of the United States or defense-dominant technologies. Grounds for criticizing the democratic peace argument also stem from studies that distinguish between consolidated and democratizing states. Since most of Latin America is made up of new democracies that are not consolidated, evidence suggests that non-consolidated democracies are not peaceful whereas consolidated democracies are. The fact that military **dictatorships** have harmonious relations with each other also demonstrates the fallacy that only democracies bring a low propensity for war. The historical pattern of peaceful inter-American relations suggests that the Western Hemisphere was extremely peaceful in the absence of democracy, a pattern that adds further skepticism to the democratic peace argument. In a recent study of democracy and democratization in Latin America, Smith (2005: 327–332) points out that electoral democracies have expanded without authoritarian reversals or wars against each other. *See also* Domino Theory; Hegemony; Intervention and Non-Intervention.

Suggested Reading

Cole Blasier, "Democracy: Dilemmas in Promoting Democracy: Lessons from Grenada, Panama, and Haiti," *North-South Issues* 4, No. 4 (1995); Victor Bulmer-Thomas and James Dunkerley, eds., *The United States and Latin America: The New Agenda* (London: Institute of Latin American Studies, University of London, and David Rockefeller Center for Latin American Studies, Harvard University, 1999); Roderic A. Camp, ed., *Democracy in Latin America: Patterns and Cycles* (Wilmington, DE: SR Books, 1996); Thomas Carothers, *In the Name of Democracy: U.S. Policy Toward Latin America in the Reagan Years* (Berkeley: University of California Press, 1991); Elizabeth Cohn and Michael J. Nojeim, "Promoting Democracy," in David W. Dent, ed., *U.S.–Latin American Policymaking: A Reference Handbook* (Westport, CT: Greenwood Press, 1995); Michael Cox, G. John Ikenberry, and Takashi Inoguchi, eds., *American Democracy Promotion: Impulses, Strategies, and Impacts* (New York: Oxford University Press, 2000); Jorge I. Dominguez, ed., *International Security and Democracy: Latin America and the Caribbean in the Post–Cold War Era* (Pittsburgh: University of Pittsburgh Press, 1998); Juan Forero, "In Latin America, Democracy Grows Fitful," *Denver Post* (August 6, 2004); Michael J. Kryzanek, *U.S.–Latin American Relations*, 3rd ed. (Westport, CT: Praeger, 1996); Abraham F. Lowenthal, ed., *Exporting Democracy: The United States and Latin America*, Vol. 2, *Case Studies* (Baltimore, MD: Johns Hopkins University Press, 1991); Tommie Sue Montgomery, ed., *Peacemaking and Democratization in the Western Hemisphere* (Boulder, CO: Lynne Rienner, 2000); Marina Ottaway and Thomas Carothers, eds., *Funding Virtue: Civil Society and Democracy Promotion* (Washington, DC: Carnegie Endowment for International Peace, 2000); George Packer, "Dreaming of Democracy," *New York Times* (March 2, 2003); Robert A. Pastor, ed., *Democracy in the Americas: Stopping the Pendulum* (New York: Holmes and Meier, 1989); John Peeler, *Building Democracy in Latin America*, 2nd ed. (Boulder, CO: Lynne Rienner, 2004); Lars Schoultz, *Beneath the United States: A History of U.S. Policy Toward Latin America* (Chapel Hill: University of North Carolina Press, 1998); Peter Smith, *Democracy in Latin America* (New York: Oxford University Press, 2005).

Dependency Theory Disenchantment with U.S. policies in Latin America during the **Cold War** led Latin American scholars to articulate a theory of development to account for the prevalence of poverty and inequality in Latin America and the causes of its economic and political failures. Using adaptations from Marxist analysis, dependency theorists argued that structural flaws in economic relations between the metropolitan centers such as the United States and peripheral regions such as Latin America made it possible to perpetuate underdevelopment and dependency by maintaining a neo-imperialist set of relationships. There are many versions of dependency theory; some are moderate and others are radical Marxist revolutionaries; they all claim that Latin America's economic life is characterized by exploitation by powerful capitalist states in the wealthy metropolitan centers.

At the core of dependency theory is the belief among contemporary scholars in Latin America and the United States that Latin America's underdevelopment is the result of a world market system that keeps Latin American countries in economic bondage and poverty. As multinational corporations link arms with local elites, severe inequalities and rigid class structures are maintained and perpetuated. Those who believe in a radical dependency perspective argue that **revolution** is the only way to eradicate the neo-imperialist relationship and meet the social and economic needs of society. The end of the Cold War and the collapse of the Soviet Union has weakened the support that dependency theory once had among Third World scholars. With Marxist socialist systems in decline, it becomes harder to argue that a theory of dependency will provide either a solution, or an explanation, of Latin America's development dilemma. Counter-poise efforts, including the development of common markets, free trade agreements, protectionism, and privatization, have gained attention as a way to deal with Latin America's serious economic problems. The growing disillusionment with the bromides offered by the **Washington Consensus** underlies the continuing struggle between the rich capitalist states and the impoverished states in Latin America and the Caribbean. *See also* Enterprise for the Americas Initiative (EAI); Imperialism; North American Free Trade Agreement (NAFTA).

Suggested Reading

Lawrence R. Alschuler, *Predicting Development, Dependency, and Conflict in Latin America: A Social Field Theory* (Ottawa: University of Ottawa Press, 1978); Mitchell A. Seligson and John T. Passé-Smith, eds., *Development and Underdevelopment: The Political Economy of Global Inequality* (Boulder, CO: Lynne Rienner, 2003); Mary Ann Tetreault and Charles Frederick Abel, eds., *Dependency Theory and the Return of High Politics* (Westport, CT: Greenwood Press, 1986); Howard J. Wiarda, ed., *New Directions in Comparative Politics* (Boulder, CO: Westview Press, 2002).

Díaz, Porfirio. *See* Hayes, Rutherford B.

Dictatorships Latin American regimes have oscillated between two broad types of governmental systems: electoral **democracy** (usually poorly consolidated) and dictatorship (usually a military-authoritarian system), often confounding U.S. presidents as to how to respond to such governments and their leaders while at the same time protecting American interests in Latin America. The line between the two is often blurred by the extent to which power is limited, representation is pluralistic and accountable, rights and freedoms are guaranteed, and how much say the masses have in determining policy outcomes (usually very little). The history of strong-man rule has deep roots in Latin American politics and has not been completely erased with the growing efforts to democratize previously authoritarian governments. The United States has a history of supporting right-wing dictatorships because they opposed Communist regimes and left-wing dictators. Dictatorships on the left are usually the product of a revolution based on nationalism and **anti-Americanism** and, therefore, have been consistently criticized and opposed by the **Washington policymakers**.

When a military junta took over in Chile following the September 11, 1973, coup against democratically elected Salvador **Allende**, authority rested in the branches of the armed forces and police, not the Chilean people. A system of command-obedience replaced democratic principles, and authority soon came to reside in one person, General Augusto **Pinochet**, commander in chief of the armed forces. In an attempt to legitimize his regime, and lessen foreign criticism of rampant **human rights** abuses, Pinochet created a so-called "protected democracy," meaning a non-pluralistic regime designed to exclude left-wing forces, democratic or non-democratic. The full expression of democratic views would not be tolerated by the military, regardless of the magnitude of their views and opinions. Pinochet was supported by Presidents Gerald **Ford** and Ronald **Reagan**, but opposed by President Jimmy **Carter**. The majority of Latin American dictatorships deny citizens the right or power to change their rulers peacefully, although some allow for sham elections that have no real meaning in determining electoral outcomes. In most cases, the personalist style of Latin American dictatorships—of the political left and right—have competed with well-established military juntas made up of more than a single individual.

Washington policymakers have often struggled with the dilemma of how to deal with unsavory governments that lack genuinely democratic institutions. Should these governments be treated the same as those with democratic leadership and institutions? What responsibility does the United States have for arming authoritarian, repressive governments that frequently serve to keep them in power, stimulating human rights abuses and anti-American sentiments? What is the value of selling weapons to authoritarian governments if the end result is the growth of communism and **terrorism**? What is more important? Supporting Latin American dictatorships to benefit jobs and profits in the United States or undermining the meaning of American principles of "liberty and justice for all"? In 1991, the United States supplied arms (grants, training, and sales) to authoritarian governments in El Salvador, Guatemala, Guyana, Haiti, and Honduras. According to a study by the Center for Defense Information in 1992, "Urging repressive militaries to be considerate of human rights and to love democracy while at the same time arming them with jet fighters and educating them in the subtleties of firing an M-16 does not work. . . . Arming dictators, quite simply, is bad policy" (Center for Defense Information, 1992: 7).

During the nineteenth century the United States chose to recognize any government that could maintain itself in power and meet its minimum obligations regardless of regime type. However, over time other factors would come to shape the minds of Washington policymakers toward Latin American dictatorships: racial inferiority and political immaturity, the desire for stability and order where American economic interests existed, and the fear of **revolutions** and political violence. Latin Americans were seen as fundamentally undemocratic (politically immature), uncivilized, and in need of guidance and direction from the United States. After the **Spanish-Cuban-American War** and the acquisition of the Panama Canal zone, the United States became more concerned about what President **Theodore Roo-**

sevelt called "chronic wrongdoing" and developed various means of preserving order through the exercise of police and military power. After the revolutions in Mexico, China, and Russia, the United States worried about the spread of such political maladies and devised various ways to oppose them. President Woodrow **Wilson** developed a policy of non-recognition of dictatorships that came to power and ruled by force, meaning that for years the United States opposed left-wing authoritarian governments in China, Guatemala, Cuba, and Vietnam. The process of U.S. support for right-wing dictatorships started in the 1920s with U.S. support of Mussolini, believing the fascists would maintain order and stability, an antidote to the spread of Bolshevism. This logic would soon became a mainstay of U.S.–Latin American policy for the rest of the century. Once the U.S. policy of supporting right-wing dictatorships caught on, it was possible to have an imposed order from compliant authoritarians without engaging in direction military intervention. The tolerance of military and authoritarian regimes in Latin America provided short-term benefits, but in the long term these "**friendly dictators**" proved to be antithetical to U.S. interests, fostering revolutions, anti-American political leaders, and nationalization of financial interests. It was clearly a "lesser-of-two-evils" approach to Latin American policy that led the United States to back some of the most brutal regimes in the world. The antifascist coalition that prevailed in **World War II** led to a short post-war period of opposing dictatorships and pushing for greater emphasis on democracy and free enterprise.

Once the **Cold War** began in the late 1940s, the United States reversed itself and came again to champion stable right-wing dictatorships opposed to communism. President **Truman** made the distinction between authoritarian dictators on the right (acceptable) and totalitarian dictators on the left (unacceptable). This distinction took on a momentum of its own and became one of the crucial guideposts of dealing with dictators around the world. Dictators such as Anastasio Somoza García, Rafael **Trujillo**, Mannel Odría, Marcos **Pérez Jiménez**, Fugencio **Batista**, and Alfredo Stroessner were mere authoritarians and deserved support throughout most of the 1940s and 1950s. After Vice-President Richard **Nixon**'s hostile reception on his Latin American tour in 1958, and the Cuban Revolution in 1959, President John F. **Kennedy** decided to re-evaluate U.S. policy toward Latin America by withdrawing support for right-wing dictators after realizing they were ineffective bulwarks against Communist advances in the Western Hemisphere. The growing challenges of revolutionary nationalism in Latin America drew the Kennedy administration back to supporting right-wing dictators and President Lyndon **Johnson** backed away from the overly optimistic **Alliance for Progress** and resorted to military **intervention** in the Dominican Republic in 1965.

During and after the Cold War the United States made numerous efforts to distance itself from the odious practices of right-wing dictatorships and promote democracy in Latin America. President Truman's secretary of state, James F. Byrnes, proclaimed in 1945 that non-intervention does not mean support for dictatorships and endorsed a multilateral effort against autocratic regimes. However, with the outbreak of the Cold War right-wing dictators gained a new lease on life by siding with the United States in the crusade against communism. The debate shifted again from dictatorship versus democracy to anti-communism versus communism. Latin American dictators such as Somoza, Trujillo, Batista, and the Duvaliers were the beneficiaries of U.S. anti-Soviet and anti-Cuban foreign policy. Peter H. Smith, *Talons of the Eagle* (2000: 200) argues that Latin American dictators were encouraged by the United States to take several steps to ensure their perpetuation in power:

- Declare fervent opposition to communism in all its forms and expressions.
- Provide support for the United States in international forum, especially the **United Nations (UN)** (where the costs of compliance were virtually zero).
- Endorse the **Monroe Doctrine**.
- Denounce all domestic opponents as communists, as communist-inspired, or as unwitting dupes of communist conspiracies; outlaw the local communist party.
- Subscribe to the **domino theory**, which meant that domestic subversion presented a threat to neighboring countries as well as to their own governments.
- Open the economy to U.S. investments and commercial interests.
- Express support for U.S. military, paramilitary, and covert actions against "communist threats" throughout the hemisphere.
- Maintain close relations with the U.S. military establishment (Somoza Sr. went so far as to send Somoza Jr. to West Point).
- Curry friendships with members of the U.S. Congress (Somoza Jr. had perhaps the closest friend of all in Representative John Murphy, D–New York).
- Cultivate close personal relations with U.S. ambassadors.

The policy pendulum swung back and forth toward dictators through the Vietnam War to the presidency of Jimmy **Carter**. After the Senate Select Committee on Intelligence, chaired by Frank Church of Idaho, criticized American covert actions, including **assassination** plots, **Central Intelligence Agency (CIA)**–orchestrated coups, and blind support of right-wing dictators, Jimmy Carter embraced a new foreign policy based on human rights. Speaking of the importance of **democracy** and human rights, Carter asserted that the United States was "now free of that inordinate fear of communism which once led us to embrace any dictator who joined us in that fear." When two friendly dictators—Somoza and the Shah of Iran—were toppled by revolutions in 1979, advocates of the old policy of backing right-wing dictators blamed Carter, particularly Ronald Reagan and Jeane **Kirkpatrick**. With the election of Ronald Reagan in 1980, the United States returned to supporting right-wing dictators, heightened Cold War tensions, and undermined Reagan's moral foundation for opposing Communist regimes because of their denial of political rights to their citizens while Washington supported governments that were equally as guilty of political abuses and denials. The end of the

Cold War removed the primary justification for supporting right-wing dictators and opposition to left-wing regimes, namely anti-communism and economic development. Without an evil empire to worry about, Washington policymakers put more emphasis on democracy promotion as a means of protecting American interests abroad. During the **Clinton** administration thousands of documents on U.S. relations with the dictatorships it supported in Latin America during the Cold War reveal that efforts were made to approach South American dictators about ending their use of **death squads** at home and abroad. Most of these efforts were half-hearted or were not carried through at all. Nevertheless, the United States continued to support dictators when they provided stability and enhanced economic development. Once President **George W. Bush** declared a global war on terrorism in the wake of the terrorist attacks on **September 11, 2001**, the commitment to democracy promotion and human rights once again slipped as a foreign policy priority, and right-wing dictators deemed useful to the anti-terrorist fight gained prominence again. *See also* Democracy and Democracy Promotion; Friendly Dictators; Intervention and Non-Intervention; Regime Change; Revolutions.

Suggested Reading

Center for Defense Information, "Arming Dictators," *The Defense Monitor,* Vol. 21, No. 5 (Washington, DC: Center for Defense Information, 1992); John Dinges, *The Condor Years: How Pinochet and his Allies Brought Terrorism to Three Continents* (New York: New Press, 2004); Peter Kornbluh, *The Pinochet File: A Declassified Dossier on Atrocity and Accountability* (New York: The New Press, 2003); Michael E. Latham, *Modernization as Ideology: American Social Science and "Nation Building" in the Kennedy Era* (Chapel Hill: University of North Carolina Press, 2000); David F. Schmitz, "Dictatorships," in Alexander DeConde, et al., eds., *Encyclopedia of American Foreign Policy*, 2nd ed. (New York: Charles Scribner's Sons, 2002); Peter H. Smith, *Talons of the Eagle: Dynamics of U.S.–Latin American Relations*, 2nd ed. (New York: Oxford University Press, 2000); Tony Smith, *America's Mission: The United States and the Worldwide Struggle for Democracy in the Twentieth Century* (Princeton, NJ: Princeton University Press, 1994).

Dirty War. *See* Death Squads (Escuadrones de Muerte); Operation Condor; Perón, Juan Domingo

Doctrines The foreign policy declarations emphasizing intentions, warnings, and purposes associated with U.S. presidents have played a significant role in U.S.–Latin American relations since the early nineteenth century. Unlike treaties that are considered a legal foundation for international relations, doctrines are merely statements or pronouncements, albeit often infused with a millennial vision of the world, a sense of exceptionalism, and a strong ideological content to persuade a doubtful or disinterested public. The presidential declarations dealing specifically with Latin America include the following: **Monroe Doctrine** (plus a number of major corollaries), Kennedy Doctrine, **Johnson Doctrine**, **Reagan Doctrine**, and the Bush Doctrine. Although presidential doctrines are nothing more than diplomatic statements of national intent, grounded in the language of national security, they are not considered legal and are often ignored, or repudiated, by governments that have been warned or admonished for their behavior.

The Monroe Doctrine of 1823 is considered one of the most significant and enduring policy declarations by a U.S. president. The purpose of the Monroe Doctrine was to provide a demonstration of U.S. power by telling Europe to keep its hands off the Americas, either by re-colonization or intervention. At first the Monroe Doctrine was ignored, but over time it assumed the status of a "doctrine," useful as a justification for intervention in Latin America and the Caribbean, a warning to European governments to stay out of the U.S. sphere of influence, and became mythologized in Washington and among the general public. Despite its malleability and popularity in the United States, the Monroe Doctrine is not considered a positive feature of U.S.–Latin American relations and is rarely mentioned in diplomatic discourse.

President John F. **Kennedy** campaigned as a Cold Warrior in 1960, arguing that the United States would have to use military force and covert action to prevent a second Communist state in the Western Hemisphere. Kennedy's fervent anti-communism was directed at Fidel **Castro**'s Cuba and British Guiana, a British colony embroiled in the transformation from home rule to independence. Kennedy feared that British Guiana's leader at the time, Cheddi Jagan, was too close to Fidel Castro and would endanger Latin America and the **Alliance for Progress** and threaten the security of the United States. If Jagan and his followers achieved independence, the Kennedy administration believed they would embrace communism and join hands with the Soviet Union. Fearing a Communist takeover on the South American mainland after Jagan's PPP (People's Progressive Party) won the 1961 parliamentary elections, President Kennedy developed a two-track policy toward Jagan: on one track the United States would offer economic and technical assistance; on the other the United States would promote a covert program of support for anti-Communist forces to bring about the downfall of Cheddi Jagan. Between 1961 and 1964 the United States worked to undermine Jagan's pro-independence and socialist program. Kennedy also worried that a Communist takeover in Guyana could jeopardize his re-election bid in 1964. In May 1963, President Kennedy asked a special **National Security Council (NSC)** task force to prepare a declaration or doctrine that would warn the Russians and Cubans that the United States would not accept a second Fidel Castro in this hemisphere. Known as the Kennedy Doctrine, it offered the president exceptions to the non-intervention clause in the **Organization of American States (OAS)** charter and provided a public statement that amounted to the right of the United States to exercise international police power in the Americas. The Kennedy Doctrine was the first effort to establish a policy of no-second Cubas in the Western Hemisphere. After Kennedy's **assassination**, President Lyndon B. **Johnson** reiterated the doctrine with his own, this time with a statement similar to President Kennedy's: "the American nations cannot, must not, will not permit the establishment of another Communist government in the Western Hemisphere." Eventually the Kennedy Doctrine succeeded in destabilizing (with the help of Great Britain) Guyana to the point that Jagan was overthrown in 1964. Efforts to prevent second Cubas were also part of U.S. efforts to undermine and overthrow Chile's Salvador **Allende**, the **Sandinistas** in Nicaragua, Haiti's Jean-Bertrand **Aristide**, and Venezuela's Hugo Chávez.

The Reagan Doctrine emerged from a world-view based on the perception that the Soviet Union and its allies were gaining influence as a result of support for Marxist movements around the world, particularly in the Horn of Africa and Central America. Containment was not working, and what the United States needed was an augmented rationale for earlier efforts to defeat communism. During the 1980 presidential campaign Reagan claimed that "the Soviet Union underlies all the unrest that is going on. If they weren't engaged in this game of dominoes, there wouldn't be any hot spots in the world." To arrest these evil trends, often blaming President Jimmy **Carter** for the new crisis, President Reagan set forth a number of measures to defy Soviet-supported aggression by supporting anti-Communict forces on every continent from Afghanistan to Nicaragua. In ways similar to the **Roosevelt Corollary to the Monroe Doctrine** in 1904, Reagan believed that American foreign policy needed an offensive component to containment, something more aggressive and wide-ranging that would confront the Brezhnev Doctrine of the irreversibility of Soviet-backed socialist gains, particularly in the Third World.

To sell his bold and assertive policies, Reagan adopted a rhetorical strategy that described anti-Communist forces as moral crusaders, revolutionary patriots, and freedom fighters for democracy. However, it was neither Reagan nor his advisers who coined the term "Reagan Doctrine," but Charles Krauthammer, a journalist and foreign policy commentator in a *Time* magazine article in April 1985. Although Reagan was clearly in sync with the doctrine's precepts, he left the role of formulation and implementation to key advisers such as **Central Intelligence Agency (CIA)** director William **Casey**, **United Nations (UN)** ambassador Jeane **Kirkpatrick**, and others who assumed the role of publicists for selling the message to the American people. The Reagan administration offered his anti-Soviet guerrillas substantial amounts of military assistance to unseat governments considered a threat to the United States. While there are those who praise the Reagan Doctrine for its role in helping to bring down the Soviet empire, others are far less generous in their assessments of what the doctrine accomplished. In the case of Nicaragua, emphasis on clandestine activity backfired, producing a scandal that did serious damage to President Reagan's legitimacy. Reagan's anti-Communist guerrillas were often involved in **human rights** abuses and displayed little interest in democratic outcomes. The death and destruction caused by the Contra war in Nicaragua did not defeat the Sandinistas, although they lost at the ballot box in 1990 with heavy U.S. support for the electoral opposition. Some argue that the Reagan Doctrine actually retarded the emergence of stability in Nicaragua and played a role in fostering the growth of **anti-Americanism** throughout the region.

The Bush Doctrine of 2001 was part of the president's war on **terrorism** in which **George W. Bush** declared that containment, and toleration, of "evil" nations was not working to the betterment of the United States. To wage a war on terrorism, Bush argued that "pre-emptive war" would now be the guide to deal with hostile forces. Although not directed at Latin America, some of his advisers interpreted the Bush Doctrine as a means of warning countries like Cuba, Colombia, Haiti, and Venezuela that the United States would have far less tolerance for hostile acts that threatened the security of the United States. The Bush Doctrine put Fidel Castro on the defensive, warning the Cuban people to prepare for a possible invasion of the island to remove Castro from power so that the Bush administration could then start the process of redesigning Cuba's economic and political system. Despite the underlying message of the Bush Doctrine, after **September 11, 2001**, the United States paid little attention to Latin America.

Presidential doctrines are not only declarations of foreign policy principles, they are also statements designed to pre-empt actions deemed hostile to the United States. By warning potential aggressors, presidential doctrines offer a way to reinject a moral component to American foreign policy. If there is truly an "evil empire" or a threatening "axis of evil," how can the president's motives be questioned? When doctrines reflect the values of a nation based on the defeat of evil regimes and a missionary zeal to create a more democratic world with greater security, prosperity, and peace, it becomes difficult to challenge these views unless the policies emanating from the doctrine backfire and American interests are clearly undermined by the failure of pre-emptive measures to produce what the president promised in his public rhetoric. *See also* Contras; Intervention and Non-Intervention; Regime Change; Threat Perception/Assessment.

Suggested Reading

Cecil Van Meter Crabb, Jr., *The Doctrines of American Foreign Policy: Their Meaning, Role and Future* (Baton Rouge: Louisiana State University Press, 1982).

Dollar Diplomacy The Latin American policy of President William Howard **Taft** (1909–1913) was defined by what became known as Dollar Diplomacy, an attempt to substitute financial control for President Theodore **Roosevelt**'s **Big Stick diplomacy**. Devised by President Taft and his secretary of state, Philander C. **Knox**, Dollar Diplomacy contained the idea that the United States needed to encourage and protect overseas investment to both expand U.S. power and serve as a brake on rival European interest in Latin America and the Far East. Francis Mairs Huntington Wilson, Taft's assistant secretary of state for Latin America, provided the public justification for U.S. financial control of Latin American customs offices to guarantee payments to American lenders. Huntington Wilson argued that Dollar Diplomacy was "common sense diplomacy" because it would eventually create a material prosperity that would wean the Latin American countries—known for their chronic fiscal instability—from their pre-occupation with **revolutions** and dictators. The Taft administration believed that political turmoil in places such as the Dominican Republic, Haiti, Honduras and Nicaragua threatened U.S. interests by increasing the likelihood of European military **intervention** in the region. However, to achieve this goal Latin Americans must accept the "guiding hand" of the

United States to prevent foreign involvement, something that affects the security of the United States. In a form of Social Darwinism, Huntington Wilson resorted to analogies between biology and international relations, arguing that "sick nations" such as Latin America will always be dominated by "strong neighbors" (United States) using the genius of Yankee capitalism and enlightened diplomacy.

The fiscal architects of Dollar Diplomacy devised a plan for fiscal reform in which financially troubled Caribbean republics would satisfy their obligations to European creditors through loans obtained from U.S. banks. By establishing U.S.–administered customs receiverships in borrowing countries, with a percentage of customs revenues set aside for repayment to American lenders, the United States hoped to provide a fiscal substitute for U.S. military **intervention**. With the completion of the Panama Canal only a few years away, President Taft postured that his Latin American policy would substitute "dollars for bullets," and in doing so create more prosperity, peace, and security for the United States and the struggling Caribbean nations.

It was a policy with inherent risks and a flare for economic morality and good will; however, Dollar Diplomacy failed to eliminate the use of U.S. military power whenever it was necessary to prevent foreign intervention and restore some semblance of political stability. In each case where a financial protectorate was put in place, charges of Yankee economic **imperialism** and **anti-Americanism** surfaced and brought greater criticism of American foreign policy. It was frequently criticized by Democrats as a device to protect American bankers and another way to facilitate U.S. economic exploitation of the region. In the 1912 election for president, Woodrow **Wilson** criticized the Big Stick and Dollar Diplomacy and adopted a more idealistic position in dealing with problems of revolution and financial instability in Latin America. In practice, Wilson's Latin American policy—stressing a defense of liberty and democracy—differed little from that of his predecessors. As political party leaders in the United States attempted to justify their mandate for change in the Latin American policy of the United States by criticizing the other, U.S. financial and military intervention in Latin America continued, adding to the legacy of U.S. interventionism in Latin America from 1898 to the 1930s. U.S. presidents continue to search for ways to protect economic and security interests through policies that contain some of the original ingredients of the Taft-Knox formula during the early part of the twentieth century. *See also* Butler, Smedley Darlington; Imperialism.

Suggested Reading

Francis Adams, *Dollar Diplomacy: United States Economic Assistance to Latin America* (Aldershot: Ashgate, 2000); Wilfred Hardy Callcott, *The Caribbean Policy of the United States, 1890–1920* (Baltimore, MD: Johns Hopkins University Press, 1942; Paul Drake, ed., *Money Doctors, Foreign Debts, and Economic Reforms in Latin America from the 1890s to the Present* (Wilmington, DE: SR Books, 1994); Herbert Feis, *The Diplomacy of the Dollar; First Era, 1919–1932* (Hamden, CT: Archon Books, 1965); Simon Gabriel Hanson, *Dollar Diplomacy Modern Style: Chapters in the Failure of the Alliance for Progress* (Washington, DC: Inter-American Affairs

Press, 1970); Benjamin T. Harrison, *Dollar Diplomat: Chandler Anderson and American Diplomacy in Mexico and Nicaragua, 1913–1928* (Pullman: Washington State University Press, 1988); Howard Hill, *Roosevelt and the Caribbean* (Chicago: University of Chicago Press, 1927); Robert H. Holden and Eric Zolov, eds., *Latin America and the United States: A Documentary History* (New York: Oxford University Press, 2000); Dana Munro, *Intervention and Dollar Diplomacy in the Caribbean, 1900–1921* (Princeton, NJ: Princeton University Press, 1964); Scott Nearing and Joseph Freeman, *Dollar Diplomacy: A Study of American Imperialism* (New York: Huebesch and Viking, 1925); Emily S. Rosenberg, *Financial Missionaries to the World: The Politics and Culture of Dollar Diplomacy, 1900–1930* (Cambridge, MA: Harvard University Press, 1999); Lars Schoultz, *Beneath the United States: A History of U.S. Policy Toward Latin America* (Cambridge, MA: Harvard University Press, 1998); Cyrus Veeser, *A World Safe for Capitalism: Dollar Diplomacy and America's Rise to Global Power* (New York: Columbia University Press, 2002); Veeser, "Dollar Diplomacy: The Guilded Age Origins of the Roosevelt Corollary to the Monroe Doctrine," *Diplomatic History*, Vol. 27, No. 3 (June 2003); Bryce Wood, *The Making of the Good Neighbor Policy* (New York: Columbia University Press, 1961).

Domino Theory A theory of **threat perception** developed by **Washington policymakers** during the **Cold War** based on what purportedly happens to Third World nations that "fall" to communism. The domino theory was constructed on the fearful belief that communism was monolithic, directed from Moscow, capable of global expansion, and politically infectious to immature and undemocratic nations. Because of its inherent expansionism, foreign policy analysts argued that if one nation were to suddenly fall to communism, then neighboring countries would quickly become susceptible to Communist influence and also fall—as with a row of dominoes—one after another. The metaphor of falling dominoes was first spelled out by President **Dwight D. Eisenhower** in April 1954, explaining what would happen if the United States abandoned Southeast Asia to the Communists. The domino theory provided a rationale for cultivating non-Communist allies (often right-wing **dictatorships**), a justification for covert action and military **intervention**, and the need for larger defense budgets to demonstrate Washington's level of commitment to fighting communism. The domino theory made sense to many who experienced the trauma of fascist expansion prior to **World War II** in which Adolf Hitler annexed Austria and Czechoslovakia and then moved to take control of Poland and France.

Since the end of the Cold War, foreign policy analysts have worried that the growing spread of Islamic fundamentalism contains elements of the domino theory. Proponents of humanitarian intervention have argued that to stop the spread of a "wider war," in places like the Balkans, military intervention may be required to prevent other conflicts in Europe. Neo-conservatives in Washington who favored war with Iraq developed a new version of the domino theory in which they argued that with the removal of Saddam Hussein, followed by the creation of a pro-Western democratic regime, Iraq will serve as a demonstration regime for others in the region. Instead of exporting authoritarian and anti-American regimes, a transformed Iraq would help spread **democracy** to closed societies such as Saudi Arabia, Iran, and Syria. For decades after 1959, Washington's efforts to destroy Fidel **Castro** and the Cuban Revolution have been rooted in the fear that any success of Cuban socialism might have a demonstration, or domino, effect on the rest of Latin America. Unable to rid Cuba of Fidel Castro, the United States intervened in Chile, Nicaragua, El Salvador, and Grenada convinced that any additional foothold gained by Communists in the region endangered the hemisphere.

Although not articulated as a domino theory per se, President Woodrow **Wilson**'s Latin American policy rested on the necessity of intervention to prevent "bad" revolutions (Mexico and Soviet Russia) from "infecting" neighboring countries. During the 1960s the **Kennedy** and **Johnson** administrations used the domino theory to justify the U.S. military response to Soviet- and Chinese-sponsored aggression in Southeast Asia. Most foreign policy analysts discredited the domino theory as having little relevance to explaining the conflict in Vietnam, arguing it was essentially a civil war over the reunification of Indo-China, not a case of Communist expansionism. **Nixon**'s national security adviser, Henry **Kissinger**, used the domino theory to justify the destabilization of Chile under President Salvador **Allende**. President **Reagan**'s interventionist policies in Central America and the Caribbean were influenced by domino analogies and related thinking in dealing with the Communist threat from El Salvador and Nicaragua on Mexico. Mexico's economic downturn and debt problems in the early 1980s stirred a lot of alarmist talk about security threats in Washington at the time, including statements about Central American countries falling like "Communist" dominoes and the possibility of a Castro-type revolution in Mexico. With little understanding of Mexico and political events in Central America, the Reagan administration tried to demonstrate a connection between Mexico and the revolutionary turmoil in "neighboring" Nicaragua and El Salvador. By portraying Mexico as a "weak domino" subject to revolutionary forces from Cuba, Central America, and elsewhere, President Ronald Reagan and conservative members of Congress hoped to gain support for a military solution to perceived security threats in the region.

Although many considered the domino theory—when applied to either Southeast Asia or Central America—a crude and false analogy, it provided policymakers in Washington with a powerful metaphor in which to present foreign policy threats in highly simplistic terms to the American people. It was not uncommon for Washington policymakers to use inflammatory rhetoric such as "Soviet beachheads," "export of revolution," "subversive-terrorist threats," "Communization," and "Cuban-inspired Marxist guerrillas" to accompany the forecast of countries "falling" into the hands of a foreign or domestic enemy. In the controversial report by the Committee of Santa Fe, *Santa Fe II: A Strategy for Latin America in the Nineties* (1988: 23), the authors warned that "The Soviet Bloc is successfully projecting its power into every country of this hemisphere and all the indicators are that these [alarming] trends will continue." Despite the fact that predictions of a Marxist revolutionary Nicaragua spreading like a wave of Communist victories throughout the region proved false, the domino theory has not lost its utility as a powerful metaphor for pursuing strategic objectives in regions of the world where U.S. interests are threatened. The imagery of framing the strategic environment as composed of states aligned as identical dominoes placed the blame for each domino's fall on external forces. This reinforced a tendency of Washington policymakers to see Latin American revolutions with leftist and anti-American orientations as being instigated and manipulated by Germany, the Soviet Union, Cuba, and others that fit the explanation. The domino metaphor said nothing about how to stop the dominoes from falling; its major value was to heighten the nature of the strategic threat and emphasize the consequences of failing to intervene to stop other dominoes from falling.

President **George W. Bush**'s doctrine of "pre-emptive war" against purported terrorist threats is based on some of the same logic that once made the domino theory a cornerstone of American foreign policy. As with other presidential **doctrines** aimed at achieving foreign policy objectives, the predictive capacity of the domino metaphor is quite narrow and often misleading. The domino metaphor was at first invoked to justify ways of challenging the ability of Soviet communism to gain adherents during the Cold War. After the United States assumed the role of the world's sole superpower, a different domino theory emerged. Instead of operating on the basis of negative assumptions about the possibilities of change due to the expansion of Soviet communism, the new domino theory envisions democracy as the cornerstone of wholesale political change in regions of the world devoid of democratic rule. When the United States faced wobbly dominoes in Latin America and elsewhere during the Cold War, it felt obligated to intervene militarily in one country to avoid having to fight in another. Today's more optimistic vision of falling dominoes (autocratic dictatorships) is derived in part from the unparalleled power of the United States in a unipolar world. When confronted with hemispheric problems such as drugs and **terrorism**, the United States has employed the metaphor of "war" to frame the policy issue. This has advantages for those foreign policy elites who are looking for a readily acceptable concept that will make it easier to militarize the problem and gain the support of an otherwise uninformed or skeptical public. *See also* Friendly Dictators; Threat Perception/Assessment.

Suggested Reading

Committee of Santa Fe, *Santa Fe II: A Strategy for Latin America in the Nineties* (Washington, DC: Committee of Santa Fe, 1988); Ross Gregory, "The Domino Theory," in Alexander de Conde, ed., *Encyclopedia of American Foreign Policy* (1979); Michael J. Hogan and Thomas G. Paterson, ed., *Explaining the History of American Foreign Relations* (New York: Cambridge University Press, 1991); Walter LaFeber, *America, Russia, and the Cold War, 1945–1975* (New York: Wiley, 1976); Frank A. Ninkovich, *Modernity and Power: A History of the Domino Theory in the Twentieth Century* (Chicago: University of Chicago Press, 1994); David F. Schmitz, *Thank God They're on Our Side: The United States and Right-Wing Dictatorships, 1921–1965* (Chapel Hill: University of North Carolina Press, 1999); Keith L. Shimko, "Foreign Policy Metaphors: Falling 'Dominoes' and 'Drug Wars,' " in Laura Neack, Jeanne A.K. Hey, and Patrick J. Haney, eds., *Foreign Policy Analysis: Continuity and Change in Its Second Generation* (Englewood

Cliffs, NJ: Prentice Hall, 1995); Sam Tanenhaus, "The Rise and Fall and Rise of the Domino Theory," *New York Times* (March 23, 2003).

Drago Doctrine A principle of **international law** opposing the use of military **intervention**, or occupation, in Latin American states for the purpose of collecting a public debt. The Drago Doctrine was enunciated in 1902 by Argentine Foreign Minister Luis María Drago after a 1902 naval blockade was imposed on Venezuela by Germany, Great Britain, and Italy for defaulting on bonds issued to nationals of those countries. The "doctrine" was contained in a diplomatic note to the Argentine minister in Washington which stated "There can be no territorial expansion in America on the part of Europe. . . . The public debt cannot occasion armed intervention, nor even the actual occupation of the territory of American nations by a European power." Drago's emphasis on sovereignty and territorial inviolability actually was a restatement of the Calvo Clause of 1868 and proscription against European intervention in the Americas stated in the **Monroe Doctrine**. The Drago Doctrine was at first supported by the United States because of its emphasis on the payment of foreign debts and the non-intervention language that reminded Washington of the Monroe Doctrine. It received wide support throughout Latin America. At the Second Hague Conference in 1907 the United States managed to soften the anti-interventionist language prior to the adoption of the doctrine. However, when the United States discovered that an international legal policy was not sufficient to avoid European intervention in the Americas, it established custom receiverships to ensure the payment of debts so as to avoid European involvement. In contemporary international law, intervention by one state to collect debts owed to its citizens by another state is prohibited; however, diplomatic intervention by a state on behalf of its citizens is still an acceptable practice. *See also* Calvo Clause; Intervention and Non-Intervention.

Suggested Reading

Calvin D. Davis, *The United States and the Second Hague Peace Conference: American Diplomacy and International Organization, 1899–1914* (Durham, NC: Duke University Press, 1976); Robert H. Holden and Eric Zolov, eds., *Latin America and the United States: A Documentary History* (New York: Oxford University Press, 2000); Lester D. Langley, *The United States and the Caribbean in the Twentieth Century*, 4th ed. (Athens: University of Georgia Press, 1989).

Drug Trafficking Although the problem of illicit narcotics trafficking has been an international issue since the 1890s, it did not become a contentious political issue in U.S.–Latin American relations until the late 1970s. As many illicit drug products—cocaine, heroin, marijuana, and others—became more potent and sophisticated, the United States and Latin American governments came to realize that the enormity of the drug business required more than individual or bilateral responses to different aspects of the problem. After **World War I**, the **League of Nations** became the center of international efforts to control illicit drugs. Since the United States was a non-member of the League of Nations, it remained indifferent to the effort and inflexible to how best to enforce certain treaty provisions. The Latin American states did not take the problem of drug regulation seriously, and efforts to comply with key regulations were often erratic. After **World War II** the **United Nations (UN)** succeeded the League of Nations and became the major international body to counter drug trafficking. The UN sponsored several conventions that provided a worldwide legal framework to counter the illicit traffic in narcotics drugs and other psychotropic substances. The emergence of powerful, private drug cartels in the 1970s and 1980s prompted the **Organization of American States (OAS)** to take collective action against drug trafficking and cartels located throughout the hemisphere. The creation of the Inter-American Drug Abuse Control Commission (CICAD) in the 1980s became the center of collaborative efforts to reduce the supply and demand for illicit drugs. Both the OAS and the United Nations have been in favor of reducing supply and demand on a more equal basis, but progress is limited by the fact that international cooperation is voluntary.

The saliency of drugs as an issue of national concern in the United States prompted the U.S. government to mobilize its resources to fight the drug cartels and tighten law enforcement efforts in the United States. The enormous size of the world drug market added to the urgency of placing drug trafficking on the foreign policy agenda of the United States and Latin American countries because of its "intermestic" impact, that is, drug trafficking bridges both domestic and international politics. Estimates place the world's volume of trade in illicit drugs to be close to $190 billion annually. Despite the recognition of the importance of trying to eliminate drug trafficking in Latin America and the United States, there is no consensus on the best approach to the drug trade. The United States has put more emphasis on limiting production and curtailing the amount of drugs entering the United States from Latin America and elsewhere. This means the U.S. government has framed the issue of drug trafficking as a "war" with only a military solution. The Latin American states caught in the drug trade, particularly Mexico, Colombia, Peru, Bolivia, and Panama, have approached the issue from a domestic policy perspective where the voracious appetite for drugs in the United States and Europe is more to blame than the supply from poor Latin American countries. Those who consider drug trafficking a demand problem want improved law enforcement measures, drug education, meaningful treatment programs, and decriminalization. A few Latin American presidents have even gone so far as to suggest that some form of "legalization" is the only way to stop the illicit drug trade that produces tremendous profits and plagues the Western Hemisphere with social, political, and legal problems. While these different perspectives are not absolute in separating the United States and Latin America, they do complicate any meaningful collaborative effort to fight the problem. **Washington policymakers** must also deal with the domestic perception of not being tough enough in dealing with drugs and drug trafficking. For example, President Bill **Clinton**'s claim that as a youth he tried marijuana but did not inhale served to undermine his anti-drug rhetoric and symbolism, both in his public statements and his political appointments to the national drug control office.

There are three drugs that are the main source of smuggling into the United States from Latin America: cocaine, heroin, and marijuana. In a March 2005 report, the Office of National Drug Control Policy (ONDCP) found that in Los Angeles, California, the largest market for illicit drugs in the United States, drug trafficking has not slowed and the street value of drugs is rising. Cocaine, with a 2003 street value (dependent on purity and ultimate destination) that ranged from $21,000 to $80,000 a pound, is brought to the United States by Colombian, Mexican, and Dominican organizations with more than two-thirds smuggled across the southwestern border of the United States. Latin American heroin smuggled into the United States comes mainly from Mexico and Colombia. Colombian heroin arrives mostly by air, either through direct commercial flights from Colombia, or other Latin American countries such as the Dominican Republic, Panama, Venezuela, and Ecuador. Mexican heroin is cheaper than heroin from South Africa or Southwest Asia because it is the least pure. Nevertheless, it still costs between $8,000 and $13,000 per pound. In its purest form, heroin can be valued at $1 million per pound. Marijuana is the most readily available illegal drug in the United States, with close to 12 million current users. Most of the marijuana is from Mexico and Colombia and is smuggled in from Mexico. The high demand for marijuana in the United States has increased domestic production at home as well as greater production of high potency marijuana from Canada. Marijuana prices range between $960 and $4,000 per pound with much higher prices for some West Coast imports from Canada.

Inter-American drug trafficking has complicated American foreign policy because the United States has played a key role in the militarization of counternarcotics efforts in Latin America. By insisting on the use of military force as an anti-drug instrument, particularly in breaking the link between drug traffickers and terrorist groups who protect them, the United States has found itself on the side of repressive governments and **human rights** violaters. Many critics of U.S. drug policy claim that the militarization of the drug war has not addressed the social and economic factors that give rise to drug production in Latin America or its consumption in the United States. Moreover, the current approach to drug trafficking has not had a discernible impact on the amount of drugs entering the United States or in the elimination of drug cartels south of the border. In many cases, the militarization of the drug war is an obstacle to democracy-building and respect for human rights. Mexican President Vicente **Fox** has been handing over more responsibility for fighting the drug war to the Mexican military because it is perceived as less corrupt; however, this approach has not had a significant impact on the flow of illicit drugs into the United States. According to the **Washington Office on Latin America (WOLA)**, "A steady stream of cocaine, marijuana and heroin continues to move north in every conceivable way, through maritime containers, shipping vessels, small planes landing on clandestine airstrips, human 'mules,' and 'air bombardment' to speed boats." The United States and Colombia signed an extradition treaty in 1979 and the United States increased funding for drug-related programs that included interdiction, crop eradication programs, legal training and assistance for Colombian police and judicial authorities, and military assistance for security. Although Bolivia was the source of coca leaves, the precursor material for cocaine, it was estimated in the 1980s that close to 80 percent of cocaine and marijuana consumed in the United States originated in or was processed in Colombia. The 1979 extradition treaty demonstrated the urgency of the drug issue and the necessity of regional cooperation, but it also became a source of considerable debate, particularly in Colombia were drug kingpins like Pablo Escobar exercised tremendous power. The merger of leftist guerrilla activity with the Colombian narcotics industry added a major dimension to how the problem was framed by government officials in Bogotá and Washington. Once the problem of drug trafficking was viewed as a security threat to Colombia, the United States, and the region as a whole, the solution quickly gravitated to a "war" requiring huge amounts of military assistance from the United States.

To strengthen U.S. anti-narcotics efforts at home and abroad, the U.S. Congress passed the Anti-Drug Abuse Act of 1986, a law that mandated annual reports to assess, or certify, anti-narcotics efforts in the drug-producing and trafficking nations around the world, nineteen of which were in Latin America and the Caribbean. When the U.S. government judged that a target government was not sufficiently aggressive in its efforts to eradicate illicit drugs and drug-related corruption, the country ran the risk of being "decertified" and susceptible to drastic reductions in U.S. aid. For example, the Clinton administration decertified Colombia in 1996 and 1997 and canceled its president's visa. Although the **George W. Bush** administration has backed Mexico and Colombia in their efforts to carry out anti-narcotics policies based on extensive use of the military combined with the direct support and intervention of U.S. police, military agencies, and private military contractors, the absence of adequate mechanisms of civilian control and legislative oversight in Latin America are causing more problems than solutions to drug trafficking in the Americas. *See also* Bush, George Herbert Walker; Plan Colombia; Private Military Contractors.

Suggested Reading

Bruce M. Bagley and William O. Walker, eds., *Drug Trafficking in the Americas* (Coral Gables, FL: North-South Center, University of Miami, 1996); Ted Galen Carpenter, *Bad Neighbor Policy: Washington's Futile War on Drugs in Latin America* (New York: Macmillan, 2003); *Colombia Monitor*, "Taking Stock: Plan Colombia's First Year," (Washington Office on Latin America, March 2002); Office of National Drug Control Policy, "Los Angeles, California: Profile of Drug Indicators" (March 2005); Jorge Luis Sierra Guzmán, "Mexico's Military in the War on Drugs," *Drug War Monitor* (Washington Office on Latin America—WOLA, April 2003); Peter H. Smith, *Talons of the Eagle: Dynamics of U.S.–Latin American Relations*, 2nd ed. (New York: Oxford University Press, 2000).

Dulles, Allen Welsh (1893–1969) Lawyer, diplomat, and intelligence official who developed a fascination with espionage and **covert operations** and played a major role in U.S.–Latin American relations after **World War II**. He was one of the dominant figures in the **Cold War** because of his work for the **Central Intelligence Agency (CIA)** (first as deputy director and then as director) from 1951 to 1961. Allen Dulles viewed the Cold War as a life or death struggle, which at times led him to engage in actions that violated the law. He subscribed to a bipolar view of the world in which the threat of Soviet despotism required a desperate effort to convince Latin Americans that to stop communism in the Western Hemisphere would require a new and different Latin American policy. Like many **Washington policymakers**, Dulles spent many years in Europe but had never traveled to Latin America and knew very little of the social and political conditions that existed in hemispheric "trouble spots."

Dulles was a controversial figure because of his methods and far-right views of what constituted security threats to the United States, both in Latin America and other parts of the Third World. He was involved heavily in the overthrow of Guatemalan president Jacobo **Arbenz** in 1954, anti-**Castro** Central Intelligence Agency (CIA) activities in Cuba including **assassination** plots, the failed **Bay of Pigs** invasion, and CIA support for Dominican dissidents in their effort to assassinate Rafael **Trujillo**, dictator of the Dominican Republic. His influence over American foreign policy was greatly enhanced by his brother, **John Foster Dulles**, President **Dwight Eisenhower**'s secretary of state and one of the leading figures in America's fight against world communism.

After graduating from Princeton University in 1916, Dulles entered the diplomatic service and served in Switzerland where he began a lifetime of interest in espionage and intelligence. He worked for the Office of Strategic Services (OSS) during World War II before joining the Central Intelligence Agency. He was instrumental in the creation of the office within the CIA that dealt with covert operations that practiced **regime change** by overthrowing left-wing governments (Iran, 1953; Guatemala, 1954) whose economic reforms threatened American commercial interests.

The high mark of Dulles' career in U.S. intelligence was the failed Bay of Pigs invasion. As director of the CIA, Dulles placed Richard **Bissell**, deputy director of plans, in charge of training a Cuban guerrilla army as well as several plots for the assassination of Fidel Castro and his brother, Raúl. After John F. **Kennedy** was elected president in 1960, Allen Dulles was retained as head of the CIA because Kennedy wanted proof that as president he was not "soft on communism." The Bay of Pigs plans continued under Kennedy and his failure to oppose the ill-fated plans for an invasion may have been part of his thinking that Castro must be overthrown for domestic political reasons. After the aborted invasion blunder, Dulles served on a committee that carried out a postmortem into CIA involvement in the affair, but it failed to agree on whether the CIA was to blame for the foreign policy failure. With his reputation as a spymaster seriously tarnished after the Bay of Pigs invasion, President Kennedy took steps to curb Dulles' influence and within months Dulles had retired from the CIA. Dulles returned to his law practice and served on the Warren Commission after the assassination of President Kennedy. After his death in 1969, historians reviewed his private papers and found evidence that Allen

Dulles realized the Cuban invasion plan had serious flaws, but was convinced that once the operation was underway President Kennedy would violate his previous pledge and provide overt U.S. support for the exiles. Dulles was proud of his covert operations that resulted in **regime change** beneficial to the United States; he had little concern with the "blowback" from policies of overthrowing left-wing governments and the support of anti-Communist, and friendly, right-wing **dictatorships** that invariably followed in the wake of these efforts. *See also* Blowback; Scandals and Blunders; Threat Perception/Assessment.

Suggested Reading

David Green, "The Cold War Comes to Latin America," in Barton Bernstein, ed., *Politics and Policies of the Eisenhower Administration* (Chicago: Quadrangle, 1970); Peter Grose, *Gentleman Spy: The Life of Allen Dulles* (Boston: Houghton Mifflin, 1994); Stephen G. Rabe, *Eisenhower and Latin America: The Foreign Policy of Anticommunism* (Chapel Hill: University of North Carolina Press, 1988); James Srodes, *Allen Dulles: Master of Spies* (Washington, DC: Regnery Publishing, 1999); Lucien S. Vandenbroucke, "The 'Confessions' of Allen Dulles: New Evidence on the Bay of Pigs," *Diplomatic History*, Vol. 8 (fall 1984).

Dulles, John Foster (1888–1959) Lawyer, diplomat, conservative politician, and intelligence officer who played a key role in orchestrating the **Cold War** foreign policy of the **Truman** and **Eisenhower** administrations. He was one of the major figures in the post–**World War II** United States who believed in the existence of a monolithic Communist conspiracy to overthrow the West and undermine U.S. influence in the Third World. He developed a reputation as a tough anti-Communist crusader, believing in a strong military establishment, support for right-wing **dictatorships**, and the United States as a leading force for good against the evils associated with the Soviet Union. His world-view was confirmed by statements made during his Senate Foreign Relations Committee hearings in which he stated that Soviet communism was "not only the gravest threat that ever faced the United States, but the gravest threat that has ever faced what we call western civilization, or indeed, any civilization which was dominated by a spiritual faith" (quoted in Rabe, 1988: 29). Dulles believed that in Latin America totalitarians (fascists and Communists) were allied in their effort to undermine U.S. **hegemony** in Central and South America. To combat Soviet aggression in Latin America, Dulles advised Eisenhower that the increasing influence of the Soviet menace must be stopped before it "infects" the whole hemisphere.

John Foster Dulles graduated from Princeton University and earned a law degree from George Washington University in 1911. He then joined the influential law firm of Sullivan and Cromwell, which served as a base for his work in international relations and American foreign policy. Sullivan and Cromwell represented the **United Fruit Company** in Latin America, and members of this firm often served in the Latin American section of the **State Department**. Dulles chose John Moors **Cabot**, a career foreign service officer with two decades of experience in a number of Latin American posts, to be assistant secretary of state for inter-American affairs. He was one of the delegates to the San Francisco Conference in 1945 that created the **United Nations (UN)**. He spent a year in the U.S. Senate after being nominated by New York Governor Thomas E. Dewey after the seat was vacated by Robert Wagner. After Dwight D. Eisenhower was elected president in 1952, Dulles was first in line to become the next secretary of state. In this role he served as chief foreign policy adviser during the Eisenhower era. Dulles was diagnosed with terminal cancer in 1958 at a time when American foreign policy was shifting away from the moral crusade against communism advocated by Dulles to more prudent forms of policy to confront the Soviet threat.

By 1954 anti-communism was the core of the Eisenhower administration's Latin American policy. This meant that anti-Communist military dictatorships were embraced and repressive policies were either ignored or tolerated. This policy eventually produced a breakdown in U.S.–Latin American relations as popularly elected leaders in Latin America criticized the United States for its tolerance of right-wing dictatorships in the region. José Figueres, president of Costa Rica, charged that "our main enemy was Mr. John Foster Dulles in his defending of corrupt dictatorships" (Rabe, 1988: 40). His bout with cancer forced his resignation in 1958, and he died on May 24, 1959. *See also* Dulles, Allen Welsh; Domino Theory; Friendly Dictators.

Suggested Reading

Stephen G. Rabe, *Eisenhower and Latin America: The Foreign Policy of Anticommunism* (Chapel Hill: University of North Carolina Press, 1988).

E

EAI. *See* Enterprise for the Americas Initiative

Earth Summit, Rio de Janeiro (1992) A large and forward-looking meeting of individuals and organizations in 1992 to address the problems of the environment and development. Building on the 1987 **United Nations (UN)** report in favor of "sustainable development," participants in the conference included more than 100 heads of state, 8,000 delegates from around the world, 9,000 members of the media, and 3,000 accredited representatives from non-governmental organizations. Dubbed the Earth Summit, it turned into the largest international conference ever held on environmental and developmental issues, a reflection of the growing importance of the environment as a political, economic, and moral issue. Under the sponsorship of the United Nations Conference on Environment and Development, participants adopted Agenda 21, a plan to guide the policies of governments as they approached the twenty-first century. With over 400 pages of text, Agenda 21 emphasized the need for a partnership between developed and developing countries in search of sustainable development. Although the Earth Summit did not fully reconcile different views on how to distribute the costs of environmental protection programs, it did manage to address a broad range of environmental and developmental issues, including the importance of reducing poverty and altering consumption patterns in rich northern countries.

Suggested Reading

Ranee K.L. Panjabi, *The Earth Summit at Rio: Politics, Economics, and the Environment* (Boston: Northeastern University Press, 1997); Daniel Sitarz, ed., *Agenda 21: The Earth Summit Strategy to Save Our Planet* (Boulder, CO: Earth Press, 1993).

Economic Sanctions A common tool of diplomacy where coercive measures are administered by governments and international organizations for the purpose of changing the leadership and/or policies of the affected state. Its appeal stems from the fact that it can be applied in different dosages to the target state. U.S. policymakers have also found punitive trade embargoes appealing because of the appearance of public officials taking action. This often enables policymakers to avoid, or postpone, more controversial policy choices. Whether they are implemented to stop **terrorism**, remove a dictator, halt the drug trade, improve **human rights**, or help promote **democracy**, economic sanctions provide a powerful opiate to punish and control other nations without having to use armed force. Economic sanctions frequently involve the withdrawal of government granted privileges—foreign aid, loan guarantees, most favored nation status—or the application of more restrictive measures such as the freezing of a nation's assets, a total trade embargo, and the removal of access to important capital markets. Although the United States used economic sanctions against Latin American countries repeatedly during the twentieth century, more often than not they failed to convince a target country to alter its political behavior in compliance with Washington's wishes. Nevertheless, faith in economic sanctions during the **Cold War** increased because of multilateral provisions in the **United Nations (UN)** Charter and the battle over the hearts and minds of uncommitted, or non-aligned, states.

Over the past fifty years the United States has used economic sanctions against Chile, the Dominican Republic, Colombia, Cuba, Grenada, Guatemala, Guyana, Haiti, Nicaragua, and Panama. The U.S. economic sanctions against Fidel **Castro**'s Cuba began in the last year of the **Dwight Eisenhower** administration and continues to this day, albeit in modified form. The goal was to reverse the course of the Cuban Revolution and retaliate for measures contained in Castro's socialist revolution. At first, Washington drastically reduced the sugar quota; when Castro expropriated U.S. property in 1960, economic sanctions increased, prohibiting all exports to Cuba except for food and medicine. After President John F. **Kennedy** instructed his staff to round up as many boxes of Cuban cigars possible, he signed legislation further tightening the economic screws on Cuba. Economic sanctions were broadened when the **Organization of American States (OAS)** applied collective sanctions on Cuba from 1964 to 1975. With the collapse of the Soviet Union in 1991, and the termination of large subsidies from Moscow, pressure from the **Cuba Lobby** increased to try to bring down the Castro regime with further economic sanctions. The Torricelli bill was passed in 1992 increasing trade sanctions against Cuba by prohibiting U.S. subsidiaries in third countries from trading with Cuba. Four years later, in the heat of an election year, President Bill **Clinton** signed the **Helms-Burton Law**, which put additional restrictions on Cuba by promising to punish foreign businesses that use properties in Cuba formerly owned by U.S. citizens and corporations. The controversy that erupted over the extra-territorial provisions of this legislation, and counter-Helms-Burton legislation passed in Canada and Mexico, led Presidents Bill Clinton and **George W. Bush** to postpone continually its full implementation.

Since the mid-1980s, the United States has mandated an annual certification process where thirty-two countries are judged according to their aggressiveness in combating **drug trafficking**. The most prominent cases in Latin America include Bolivia, Colombia, Ecuador, Guatemala, Haiti, Mexico, Panama, Paraguay, and Peru. Until the introduction of **Plan Colombia**, Colombia was the main target of U.S. decertification efforts. In 1996 and 1997 it suffered economic sanctions, including dramatic aid reductions and an automatic "no" vote on any loan requests to international lending agencies such as the World Bank and the International Monetary Fund. However, Mexico has never been decertified when many doubt the degree of its actual cooperation with the United States and level of commitment to drug control. Despite the shortcomings in Mexico's drug control efforts, **Washington policymakers** refuse to decertify Mexico because of its importance to trade and immigration in the United States.

The United States and Latin America are more in sync with the propriety of economic sanctions when it comes to multilateral diplomacy. Economic sanctions are permitted in the multilateral arena because they must be applied with the consent of the organization's members according to international law. Both the United Nations Charter and the Charter of the Organization of American States provide mechanisms for the use of economic sanctions. Article 19 of the OAS Charter states that "No State may use or encourage the use of coercive measures of an economic or political character to force the sovereign will of another State and obtain from it advantages of any kind." However, economic sanctions can be applied to a member state if the OAS approves collective economic sanctions by a two-thirds vote. In an effort to promote democracy throughout the hemisphere, the OAS approved a resolution that requires the OAS secretary-general to call a meeting of the Permanent Council if a democratically elected government is overthrown. It can then decide if economic sanctions are warranted to assist in the restoration of representative democracy in a member state.

While punitive economic sanctions—either unilateral or multilateral—are often seductive forms of diplomacy and statecraft, they rarely achieve their stated objectives. When the U.S. Congress debated the trade embargo against Cuba in the early 1960s, those who argued for cutting off the importation of sugar believed that by "hitting Castro where it hurts, his pocketbook," the regime would fall quickly. The trade embargo against Castro's Cuba has been in effect for more than forty-five years, yet it has not toppled Castro nor destroyed the Cuban Revolution. Economic sanctions did not bring down the **Noriega** regime in Panama nor the military government in Haiti under René Préval. In both cases, U.S. military force, not the pain of economic restrictions, was required to bring about the results Washington desired.

The relative inefficiency and failure of economic sanctions can be explained by the following factors. First, economic sanctions hurt business interests and generate tensions with important and friendly trading partners, particularly if economic sanctions contribute to human rights violations, starvation, and loss of life of innocent civilians. Second, most target countries can find alternative sources of supply or other foreign markets to compensate for the trade embargo. After President Dwight Eisenhower stopped importing Cuban sugar, Fidel Castro turned to the Soviet Union for a more favorable arrangement than what he had while dominated by the United States. Third, when sanctions are imposed, either unilaterally or multilaterally, they tend to undermine the legitimacy of the state or international organization applying them. U.S.–Cuba policy remains in a Cold War mindset despite the fact that the economic sanctions are seen as a violation of international law and repeated resolutions condemning the United States in the United Nations pass by large margins. Fourth, economic sanctions fail when the target government is heavily invested in objectionable political or military behavior that is judged to be crucial to its national interest. Clearly, decades of economic hardship have not forced Fidel Castro to conclude that Cuba should abandon revolutionary principles and accede to U.S. demands that it change its behavior. Finally, once punitive sanctions are imposed, state-to-state hostility increases, and the target country becomes less willing to compromise to relax the economic restrictions. After the Clinton administration imposed economic sanctions on Colombia in 1996 because of strong evidence that its president was involved in the drug trade, U.S.–Colombian cooperation in the drug war declined. Drug certification measures designed as a means to increase cooperation and hemispheric good will have often produced the opposite effects. When the United States insists on imposing economic sanctions through the process of decertification, **anti-Americanism** (many think the United States should be decertified) increases along with charges that the United States is a hypocritical bully for judging others while refusing to subject itself to the same review process. Doubts about the efficacy of economic sanctions as a foreign policy tool have spurred some policymakers to consider alternatives to what many consider a failed policy. Backed by Senators Christopher Dodd (D-Conn.), John McCain (R-Ariz.), and Charles Hagel (R-Neb.), the U.S. Congress amended the certification process in 2002, effective for one year. During this period certification will be based on a nation's adherence to international agreements rather than their level of cooperation with Washington on the drug war.

Despite the number of cases in inter-American relations that suggest that economic sanctions often fail to achieve their objectives, there is often sufficient rhetorical support to apply punitive sanctions because they often serve as a shield against domestic and foreign criticism. In a span of three years—1993–1997—the United States imposed economic sanctions or passed legislation that threatened to do so sixty times against thirty-five countries, seven of which were located in the Latin American or Caribbean region. The war on terrorism offers an additional rationale for using economic sanctions as a diplomatic weapon, regardless of the historical record of failure and the public's support of economic sanctions if they serve as a substitute for aggressive military action. *See also* Dictatorships; International Law.

Suggested Reading

Hossein G. Askari, et al., *Economic Sanctions: Examining Their Philosophy and Efficacy* (Westport, CT: Praeger, 2003); Ted Galen Carpenter, *Bad Neighbor Policy: Washington's Futile War on Drugs in Latin America* (New York: Palgrave, 2003); David Cortright and George A. López, eds., *Smart Sanctions: Targeting Economic Statecraft* (Lanham, MD: Rowman and Littlefield, 2002); Alan P. Dobson, *U.S. Economic Statecraft for Survival, 1933–1991: Of Sanctions, Embargoes and Economic Warfare* (New York: Routledge, 2002); Diane Kunz, "Economic Sanctions," in Bruce W. Jentleson and Thomas G. Paterson, eds., *Encyclopedia of U.S. Foreign Relations*, Vol. 2 (New York: Oxford University Press, 1997); Michael P. Malloy, *United States Economic Sanctions: Theory and Practice* (Boston: Kluwer Law International, 2001); Makio Miyagawa, *Do Economic Sanctions Work?* (New York: St. Martin's Press, 1992); Meghan L. O'Sullivan, *Shrewd Sanctions: Statecraft and State Sponsors of Terrorism* (Washington, DC: Brookings Institution Press, 2003); Sidney Weintraub, ed., *Economic Coercion and U.S. Foreign Policy* (Boulder, CO: Westview, 1982); Larman C. Wilson and David W. Dent, *Historical Dictionary of Inter-American Organizations* (Lanham, MD: Scarecrow Press, 1998).

Eisenhower, Dwight David (1890–1969) Decorated Army officer and president of the United States (1953–1961) who emerged as a national hero after his stewardship during **World War II**. The **Cold War** emphasis on containing Communist aggression, particularly the possibility of a Soviet attack, formed the dominant context for American foreign policy in general and U.S.–Latin American policy in particular. To prevent the Soviets from obtaining strategic advantages in Latin America, the Eisenhower administration used covert action to orchestrate a **Central Intelligence Agency (CIA)** backed plot to overthrow the democratically elected government of Jacobo **Arbenz** in Guatemala in 1954 that signaled an end to the **Good Neighbor Policy**. During his second term, interest in Latin America mounted as right-wing **dictatorships** were toppled by progressive and revolutionary forces that were perceived as security threats to the United States. After Vice-President Richard M. **Nixon**'s tour of Latin America in 1958, which included attacks by violent anti-American mobs in Lima and Caracas, the Eisenhower administration increased U.S. diplomatic and economic interest in the region. After Fidel **Castro**'s successful revolution in Cuba in 1959, the Eisenhower administration began the politics of hostility between the United States and Cuba that has lasted to this day. In an effort to rid Cuba of Castro, Eisenhower instituted a trade embargo, severed diplomatic ties, and put in place a covert plan to invade Cuba using Cuban exiles that would put an end to Castro and the Cuban Revolution.

Eisenhower's Latin American policy developed in response to Cold War anticommunism combined with the difficulty of distinguishing between homegrown revolutionaries, nationalist reformers, and Soviet-inspired Communists. The other issues that caused the Eisenhower administration problems was how to move Latin America toward modernization. The genesis of Eisenhower's Latin American policy occurred during the 1952 presidential campaign when President Harry S. **Truman** was criticized for neglecting Latin America in the aftermath of the Good Neighbor Policy and collaboration during World War II. By accusing Truman of conducting a "poor neighbor policy," the Eisenhower administration moved quickly to carry out corrective measures, particularly the emphasis on hemispheric solidarity to reduce the threat of internal Communist subversion. Latin American leaders who embraced the doctrine of anti-communism could count on support from Washington, even repressive dictators.

President Eisenhower came to office with little experience with Latin America. After graduating from West Point in 1915, Eisenhower visited Mexico while serving at Fort Sam Houston in San Antonio, Texas. He developed a sensitivity for Panamanians in the Canal Zone who experienced racial discrimination under U.S. control. Eisenhower believed that it was more important to support anti-Communist dictators who could maintain order and stability in societies that were unlikely to embrace pluralist **democracy** and **human rights**. With a strong foundation for poverty-induced communism in Latin America, it was important that the United States support "strong men" because of the belief that whenever a dictator is removed, Communist forces gain power. Eisenhower made up for his modest experience in Latin America by relying on his secretary of state, **John Foster Dulles**, and his youngest brother, Dr. **Milton S. Eisenhower** for information about the region. Although neither one of these close advisers possessed Latin American expertise, brother Milton was sent on several fact-finding missions to Latin America that formed the basis for his advice on how to handle the growing **anti-Americanism** and the causes of political instability. Officials in the Eisenhower administration were united in the belief that communism posed a worldwide danger to the United States. In constant search for enemies, Milton Eisenhower's reporting was often far off base in portraying trends in Latin America. On one visit in 1953 he claimed that most Latin American nations were moving from dictatorship to democracy despite the fact that military dictators ruled in two-thirds of the countries and enjoyed favors and cordial relations with Washington.

After leaving office in 1961, Eisenhower retired to his farm in Gettysburg, Pennsylvania, authored several books on his life and times as president, and remained active in Republican politics. In his farewell address he warned against the danger of a U.S. military-industrial complex, a subject that has remained a part of domestic political debate ever since. *See also* Doctrines; Domino Theory; Economic Sanctions; Friendly Dictators; Threat Perception/Assessment.

Suggested Reading

Robert R. Bowie and Richard H. Immerman, *Waging Peace: How Eisenhower Shaped an Enduring Cold War Strategy* (New York: Oxford University Press, 1998); H.W. Brands, Jr., *Cold Warriors: Eisenhower's Generation and American Foreign Policy* (New York: Columbia University Press, 1988); Jeff Broadwater, *Eisenhower and the Anti-Communist Crusade* (Chapel Hill: University of North Carolina Press, 1992); Richard Damms, *The Eisenhower Presidency, 1953–1961* (Harlow, U.K.: Longman, 2002); Dwight D. Eisenhower, *Waging Peace, 1956–1961: The White House Years* (Garden City, NY: Doubleday, 1965); Eisenhower, *Mandate for Change, 1953–1956* (New York: Doubleday & Co., 1963); Michael D. Gambone, *Eisenhower, Somoza, and the Cold War in Nicaragua, 1953–1961* (Westport, CT: Praeger, 1997); Lewis L. Gould, *The Modern American Presidency* (Lawrence: University Press of Kansas, 2003); Trumbull Higgins, *The Perfect Failure: Kennedy, Eisenhower, and the CIA at the Bay of Pigs* (New York: W.W. Norton, 1987); Richard Immerman, *John Foster Dulles: Piety, Pragmatism, and Power in U.S.*

Foreign Policy (Wilmington, DE: Scholarly Resources, 1999); Immerman, *The CIA in Guatemala: The Foreign Policy of Intervention* (Austin: University of Texas Press, 1982); Shawn J. Parry-Giles, *The Rhetorical Presidency, Propaganda, and the Cold War, 1945–1955* (Westport, CT: Praeger, 2002); Stephen G. Rabe, *Eisenhower and Latin America: The Foreign Policy of Anticommunism* (Chapel Hill: University of North Carolina Press, 1988); Bernardo Vega, *Eisenhower Y Trujillo* (Santo Domingo, Dominican Republic: Fundación Cultural Dominicana, 1991); Tom Wicker, *Dwight D. Eisenhower* (New York: Times Books, 2002).

Eisenhower, Milton S. (1899–1985) Brother of **Dwight D. Eisenhower** who served as a presidential adviser on Latin America during his time in the White House. President Eisenhower used his brother Milton to gain policy feedback and critical analysis while Milton served as special envoy to Latin America. Milton S. Eisenhower began his lengthy government career in the foreign service followed by positions in the Agriculture Department and a special assignment by President **Franklin D. Roosevelt** relocating Japanese Americans from the West Coast during **World War II**. During this assignment and later as associate director of the Office of War Information (OWI), Milton Eisenhower became acutely aware of flaws in American foreign policy. He carried these thoughts and how to improve American foreign policy into his appointment as his brother's special envoy to Latin America in the 1950s. He was sensitive to the drawbacks of supporting **friendly dictators** for the sake of furthering an anti-Communist foreign policy and recommended in his book *The Wine is Bitter*, that the United States needs to recognize the difference between communism and Latin American nationalism and the best remedy against Communist advancement in Latin America is to offer assistance to liberal reformers and contribute more to foreign economic assistance programs that alleviate poverty and **anti-Americanism**. In addition to his government service, Milton Eisenhower had successful tenures as president of Kansas State, Penn State, and Johns Hopkins University (where its main library carries his name). He continued to advise U.S. presidents of both parties on Latin American issues until his death in 1985. *See also* Dictatorships; Nixon, Richard Milhous.

Suggested Reading

Milton S. Eisenhower, *The Wine Is Bitter: The United States and Latin America* (Garden City, NY: Doubleday, 1963).

Elián González Incident In November 1999, a young Cuban boy was rescued off the coast of Florida in an attempt to flee Cuba and illegally enter the United States. Elián González left by boat with his mother and ten other Cubans seeking exile in the United States; however, the boat capsized, killing everyone on board except the five-year-old boy who was later found floating on an inner tube in the ocean near Florida. After he was given to his Miami relatives by the Immigration and Naturalization Service (INS), his father, Juan Miguel González, who was still living in Cuba, demanded custody of his child. The incident became a heated and emotional battle between Elián's relatives in Miami and his father in Cuba over custody of the child that lasted seven months. The U.S. government found itself in a quandary over the law, family values, and U.S.–Cuban relations in the aftermath of recent legislation aimed at **regime change** on the island. Should his natural parent be given custody of the child, or should he be treated as a political refugee whose life would be endangered if he returned to Cuba? The anti-Castro **Cuba Lobby** took the side of his Miami relatives and financed his stay and the cost of the lawyers hired to keep Elián in the United States. The international custody dispute soon became highly politicized with a **media** frenzy, mass protests in Miami and Havana, court battles, and pressures on the White House and Congress to either let Elián return to his father or grant the boy asylum. Fidel **Castro** turned the episode into an anti-American crusade by organizing "Free Elián" marches and demonstrations and vowed that the Cuban government would do everything possible for his return. Janet Reno, U.S. attorney general in the **Clinton** administration argued that the Cuban boy should be reunited with this father; both of the leading Republican presidential candidates, **George W. Bush** and John McCain, supported the efforts of Miami Cubans to prevent the child from being returned to the island. The emotional and political standoff ended when U.S. federal agents entered the relatives' home in Miami on April 22, 2000, and removed the boy at gunpoint. The father, along with his new wife and family, came to the United States to retrieve the child and return to Cuba; however, Elián did not return to Cuba until June 28, 2000, after the U.S. Supreme Court affirmed the father's right to custody of his son. Elián González achieved national hero status after his return to his hometown of Cárdenas where his school was turned into a newly repainted shrine, a symbol of Cuban defiance of Yankee interference in Cuban affairs. The Elián González incident also served as a catalyst for weakening the political clout of the Cuban American National Foundation (CANF) by exposing the intransigence of the older hardliners and the greater willingness of the new CANF leadership to reach beyond the Cuban exile community for a policy of dialogue over confrontation. On the fifth anniversary of his reunion with his father in April 2000, Elián González spoke to the Cuban nation and thanked the American people for backing his wishes to return to his family. *See also* Anti-Americanism; Cuba Lobby; Mas Canosa, Jorge L.; Partisanship and Policy.

Suggested Reading

Ann Louise Bardach, *Cuba Confidential: Love and Vengeance in Miami and Havana* (New York: Random House, 2002); Rick Bragg, "Fight Over Cuban Boy Leaves Scars in Miami," *New York Times* (June 30, 2000); Karen De Young, "Cuba Triumphant Over Elián," *Washington Post* (June 29, 2000).

Enterprise for the Americas Initiative (EAI) One of the hallmarks of the **George H.W. Bush** administration to expand trade and advance business opportunities in Latin America. President Bush announced the EAI in 1990 when Latin America was in the throes of debt and economic woes. The EAI attempted to link significant public sector debt reduction with increased economic aid and the promise of a free trade area for the entire Americas. It called for free and fair trade, debt service reduction, domestic and foreign investment, new capital flows, a reduction in debt burdens, and efforts to improve the environment. Latin American leaders welcomed Bush's initiative because they believed the United States was finally willing to recognize Latin America's economic needs and create a working regional partnership to forge the new economic (and political) relationship. Washington's hope for a more productive relationship was based on forgiving significant amounts of public aid debts and negotiating a series of agreements that would lay the foundation for future trade negotiations and the eventual goal of establishing hemispheric-wide trade zones. The whole process of recognizing the Latin American debt crisis with a plan to open markets and facilitate investment helped to mitigate financial collapse and helped bring some improvement in prosperity through economic integration and cooperation between Latin America and the United States. President Bush visited the debt-ridden countries of South America in December 1990 where he found enthusiastic support among the Latin American governments. Although the EAI worked its way through the U.S. Congress rather slowly, Bush's economic initiative helped improve U.S.–Latin American relations for the first time in decades. *See also* Brady Plan (1989); North American Free Trade Agreement (NAFTA).

Suggested Reading

Michael Kryzanek, *U.S.–Latin American Relations*, 3rd ed. (Westport, CT: Praeger, 1996); Michael LaRosa and Frank O. Mora, eds., *Neighborly Adversaries: Readings in U.S.–Latin American Relations* (Lanham, MD: Rowman and Littlefield, 1999).

Escuadrones de Muerte. *See* Death Squads

Estrada Doctrine (1930) A recognition policy formulated by Mexican Foreign Minister Genaro Estrada after the Mexican Revolution to deal with the problem of legitimacy for governments, particularly those that came to power through revolutionary means. The Estrada Doctrine argued that diplomatic recognition should be *de facto*, fully accepting the government in actual control and not based on political considerations one finds in the selective application of legal (*de jure*) recognition of the new government. Estrada's proposition challenged the **Tobar Doctrine**—collective non-recognition of governments coming to power by other than democratic means and the use of collective **intervention** if necessary—by asserting the principle of continuous diplomacy in the recognition process. By automatically recognizing new governments it was possible to acknowledge the reality of a revolutionary government without indicating approval of the regime that had just come to power. The interplay between the interventionist language of the Tobar Doctrine and the avoidance of intervention in the Estrada Doctrine show how long the United States and Latin America have been concerned with the conflicting demands and interpretations of **democracy**, **human rights**, **revolutions**, and inter-American security in the Americas. If the basic principle of non-intervention is the cornerstone of the inter-American system, how can representative democracy be promoted and human rights enforced without violating the hallowed principle of non-interference? Since the end of the **Cold War** and the war on **terrorism** there has been more emphasis on some sort of collective intervention, particularly under the auspices of the **United Nations (UN)**, the **Organization of American States (OAS)**, or the North Atlantic Treaty Organization (NATO), to oppose dictators that are associated with acts of terrorism and possess weapons of mass destruction. Mexico's sympathy for the plight of other revolutionary governments—Cuba, Nicaragua, Grenada—has declined as it has become more democratic and developed closer ties with the United States. *See also* Dictatorships; Intervention and Non-Intervention; Recognition and Non-Recognition.

Suggested Reading

G. Pope Atkins, *Latin America in the International Political System*, 2nd ed. (Boulder, CO: Westview Press, 1989); Larman C. Wilson and David W. Dent, *Historical Dictionary of Inter-American Organizations* (Lanham, MD: Scarecrow Press, 1998).

F

Fair Play for Cuba Committee (FPCC). *See* Beals, Carleton; Yankee *Fidelistas*

Falklands/Malvinas War (1982) War over disputed islands between the British and Argentines in 1982 that had a major impact on U.S.–Latin American relations at the time. The basis of the war was Argentina's long-standing legal and historical claim to title since independence in 1816 and the counter-claims by Great Britain, an occupier of the islands since 1833. Prior to the outbreak of war in 1982, Argentina pressed its claim of ownership and expressed optimism that a restoration of Argentine sovereignty could be achieved. Argentina's military government ordered an invasion on April 2, 1982, apparently an effort to fan nationalism and turn attention away from a disastrous economic situation. The few British marines were quickly overcome, and the war dragged on for almost two months. In the meantime, both the **United Nations (UN)** Security Council and the **Organization of American States (OAS)** Permanent Council met to forge a response to the war. A debate ensued over which organization—the OAS as a regional body or the UN as a global organization—was appropriate for resolving the dispute. At first the United States supported the OAS in opposition to its European ally Great Britain. However, once it became clear that Britain would support the UN position, the United States switched from a neutral position to one in favor of what the UN was trying to do. The Latin American states also wavered in support for Argentina: at first they opposed on the grounds that Argentina had violated the OAS charter by violating the non-intervention pledge; but after it became apparent that U.S. Secretary of State Alexander Haig was not neutral, the Latin American states shifted their position, opposing the United States and supporting Argentina. Thereafter, the

European Community (EC) imposed sanctions on Argentina, but the OAS gathered in a Meeting of Consultation and the majority attending shifted to support Argentina based on the provisions of the Rio Treaty, a collective security treaty administered by the OAS. As the battle over the Falklands raged, the OAS called on the British to withdraw and passed a pro-Argentina resolution. At this point the United States decided to give military aid to Britain, impose sanctions on Argentina, and wait for the inevitable victory of British forces over the poorly trained and unenthusiastic Argentine conscripts. The United States was criticized by the OAS for "abandoning and betraying" the inter-American system for its support of the British and the EC sanctions. After winning several battles at sea and in the air, the Argentines surrendered on June 14, 1982.

The costly and humiliating loss brought about the rapid downfall of General Leopoldo F. Galtieri, the Argentine military dictator responsible for the disastrous war with Britain over the remote and disputed Falkland Islands. The Argentine military junta was later found responsible for the death and disappearance of up to 30,000 people in Argentina's "Dirty War" against purported opponents of the regime. Key members of the junta were tried for **human rights** crimes and General Galtieri was convicted in 1986 for negligence during the war in the Falklands. However, Galtieri and other leaders were given amnesties and freed in the late 1980s and early 1990s. Many critics of the war claim that the war was designed as a means of diverting attention from the crimes of the junta and the rapidly deteriorating economic situation. Rex Hunt, the former governor of the Falklands, claims that the seventy-four–day war, in which nearly 1,000 died, was Galtieri's blunder and ensured that the islands remained under British control. The Falkland Islands remain a source of contention between Argentina and Britain as evidenced by public notices proclaiming "The Malvinas are Argentine." *See also* Intervention and Non-Intervention; Reagan, Ronald; Scandals and Blunders.

Suggested Reading

Jack Child, *Geopolitics and Conflict in South America: Quarrels Among Neighbors* (New York: Praeger, 1985); Alberto R. Coll and Anthony C. Arend, eds., *The Falklands War: Lessons for Strategy, Diplomacy and International Law* (Winchester, MA: Allen and Unwin, 1985); "Leopoldo Galtieri, 76, of Falklands Rout, Dies," *New York Times* (January 13, 2003); Andrew Orgill, *The Falklands War: Background, Conflict, Aftermath: An Annotated Bibliography* (London: Mansell Publishing, 1993); Larman C. Wilson and David W. Dent, *Historical Dictionary of Inter-American Organizations* (Lanham, MD: Scarecrow Press, 1998).

***Father Roy: Inside the School of Assassins* (1997)** *Father Roy* is a 1997 PBS documentary on the U.S. Army **School of the Americas (SOA)** and the efforts of Father Roy Bourgeois to close the school. The film documents the political struggle to shut down the training facility, located at Ft. Benning, Georgia, and the transformation of a patriotic citizen and Vietnam verteran with an exemplary record and Purple Heart into a Catholic missionary committed to the plight of the poor and suffering in Latin America. After witnessing the violence, poverty, and suffering in Vietnam—and the role of the U.S. military in that tragedy—Father Roy entered the Maryknoll Order of the Catholic Church where he spent four years studying to be a priest. During this time he joined the Vietnam Veterans Against the War, turned in his Purple Heart award, and after being ordained left for Bolivia. After five years of working to alleviate the suffering of *campesinos* and indigenous groups there, he was kicked out by the military government. When the anti-Communist violence and revolutionary turmoil started in the 1970s, Father Roy became aware of the connection between the plight of the poor in Latin America and the role of the U.S. military in the training of Latin American military officers at the U.S. Army School of the Americas (SOA).

One of the primary educational benefits of the film is the way it explains the metamorphosis of a priest through direct contact (and later political action) with Latin American societies at the grass-roots level and the determination to find out the truth about U.S. military doctrine as revealed in the activities of the army training school. The history of the school is presented, from its founding in Panama in 1946 to the recent congressional efforts to shut down the school now located near Columbus, Georgia. After years of organized protest against the school and the struggle of Father Roy and members of the U.S. Congress to close the SOA, the school changed its name in 2000 to the Western Hemisphere Institute for Security Cooperation and revised its mission and curriculum. With a new emphasis training both civilian and military officials (it is the only military institution in the United States that offers instruction solely in Spanish), democratic values, and other benign subjects, the institute continues to operate at its Ft. Benning location. With the argument that "You can't teach democracy through the barrel of a gun," opponents of the SOA have not given up in their quest to remove the school from U.S. soil. With the **George W. Bush** administration now embroiled in a global war against **terrorism**, it is possible that the SOA will gain added value and budgetary legitimacy because of the close fit between what happens at the school and the need to eliminate terrorism and insurgency in the Western Hemisphere. The school's curriculum at Ft. Benning includes counter-insurgency, military intelligence, interrogation techniques, sniper fire, commando tactics, psychological warfare, and jungle operations. All of this learning is now being applied in Colombia against leftist guerrillas and in Southern Mexico where the Zapatistas are opposed to the **North American Free Trade Agreement (NAFTA)** and the mistreatment of indigenous rural communities.

There is no doubt that the causes of Latin American turmoil and violence have been largely kept from American eyes, making it difficult to make the necessary connection between what the United States actually does abroad and the consequences at home. Critics of the SOA see the inevitable consequences of a military school that does not serve American national security interests and is harmful to productive relations between the United States and Latin America. Since its founding, the SOA has trained over 60,000 military and police officers from Latin American and Caribbean countries. The cries for the elimination of what many call a "national obscenity" are broad and reach into the highest levels of the U.S. Congress, yet the Pentagon and the White House have always found ways to keep the SOA in the budget. People like Father Roy and **human rights** organizations that have taken the time to find out more of the consequences of SOA training, see a training school that provides a base for destabilization in Latin America, particularly the evidence that shows the connection between graduates of the school and **drug traffickers**, human rights abusers, dictators, political corruption, and the rise of **anti-Americanism**. The defenders of the school within the military and on Capitol Hill argue that the positives outweigh the negatives: The school serves a national security purpose, and you can't close the school because of "a few bad apples." In any case, the school continues to operate with a new name and curriculum, but protesters also continue to gather every fall to generate public pressure to end the school and its military mission in Latin America.

The tradition of peaceful resistance is now an annual affair designed to protest U.S. policy and the consequences of training military personnel for repressive regimes in Latin America. According to Father Roy, the founder of SOA Watch, "We [United States] are fighting terrorism out there in other parts of the world, but we are harboring and training terrorists [on our own soil]." The U.S. Department of Defense still maintains that the institute's new mission (and name) is to focus on twenty-first-century challenges facing the United States. With the passage of the USA Patriot Act in 2001, those who engage in peaceful democratic dissent of this kind now face a government that is less concerned about constitutional freedoms and privacy rights than was the case before **September 11, 2001**. There is a precedent for ending government programs involved in training security personnel in Latin America when growing negative publicity reveals evidence of torture and murder by U.S.–assisted security forces. The Office of Public Safety (OPS), a global police training program between 1962 and 1974, was closed by Congress in 1974 because the **Agency for International Development (AID)** program was shown to have made repressive regimes even more repressive. Whether the SOA is destined to suffer the same fate remains to be seen. *See also* Southern Command.

Suggested Reading

Robert H. Holden and Eric Zolov, eds., *Latin America and the United States: A Documentary History* (New York: Oxford University Press, 2000); Martha Huggins, *Political Policing: The United States and Latin America* (Durham, NC: Duke University Press, 1998); Robert Richter (Producer/Director), "Father Roy: Inside the School of Assassins" (PBS documentary, 1997).

Filibusters/Filibustering Private mercenaries and daring adventurers from the United States, many of whom went to Latin American and Caribbean countries in the middle of the nineteenth century for the sake of acquiring territory, glory, and financial enrichment. The term came into currency in the 1840s and was derived from the Spanish *filibustero*, meaning a freebooter or pirate. There was a close connection between their armed forays against Latin American nations or colonies and the financial and material backing they received from sympathetic private sponsors, most of whom were interested in capturing additional slave territory and establishing governments amenable to being annexed to the United States.

Filibustering flourished in the mid-nineteenth century due to the ideology of **Manifest Destiny** and its strong spirit of expansionism and nationalism. Southern expansionists desired new slave territory as a way to solidify the South's power and to safeguard slavery against the growing movement toward abolition. Many believed that acquiring more territory in Latin America was needed to maintain a balance of power in Congress between slave and free states. The most noteworthy filibusters were Narciso López and William **Walker**, both of whom launched expeditions from U.S. soil. López was a Venezuelan and former Spanish general who carried out three unsuccessful expeditions from New Orleans against Spanish-controlled Cuba. On his last attempt at freeing Cuba from Spanish rule, López and his American and Cuban exile volunteers were captured and executed by Spanish forces in 1851. William Walker—perhaps the most daring and notorious of the *filibusteros*—led armed expeditions into Mexico in 1853 that ultimately failed and in 1855 mounted an invasion of Nicaragua. With only fifty-seven men he managed to capture Grenada and briefly established a rogue regime with the help of the United States. With the support of pro-slavery Southerners, Walker had himself "elected" president of Nicaragua, the only time a U.S. citizen ruled as chief of state in Latin America. Only the United States recognized the fraudulent government. Walker did not last long before the Central Americans drove him from office; he was killed by a Honduran firing squad in 1860.

The adventuresome American filibusters were in constant trouble with U.S. courts and anti-slavery political forces since their filibustering forays into Latin America violated federal neutrality laws forbidding such activities. Despite the illegality of filibustering, it was virtually impossible to convict them at trial due to widespread public sympathy in the American South and Far West. By the early 1860s filibustering had become a problem in U.S.–Latin American relations and a divisive issue in domestic politics prior to the U.S. Civil War. With pressure from anti-slavery political forces in the North, President Franklin **Pierce** and President James **Buchanan** initiated measures to stop filibustering in Central America. For example, President Buchanan in 1857 ordered U.S. ships to patrol Central American ports to prevent the landing of marauding filibusters. By the time of the U.S. Civil War, forces of abolition and the declining interest in Manifest Destiny put the filibusters and their followers out of business.

Although the filibusters were failures in their efforts to extend American influence over Central America, their forays into Latin America served to expand the popularity of the **Monroe Doctrine**. For those on the receiving end of American efforts to achieve a tropical empire, filibustering proved to be of little benefit. These mercenaries did not bring prosperity, and their distinct racial attitudes contributed to the reinforcement of common negative stereotypes of Central Americans as immature and inferior to Anglo-Saxon North Americans. *See also* Race and Racism.

Suggested Reading

Karl Berman, *Under the Big Stick: Nicaragua and the United States since 1848* (Boston: South End Press, 1986); Charles H. Brown, *Agents of Manifest Destiny: The Lives and Times of the Filibusters* (Chapel Hill: University of North Carolina Press, 1980); Tom Chaffin, *Fatal Glory: Narciso López and the First Clandestine U.S. War Against Cuba* (Charlottsville: University of Virginia Press, 1996); Richard Harding Davis, *Real Soldiers of Fortune* (New York: Charles Scribners, 1906); Robert E. May, *Manifest Destiny's Underworld: Filibustering in Antebellum America* (Chapel Hill: University of North Carolina Press, 2002); William O. Scroggs, *Filibusters and Financiers; the Story of William Walker and his Associates* (New York: Macmillan, 1916); Joseph Allen Stout, Jr., *Schemers and Dreamers: Filibustering in Mexico, 1848–1921* (Forth Worth: Texas Christian University Press, 2002); Edward Seccomb Wallace, *Destiny and Glory* (New York: Coward-McCann, 1957).

Flood, Daniel. *See* Panama Canal Treaties

Ford, Gerald R. (1913–) Lawyer, Republican politician, and president of the United States (1974–1977) during the height of détente with the Soviet Union. The fact that Ford had not been elected to the White House (he was appointed vice-president by President Richard M. **Nixon** and replaced Nixon after he was forced to resign the presidency because of the threat of impeachment for his role in the Watergate affair) created many obstacles to his capacity to pursue a separate foreign policy in the post-Watergate and post-Vietnam era. Gerald Ford had little experience, or interest in Latin American affairs, and his administration focused mainly on global strategies designed to restrain Soviet expansionism in the Third World. Gerald Rudolph Ford was born in Omaha, Nebraska, but spent most of his life in Grand Rapids, Michigan. After graduating from the University of Michigan where he won All-American football honors in the 1930s, Ford attended Yale Law School after which he served in the navy during **World War II**. From 1948 until his selection to replace Nelson Rockefeller as vice-president in 1973, Ford served in the U.S. House of Representatives where he adopted conservative, but internationalist, Republican foreign policies. During his time in Washington Ford developed an expertise in military spending and backed military assistance to pro-American countries. While president, Ford announced a new doctrine for the Pacific in 1975 based on a pledge to strengthen the self-reliance and regional security of pro-American friends and allies in Asia, particularly Indonesia and the Philippines.

Gerald R. Ford inherited Nixon's foreign-policy agenda and retained Henry A. **Kissinger** as his secretary of state. The Nixon-Ford policy of détente was hamstrung by congressional suspicion of executive leadership in the wake of the defeat in Vietnam. Ford's efforts to counter Soviet-Cuban advances in Africa with covert aid to pro–U.S. forces was frequently undermined by congressional resistance. President Ford also battled with Congress over sensitive investigations of criminal behavior at home and abroad of the **Central Intelligence Agency (CIA)**.

Worried about the fallout from investigations of CIA illegal activity, President Ford tried to pre-empt the revelations uncovered by the **Church Committee Report** by creating his own commission headed by Vice-President Nelson **Rockefeller** who sided with Ford's wishes in his final report by removing all references to CIA efforts to assassinate foreign leaders, including Fidel **Castro** and Rafael L. **Trujillo**. Despite Ford's efforts to provide cover for the CIA, the Church Committee went ahead and included the names of foreign leaders the CIA had targeted for **assassination** in the 1950s and 1960s while following presidential directives and orders. However, by firing CIA Director William Colby for his critical testimony about the CIA's activities to the Church Committee, President Ford was able to provide some damage control and Congress failed to provide the leadership to reform the CIA to prevent similar violations under future administrations. Ford issued an executive order banning the use of assassination as an instrument of American foreign policy that served to bolster his legitimacy in Congress. Some critics argue that the congressional failure of any serious agency reform later set the stage for future violations and ruthless disregard for Congress during the **Reagan** administration that led to the **Iran-Contra scandal**.

The Ford/Kissinger years in Washington made a number of promises for a new dialogue and new partnership with Latin America designed to convince Latin American and Caribbean leaders that the United States was going to make the region a top priority. Unfortunately for U.S.–Latin American relations, the Ford-Kissinger team had few opportunities to engineer such changes due to growing domestic and international problems and the electoral loss to Jimmy **Carter** in 1976. Although President Ford had several opportunities to change U.S. policy toward Latin America during his short term in office, he continued to support **dictatorships** in Latin America that were widely known for committing human rights violations. When President Isabel Perón was overthrown by the anti-democratic junta in Argentina in 1976, President Ford granted prompt recognition and refused to provide Congress with information concerning Latin American governments that were receiving U.S. military assistance while simultaneously engaged in "gross violations" of human rights. To do so, in Ford's view, was to not serve the security interests of the United States. Henry Kissinger responded that military aid should continue despite the reported violations to enable the United States to "influence" the military establishment. After losing to Washington outsider Jimmy Carter in the 1976 presidential election, Gerald Ford wrote his memoirs, *A Time to Heal* (1979), built the Ford Presidential Library in Ann Arbor, Michigan, and continued to voice his opinions on American foreign policy. According to Gaddis Smith (1994: 137), "Nothing of great significance involving Latin America or the **Monroe Doctrine** occurred in the short presidency of Gerald Ford."

Suggested Reading

David W. Dent, *The Legacy of the Monroe Doctrine: A Reference Guide to U.S. Involvement in Latin America and the Caribbean* (Westport, CT: Greenwood Press, 1999); Gerald R. Ford, *A Time to Heal: The Autobiography of Gerald R. Ford* (New York: Harper and Row, 1979); John

Robert Green, *The Presidency of Gerald R. Ford* (Lawrence: University Press of Kansas, 1994); Gaddis Smith, *The Last Years of the Monroe Doctrine, 1945–1993* (New York: Hill and Wang, 1994).

Fox Quesada, Vicente (1942–) Businessman, politician, and Mexican president (2000–2006) who succeeded in defeating the ruling party (Partido Revolucionario Institucional, PRI) after seventy-one years of uninterrupted state-party domination. Vicente Fox was born in Guanajuato to a father of Irish descent and a Spanish-born mother. He studied business and management—first at the Jesuit-run Iberoamerican University in Mexico and later at Harvard University in the United States—before using his successful career as head of Coca-Cola as a stepping stone to state and national politics. He developed a loose connection with the Partido Acción Nacional (PAN), formed an alliance with other small parties, and ran an aggressive political campaign in 2000 in which he declared himself a progressive modernizer who would change Mexico by rooting out the evils of the old regime.

Although Fox provided a new vision of Mexico with his reform promises, his presidency faced a plethora of problems he was unable to solve: a sluggish economy and trade competition with China, a hostile Congress dominated by members of the PRI, controversial domestic **human rights** cases, and political tensions with Washington after he was criticized for his reaction to the events of **September 11, 2001**. The successful four-day visit with President **George W. Bush** in early September 2001 seemed to augur well for a more productive and friendly relationship with the United States that would address such important bilateral issues as **drug trafficking**, corruption, crime, and the status of Mexican immigrants living and working in the United States. However, Fox's reaction to the terrorist attacks and his refusal to join the "Coalition of the Willing" to support the war against Saddam Hussein undermined U.S.–Mexican relations throughout Bush's first term as president. As the 2004 presidential election approached, President Bush revived his immigration reform package to attract more Hispanic voters and set the stage for a new guest-worker program that he and President Fox supported. In an effort to bolster his own flagging presidency, President Fox has proposed legislation that would grant Mexicans living in the United States the right to vote in Mexican elections. Despite general agreement on the importance of immigration reform, Mexico's interest in "preventative diplomacy" did not dovetail with the Bush administration's emphasis on pre-emptive war and unilaterialism in dealing with the global war on **terrorism**. For example, Mexico remains committed to a non-military solution to the civil war in Colombia, a "hands-off" response to the populist leader of Venezuela, Hugo Chávez, and a policy of normalization—trade, tourism, and investments—toward Fidel **Castro**'s Cuba. It is very likely that the enthusiasm and euphoria that greeted Vicente Fox when he defeated the PRI in 2000 will not be matched by the reaction of the majority of Mexicans when his term of office ends in December 2006. Nevertheless, the 2000 defeat of the ruling party and the growing sense of democratic legitimacy in Mexican politics will form the core of Fox's political legacy. *See also* Democracy and Democracy Promotion.

Suggested Reading

Roderic Ai Camp, *Politics in Mexico*, 4th ed. (New York: Oxford University Press, 2003); David W. Dent, *Encyclopedia of Modern Mexico* (Lanham, MD: Scarecrow Press, 2002); Robert S. Leiken, "With a Friend Like Fox," *Foreign Affairs* (September–October 2001).

Frente Sandinista de Liberación Nacional. *See* Sandinistas

Free Trade Area of the Americas (FTAA) Hemispheric trade zone akin to the **North American Free Trade Agreement (NAFTA)** between the United States, Canada, and Mexico. First proposed at the first **Summit of the Americas** in 1994, the FTAA offered to eliminate tariffs on goods imported from Latin America, excluding Cuba, by 2015. In a move to accelerate some tariffs, the **George W. Bush** administration, working through the office of the U.S. Trade Representative, offered to eliminate tariffs on clothing and textiles imported from Latin America by 2010. Although free trade advocates argue that a trade deal with Latin America will benefit U.S. consumers by giving them access to cheaper goods, textile executives in the United States maintained that the elimination of tariffs will only hasten the economic decline of a troubled industry in the United States. Supporters of the FTAA hope that it will be made final in 2005, but U.S. domestic opposition and reluctance by some Latin American countries, especially Brazil, may slow the process. Unless the United States lowers subsidies on agriculture, convincing Latin Americans of the benefits of free trade may be next to impossible. And textile companies that would be forced to compete with cheap labor and lower production costs in Latin America are likely to resist the move to lower tariffs on apparel and textiles. According to **Robert A. Pastor**, there are currently such huge differences between the United States and Latin America over the importance of the FTAA that the trade negotiators are unlikely to succeed by the target date.

Suggested Reading

Patrice M. Franco, *Toward a New Security Architecture in the Americas: The Strategic Implications of the FTAA* (Washington, DC: Center for Strategic and International Studies, 2000); Ambler H. Moss and Stephen Lande, *Free Trade in the Americas: Fulfilling the Promise of Miami and Santiago* (Coral Gables, FL: University of Miami Press, 1998); Jeffrey Stark, ed., *The Challenge of Change in Latin America and the Caribbean* (Coral Gables, FL: University of Miami Press, 2001).

Frelinghuysen, Frederick Theodore (1817–1885) Republican senator (1866–1869; 1871–1877) after the U.S. Civil War who succeeded James G. **Blaine** as secretary of state (1881–1885) under Chester A. Arthur. Frelinghuysen graduated from Rutgers College in 1836 and spent the next thirty years as a corporate lawyer and as attorney general of New Jersey. A cautious diplomat, Frelinghuysen displayed little interest in improving U.S.–Latin American relations during the 1880s. He put a halt to Blaine's efforts to mediate the dispute between Chile and Peru over the War of the Pacific and failed to convince the British that it would be in their best interest to abrogate the **Clayton-Bulwer Treaty** (1850) giving them rights over any future canal through Central America. He negotiated a protectorate over Nicaragua in 1884 that included a provision that the United States would become co-owner of any future canal in Nicaragua, but it failed to win Senate approval and President Grover **Cleveland** withdrew the proposal in 1885. His cautious approach to foreign policy led him to turn down protectorate offers made by Haiti and Venezuela in 1883. Frelinghuysen was successful in negotiating commercial reciprocity agreements with Mexico, Spain (concerning Cuba and Puerto Rico), and the Dominican Republic, but all were terminated by Congress. The frustrations that occurred in U.S.–Latin American relations in the 1880s set the stage for the push for Pan American unity and hemispheric expansion in the 1890s. *See also* Pan-Americanism.

Suggested Reading

Justus D. Doenecke, *The Presidencies of James A. Garfield and Chester A. Arthur* (Lawrence: Regents Press of Kansas, 1981); David A. Pletcher, *The Awkward Years: American Foreign Relations Under Garfield and Arthur* (Columbia: University of Missouri Press, 1962).

Frente Sandinista de Liberación Nacional. *See* Sandinistas

Friendly Dictators Those who conduct American foreign policy—despite their frequent references to the importance of **democracy**, liberalism, **human rights**, freedom, and hemispheric solidarity—have often supported right-wing dictators in Latin America. Beginning in the early part of the twentieth century, the U.S. support for "friendly dictators" in Latin America and the Caribbean became a frequent theme in U.S.–Latin American relations. Ideological support for authoritarian regimes developed out of the belief that U.S. national interests were more important than trying to classify Latin American rulers as dictators or democrats. As a result, **Washington policymakers** put a great deal of emphasis on the leader's ability to control the country effectively and largely ignored questions about the long-term negative impact of dictatorship on civic participation and on the building of democratic institutions.

The dictators who emerged at the time of the **Good Neighbor Policy** in the 1930s—Rafael **Trujillo**, Fulgencio **Batista**, Anastasio Somoza García—took advantage of the U.S. pledge of non-intervention, recognizing that whatever they did to squash their opponents would most likely be ignored or shielded in Washington. Those in the White House and **State Department** often chose right-wing autocracies because they served as a bulwark against governments and political leaders that appeared unstable, weak, or susceptible to Communist ideology. The concern for quick solutions to Latin American problems and the importance of order and political stability led American policymakers to support numerous right-wing **dictatorships**. At times it didn't seem to matter that many of these dictators were often greedy, venal, and ruled with an iron fist. It was also important to the United States that Latin American governments supported its prevailing ideology and world-view so as to enhance the ability to prevail during times of international conflict.

Since the time of the **Monroe Doctrine**, there have been over forty "friendly dictators" who formed close alliances with the United States in an effort to expand and perpetuate their autocratic rule (see Table 1). Although there were times when the United States tried to "scold" the behavior of Latin American dictators and the once harmonious relationship came to an end, there were few cases in which the United States conspired to bring an end to right-wing dictatorships. For example, the **Central Intelligence Agency (CIA)** provided information and weapons to Dominican conspirators to rid the Dominican Republic of the aging tyrant Rafael L. Trujillo in 1961. In 1989, the **George H.W. Bush** administration orchestrated a military invasion of Panama to remove and capture General Manuel **Noriega**, once a key ally and friendly supporter of the U.S.–backed **Contra** forces, the war on drugs, and protector of the Panama Canal during the 1980s. The importance of some dictators to the **Cold War** fight against communism led the **Eisenhower** administration to bestow medals and honors on some Latin American autocrats, despite their corruption, greed, lack of democracy, and human rights violations.

During the 1950s, while Venezuelan General Marcos **Pérez Jiménez** was in power, U.S. military officers instructed Venezuelan officers on the importance of Cold War ideology and accepted rampant corruption, the absence of civil liberties, and human rights abuses as one of the necessary evils in keeping the Soviets out of the hemisphere and protecting Venezuela's oil supply for U.S. consumers. Diplomats who represented the United States in Venezuela during the Eisenhower years either ignored the excesses of the dictatorship or offered old shibboleths about immature voters not adequately prepared to handle democratic rule. A report on Venezuela written by the State Department for the **National Security Council (NSC)** in 1953 indicated that "the present dictatorship . . . is not generally liked by the people, but is popular with the majority of the armed forces and of the business interests and privileged classes who prefer a government friendly to them rather than greater civil liberties" (Schoultz, 1998: 348). In November 1954 General Pérez Jiménez was awarded the Legion of Merit by the United States for "special meritorious conduct in the fulfillment of his high functions, and anti-Communistic attitudes." The single act of embracing right-wing dictators would haunt Washington policymakers for years to come, but it served short-term economic interests while allowing new petroleum concessions to be awarded to U.S. investors in 1956 and protected U.S. exports to Venezuela at the time. As the Eisenhower administration came to a close, Democrats in Washington used Pérez Jiménez as a symbol of brutal dictatorship and a failed Latin American policy of the United States.

The decision to support friendly tyrants in the Cold War period flowed naturally from the prevailing belief that democracy was not desirable or even possible in

Latin America, and besides, anti-Communist stability was considered more important to policymakers in Washington. Any serious effort at democracy-building took a back seat to the myopic view that anti-Communist right-wing dictators were better able to maintain order and stability than disorderly democrats. While there were some policymakers in Washington who doubted this formula, arguing that while dictators may be able to handle Communists more effectively in the short run, and the best policy in the long run is the encouragement of democratic rule to root out communism, others were adamant about the importance of supporting right-wing dictators. "Do nothing to offend the dictators," John Foster **Dulles** told his State Department staff, "they are the only people we can depend on." Those on the receiving end of this policy—the Latin Americans themselves—had little opportunity to challenge or modify the "friendly dictator" policy of the United States except through demonstrations, riots, strikes, and **revolutions**, hardly a prescription for a foreign policy of progress or improvement, or in fostering good neighborliness in the Americas. Their voices would not be heard until a revolution managed to topple a dictator and address their needs.

Critics of American support for right-wing dictators began to take hold after 1965, particularly among outspoken members of Congress like Frank Church and William Fulbright and by various grass-roots organizations and political groups opposed to U.S. policy in Vietnam and Latin America. The **Church Committee Report** uncovered many of the negative consequences of covert activities, including **assassinations** and support for anti-Communist autocrats. Scholars who examined U.S. foreign police assistance and military training found that this kind of assistance contributed to the creation of the bureaucratic-authoritarian states whose internal security apparatus had the capacity to penetrate more deeply than ever before into the heart of civil society. President Jimmy **Carter** reversed U.S. support for right-wing dictators in favor of a foreign policy based on human rights. President Ronald **Reagan** returned American foreign policy to one of support for a variety of dictators throughout the world under the guise of the **Reagan Doctrine**. Until the global war on **terrorism** declared by President **George W. Bush** in 2001, the Bush and **Clinton** presidencies—thanks to the absence of anti-communism as a unifying theme for American foreign policy—found it more difficult to justify support for right-wing dictators. The increasing role of the **Organization of American States (OAS)** in supporting democratic rule while condemning military takeovers and unconstitutional manipulation of power has made it far more difficult for the United States to rationalize support for authoritarian regimes. However, many American officials still find benefits in supporting right-wing dictatorships around the world, often the result of threat perceptions based on terrorism, energy needs, and an assortment of ideological, economic, regime, and racial arguments stretched to fit the proclivities of those who occupy the White House. The recent global war on terrorism has moved the pendulum back to supporting autocratic regimes, particularly those in the Middle East that maintain a pro–United States outlook on the world, permit the establishment of U.S. military bases and operations on their soil, and provide ade-

Table 1
Friendly Dictators in Latin America and the Caribbean

Name	Country	Time Period
Alfaro, Eloy	Ecuador	1895–1901; 1906–1911
Arias, Arnulfo	Panama	1968
Arroyo del Río, Carlos	Ecuador	1940–1944
Balaguer, Joaquín	Dominican Republic	1966–1978; 1986–1996
Banzer, Hugo	Bolivia	1971–1979
Barrios, Justo Rufino	Guatemala	1871–1885
Batista, Fulgencio	Cuba	1933–1944; 1952–1958
Bonilla, Manuel	Honduras	1903–1907; 1911–1913
Carías Andino, Tiburcio	Honduras	1932–1948
Castello Branco, Humberto	Brazil	1964–1967
Castillo Armas, Carlos	Guatemala	1954–1957
Díaz, Porfirio	Mexico	1876–1911
Duvalier, Françoise	Haiti	1957–1971
Duvalier, Jean-Claude	Haiti	1971–1986
Estrada Cabrera, Manuel	Guatemala	1897–1920
Flores, Juan José	Ecuador	1830–1835; 1839–1845
Gairy, Eric	Grenada	1974–1979
Gómez, Juan Vicente	Venezuela	1908–1935
Hernández Martínez, Maximiliano	El Salvador	1931–1944
Leguía, Augusto	Peru	1908–1912; 1919–1930
López Arrellano, Oswaldo	Honduras	1963–1971; 1972–1975
López Contreras, Eleazar	Venezuela	1935–1940
Lucas García, Romero	Guatemala	1979–1982
Machado, Gerardo	Cuba	1924–1933
Morínigo, Higinio	Paraguay	1940–1948
Noriega, Manuel Antonio	Panama	1981–1989
Odría, Manuel	Peru	1948–1956
Pacheco Areco, Jorge	Uruguay	1967–1972
Paéz, José Antonio	Venezuela	1830–1848
Pérez Jiménez, Marcos	Venezuela	1949–1957
Pinochet, Augusto	Chile	1973–1989
Ríos Montt, Efraín	Guatemala	1982–1983
Rojas Pinilla, Gustavo	Colombia	1954–1957
Sánchez Hernández, Fidel	El Salvador	1967–1972
Somoza Debayle, Anastasio	Nicaragua	1967–1979
Somoza Debayle, Luis	Nicaragua	1956–1967
Somoza García, Anastasio	Nicaragua	1936–1956
Stroessner, Alfredo	Paraguay	1954–1989
Suazo Córdoba, Roberto	Honduras	1981–1985
Trujillo, Rafael Leónidas	Dominican Republic	1930–1961
Ubico, Jorge	Guatemala	1930–1944
Vargas, Getulio	Brazil	1930–1945; 1951–1954
Velasco Ibarra, José María	Ecuador	1933–1934; 1944; 1952; 1968–1972
Videla, Jorge Rafael	Argentina	1976–1981

quate security measures to make sure that oil production and exports to the United States and its allies are not interrupted. In the aftermath of the war with Iraq in 2003, a *New York Times*/CBS News Poll found that 48 percent of respondents said that it was wrong for the United States to change a dictatorship to a democracy and it is better for the United States to "stay out" of the affairs of other countries. However, in a speech marking the twentieth anniversary of the **National Endowment for Democracy (NED)** in November 2003, President George Bush spoke of a new policy he called a "forward strategy of freedom in the Middle East." Although he called Cuba "an outpost of oppression," the speech said nothing about Latin America or Washington's support for Latin American dictators for the past 100 years. In making a commitment to democracy, President Bush did admit that "sixty years of Western nations excusing and accommodating the lack of freedom in the Middle East did nothing to make us safe, because in the long run stability cannot be purchased at the expense of liberty." The same flaw in American foreign policy is evident in how the United States has approached nondemocratic governments in Latin America.

The legacy of the U.S. creation and support of dozens of friendly dictators in Latin America make even the most carefully crafted statements about democracy, human rights, and anti-terrorism seem dubious and hypocritical in light of past policies and the complacency and arrogance that characterize Washington's attitudes toward Latin America today. To make matters worse, the United States developed the habit of harboring refugee dictators once they were deposed by coups, revolutions, or other means. When unexpected **blowback** disasters occur because of past support for friendly dictators in Latin America, American citizens should not be shocked or mystified about the negative consequences of what the United States does abroad in the name of American foreign policy. If President Bush is sincere about ending the tradition of excusing and accommodating dictators, many in Latin America will be looking for the day when the United States denies economic and military aid to a dictator who is pro-American and in sync with U.S.–Latin American policy instead of a freely elected anti-American democrat. At the present time the Central Intelligence Agency has no restrictions on recruiting criminals, human rights abusers, and unsavory characters if CIA officers believe that such individuals have access to information considered a threat to the United States or its allies. The war on terrorism seems to have removed any concern within the intelligence community for the unintended negative consequences of dealing with such nefarious individuals. The folly of supporting friendly dictators was recognized by the 9/11 Commission report that recommended that the United States should be much more critical of autocratic regimes, even friendly ones, if for no other reason than to demonstrate the importance of stated principles of American foreign policy. If this recommendation came to pass, U.S. relations with Latin America would improve dramatically within a short period of time. *See also* Intervention and Non-Intervention; Threat Perception/Assessment.

Suggested Reading

Robert D. Crassweller, *Trujillo: The Life and Times of a Caribbean Dictator* (New York: Macmillan, 1956); Eduardo Crawley, *Dictators Never Die: A Portrait of Nicaragua and the Somozas* (New York: St. Martin's Press, 1979); David W. Dent, *The Legacy of the Monroe Doctrine: A Reference Guide to U.S. Involvement in Latin America and the Caribbean* (Westport, CT: Greenwood Press, 1999); Paul J. Dosal, *Doing Business with the Dictators: A Political History of United Fruit in Guatemala, 1899–1944* (Wilmington, DE: Scholarly Resources, 1993); Adam Garfinkle, et al., *The Devil and Uncle Sam: A User's Guide to the Friendly Tyrants Dilemma* (New Brunswick, NJ: Transaction, 1992); John Mason Hart, *Empire and Revolution: The Americans in Mexico Since the Civil War* (Berkeley: University of California Press, 2002); Martha K. Huggins, *Political Policing: The United States and Latin America* (Durham, NC: Duke University Press, 1998); Frederick Kempe, *Divorcing the Dictator: America's Bungled Affair With Noriega* (New York: G.P. Putnam's Sons, 1990); Jeane Kirkpatrick, *Dictatorships and Double Standards* (New York: Harpers, 1980); Jonathan Kwitney, *Endless Enemies: The Making of an Unfriendly World* (New York: Congdon and Weed, 1984); Carlos R. Miranda, *The Stroessner Era: Authoritarian Rule in Paraguay* (Boulder, CO: Westview Press, 1990); Daniel Pipes and Adam Garfinkle, eds., *Friendly Tyrants: An American Dilemma* (New York: St. Martin's Press, 1991); Stephen G. Rabe, *The Most Dangerous Area of the World: John F. Kennedy Confronts Communist Revolution in Latin America* (Chapel Hill: University of North Carolina Press, 1999); Rabe, *Eisenhower and Latin America: The Foreign Policy of Anticommunism* (Chapel Hill: University of North Carolina Press, 1988); David F. Schmitz, *Thank God They're on Our Side: The United States and Right-Wing Dictatorships, 1921–1965* (Chapel Hill: University of North Carolina Press, 1999); Lars Schoultz, *Beneath the United States: A History of U.S. Policy Toward Latin America* (Cambridge, MA: Harvard University Press, 1988); Gaddis Smith, *The Last Years of the Monroe Doctrine, 1945–1993* (New York: Hill and Wang, 1994); Roger R. Trask, "George F. Kennan's Report on Latin America (1950)," *Diplomatic History* 2 (summer 1978): 307–311; Robin Wright, "Idealism in the Face of a Troubled Reality," *Washington Post* (November 7, 2003).

FTAA. *See* Free Trade Area of the Americas

G

Garfield, James A. (1831–1881) Republican politician (state senator and congressional representative from Ohio) and president of the United States (1981) who championed free trade and commercial expansion. Born in Cuyahoga County, Ohio, Garfield attended Western Reserve Eclectic Institute before graduating from Williams College in 1856. He made his mark in the U.S. Congress by pushing for new markets in Latin America, in part to keep the British out of the Western Hemisphere. He repudiated territorial expansion, arguing against the acquisition of Cuba and the West Indies. During his brief presidency, he called for U.S. control over any canal built across the Isthmus of Panama, intervened on the side of Peru during the War of the Pacific (1879–1883), and supported Guatemala in a border dispute with Mexico. Although Garfield left the running of foreign affairs to his secretary of state, James G. **Blaine**, his administration helped pave the way for greater U.S. involvement in Latin America after his death by an assassin's bullet after only six months into his presidency. *See also* Manifest Destiny.

Suggested Reading

Hendrik Booraem, *The Road to Respectability: James A. Garfield and his World, 1844–1852* (Lewisburg, PA: Bucknell University Press, 1988); Justus D. Doenecke, *The Presidencies of James A. Garfield and Chester A. Arthur* (Lawrence: Regents Press of Kansas, 1981); Allan Peskin, *Garfield: A Biography* (Kent, OH: Kent State University Press, 1978); David M. Pletcher, *The Awkward Years: American Foreign Relations Under Garfield and Arthur* (Columbia: University of Missouri Press, 1962).

German Threat With over a million and a half ethnic Germans residing in Latin America at the start of **World War II**, U.S. military strategists feared the possibility of German destabilization of Latin America at a time war seemed inevitable in Europe. To keep the continent safe, the United States began blacklisting and expelling Germans in Latin America because of: rumors of Nazi involvement in numerous coup attempts, Germans in Latin America were unassimilated, Nazi propagandists claimed the allegiance of every German, and the prevailing mindset in Washington that Latin Americans were inferior and therefore incapable of managing their own affairs without outside guidance. The U.S. view of the thousands of Germans residing in the United States was different, according to Max Paul Friedman (2003: 4), "because of the U.S. view of Latin America as a vulnerable, dependent region where latinos are helpless and foreigners are the real actors; because of the poor quality of the intelligence operation that was supposed to find subversives to the south; and because Germans living in Latin America presented another challenge: they were making inroads into Latin American markets." While some **Washington policymakers** may have had some recollection of the threat posed by Germany at the turn of the century and during **World War I**, most did not argue that the threat in the 1930s and the 1940s had anything to do with prior German interest and involvement in Latin America.

In a recent study of the U.S. pursuit of German nationals in Latin America, Friedman finds irony and incompetence in dealing with the German threat during World War II. The widespread but exaggerated fears of German immigrant subversion resulted in a program that did little to combat an ostensible external threat to Latin America and cost the United States in international credibility and esteem. As Friedman (2003: 234) points out in his landmark study, "If governments were to base their security measures on evidence of *suspicious activity*, rather than on perceived *suspicious identity* determined by ethnicity, religion, or nationality, they might well be able to learn something from the past, instead of being condemned to repeat it." The lack of evidence substantiating the German threat came in large part from individuals with little knowledge or understanding of Latin America. When individuals in positions of power are trained and experienced in the region, they are less likely to rely on negative stereotypes and political ideology to assess threats to national security. The search for enemies of German background was replaced after World War II by the **Cold War** focus on Communists and subversives who could be labeled easily as Communists. *See also* Roosevelt, Franklin Delano; Threat Perception/Assessment.

Suggested Reading

Stephen Fox, *America's Invisible Gulag: A Biography of German American Internment and Exclusion in World War II* (New York: Peter Lang, 2000); Max Paul Friedman, *Nazis and Good Neighbors: The United States Campaign Against the Germans of Latin America in World War II* (New York: Cambridge University Press, 2003); David G. Haglund, *Latin America and the Transformation of U.S. Strategic Thought, 1936–1940* (Albuquerque: University of New Mexico Press, 1984); Lester D. Langley, *The Cuban Policy of the United States: A Brief History*

(New York: John Wiley, 1968); Brian S. McBeth, *Gunboats, Corruption, and Claims: Foreign Intervention in Venezuela, 1899–1908* (Westport, CT: Greenwood Press, 2001); Nancy Mitchell, *The Danger of Dreams: German and American Imperialism in Latin America* (Chapel Hill: University of North Carolina Press, 1999).

González, Elián. *See* Elián González Incident

Good Neighbor Policy U.S. policy toward Latin America designed to transform the image of the United States as a "bad neighbor" based on the principles of **intervention** and **hegemony** into one that emphasized equality, partnership, **non-intervention**, and trade reciprocity. While the policy is most closely associated with **Franklin D. Roosevelt** (1933–1945), its origins can be traced back to his three Republican predecessors who were anxious to do something about the growing **anti-Americanism** (Yankeephobia) in the Americas. By renouncing intervention and treating Latin Americans as friends and equals, the Good Neighbor Policy sought to reverse a pattern of U.S. intervention, commercial domination, and military occupation going back to the nineteenth century. During the presidencies of Herbert **Hoover** (1929–1933) and Franklin D. Roosevelt the policy change helped to improve U.S.–Latin American relations, restore trade flows in the Western Hemisphere, create a unified hemispheric bloc against the Axis powers during **World War II**, and build the inter-American system. It was President Hoover's idea to repudiate the **Roosevelt Corollary to the Monroe Doctrine**—the principal justification for U.S. intervention going back to 1904—by issuing the **Clark Memorandum** in 1930. Written by Undersecretary of State J. Reuben Clark in 1928, the document rejected the Roosevelt Corollary as a false and counter-productive interpretation of Monroe's principles and signaled a major shift in the Latin American policy of the United States. The Good Neighbor Policy served as a means of "pre-emptive cooperation" that helped to diminish the negative effects of the **Monroe Doctrine** and interventionism reaching back to the 1890s. The failures associated with U.S. military occupation of Caribbean and Central American nations, **gunboat diplomacy**, and rising anti-Yankeeism contributed to the origins of the Good Neighbor Policy.

Franklin D. Roosevelt applied the principles of the Good Neighbor Policy during the 1930s and World War II in an effort to demonstrate the importance of hemispheric cooperation (partnership) and non-intervention. He was also interested in banishing the fear of some Latin Americans that the United States was only interested in acquiring more territory and gaining financial advantage over the economies of Latin America. Roosevelt refused to intervene in Cuba during the 1933 Revolution and resisted corporate and political appeals to reverse the oil expropriation initiatives of Mexican President Lázaro Cárdenas in 1938. President Roosevelt also instructed Secretary of State Cordell **Hull** to sign non-intervention pledges at inter-American conferences held in Montevideo, Uruguay, in 1933 and Buenos Aires, Argentina, in 1936. However, the rhetoric of the "good neighbor" and "non-intervention" did not mean that Washington would forego its right to protect its nationals and U.S. corporations operating in Latin America. In Washington's view, "intervention" was narrowly construed to mean the use of armed force; "internal affairs" meant the domestic politics of the United States. In fact, the United States always recognized that it could balance its national interests and international legal principles through diplomatic pressure and the use of surrogates in positions of political power in Latin America. The Good Neighbor Policy did contribute to less military intervention and more multilateralism, an approach that helped pave the way for the creation of the **Organization of American States (OAS)** in 1948; however, once the Cold War started the United States reverted to more subtle forms of intervention and unilateralism in dealing with **revolutions** in Guatemala, Cuba, and Chile. It is also important to point out that the attempt to reverse previous policies in Latin America was made possible by internationalizing U.S. assistance through police training and cooperation with U.S.–established constabularies that were in the process of consolidating power over political and social life in Latin America. *See also* Ambassadors; Friendly Dictators.

Suggested Reading

Earl R. Curry, *Hoover's Dominican Diplomacy and the Origins of the Good Neighbor Policy* (New York: Garland, 1979); Fred Fejes, *Imperialism, Media and the Good Neighbor: New Deal Foreign Policy and United States Short Wave Broadcasting to Latin America* (Norwood, NJ: Ablex Publishing, 1986); David Green, *The Containment of Latin America: A History of the Myths and Realities of the Good Neighbor Policy* (Chicago: Quadrangle Books, 1971); Michael Grow, *The Good Neighbor Policy and Authoritarianism in Paraguay* (Lawrence: Regents Press of Kansas, 1981); Edward O. Guerrant, *Roosevelt's Good Neighbor Policy* (Albuquerque: University of New Mexico Press, 1950); Frederick B. Pike, *FDR's Good Neighbor Policy: Sixty Years of Generally Gentle Chaos* (Austin: University of Texas Press, 1995); Eric Paul Roorda, *The Dictator Next Door: The Good Neighbor Policy and the Trujillo Regime in the Dominican Republic, 1930–1945* (Durham, NC: Duke University Press, 1998); Dick Steward, *Trade and Hemisphere: The Good Neighbor Policy and Reciprocal Trade* (Columbia: University of Missouri Press, 1975); Bryce Wood, *The Dismantling of the Good Neighbor Policy* (Austin: University of Texas Press, 1985; Wood, *The Making of the Good Neighbor Policy* (New York: Columbia University Press, 1961); Randall Bennett Woods, *The Roosevelt Foreign-Policy Establishment and the "Good Neighbor": The United States and Argentina, 1941–1945* (Lawrence: Regents Press of Kansas, 1979).

Gordon, [Abraham] Lincoln (1913–) Government official, professor of government, and U.S. ambassador to Brazil from 1961 to 1966. Lincoln Gordon was born in New York City in 1913, graduated from Harvard and Oxford universities, and throughout his life mixed academic life with a variety of government and diplomatic posts. Gordon's view of Latin America was influenced by **World War II** and the early efforts of Washington to counter Soviet advances in the Third World. He was one of the most enthusiastic and articulate advocates for supporting the military as a bulwark against communism and a progressive force capable of transforming Latin American society by combating **terrorism**, rooting out corruption, improving health conditions, and building schools and roads. Considered one of President John F. **Kennedy**'s cadre of the "best and brightest," Gordon is best known in the history of U.S.–Latin American relations for his interventionist actions in Brazil, first in undermining President João Goulart's legitimacy and then in helping the anti-Goulart conspirators remove the president in April 1964. His successful role of proconsul against Goulart was not matched by his concerns for the consequences of supporting Brazil's military. Gordon's avid support of the military was based on his convictions that they were imbued with the following positive attributes: moderately nationalistic, pro–United States, anti-Communist, anti-fascist, pro-democratic, constitutionalist, and an important source of trained public administrators for government civil service. As such, Gordon believed the military would provide the perfect form of government to protect U.S. interests in Latin America. Like many **Cold War** ambassadors, Lincoln Gordon worried about poorly governed countries "falling" to communism, the "death" of the **Monroe Doctrine**, immature and misguided democracies, and the unwillingness of Washington to adequately support right-wing anti-Communist governments in the Western Hemisphere. The **regime change** he helped engineer in getting rid of Goulart led ambassador Gordon to declare Goulart's removal "a great victory for the free world."

After serving with the War Production Board during World War II, Lincoln Gordon taught government and public administration at Harvard from 1947 to 1950. During the 1950s he was minister for economic affairs and director of the aid mission at the U.S. embassy in London and professor of international economic relations at Harvard. From 1961 to 1967, Gordon was the most active in Latin American affairs, first as ambassador to Brazil (1961–1966) and then as assistant secretary of state for inter-American affairs (1966–1967). After leaving the **State Department** in 1967, Gordon became president of Johns Hopkins University from 1967–1971, a research fellow at the Woodrow Wilson International Center for Scholars (1972–1975), and a senior fellow of Resources for the Future in Washington, D.C. (1975–1980). After leaving government service at the end of the **Johnson** presidency, Lincoln Gordon became a lightening rod for critics of U.S.–Latin American policy, particularly the policy of supporting right-wing **dictatorships** that provided stability at the expense of innocent civilian lives. *See also* Alliance for Progress; Ambassadors; Friendly Dictators.

Suggested Reading

Jan K. Black, "Lincoln Gordon and Brazil's Military Counterrevolution," in C. Neale Ronning and Albert P. Vannucci, eds., *Ambassadors in Foreign Policy: The Influence of Individuals on U.S.–Latin American Policy* (New York: Praeger, 1987); Lincoln Gordon, *Brazil's Second Chance: En Route Toward the First World* (Washington, DC: Brookings Institution Press, 2001); Gordon, *A New Deal for Latin America: The Alliance for Progress* (Cambridge, MA: Harvard University Press, 1963); Edward S. Mihalkanin and Warren Keith Neisler, "The Role of the Ambassador," in David W. Dent, ed., *U.S.–Latin American Policymaking: A Reference Handbook* (Westport, CT: Greenwood Press, 1995); Stephen G. Rabe, *The Most Dangerous Area in the World: John F. Kennedy Confronts Communist Revolution in Latin America* (Chapel Hill: University of North Carolina Press, 1999); Gaddis Smith, *The Last Years of the Monroe Doctrine, 1945–1993* (New York: Hill and Wang, 1994); W. Michael Weiss, *Cold Warriors and Coups d'Etat: Brazilian-American Relations, 1945–1964* (Albuquerque: University of New Mexico Press, 1993).

Grace, William Russell (1832–1904) Irish-born entrepreneur who established one of the leading foreign enterprises in Latin America during the nineteenth century. Grace sailed to Peru in 1851 and became involved in shipping, guano exports, sugar cultivation and refining, and other commercial endeavors. After launching New York–based W.R. Grace & Co. in 1871, Grace built a business empire that would play a major role in the Peruvian economy for decades. Working with his younger brother, Michael, and Charles R. Flint, William Grace became one of Peru's leading merchants, first in the guano trade and later in shipping, telegraph cables, silver mining, railroads, and sugar. Like many of the American merchants who carried out successful business ventures in Latin America and were convinced of the superiority of their values and methods, the Grace brothers became deeply involved in the internal political affairs of their hosts and in inter-American relations. Confident that their business interests would serve the long-term reform and development of Latin America, Grace and other entrepreneurs set out to open economies to the forces of U.S. capital and technology. According to Thomas O'Brien (1999: 22), "Their capital and technology, combined with their acumen and a set of values championing individualism, hard work, and sobriety would reform Latin American societies much as in the United States." In response to these entrepreneurs with a mission, Latin Americans endorsed some of their influence, but also strongly resisted encroachments on their economic and political sovereignty.

W.R. Grace Company played a major role in Peru's economy from the 1880s until 1930, opening the door to foreign capitalists while working hand-in-glove with Peru's oligarchy. After the humiliating defeat in the War of the Pacific, Peru faced civil war and a huge foreign debt. To escape from their dilemma, Peruvians signed the Grace Contract in 1888, an arrangement that provided for the cancellation of foreign debt in exchange for lucrative business opportunities. The Grace Contract granted foreigners control over its railroads, a steamer franchise, guano and jungle land as well as large annual payments for a period of thirty years. Peruvians were offended by the Grace Contract's assault on national pride; **Washington policymakers** chafed at being manipulated by private interests with the power to manipulate the **State Department** and circumvent U.S. diplomats. The power of W.R. Grace Company continued to expand into the twentieth century by trying to identify itself with Peruvian national interests. However, by the end of the twentieth century the company was no longer active in Latin America. After William R. Grace's death in 1904, Grace enterprises remained under the control of the family. The aggressive entrepreneurs of the second half of the nineteenth century were helped by Europeanized elites in Latin America who shared the views of U.S. businesspeople about the people of Latin America and the best development strategy for the region. The liberal elite of Latin America, according to O'Brien (1999: 23), "viewed their Indian and Mestizo populations as inherently inferior to themselves . . . and promoted a development strategy that included European immigration, the breakup of communal rural land holdings, and foreign trade and investment." W.R. Grace was one of many nineteenth-century entrepreneurs who exploited these opportunities. *See also* Race and Racism.

Suggested Reading

William V. Bishell, "Fall from Grace: U.S. Business Interests versus U.S. Diplomatic Interests in Peru, 1885–1890," *Diplomatic History*, Vol. 20 (spring 1996); David W. Dent, *The Legacy of the Monroe Doctrine: A Reference Guide to U.S. Involvement in Latin America and the Caribbean* (Westport, CT: Greenwood Press, 1999); Thomas O'Brien, *The Century of U.S. Capitalism in Latin America* (Albuquerque: University of New Mexico Press, 1999); Jimmy M. Skaggs, *The Great Guano Rush: Entrepreneurs and American Overseas Expansion* (New York: St. Martin's Press, 1994).

Grenada Invasion (1983) The U.S. invasion of Grenada occurred in October 1983, preceded by a number of events that triggered the **Reagan** administration's decision to send in an invasion force of 5,300 to the tiny Caribbean island. First, Washington grew increasingly concerned about the People's Revolutionary Government and its socialist and charismatic leader, Maurice Bishop. Of particular concern at the time was Bishop's open support of the Soviet bloc, close ties between Grenada and Cuba and the construction of a long runway at the Point Salines airport. Second, President Reagan justified the invasion on his concern about the safety of approximately 1,000 U.S. citizens on the island, mostly medical students and tourists. Third, the military intervention against such a weak adversary underscored the possibility of similar treatment for Nicaragua, although the Reagan administration never formally made such a connection. Although the U.S. invasion succeeded in its purpose, it provoked great controversy among the Latin American states and at the **Organization of American States (OAS)** and the **United Nations (UN)** General Assembly where a resolution critical of the United States passed 108 to 9. Critics of the invasion argued that exaggerated security concerns and the level of danger to Americans was never serious enough to justify the costs in American lives (18 dead and 106 wounded) and the damage to U.S.–Latin American relations. Moreover, many contended that the use of force lacked legal justification based on the non-intervention language of the charters of the UN and the OAS. While defenders of **Operation Urgent Fury** argued that **international law** allowed for this type of **intervention** to protect nationals or restore order, particularly when the Organization of East Caribbean States requested the invasion and the majority of people in Grenada welcomed the invasion and often referred to it as a rescue operation. Despite the deaths of Americans and hundreds of Cuban (84) and Grenadian (400) casualties, the invasion did provide a military rescue for the U.S. citizens on the island and the restoration of order in the aftermath of the assassination of Prime Minister Bishop by a rival faction within the New Jewel Movement. U.S. troops only remained for two months, and new elections were held in 1984. As with previous military invasions of Latin American countries, Operation Urgent Fury was preceded by destabilization tactics against the Bishop government, including outrageous disinformation campaigns and lies about the dangers posed by its fear of "another Cuba" in the Caribbean with links to the Soviet Union and its allies. Some argue that the Reagan administration had plans for an invasion of Grenada in place since 1981 and had used the Puerto Rican island of Vieques to simulate an invasion of Grenada. The American public had no trouble believing the official rhetoric from Washington, particularly when it was couched in Reagan and **Monroe Doctrine** language. To make sure the images of the invasion were favorable to U.S. objectives, reporters and photographers were quarantined in Barbados and prohibited from landing on the island for almost a week after the invasion started. The success of this Pentagon prohibition on **media** war coverage was continued afterward whenever U.S. troops intervened abroad. President Reagan wrote in his memoirs that, "I probably never felt better during my presidency than I did that day." In Reagan's mind the United States was "back and standing tall" in Latin America and the world, a stature not experienced since **World War II**.

The U.S. invasion of Grenada in 1983 marked the first time the United States had sent troops to an English-speaking Caribbean country and the first U.S. military intervention in the Caribbean since the Dominican crisis of 1965. In the aftermath of the U.S. defeat in Vietnam, the Grenada invasion proved to be a valuable symbolic act. The invasion could be interpreted as a "defeat" of the Soviets and Cubans, a sign that the United States was the most powerful player in world politics, and a warning to other enemies of Washington that they could be next on the invasion hit list. *See also* Intervention and Non-Intervention; Reagan Doctrine.

Suggested Reading

Mark Adkin, *Urgent Fury: The Battle for Grenada* (Lexington, MA: Lexington Books, 1989); Robert J. Beck, *The Grenada Invasion: Politics, Law, and Foreign Policy Decisionmaking* (Boulder, CO: Westview Press, 1993); Reynold A. Burrowes, *Revolution and Rescue in Grenada: An Account of the U.S.–Caribbean Invasion* (New York: Greenwood Press, 1988); Scott Davidson, *Grenada: A Study in Politics and the Limits of International Law* (Brookfield, VT: Gower, 1987); Peter M. Dunn and Bruce W. Watson, *American Intervention in Grenada: The Implications of Operation "Urgent Fury"* (Boulder, CO: Westview Press, 1985); Raymond English, ed., *The Grenada Mission: Crisis Editorializing in the* New York Times, Wall Street Journal, Washington Post *and* Washington Times (Washington, DC: Ethics and Public Policy Center, 1984); William C. Gilmore, *The Grenada Intervention: Analysis and Documentation* (New York: Mansell Books, 1984); *Heartbreak Ridge* (video), (Burbank, CA: Warner Home Video, 2002); *Lessons of Grenada* (Washington, DC: U.S. Department of State, 1985); Gordon K. Lewis, *Grenada: The Jewel Dispoiled* (Baltimore, MD: Johns Hopkins University Press, 1987); John Norton Moore, *Law and the Grenada Invasion* (Charlottsville: Center for Law and National Security, University of Virginia, 1984); Hugh O'Shaughnessy, *Grenada Revolution, Invasion, and*

Aftermath (London: Sphere Books, 1984); O'Shaughnessy, *Grenada: An Eyewitness Account of the U.S. Invasion and the Caribbean History that Provoked it* (New York: Dodd Mead, 1984); Anthony Payne, et al., *Grenada: Revolution and Invasion* (London: Croom Helm, 1984); "Whose News is it?" (video) (Alexandria, VA: 1984).

Guadalupe Hidalgo, Treaty of (1848) An onerous treaty between the United States and Mexico that ended the **Mexican-American War** in 1848. President James K. **Polk** appointed Nicholas **Trist** to travel to Mexico with a draft treaty containing a list of demands and concessions. On arrival in Mexico, Trist found himself embroiled in a feud with Winfield Scott, the U.S. commander in central Mexico who resented having to take orders from a civilian employee, and the disarray within the Mexican Congress. Later he would suffer from the loss of confidence in his negotiating skills back in Washington. In his efforts to negotiate a peaceful end to the conflict, Scott and Trist dispensed a million dollars to Mexican officials as a monetary inducement to begin peace talks. The "bribery" plan failed, but Trist continued his efforts to bring an end to the conflict even though there was no authorized body with which to negotiate. Trist defied President Polk's orders to return home and eventually brought representatives of a newly organized government to Guadalupe Hidalgo, a suburb of Mexico City, where the treaty was signed on February 2, 1848. The document required Mexico to give up any claim to Texas, recognize the Rio Grande as the international boundary, and cede New Mexico and upper California to the United States along with other parts of the Southwest. Mexico denied the United States the right of transit across the Isthmus of Tehuantepec and the cession of lower California, but it did relinquish title to 55 percent of Mexican territory. In return the United States paid Mexico $15 million and assumed responsibility for $3.5 million in claims against the Mexican government by U.S. citizens. President Polk sent the Treaty of Guadalupe Hidalgo to the U.S. Senate where it was ratified on March 10, 1848. Mexico approved the treaty in May, and U.S. troops left Mexico soon after and returned home. *See also* Manifest Destiny.

Suggested Reading

Richard Griswold del Castillo, *The Treaty of Guadalupe Hidalgo: A Legacy of Conflict* (Norman: University of Oklahoma Press, 1990); Charles E. Hill, *Leading American Treaties* (New York: The Macmillan Company, 1922); Wallace Ohrt, *Defiant Peacemaker: Nicholas Trist in the Mexican War* (College Station: Texas A&M University Press, 1997).

Guantánamo Bay A prime piece of coastal property in southeast Cuba where the United States has held an indefinite lease for over 100 years. The continued existence of a U.S. military base within Communist territory is one of the anomalous aspects of contemporary U.S.–Cuban relations. It is the oldest U.S. overseas military base and a constant reminder of Washington's traditional relationship with Cuba. Those in the U.S. military refer to it affectionately as "Gitmo" while the

Cubans refer to it as *Caimanera*, the name of the Cuban town on the western side of the bay. Fidel **Castro** has always referred to the U.S. occupation of his island as "illegal" and insisted that the status of the base be part of any agenda devoted to the normalization of relations between the two countries. There have been very few flare ups over the U.S. occupation of Guantánamo, even with the use of the naval base to detain over 650 "enemy combatants" in the early stages of the war on **terrorism** announced by President **George W. Bush**. In Castro's view, "There is a base on our island territory directed against Cuba and the revolutionary government of Cuba, in the hands of those who declare themselves enemies of our country, enemies of our revolution, and enemies of our people" (Bender, 1975: 110). While Castro uses the occupation of Guantánamo to stir up national resentment against the United States, U.S. presidents have always insisted that the United States has treaty rights that allow it to exercise complete jurisdiction and control over the area. Now that Guantánamo serves a vital role in the U.S. war against terrorism, Washington has no reason to abandon the base to the Cubans. Fidel Castro realizes that Cuba is powerless to remove the United States and has insisted that it would be the height of stupidity to attempt to use force against U.S. military forces. With the war on terrorism and the withdrawal of U.S. military bases from Panama in 2000, Guantánamo has increased its value as a strategic asset and symbol of U.S. imperial power in the Caribbean region.

The United States obtained Guantánamo Bay shortly after the end of the **Spanish-Cuban-American War** when the United States possessed the power to dictate the future of an independent Cuba. The **Platt Amendment** (1902) contained a provision that enabled the United States to create a protectorate over the island, including the right to buy or lease lands necessary for coaling or naval stations. The Platt Amendment established the legal basis for leasing the 45 square miles of land and water found in the agreement signed by the two countries in February 1903 and later amended and reaffirmed in the Treaty of Relations of 1934. The original lease stipulated that the United States would agree to pay Cuba $2,000 in gold per year. When gold coins were discontinued in 1934 the rent was increased to $4,085, payable on an annual basis by U.S. Treasury check. During the first several years of the Revolution Fidel Castro cashed the paltry check, but the **Cuban missile crisis** so angered him that he has since refused to cash the checks as a form of protest against the provisions of the treaty and U.S. imperialism. The checks are delivered through the Swiss Embassy in Havana to the Cuban government, but they have not been cashed. Since the modifications of the treaty in 1934, the United States has the benefit of a treaty based on an "indefinite lease," which only both parties can modify and terminate. The base has been closed to Cubans since January 1, 1959, but over the years it has served as an immigration processing center, first for Haitian refugees fleeing the island's turmoil in 1992 and then for housing more than 20,000 *balseros* in 1994. Since 2001, it has been converted into a prison camp for suspected "enemy combatants" in the war on terrorism. U.S. servicemen on the base monitor Cuban air space, maintain warships, conduct defense exercises, and practice amphibious landings and underwater demolition techniques. The Defense Department chose Guantánamo because it was remote and in a foreign country, where prisoners would be outside the reach of U.S. constitutional protections.

The current status of Guantánamo Bay as a secret overseas facility for prisoners suspected of committing terrorist acts has complicated the possibility of negotiating an end to the U.S. presence on the island. In 2003, about 660 prisoners were held at Guantánamo Bay, anonymously and under rather harsh conditions. These detention camps outside the United States are kept as secret as possible to avoid criticism by Congress, the press, private citizens, or international **human rights** organizations. While the alleged security benefits from the "enemy combatants" held at Guantánamo Bay seem minimal, it now seems obvious that under the current circumstances negotiating a new relationship with Cuba is likely to be far more difficult than when Guantánamo Bay was on the chopping block for base closings to save the taxpayers money. After two years of legal limbo, the U.S. Supreme Court agreed to consider whether federal courts have any power over the non-American detainees at Guantánamo Bay. The secrecy involved in holding "unlawful combatants" and the refusal of the Bush administration to disclose who is being held and on what charges has added to the saliency of the U.S. military base on Cuban soil. After the prisoner abuse scandals in Iraq rocked Washington in 2004, the U.S. Supreme Court ruled that the detainees at Camp Delta have the right to challenge their detentions in U.S. courts and pretrail proceedings commenced in August 2004.

Between 5,000 and 7,000 U.S. servicemen and their dependents live on the Guantánamo Bay naval base where they enjoy all the comforts of a small town in the United States. They have access to the only McDonald's and Subway in Cuba, a school, health spa, golf course, five swimming pools, a bowling alley, and four outdoor movie houses. A small number of Cubans reside on the base, a choice that some made following the Revolution and others known as "fence-jumpers" who have risked their lives by swimming in the shark-infested waters to reach the base. Although clashes are infrequent between Cubans and Americans along the heavily mined boundary, Guantánamo remains one of the strange remnants of ongoing hostility between the United States and Cuba. For Washington, Guantánamo serves a dual purpose: a thorn in the side of Fidel Castro and a convenient base on foreign soil where prisoners remain beyond the reach of courts that might review the American president's decision to label individuals captured in a military zone as "enemy combatants." In the meantime, the Guantánamo lease agreement remains in effect until both parties agree to change it, and the United States enjoys one of its best real estate bargains for an overseas military base. The Cubans maintain a large sign in front of the U.S. base proclaiming defiance against the U.S. occupation of Cuban soil and a reaffirmation of "Socialism or Death," the motto of the Cuban Revolution.

Suggested Reading

Lynn Darrell Bender, *The Politics of Hostility: Castro's Revolution and United States Policy* (Hato Rey, Puerto Rico: Inter American University Press, 1975); Editorial, "Justices at Guantánamo," *Washington Post* (November 11, 2003); Joseph Lelyveld, "In Guantánamo," *The New*

York Review (November 7, 2002); *The History of Guantanamo Bay* (http://purl.access.gpo.gov/GPO/LPS17563); Theodore K. Mason, *Across the Cactus Curtain: the Story of Guantánamo Bay* (New York: Dodd Mead, 1984); Roger Ricardo, *Guantánamo: The Bay of Discord* (New York: Ocean Press, 1994).

Guatemala, U.S. Invasion of (1954) The **Central Intelligence Agency (CIA)** coup in Guatemala in 1954 followed the successful overthrow of Iran's secular-nationalist leader Mohammad Mossadegh the previous year. In both cases, the success of **covert operations** in bringing about **regime change** emboldened those in the intelligence community to repeat similar instances of secret covert action against distasteful regimes, particularly in Latin America where the White House believed the Communists might takeover. As more and more previously classified documents become available, clear parallels can be seen between neo-conservatives in the **George W. Bush** administration who see "regime change" in the same way brothers **Allen Welsh** and **John Foster Dulles** in the **Dwight D. Eisenhower** administration viewed the turbulent world at the time. To convince Eisenhower that **intervention** and regime change was necessary in Iran, John Foster Dulles explained to the president that the problem was not so much a **dictatorship** under a popular nationalist like Mossadegh, but the possibility of Communists succeeding him if he was assassinated or removed from power. In each case, the decision to remove pre-emptively Jacobo **Arbenz** in Guatemala and Mohammad Mossadegh in Iran had far less to do with threats to the owners of banana plantations and oil refineries than what might follow these leaders if allowed to remain in power. The Bush doctrine of pre-emption—waging preventative wars because of possible terrorist threats, not actual ones—contains the same logic that existed at the beginning of the **Cold War** when Washington worried about communism and claimed the right to remove pre-emptively the perceived threat to U.S. security interests. When **Washington policymakers** believed that a Third World country was about to succumb to Moscow's or Cuba's influence, covert operations offered a relatively safe and inexpensive substitute to armed intervention against Communist influence in the Third World. Beginning with the U.S. invasion of Panama in 1989, classic Cold War motivations evaporated while the use of armed forces increased. *See also* Hegemony; Threat Perception/Assessment.

Suggested Reading

Nick Cullather, *Secret History: The CIA's Classified Account of its Operations in Guatemala, 1952–1954* (Stanford, CA: Stanford University Press, 1999); Piero Gleijeses, *Shattered Hope: The Guatemalan Revolution and the United States, 1944–1954* (Princeton, NJ: Princeton University Press, 1991); Richard H. Immerman, *The CIA in Guatemala: The Foreign Policy of Intervention* (Austin: University of Texas Press, 1982); Susanne Jonas, *The Battle for Guatemala: Rebels, Death Squads, and U.S. Power* (Boulder, CO: Westview Press, 1991); Stephen C. Schlesinger and Stephen Kinzer, *Bitter Fruit: The Untold Story of the American Coup in Guatemala* (Garden City, NY: Anchor Press/Doubleday, 1983); James F. Siekmeier, *Aid, Nationalism, and Inter-American Relations: Guatemala, Bolivia, and the United States, 1945–1961*

(Lewiston, NY: E. Mellen Press, 1999); Stephen M. Streeter, *Managing the Counter-Revolution: The United States and Guatemala, 1954–1961* (Athens: Ohio University Center for International Studies, 2000).

Guerrilla Warfare A Spanish term that means "small war" that is often used as a tool of the weak against the strong. The concept and strategy has ancient roots, but it has been applied most successfully in the twentieth century. Latin American governments have had to engage in anti–guerrilla warfare, often working with the United States to subdue rebellions aimed at overthrowing corrupt regimes and brutal **dictatorships** friendly to Washington. At times the U.S. government has created and sustained guerrilla forces as part of a national security strategy that appears to have less risk and more cost-effective means of achieving U.S. objectives. During the era of **intervention** (1895–1930) the U.S. military often faced guerrillas who resented U.S. occupation and domination. This occurred in Haiti, Cuba, and Nicaragua, often stimulating nationalism and **anti-Americanism** in the process. Augusto **Sandino** used guerrilla tactics to drive the U.S. Marines from Nicaragua in the 1920s and early 1930s. The Cuban Revolution under the leadership of Fidel **Castro** and Che **Guevara** used guerrilla warfare to defeat Fulgencio **Batista**'s conventional forces. In his most influential work, *Guerrilla Warfare* (1960), Che Guevara developed his *foco* theory and vowed that Cuba would export the revolution to the entire continent. He falsely predicted imminent "explosions" in which insurrectional *focos* (guerrillas operating in small bands in the countryside) would liberate Latin America from oppression and **imperialism**.

The "freedom fighters" created by the **Reagan** administration to defeat the **Sandinistas** in Nicaragua used classic techniques of guerrilla warfare: sabotage, severing lines of communication, surprise attacks, and ambushes, and **propaganda** at home and abroad. Guerrilla warfare uses superior agility and small armed bands to attack and disperse as necessary. The heavy cost of direct, sustained encounters with larger conventional forces that have far more firepower and logistical support are avoided at all costs. Over the past three decades, the nature of insurgencies has changed dramatically with the growing involvement of insurgent forces with narcotraffickers intent on overthrowing existing governments. With the growing risk of fragile democracies in Latin America, the United States continues to face a variety of threats posed by insurgents, guerrillas, and narcotraffickers who undermine the security of the United States.

Those who rely on guerrilla warfare often have different motives and objectives; this means that it is not always possible to clearly distinguish between "bandits," "partisans," "insurgents," "raiders," "terrorists," and "guerrillas." Obviously, the terminology and rhetoric is used to gain political and moral advantage over those who employ small war tactics. Over the course of U.S.–Latin American relations, the United States has faced bandits (small forces that seek pecuniary gain, but employ guerrilla tactics), insurgents (guerrillas fighting their own government), and terrorists (small cell-like organizations that rely on secrecy, fear, and violence to successfully oppose national, religious, and ideological adversaries). Many of the guerrilla adversaries the United States encountered during its Caribbean interventions were exterminated during military campaigns that often resorted to merciless counter-guerrilla strategies and tactics. During the **Cold War**, the United States invested heavily in figuring out ways to counter anti-Communist guerrilla forces, particularly in Guatemala, El Salvador, Honduras, Nicaragua, Cuba, and Vietnam. The **Kennedy** administration gave special attention to the creation and support of the U.S. Army Special Forces as the best and the brightest of counter-insurgency warriors. Counter-insurgency warfare is taught at many of the nation's military installations, particularly the U.S. Army **School of the Americas (SOA)** at Ft. Benning, Georgia. The failure of counter-insurgency warfare in Vietnam did not damper the military's interest in its desire to use and succeed with counter-guerrilla warfare. In fact, it contributed to the development of "low-intensity" warfare as a means of fighting insurgents where U.S. interests are involved. Recent confrontations with corrupt, dangerous, and distasteful leaders in Haiti, Panama, Iraq, and Cuba have led some critics to conclude that the responsibility of removing dictators, or **regime change**, should not be the primary responsibility of the United States, but should reside with the people themselves. Whatever the case, the United States is handicapped in fighting guerrilla insurgencies because of the nature of democratic authority and restrictions, as well as employing military power in heavily populated civilian areas. In turn, this means that U.S. adversaries will continue to find guerrilla warfare as the only way the weak can oppose the strong in today's chaotic and unjust world. *See also* Drug Trafficking; Friendly Dictators; Terrorism.

Suggested Reading

Yildiz Atasoy and William K. Carroll, eds., *Global Shaping and its Alternatives* (Bloomfield, CT: Kumarian Press, 2003); I.F.W. Beckett, *Encyclopedia of Guerrilla Warfare* (Santa Barbara, CA: ABC-CLIO, 1999); Roger Burbach, *Globalization and Postmodern Politics: From Zapatistas to High-Tech Robber Barons* (Sterling, VA: Pluto Press, 2001); Daniel Castro, ed., *Revolution and Revolutionaries: Guerrilla Movements in Latin America* (Wilmington, DE: SR Books, 1999); Paul J. Dosal, *Comandante Che: Guerrilla Soldier, Commander, and Strategist, 1956–1967* (University Park: Pennsylvania State University Press, 2003); Ernesto Che Guevara, *Guerrilla Warfare*, 3rd. ed. (Wilmington, DE: Scholarly Resources, 1960, 1997); Ernst Halperin, *Terrorism in Latin America* (Beverly Hills, CA: Sage Publications, 1976); John Holloway and Eloína Peláez, *Zapatista!: Reinventing Revolution in Mexico* (Sterling, VA: Pluto Press, 1998); Anthony James Joes, *America and Guerrilla Warfare* (Lexington: University Press of Kentucky, 2000); James Kohl and John Litt, *Urban Guerrilla Warfare in Latin America* (Cambridge, MA: MIT Press, 1974); Brian Loveman and Thomas M. Davies, Jr., *Guerrilla Warfare/Che Guevara* (Wilmington, DE: SR Books, 1997); Max G. Manwaring, *Internal Wars: Rethinking Problem and Response* (Carlisle, PA: U.S. Army War College, 2001); Bard E. O'Neil, *Insurgency and Terrorism: Inside Modern Revolutionary Warfare* (Dulles, VA: Brassey's, 2000); Paul B. Rich and Richard Stubbs, eds., *The Counter-Insurgent State: Guerrilla Warfare and State Building in the Twentieth Century* (New York: St. Martin's Press, 1997); Keith Suter, *An International Law of Guerrilla Warfare: The Global Politics of Law Making* (New York: St. Martin's Press, 1984); Tayacán, *Psychological Operations in Guerrilla Warfare* (New York: Vintage Books, 1985).

Guevara, Ernesto "Che" (1928–1967) Argentine-born physician, Marxist revolutionary theoretician, and guerrilla fighter who joined Fidel **Castro** in the successful overthrow of Cuba's dictator Fulgencio **Batista** on January 1, 1959. Born in Rosario, Argentina, to middle-class parents of Irish and Spanish descent, Che Guevara attended school there; after completing high school, Guevara entered the University of Buenos Aires where he studied medicine. In late 1952 he interrupted his studies to embark on an eight-month, 7,500-mile odyssey across five South American countries along with a brief stop in Florida. It was a voyage of adventure and self-discovery for the asthmatic twenty-three-year-old medical student. After returning to Argentina he finished his studies and graduated as a surgeon in 1953 but with little interest in practicing medicine.

Che Guevara's political orientation was the product of his mother's politics in Peronist Argentina, the writings of Chilean Communist poet Pablo Neruda, Peruvian Marxist friend (and later wife), Hilda Gadea, travel experiences in the poorest of Latin American countries, and his conviction that much of Latin America's economic and political ills was due to American **imperialism**. After leaving Argentina for good in 1953, the young Guevara traveled to Guatemala to participate in the reformist regime of Jacobo **Arbenz**. He witnessed the CIA-backed overthrow of the Arbenz regime and came to despise the United States for putting an end to revolution in one of Central America's most backward countries. In the turmoil of the overthrow of Arbenz in 1954, Guevara sought refuge in the Argentine embassy until he was allowed to leave for Mexico City in 1955. While in Mexico City he was introduced to Fidel and Raúl Castro and other members of the July 26th Movement who were planning an expedition to rid Cuba of dictator Batista. He joined Castro's group and became part of a small guerrilla force that traveled by boat to Cuba in 1956. The unsuccessful naval attack resulted in the death of most of the expedition but a few escaped to the Sierra Maestra mountains to continue the revolution. Handsome, selfless, and charismatic, Che Guevara quickly became one of the revolution's top leaders and participated in the final battle that ended the Batista **dictatorship**. After the Battle of Santa Clara, Che Guevara was one of the first rebel commanders to reach Havana and take control of the city.

Although Che Guevara only lived in Cuba for eight years, he played a key role in the early decisions that set the course of the Cuban Revolution. As director of the Industrial Department of the National Institute of Agrarian Reform, president of the National Bank of Cuba, and Minister of Industry, Guevara initiated central economic planning and state ownership of productive enterprises. In the realm of a revolutionary work ethic, Che Guevara pushed for the creation of a "new socialist man" who would be motivated by moral rather than material incentives. His plans to convert Cuba from a sugar-based economy to an industrial one failed, and his moral incentives only had limited appeal. During the first five years of the Cuban Revolution, Che Guevara carried out numerous diplomatic missions—mainly to the Soviet Union and Eastern Europe—to spread his vision of socialist economic development, **anti-imperialism**, and Marxist revolution. The Cuban economy—in the hands of Che Guevara—dismantled the old capitalist system and market-based principles in favor of an economic system of public ownership and state plans. When it became apparent that his economic policies were failing, Che Guevara was removed from his government posts and allowed to put his revolutionary energy into efforts in other parts of the Third World. He traveled to Central Africa where his efforts focused on organizing Congolese rebels; when this proved fruitless, Che Guevara returned to Cuba in 1966, bid Castro and his family farewell, and then left to apply his *foco* theory to Bolivia. He formed an international brigade with the intention of toppling the military government in Bolivia and, in the process, he believed more guerrilla operations would spread across the Andes. According to Guevara, this would force the United States to intervene and spark more Vietnams in the Andes mountains. The Bolivian episode was executed poorly and built on weak assumptions about the exportability of the Cuban experience, and it eventually contributed to Che Guevara's death at the hands of the Bolivian army with the help of supplies and military advisers from the United States. The decision to execute Che was carried out by the Bolivian military, and noncommissioned officers were instructed to carry out the order by drawing straws to see who would put to death the Argentine revolutionary. Although there are several accounts of who actually executed Che, Anderson (1997) claims that when Sergeant Jaime Terán was about to kill Che he exclaimed, "I know you've come to kill me. Shoot, you are only going to kill a man."

The **Clinton** administration declassified a few once-secret documents that reveal a determined effort of U.S. intelligence and military personnel to track and "destroy" Che Guevara's guerrillas in Bolivia. After being captured and executed, his body was buried in a secret grave until 1997 when it was recovered and returned to Cuba. Why did Che Guevara renounce his Cuban citizenship, leave his government posts, and embark on other revolutionary pursuits in Africa and Latin America? In a recent book, Manuel Piñeiro (2001) questions the theories that stress the growing separation/isolation between Che and Fidel and puts more emphasis on a mutual understanding between the two that Che's leadership was required elsewhere. In his farewell letter to Fidel Castro in 1965 (HistoryofCuba.com), Che said, "I feel that I have fulfilled the part of my duty that bound me to the Cuban Revolution on its territory, and I take my farewell of you, my comrades and your people who are now my people." After warm tributes to Fidel for giving him a "revolutionary spirit," Che said, "Other regions of the world claim the support of my modest efforts" and on "new battlefields I [will continue] to fight against imperialism."

For Che Guevara, the Cuban Revolution was the defining experience that confirmed his belief that insurrection was the only way to get rid of dictatorial governments and the oppressive power of the United States over Latin American societies. In *Guerrilla Warfare* (1960) he stressed what he called the *foco* theory of revolutionary development in which he argued that the presence of revolutionary conditions would spark the need for an insurrection. The Cuban experience contributed to the growth of revolutionary movements across Latin America in the 1960s, many of which were crushed by repressive military regimes backed by the

United States. Nevertheless, Che Guevara continues to be an inspiration for mass movements and revolutionaries, as well as a cult figure among many young people, most of whom were born after his death.

The Cubans have devoted a great deal of energy and funds to memorialize Che Guevara, including the Che Guevara Memorial in Santa Clara and the Havana-based Che Guevara Studies Center devoted to the thought, life, and works of the Argentine-Cuban revolutionary. The center is located in the house where Che lived with his family from 1962 until his final departure from Cuba in 1966. The director of the center is Aleida March, his widow and second wife. His son, Camilo, also lives in Havana and helps maintain the true spirit and positive image of his father.

Despite the efforts of many to cash in on Che Guevara's heroic image, his revolutionary legacy is changing with time. While some still remember Che Guevara as a revolutionary figure (heroic Christ-like martyr), others see him as the embodiment of a failed ideology that did more harm than good for Latin America. Others remember him as nothing more than a commercialized image on a T-shirt, watch, key chain, or poster. With the publication of his long-suppressed memoir known as *The Motorcycle Diaries* (1995), Che Guevara is now being portrayed as a romantic and tragic adventurer. The malleability of Che's character and experience suggests that he is a cult figure who can constantly be examined and re-examined as someone who embodies a potent figure of protest and idealism. As much as the Cubans try to exclude everything about Che Guevara that is not heroic, pure or revolutionary, there are those who insist he reflects different qualities. Part of this is the result of a generational split among Latin Americans, particularly younger Latin Americans who consider him too remote and part of a political past of which they have few memories. *See also* Central Intelligence Agency (CIA); Covert Operations; Guerrilla Warfare; Revolutions.

Suggested Reading

Jon Lee Anderson, *Che Guevara: A Revolutionary Life* (New York: Grove Press, 1997); Christopher P. Baker, *Moon Handbooks: Cuba*, 2nd ed. (Emeryville, CA: Avalon Travel, 2000); Jorge Castañeda, *Compañero: The Life and Death of Che Guevara* (New York: Knopf, 1997); Fidel Castro, *Che: A Memoir* (Melbourne, Australia: Ocean Press, 1983); HistoryofCuba.com, "Che's Farewell Letter to Fidel Castro," (www.historyofcuba.com/history/cheltr.htm); Paul S. Dosal, *Comandante Che: Guerrilla Soldier, Commander, and Strategist, 1956–1967* (University Park: Pennsylvania State University Press, 2003); Ernesto Che Guevara, *Guerrilla Warfare*, 3rd ed. (Wilmington, DE: Scholarly Resources, 1960, 1997); Guevara, *The Motorcycle Diaries: A Journey Through South America* (London: Verso, 1995); Guevara, *Reminiscences of the Cuban Revolutionary War* (New York: Pathfinder, 1969); Richard L. Harris, *Death of a Revolutionary: Che Guevara's Last Mission*, rev. ed. (New York: W.W. Norton, 2000); Peter Kornbluh, *The Death of Che Guevara: Declassified* (Washington, DC: George Washington University; National Security Archive, 1997); George Lavan, ed., *Che Guevara Speaks: Selected Speeches and Writings* (New York: Merit Publishers, 1967); Manuel Piñeiro, *Che Guevara and the Latin American Revolutionary Movements* (Melbourne, Australia: Ocean Press, 2001); Michael Ratner and Michael

Steven Smith, eds., *Che Guevara and the FBI: The U.S. Political Police Dossier on the Latin American Revolutionary* (Brooklyn: Ocean Press, 1997); Felix Rodríguez and John Weisman, *Shadow Warrior* (New York: Simon and Schuster, 1989); Henry Butterfield Ryan, *The Fall of Che Guevara* (New York: Oxford University Press, 1997).

Gunboat Diplomacy A form of U.S. **intervention** based on dispatching naval gunboats to hostile ports or coastlines in Latin America and the Caribbean to protect national interests, pursue diplomatic objectives, or avert a loss in an international dispute. Between 1898 and 1934, U.S. naval vessels were ordered to patrol the seas off Caribbean and Central American countries in the throes of revolution or internal political turmoil to quell threats to U.S. strategic or economic interests. The display of force and military resolve was designed to bolster pro–U.S. governments, coerce obedience among warring factions, and help restore order. As a Latin American policy of the United States, many in Washington believed that with a show of U.S. Navy gunboats there would be no need for direct military intervention and occupation. Unfortunately, the threat of naval power did not prevent many of these vessels from acting as agents of armed intervention in early twentieth-century Cuba, Haiti, Honduras, Nicaragua, Mexico, and the Dominican Republic. Although this catchphrase was particularly important during the era of intervention, it has been employed by **Washington policymakers** ever since. Paradoxically, the gunboat diplomacy that provided the United States with its microstate in Panama from 1903 to 2000 did not carry over into further efforts to acquire more territory in Latin America. Although the United States has most frequently resorted to gunboat diplomacy in Latin America and the Caribbean, the application of limited naval force has also occurrred in China, the Mediterranean, Taiwan Straits, Beirut, Iraq, and Serbia.

The use of gunboat diplomacy in Latin America, mostly in the early twentieth century, was attractive to policymakers in Washington because of the small size and weakness of the Latin American states, the legitimacy provided by the **Roosevelt Corollary to the Monroe Doctrine** of 1904, the imperialist attitudes rooted in the expansionism of **Manifest Destiny** and the White Man's Burden, the excitement generated by the drive for national power through naval power, and the strategic importance of the Panama Canal during construction and after its opening in 1914. The use of gunboat diplomacy declined with President **Franklin D. Roosevelt**'s **Good Neighbor Policy** and the creation of other methods such as **covert operations** during the **Cold War**. However, gunboat diplomacy has not disappeared with the end of the Cold War; its frequency and utility have been affected by the growing power of small states to resist and retaliate against the limited use of naval force, technological developments in weaponry, the declining acceptance of outside intervention by international public opinion, and the expanding role of international organizations such as the **United Nations (UN)** and the **Organization of American States (OAS)** that stand in opposition to such violations of national sovereignty. The principal use of gunboat diplomacy today is associated with the enforcement of economic sanctions, particularly where limited naval vessels have access to ports, waterways, and population centers. *See also* Imperialism; Monroe Doctrine (1823); Roosevelt, Theodore.

Suggested Reading

Andrew Graham-Yooll, *Imperial Skirmishes: War and Gunboat Diplomacy in Latin America* (New York: Olive Branch Press, 2002); David Healy, *Gunboat Diplomacy in the Wilson Era: The U.S. Navy in Haiti, 1915–1916* (Madison: University of Wisconsin Press, 1976); Miriam Hood, *Gunboat Diplomacy: Great Power Pressure in Venezuela* (Boston: Allen and Unwin, 1983); Dana Gardner Munro, *Intervention and Dollar Diplomacy in the Caribbean, 1900–1921* (Princeton, NJ: Princeton University Press, 1964).

H

Harding, Warren (1865–1923) Republican politician from Ohio and president of the United States (1921–1923) who rejected progressive reform at home and military involvement in Latin America, which had characterized U.S. policy since the administration of **Theodore Roosevelt**. With a chairman of the board style of governing similar to that of Ronald **Reagan**, Harding would set broad policy guidelines and then leave the details and implementation to members of his cabinet and a few other subordinates. He directed Secretary of State Charles Evans Hughes to initiate a new direction in U.S.–Latin American relations by terminating previous military interventions and occupations, set a tone of conciliation, and shifted the supervision of U.S. troops in the Caribbean from the Department of the Navy to the **State Department**. By dispatching presidential commissions to the Dominican Republic, Haiti, and Cuba, Harding managed to improve the political situation so that U.S. troops could be withdrawn in a peaceful manner. He was only successful in the Dominican Republic where a provisional government paved the way for the withdrawal of U.S. troops in 1924. He also played a key role in settling the oil-claims issue with the revolutionary government of Mexico through the **Bucareli Agreements**, using direct communication with his Mexican counterpart and intermediaries outside of regular diplomatic channels. Although Harding's presidential term was brief, he exerted considerable influence over U.S.–Latin American policy, laying the foundation for the **Good Neighbor Policy** of President **Franklin D. Roosevelt**. *See also* Hoover, Herbert.

Suggested Reading

Warren I. Cohen, *Empire Without Tears: America's Foreign Relations, 1921–1933* (Philadelphia: Temple University Press, 1987); Kenneth J. Grieb, *The Latin American Policy of Warren G. Harding* (Ft. Worth: Texas Christian University Press, 1977).

Hay, John Milton (1838–1905) Historian, diplomat, and secretary of state under Republican presidents William **McKinley** and **Theodore Roosevelt** who influenced U.S.–Latin American relations through the 1903 **Hay-Bunau-Varilla Treaty** with Panama. During the last half of the nineteenth century Hay became a key figure in Republican Party circles, serving as assistant private secretary to President Abraham Lincoln (1861–1865); adviser, ambassador to Great Britain, and secretary of state to William McKinley (1896–1901); and secretary of state in the Theodore Roosevelt administration (1901–1905). As a writer, he worked as an editorialist for the *New York Tribune* and crafted multivolume works on Abraham Lincoln. Born in Salem, Indiana, in 1838, John Hay graduated from Brown University and then studied law in Springfield, Illinois, where he came in contact with Abraham Lincoln. His early connection with Lincoln proved invaluable for advancing his career as a diplomat and writer. Hay's most notable accomplishments were in settling conflicts with Great Britain and the diplomacy associated with the Panama Canal while secretary of state under Theodore Roosevelt.

Working with President Roosevelt, Hay negotiated with Britain, Nicaragua, Colombia, and Panama to unravel the complicated diplomatic knot that would allow the United States to build the canal. First, the United States had to confront the **Clayton-Bulwer Treaty** that called for a joint project with the British in the event a canal was to be constructed. Second, the Colombians displayed little interest in getting rid of their northern province, despite the fact the Panamanians had long struggled to separate from Colombia. The Hay-Pauncefote Treaty (1901) removed the mandated Anglo-American action on the waterway through the isthmus; the Hay-Bunau-Varilla Treaty (1903) provided for an extremely favorable arrangement giving the United States the right to intervene militarily to quell riots and maintain order and the right to take additional lands necessary for the canal's defense. It was Hay's diplomatic work that provided the favorable terms of the treaty for the United States, and the not so favorable terms for the newly independent Panamanians. In a letter to Senator Spooner he confided that the new treaty was "very satisfactory, vastly advantageous to the United States, and we must confess, with what face we can muster, not so advantageous to Panama. . . . You and I know too well how many points there are in this treaty to which a Panamanian patriot could object" (McCullough, 1977: 392). Secretary of State John Hay remained in his post until his death in 1905. *See also* Mahan, Alfred Thayer; Panama Canal Treaties.

Suggested Reading

Kevin Buckley, *Panama: The Whole Story* (New York: Simon and Schuster, 1991); Kenton J. Clymer, *John Hay: The Gentleman as Diplomat* (1975); Walter LaFeber, *The Panama Canal: The Crisis in Historical Perspective*, expanded Ed. (New York: Oxford University Press, 1978); David McCullough, *The Path Between the Seas: The Creation of the Panama Canal, 1870–1914* (New York: Simon and Schuster, 1977); Warren Zimmerman, *First Great Triumph: How Five Americans made Their Country a World Power* (New York: Farrar, Straus, and Giroux, 2002).

Hay-Bunau-Varilla Treaty (1903) Treaty between Panama and the United States that provided for the construction and defense of a isthmian canal across Panama that followed Panama's independence from Colombia. In a strange mixture of diplomacy and intrigue, Secretary of State John **Hay** negotiated a treaty highly favorable to the United States with Panama's French representative Philippe **Bunau-Varilla**. The United States paid Panama $10 million in gold and $250,000 per year beginning nine years after the treaty was ratified by Panama (December 3, 1903). The treaty amounted to a U.S. protectorate over Panama, given the fact that it contained the right to **intervention** and rights as if it were sovereign in perpetuity over a ten-mile wide Canal Zone. The U.S. Senate ratified the treaty in 1904, and it remained in effect—despite controversy, tension, and small adjustments in the annual lease payments—until the **Carter** administration signed two new **Panama Canal Treaties** in 1977 that terminated U.S. control and operation of the canal on December 31, 1999. The U.S. Senate ratification of the new treaties in 1978 contributed to considerable improvement in U.S.–Latin American relations, although relations deteriorated after the election of Ronald **Reagan** in 1980, a staunch foe of those who favored turning over the canal to the Panamanians. *See also* Roosevelt, Theodore.

Suggested Reading

Gustave A. Anguizola, *Philippe Bunau-Varilla: The Man Behind the Panama Canal* (1980); Anguizola, *The Panama Canal: Isthmian Political Instability from 1821–1976* (Washington, DC: University Press of America, 1977); Walter LaFeber, *The Panama Canal: The Crisis in Historical Perspective* (New York: Oxford University Press, 1979); Sheldon Liss, *The Canal: Aspects of United States–Panamanian Relations* (Norte Dame, IN: University of Notre Dame Press, 1976).

Hayes, Rutherford B. (1822–1893) Lawyer, politician, and U.S. president (1877–1881) who devoted most of his single presidential term to domestic issues related to post–Civil War reconstruction. The problems that Hayes faced in Latin America centered on Mexico, U.S. control over any future canal in Panama, and territorial disputes in Venezuela and Paraguay. Rutherford B. Hayes was born in Ohio, graduated from Kenyon College in 1842, and Harvard Law School in 1845. After being admitted to the Ohio bar, Hayes practiced law, and entered politics in Ohio, first as a Whig and later as a member of the new Republican Party in the 1850s. During the U.S. Civil War he rose to the rank of brigadier general and used his war service to launch his political career, first as a representative to the House of Representatives from Ohio followed by two full terms as governor of Ohio. After being elected for a third term in 1875, Hayes' reputation as a national political figure helped him gain the Republican presidential nomination in 1876. The bitter dispute over the outcome of the election required Congress to determine the winner, and Hayes was awarded the presidency by a single electoral vote.

President Hayes had to deal with Mexico after Porfirio Díaz deposed the established government in 1876, but proved to be unable, or unwilling, to stop cross-border raids by Mexicans into U.S. territory. Hayes decided to deal with the problem by withholding diplomatic **recognition**, sending Texas army units in pursuit of the marauders back across the border into Mexico. Hayes' policy of "hot pursuit" helped to convince President Díaz of the seriousness of the conflict, and in 1878 Hayes granted recognition to the dictatorship despite the fact that the raids were not fully suppressed until 1880. The U.S. policy of sending troops to Mexico with the intention of capturing unruly bandits did not result in armed clashes with Mexican forces, a remarkable achievement given the fact that U.S. troops entered Mexican territory at least a dozen times over a span of two years. President Hayes revoked the "hot pursuit" policy in 1880, convinced that the Díaz dictatorship was finally capable of controlling the border raids. The United States insisted that recognition would require an election approved by the Mexican people, an unprecedented move since up until this time the United States had followed Thomas Jefferson's policy of *de facto* recognition of new governments. After Díaz held a legitimizing election, he expressed a desire to cooperate with the United States by signing a treaty stipulating that federal troops from both countries may engage in cross-border raids "when they are in close pursuit of a band of savage Indians" (quoted in Schoultz, 1998: 236). This cooperative spirit improved U.S.–Mexican relations by opening the door to U.S. investors, allowing a vast number of U.S. citizens to gain financial control over the Mexican economy (mining, railroads, land, and petroleum) and considerable political power in both countries. This intrusion of foreign capital and political control during the *Porfiriato* (the long period of the Porfirio Díaz dictatorship) set the stage for the Mexican Revolution beginning around 1910. Poor diplomatic representation and the importance of stability to protect U.S. investments helped prolong the Díaz dictatorship and the eventual uprising that drove him from office in 1911.

The question of who would build a future Central American canal and where became another issue in U.S.–Latin American relations during the Hayes administration. While those in Washington assumed the canal would be built with private U.S. capital, and located in Nicaragua, a French company under the leadership of Ferdinand de Lesseps started to raise funds to build the canal in Panama. President Hayes mounted a challenge to the French project by using **gunboat diplomacy**, demanding full U.S. control of any passageway, and seeking modification of the **Clayton-Bulwer Treaty**.

The territorial disputes between Venezuela and Great Britain over the boundary with British Guiana and Paraguay and Argentina resulted in U.S. involvement because of possible violations of the **Monroe Doctrine** and fear of European threats to U.S. **hegemony** in the Western Hemisphere. After Paraguay's defeat in the Triple Alliance War (1865–1870), it faced the daunting task of rebuilding its economy after one of the greatest military disasters in modern history. According to Wilson and Dent (1998: 175), "Paraguay lost nearly half of its population of 400,000 and close to 80 percent of its male population." To aid in the reconstruction, Paraguay, under a succession of military leaders, courted thousands of immigrants and foreign capital from Europe; however, it continued to be plagued with border disputes, dependency on external development funds, and authoritarian rule. After a border dispute with Argentina in 1878, President Hayes was invited to arbitrate the right of sovereignty over the disputed territory. He ruled in favor of Paraguay, both sides approved the decision, and expressed their appreciation to the United States. As a final gesture of gratitude, Paraguay named a city Villa Hayes and one of its nineteen provinces after the American president. After promising he would not consider a second presidential term, Hayes retired to his Ohio home in 1881 and devoted the rest of his life to philanthropy and public speaking on issues of personal concern to him. *See also* Dictatorships.

Suggested Reading

Joseph Nathan Kane, Janet Podell, and Steven Anzovin, eds., *Facts about the Presidents: A Compilation of Biographical and Historical Information* (New York: H.W. Wilson, 2001); Hans L. Trefousse, *Rutherford B. Hayes* (New York: Times Books, 2002); Larman C. Wilson and David W. Dent, *Historical Dictionary of Inter-American Organizations* (Lanham, MD: Scarecrow Press, 1998).

Hegemony Asymmetries in power have resulted in a state of affairs in U.S.–Latin American relations in which the United States dominates the region through economic, political, and military power. U.S. hegemony has prevailed since the era of **intervention** (1895–1930) when U.S. power in the region replaced British, French, and German influence. With unrivaled hegemony in Latin America and the Caribbean, the United States sought to impose its economic system, social and cultural values, and political ideology. From **World War I** through the **Cold War** the United States was the major hegemon in Latin America. However, after the Cold War ended, the United States experienced a decline in hegemony as the Latin American states began to challenge the United States, offering resistance and disagreement to U.S. policies. The signs of waning U.S. hegemony were evident in the overthrow of dictatorial but pro–U.S. regimes by revolutionary forces in places like Cuba, Nicaragua, Grenada, and Iran. President Jimmy **Carter**'s diplomatic success in altering the hegemony of the United States in Panama also included a provision in the new treaties that permitted unilateral intervention in Panama "in perpetuity." The Cuban Revolution under Fidel **Castro** quickly led to countermeasures to undermine Castro and his constant humiliation of U.S. government officials. Different perceptions of U.S. hegemony were most acute during the presidencies of Jimmy Carter and Ronald **Reagan**. President Carter was often blamed for undermining the hegemony of the United States in Latin America by focusing on human rights and non-intervention; President Reagan tried to counter his predecessor's diplomatic impotency through a controversial doctrine of "peace through strength." Reagan sought to revive U.S. hegemony by promising to rearm the United States, employing military force in support of foreign policy objectives, and exaggerating the security threat posed by the Soviet Union and Cuba. Nevertheless, by the end of Reagan's second term the hegemony of the United States in Latin America was less than when he came to office eight years earlier. The **Iran-**

Contra scandal damaged the United States in Latin America and undermined its ability to provide moral leadership in its opposition to revolutionary regimes associated with what Reagan called the "evil empire."

After the **George W. Bush** administration declared war on **terrorism** in 2001, Latin American and Caribbean leaders resisted Washington's arm-twisting initiatives. The Bush administration found it could not bully Mexico and Chile to support its efforts in dealing with Saddam Hussein's Iraq and only a few countries (El Salvador, Honduras, Nicaragua, and the Dominican Republic) sent small token forces to join the U.S.–led coalition of military forces in Iraq. Foreign policy failures in Haiti, Panama, and Cuba provided ample evidence to critics of U.S.–Latin American policy that the United States faced numerous limits to its ability to dominate Latin American affairs. If a pattern exists in how the United States exercises control over Latin America, the most obvious is that there continues to be a great deal of hegemony over Latin American countries although the level of influence varies based on geographical proximity, U.S. presidential leadership, perceived threats, and the willingness of Latin Americans to take charge of their own destiny. The hegemony of the United States in Latin America is also influenced by how American citizens view the people of Latin America. As Gilderhus (2000: 247) points out, "A sense of menace from the outside seems to have made it easier for them [U.S. leaders] to act upon attitudes characterized by condescension if not outright distaste for Latin Americans." The fact that these negative attitudes have changed little with time means that U.S. hegemony is rooted in both power and cultural attitudes. The staying power of the **Monroe Doctrine** in U.S.–Latin American relations can also be attributed to the perceived connection between hegemony and international credibility. As Lars Schoultz (1998: 368–369) argues, "Once the United States had asserted its hegemony in Latin America, officials in Washington quickly concluded that it was important to retain control for a *symbolic* reason: hegemony over the region became an indicator of U.S. credibility in international relations." Abraham F. **Lowenthal** argues that U.S. policies toward Latin America before the 1980s were based on a "hegemonic presumption" in which practically all aspects of hemispheric life were dominated by the United States. The future of U.S.–Latin American relations is likely to rest on how far the United States is willing to assert its hegemony over the region and the ability of the Latin Americans to assert their independence from the prevailing paternalism in Washington. *See also* Anti-Americanism; Imperialism; Intervention and Non-Intervention; Threat Perception/Assessment.

Suggested Reading

Rosemary Foot, S. Neil MacFarlane, and Michael Mastanduno, eds., *U.S. Hegemony and International Organizations: The United States and Multilateral Institutions* (New York: Oxford University Press, 2003); Mark T. Gilderhus, *The Second Century: U.S.–Latin American Relations Since 1889* (Wilmington, DE: Scholarly Resources, 2000); Robert O. Keohane, *After Hegemony, Cooperation and Discord in International Politics* (Princeton, NJ: Princeton University Press, 1984); Charlotte Ku and Harold K. Jacobson, eds., *Democratic Accountability and the Use of*

Force in International Law (New York: Cambridge University Press, 2003); Walter LaFeber, *The New Empire: An Interpretation of American Expansion, 1860–1898* (Ithaca, NY: Cornell University Press, 1998); LaFeber, *Inevitable Revolutions: The United States in Central America*, 2nd ed. (New York: W.W. Norton, 1993); Thomas J. McCormick and Walter LaFeber, eds., *Behind the Throne: Servants of Power to Imperial Presidents, 1898–1968* (Madison: University of Wisconsin Press, 1993); Joseph L. Nye, *Bound to Lead: the Changing Nature of American Power* (New York: Basic Books, 1990); Lars Schoultz, *Beneath the United States: A History of U.S. Policy Toward Latin America* (Cambridge, MA: Harvard University Press, 1998); Larman C. Wilson and David W. Dent, *Historical Dictionary of Inter-American Organizations* (Lanham, MD: Scarecrow Press, 1998).

Helms, Jesse Alexander, Jr. (1921–) U.S. senator (1974–2003) and a key foreign policy spokesman for a wide range of conservative causes. Although Helms lacked a strong background in foreign policy, he gained notoriety with his arch–anti-Communist beliefs and blunt utterances, and a right-wing staff that helped him block presidential nominations to diplomatic posts and within the **State Department**. During his career, he was bitterly opposed to the **Panama Canal Treaties**, the Nicaraguan **Sandinistas**, Fidel **Castro**'s Cuba, and dozens of appointees who he considered too liberal and not sufficiently anti-Communist to be in charge of U.S.–Latin American relations. At the same time he supported "**friendly dictators**" such as Anastasio **Somoza** Debayle (Nicaragua), Augusto **Pinochet** (Chile), military strongmen in El Salvador such as Major Roberto D'Aubuisson, and the Argentine military junta because of their anti-communism and free-market beliefs. He admired the Nicaraguan **Contras** as much as Ronald **Reagan** and Oliver **North**. Jesse Helms and other conservatives in the U.S. Senate viewed **Carter**'s efforts to revise the U.S. treaty relationship with Panama as another post-Vietnam retreat by those unwilling to exercise the full power of the United States abroad. Whenever Helms thought a State Department nominee was from the **Kissinger** wing of the Republican Party (he called them "Kissinger retreads") and soft on communism, or anyone associated with the Panama Canal "give away," he would engage in delaying tactics to kill their nomination. His open criticism of Thomas Pickering, U.S. ambassador in El Salvador in 1984, over **Central Intelligence Agency (CIA)** interference in the Salvadoran presidential election, sparked a plot by D'Aubuisson supporters to assassinate the ambassador.

Jesse Helms was born in Monroe, North Carolina, attended Wake Forest University, but never graduated. He worked in journalism and broadcasting in Raleigh, North Carolina, before serving as administrative assistant to arch-conservative Senator Wallis Smith. After being elected to the U.S. Senate in 1973, Jesse Helms built a career as a member of the Senate Foreign Relations Committee, first as Republican minority member and then chair of the committee in 1995 after the Republicans won the 1994 congressional elections. With close ties to the anti-Castro **Cuba Lobby** in Miami, Helms managed to capture national attention by crafting the **Helms-Burton** Act, a complex law that passed in 1996 tightening the U.S. embargo against Cuba.

Jesse Helms made up for his lack of knowledge of Latin America—he spoke no Spanish and made few trips to the region—by relying on aides who reflected his Christian fundamentalist beliefs and anti-communism agenda. For over a decade he relied on Deborah De Moss, the daughter of a multimillionaire insurance executive and influential evangelical Christian who traveled to Latin America on her own funds to investigate leaders she considered harmful to U.S. interests. Over the years De Moss put together an information network of generals, politicians, anti-Communist guerrillas, and business executives in Miami and Central America with which she used to advise Helms on appointments and policy issues. With the private investigative information provided by De Moss, Senator Helms could raise hell on a whole host of Latin American issues, from Jean-Bertrand **Aristide** to Fidel Castro and General Manuel **Noriega**. Senator Helms supported brutal right-wing **dictatorships**, and Reagan's Contras, because he believed they provided a bulwark against communism in the Western Hemisphere. Deborah De Moss acquired the name "Death Squad Debbie" for her advice and admiration for despots who agreed with her **Cold War** strategy and tactics. During the eighties and early nineties she traveled to Central America with her own money, often bumping into Helms' paid staffers such as John Carbaugh, Jim Lucier, and Chris Manion while ignoring the advice of respected U.S. ambassadors in the field. De Moss played a key role in helping Helms expose General Noriega's **drug-trafficking** operation in Panama in 1986 and in skewering the **George H.W. Bush** administration in 1989 for botching the attempted October coup against Noriega by Panamanian soldiers. In 1992 she produced a Senate report critical of President Violeta Chamorro's Nicaragua that led President Bush to cut off more than $100 million to the impoverished Central American nation. After marrying a divorced Honduran military officer, De Moss moved to Tegucigalpa where she helps her husband run a political consulting firm. She maintains, "History will prove Helms's position was right on in Latin America—every issue," although it's hard to imagine that the thousands who suffered from the brutality of the **death squads** would agree with her views (Monk, 1994: 51). After retiring in 2003, Jesse Helms continued his vitriol against Fidel Castro through his contacts with the Cuban exile community and derogatory radio messages carried on **Radio Martí**. *See also* Ambassadors; Economic Sanctions; Washington Policymakers.

Suggested Reading

Peter Applebome, "Pit Bull Politician," *New York Times Magazine* (October 28, 1990); Ernest B. Ferguson, *Hard Right: The Rise of Jesse Helms* (New York: W.W. Norton, 1986); Charles Horner, "The Senator They Love to Hate," *Commentary* 93 (January 1992): 51–53; John Monk, "Jesse's Secret Weapon," *The Washingtonian* (September 1994): 41–51.

Helms, Richard McGarrah (1913–2002) Career intelligence and espionage officer who joined the newly formed **Central Intelligence Agency (CIA)** in 1947 and later went on to lead the agency between 1967 and 1973. Considered a **Cold**

War patriot by many, Helms believed in action and maximum loyalty to his intelligence colleagues and his superiors, particularly Presidents Lyndon **Johnson** and Richard **Nixon**. While CIA director he resisted congressional inquiry and oversight and tended to favor covert operations over standard intelligence analysis. He played a role in the foreign policy blunder at the **Bay of Pigs**, assassination plots against Cuban revolutionary Fidel **Castro**, covert action against Chile, and the Watergate affair that destroyed the presidency of Richard M. Nixon.

Richard Helms was born in St. Davids, Pennsylvania, to a wealthy family. His father was a top executive for Alcoa and his maternal grandfather a respected international banker. He grew up in South Orange, New Jersey, but attended high school in Switzerland where he learned to speak German. Helms graduated with top honors from Williams College in 1935, and then began his career as a journalist for the United Press and the *Indianapolis Times*. With an ability to speak German and first-hand knowledge of Europe, Helms was introduced to Adolf Hitler in 1936 and later wrote several articles on the German leader and events in Europe. During **World War II** he served as a navy lieutenant commander and was recruited by the Office of Strategic Services (OSS) to engage in intelligence work on both sides of the Atlantic. His OSS experience and friendships with William J. Donovan and **Allen W. Dulles** helped pave the way for his career as an intelligence professional. Helms' obsession with executive branch secrecy, covert actions, and the protection of those with whom he worked would lead to conflicts inside the executive branch and serious charges from Congress that he failed to give complete and accurate information regarding CIA operations against Chilean president Salvador **Allende**. After being fired from the CIA in 1972, President Nixon nominated him to serve as ambassador to Iran. He served three years in Tehran before ending his career in government service in 1976. Helms claims that he was fired from his CIA post because of his refusal to join the Watergate coverup, then in the hands of Nixon and many of his top officials.

The secret efforts of the United States to prevent the election of socialist Salvador Allende of Chile, and work behind the scenes to undermine his presidency, would generate demands for congressional investigations about the CIA role in the Allende affair. Helms was more interested in protecting sources and secrets than answering probing questions about the U.S. role in Chile. In October 1977, Helms pleaded no contest to federal charges of failing to testify fully before Congress about CIA involvement in Chile and the overthrow of President Allende. He received a suspended two-year prison sentence and a $2,000 fine—paid in full by retired CIA agents—for his inaccurate and incomplete testimony in 1973. Helms felt he was exonerated six years later when President Ronald **Reagan** awarded him the National Security Medal for "exceptionally meritorious service." For many, Richard Helms represents the "dark side" of U.S.–Latin American relations, a top-level policymaker who felt the United States could only feel secure if it tracked down and eliminated "Communists" and other suspected enemies of America. *See also* Assassination; Church Committee Report; Covert Operations; Kissinger, Henry Alfred; Pinochet Ugarte, Augusto.

Suggested Reading

Bart Barnes, "Longtime CIA Director Richard Helms dead at age 89," *Washington Post* (October 24, 2002); William Colby and Peter Forbath, *Honorable Men: My Life in the CIA* (New York, 1978); Richard Helms, *A Look Over My Shoulder: A Life in the Central Intelligence Agency* (New York: Random House, 2003); Thomas Powers, *The Man Who Kept Secrets: Richard Helms and the CIA* (New York: Knopf, 1979); John Prados, *Lost Crusader: The Secret Wars of CIA Director William Colby* (New York: Oxford University Press, 2003); Prados, *Presidents' Secret Wars: CIA and Pentagon Covert Operations from World War II through the Persian Gulf* (New York: W. Morrow, 1986); John Ranelagh, *The Agency: The Rise and Decline of the CIA* (New York: Simon and Schuster, 1986).

Helms-Burton Law (1996) In an effort to punish Fidel **Castro** and overthrow his regime after Soviet troops departed in 1993, members of Congress and Cuban American exiles teamed up to tighten significantly the U.S. embargo against Cuba in 1995–1996. Those in the exile community joined hands with members of Congress to undermine Cuba's economy at a time when it was in its most severe crisis due to the cutoff of Soviet subsidies. By "hitting Castro in the pocketbook," many argued that the regime would collapse and Castro would be deposed at last. In 1995, Senator Jesse **Helms** (R-NC) and Representative Dan Burton (R-Ind.) introduced the Cuban Liberty and Democratic Solidarity Act, a controversial proposal to modify the U.S. embargo and define the future government of Cuba. At first President Bill **Clinton** said he opposed the legislation and would not sign it because its contents clearly violated international law. However, following the Brothers to the Rescue incident in which Cuban jet fighters shot two Cessna aircraft down that had violated Cuban air space, Clinton signed the bill into law knowing how important the state of Florida would be to his re-election that year. The timing could not have been worse for the Clinton administration as its Cuba policy to promote democracy was now in jeopardy. The outcry forced President Clinton to sign the Helms-Burton Act even though the legislation significantly limited the president's power to change U.S. policy toward Cuba in the future. After passage of Helms-Burton, future American presidents would have to seek congressional approval before the embargo could be modified or lifted. After the passage of Helms-Burton, U.S.–Cuba policy was in the hands of the anti-Fidel (pro-embargo) component of the **Cuba Lobby**.

Although Jesse Helms and Dan Burton were able to take credit for the legislation and received large campaign donations from the anti–Castro Lobby in Miami, the law is designed to represent the interests of wealthy Cuban Americans in Florida, including the Bacardi Corporation and the Fanjul family. Both lost considerable property in Cuba and with the help of the U.S. Congress were now looking for retaliatory legislation that would further squeeze the Cuban economy. The Helms-Burton Law (some dubbed it the "Bacardi Rum Protection Law") was concocted by congressional staffers of Jesse Helms and Dan Burton working closely with three Cuban American members of Congress: Ileana Ros-Lehtinen (Florida), Lincoln Díaz-Balart (Florida), and Robert Menéndez (New Jersey). Those who were major property owners in Cuba prior to the nationalization process in the 1960s had a major hand in drafting the legislation, particularly the National Association of Sugar Mill Owners of Cuba and the Bacardi Corporation, one of the largest rum companies in the world. Helms-Burton satisfied those who wanted **regime change** in Cuba, but in doing so the law has brought condemnation upon the United States and international support for the Cuban side of the issue. The legal experts at the **Organization of American States (OAS)** found ten parts of Helms-Burton that violated **international law** and the Pope condemned the law as a violation of **human rights**. Former President Jimmy **Carter** called the law the "stupidest thing my country has done." The law was well publicized in Cuba and helped unite the Cuban people behind the Castro government. Clearly, it was now easier for Fidel Castro to revive the banner of anti-Yankeeism, jail pro-democracy dissents, and blame the United States. According to Jatar-Hausmann (1999: 136), "The Helms-Burton Law in Cuba has had paradoxical results. A law designed to destroy Fidel Castro has in fact done wonders to rally support for his regime at home and abroad."

The Helms-Burton Act is a thirty-nine-page law consisting of four titles. Title I seeks additional sanctions against Cuba, including directives to the secretary of the Treasury to make sure that U.S. directors of international financial institutions like the World Bank or the **Inter-American Development Bank (IADB)** oppose Cuba's admission to those organizations. Title II requires the U.S. president to develop an assistance plan for a future transitional government. In a far-reaching set of "requirements," Title II attempts to dictate the future of Cuba from Washington, not Havana. For example, both Fidel and Raúl Castro are prohibited from participating in the transition government. Title II requires that the new government must make clear commitments to return the properties taken early in the revolution, including those belonging to U.S. citizens and those who were Cuban citizens when their properties were expropriated. Title II also calls for the transition government to cease any interference with **Radio Martí** and Television Martí broadcasts. Title III has generated the most conflict with other nations because of the legal issue of extra-territoriality contained in the law. In one provision, it allows U.S. citizens, former owners of property expropriated by the Castro government, to sue the current investor in the property. U.S. courts can be used to litigate cases that involve "trafficking" in expropriated property. Title IV denies entry into the United States officers of foreign companies that are found to be violation of the Helms-Burton Law. The arrogance of this type of punitive legislation does not seem to bother the United States, despite the fact that it has further legitimized Castro's authority, deepened feelings of distrust against the United States, and revived Cuba's decades of frustrated nationalism. These feelings are captured by the comments of Ricardo Alarcón, president of Cuba's National Assembly: "These Americans, they do not learn. They are now going to tell us how according to *them* we should make a transition and *what* is accepted as a transitional government for them. First, we are not in transition to anything; second, who are they to tell us what we have to do and; third, how can they write in a Law that a transition government should not, I repeat, should not include Fidel or Raúl Castro? What kind of conditioning over a sovereign country is this?" (quoted in Jatar-Hausmann, 1999: 138). It is an open question whether the detailed list of provisions in the Helms-Burton Law will have any impact on a Cuba without Fidel Castro. Over the more than four decades the embargo has been in effect the United States has paid a heavy economic price in keeping U.S. companies from doing business with Cuba. A report by the International Trade Commission in 2001 showed that the U.S. trade embargo against Cuba costs U.S. companies between $652 million and $990 million in potential exports every year. Throughout the duration of the U.S. trade embargo against Cuba—reaching back to the **Dwight D. Eisenhower** administration—estimates place the total financial loss to the United States at $33 billion dollars. The Helms-Burton Law has helped to increase the losses to American businesses. *See also* Economic Sanctions.

Suggested Reading

Julia Jatar-Hausmann, *The Cuban Way: Capitalism, Communism and Confrontation* (West Hartford, CT: Kumarian Press, 1999); Patrick J. Kiger, *Squeeze Play: The United States, Cuba, and the Helms-Burton Act* (Washington, DC: The Center for Public Integrity, 1997); Stephen J. Randall, *A Not So Magnificent Obsession: The United States, Cuba, and Canada from Revolution to the Helms-Burton Law* (Orono, ME: Canadian-American Center, University of Maine, 1998); Joaquín Roy, *Cuba, the United States, and the Helms-Burton Doctrine: International Reactions* (Gainesville: University Press of Florida, 2000); Lars Schoultz, "Blessings of Liberty: The United States and the Promotion of Democracy in Cuba," *Journal of Latin American Studies*, 34 (2002).

Heritage Foundation Washington-based **think tank** with a conservative point of view that was particularly important in defining domestic and foreign policy during the first years of the **Reagan** administration. The hallmark of Heritage advocacy has been a consistent advocate of free-market, supply-side economics, federal tax cuts, a strong national defense, and free trade pacts in the Americas. During the Reagan years it was a strong supporter of Reagan's anti-Communist "freedom fighters" in Nicaragua and advocated a consistent hard-line policy toward **Castro**'s Cuba. It was organized in 1973 by former congressional staffers Edwin Feulner and Paul Weyrich to compete with the more liberal Brookings Institution. With a conservative research agenda, the Heritage Foundation pushed a strong national security position through major conferences and publications, particularly *Policy Review*, the *Executive Memoranda*, and *Backgrounders*. With thousands of experts in its Resource Bank, Heritage managed to get widespread press coverage for its personnel. Known for its ideological zeal, Heritage monographs emphasized international threats to U.S. national security. Until the end of the **Cold War**, the Soviet Union was the major threat to U.S. security in Central America. In *The Bear in the Back Yard: Moscow's Caribbean Strategy* (1987), Timothy Ashby describes the threats posed by the Soviets in Central America and the Caribbean.

The Heritage Foundation gained power over Latin American policy by having a liaison office with the executive branch and various parts of Congress. It produced short, quick analyses that reached the desk of members of Congress on an overnight basis telling them how to vote on key issues. Those who questioned Heritage's methods claimed its research was often unreliable, and it became known more as a lobbying organization than a think tank with a respected group of regional specialists and academic scholars. According to Howard **Wiarda** (1995: 107), "Heritage did not hire senior, established scholars but persons at the senior graduate student level whom it could work hard for several years, pay little, and then discard when it was ready to move on to other issues. In other words, Heritage already had the answers, which could be found in its conservative ideology; it wanted low-level scholars who could provide the rationalizations for policy solutions already decided by Heritage's professional staff."

The Heritage Foundation does not accept any government funding, but it has received generous contributions from prominent individuals and conservative foundations in the United States. In the beginning, Heritage received a $250,000 grant from the Coors Foundation and Company. The John M. Olin Foundation has also been a long-time supporter of the conservative think tank. During the 1980s the Board of Trustees included some of the major conservatives in the United States: Clare Boothe Luce, Lewis E. Lehrman, Cullom Davis, Joseph Coors, Midge Decter, and William E. Simon. Jack Kemp, Jeane **Kirkpatrick**, Richard Allen, and Edwin Meese have been Distinguished Fellows of the foundation. Many attribute the success of Heritage to Edwin Feulner, president of the foundation since 1978. He manages Heritage as a business enterprise and believes the first responsibility of a think tank in Washington is to influence policy. The whole purpose of the Heritage Foundation, according to Feulner, is to tell **Washington policymakers** what we think about the subject, explain what should be done (that is, how to vote), and then tell them why.

Suggested Reading

Timothy Ashby, *The Bear in the Back Yard: Moscow's Caribbean Strategy* (Washington, DC: Heritage Foundation, 1987); Russ Bellant, *The Coors Connection: How Coors Family Philanthropy Undermines Democratic Pluralism* (Boston: South End Press, 1991); Edwin J. Feulner, *Ideas, Think Tanks, and Governments* (Washington, DC: Heritage Foundation, 1985); David M. Ricci, *The Transformation of American Politics: The New Washington and the Rise of Think Tanks* (New Haven: Yale University Press, 1993); James Allen Smith, *The Idea Brokers: Think Tanks and the Rise of the New Policy Elite* (New York: The Free Press, 1991); Cynthia Watson, *U.S. National Security Policy Groups: Institutional Profiles* (Westport, CT: Greenwood Press, 1990); Howard J. Wiarda, "Think Tanks," in David W. Dent, ed., *U.S.–Latin American Policymaking: A Reference Handbook* (Westport, CT: Greenwood Press, 1995).

Herring, Hubert Clinton (1889–1967) Educator, writer, and minister of Congregational churches in the American midwest. He was one of several prominent historians who played a role in the creation and implementation of Latin American policy from 1930 to 1960. Born in Winterset, Iowa, Hubert Herring received his B.A. from Oberlin College in 1911 and his M.A. from Columbia University in

1912. In 1913 he graduated from Union Theological Seminary. Throughout his long career he combined an interest in Latin American history with church-based social activism in Latin America. From 1913 to 1967, he coordinated social awareness and cultural relations for Congregational churches in Wisconsin and Kansas. Beginning in the late 1920s, he directed annual seminars in Mexico, Central America, and the Caribbean. Between 1944 and 1967 he was professor of Latin American civilization at Claremont College and Pomona College in California. While working for the Congregational Church in 1926, Professor Herring organized one of the early solidarity groups opposed to U.S. **intervention** in Mexico. Under the auspices of the Congregational Church, Herring's idea was to take opinion leaders to Mexico where they would meet with Mexican citizens and public officials and then return home to lobby Congress on behalf of non-intervention. Herring's Committee on Cultural Relations with Latin America (CCRLA) was credited with taking over 200 opinion leaders to witness Mexico first hand and then serve as advocates for peace and non-intervention.

Hubert Herring wrote several books on Latin America, including *America and the Americas* (1944) and *A History of Latin America* (1955; revised edition, 1967), each reflecting his wide-ranging interest and frequent visits to the region where he made friends with Latin American political leaders and a cross-section of people in the Western Hemisphere. His unorthodox educational background, constant travel in the region, and excellent teaching skills allowed him to introduce countless students to the study of Latin American history and politics.

Although considered left-of-center by most historians, Herring's beliefs of Latin American inferiority and immaturity were in line with most writers at the time. Herring's lectures seemed tailor-made to form a positive view of Mexico and Mexicans, but he joined in the chorus of repeating the negative stereotypes of Mexicans in *Good Neighbors: Argentina, Brazil, Chile and Seventeen Other Countries* (1941: 306):

> There are some things which any American knows about all Mexicans: Mexicans are bandits, they carry guns, they make love by moonlight, they eat food which is too hot, and drink which is too strong, they are lazy, they are communists, they are atheists, they live in mud houses and play the guitar all day. And there is one more thing which every American knows: that he is superior to every Mexican. Aside from these items the atmosphere between Mexico and the United States is mild and friendly.

Some of his students admired his enthusiasm, clear presentation of material, and non-prejudicial views of the people of Latin America. However, the citation printed above does suggest that his firsthand knowledge of Mexico did not prevent him from passing along negative stereotypes of the people and culture of Mexico. Hubert C. Herring died of a heart attack in 1967. *See also* Intervention and Non-Intervention; Propaganda; Race and Racism.

Suggested Reading

Britton, John A., *Carleton Beals: A Radical Journalist in Latin America* (Albuquerque: University of New Mexico Press, 1987); Hubert C. Herring, *A History of Latin America from the Beginning to the Present*, 2nd ed., revised (New York: Knopf, 1961); Herring, *America and the Americas* (Claremont, CA: Claremont College, 1944); Herring, *Good Neighbors: Argentina, Brazil, Chile and Seventeen Other Countries* (New Haven: Yale University Press, 1941).

Hickenlooper Amendment (1962) After the Cuban Revolution the United States faced the problem of expropriation of U.S.–owned property in Latin America and sought ways to remedy the situation with punitive legislation. These were driven by corporate lobbying efforts to use the power of the U.S. government to resist and punish expropriation attempts. The Hickenlooper Amendment to foreign assistance legislation tried to prevent a recurrence of such acts. In response to legal efforts to protect the **United Fruit Company** from possible expropriation by the Honduran government, Monroe Leigh, a Washington lawyer, was hired to protect the interests of the company with the assistance of the U.S. government. Senator Bourke Hickenlooper (R-Iowa) sponsored an amendment to the Foreign Assistance Act of 1961 that tried to prevent uncompensated nationalizations by giving the president of the United States the power to "suspend assistance to the government of any country to which assistance is provided under the Act when the government of such country has" nationalized or seized control of the property of a U.S. citizen or corporation. The Hickenlooper Amendment also called for suspension when the government "has imposed or enforced discriminatory taxes or other exactions" and failed to provide for speedy compensation within a reasonable time. The **Kennedy** administration tried to prevent the passage of the amendment, arguing that it would impede the implementation of the **Alliance for Progress**; however, the amendment passed and expanded in 1994 when Congress required U.S. government representatives serving on the boards of international lending agencies (World Bank, **Inter-American Development Bank [IADB]**, etc.) to vote against providing funds to governments caught in a suspension according to the original 1962 legislation. *See also* Calvo Clause; Dollar Diplomacy.

Suggested Reading

Robert H. Holden and Eric Zolov, eds., *Latin America and the United States: A Documentary History* (New York: Oxford University Press, 2000); Harold Molineu, *U.S. Policy Toward Latin America: From Regionalism to Globalism* (Boulder, CO: Westview Press, 1986).

Hoover, Herbert (1874–1964) Engineer, international relief administrator, and president of the United States (1929–1933) who repudiated U.S. **intervention** in Latin America and spoke of the importance of being a good neighbor in the region. As secretary of commerce (1921–1928), Hoover developed an increasing dissatisfaction with previous Latin American policies, particularly the right to pre-emptive military intervention contained in the **Roosevelt Corollary to the Monroe Doctrine**. However, Hoover's foreign policy initiatives were halted by the October 1929 stock market crash and the economic downturn that returned the House of Representatives to the Democratic Party. Herbert Hoover's efforts to improve U.S. relations with Latin America are often overshadowed by the Great Depression, but he is recognized for being one of the main contributors to the **Good Neighbor Policy**. He was the first president to directly challenge **Big Stick diplomacy** by redirecting U.S. policy away from military occupation toward increased economic relations. By denouncing pre-emptive military intervention in favor of wide-ranging foreign trade and investment, Hoover helped improved economic and diplomatic relations.

Born in Iowa, Herbert Hoover was orphaned after the death of his mother in 1884 and moved to Oregon where he was raised by relatives. He graduated from Stanford University in 1895 and began a career as a mining engineer. His independent mining ventures took him to far off lands where he gained considerable wealth and international recognition. According to Gilderhus (2000: 72), "During his career as an engineer working in other countries, he had acquired more international experience than any president since **John Quincy Adams**." During **World War I** he served as head of the Private American Relief Committee that provided assistance for the 120,000 Americans stranded in Europe by the war hostilities. He formed a committee to provide humanitarian assistance to German-occupied Belgium. Before becoming secretary of commerce in 1921, Hoover served as U.S. wartime food administrator and head of the America Relief Administration that provided emergency food assistance to war-ravaged Europe. He ran on the Republican ticket for president in 1928 and easily won over his Democratic rival Alfred E. Smith. Before his inauguration he made a tour of Latin America—Honduras, El Salvador, Nicaragua, Costa Rica, Ecuador, Peru, Chile, Argentina, Uruguay, and Brazil—for the purpose of establishing friendly relations with what he called "our neighbors to the south." His positive rhetoric—shared understanding, mutual respect, non-intervention, and equality among states—brought disbelief to those who listened to the future president, but the actual deeds that followed established Hoover as one of the principal founders of the Good Neighbor Policy.

Hoover's Latin American policy, albeit short in duration, was considered highly successful. One of the most forceful advocates of non-intervention, Hoover refused all requests for armed intervention, disengaged militarily from Nicaragua and developed similar plans for Haiti, and criticized diplomats and businessmen for political meddling. As a proponent of peace, Hoover attempted to settle border disputes in South America but was not successful. The Hawley-Smoot tariff of 1930 that was enacted by the Republican-controlled Congress to safeguard domestic markets was a disaster for Latin American economies that suffered export earning declines and the lack of access to international money markets. After some delay in making the report public, Hoover instructed the U.S. **State Department** to publish the **Clark Memorandum** repudiating the Roosevelt Corollary to the Monroe Doctrine that had justified U.S. intervention in Latin America since 1904. Herbert Hoover won renomination for president by the Republican Party but was defeated by **Franklin D. Roosevelt** in the 1932 election. After leaving office, he oversaw the development of the Hoover Institution on War, Revolution, and Peace at Stanford University and served as chairman of a number of committees that recommended ways to improve the organization of the federal government. *See also* Friendly Dictators; Intervention and Non-Intervention.

Suggested Reading

Earl R. Curry, *Hoover's Dominican Diplomacy and the Origins of the Good Neighbor Policy* (New York: Garland, 1979); Alexander DeConde, *Herbert Hoover's Latin-American Policy* (Stanford, CA: Stanford University Press, 1951); Mark T. Gilderhus, *The Second Century: U.S.–Latin American Relations Since 1889* (Wilmington, DE: Scholarly Resources, 2000); Lewis L. Gould, *The Modern American Presidency* (Lawrence: University Press of Kansas, 2003).

Hull, Cordell (1871–1955) Lawyer and secretary of state for twelve years during the presidency of **Franklin D. Roosevelt** who used his power and influence over the U.S. Congress to push for better relations with Latin America. Hull was an energetic supporter of reciprocal trade agreements and a firm believer in the importance of demonstrating to Latin American nations the U.S. commitment to a policy of non-intervention. As one of the architects of Roosevelt's **Good Neighbor Policy**, Hull was instrumental in providing a foundation for the high degree of solidarity in inter-American relations that occurred during **World War II**. Although his clout in Washington was diminished by his quarrels with Undersecretary of State Benjamin Sumner **Welles**, Hull played a major role in planning for the **United Nations (UN)** and received the Nobel Prize in 1945 for his work on this important organization. Hull was often cautious in his diplomatic work, always in search for ways to meet the concerns of the Latin American states while at the same time ensuring that U.S. interests were protected. For example, he accepted the idea of non-intervention in principle, but he also insisted on ambiguous language that retained for the United States the right to intervene militarily in the event that U.S. citizens and property were threatened. Hull was not bothered by consequences of withdrawing U.S. military forces as part of the Good Neighbor Policy, namely, the replacement of U.S. military forces with corrupt and repressive **dictatorships** such as Anastasio Somoza García (Nicaragua) and Rafael **Trujillo** (Dominican Republic), now protected by Washington's pledge to avoid the interventionist mistakes of the past. Cordell Hull continued his interest in foreign affairs after retiring from the **State Department** in 1944 until his death in Bethesda, Maryland in 1955. *See also* Intervention and Non-Intervention.

Suggested Reading

Michael A. Butler, *Cautious Visionary: Cordell Hull and Trade Reform, 1933–1937* (Kent, OH: Kent State University Press, 1998); Justo Carillo, *Cuba 1933: Students, Yankees, and Soldiers* (New Brunswick, NJ: Transaction Publishers, 1994); Harold Boaz Hinton, *Cordell Hull, A Biography* (Garden City, NY: Doubleday, 1942); Randall B. Woods, *The Roosevelt Foreign Policy Establishment and the "Good Neighbor": The United States and Argentina, 1941–1945* (New York: Cambridge University Press, 1979).

Human Rights The history of U.S.–Latin American relations has always contained some reference to human rights, usually understood as the right of humans to enjoy certain protections by virtue of being human. The rights of man are often complicated by contrasting definitions, political ideologies, and methods of application. The United States has made the protection of human rights a part of its national identity, emphasizing the individual's right to pursue religious, political, and personal liberty. These are enshrined in the Declaration of Independence and the first ten amendments of the U.S. Constitution. Americans are taught to believe that the United States is so advanced in its pursuit of political freedom, civil liberties, and individual rights that it can easily serve as a model of human rights protection around the globe. In its relations with Latin America, the United States has found that its security interests must often outweigh any ethical considerations in dealing with foreign governments that place less value on freedom and democracy in favor of collective well-being and social harmony. Furthermore, **Washington policymakers** are often tempted to use the rhetoric of freedom, democracy, and self-determination to mask policies that involved **intervention** and support for repressive authoritarian regimes.

During the nineteenth century the United States paid little attention to the internal rights that existed among Latin American governments, reasoning that it was better to remain uninvolved in the affairs of independent states. The expansion of the frontier emphasized America's civilizing mission under the banner of **Manifest Destiny** and the White Man's Burden; until the **Spanish-Cuban-American War** of 1898, there was little interest in human rights and political freedom. Of primary concern was to protect U.S. economic interests and prevent European powers from intruding on the U.S. sphere of influence. Local oligarchs and military dictators were acceptable as long as they supported U.S. objectives in Latin America.

Between **World War I** and **World War II** human rights remained an insignificant issue in dealing with Latin America. Latin American governments that mistreated their own citizenry within their own boundaries were considered to be exercising a sovereign prerogative. The horrors of World War II brought human rights into the main stream of American foreign policy, resulting in changes in international law to protect the rights of humans. The U.S. commitment to human rights has evolved over the past sixty years from the passing of resolutions declaring human rights to be important and their protection desirable, to binding legal obligations approved by international organizations' that apply to all member states, for example, the **Organization of American States (OAS)**. The initial major American commitment to human rights was made near the end of World War II in a resolution adopted on the "International Protection of the Essential Rights of Man" at the inter-American conference in Mexico City in 1945. It was approved as a declaration, but not as a convention, in 1948 at the same time the OAS was being created in Bogotá, Colombia. It marked a major step in transforming human rights from a morally to a legally binding commitment. The **United Nations (UN)** adopted the Universal Declaration of Human Rights, but there are democratic governments, including the United States, Britain, and France that have refused to incorporate many of the declaration's principles into their own constitutional structures.

While the OAS and the UN turned their attention to the protection and promotion of human rights during the **Cold War**, the United States adopted a rhetorical and self-interest approach to international human rights. When the values inherent in the **Good Neighbor Policy** gave way to Cold War realism, the United States emphasized anti-communism over human rights. The **friendly dictators** who supported the United States during the Cold War were considered "evil" and unfortunate, but they served a vital national purpose and their human rights abuses were excused as the price for preserving economic and political freedom. The Vietnam War, support for friendly autocrats, and covert interventions to democratically elected heads of state, brought human rights back to domestic politics and in the pursuit of morality in foreign policy. After the debacle over Salvador **Allende**'s Chile, Congress recommended linking human rights concerns to U.S. foreign policy. The use of **covert operations** to remove Allende and the military violence that followed increased the saliency of human rights in American foreign policy.

It took the Jimmy **Carter** administration to elevate human rights concerns in dealing with Latin America. He made it a cornerstone of his foreign policy, reducing military aid to Argentina and Uruguay, publicly denouncing governments that violated human rights, and using international organizations to condemn military regimes. President Carter's attention to human rights stood in stark contrast to statements by Secretary of State Henry **Kissinger** who publicly reprimanded the U.S. ambassador to Chile for even addressing the issue of human rights in private discussions. In Central America, Carter distanced the United States from its traditional support of the **Somoza dictatorship** and supported the 1979 coup by reformist military officers in El Salvador. Carter's human rights efforts were only partially successful, as the United States continued to support "friendly dictators" around the world because of geopolitical and economic interests.

When Ronald **Reagan** came to power in 1981, his administration tried to reverse the Carter policy on human rights by stressing security, **terrorism**, and stability. Relations with the often brutal military dictatorships in Central and South America returned to cordiality and cooperation. The Reagan administration found that it was not possible to avoid human rights issues in its foreign policy as the language of human rights in international relations had been changed permanently by the Carter presidency. The policymaking environment now consisted of newly created non-government organizations with advocacy skills that countered Reagan's new Cold War vision. The U.S. Congress also weighed in by insisting that the executive branch certify that massive human rights violations were not taking place before economic and military assistance could be provided. President Reagan faced some of the same difficulties in applying human rights principles as Jimmy Carter. In fact, Reagan was more selective than Carter in condemning human rights violations in the Soviet Union, Cuba, and Nicaragua while excusing human rights violations in other parts of the world. By the time **George H.W. Bush** took over in 1989, human rights principles had achieved a permanent place in American foreign policy. Many questioned whether Ronald Reagan's interest in applying human rights to foreign policy was authentic or merely a rhetorical prop to achieve other objectives. As Cohn points out (1995: 443), President Reagan's "objective in Nicaragua was always to oust the **Sandinistas**, not to improve their human rights record, and in El Salvador, Reagan was more concerned with prosecuting the war against guerrillas than with ending abuses. Reagan employed human rights as a tool in a larger war, not simply an end in itself."

The rhetoric of American foreign policy changed after the Cold War as Presidents George H.W. Bush, Bill **Clinton**, and **George W. Bush** faced new challenges and devised different ways to further U.S. interests in Latin America. George H.W. Bush made few references to the value of human rights and instead spoke of the importance of "free trade" and the importance of militarizing the war on drugs, particularly in South America. Latin America's importance to the United States declined further during the Clinton and George W. Bush presidencies, although Clinton was forced to deal with problems of immigration, drugs, and trade. Beginning with President Clinton, American presidents began to grapple with a "use of force" doctrine and the question of how to expand democratic rule in the post–Cold War world. There are elements of President Woodrow **Wilson**'s civilizing missions to bring "freedom" and "democracy" to Latin America in the rhetorical ploys carried out by Clinton and Bush. Unfortunately, it is far more difficult to spread democracy when the global trends show less interest in market-oriented democracies than many of the military-minded civilians in the government understand or want to admit. U.S.–Latin American relations are undermined by the fact that human rights are of much less importance than economic, security, and domestic political interests. Latin American leaders find it difficult to accept official human rights and freedom rhetoric when individuals such as Elliott **Abrams** and John **Negroponte** and Otto **Reich** are appointed repeatedly to foreign policy positions after having helped administer policies devised in Washington that violated human rights in Latin America. To make matters worse, some of those responsible for human rights violations in Latin America have been allowed to establish residency in the United States. In its 2003 human rights report, Amnesty International estimated that 1,000 human rights violators were living in the United States, including many from Latin American countries.

Suggested Reading

Jaime Behar, ed., *Inequality, Democracy, and Sustainable Development in Latin America* (Stockholm, Sweden: Institute of Latin American Studies, 2000); Virginia Bouvier, ed., *The Globalization of U.S.–Latin American Relations: Democracy, Intervention and Human Rights* (Westport, CT: Praeger, 2002); Colin Campbell and Bert A. Rockman, eds., *The Clinton Legacy* (New York: Chatham House, 2000); Elizabeth Cohn, "Human Rights," in David W. Dent, ed., *U.S.–Latin American Policymaking: A Reference Handbook* (Westport, CT: Greenwood Press, 1995); Tom J. Farer, *The Grand Strategy of the United States in Latin America* (New Brunswick,

NJ: Transaction Books, 1988); Manuel Antonio Garretón and Edward Newman, eds., *Democracy in Latin America: (re) constructing Political Society* (New York: United Nations University Press, 2001); Richard S. Hillman, John A. Peeler, and Elsa Cardozo da Silva, eds., *Democracy and Human Rights in Latin America* (Westport, CT: Praeger, 2002); Julie A. Mertus, *Bait and Switch: Human Rights and U.S. Foreign Policy* (New York: Routledge, 2004); Guillermo O'Donnell, *Polyarchies and the (un)rule of Law in Latin America* (Notre Dame: Helen Kellogg Institute for International Studies, 1998); Riordan Roett, ed., *Latin America in a Changing Global Environment* (Boulder, CO: Lynne Rienner, 2003); Lars Schoultz, *Human Rights and United States Policy Toward Latin America* (Princeton, NJ: Princeton University Press, 1981); David Sheinin, ed., *Beyond the Ideal: Pan Americanism in Inter-American Affairs* (Westport, CT: Greenwood Press, 2000).

I

IADB. *See* Inter-American Development Bank

ICC. *See* International Criminal Court

ICJ. *See* International Court of Justice

Imperialism Imperialism is a multifaceted concept in international relations that refers to a nation's forcible extension of its control over other societies through such means as military occupation, colonization, protectorates, favorable treaties, friendly elites, proconsul **ambassadors**, economic exploitation, and cultural domination. At the time of its independence, President George Washington warned of the dangers of the United States becoming involved in "foreign entanglements." However, signs of an imperialist foreign policy began to take shape in the early part of the nineteenth century as the U.S. desire to move westward expanded. Despite times in which the American people endorsed the concept of empire, most Americans feel ambivalent about imperial possessions. Prior to the **Spanish-Cuban-American War** in 1898, imperialism flourished under the expansionist doctrine of **Manifest Destiny** as the United States acquired a taste for more territory and control over Latin America and the Caribbean. Racist theories contributed to the imperialist sentiments of the time with many arguing that Anglo-Saxon superiority obligated the United States to assume the White Man's Burden of carrying civilization and progress to "backward" areas and "inferior" peoples in Latin America. This early form of American imperialism—learned from the Europeans—justified itself as a civilizing mission, one that would take time to inculcate the habits of self-discipline in "lesser breeds" for the eventual capacity of self-rule. By the 1890s, a group of top-level business executives, politicians, newspapermen, and naval officers pushed for territorial expansion in an effort to establish the U.S. claim to hegemony in the Western Hemisphere. Zimmermann (2002) examines the lives of five powerful figures of the time—Alfred T. **Mahan**, **Theodore Roosevelt**, Henry Cabot **Lodge**, John **Hay**, and Elihu **Root**—who endorsed expansionism, war, overseas possessions, and naval bases because of strategic and commercial considerations. The explosion that destroyed the battle ship *Maine* while in Havana harbor in 1898, killing 242 sailors, gave U.S. imperialists the opportunity they had been waiting for in the same way neo-conservatives were energized to pursue hegemonic control overseas by the attacks on the United States on **September 11, 2001**.

The major imperial interests of the United States lay in the Caribbean basin where the chronic disorder and fiscal instability were drawing European powers into the U.S. sphere of influence. It was during the nineteenth century that the United States fought a war with Mexico (1846–1848), launched **filibustering** expeditions to acquire more slave territory in Cuba, Mexico, and Nicaragua, and attempted to purchase more national territory. The **Mexican-American War** brought the United States victory and close to a doubling of its national territory. However, the filibustering expeditions were failures as were other imperialist ventures in Latin America. These early imperialist policies spawned opposition and divided the nation into imperialist and anti-imperialist factions. Anti-imperialists opposed the war with Mexico, President Ulysses Grant's efforts to annex the Dominican Republic, filibustering expeditions, **intervention**, and presumptions of American hegemony. President Theodore Roosevelt supported a Panamanian rebellion against Colombia in hopes that the rebels would cede rights for land to build a canal across the Isthmus of Panama.

In the quest for order in Latin America and the Caribbean, some **Washington policymakers** rejected the notion that the United States conducted an imperialist foreign policy, arguing that it was the shortcomings of Latin Americans that obligated the United States to intervene. Dana Munro, a **State Department** specialist on Latin America in the early twentieth century, argued that **revolutions** and financial crises were the cause of U.S. intervention. In other words, the United States intervened for the benefit of Latin Americans, not because of an American desire for control or domination. The anti-imperialists argued that it was immoral and inhumane to impose a government on foreign lands.

The imperialists who controlled Latin American policy at the turn of the nineteenth century embraced the theories of Social Darwinism, the assertion of Anglo-Saxon superiority, and the need for expanded sea power to seek out overseas markets, raw materials, and investment opportunities. The Spanish-Cuban-American War brought the United States victory over Spain that would contribute to U.S. control over Cuba, Puerto Rico, Guam, and the Philippine Islands. Between 1902 and 1904, the United States had created protectorates over Cuba and Panama, both through treaties that granted Washington the right of military intervention. After 1900, U.S. imperialism was characterized by the extension of influence rather than territorial aggrandizement. With the **Roosevelt Corollary to the Monroe Doctrine**, the United States embarked on a policy of protective imperialism for Latin America, carrying a Big Stick to assert U.S. dominance in the region (see **Big Stick Diplomacy**). The goal for much of the twentieth century was to prevent the expansion of hostile foreign influence in the chronically unstable and fiscally corrupt Latin American nations. This was accomplished with the **Monroe Doctrine** and its various corollaries, U.S. military intervention and occupation, **Dollar Diplomacy**, customs receiverships, protectorates, and economic dominance. Early twentieth-century imperialism in Latin America was also concerned with protecting the Panama Canal and the vital sea lanes that connected Latin America's raw materials to the industrial demands of the United States.

The imperialists at the turn of the century were mostly Washington insiders committed to making the United States into a world power. However, there were numerous anti-imperialists who argued against the motives and goals of the imperialists. The anti-imperialists included such dignitaries as Andrew **Carnegie**, Mark Twain, Samuel Gompers, Charles W. Elliot, and Carl Shurz. The anti-imperialists believed that the United States would surrender its heritage by denying freedom and self-government to people who deserved it. For Roosevelt and his imperialist friends, it was too late to reverse the noble consequences of Manifest Destiny and the desire for global power. Until recently, the American left has been the most vociferous critic of imperialist ventures while the right has been far less likely to oppose imperialist ventures in Latin America. After **World War I** and the Mexican Revolution, U.S. imperialism went through a metamorphosis in which financial protectorates were abolished, military occupations were ended, and the right to intervention embodied in the Monroe Doctrine and various treaties was denounced and repudiated. This retrenchment came about as the result of growing **anti-imperialism**, the Great Depression, the **Good Neighbor Policy**, and the creation of **friendly dictators**. The U.S. support for right-wing **dictatorships** was based on the belief that authoritarian rule was the best route to democracy and stability. Many in Washington failed to grasp the inherent contradiction in supporting authoritarians solely on the basis that they were perceived to be on our side. Secretary of State Charles Evans Hughes rejected the suggestion that U.S.–Latin American policy was imperialistic. Our interests, he often explained, are rooted in having prosperous, peaceful, and law-abiding neighbors in Latin America; the United States was forced to intervene, not because it was interested in controlling peoples, but because of the shortcomings—revolution, bloodshed, disorder, inferiority—of Latin Americans. It was only because of revolutions and financial crises that the United States intervened in Latin America and only for the benefit of the Latin Americans.

During the **Cold War**, the Good Neighbor Policy was replaced with imperialism based on anti-communism, foreign policies that required **covert operations**, military intervention, and counter-revolutions against perceived Soviet, Chinese, and Cuban threats to Latin America. To protect the Western Hemisphere from the threat of communism, the United States resurrected the Monroe Doctrine and returned to imperialist policies of the past. Anti-communism became the unifying theme of American foreign policy, and the principal justification for supporting right-wing dictators such as Fulgencio **Batista** (Cuba), Rafael **Trujillo** (Dominican Republic), Alfredo Stroessner (Paraguay), the Duvaliers (Haiti), and Anastasio Somoza García (Nicaragua). Despite the end of the Cold War in 1989–1990, the ideological, economic, and racial arguments used to justify U.S. imperialism in Latin America and elsewhere have not disappeared from the minds of Washington policymakers.

After President **George W. Bush** became president in 2001 a new form of imperialism took shape to deal with terrorist threats. The new form of imperialism offered several goals and objectives that suggested a radically different foreign policy for the twenty-first century. The first focused on the need to empower local elites while at the same time making sure that real power remained in Washington or in military enclaves abroad. Driven by a tight-knit group of military-minded civilian neo-conservatives, a new imperial fever swept Washington while pushing for a vision of global U.S. military dominance. Instead of the U.S. Department of State as a key player in defining American foreign policy, the Pentagon would now be the major player in world politics. The war on **terrorism** and efforts to dismantle Saddam Hussein's military power would replace the old imperialism, domination based on deterrence, sporadic military intervention, economic assistance, military alliances, and **propaganda**. The new imperialism would require new military alliances (and overseas bases), new legal institutions, a new model of international development organizations, and a heightened awareness of "**blowback**" from misguided official rhetoric and policies. Since September 11, 2001, the United States has asserted a level of global power and imperialism designed to suit American objectives. The places where the new imperialism has been at work to restore order and eliminate terrorism is faced with much of the dilemmas of the past, but with far more emphasis on an exit strategy that will return the imperial conquest back to the locals while at the same time retaining real power in Washington. The failure to stabilize Iraq in the aftermath of the U.S. invasion in 2003 brought forth a second principle directed at Bush's imperialist adventures in the Middle East. In a speech commemorating the twentieth anniversary of the **National Endowment for Democracy (NED)**, President Bush announced a grand theory of democratic imperialism where the United States would cease supporting non-democratic allies "because stability cannot be purchased at the expense of liberty." At the core of his speech was a repudiation of "sixty years of accommodating the lack of freedom in the Middle East," claiming that Cold War realism "did nothing to make us safe." Liberal **human rights** activists applauded the president's critique of supporting friendly tyrants in the name of security and stability, but pointed out that proposing a theory of world democratization is likely to be far easier than putting such a radical policy into effect.

This new empire-building tied to the invasion and occupation of Iraq has sparked a growing body of foreign policy scholars and analysts—whose political views cover the whole ideological spectrum—opposed to the imperial policies pursued by President George W. Bush. This coalition of anti-imperialists hopes to challenge those who support President Bush's imperial policies, beginning with its national security strategy of "pre-emptive" war aimed at U.S. military domination. The basic critique of the new anti-imperialists is that the pursuit of empire both subverts the freedoms and liberties of citizens at home, undermines the will of people abroad, and threatens to entangle the United States in a wide variety of unnecessary and unrewarding wars. The new coalition of anti-imperialists hopes to counter the pro-imperial and pro-war voices that have dominated television and radio since September 11, 2001.

After more than four decades, the U.S. desire to punish and humiliate Fidel **Castro** has not ended and the desire to maintain (imperial) control over the island still radiates from Washington. At the time of any future **regime change** in Cuba, the United States has passed legislation (**Helms-Burton Act**) stating that Fidel, and his brother Raúl, are to be ineligible for leadership positions in a new Cuba. If Fidel Castro dies, or is toppled by some internal revolt, the essence of the new imperialism would be to make sure that the new Cuban elites are receptive to the dictates of American imperial forces once they have departed the island. If this is the outcome, Cuban nationalism will once again face the same dilemma of their forefathers who were forced to swallow the **Platt Amendment**, a serious compromise to the strong-felt desire of Cubans to free themselves of alien domination, and the task of the United States to elevate its interests above the sovereignty of the Cuban state.

The war on terrorism has helped to expand the imperial power of the United States around the globe; however, Washington is having a hard time figuring out how to be a successful empire while pretending that one does not exist. Critics charge that the United States is afraid to raise the flag of imperial domination or remain too long on foreign soil. Niall Ferguson, author of *Empire*, argues that the United States has systematically pursued an imperial policy since the Spanish-Cuban-American War in 1898 while at the same time trying to hide or mask its hegemonic efforts. "It's simply a suspension of disbelief by Americans. They think they're so different that when *they* have [military] bases in foreign territories, it's not an empire. When *they* invade sovereign territory, it's not an imperial policy" (quote in Dowd, 2003: A31). There has always been a certain ambivalence among the American public and Washington policymakers toward imperialistic policies. The American public is willing to support policies that prevent the outbreak of conflicts and maintain stability in the world because they feel a moral imperative to act against violence, aggression, and harmful dictators. There has never been a broad public outcry over U.S. actions to police events in Latin America. However, the American public is distrustful of economic assistance, costly foreign adventures, and the folly of military domination and occupation of foreign lands. There is also little public support for the difficult job of converting dictatorships into pluralist democracies, either in Latin America or around the world. Nevertheless, some believe that the United States has developed into a "liberal empire" based on the morality and truth of its imperial mission abroad. According to legal scholar Linda

Bishai (2004: 51), "In this form of liberalism, which has taken root particularly in America, might does not *make* right, might *is* right (because it is in the hands of the good)." *See also* Democracy and Democracy Promotion; International Law; Intervention and Non-Intervention.

Suggested Reading

Jules R. Benjamin, *The United States and Cuba: Hegemony and Dependent Development* (Pittsburgh: University of Pittsburgh Press, 1977); Linda Bishai, "Liberal Empire," *Journal of International Relations and Development*, Vol. 7 (2004); Maureen Dowd, "Hypocrisy & Apple Pie," *New York Times* (April 30, 2003): A31; Philip S. Foner and Richard C. Winchester, eds., *The Anti-Imperialist Reader: A Documentary History of Anti-Imperialism in the United States* (New York: Holmes and Meier, 1984); Richard N. Haass, *Intervention: The Use of American Military Force in the Post–Cold War World*, rev. ed. (Washington, DC: Brookings Institution Press, 1999); David Healy, *U.S. Expansionism: The Imperialist Urge in the 1890s* (Madison: University of Wisconsin Press, 1970); Reginald Horsman, *Race and Manifest Destiny: The Origins of American Racial Anglo-Saxonism* (Cambridge, MA: Harvard University Press, 1981); Michael Ignatieff, "The Burden," *New York Times* (January 5, 2003); Walter LaFeber, *Inevitable Revolutions* (New York: W.W. Norton, 1983); David M. Malone and Yuen Foeng Khong, eds., *Unilateralism and U.S. Foreign Policy: International Perspectives* (Boulder, CO: Lynne Rienner, 2003); Frederick Pike, *The United States and Latin America: Myths and Stereotypes of Civilization and Nature* (Austin: University of Texas Press, 1992); Emily S. Rosenberg, *Spreading the American Dream: American Economic and Cultural Expansionism, 1890–1940* (New York: Hill and Wang, 1982); David F. Schmitz, *Thank God They're on Our Side: The United States and Right-Wing Dictatorships, 1921–1965* (Chapel Hill: University of North Carolina Press, 1999); Thomas D. Schoonover, *The United States in Central America, 1860–1911: Episodes of Social Imperialism and Imperial Rivalry in the World System* (Durham, NC: Duke University Press, 1991); Steven Schwartzberg, *Democracy and U.S.–Latin American Policy During the Truman Years* (Gainesville: University of Florida Press, 2003); Josiah Strong, *Our Country: Its Possible Future and Its Present Crisis* (New York: Baker and Taylor, 1885); Sumner Welles, "Is America Imperialistic?" *Atlantic Monthly* (September, 1924): 412–423; Warren Zimmermann, *First Great Triumph: How Five Americans Made Their Country a World Power* (New York: Farrar, Straus & Giroux, 2002).

Inter-American Development Bank (IADB) The oldest and largest of the regional multilateral development banks created to foster economic and social development in Latin America and the Caribbean. The agreement creating the IADB (sometimes the IDB acronym is used) was drawn up by a special committee of the **Organization of American States (OAS)** and signed in 1959 by nineteen Latin American republics and the United States. It began its operations as a regional lending institution in October 1960. The bank, headquartered in Washington, D.C., has a membership of forty-six nations, including the United States, Canada, Japan, Israel, and sixteen European nations. During the 1990s the IADB approved loans for agriculture, energy production, transportation and communications; the environment and public health, education, science and technology; and urban development. The bank encourages private investment and provides technical expertise for planning economic growth. To provide loans to private enterprises, the IADB sponsored the formation of the Inter-American Investment Corporation in 1989, which is composed of most members.

The bank's guaranteed loan fund is financed by member contributions, especially those of the United States, and by the sale of bank bonds to finance Latin American projects. Loans are made to governments or government-guaranteed entities such as the Social Progress Trust Fund, a $500 million endowment established by the United States in 1961 under the Charter of the **Alliance for Progress**. The organizational powers of the IADB are vested in a board of governors, which consists of one representative and one alternate from each member country. Voting strength in the IADB is based on the size of a member's contributions; as the largest shareholder, the United States holds 35 percent of total voting power, one vote for each share of the bank's capital stock it holds. The Inter-American Development Bank served as a model of regional lending and financing for the Asian and African Development Banks. The current president of the IADB is Enrique V. Iglesias of Uruguay.

Suggested Reading

Sidney Dell, *The Inter-American Development Bank: A Study in Developing Financing* (New York: Praeger, 1972); R. Peter DeWitt, *The Inter-American Development Bank and Political Influence, With Special Reference to Costa Rica* (New York: Praeger, 1977); Manuel Sánchez and Rossanna Corona, eds., *Privatization in Latin America* (Washington, DC: Inter-American Development Bank, 1993); Diana Tussie, *The Inter-American Development Bank* (Boulder, CO: Lynne Rienner, 1994).

Inter-American Dialogue (IAD) Moderate Washington-based **think tank** founded in 1982 to provide a counter-weight to the more conservative think tanks that dominated President Ronald **Reagan**'s Latin American policy in the 1980s. The IAD grew out of Abraham F. **Lowenthal**'s work at the Woodrow Wilson Center for Scholars where he was secretary of the Latin American program in the late 1970s and early 1980s. With Lowenthal's organization and fund-raising skills, the Inter-American Dialogue gained in stature as the premier think tank handling U.S.–Latin American relations. In creating the IAD, Lowenthal employed the clever device of having compatible participants join together from the United States and Latin America in roughly equal numbers. Without having to pay members to join the IAD, his recommendations gained legitimacy and media attention from the simple fact that they emerged from its prestigious membership and cross-national modus operandi. Despite the rapid success—due in large part to its large membership, organizational structure, and method of operation—in the Latin American policymaking arena, conservatives in Washington and beyond criticized the Inter-American Dialogue for not having sufficient representation from those on the political right.

At first the IAD served mainly as a coordinator and disseminator for an already established policy agenda. Over time, with serious fund-raising efforts, the Inter-

American Dialogue was converted into a full-scale think tank with leadership, staff, and resources to develop a serious research agenda devoted to the major issues confronting the United States and Latin America. Sol Linowitz was a prime mover of the IAD and served as chair of the organization for many years. Some Latin America scholars argue that the impact of the IAD improved after it moved closer to the center of the ideological spectrum. Others insist that the Inter-American Dialogue belongs on the left given the attention it pays to such topics as equity, social movements, indigenous peoples, Cuba, **democracy promotion** and sustainable development.

Since 1996 the Inter-American Dialogue has stressed more inter-Americanism by ensuring effective communication with hemispheric leaders across a broad spectrum of activities. Currently, the IAD's research is focused on four areas: democratic governance, multilateral governance, trade and economics, and social policy. Through a variety of policy reports and seminars, the dialogue has remained critical of the **George W. Bush** administration for not paying enough attention to Latin America during his first term. Other than regional trade and the militarization of Colombia, the Bush administration has chosen to ignore Latin America. In contrast to earlier periods of inter-American history, where the United States paid attention to the region only in times of crisis, the Bush administration has largely ignored the trouble spots in the hemisphere, namely Colombia, Venezuela, Argentina, Haiti, and Paraguay.

The Inter-American Dialogue is run by a staff of thirty and is funded by the federal government, international organizations, private foundations, and individual donations. Peter Hakim replaced Richard Feinberg as president of the Inter-American Dialogue in the second Bill **Clinton** presidency and has put more emphasis on expanding and diversifying its activities to include smaller conferences, working groups, congressional seminars, forums for visiting Latin Americans, and individually authored articles for mass consumption. President Hakin focuses on trade and economics, Mexico and Brazil; Chief Researcher Michael Shifter writes on democracy, **human rights**, freedom of the press, and Colombia. Like other specialized Latin America–focused think tanks in Washington, the Inter-American Dialogue is part of a policymaking environment where think tank influence depends on the ideology and leadership style of the president. Since 2001, the IAD has organized monthly sessions with Congress to address trade issues. It is now meeting with Latin American legislators (El Salvador and Colombia) to talk about hemispheric issues. The IAD published *Hemispheric Leaders Advise Next U.S. President: Reshape Policy Agenda Toward Colombia, Mexico* in 2001, but the recommendations in the report did not get major attention from the White House or the U.S. **State Department**. The IAD works closely with the Carnegie Endowment for International Peace and the Brookings Institution despite the fact that both of these Washington-based think tanks are not exclusively devoted to inter-American relations. The IAD published *Agenda for the Americas in 2005* in an effort to force the George W. Bush administration to devote more attention to the problems and opportunities in Latin America. Fernando Henrique Cardoso, former

Brazilian president, is now co-chair of the IAD. *See also* Washington Policymakers.

Suggested Reading

Inter-American Dialogue, *Agenda for the Americas* (Washington, DC: IAD, 2005); Inter-American Dialogue, *Hemispheric Leaders Advise Next U.S. President: Reshape Policy Agenda Toward Colombia, Mexico* (Washington, DC: IAD, 2001); Andres Oppenheimer, "Think Tank Can Shape Clinton's Latin Policy," *Miami Herald* (February 1, 1993); Howard J. Wiarda, "Think Tanks," in David W. Dent, ed., *U.S.–Latin American Policymaking: A Reference Handbook* (Westport, CT: Greenwood Press, 1995).

Inter-American System. *See* Bogotá Conference (1948)

Inter-American Treaty of Reciprocal Assistance (1947) One of the outcomes of the Act of Chapultepec in 1945 was the American commitment to negotiate a mutual security treaty, a task that was carried out two years later when delegates from the United States and nineteen Latin American countries met at the Inter-American Conference for the Maintenance of Continental Peace and Security at Petrópolis, Brazil, near Rio de Janeiro. Also known as the Rio Treaty, the Inter-American Treaty of Reciprocal Assistance created a means of providing collective security for the Americas. It became important during the **Cold War**, especially for diplomatic and military methodology for defining and acting upon perceived threats to national security. The notion of shared responsibility was overshadowed by the overwhelming economic and military superiority of the United States following **World War II**. The United States became the principal power in deciding what constituted aggression and how to apply the Rio Treaty to specific situations. It was particularly important for handling Cuba in the aftermath of the Cuban Revolution. The two most important articles—one specifying the basis for action and the other with measures to be taken—addressed threats to a state's territorial integrity, sovereignty, or independence from either an armed attack, or conflict, from either outside (extra-territorial) or inside (intra-continental) the Western Hemisphere that might endanger the peace and security of the region. In the event of such a threat, the Organ of Consultation was to meet at once to agree to a range of measures to be taken for the defense of the Americas. These measures—from recalling chiefs of diplomatic missions to the use of armed force—required a two-thirds vote and were binding on all Rio Treaty parties. However, no state would be required to use armed force without its explicit consent, a provision that weakened the ability to achieve consensus on the proper measures to be taken at the time of the crisis. Furthermore, the legal approach of the United States treated the central concepts—armed attack, threat to the peace, act of aggression—as essentially political categories open to broad interpretation. The Rio Treaty became a Cold War instrument of the United States, particularly in dealing with the connection between the Soviet Union and Cuba. Since its inception in 1947 there have been several efforts to amend the Rio Treaty. The military government of Peru, with strong support from Ecuador and Panama, failed to pass resolutions aimed at addressing issues such as "collective economic security for development" and "integral development" in Latin America. Prior to the terrorist attacks on the United States on **September 11, 2001**, Mexican President Vicente Fox tried unsuccessfully to have the Rio Treaty abolished, arguing that it had outlived its purpose and was a relic of the Cold War. *See also* Organization of the American States (OAS); Threat Perception/Assessment.

Suggested Reading

G. Pope Atkins, *Encyclopedia of the Inter-American System* (Westport, CT: Greenwood Press, 1997); Jorge I. Domínguez, ed., *International Security and Democracy: Latin America and the Caribbean in the Post–Cold War Era* (Pittsburgh, PA: University of Pittsburgh Press, 1998); William Perry and Max Primorac, "The Inter-American Security Agenda," *Journal of Inter-American Studies and World Affairs* 36 (fall 1994); Jerome Slater, *A Reevaluation of Collective Security: The OAS in Action* (Athens: Ohio State University Press, 1965); Thomas G. Weiss, ed., *Collective Security in a Changing World* (Boulder, CO: Lynne Rienner, 1993).

International Court of Justice (ICJ) The ICJ is the judicial organ of the **United Nations (UN)**; often referred to as the World Court, which has jurisdiction over disputes between states. It succeeded the Permanent Court of International Justice of the **League of Nations** and began functioning in 1946 as the "principal judicial organ" of the UN. The ICJ is a fifteen-member body with two categories of seats: five permanent and ten non-permanent. Terms on the bench are nine years for a permanent seat judge and two years for a non-permanent judge. At the time the ICJ was constituted, an agreement was reached where there would be two judges from the Latin America states that would rotate among the twenty states. With the growing independence and UN membership of the Commonwealth Caribbean states in the 1960s, it was decided that one judge should come from the Commonwealth Caribbean, a decision that was carried out in the 1980s. During the **Cold War** the ICJ faced numerous difficulties over the enforcement of its decisions, particularly when they ran contrary to the more powerful permanent members of the court. For example, when Nicaragua brought a case before the ICJ in 1984, charging the United States with "training, supplying and directing military and paramilitary actions against . . . [Nicaragua]" for the purpose of overthrowing its government, Managua asked the ICJ to rule that the United States had violated **international law** and requested that it pay reparations for damages done during the **Central Intelligence Agency (CIA)** mining of its harbors. The ICJ handed down its major decision in 1986, ruling against the United States and in favor of Nicaragua's claims of **intervention** and violation of international law. The United States refused to accept the ruling and failed to appear in court when it was scheduled to assess the amount of reparations to be paid. This questionable action left the ICJ helpless to enforce its major findings in the case and undermined the Central American peace efforts in process at the time. *See also* International Criminal Court (ICC); Intervention and Non-Intervention; Reagan Doctrine.

Suggested Reading

Evan Luard, *The United Nations: How it Works and What it Does* (Basingstoke, England: Macmillan, 1989); Larman C. Wilson and David W. Dent, *Historical Dictionary of Inter-American Organizations* (Lanham, MD: Scarecrow Press, 1998).

International Criminal Court (ICC) A controversial international tribunal that came into existence in 2002 to address the most heinous cases of genocide, war crimes, and crimes against humanity. The United States was active in the tense and emotional negotiations that preceded the signing of the treaty at the Rome Conference in 1998, but did not sign the Rome Statute of the ICC along with seven other nations including Cuba, Israel, and China (120 nations voted in favor; 21 abstained). President Bill **Clinton** eventually recognized the merits of having such a juridical body and signed the Rome Treaty in December 2000, but the **George W. Bush** administration "unsigned" the treaty in 2001 and has opposed actively the organization ever since. The Bush administration fears that the International Criminal Court could become an anti-American body that might subject Americans to international tribunals on politicized charges. The United States objected to the ICC's jurisdiction over non-party states' nationals and wanted to have **United Nations (UN)** Security Council control over court cases. In an effort to protect American interests abroad, President Bush has threatened to withdraw from United Nations peacekeeping if American soldiers (and by implication, all American citizens) are not exempted from the court's jurisdiction and has tried to strong-arm other nations into signing bilateral agreements with Washington not to send Americans to the court. The Bush administration has gone so far as to threaten the termination of U.S. military assistance if countries refuse to comply with U.S. demands. Under a provision of a 2002 American anti-terrorism law, any country that became a member of the ICC but failed to give exemptions to Americans serving within its borders automatically would lose such aid.

The ICC became operational after sixty states deposited instruments of ratification, meaning that the court can only prosecute crimes occurring *after* July 1, 2002. The ICC's work is guided by the ninety-two countries that have agreed to take part in the court, not the UN Security Council. Luis Moreno Ocampo, an Argentine lawyer, insists that the ICC is not an arbitrary political weapon and it is not designed "to replace national judicial systems." He added, "We [ICC] will act only if they need us." In August 2002, Marc Grossman, undersecretary of state for political affairs, requested that U.S. military personnel in Colombia be granted immunity from prosecution by the International Criminal Court for any **human rights** abuses committed while in the line of duty. Many see this as a bad example of allowing U.S. military personnel to ignore human rights and the rule of law while condemning the Colombians for human rights abuses and the absence of **democracy**. The Bush administration continues to pressure other nations into signing bilateral agreements not to send Americans to the court. Angry over the refusal of many countries to bow to U.S. demands, the Bush administration suspended all American military assistance to thirty-five countries on July 1, 2003, because of their refusal to pledge to give American citizens immunity before the ICC. The U.S. policy requiring the exemption of U.S. citizens from the ICC has raised concerns about U.S. security interests with the growing influence of the Chinese military in the region.

Despite the fact that the ICC has jurisdiction over cases only if a nation's own judicial system *cannot* or *will not* prosecute them, and only if the perpetrator or the territory of the crime involve a state party, and the undisputed high quality of the jurists elected to serve on the court, the Bush administration has yet to be persuaded of the merits of the court. Ocampo has been named prosecutor; Philippe Kirsch, a Canadian, was elected president of the court. All of the judges elected by the member nations come with a serious concern for dealing with the world's most serious crimes and those who commit them. Although some critics of the court feared that the formation of the court would facilitate the prosecution of former **Nixon** aide Henry **Kissinger** for war crimes, the beginning date of the court's mandate over such matters would seem to put to rest concerns about his future prosecution. While the ICC's jurisdiction will not be retroactive as some countries had hoped, many argue that it will be far more difficult for future Latin American tyrants such as Augusto **Pinochet** (Chile), the Duvaliers (Haiti), Rafael **Trujillo** (Dominican Republic), the **Somoza** dynasty (Nicaragua), and Alfredo Stroessner (Paraguay) to escape justice as was the case prior to the establishment of the court. It remains to be seen what impact the deterrence value of the ICC will have on the important connection between corrupt and venal right-wing dictators and leftist-nationalist **revolutions** in the Western Hemisphere. Although it is doubtful that the Bush administration's campaign against the ICC will lead to its demise, many Latin American countries recognize the merits of having an international body to deal fairly and judiciously with individuals and governments that commit human rights abuses and see no reason to grant the United States immunity before the court. The ICC is now completely staffed with lawyers, researchers, and investigators and has already started investigating referred cases. In 2005, the first case to be referred to the ICC by the UN Security Council concerned the atrocities in Darfur (Sudan). *See also* International Court of Justice (ICJ); International Law.

Suggested Reading

M. Cherif Bassiouni, *The Statute of the International Criminal Court and Related Instruments: Legislative History, 1994–2000* (Ardsley, NY: Transnational Publishers, 2001); Michael Scharf, "The Politics of the U.S. Opposition to the International Criminal Court," *New England International and Comparative Law Annual* (1999); David J. Scheffer, "The United States and the International Criminal Court," *American Journal of International Law*, 93 (1999): 12–22; International Criminal Court Now (www.iccnow.org).

International Law The international relations between the United States and Latin America are shaped in a variety of ways by the use (and abuse) of international law—the body of customs, practices, agreements, and treaties that constitute a legal foundation for conducting relations among sovereign states. International law is important because it provides institutions, concepts, principles, and procedures by which hemispheric states maintain diplomatic relations, carry on trade and commerce, and resolve inter-state disputes. The asymmetries in power between the United States and the Latin American states means that such concepts as sovereignty, and its important corollary, non-intervention—designed to constrain hostile actions and promote harmonic relations—have played an important role in hemispheric relations. Throughout most of the twentieth century the weaker Latin American states stressed the importance of sovereignty and its non-intervention corollary in an effort to curtail the power and blatant **interventions** in their internal affairs by the United States reaching back to the nineteenth century. The United States did not justify its earlier interventions on legal grounds; rather, these interventions were based on policies and presidential pronouncements designed to promote the national interest. After the 1820s, the **Monroe Doctrine** (and its many corollaries) became an important part of U.S.–Latin American policy and was buttressed at times by the ideas of **Manifest Destiny** and the White Man's Burden. Beginning in the early decades of the twentieth century, U.S. interventions were justified in terms of maintaining stability, collecting debts, promoting economic development, exporting **democracy**, protecting **human rights**, fighting communism, and combating **drug trafficking** and **terrorism**. After the era of intervention (1898–1934), the United States began to pay more attention to international law. However, there were times throughout the twentieth century when the United States reverted to earlier policies that placed national security interests above the principles of international law.

During the **Cold War**, relations between the United States and Latin America suffered because of the lack of U.S. respect for and reliance on international law. **Washington policymakers** often acted to meet the needs of national security as they saw them, rather than concern themselves with a scrupulous regard for international legal principles. During the 1980s, **covert operations** and military interventions in Central America and the Caribbean were condemned widely as violations of international law. The invasion of Grenada and covert military measures against **Sandinista** Nicaragua (including the creation and support of the **Contras**), which the **International Court of Justice (ICJ)** found to be illegal, provide several examples of how the Cold War damaged international law and the conduct of U.S.–Latin American relations. Recent attempts to apply U.S. domestic law extraterritorially in the case of the **Helms-Burton Law** aimed at Cuba have been condemned widely as a violation of international law by inter-American and international organizations. The enactment of the Helms-Burton Law in 1996 was evaluated by a body of international jurists who concluded it violated international law in ten different areas. In the area of human rights, the United States, while insisting on monitoring the human rights obligations of other states, has resisted adhering to international covenants and conventions, and international surveillance of human rights conditions at home. Globalization has eroded the concept of national sovereignty making it more difficult to apply international legal principles contained in the **United Nations (UN)** Charter and the **Organization of American States (OAS)** Charter to hemispheric relations.

In response to U.S. intervention in Latin America, there was a Latin American effort to develop a regional legal approach that would have made the non-intervention principle much more absolute. The United States refused to accept such an approach, but did finally agree to the non-intervention principle enshrined in the 1948 OAS Charter. Nevertheless, where individuals have become the subjects of international law (human rights) and are entitled to certain legal protections, the United States is often reluctant to apply restrictive standards that impair its foreign policy goals. This became apparent during the war against Iraq in 2003–2004 when the Defense Department claimed that President Bush's authority to order torture could not be checked even by American lawmakers. By acting as if the Geneva Conventions do not apply to the United States, the Bush administration has opened a pandora's box by attempting to legalize torture in the name of higher national interests and in violation of international law. *See also* International Criminal Court (ICC); Intervention and Non-Intervention.

Suggested Reading

William Everett Kane, *Civil Strife in Latin America: A Legal History of U.S. Involvement* (Baltimore, MD: Johns Hopkins University Press, 1972); Donald R. Kelly, ed., *After Communism: Perspectives on Democracy* (Fayetteville: University of Arkansas Press, 2003); Charlotte Ku and Harold K. Jacobson, eds., *Democratic Accountability and the Use of Force in International Law* (New York: Cambridge University Press, 2003); Ivan Musicant, *The Banana Wars: A History of United States Military Intervention in Latin America from the Spanish-American War to the Invasion of Grenada* (New York: Macmillan, 1990); John Torpey, ed., *Politics and the Past: On Repairing Historical Injustices* (Lanham, MD: Roman and Littlefield, 2003).

Intervention and Non-Intervention U.S.–Latin American relations have been dominated by the themes of intervention and non-intervention, both of which have been constants in the history of U.S. involvement in Latin America. Although there are periods in the U.S.–Latin American relationship when intervention has not occurred, intervention in various guises continues and is still one of the most common complaints of the Latin American and Caribbean states. In *Civil Strife in Latin America* (1972: 1), William Everett Kane argues that "If one had to choose a one-word characterization of U.S.–Latin American relations since the turn of the [twentieth] century, 'intervention' would probably be the choice of a majority of Latin American scholars." In terms of American foreign policy, the United States has intervened more in Latin America and the Caribbean than any other world region. Although exact numbers are hard to come by, more than several hundred U.S. military interventions have been recorded since Latin American independence in the 1820s. After the **Mexican-American War** in the late 1840s, intervention gained in importance to the United States. The era of intervention between 1895 and 1930 marked a period in which U.S. presidents—William **McKinley**, **Theodore Roosevelt**, William H. **Taft**, and Woodrow **Wilson**—felt obliged to act as the hemisphere's peacemaker, debt collector, political reformer, and economic modernizer. Intervention declined with the advent of the **Good Neighbor Policy** of Presidents Herbert **Hoover** and **Franklin D. Roosevelt**, but expanded dramatically with the **Cold War** when the United States intervened in Guatemala, British Guiana/Guyana, Brazil, Cuba, the Dominican Republic, Chile, Nicaragua, Grenada, Panama, Haiti, El Salvador, Honduras, and Venezuela. In *Rogue State* (2000), William Blum examines twenty–one cases of U.S. intervention in Latin America and the Caribbean between 1945 and 2000. These interventions have varied in terms of rationale, duration, and level of violence. Some scholars speculated at the end of the Cold War that U.S. military intervention would cease because of the absence of an extra-hemispheric power at odds with the United States in Latin America. However, intervention continues in ways that suggest the need for different approaches to fulfill U.S. goals and interests in the Latin American and Caribbean region.

United States intervention in Latin America has undergone a series of adjustments over the past 100 years. Political scientist Michael J. Kryzanek argues that a "political metamorphosis" has taken place in which the shape and direction of U.S. intervention has changed to advance and protect U.S. interests. He explains this as an evolutionary process "beginning with the raw use of military intervention [and occupation] for stabilizing purposes during the early stages of the rise of the United States as a world power, changing over to a reliance on **covert operations** to stem the tide of Communist influence, and ending with series of redefined techniques as the United States in the 1980s sought to reassert its preeminent position in the region" (Kryzanek, 1995: 402). U.S. intervention after the Cold War has relied more on multilateral forms of intervention, using international organizations such as the **United Nations (UN)** and the **Organization of American States (OAS)** when it best suited its interests but often ignoring prescribed legal constraints when U.S. interests required modification and "great power" interpretations. The current global war on **terrorism** announced by President **George W. Bush** has revived Washington's interest in pursuing interventionist policies, particularly in cases such as Cuba, Haiti, Colombia, and Venezuela when they engage in international activity that is not acceptable to the United States.

Latin Americans have not been quiescent when it comes to the issue of intervention, particularly when it comes to U.S. policy. The **doctrines** of **Calvo** and **Drago** were deliberate efforts to challenge the United States by articulating the importance of sovereign rights and non-intervention responsibilities among unequal states. The smaller and weaker Latin American states stressed **international law** and the role of international organizations to counter-balance the international power of the United States in Latin America. The Latin American perspective on non-intervention was incorporated into the OAS Charter in 1948 and is often given considerable weight in the conduct of inter-American relations. Although Washington accepted the principle of non-intervention, during periods of conflict when security threats emerged it was not uncommon for the United States to embark on interventionist measures that undermined the importance of international law. When the **Clinton** administration was preparing to invade Haiti to restore President **Aristide** to power in 1994, it sought, and obtained, UN approval for the use of force to remove the Haitian generals who were obstructing "democracy" by keeping Aristide out of Haiti. U.S. intervention is now more likely to be multilateral in form than the unilateral intervention of previous eras.

In 1975 the Commission on United States–Latin American Relations (Linowitz Commission, named after its chairman, Sol Linowitz) made the following recommendations in *The Americas in a Changing World* (1975: 24–25): "The United States should refrain from unilateral interventions in Latin America, and covert interventions in the internal affairs of Latin American countries should be ended. The President and Congress should ensure that all agencies of the U.S. government fully respect the sovereignty of the countries of Latin America." This recommendation came after the **Nixon** administration orchestrated the removal of Chilean President Salvador **Allende** and revelations of previous efforts to carry out plans to assassinate Latin American political figures, including Fidel **Castro**, Che **Guevara**, and Rafael **Trujillo**. While others have made similar pledges to refrain from unilateral interventions since the commission made its recommendations, the interventionist impulse still prevails among **Washington policymakers**. Since 1975, this has been evident in Nicaragua, Honduras, El Salvador, Grenada, Haiti, and Panama. In his historical inventory of U.S. intervention in Latin America, Etheredge (1985: 135) finds "the recurrent pattern of American interventions in the Central American region" part of a pattern going back to the nineteenth century. What is most striking in the pattern is not simply the number of military interventions—particularly in Cuba, Panama, Mexico, Nicaragua, Haiti, and the Dominican Republic—but the initial phase of intervention to deal with a "political disorder" was followed by long periods of occupation to maintain American **hegemony**. *See also* Calvo Clause; Covert Operations, Drago Doctrine; Friendly Dictators; German Threat; International Law; Recognition and Non-Recognition; Threat Perception/Assessment; Tobar Doctrine.

Suggested Reading

Robert Beck, *The Grenada Invasion: Politics, Law and Foreign Policy* (Boulder, CO: Westview Press, 1993); William Blum, *Rogue State: A Guide to the World's Only Superpower* (Monroe, ME: Common Courage Press, 2000); Max Boot, *The Savage Wars of Peace: Small Wars and the Rise of American Power* (New York: Basic Books, 2002); Seyom Brown, *The Illusion of Control: Force and Foreign Policy in the Twenty-First Century* (Washington, DC: Brookings Institution Press, 2003); Commission on United States–Latin American Relations, *The Americas in a Changing World* (New York: Quadrangle, 1975); Peter M. Dunn and Bruce W. Watson, eds., *American Intervention in Grenada: The Implications of Operation "Urgent Fury"* (Boulder, CO: Westview Press, 1985); Lloyd S. Etheredge, *Can Governments Learn? American Foreign Policy and Central American Revolutions* (New York: Pergamon Press, 1985); Michael Ignatieff, "A Mess of Intervention: Peacekeeping, Pre-emption, Liberation, Revenge," *New York Times Magazine* (September 7, 2003); William Everett Kane, *Civil Strife in Latin America: A Legal*

History of U.S. Involvement (Baltimore, MD: Johns Hopkins University Press, 1972); Michael J. Kryzanek, "Intervention and Interventionism," in David W. Dent, ed., *U.S.–Latin American Policymaking: A Reference Handbook* (Westport, CT: Greenwood Press, 1995); U.S. Department of State, *U.S. Policy Toward Latin America: Recognition and Non-Recognition of Governments and Interruptions in Diplomatic Relations, 1933–1974* (Washington, DC: Department of State, 1975); Larman C. Wilson and David W. Dent, *Historical Dictionary of Inter-American Organizations* (Lanham, MD: Scarecrow Press, 1998).

Iran-Contra Scandal The merging of two secret foreign policy initiatives carried out by the administration of Ronald **Reagan** produced the Iran-Contra affair in the mid-1980s, the most serious constitutional crisis since Watergate. The whole affair raised troubling questions about the use of secrecy and deception in foreign policy, the source of responsibility for legal violations committed under superior orders, and inter-branch control over Latin American policy. The scandal came to public attention during the second term of President Reagan in which it was revealed that American arms had been sold secretly to Iran (then defined as a "terrorist state") in exchange for the freeing of American hostages held in Lebanon combined with the profits used to provide secret support (after the **Boland Amendments** halted funding) for the **Contras** fighting against the leftist **Sandinista** government in Nicaragua. Reagan's credibility in foreign policy was undermined as the growing revelations brought to light the magnitude of abuses of governmental authority. At first President Reagan denied there was an arms-for-hostages swap and those in the **National Security Council (NSC)** handling Central American affairs denied that they were providing any assistance to the Contras. Following public disclosures and an investigation by a presidential review board, a congressional investigation, and a seven-year criminal inquiry by an independent counsel, the major participants in the affair—National Security Adviser Robert McFarlane, his successor, John Poindexter, NSC aide Oliver **North**, and assistant secretary for Inter-American affairs, Elliott **Abrams**, and others were tried and convicted for lying to Congress and diverting public funds. During the year-long congressional testimony, several key Iran-Contra figures maintained that the ends they sought justified the means they employed, their activities were consistent with President Reagan's explicit and implicit goals, and they did not violate any laws.

Although neither Congress nor the independent counsel found evidence that President Reagan knew of the diversion, the president did authorize the sale of arms to Iran and the solicitation of private funds for the Contras. The Tower Commission, chaired by former Senator John Tower, attributed the Iran-Contra affair to bureaucratic failures inside the White House and criticized President Reagan for poor management and direction of his staff. Reagan was also criticized for deceiving the public on his opposition to Iran, and of doing an end-run around congressional opposition to continued U.S. aid to the Contras. The final report by the Senate and House investigating committees concluded that unelected officials repeatedly defied Congress' efforts to carry out its oversight role, and the defiance of Congress led to policy failure. President Reagan was criticized for creating a policy-making environment in which senior foreign policy officials felt justified in breaking the law and misleading Congress.

Vice-President **George H.W. Bush** was also implicated in the Iran-Contra affair but claimed at the time that he was "out-of-the-loop" of decision-making authority. Nevertheless, a Bush-Contra link came to light when Eugene Hasenfus' **Central Intelligence Agency (CIA)** cargo plane was shot down and his capture in Nicaragua provided evidence of Bush's involvement in the undercover operation. After Hasenfus told his Nicaraguan captors the names of those directing the Contra-aid operation from an air base in El Salvador, the trail of involvement quickly led to Félix Rodríguez (Cuban-American operative in El Salvador), Donald P. Gregg (Vice-President Bush's national security adviser), and George H.W. Bush himself. Further evidence of Bush's involvement with the scandal came from several memos documenting meetings between Bush and those involved in the Contra war. After becoming president, Bush tried to put a close to the sordid affair by pardoning six Iran-Contra defendants—including Secretary of Defense Casper Weinberger and former Assistant Secretary of State Elliott Abrams—and hiding incriminating documents.

One of the key planners of the Iran-Contra operation was John Poindexter, a career navy officer who served on the staff of the National Security Council from 1981 to 1985. When Robert McFarlane resigned as National Security Adviser to Ronald Reagan in 1985, Poindexter replaced him and made many of the key decisions until Poindexter resigned when the Iran-Contra scandal became public knowledge in 1986. To provide President Reagan with "plausible deniability," Poindexter blocked the decision-making evidence from reaching the president. During the Senate hearings in 1987, Poindexter defended his actions by claiming he was carrying out the president's wish to keep the Contras a viable fighting force and his belief that he was working to protect the long-term interests of the United States in Central America. The lengthy investigations removed any possibility that the United States could continue the covert war against Nicaragua; however, Ronald Reagan left the presidency on a positive note with a high approval rating and the national **media** barely mentioned the scandal when he died in June 2004. There is no doubt the 30,000 Nicaraguans and 70,000 Salvadorans who died because of the **Reagan Doctrine** would remember a different president than the one eulogized in the United States. The Iran-Contra investigation also revealed a pattern of secrecy, elitism, deception, and arrogance among **Washington policymakers** in other Latin American policies, particularly Cuba, Chile, and Panama. *See also* Reich, Otto Juan; Scandals and Blunders.

Suggested Reading

Theodore Draper, *A Very Thin Line: The Iran-Contra Affairs* (New York: Hill and Wang, 1991); Oliver Trager, ed., *The Iran-Contra Arms Scandal: Foreign Policy Disaster* (New York: Facts on File, 1988); Lawrence Walsh, *Final Report of the Independent Counsel for Iran/Contra Matters* (Washington, DC: Government Printing Office, 1993).

J

Jagan, Cheddi. *See* Kennedy, John Fitzgerald (1917–1963)

Johnson, Lyndon Baines (1908–1973) Master politician and thirty-sixth president of the United States whose most important accomplishments were in the field of domestic policy. Because he did not consider himself an expert in foreign affairs, Lyndon B. Johnson relied to an extraordinary degree on advisers he inherited from the **Kennedy** administration. Although Johnson and his advisers—mainly Robert McNamara, Dean Rusk, Thomas **Mann**, and McGeorge Bundy—shared the **Cold War** doctrine of containment and fear of Soviet expansionism, they often misinterpreted events in Latin America by falsely linking political events in the Western Hemisphere as part of a Soviet-Cuban conspiracy to dominate the world. A firm believer in the **domino theory**, President Johnson found a connection between what was happening in Vietnam and Latin America. His perception of threats from Fidel **Castro**'s Cuba and anti-American nationalism in Latin America fueled his concern of Communist encroachment in Latin America and the Caribbean.

Lyndon Johnson was born near Stonewall, Texas, graduated from Southwest State Teachers College, and taught briefly in public schools before deciding on a career in politics. After being elected to the House of Representatives in 1937, Johnson rose to U.S. senator in 1948. He ran for president in 1960, but was defeated for the Democratic nomination by John F. Kennedy. Kennedy named him as his running mate the same year, and they went on to defeat Richard **Nixon** and Henry Cabot Lodge in a very close election. Johnson's political career taught him the importance of face-to-face relations in solving domestic disputes and foreign disagreements. However, Johnson's faith in compromise and diplomatic negotiation often gave way to military **intervention** and violent confrontation.

Although Lyndon Johnson is best known for his blunders in fighting communism in Vietnam, he also faced problems in Latin America and was keenly interested in the Western Hemisphere. He continued Kennedy's Latin American policy by supporting the **Alliance for Progress** and sustaining the policy of isolating Cuba to diminish its influence in the region. After taking over the presidency after the **assassination** of John F. Kennedy, Johnson dismissed Kennedy's team of Latin Americanists in the **State Department** and the **Agency for International Development (AID)**. To put his own stamp on U.S.–Latin American relations, Johnson turned to veteran diplomat and fellow Texan Thomas Mann to deal with Latin America. Mann believed it was essential that the United States work with non-democratic governments in the Americas and declared in the so-called **Mann Doctrine**, that Washington would work with all non-Communist governments, including military ones, in the Western Hemisphere. Although some interpreted this as a radical break with the principles of the Alliance for Progress and Kennedy policies, Mann's views were not at odds with Kennedy's Latin American policy.

Lyndon Johnson left his mark on Latin American policy by continuing to fight the Cold War in Latin America, particularly with regard to Panama, Brazil, and the Dominican Republic. In Panama, Johnson recognized the importance of negotiations that would culminate in the return of Panamanian sovereignty over the Panama Canal. In Brazil, Johnson and his advisers worked to encourage the Brazilian military to remove João Goulart, a constitutionally elected president that U.S. officials judged to be a secret Communist. In the spring of 1965, Lyndon Johnson responded to a civil war in the Dominican Republic by sending over 20,000 U.S. troops to prohibit the establishment of "another Communist government in the Western Hemisphere." Most scholars have judged Johnson's reaction to Communist influence in the Dominican Republic to be exaggerated and based on faulty intelligence. While the negative consequences of such a return to **Big Stick diplomacy** damaged U.S.–Latin American relations, Johnson was able to claim a rhetorical victory over communism close to home. The **Johnson Doctrine** (no second Cubas) did not go over well in Latin America, but it taught President Johnson that with enough military power the Communists could be defeated in the Third World. His application of the Dominican lesson to Vietnam—as measured by the dramatic escalation of U.S. troops after April 1965—proved to be disastrous, but few would attribute the failure in Vietnam to the success in the Dominican invasion. Johnson tempered his use of military force with his belief that economic and social development are also important to defeat communism. In April 1967 Johnson went to Punta del Este, Uruguay, to meet with Latin American leaders about the idea of a closer relationship with Latin America that would diminish the image of the United States as the "colossus of the north." However, Johnson failed to obtain increased appropriations from Congress required for his development plan, and it never went into effect. After deciding to not run for re-election in 1968, Johnson returned to Texas, wrote his memoirs, and opened the Lyndon Baines Johnson Presidential Library in Austin. Johnson died at his ranch in Johnson City, Texas, in 1973. *See also* Scandals and Blunders; Threat Perception/Assessment.

Suggested Reading

Michael Beschloss, ed., *Reaching for Glory: Lyndon Johnson's Secret White House Tapes, 1964–1965* (New York: Simon and Schuster, 2001); H.W. Brands, ed., *The Foreign Policies of Lyndon Johnson: Beyond Vietnam* (College Station: Texas A&M University Press, 1999); Robert A. Caro, *The Years of Lyndon Johnson* (New York: Knopf, 1982); Warren I. Cohen and Nancy Bernkopf Tucker, eds., *Lyndon Johnson Confronts the World: American Foreign Policy, 1963–1968* (New York: Cambridge University Press, 1994); Robert Dalleck, *Flawed Giant: Lyndon Johnson and His Times, 1961–1973* (New York: Oxford University Press, 1998); Lyndon B. Johnson, *The Vantage Point: Perspectives on the Presidency, 1963–1969* (New York: Holt, Rinehart, and Winston, 1971); Alan McPherson, "Misled by Himself: What the Johnson Tapes Reveal about the Dominican Intervention of 1965," *Latin American Research Review*, Vol. 38, No. 2 (June 2003); *The Lyndon B. Johnson National Security File. Latin America* [microfilm]: National Security Files, 1963–1969 (Frederick, MD: University Publishers of America, 1987); Irwin Unger and Debi Unger, *LBJ: A Life* (New York: Wiley, 1999); Thomas C. Wiegele, et al., *Leaders Under Stress: A Psychophysiological Analysis of International Crises* (Durham, NC: Duke University Press, 1985).

Johnson Doctrine Declaration by President Lyndon B. **Johnson** in 1965 stating that the U.S. government would not allow the establishment of a "second Cuba" in the Western Hemisphere. In one of several speeches made at the time of U.S. military **intervention** in the Dominican Republic in April 1965, President Johnson pledged that "the American nations cannot, must not, and will not permit the establishment of another Communist government in the Western Hemisphere." In declaring that military intervention was an acceptable and ready means to defeat communism, and change the regime in the Dominican Republic, Johnson's speech was soon characterized as a doctrine bearing his name. Johnson's pledge also reflected his determination to back rightist governments aligned with the United States in the war against communism, something that paved the way for the dramatic escalation of U.S. military involvement in Vietnam the same year.

Latin America held a much lower priority in Johnson's administration than during the short tenure of the Kennedy administration. Even the hallmark of Kennedy's Latin American policy, the **Alliance for Progress**, became a political instrument for maintaining the status quo and a greater tolerance for military-authoritarian regimes. The quick success of defending a right-wing government against a bloody popular revolt had serious repercussions for American foreign policy. Johnson's decision to send over 20,000 U.S. troops to thwart the alleged Castro-style takeover tarnished the image of the United States in Latin America. The use of such a blunt instrument—massive military intervention—in the Dominican Republic was deplored in Latin America as a violation of the non-intervention clause of the **Organization of American States (OAS)** charter and as resurgent "Yankee imperialism." When President Johnson was unable to back his claims about the Communist connection in the Dominican revolt, he lost a considerable amount of legitimacy among his liberal allies in Congress. In what some analysts perceived to be an even darker side to the Johnson Doctrine, the heavy use of force to "defeat" communism in the Caribbean in 1965 led to the rapid U.S. troop buildup in Vietnam over the following year. After its troops landed, the United States turned to the OAS to obtain its multilateral endorsement of unilateral action. This in turn led to the creation of an Inter-American Peace Force, the gradual withdrawal of U.S. troops, a peace agreement between the two sides in the civil war, and preparations for national elections in 1966. The 1965 Dominican intervention marked the beginning of a new form of **imperialism** in which the use of force was followed quickly by the re-establishment of national sovereignty and rapid exit of U.S. military forces. The invasion also gave those trained in psychological warfare an opportunity to test their newly acquired skills of written and verbal deception. The Johnson Doctrine's overreach worried those who feared that the United States would now try to remove a socialist government in Peru or Chile by military force in the event that it was perceived as serving as a base for a foreign state or for the subversion of other states in the Western Hemisphere. Although President Richard **Nixon** spoke in 1971 of "the right of any country to have internal policies and an internal government quite different from what we approve of," plans were well underway to bring down the government of Salvador **Allende** in Chile to prevent a "second Cuba." The U.S. invasion of Grenada in 1983 had all of the earmarks of another application of the Johnson Doctrine to a small, weak Caribbean island. Anything that resembled a "second Cuba" in the Western Hemisphere would not be tolerated by **Washington policymakers**, regardless of party affiliation. *See also* Doctrines; International Law; Intervention and Non-Intervention.

Suggested Reading

G. Pope Atkins and Larman C. Wilson, *The Dominican Republic and the United States: From Imperialism to Transnationalism* (Athens: University of Georgia Press, 1998); Isaak I. Dore, "The U.S. Invasion of Grenada: Resurrection of the 'Johnson Doctrine,'?" *Stanford Journal of International Law* 20 (1984); Thomas M. Franck and Edward Weisband, *Word Politics: Verbal Strategy Among the Superpowers* (New York: Oxford University Press, 1972); Jonathan Hartlyn, "The Dominican Republic: Legacy of Intermittent Engagement," in Abraham F. Lowenthal, ed., *Exporting Democracy: The United States and Latin America* (Baltimore, MD: Johns Hopkins University Press, 1991); Jerome Slater, *Intervention and Negotiaton: The United States and the Dominican Intervention* (New York: Harper and Row, 1970).

K

Kennan, George Frost (1904–2005) A highly respected diplomat and one of the principal architects of the **Cold War** doctrine of containment of the Soviet Union and its Communist allies. After entering the Foreign Service in 1925, Kennan specialized in Russian affairs, mastered the Russian language, traveled widely in the Soviet Union and Eastern Europe, and wrote detailed reports warning Washington of the dangers of Soviet expansionism, subversion, and commitment to spread Communist ideology around the globe. His dispatches from Moscow and the publication of the anonymous "X" article in *Foreign Affairs* in July 1947 helped establish Kennan as the key foreign policy intellectual behind the containment consensus. Between 1947 and 1950 he headed the new **State Department** Policy Planning Staff (PPS), but clashed frequently with President **Truman**'s policy of militarizing containment, a strategy that ran counter to his belief that containment should be "ideological-political" rather than military. After resigning from the State Department in 1950, Kennan made a brief visit to Latin America where he found a region of feeble governments and hopeless people, too immature and weak to contain the Communists. In what Gaddis Smith calls the Kennan Corollary to the **Monroe Doctrine**, Kennan's secret report stated:

> We cannot be too dogmatic about the methods by which local communists can be dealt with . . . where the concepts and traditions of popular government are too weak to absorb successfully the intensity of communist attack, then we must concede that *harsh measures of government repression* may be . . . the only alternative to further communist success. (Smith, 1997: 164, emphasis added)

The first application of the Kennan Corollary occurred in Guatemala in 1954 when the U.S. government and the **United Fruit Company** conspired to remove the democratically elected Jacobo **Arbenz** and arranged for his replacement with Carlos Castillo Armas, a military leader who installed a "harsh" regime advocated by George F. Kennan in his memorandum on U.S.–Latin American relations. After resigning from the State Department in 1950, he began what would become an accomplished career as an historian and critical analyst of U.S. foreign policy. His books condemned "idealistic diplomacy" and emphasized the importance of national interest and power politics in the conduct of foreign relations. Following the election of John F. **Kennedy**, Kennan was appointed ambassador to Yugoslavia, but resigned after two years when the U.S. Congress revoked the host country's most-favored nation trade status. After quitting the diplomatic service in 1953, he joined the Institute for Advanced Study in Princeton and devoted his time to strategic thinking and analysis. He was disturbed by the gradual expansion of U.S. military involvement in Vietnam, wrote a scathing critique of U.S. policy in 1966, but opposed U.S. withdrawal from the conflict. His reasoning was based on the fear that any capitulation to Communists could undermine U.S. credibility and energize Marxist subversives around the globe. As both an architect and critic of the Cold War, Kennan faced a number of internal conflicts over how to deal with domestic priorities and prevent a devastating global conflict because of the militarization of containment. Kennan criticized President **Carter** for his emphasis on human rights and avoidance of military involvement abroad, arguing that other interests—international stability and arms control—deserve far more attention. Although Kennan paid little attention to Latin American diplomacy after his travels and reports in 1950, his "realist" perspective influenced how **Washington policymakers** decided to handle revolutionaries, dictators, and democrats in Guatemala, Cuba, the Dominican Republic, Chile, Nicaragua, and Panama. His diaries—started at age eleven—cover more than ninety years of his life and thoughts on American foreign policy. Princeton University celebrated his 100th birthday in 2004 with notable speakers including Secretary of State Colin L. Powell and John Lewis Gaddis, professor of history and political science at Yale. Kennan died at his home in Princeton, N.J., at the age of 101. *See also* Friendly Dictators; Guatemala, U.S. Invasion of (1954).

Suggested Reading

Douglas Brinkley, "Celebrating a Policy Seer and his Cold War Insight," *New York Times* (February 17, 2004); George Frost Kennan, *Memoirs, 1950–1963* (Boston: Little Brown, 1972); Wilson D. Miscamble, *George F. Kennan and the Making of American Foreign Policy, 1947–1950* (Princeton, NJ: Princeton University Press, 1992); Gaddis Smith, *The Last Years of the Monroe Doctrine, 1945–1993* (New York: Hill and Wang, 1994); Anders Stephanson, *Kennan and the Art of Foreign Policy* (Cambridge, MA: Harvard University Press, 1989); Tim Weiner and Barbara Crossette, "George F. Kennan, Leading U.S. Strategist of the Cold War Dies at 101," *New York Times* (March 19, 2005).

Kennan Corollary to the Monroe Doctrine. *See* Kennan, George Frost; Monroe Doctrine (1823)

Kennedy, John Fitzgerald (1917–1963) Popular **Cold War** politician (U.S. congressman, 1946–1952; U.S. senator, 1952–1960; and thirty-fifth president, 1961–1963) with an avid and detailed interest in foreign affairs. Although he spoke no Spanish and had made few trips to the region, his brief presidency focused a great deal of attention on Latin America and the Caribbean, particularly Cuba and Guyana. In an extremely close election based heavily on who could best stand up to the Soviet Union, Kennedy beat Republican Richard **Nixon** and inherited a Latin American policy that had already targeted the removal of Fidel **Castro** in Cuba. Although Kennedy inherited from President Dwight **Eisenhower** a foolhardy plan to use **Central Intelligence Agency (CIA)**-trained Cuban exiles to invade Cuba and put an end to Castro's revolution, he permitted the expedition to go forward with the proviso that no U.S. forces be used in the counter-revolution. This flawed **covert operation** resulted in the **Bay of Pigs** invasion, a foreign policy blunder that resulted in a humiliating defeat for Kennedy and his new administration and a boon to Castro's legitimacy as a revolutionary leader capable of repelling Yankee **imperialism**. Kennedy's Latin America policy reflects many of the objectives that other presidents have pursued in the region, namely the exclusion of extra-continental powers from the Western Hemisphere, the creation of stable regimes that acquiesced to Washington's foreign policy goals, the authorization of dozens of covert interventions, the use of **gunboat diplomacy** against distasteful regimes, and the application of a doctrine of exercising international police power to prevent the emergence of Communist regimes.

Born in Brookline, Massachusetts, to a wealthy and well-connected family, Kennedy's first experience with foreign relations occurred while he traveled about Europe in 1937, observing political developments in the wake of **World War II**. Kennedy's father was a foreign policy isolationist, both during World War II and during the Cold War. His son opposed this view, believing that only an enlightened internationalism could save the world. After finishing his studies at Harvard in 1940, he joined the U.S. Navy during World War II where he served in the Pacific. He returned as a war hero, which helped him win his election to Congress in 1946. Throughout his political career he shared the consensus view of the Cold War in Washington, meaning that the United States must do everything possible to protect U.S. interests from local Communists, whether in Latin America, Africa, or Asia. To that end he presided over the largest arms buildup, to that point, in U.S. peacetime history and dramatically increased the number of U.S. advisers in Vietnam from 500 to 16,500.

Despite a political campaign in 1960 that put little emphasis on inter-American relations, during his first year in office Kennedy tried to realign relations with Latin America. In many ways, Kennedy's Latin American policy emerged with many contradictions. Kennedy announced in a speech in San Juan, Puerto Rico, in December 1958 that he was sympathetic to nationalist movements, favored financial assistance to poor regions in the world, and supported the principle of non-intervention in inter-American relations. On the other hand, he stated "that should any Latin American country be driven by repression into the arms of the Communists, our attitude on non-intervention would change overnight" (Rabe, 1999: 13). Kennedy adopted a hard-line view on Castro's Cuba during his campaign against Vice-President **Nixon**, arguing that Cuba threatened the security of the United States by serving as a base from which to advance Communist influence and subversion throughout the hemisphere.

With the help of Adolf A. **Berle**, Jr., Kennedy used the failures of the Eisenhower administration to build a case for articulating a blueprint for Latin America. He began by putting more emphasis on the importance of democratic reform and economic development, but refused to eliminate military aid to Latin American governments. He criticized Eisenhower for supporting **friendly dictators**, called military aid to Latin America a disaster, and convinced many people that Latin America was vital in the context of the Cold War. He proposed an **Alliance for Progress** to promote economic development and democratic reform, reflecting his penchant for bold and decisive initiatives from the White House. Kennedy received most of his advice on Latin American affairs from individuals—Richard N. Goodwin, Arthur M. Schlesinger, Jr., Adolf Berle, Teodoro Moscoso, and C. Douglas Dillon—who believed that promoting economic development (modernization) and democratization would solve Latin America's problems. However, with the exception of Berle, none had any special training or expertise in Latin American culture or history. With New Frontier optimism, Kennedy and his advisers believed that the United States could stem the growing popularity for national liberation strategies following the Castro model of **guerrilla warfare**. The April 1961 fiasco at the Bay of Pigs did not stop Kennedy's determination to rid the hemisphere of Fidel Castro, oppose Soviet initiatives in the region, and pursue progressive development policies. With a fascination for counter-insurgency and special forces, Kennedy continued to back efforts to rid the Caribbean of Fidel Castro. He urged the CIA to mount **Operation Mongoose**, an attempt to infiltrate the island with saboteurs to overthrow Fidel Castro. On its own, but with the apparent acknowledgment of the president, the CIA continued plotting to assassinate Fidel Castro. His emphasis on unconventional war to counter national liberation insurgencies in Latin America and the Third World led to several blunders that stemmed from the belief in the right to **intervention** and **regime change** in other countries. To further his goal of pursuing "peaceful revolution" in Latin America, Kennedy organized the Alliance for Progress, created the Peace Corps as a symbol of U.S. idealism, and shifted the emphasis of U.S. aid programs from military assistance to economic and social development.

Kennedy's own inexperience in inter-American affairs did not prevent him from his campaign pledge to take charge of the Latin American policy of the United States. During his brief presidency, he visited Latin America three times, stayed in contact with most heads of state in the region, worked closely with his U.S. advisers, and spent time studying his briefing papers to better understand the region.

Kennedy possessed some core beliefs that he carried into his discussions about inter-American relations. He often expressed a sincere sympathy with the plight of average Latin Americans, felt that past mistakes needed to be corrected, and responded quickly to Latin American problems when he thought he could make a difference. He wanted to improve the legitimacy of U.S. policy in the region by making it clear that "we can't embrace every tinhorn dictator who tells us he's anticommunist while he's sitting on the necks of his own people" (Rabe, 1999: 17). Kennedy recognized the importance of trade and economic investment in Latin America, but realized that government planning and national development plans may be needed instead of a mindless application of free markets and privatization. Like many of his successors, Kennedy paid close attention to the domestic consequences of U.S.–Latin American policy and labored to keep controversial Latin American issues—the future of the Panama Canal, Castro and the Soviets, and independence for British Guiana—from harming the electoral chances of the Democratic Party. Although Cheddi Jagan's (the father of British Guiana/Guyana independence) goal was to create a socialist state by non-violent means, Kennedy was convinced that Jagan and his wife were hell bent on tying Guyana to the international Communist movement. Later, Kennedy administration officials involved in the downfall of Jagan admitted that the intense domestic fear of communism distorted the administration's thinking when dealing with revolutionaries such as Jagan. Nevertheless, according to Rabe (1999: 198), "The ouster of Goulart [Brazil] and Jagan in 1964 helped insure the reelection of a Democrat to the presidency that year." It is hard to overstate the importance of domestic politics for **Washington policymakers** dealing with Latin American political figures.

Kennedy was the first president to worry about the effects of a "second Cuba" on fighting and winning the Cold War in Latin America. Shortly before his death in Dallas, Texas, in 1963, Kennedy warned that Latin American was now "the most dangerous area in the world" because of Soviet attempts at penetration of the region. Kennedy's humiliation over his defeat at the hands of Fidel Castro produced a feeling of obsession with getting rid of Castro that influenced how the administration handled Latin American affairs. Although Kennedy wanted to rectify the mistakes of the past, he never appeared to make the connection between his failures over Cuba and the magnitude of the Communist threat throughout the region. The fate of Latin America was tied to the Cold War mind-set that the future of Western Civilization rested on victory in the Cold War. Failing to maintain a secure sphere of influence in Latin America would endanger the ability of the United States to deal with challenges in other parts of the world and give the Soviets an open door to meddle "in our own backyard." The Soviet-Cuban threat was often exaggerated for domestic political reasons, but Kennedy established the battle plan for combating communism in Latin America. Many of the reports that Kennedy received dealing with Latin America contained the same message: poverty and injustice, entrenched oligarchs reluctant to change, growing extremism and prospects for revolution, and the need to build nations that were progressive, socially just, and anti-Communist. The sturdy, self-reliant, anti-Communist societies that

Kennedy wished for proved to be far more challenging than he and his advisers envisioned at the time. Unfortunately, hardliners in the national security establishment pushed Kennedy's commitment in Vietnam and Laos, setting in motion the policies that would take the United States much deeper into one of its worst Third World quagmires. Despite Kennedy's mistakes, he remains popular in Latin America for his sympathy and understanding of the major problems facing the region and his noble efforts to forge a policy aimed at creating more liveable societies south of the border. Nevertheless, his lofty ideals and noble goals often led him and his foreign policy advisers in his administration to ultimately undermine many of his objectives in the Western Hemisphere. By the time of his **assassination** (November 22, 1963), President Kennedy had established a reputation as staunch defender of U.S. interests in the Americas and a leader to be admired at home and abroad. That reputation would decline with the declassification of government documents associated with his presidency. *See also* Cuban Missile Crisis (1962); Intervention and Non-Intervention; Scandals and Blunders; Threat Perception/Assessment.

Suggested Reading

Adolf A. Berle, Jr., *Latin America: Diplomacy and Reality* (New York: Harper and Row, 1962); Michael R. Beschloss, *The Crisis Years: Kennedy and Khrushchev, 1960–1963* (New York: Edward Burlingame Books, 1991); Hugh Brogan, *Kennedy* (London: Longman, 1996); James N. Giglio, *The Presidency of John F. Kennedy* (Lawrence: University Press of Kansas, 1991); John Hellmann, *The Kennedy Obsession: The American Myth of JFK* (New York: Columbia University Press, 1997); Seymour M. Hersh, *The Dark Side of Camelot* (Boston: Little, Brown, 1997); Walter LaFeber, "Thomas C. Mann and the Devolution of American Foreign Policy: From the Good Neighbor to Military Intervention," in Thomas J. McCormick and Walter LaFeber, eds., *Behind the Throne: Servants of Power to Imperial Presidents, 1898–1968* (Madison: University of Wisconsin Press, 1993); Herbert S. Parmet, *JFK: The Presidency of John F. Kennedy* (New York: Dial Press, 1983); Thomas G. Paterson, ed., *Kennedy's Quest for Victory: American Foreign Policy, 1961–1963* (New York: Oxford University Press, 1989); Stephen G. Rabe, *The Most Dangerous Area in the World: John F. Kennedy Confronts Communist Revolution in Latin America* (Chapel Hill: University of North Carolina Press, 1999); Thomas C. Reeves, *A Question of Character: A Life of John F. Kennedy* (New York: Free Press, 1991); Michael D. Shafer, *Deadly Paradigms: The Failure of U.S. Counterinsurgency Policy* (Princeton, NJ: Princeton University Press, 1988); Kenneth W. Thompson, ed., *The Kennedy Presidency* (New York: University Press of America, 1985); Lucien S. Vandenbroucke, *Perilous Options: Special Operations as an Instrument of U.S. Foreign Policy* (New York: Oxford University Press, 1993); William O. Walker III, "Mixing the Sweet with the Sour: Kennedy, Johnson, and Latin America," in Diane B. Kunz, ed., *The Diplomacy of the Crucial Decade* (New York: Columbia University Press, 1994); Richard J. Walton, *Cold War and Counterrevolution: The Foreign Policy of John F. Kennedy* (New York: Viking Press, 1972).

Kerry, John F. (1943–) Democratic senator from Massachusetts and presidential candidate in 2004 whose life in the U.S. Senate was devoted to efforts to deal with **terrorism** and narco-trafficking. Born in Aurora, Colorado, while his father was in the military, Kerry spent time in various parts of the United States before settling in the East. After graduating from Yale University in 1966, Kerry joined the U.S. Navy, where he became an officer on a gunboat in the Mekong Delta in Vietnam. He condemned the Vietnam War on return to the United States, spoke out in favor of those who served in the armed forces, entered Yale Law School in 1976, and embarked on a career as a prosecuting attorney in Boston. He was lieutenant governor of Massachusetts (1982–1984) before entering the U.S. Senate in 1984. Kerry made his mark in the U.S. Senate as chairman and ranking Democrat on the U.S. Senate Subcommittee on Terrorism, Narcotics, and International Operations, investigating White House efforts to aid the Nicaraguan **Contras**, **human rights** violations, and probed allegations that profits from Colombian drug cartels were being channeled to the Contras. He also used his legal talent and senatorial power to investigate other cases of drug corruption in the United States and other misdeeds. He emerged from a large field of Democratic challengers to President **George W. Bush** in the democratic primaries, picked a fellow senator, John Edwards (D–NC) as his running mate, and ran a cautious campaign, saying very little about U.S.–Latin American relations. During the 2004 presidential campaign Kerry criticized George W. Bush for ignoring Latin America—particularly **drug trafficking**, high unemployment, and political and economic crises connected with failed economic models of development—and promised to change this if elected president. He also emphasized that he would work to bring the United States closer to its Latin American neighbors by developing a "community of the Americas" that would provide for cooperation to protect the nations' security and laws, and other measures to reduce the risk of terrorist attacks in the region. However, the more moderate and principled Latin American policy that Kerry spoke of earlier in his political campaign soon disappeared by moving to the right for short-term political objectives later in the campaign.

While campaigning for president, Kerry issued a number of statements on Latin American designed to outflank Bush's reactionary and right-wing policies. To garner the support of wealthy anti-**Castro** exiles in South Florida, Kerry called for the continuation and intensification of the failed embargo policy of previous U.S. presidents. Kerry voted for the **Helms-Burton Law** in 1996 because he felt it was important to be tough on companies that deal with Fidel Castro. Kerry also attacked Venezuelan President Hugo Chávez, claiming he was a threat to **democracy**, a supporter of "narco-terrorists" in neighboring Colombia, and a close friend of Fidel Castro. It is obvious that Kerry's motives in trying to take votes from President Bush were aimed at winning Florida's twenty-seven electoral votes by pandering to Miami's Cuban-American community and wealthy Venezuelan expatriates living in Florida. Despite this maneuver, the Kerry-Edwards ticket lost Florida and lost more Latino votes to the Bush election. Kerry attracted more Latino votes than Republican George W. Bush, but the president made inroads into the Hispanic community by getting 45 percent of the vote, a small gain from the 2000 election. It's hard to gauge what Kerry's narrow loss (51 to 48 percent) to Bush means in terms of improving the U.S.–Latin American relationship, but the success of trumpeting the war on terrorism will no doubt influence what George W. Bush does in the White House during his second term. After his electoral loss in 2004, John F. Kerry returned to the U.S. Senate to challenge Bush's policies and consider plans for another presidential bid in 2008.

Suggested Reading

Larry Birns and Jessica Leight, "Disturbing Signals: Kerry and Latin America," *Counterpunch* (March 27/28, 2004); Lois Romano, "Kerry: Bush Has Neglected Latin America," *Washington Post* (June 27, 2004); Ginger Thompson, "Mexico to Press U.S. on Stalled Migration Plan," *New York Times* (November 8, 2004).

Kirkpatrick, Jeane Jordan (1926–) Political scientist, diplomat, and conservative ideologue whose career was launched by her views on how to correct the foreign policy dilemma of how best to deal with dictatorial (authoritarian) but pro–U.S. regimes in the Third World. As an antidote to the foreign relations failures that ruined the **Carter** presidency in 1979–1980, Kirkpatrick argued that the United States had a responsibility to support and maintain authoritarian rulers because they were redeemable and served as bulwarks against the more insidious forms of totalitarian communism. In the November 1979 issue of *Commentary*, she argued in "Dictators and Double Standards" that the Carter administration failed to distinguish between authoritarian and totalitarian rulers, arguing that Anastasio **Somoza** in Nicaragua and the Iranian Shah provided friendship and respect for U.S. interests abroad and were capable of moving toward **democracy**, traits unknown to "totalitarians" such as the **Sandinistas**, Fidel **Castro**, and other rulers from the past such as Hitler or Stalin. Her academic writings led to her appointment as U.S. ambassador to the **United Nations (UN)** in 1981 where she was known for her staunch anticommunism and inflexibility in dealing with East-West issues. Despite little experience in Latin America, aside from a doctoral dissertation on Peron's Argentina, Kirkpatrick quickly emerged as one of the principal intellectual architects of President Ronald **Reagan**'s Latin American policy. Eldon Kenworthy argued in 1984 that Kirkpatrick's expertise as a political theorist did not warrant her transformation by the Reagan administration as a knowledgeable official on matters related to Central America. Nevertheless, it was the simplification of Central American realities—democracy (friend); totalitarianism (foe)—that attracted the Reagan administration to Kirkpatrick's thinking and made her popular in anti-Communist circles.

Jeane Jordan was born in Duncan, Oklahoma, in 1926, graduated from Barnard College in 1948 and then attended Columbia University where she received her M.A. in 1950. After marrying Evron Kirkpatrick in 1955, she did research work for the **State Department** before returning to earn a Ph.D. from Columbia in 1967. She has taught political theory and foreign policy at Georgetown University since 1967, except when she engaged in government service. Her politics remained attached to the Democratic Party through the 1970s, but like other neo-conservatives at the time, she shed these ideological roots and gravitated toward the Republican Party and its more muscular anti-communism and realist foreign policy. With little knowledge of Central America, Kirkpatrick's insights relied on the work of others and simplistic notions of political culture to explain political instability, **human rights** violations, and the foundations of democracy. Despite evidence to the contrary, she remained convinced that the conflicts in El Salvador and Nicaragua were easily explained by the East-West struggle for world domination. Jeane Kirkpatrick was one of a number of Reagan administration policymakers who had never set foot in Central America, or seriously examined its history, but were given positions of enormous power to conduct policy and serve as polemicists for misguided policies under increasing attack from the **media** and Democrats in Congress. She left the Reagan administration in 1985 and returned to teaching and writing and remains as a fellow at the conservative **American Enterprise Institute (AEI)**. *See also* Cold War; Dictatorships; Reagan Doctrine; Scandals and Blunders; Threat Perception/Assessment.

Suggested Reading

Ronald Brownstein and Nina Easton, *Reagan's Ruling Class: Portraits of the President's Top One Hundred Officials* (New York: Pantheon Books, 1983); Judith Ewell, "Barely in the Inner Circle: Jeane Kirkpatrick," in Edward Crapol, ed., *Women and American Foreign Policy: Lobbyists, Critics, and Insiders*, 2nd ed. (Wilmington, DE: SR Books, 1992); Allan Gerson, *The Kirkpatrick Mission: Diplomacy Without Apology: America at the United Nations, 1981–1985* (New York: Free Press, 1991); Eldon Kenworthy, "Our Colleague Kirkpatrick," *LASA Forum*, Bulletin of the Latin American Studies Association 14, 4 (winter, 1984); Jeane J. Kirkpatrick, *The Withering Away of the Totalitarian State . . . and Other Surprises* (Washington, DC: AEI Press, 1990); Kirkpatrick, *Legitimacy and Force* (New Brunswick, NJ: Transaction Books, 1988); Kirkpatrick, *Dictatorships and Double Standards: Rationalism and Reason in Politics* (New York: Simon and Schuster, 1982); Kirkpatrick, *The Strategy of Deception: A Study in World-Wide Communist Tactics* (New York: Farrar, Straus, 1963).

Kissinger, Henry Alfred (1923–) Harvard political scientist and foreign policy consultant, national security adviser (1969–1975), and secretary of state (1973–1977) who was a major architect of American foreign policy in the administrations of Richard M. **Nixon** and Gerald R. **Ford** from 1969 to 1977. A German-born, Jewish refugee from Nazi Germany, Kissinger and his family settled in New York City where he attended high school and the City College of New York in 1940. After Pearl Harbor, he was drafted into the U.S. Army where he spent time in Europe before returning to the United States to enter Harvard University. There he became more Americanized while completing both undergraduate and graduate studies in political science and international relations. According to some who have studied Kissinger and written biographies of the man, his boyhood experience as a Jew in Hitler's Germany influenced Kissinger's views of diplomacy, nuclear warfare, covert operations, domestic turmoil, and the policymaking process. While teaching at Harvard after finishing his doctoral dissertation, Kissinger developed contacts with important politicians and business executives from the United States and other countries that proved invaluable for expanding his base of power within both political parties. As an adviser to Republican Governor Nelson A. **Rockefeller** in the 1960s, Kissinger managed to open a recruitment channel to prominent politicians seeking the presidency, including Rockefeller, Hubert H. Humphrey, and Richard Nixon. Shortly after Nixon won the 1968 presidential race, Kissinger was appointed as national security adviser.

While working inside the Nixon White House, Kissinger was able to apply his foreign policy intelligence and realist perspective on how the world should work in favor of U.S. interests. Latin America was of little importance to Kissinger, who viewed the axis of world power running in an East-West direction, not North-South. Nevertheless, Kissinger conducted a secretive foreign policy, often with little regard for congressional oversight and the protection of human rights abroad, that drew criticism from those who considered the Harvard professor arrogant and a self-promoter. His time in the limelight because of his handling of the Vietnam War, and the secret diplomacy that led to the opening of relations with the People's Republic of China, contributed to an aura of legitimacy and celebrity status that has stuck with him despite repeated attacks on his style, policies, credibility, bureaucratic power, and old-fashioned approach to international relations. Henry Kissinger shared the Nobel Peace Prize with his Vietnamese counterpart for his efforts to end the Vietnam War.

His career in government was marked by many deceits and obfuscations designed to circumvent bureaucratic and constitutional limits on the use of force and power. As more and more documents are declassified from Kissinger's work as national security adviser and secretary of state, we learn that his multivolume memoirs don't even begin to tell the full story of how he helped destroy the democratically elected government of Salvador **Allende** and bring decades of fascism to Chile and Argentina. In approving the covert plan to get rid of Allende, Kissinger told the secret committee in charge of approving covert actions, "I don't see why we need to stand by and watch a country go communist due to the irresponsibility of its own people."

Henry Kissinger's involvement in various Latin American policies is less known to the public than his policies directed at other parts of the world. As scholars and journalists gain access to government documents from the Kissinger era, what emerges is a sullied record of secrecy and duplicity in the conduct of foreign relations, distrust of democratic institutions, manipulation of subordinates, and his general indifference to the fate of individuals suffering abuse at the hands of tyrannical governments. These lesser-known activities have clearly clouded some of his diplomatic and global achievements. Few in the upper reaches of the Nixon and Ford presidencies knew or cared about Latin America. Nevertheless, Kissinger applied his realist vision to several trouble spots, including the White House decision to destabilize and remove Allende in Chile, negotiations designed to return the Panama Canal to Panama, **assassination** plots, support for Augusto **Pinochet**, and the secret work of **Operation Condor**, a multination effort by right-wing military governments in Latin America to share intelligence and manpower for the purpose of arresting and intimidating political opponents. At the height of Pinochet's repression three years after the coup against Allende, Kissinger met with Pinochet and told him "we are sympathetic to what you are trying to do here [in Chile]." After apologizing for congressional opposition to arms sales to General Pinochet, he applauded the 1973 coup by telling Pinochet, "You did a great service to the West in overthrowing Allende. Otherwise Chile would have followed Cuba." In the same year, Kissinger met with Argentina's foreign minister who received what he believed was tacit encouragement for his government's violent and repressive efforts; two years later Kissinger praised the Argentine junta for its outstanding job of wiping out **terrorism**. When Kissinger and Nixon were reminded of the moral and legal bankruptcy of their actions in Chile by their own advisers, they often defended Pinochet because he was "pro-American" and did not jeopardize U.S. interests.

Kissinger left government service when Jimmy **Carter** assumed the presidency in 1977 and devoted his private life to writing about the practice of international relations, voicing his conservative opinions on foreign crises in the mass **media**, and providing advice on foreign affairs to his clients at Kissinger Associates, a lucrative consulting firm in New York. Two U.S. presidents invited him to lend his prestige to two presidential commissions, but the only one he chaired and guided was an effort to find solutions and offer useful policy recommendations in Central America. Ronald **Reagan** appointed Kissinger to chair the National Bipartisan Commission on Central America in 1983, also known as the **Kissinger Commission**; it produced a biased report that came out in time for Reagan's re-election bid, which provided cover for the Reagan administration's secret war in Nicaragua.

Under pressure from victims' families of the 9/11 tragedy, President **George W. Bush** appointed Henry Kissinger in November 2002 to head a commission to investigate the attacks and make recommendations that might prevent such attacks in the future. At the time of his appointment, many in the media expressed doubts that the truth about what the president learned in his August 2001 briefing about Al-Qaeda operatives and plans, and what bureaucratic wires were crossed at the **Central Intelligence Agency (CIA)**, FBI, and Immigration and Naturalization Service (INS), would come to light from a chairman whose *modus operandi* has been secretiveness and the protection of Republican presidents. Kissinger's appointment was made even more controversial by the 2002 release of *The Trials of Henry Kissinger*, a documentary movie that indicts the former national security adviser as a war criminal for his involvement in prolonging the war in Vietnam, the secret bombing of Cambodia, the slaughter in East Timor, and the destruction of democracy in Chile during the Allende years. Several weeks after his appointment to head the 9/11 Commission, Kissinger resigned and returned to his work at Kissinger Associates, citing difficulties with the rule that members reveal the names of business clients that might suggest a conflict of interest. Many Americans questioned why Henry Kissinger would accept such a position in the first place, particularly given his obvious partisanship and proclivity for secrecy and deception.
See also Cold War; Human Rights; September 11, 2001.

Suggested Reading

Dan Caldwell, ed., *Henry Kissinger, His Personality and Politics* (Durham, NC: Duke University Press, 1983); Richard A. Falk, *What's Wrong with Henry Kissinger's Foreign Policy* (Princeton, NJ: Center of International Studies, Princeton University, 1974); Melvin A. Goodman, "Choice of Kissinger Discredits 9/11 Probe," *Baltimore Sun* (December 5, 2002); Seymour Hersh, *The Price of Power: Kissinger in the Nixon White House* (New York: Summit Books, 1983); Christopher Hitchens, *The Trial of Henry Kissinger* (London: Verso, 2001); Walter Isaacson, *Kissinger: A Biography* (New York: Simon and Schuster, 1992); Henry Kissinger, *Diplomacy* (New York: Touchstone, 1995); Kissinger, *Years of Upheaval* (Boston: Little, Brown, 1983); Kissinger, *White House Years* (Boston: Little, Brown, 1979); Kissinger, *Major Statements on Latin America* (Washington, DC: U.S. Department of State, Bureau of Public Affairs, 1976); "The Kissinger Deceit," *The Nation* (December 23, 2002); Peter Kornbluh, *The Pinochet File: A Declassified Dossier on Atrocity and Accountability* (New York: New Press, 2003); Diana Jean Schemo, "Latin Death Squads and the U.S.: A New Disclosure," *New York Times* (October 23, 2002); Robert D. Schulzinger, *Henry Kissinger: A Doctor of Diplomacy* (New York: Columbia University Press, 1989); Tad Szulc, *The Illusion of Peace: Foreign Policy in the Nixon Years* (New York: Viking Press, 1978).

Kissinger Commission (1983) President **Ronald Reagan** set up a bipartisan blue-ribbon panel in 1983 to justify his Central American policy and undermine liberal Democrats' opposition to policies aimed at El Salvador and Nicaragua. The brainchild of two neo-conservatives—**United Nations (UN)** ambassador Jeane **Kirkpatrick** and the late Senator Henry Jackson—and chaired by Henry **Kissinger**, the National Bipartisan Commission on Central America was aimed at defusing Central America as an election issue in 1984. Its major purpose was to provide a rationale for current policy rather than a new one. The selection of Henry Kissinger to chair the commission was not universally popular, given the fact that he had presided over the CIA's successful overthrow of Chilean President Salvador **Allende**, the bombing of Hanoi, the Panama Canal "giveaway," and the diplomacy of detente and the loss of U.S. military prestige. But Kissinger still retained credibility with the public and agreed completely with Reagan's hard-line Central American policy. Critics of the commission, and later its report, point out that its bipartisanship was only nominally divided between Republicans and Democrats; the Democrats were mostly **Cold War** liberals and the Republicans were all conservatives. Only two of the twelve-member panel could be considered moderately liberal in their political orientation. Yale economics professor Carlos Díaz-Alejandro, was appointed without the president's advisers knowing that his Cuban-American heritage did not represent the views of Cuban exiles in the United States. He was the only member who had any experience or expertise in the region, although he specialized in South America. The rest of the commissioners were uninformed about Central America and were heavily dependent on the information they gathered from hearings and analysis that was contracted to consultants in Washington with Central American experience. When the Kissinger Commission traveled to Latin America, they spent less than one day in each Central American country they visited. As William LeoGrande (1998) points out in his exhaustive study of the period, "With Kissinger in charge, there was never any doubt that the commission's report would frame the Central American crisis in East-West terms and call for increased military assistance."

Political scientist Howard J. **Wiarda** prepared two submissions as "Senior Consultant" to the Kissinger Commission while working for the **American Enterprise Institute (AEI)**, a conservative **think tank** with ties to the Reagan administration. Many AEI scholars testified to the Kissinger Commission and helped craft what many considered to be an alarmist report on the "Communist challenge" in Central America and the danger of doing nothing to stop the Soviets and Cubans south of the border. A strong believer in corporatist theories of political development in Latin America, Wiarda realized that U.S.–Latin American policy was often devoid of useful theories and often misguided due to "ethnocentrism" and false analogies in the decision-making process. Nevertheless, Wiarda was a staunch defender of the Reagan Doctrine and the conclusions and recommendations set forth in the Kissinger Commission Report.

The report, like the policy, contained elements of fantasy concerning the problems and magnitude of the threat that existed in El Salvador and Nicaragua. With Kissinger in charge, the commission report provided a clever and sophisticated brief for Reagan's Central American policy and the stamp of bipartisan consistency and truth. When the report appeared in January 1984 it contained four dubious premises: the Cubans and Soviets were behind the crisis in Central America and therefore a threat to the security of the United States; the United States was supporting genuine democrats and functioning democracies in the region; Washington favored serious social and economic reform to remedy past injustices; and that the United States favored a political rather than a military solution to the Central American crisis. The report had little impact on the growing debate over Central America and the reactions were predictably partisan: liberal Democrats criticized the report for its flawed logic; supporters of the president approved the report, finding nothing of substance to criticize. The American public was overwhelmingly opposed to providing El Salvador with economic aid, even when told that the president's commission had recommended it. The content of the report and later its implementation was influenced by Lt. Colonel Oliver L. **North** when he worked as the **National Security Council**'s **(NSC)** liaison to the Kissinger Commission. Like most other members of the commission, North spoke no Spanish and had no expertise or experience in Central America. While on the commission's trip through Central America he would often jokingly refer to himself as "the advance man for the U.S. invasion." At its core the Kissinger Commission report was a Cold War document designed to contain the spread of revolution by ostensibly addressing the causes of Latin American **revolutions**: poverty, injustice, economic decay, and repressive and corrupt governments. But unlike other presidential commissions during the Cold War and after, the Kissinger Commission report exaggerated the threats to U.S. security by using emotionally charged language and presented to the American people and Congress an unrealistic and overly confident guide to

American foreign policy. It also contained a managerial, problem-solving mind-set convinced that it would be quick and easy to transform Central American societies into smaller versions of the United States: liberal, democratic, progressive, and prosperous. Despite the lofty aspirations found in the report, the key findings had little impact on the conduct of U.S.–Central American policy throughout the Reagan era. It did little to gain bipartisan support in the Senate and House, despite the fact that it contained two separate ideological prescriptions for Central America: a liberal-reformist component stressing **human rights** and political and economic reform along with a conservative section emphasizing the importance of private-sector development programs and the importance of U.S. military aid to stop the spread of communism in Latin America. *See also* Arias Sánchez, Oscar; Washington Policymakers.

Suggested Reading

Larry G. Hufford, *The United States in Central America: An Analysis of the Kissinger Commission Report* (Lewiston, NY: E. Mellen Press, 1987); William M. LeoGrande, *Our Own Backyard: The United States in Central America, 1977–1992* (Chapel Hill: University of North Carolina Press, 1998); Robert Parry, *Fooling America: How Washington Insiders Twist the Truth and Manufacture the Conventional Wisdom* (New York: William Morrow, 1992); *The Report of the President's National Bipartisan Commission on Central America* [Kissinger Commission Report] (New York: Macmillan, 1984).

Knox, Philander Chase (1853–1921) Corporate lawyer, U.S. senator, and secretary of state during the presidency of William Howard **Taft** (1909–1913). Philander C. Knox was born in Brownsville, Pennsylvania, graduated from Mount Union College in Ohio, studied law and was admitted to the bar in 1875. The fact that Knox had almost no knowledge of foreign affairs did not prevent President Taft from nominating him to be his secretary of state in 1909. Knox's Latin American policy was based on his negative beliefs about Latin American culture, the necessity of the **Monroe Doctrine** to maintain U.S. **hegemony** in Latin America, and **Dollar Diplomacy**, defined as the substitution of dollars for bullets, to improve U.S.–Latin American relations. With better supervision and public relations, Knox envisioned a more stable and prosperous region in tune with U.S. security and financial interests. The efforts to remake Latin America in the image of the United States were resented in Latin America and Dollar Diplomacy proved to be far too simplistic to solve the problems of development as defined by those in favor of U.S. paternalism (diplomacy) and the infusion of capitalist principles (dollars). The principal motivation behind Dollar Diplomacy came from Knox's belief in the wisdom of blending economic and security issues and the moral duty of the United States to enhance its security in the Caribbean by ensuring Latin Americans paid their debts. Knox's diplomacy of the dollar was applied most forcefully in Haiti, Nicaragua, and the Dominican Republic. As political scientist Lars Schoultz (1998: 209) points out, "every case [in which Dollar Diplomacy was implemented] began with U.S. government **intervention**, after which government officials brokered a financial arrangement between the intervened Latin American government and the U.S. private sector." Philander Knox left the **State Department** in 1913 and returned to his law practice until 1917 when he was elected again to the U.S. Senate. During his final years in the Senate, Knox opposed America's joining the **League of Nations**, arguing that it was unconstitutional. He died in 1921 while still in the Senate. *See also* Threat Perception/Assessment.

Suggested Reading

Walter F. Scholes, "Philander C. Knox," in Norman A. Graebner, ed., *An Uncertain Tradition* (New York: McGraw-Hill, 1961); *New York Times* (October 13, 1921); Lars Schoultz, *Beneath the United States: A History of U.S. Policy Toward Latin America* (Cambridge, MA: Harvard University Press, 1998).

L

Lansky, Meyer (1902–1983) Major underworld criminal figure whose money laundering and casino gambling enterprises in Cuba and the Bahamas played a key role in the events leading up to the Cuban Revolution in 1959. Known as the "Jewish Godfather," Lansky concentrated much of his activity in Cuba during the 1950s. Once Fidel **Castro** came to power in 1959, revolutionary leaders banned gambling and Lansky's plush casino operations at his Hotel Nacional were lost forever. Meyer Lansky realized that for the mob to resume its lucrative gambling activities in Cuba, Castro would have to be removed. Once the **Central Intelligence Agency (CIA)** advocated the murder of Fidel Castro, Lansky offered to assist with **Operation Mongoose**, the CIA-Mafia plot to assassinate Fidel Castro.

Lansky was born Maier Suchowljansky in Grodno, Byelorus, and came to the United States as a youth in 1911. He attended public schools in New York City where he was considered a good student and skilled with numbers. However, he dropped out of school at age sixteen and entered the world of violent crime, something he was accustomed to through life on the volatile streets of the Lower East Side of the city. He forged a friendship with "Bugsy" Siegel, another Jewish hoodlum, and together they engaged in hijacking, robberies, burglaries, and extortion. After forming alliances with other criminals and racketeers, Lansky developed a specialty in gambling and was the key figure in arranging casino gambling in Florida and Cuba during the 1930s and 1940s.

Lansky established a relationship with Fulgencio **Batista** in 1939 that allowed him to take over the Oriental Park racetrack and the lucrative casinos at Havana's Casino Nacional. Tourist travel slowed to a trickle during **World War II** so Lansky decided to return to Florida where he was joined by Batista after the end of his term in 1944. With Lansky gone, national crime syndicate boss Salvatore "Lucky" Luciano moved to Cuba in 1946 with the intention of establishing a gambling and narcotics operation that would afford him the possibility of regaining his status as head of the U.S. mob. Washington pressured the government of Dr. Ramón Grau (1944–1948) to deport Luciano back to Italy, thus opening the door again for the return of Meyer Lansky. After the state of Florida voted against legalized gambling and the state's casinos were closed down, the mob worked hand-in-glove with Batista and other Cuban politicians and military officials to help Batista regain power once again. This would allow for the return of Batista and key North American crime figures. After Batista's 1952 coup, Lansky and other mobsters took over the major hotels, nightclubs, pornography field, prostitution rings, and the illicit drug business that helped route heroin and cocaine to the United States. The large-scale corruption and incredible self-enrichment established the three-part basis of power in pre-Castro Cuba: organized crime, American business, and Batista's military.

After World War II, Lansky worked with Siegel in Las Vegas where they pioneered casino gambling and made enormous profits in high-risk enterprises. Lansky made millions from skimming operations in Las Vegas, a business that worked because of his ability to appear "fair and honest" among his fellow hoodlums. His vast criminal wealth finally attracted the attention of the Justice Department, and in 1962 it began to monitor his activities. After years of FBI surveillance, and fearing an indictment for tax evasion, Lansky fled to Israel where he hoped to claim citizenship as a Jew and avoid extradition to the United States. After a long legal battle, Lansky was denied citizenship in 1972 and forced to leave Israel. He sought sanctuary in Paraguay, but was prevented from leaving his plane in Asunción, the capital. At this point he was forced to return to the United States were he was arrested in Miami in 1972 for income tax evasion and contempt of court. He managed to escape the more serious accusations—his only conviction was for illegal gambling—and spent the rest of his life in seclusion in Miami. The close connection between the U.S. mob, the tyrant Batista, and key sectors of the U.S. business community before 1958 became a source of anger and humiliation for millions of Cubans and provided much of the legitimacy for the intense nationalism, **anti-Americanism**, and political opposition that contributed to the success of the Cuban Revolution by Fidel Castro. *See also* Assassination; Revolutions.

Suggested Reading

Robert Lacey, *Little Man: Meyer Lansky and the Gangster Life* (Boston: Little, Brown, 1991); Hank Messick, *Lansky* (New York: Putnam, 1973); Thomas G. Paterson, *Contesting Castro: The United States and the Triumph of the Cuban Revolution* (New York: Oxford University Press, 1994).

Latin American Working Group (LAWG) A coalition of non-governmental, religious, policy, and humanitarian agencies organized to promote U.S. policy toward Latin America that stresses **human rights**, justice, peace, and sustainable development. In 2003–2004 LAWG focused on three major campaigns to improve U.S.–Latin American relations: (1) a more peaceful approach to Colombia, meaning support for increased social and economic aid and no military aid; (2) removal of the trade and travel embargo on Cuba; and (3) more humane border policies designed to reduce the deaths of immigrants on the U.S.–Mexico border. The Latin American Working Group believes that by giving concerned citizens better tools to understand and change U.S. policy toward Latin America where needed, concerned and informed citizens can improve hemispheric relations. LAWG often works with the **Washington Office on Latin America (WOLA)** and the Center for International Policy in Washington, D.C., and a variety of other non-governmental organizations in the United States and Latin America to achieve its objectives. Its website on U.S. military training and aid programs in Latin America and the Caribbean (www.ciponline/facts) is the most comprehensive single source on this subject and a popular source of information for scholars, journalists, congressional staff, and policy activists. The Latin American Working Group's website (www.lawg.org) offers regular action alerts to help individuals influence U.S. policymakers and Latin American governments. LAWG publishes *The Advocate*, a bimonthly newsletter highlighting the group's activities and issues of concern to individuals in favor of a more enlightened policy toward Latin America. In 2003 it established the Latin American Working Group Education Fund to focus on education activities while LAWG engages in lobbying activities aimed at supporting human rights and a more peaceful world. The Education Fund publishes pamphlets on current policy devoted to providing citizens with facts to energize their activism in dealing with U.S.–Latin American relations. In 2004 LAWG published *Ignored Majority: The Moderate Cuban-American Community* and *Going to Extremes: The US-Funded Aerial Eradication Program in Colombia*. LAWG's work is supported by contributions from the Ford Foundation, the Christopher Reynolds Foundation, the Arca Foundation, the Stewart Mott Charitable Trust, the Open Society Institute Development Foundation, and the General Service Foundation. Several religious and humanitarian organizations also contribute to the advocacy work carried out by the Latin American Working Group. *See also* Plan Colombia; September 11, 2001.

Suggested Reading

Latin American Working Group, *Action at Home for Just Policies Abroad*. 2003 Annual Report (Washington, DC: LAWG, 2003).

LAWG. *See* Latin American Working Group

League of Nations Following **World War I**, President Woodrow **Wilson** inspired the creation of the League of Nations, the world's first permanent international security organization. The United States never joined the organization, and the league had trouble creating even the minimum conditions for collective security. Nevertheless, it was an attractive body for the Latin American members (nine Latin

American countries became charter members in 1919, and several more joined during the 1920s) because they believed it would serve as an instrument for counterbalancing the growing economic and political power of the United States and the economic power of Great Britain in the Western Hemisphere. The Latin American nations that joined the league hoped that it would provide the legal means for countering the following U.S. policies: **Big Stick diplomacy**, the various corollaries attached to the **Monroe Doctrine**, and British designs in the Caribbean. The principles of non-intervention and peaceful settlement of disputes, later incorporated into the Charter of the **Organization of American States (OAS)**, were of particular importance to the Latin Americans. However, they were disappointed to find that the Monroe Doctrine was described as a "regional understanding" instead of a unilateral declaration of policy by Washington. The League of Nations never served as an organization to check the power of the United States since the United States never joined and failed to demonstrate much interest in mediating international disputes peacefully. By 1938, most of the Latin American and Caribbean members left the league and turned to bilateral strategies for coping with the United States. *See also* Intervention and Non-Intervention; United Nations (UN).

Suggested Reading

Larman C. Wilson and David W. Dent, *Historical Dictionary of Inter-American Organizations* (Lanham, MD: Scarecrow Press, 1998).

Lodge, Henry Cabot, Sr. (1850–1924) Historian, political scientist, and Republican member of Congress from Massachusetts, first as a member of the House of Representatives and later as senator from the same state. During his long term in the U.S. Senate he served as a member of the Senate Foreign Relations Committee and exercised a major influence on U.S. foreign policy. A staunch protectionist and ardent nationalist, Lodge embraced the new imperialism of the 1890s and strongly supported the war against Spain in 1898. His impact on U.S.–Latin American relations can be seen in his support for (1) U.S. expansionism in the 1890s, (2) U.S. control over Cuba, (3) ratification of Hay-Pauncefote Treaty (1901) granting the United States an exclusive right to build and operate an interoceanic canal in Central America, (4) the **Lodge Corollary** to the **Monroe Doctrine** prohibiting private Japanese investors from purchasing strategically valuable land in Mexico's Baja California peninsula, and (5) the indemnification of Colombia for the loss of Panama.

Henry Cabot Lodge, Sr. was born in Boston into a wealthy and prominent family. After graduating from Harvard in 1871, Lodge obtained a law degree before completing his graduate studies in political science. Lodge received Harvard's first Ph.D. in political science and taught there until his academic life ended, and he turned to a career in politics as a Republican. His historical writings focused on biographies of Alexander Hamilton, Daniel Webster, and George Washington. Lodge served in the Senate until his death in 1924. *See also* Big Stick Diplomacy; Imperialism; Lodge Corollary (1912).

Suggested Reading

John Arthur Garraty, *Henry Cabot Lodge: A Biography* (New York: Knopf, 1953); Warren Zimmermann, *First Great Triumph: How Five Americans Made Their Country a World Power* (New York: Farrar, Straus, and Giroux, 2002).

Lodge Corollary (1912) An extension of the **Monroe Doctrine**, named for Senator Henry Cabot **Lodge**, Sr., that emerged from the proposed sale of an important harbor in lower California by American investors to a group of Japanese investors in 1911–1912. Senator Lodge, a firm believer in the Monroe Doctrine, introduced a resolution that stated that strategic places in Latin America could not be sold to a foreign country because of the possibility that it might make military use of the land against the United States. The U.S. Senate supported Lodge's proposed resolution by a 51–4 vote, but President William H. **Taft** opposed it. Although the sale of private property never took place, the Lodge Corollary established a remarkable principle for excluding non-American influence from the Western Hemisphere. The Lodge Corollary was significant because it represented a new application of the Monroe Doctrine by applying it to an Asian nation while at the same time prohibiting the transfer of private property between private individuals. As Federico Gil (1971: 73) points out, "It extended Monroe's principles to corporations or associations under control of a non-American government, perhaps in recognition that there existed modern subterfuges by which foreign governments could achieve indirectly what they could not do without violating the Doctrine." Thus, by infringing on the sovereignty of Mexico, the Lodge Corollary represented further evidence of U.S. claims to **hegemony** over the American states. For many critics of American foreign policy at the time, the Lodge Corollary contributed to the growing **anti-Americanism** in Latin America that followed the **Roosevelt Corollary to the Monroe Doctrine** and subsequent use of military force in the region. *See also* Imperalism; Mahan, Alfred Thayer.

Suggested Reading

Federico G. Gil, *Latin American–United States Relations* (New York: Harcourt Brace Jovanovich, 1971); Herbert F. Wright, "Philander Chase Knox," in Samuel F. Bemis, ed., *American Secretaries of State and Their Diplomacy*, Vol. 9 (New York: Knopf, 1928).

Lowenthal, Abraham F. (1941–) International relations professor, founder, and director of several prominent **think tanks** with a focus on U.S.–Latin American relations, and a prolific writer on a wide variety of subjects dealing mainly with the government and politics of Latin America and hemispheric relations. Abraham Lowenthal has pursued two distinct, but intersecting careers: as a scholar, teacher, commentator and adviser on U.S.–Latin American relations and as an institution-builder at the nexus between the world of ideas and the world of decision-making and policy implementation. Although he has testified many times before Congress, and served on commissions dealing with U.S.–Latin American relations, Abraham Lowenthal has never served in a formal government position; he was invited to join the **Ford**, **Carter**, and **Clinton** administrations, but declined to do so in each case. After much of his life on the East Coast—Cambridge, Princeton, New York City, and Washington—where he taught courses on international affairs, founded and directed Latin American programs and think tanks, including the Latin American Program at the Woodrow Wilson International Center for Scholars and the well-known **Inter-American Dialogue**, he moved for personal reasons to the University of Southern California where he continued to teach, consult, and to direct research projects and centers. In 1995, he founded the Pacific Council on International Policy, an independent and non-partisan leadership forum that focuses on global trends of particular importance to the western United States. He is currently (2005) professor of international relations at the University of Southern California (USC), and vice-president of the Council on Foreign Relations in New York.

His early work on Latin America focused on the Dominican Republic and Peru, two countries where he was employed by the Ford Foundation. His first book (and Ph.D. dissertation) on the Dominican Republic focused on the impact of ideas on foreign policy; a theme he returns to in *Partners in Conflict* (1990). During the 1970s he wrote two influential articles on U.S.–Latin American relations. His 1973 article on "United States Policy Toward Latin America: 'Liberal,' 'Radical,' and 'Bureaucratic' Perspectives" in the *Latin American Research Review* made a significant contribution to the academic literature on hemispheric relations. The second one—"The United States and Latin America: Ending the Hegemonic Presumption"—appeared in *Foreign Affairs* in 1976 and had a measurable impact on Latin American policy. Throughout his career he has concentrated on understanding and trying to improve "mental maps" about Latin America and its relations with the United States.

Abraham Lowenthal was born in Hyannis, Massachusetts, on April 6, 1941, the child of German Jewish refugees who came to the United States in 1939. Abraham Lowenthal attended public schools in Leominster, Massachusetts, and Harvard where he earned his A.B. (1961), M.P.A. (1964, Graduate School of Public Administration), and Ph.D. (1971, Government). While at Harvard, he studied with McGeorge Bundy (his senior honor's adviser), Hans J. Morgenthau, Henry A. **Kissinger**, Ernest R. May, Samuel P. Huntington (his main Ph.D. adviser). His interest in history, government, and public policy coincided with the growing public and private interest in Latin America associated with the Cuban Revolution, the **Alliance for Progress**, and opposition to the way Latin American policy was being formulated in the United States. In his writings, lectures, seminars, congressional testimony, consulting, and research activities, Professor Lowenthal has been a frequent critic of U.S.–Latin American policy. While working with the Linowitz Commission in the 1970s, and the Inter-American Dialogue in the 1980s, Lowenthal articulated what some considered a liberal perspective on U.S.–Latin American relations, stressing: (1) the limits of American **intervention** in seeking to influence what happens in Latin America; (2) the importance of dialogue as a means of resolving conflicts; (3) the importance of rethinking policies that have proven to be conflictual and counter-productive; (4) the need to improve the process of making policy toward Latin America; and (5) the relationship between the press, **public opinion** and education on what the United States does in Latin America. Professor Lowenthal has been a prime mover in articulating the need to search for lessons in past U.S.–Latin American relations to improve the inter-American relationship. Since moving to USC in 1984, Professor Lowenthal has developed a greater interest in Mexico and U.S.–Mexico relations, democratic governance, U.S. relations with the Pacific Basin, and California's international role in that region.

Abraham Lowenthal has written, edited and/or co-edited twelve books dealing with the government and politics of Latin America and U.S.–Latin American relations. He has also published numerous journal articles and more than 150 newspaper columns. His views of U.S.–Latin American relations are rooted in the belief that the United States and Latin America need to address issues of mutual concern through dialogue and understanding while avoiding the mistakes from the past that have contributed to a troubled relationship. This means that Latin America needs more sustained attention from Washington than has been the case among recent presidents of the United States. A key feature of his work at the Wilson Center, the Inter-American Dialogue, and USC California-Mexico project and the Pacific Council has been a commitment to the systematic exchange of ideas with Latin Americans and others from other countries and incorporating vital international perspectives into thinking about what the United States does in Latin America and the Caribbean. *See also* Democracy and Democracy Promotion; Hegemony; Partisanship and Policy.

Suggested Reading

Abraham F. Lowenthal, "Latin America at the Century's Turn," in Larry Diamond and Marc F. Plattner, eds., *The Global Divergence of Democracy* (Baltimore, MD: Johns Hopkins University Press, 2001); Lowenthal, *The Dominican Intervention* (Cambridge, MA: Harvard University Press, 1972), Reissued in paperback (with a new preface) by Johns Hopkins University Press, 1994; Lowenthal, *Partners in Conflict: The United States and Latin America in the 1990s*, rev. ed. (Baltimore, MD: Johns Hopkins University Press, 1990); Lowenthal, ed., *Exporting Democracy: The United States and Latin America* (Baltimore, MD: Johns Hopkins University Press, 1991); Lowenthal and Jorge I. Domínguez, eds., *Constructing Democratic Governance: Latin America and the Caribbean in the mid-1990s* (Baltimore, MD: Johns Hopkins University Press, 1996).

M

Mahan, Alfred Thayer (1840–1914) Officer in the U.S. Navy and prominent historian whose theories on the importance of sea power had an important role in the strategic thinking of **Theodore Roosevelt**, Henry Cabot **Lodge**, Sr., Elihu **Root** and others who believed in the transformation of the United States into a world power. After graduating from the U.S. Naval Academy in 1859, Mahan began a career of teaching and writing that brought him notoriety as a key figure in the U.S. debate over overseas expansion after the U.S. Civil War. Mahan's views followed the ideology of **Manifest Destiny** (calling for continental expansion), the rapid success of the **Mexican-American War** (territorial annexation), the superiority of the Anglo-Saxon race advocated by Josiah Strong (a Congregational minister who wrote the popular *Our Country* in 1885), and the nationalist views of Charles Darwin who believed that a strong nation has the "right to expand to survive." In Mahan's view, the United States would never be able to realize its ultimate destiny as a world power without the ability to project sea power globally. Without command of the seas, the United States would be hampered in its ability to influence world affairs.

The burst of extra-continental **imperialism** sponsored by Theodore Roosevelt and his friends in the 1890s resulted in a number of interventions, annexations, and protectorates in Latin America that relied on the geopolitical theories of Admiral Alfred T. Mahan. The period of U.S. **intervention** in Latin America and the Caribbean between 1895 and 1930 served to expand the power of the United States throughout the Western Hemisphere, but it also spawned a generation of Latin Americans who resented the encroachments on their sovereignty, independence, security, and national well-being.

While teaching at the U.S. Navy War College, Mahan wrote two works that influenced U.S. foreign policy at the turn of the century: *The Influence of Sea Power Upon History, 1660–1783* (1890), and *The Influence of Sea Power Upon the French Revolution and Empire, 1793–1812* (1892). During the 1890s he wrote numerous articles that influenced the Latin American policy of the United States, particularly the establishment of naval bases in the Caribbean, the war with Spain to liberate Cuba, and the necessity of building a transoceanic canal in Panama. Although Mahan retired in 1896, he was recalled to active duty in 1898 to direct naval operations during the **Spanish-Cuban-American War**. The Latin American policy of the United States after 1890 was constructed on the naval and political strategies of Alfred Thayer Mahan. Some historians claim that Mahan's ideas were behind the modern policy initiatives to build aircraft carriers to carry military forces to project U.S. power and control around the world. *See also* Big Stick Diplomacy; Hay-Bunau-Varilla Treaty (1903); Hegemony; Imperialism; Intervention and Non-Intervention.

Suggested Reading

Alfred Thayer Mahan, *The Influence of Sea Power Upon History, 1660–1783* (1890; reprint, New York: Dover Publications, 1987); Mahan, *The Influence of Sea Power Upon the French Revolution and Empire, 1793–1812* (1892; reprint, New York: Greenwood Press, 1968); Mahan, *The Interest of America in International Conditions* (Boston: Little, Brown, 1915); Richard W. Turk, *The Ambiguous Relationship: Theodore Roosevelt and Alfred Thayer Mahan* (New York: Greenwood Press, 1987); Warren Zimmermann, *The First Great Triumph: How Five Americans Made Their Country a World Power* (New York: Farrar, Straus, and Giroux, 2002).

Malvinas War. *See* Falklands/Malvinas War (1982)

Manifest Destiny A belief in the superiority of the United States and its institutions and values during the nineteenth and early twentieth centuries that served as the basis for America's territorial growth, including the continental expansion, a major war with Mexico, the annexation of Puerto Rico and the Panama Canal Zone (1903–2000), and the creation of protectorates over Cuba and other Caribbean countries. The term "Manifest Destiny" was coined by John L. O'Sullivan in an 1845 editorial in his *Democratic Review*. O'Sullivan was a pro-southern proponent of nationalism and expansionism prior to the U.S. Civil War. A strong believer in Cuban annexation, he backed the Narciso López expedition to the island in 1849 and was indicted twice for violating neutrality laws prohibiting such endeavors.

The earlier form of Manifest Destiny that served as a justification for American continental expansionism in the 1840s was followed by a new Manifest Destiny in the 1890s in which expansionism became transoceanic, with a regional focus on Latin America and the Far East. The New Manifest Destiny carried with it some of the original beliefs in Anglo-Saxon racial superiority and the obligation to civilize and Christianize inferior and immature peoples of the world, but it also acquired a new emphasis on economic exploitation, a market-based foreign policy to compete with the British and Germans, and a means to overcome the depression of the 1890s. *See also* Filibusters/Filibustering; Imperialism; Intervention and Non-Intervention; Mexican-American War (1846–1848); Polk, James K.; Race and Racism.

Suggested Reading

Charles H. Brown, *Agents of Manifest Destiny: The Lives and Times of the Filibusters* (Chapel Hill: University of North Carolina Press, 1981); David S. Heidler and Jeanne T. Heidler, *Manifest Destiny* (Westport, CT: Greenwood Press, 2003); Reginald Horsman, *Race and Manifest Destiny: The Origins of American Racial Anglo-Saxonism* (Cambridge, MA: Harvard University Press, 1981); Mark S. Joy, *American Expansionism, 1783–1860: A Manifest Destiny?* (Harlow: Longman, 2003); Dana Lindaman and Kyle Ward, *History Lessons: How Textbooks from Around the World Portray U.S. History* (New York: New Press, 2004); Robert E. May, *Manifest Destiny's Underworld: Filibustering in Antebellum America* (Chapel Hill: University of North Carolina Press, 2003); Frederick Merk, *Manifest Destiny and Mission in American History: A Reinterpretation* (New York: Alfred A. Knopf, 1963); James A. Morone, *Hellfire Nation: the Politics of Sin in American History* (New Haven: Yale University Press, 2003); Frank Lawrence Owsley, Jr., and Gene A. Smith, *Filibusters and Expansionists: Jeffersonian Manifest Destiny, 1800–1821* (Tuscaloosa: University of Alabama Press, 1997); Anders Stephenson, *Manifest Destiny: American Expansionism and the Empire of Right* (New York: Hill and Wang, 1995); James T. Wall, *Manifest Destiny Denied: America's First Intervention in Nicaragua* (Washington, DC: University Press of America, 1981).

Mann, Thomas Clifton (1912–) Lawyer and controversial diplomat who played a major role in U.S.–Latin American relations during the **Kennedy-Johnson** years in the 1960s. Born in Laredo, Texas, Thomas C. Mann graduated from Baylor University where he received his B.A. and LL.B. in 1934. He practiced law in Laredo until he decided to join the **State Department** in 1942. Between that year and his last State Department post in 1966, Mann worked in various diplomatic posts in Washington and Latin America. As assistant secretary of state for inter-American affairs, Mann represented the United States at many economic conferences, helped to write the Act of Bogotá (1960) and negotiate the Chamizal Treaty, and while in the Johnson administration he became the chief spokesman for the administration on Latin American relations. In this position he negotiated a settlement of the anti–United States flag riots in Panama in 1964, administered the **Alliance for Progress**, and the diplomacy related to the U.S. invasion of the Dominican Republic in 1965. However, he opposed the **Bay of Pigs** invasion because he believed (correctly) that an invasion of this kind would damage the image of the United States in Latin America. President Lyndon Johnson named Mann his "Mr. Latin America" for his knowledge of Latin American hardline anti-Communist views and U.S. corporate investment in Latin America. His failure to establish an acceptable democratic government in the Dominican Republic in 1965 led to serious criticism in the press and finally his replacement by Ellsworth **Bunker**. After leaving the State Department in 1966, Mann taught at

Johns Hopkins University's School of Advanced International Studies and served as president of the Automobile Manufacturers Association. *See also* Dictatorships; Doctrines; Friendly Dictators; Mann Doctrine.

Suggested Reading

Nelson Lichtenstein, ed., *Political Profiles: The Johnson Years* (New York: Facts on File, 1976).

Mann Doctrine President Lyndon **Johnson** disagreed with John F. **Kennedy**'s Latin American policy, arguing that the **Alliance for Progress** placed too much emphasis on social reforms and not enough emphasis on stability in the region. As a special assistant to the president, and later assistant secretary of state for inter-American affairs, Thomas **Mann** was given the task of changing Latin American policy from one of support for peaceful **revolutions** like the Alliance for Progress to one of stability and orderly evolution. A fellow Texan and longtime **State Department** expert on Latin America, Mann had a positive view of the military, which he saw as a force for stability and order. The reversal of Kennedy's policy—social reform and opposition to right-wing **dictatorships**—under Mann's direction came to be known as the Mann Doctrine. In a speech in Washington before the American diplomatic corps on Latin America, Mann outlined the new policy by claiming it would contain four basic principles: promoting economic growth, protection of U.S. investments in Latin America, non-intervention in the internal affairs of Latin American governments, and anti-communism. Mann's speech caused a string of unfavorable news stories and consternation within the State Department. The U.S. ambassador to Guatemala, John Bell, asked Mann if this new policy meant that the United States would no longer distinguish between "good guys and bad guys" in the formulation of American foreign policy. Mann's reply indicated that Bell was correct. The Mann Doctrine was first applied to the military takeover of Brazil in 1964, a switch from civilian to military rule that lasted for almost twenty years. *See also* Johnson Doctrine; Mann, Thomas Clifton.

Suggested Reading

Stephen G. Rabe, *The Most Dangerous Area in the World: John F. Kennedy Confronts Communist Revolution in Latin America* (Chapel Hill: University of North Carolina Press, 1999); David F. Schmitz, *Thank God They're on Our Side: The United States and Right-Wing Dictatorships, 1921–1965* (Chapel Hill: University of North Carolina Press, 1999).

Martí y Pérez, José Julián (1853–1895) Poet, journalist, and revolutionary thinker who organized Cuba's final war against Spain in 1895. Despite his early death at the hands of the Spanish army, Martí is considered Cuba's greatest political hero, most influential writer, and the one individual who had the greatest impact on Fidel **Castro**'s revolution in the 1950s. He evokes the spirit of freedom and independence for Cubans in the same way that George Washington and Thomas Jefferson do for people in the United States. José Martí was born in 1853 to poor

Spanish immigrant parents and during his youth came to resent Spanish domination over the island. He was arrested many times for his political dissent, controversial writings, and revelations of Spanish oppression to maintain tight control over Cuba. After being arrested for his writings advocating freedom and independence for Cuba, he spent several months in jail before being banished to Spain. He resumed his studies there and in 1874 received a degree in philosophy and law from the University of Zaragoza. From 1875 until his arrival in New York in 1881, Martí traveled through Europe, worked in Mexico as a journalist, taught literature and philosophy in Guatemala, returned to Cuba for short visits, some of which landed him in jail again and another deportation to Spain for his revolutionary activities.

It was in the United States that José Martí had his greatest impact on U.S.–Latin American relations as he continued to write about the problems of Latin American nations, publish some of his most significant poems, and argue persuasively that Cuba's destiny could only be realized through complete independence from Spain. He struggled to unite the diverse factions within Cuba—autonomists vs. annexationists—while at the same time warning of the danger of the United States intervening in Cuba in the event of a successful war of independence against the Spanish. It was during his time in the United States that Martí developed his political thought, organized Cubans in exile for the eventual war against Spain, and inspired Cubans on the island to revolt for their freedom and independence. According to Leonard (1999: 114), "His oratory inspired his listeners, his honesty and sincerity inspired faith, and his conviction in the ideas he was pursuing inspired respect and loyalty for him and his cause. His writings were not merely rhetorical exercises; rather they were moral teachings aimed at making a better person."

Martí's political ideas were largely forgotten after the **Spanish-Cuban-American War** and the adoption of the **Platt Amendment** as a U.S. protectorate over the island. However, his ideas provided nationalists in the twentieth century with the motivation to seek a new Cuban identity and a future free of foreign control. His writings that focused on humanitarianism and morality in government influenced Cuban leaders in the 1930s and 1940s and the Castro generation in the 1950s. Because his writings were often contradictory, Martí is revered by Cubans who consider themselves revolutionaries on the island and opponents of Fidel Castro in exile. Martí was not a Marxist, but believed in improving the plight of the lower classes and advocated a form of justice that included fair treatment of the working man. He was ambivalent toward the United States in his writings, worried about the expansionist desires of the United States in Latin America, and feared some of the negative consequences of the industrial revolution and the capitalist model of development; however, he also admired the United States for its economic dynamism and the entrepreneurial spirit of its people. Many of his ideas—**anti-imperialism**, morality in government, and economic equality—resonated throughout Latin America. Shortly after José Martí gave the orders to resume another war of independence in 1895, he landed in Cuba to lead the war but was killed in an insignificant battle with Spanish troops in Eastern Cuba on May 19, 1895. *See also* Anti-Americanism; Imperialism; Radio Martí.

Suggested Reading

Philip S. Foner, ed., *Inside the Monster: Writings on the United States and American Imperialism* (New York: Monthly Review Press, 1975); Richard B. Gray, *José Martí, Cuban Patriot* (Gainesville: University of Florida Press, 1962); John M. Kirk, *José Martí: Mentor of the Cuban Nation* (Gainesville: University of Florida Press, 1983); Thomas M. Leonard, *Castro and the Cuban Revolution* (Westport, CT: Greenwood Press, 1999); Louis A. Pérez, Jr., *Cuba Between Empires, 1878–1902* (Pittsburgh: University of Pittsburgh Press, 1986).

Mas Canosa, Jorge L. (1939–1997) Businessman, anti-Castro activist, and the founder of the Cuban American National Foundation (CANF), one of the most powerful ethnic lobbies devoted to maintaining hard-line opposition to Fidel **Castro** and the Cuban Revolution. A veteran of the **Bay of Pigs** invasion, Jorge Mas devoted his life to the overthrow of Fidel Castro—first as a conspirator in a number of armed plots and then, for the last two decades of his life, pressuring **Washington policymakers**—and the removal of the economic and political system Castro imposed on the Cuban people.

Born in Santiago to a major in the Cuban army, Mas was educated in Cuban schools before attending the Presbyterian Junior College in North Carolina. He returned to Cuba shortly after Castro's victory over Fulgencio **Batista** and started law school at Oriente University in Santiago, Cuba. He conspired with his fellow students against Castro, but was forced to leave Cuba in 1960 to escape punishment from the new revolutionary government. Mas was recruited by the **Central Intelligence Agency (CIA)** for the Bay of Pigs invasion, but his ship could only circle offshore while the main landing force was either killed or captured and taken prisoner. After a brief time in the U.S. Army, Mas returned to Miami where he became a successful businessman and joined several exile groups that were linked to CIA-sponsored terrorist attacks upon Cuba's economic infrastructure in the mid-1960s and 1970s. Jorge Mas became one of the many successful Cuban immigrants in the United States and through his telecommunications construction company, Church and Tower, he amassed a fortune in excess of $100 million at the time of his death in 1997. He was a prime mover in the creation, and leadership, of the CANF, one of the mainstays of the pro-embargo (anti-Castro) lobby in Miami and Washington, D.C. Until his death he was seen as a potential replacement for Fidel Castro in the event of a **regime change** on the island. His son, Jorge Mas Santos replaced him as the head of CANF, but he did not have the respect of the older members of the exile community and left the organization after a few years. *See also* Cuba Lobby; Helms-Burton Law (1996).

Suggested Reading

Americas Watch/Fund for Free Expression, *Dangerous Dialogue: Attacks on Freedom of Expression in Miami's Exile Community* (Washington, DC: Americas Watch, 1992); Gaeton Fonzi, "Who is Jorge Mas Canosa," *Esquire*, Vol. 119, no. 1 (January, 1993); George Gedda, "The Cuba Lobby," *Foreign Service Journal*, Vol. 78, No. 6 (June, 1993); Pat Jordan, "After Fidel, Mr. Mas?

From Exile the Most Influential in America Plots His Archenemy's Fall," *Los Angeles Times Magazine* (May 3, 1992); Larry Rohter, "A Rising Cuban-American Leader: Statesman to Some, Bully to Others," *New York Times* (October 29, 1992); María de los Angeles Torres, *In the Land of Mirrors: Cuban Exile Politics in the United States* (Ann Arbor: The University of Michigan Press, 2001); Torres, "Autumn of the Cuban Patriarchs: After Castro and Mas Canosa," *The Nation*, Vol. 265, No. 18 (December 1, 1997).

Matthews, Herbert (1900–1977) War correspondent for the *New York Times* most noted for his controversial interview with Fidel **Castro** in the Sierra Maestra mountains in 1957 that unsettled the **Batista** dictatorship, angered the American embassy, and propelled Castro's guerrillas into the international limelight. Through his reporting and contacts in Latin America, Matthews developed a sympathy for rebel movements opposed to **friendly dictators** supported by the United States. His fluency in Spanish gave him advantages that other foreign correspondents, and diplomats, did not possess. Matthews was neither a dupe nor politically naive; most of his reporting on Cuba was accurate at the time despite the fact that his reportage was criticized for not pinning the "Communist" label on Fidel Castro.

Born in New York City, Matthews was raised and educated there before enlisting in the U.S. Army to fight in **World War I**, but by the time he arrived in Europe the conflict was over. After his tour of duty he entered Columbia University where he studied Romance languages and medieval history. Herbert Matthews worked for the *New York Times* for forty-five years, first as a secretary in the business office and then from 1949 to 1967 on the editorial board. He wrote virtually all the *Times*' editorials on Latin America during this period of time. His reporting on the Spanish Civil War and the Cuban insurrection against Batista became the basis of a long friendship with American writer Ernest Hemingway. Matthews wrote six books while employed by the *Times* and six more after his 1957 interview with Fidel Castro. As a key figure in the Cuban story, Herbert Matthews soon came under attack for his sympathetic writings on Castro and the Cuban Revolution. By the end of 1960 he was receiving a flood of hate mail along with protesters marching outside the *Times* building in New York City. Nathaniel Weyl, author of the hateful treatment of Castro in *Red Star Over Cuba: The Russian Assault on the Western Hemisphere*, blames the Cuban Revolution on Matthews. "If there is any single American who could be responsible for the Cuban tragedy, it was Herbert L. Matthews of the *New York Times*" (Weyl, 1960: 169). The absurdity of Weyl's assertion that Matthews caused the Cuban Revolution has about the same logic as blaming a TV weatherman for a flood or tornado. Prohibited from covering Cuba for the *Times*, and constantly attacked (including death threats) by Cuban exiles, the John Birch Society, and other right-wing individuals and organizations in the United States, Matthews was forced to resign and leave the country. In the books that followed, Matthews made attempts to defend his interpretation of Castro and the Cuban Revolution and lived long enough to witness Senator George McGovern's efforts to start a detente with Cuba. There is no doubt that the Sierra Maestra interviews and photographic proof of Castro's existence contributed to the publicity and momentum that played a significant role in Castro's victory over Batista on January 1, 1959.

Castro's revolution borrowed heavily from the strategy and tactics of Cuba's nineteenth-century revolutionary hero José **Martí**. Martí arranged to have an American journalist cover his revolt against Spanish rule in 1895. *New York Herald* reporter, George E. Bryson, interviewed Martí at the start of the **Spanish-Cuban-American War** and then carried a long letter with the program of the revolutionary movement that was published in the *Herald* on his return. After suffering months of negative **propaganda** from Batista's regime that the guerrilla leader was dead, Fidel Castro sent word to Havana that he would like to meet with a foreign journalist (he feared Batista would censor any Cuban reporter) and later planned the encounter carefully to enhance the motives and size of his M-26-7 (the movement is named after the date of Castro's attack on the Moncada army barracks, July 26, 1953) movement. Felipe Pasos, a Cuban economist and early supporter of Castro, and his brother arranged the series of contacts that brought Herbert Matthews to Cuba to interview and photograph Castro in their mountain hideaway. In a bit of "guerrilla theatre" Castro and Che **Guevara** managed to convince Matthews that the movement had forty to fifty fighters in the Sierra Maestra when he actually had less than twenty. The lengthy interviews belied the claims by the Batista **dictatorship** that Castro was dead, and portrayed the M-26-7 as a rebellion fighting for a free and democratic Cuba. Two years after the Matthews interview was published in the *New York Times*, Fidel Castro had toppled Batista and was in charge of a revolutionary transformation of the island. The portrayal of Castro as a daring and energetic leader in charge of a noble cause helped shape anti-Batista opinion in the United States, but many in the journalistic profession thought Matthews had crossed the line from respected journalism into biased reporting. Some blamed Matthews for Castro's success, and he was eventually denied the opportunity to report on Cuba and fired from the *New York Times* for salvaging Castro's guerrilla band. Matthews spent much of his retirement in Australia, writing books and articles before his death in 1977. *See also* Guerrilla Warfare; Media; Revolutions; Yankee *Fidelistas*.

Suggested Reading

Jerry W. Knudson, "Herbert Matthews and the Cuban Story," *Journalism Monographs* (February 1978); Herbert L. Matthews, *Revolution in Cuba: An Essay in Understanding* (New York: Scribners, 1975); Matthews, *A World in Revolution: A Newspaperman's Memoir* (New York: Scribners, 1972); Matthews, *Castro: A Political Biography* (New York: Simon and Schuster, 1969); Matthews, *The Cuban Story* (New York: George Braziller, 1961); Herbert L. Matthews, ed., *The United States and Latin America*, 2nd ed. (Englewood Cliffs, NJ: Prentice Hall, 1963); Thomas G. Paterson, *Contesting Castro: The United States and the Triumph of the Cuban Revolution* (New York: Oxford University Press, 1994); Nathaniel Weyl, *Red Star Over Cuba: The Russian Assault on the Western Hemisphere* (New York: Devin-Adair, 1960).

McKinley, William (1843–1901) Lawyer, Republican politician, and president of the United States from 1897 to 1901. He fought in the U.S. Civil War, but the conflict left him "with an abiding hatred of war" and that the civilizing principle of arbitration "should prevail in the settlement of all disputes." He witnessed the carnage at Antietam and vowed to avoid foreign wars. McKinley's presidency coincided with the **Spanish-Cuban-American War**, a conflict that he desperately tried to avoid once he was elected in 1896. McKinley was unsuccessful in negotiating a cease-fire between Spain and the Cuban insurgents in 1897. He endorsed the **Teller Amendment** that promised that the United States would not annex Cuba in the event of separation from Spain, but was unable to hold back the tide of opinion in favor of war with Spain. A reluctant interventionist, McKinley succumbed to the imperialist urge and declared war and endured the brutality of conflict in the name of the **Monroe Doctrine**, the acquisition of territory, and the necessity of providing U.S. tutelage over the Cubans to prepare them for complete independence. To compensate for his lack of interest in foreign affairs, McKinley relied on cabinet officers for guidance in protecting business interests abroad. The group that helped him the most were Secretary of State John **Hay**, Secretary of War Elihu **Root**, and Army General Leonard Wood. After three years of U.S. military occupation he approved the **Platt Amendment** (1901, in effect, 1902), a clever piece of legislation that denied Cubans their full independence and gave the United States a valuable protectorate in the Caribbean. After being shot on September 6, 1901, McKinley died eight days later and the presidency passed on to **Theodore Roosevelt**. *See also* Imperialism; Olney, Richard.

Suggested Reading

David W. Dent, *The Legacy of the Monroe Doctrine: A Reference Guide to U.S. Involvement in Latin America and the Caribbean* (Westport, CT: Greenwood Press, 1999); John Dobson, *Reticent Expansionism: The Foreign Policy of McKinley* (Pittsburgh, PA: Duquesne University Press, 1988); Margaret Leech, *In the Days of McKinley* (New York: Harper and Brothers, 1959).

Media Since the **Spanish-Cuban-American War** in 1898, the U.S. media has played an important role in U.S. relations with Latin America and the Caribbean. The media played a major role in U.S.–Latin American relations during the **Cold War** when administration after administration played on the fears of communism by the American public. Since the war on **terrorism** announced by President **George W. Bush** in 2001, the United States has been less interested in Latin America, and the media has all but forgotten that Latin America exists. Unfortunately, the relationship between the media and foreign policy is not well understood, and the available literature on the subject is rather limited. This is compounded by the fact that most of the media's attention to Latin America is devoted to only a few countries, namely Cuba and Mexico. As Nichols (1995: 169) points out, "not only is Cuba the Latin American country most frequently mentioned in the U.S. media, the U.S. coverage of Cuba is the most thoroughly studied in the literature." With the exception of conflicts related to the drug trade in South America, the rest of Latin America receives scant attention in the mainstream media in the United States. What is reported is often tied to visually exciting crises that can be reported on American television because TV is the major source of news for the American public. There is widespread agreement that during the 1980s when the United States was deeply involved in Central America, the media did not present to the people of the United States a fair and accurate reflection of the key events and issues in the region. The reporting on the Nicaraguan revolution was biased in favor of the official position taken by Washington. The media coverage of El Salvador was criticized for being superficial, vacillating, distorted, conflict-oriented, and assessed largely in terms of U.S. interests, stereotypes, and assumptions with little in the way of historical background or meaningful political analysis.

The relationship between the U.S. media and the government's handling of U.S.–Latin American policy is influenced by several factors. First, the mass public pays little attention to the dangers and complexities of foreign policy and grants executive branch policymakers some secrecy to protect national security. Second, the conduct of U.S.–Latin American relations is highly centralized under the presidency and as such is subject to a process of making sure that the news always fits the views of the White House. The ability to control information and control what the media says about Latin America is vital to the conduct of foreign policy. Third, the public tends to have less interest in and exercises less critical evaluation of foreign news than is the case for domestic policy. Despite these advantages, the media have substantial powers that can be used to counter the "spin" offered by the president and his advisers. This is particularly acute with the information that the media collects and disseminates that cannot be controlled by the executive branch. Although President George W. Bush announced that he does not read newspapers, his staff does, and they serve as a filter for what is decided by foreign policy elites. The tug-of-war between media correspondents and government officials is probably best described as a symbiotic relationship where both parties derive considerable benefit from each other, despite the adversarial relationship that often exists. There are many examples of media-government collaboration that have produced both positive and negative types of reporting on U.S.–Latin American relations. Nevertheless, most of those who have studied U.S.–Latin American relations would agree that the president has substantial powers to manipulate the media for the purpose of winning policy debates. In the debate over aid to the Nicaraguan **Contras** during the **Reagan** administration public opposition was a salient factor in limiting aid to the rebels.

What impact does the media have on U.S.–Latin American relations? There is some empirical evidence that the U.S. media affect the policy process by agenda setting. Once the White House focused on such policies as the new **Panama Canal treaties**, conflict in Nicaragua and El Salvador, the drug war in the Andes, **human rights** in Cuba, immigration, or the **North American Free Trade Agreement (NAFTA)**, those issues quickly moved to the top of the media agenda. However, once the president's attention turns elsewhere, the media will follow, and the Latin American topic will quickly disappear. Mexico was at the top of President George W. Bush's Latin American policy agenda prior to the events of **September 11, 2001**, and he and President Vicente **Fox** praised each other as leaders and the importance of addressing the plight of illegal Mexican immigrants in the United

States. Within weeks of the terrorist attacks on New York and Washington, Bush declared a war on terrorism and Mexico quickly disappeared from the concerns of the White House until early January 2004. Many media analysts saw this as a beginning step to attract Latino voters to the president's re-election bid the same year.

After the negative impact of global television on the outcome of the Vietnam War, the presidential advisory system—**National Security Council (NSC)**, **State Department**, Pentagon, and the **Central Intelligence Agency (CIA)**—developed a contempt and hostility for the press and saw journalists as critics of the military and the White House who must be managed to control the type and volume of information from the war front. After watching British Prime Minister Margaret Thatcher manipulate the media to its advantage during the **Falklands/Malvinas War** in 1982, and the immediate domestic political advantages, the Reagan administration decided it was time to put more emphasis on controlling the briefings, the videos, and the message from foreign entanglements. President Reagan and his defense chief, Casper Weinberger, thought nothing of getting militarily involved in Lebanon in 1983, but after witnessing the slaughter of over 240 U.S. Marines in a truck-bomb explosion at the Beirut airport, they quickly decided to withdraw. In an effort to mask the negative press coverage of the U.S. Marine barracks in Lebanon, the Reagan administration dispatched over 7,000 American troops to the small Caribbean nation of Grenada and made sure reporters were banned from the invasion. Some who tried to land in an effort to cover the conflict were arrested and imprisoned and all details and photographs were controlled by the Pentagon. When **George H.W. Bush** invaded Panama in 1989 to capture General Manuel **Noriega**, journalists were once again banned, leaving few pictures, no first-hand accounts, and no accurate tally of the number of Panamanians killed in the operation. The White House has learned the importance of making sure that members of the press don't report anything that might be too upsetting to the American public, particularly the sight of bodies killed by friendly fire, video footage of U.S. troops killing enemy forces, and the arrival ceremonies at the Air Force base at Dover, Delaware, where flag-draped coffins arrive after a conflict. Although the White House feels that the media can jeopardize national security, and the safety of U.S. forces, by its critical assessment of foreign policy decisions, more often than not it is the perception that reporters are not sufficiently supportive of U.S. policy—good or otherwise. For example, Secretary of State George Shultz explained that the press were kept off the island of Grenada in 1983 because "reporters are always against us, and they're always seeking to report something that's going to screw things up." The problem for the White House is that the media is perceived as too anxious to raise vital and troubling issues that tend to undermine decisions and rhetoric that often don't match events on the ground. What this often means is that the media have more influence on Latin American policy at the evaluation stage—particularly when things are not going well for the administration—than at the earlier stages of formulation and implementation. In the aftermath of September 11, 2001, the George W. Bush administration has made numerous efforts to silence the media and prevent democratic accountability.

The use of military force has been a constant in dealing with perceived international threats in Latin America, and the media has played a critical role in framing the motivation and consequences of the use of force. This happens most frequently during a crisis when the president decides that it is in the national interest to project military force abroad. If the media depicts the crisis as a legitimate threat to the interests of the United States, the American electorate will attribute responsibility to the target country or individuals and support the president. This produces a positive effect for the president in which the mass public rallies "round-the-flag" and the president's popularity in public opinion polls rises. This phenomenon has made the media more critical of presidential motives and increased the levels of cynicism of American presidents by the mass public. However, given the lack of awareness and sophistication regarding U.S.–Latin American relations, ignorance allows the president and his advisers to manipulate the public by tapping into core beliefs central to democratic rules and free-market economics. This means that American presidents can use threatening situations (real or manufactured) to their political advantage with little fear of negative repercussions, at least in the short run. If military action is limited and few American lives are lost, the president's popularity will rise; however, if the use-of-force response fails, the media may re-frame the foreign policy action and the president's support will decline. As political cynicism grows in the United States due to the president's manipulation of the nature of the threat, the media find it much easier to question the motives of the president and his advisers and presidential power is likely to subside. Although President Reagan did not shrink from censoring, and manipulating, news about his policies in Latin America, the news media helped Reagan with its self-censorship. Reporters who uncovered stories that were critical of Reagan's Central American policies were often removed when their exposés revealed the lies and distortions being put out by the White House. According to some media critics, President Reagan was the beneficiary of the media's failure to criticize him because he was popular among the nation's elite. President Reagan helped launch a right-wing offensive that continues to shape how international events are covered in the media, particularly when journalists feel they must bend over backward to prove they're not liberals.

Journalists who cover events in Latin America for American newspapers are sometimes accused of providing coverage that is too critical of the administration or not sufficiently patriotic when Latin American insurgents are given too much legitimacy in a struggle where the United States has sided with the government. When the administration is able to dictate the terms of the coverage, and constantly refute stories they disagree with, the media have a hard time holding the government accountable. The advances in media technology and instantaneous satellite broadcasting can alter a policy due to its dramatic, real-time impact on **Washington policymakers** and the American public. When the networks obtain dramatic footage of violence or humiliating situations, the White House may have no choice but to alter its policy toward a particular country or regime. Nevertheless, when the media wanders too far from the accepted parameters of U.S. policy debate—

regardless of the accuracy of their reporting—then they can face substantial risk to their journalistic careers. There are many examples of this situation in media coverage of political and turbulent events in Latin America, including Carleton **Beals** (Nicaragua and Cuba), Herbert **Matthews** (Cuban insurrection), Raymond Bonner (massacres in El Salvador), Gary Webb (Contra-cocaine connection), Lindsay Grusen (Guatemala), and Charles Horman (Chile during the **Pinochet** coup). After more than four decades of U.S. government hostility aimed at Fidel **Castro**, and hundreds of editorials—both liberal and conservative—critical of executive branch policy toward Cuba, U.S.–Cuba policy remains virtually unchanged. The depth of hostility to Castro's Cuba has often been the product of the ability of the **Cuba Lobby** to exert influence over key members of Congress and the White House through the creation of **Radio Martí** and TV Martí, although the latter is more symbolic since it is rarely seen on the island. This suggests that the U.S. media have little power to change Latin American policy when those in power feel little constraint from a hostile press that labors to reveal the lies and distortions that flow from the "spin" offered by the newsmakers and manipulaters inside the White House. *See also Missing* (1982); Threat Perception/Assessment.

Suggested Reading

Eric Alterman, "Bush's War on the Press," *The Nation* (May 9, 2005); Landrum R. Bolling, ed., *Reporters Under Fire: U.S. Media Coverage of Conflicts in Lebanon and Central America* (Boulder, CO: Westview Press, 1985); Denise M. Bostdorff, *The Presidency and the Rhetoric of Foreign Crisis* (Columbia: University of South Carolina Press, 1994); Karl R. DeRouen, Jr., ed., *Historical Encyclopedia of U.S. Presidential Use of Force, 1789–2000* (Westport, CT: Greenwood Press, 2001); Michael J. Francis, "The U.S. Press and Castro: A Study in Declining Relations," *Journalism Quarterly*, Vol. 44 (summer 1967); Elizabeth Hannan, "Censorship During the Invasion of Grenada: The Press, the Public and the Pentagon," *International Communication Bulletin*, Vol. 23 (fall 1986); Michael Leeden, "Secrets," in Simon Serfaty, ed., *The Media and Foreign Policy* (New York: St. Martin's Press, 1991); John Spicer Nichols, "The U.S. Media," in David W. Dent, ed., *U.S.–Latin American Policymaking: A Reference Handbook* (Westport, CT: Greenwood Press, 1995); Patrick O'Heffernan, *Mass Media and American Foreign Policy: Insider Perspectives on Global Journalism and the Foreign Policy Process* (Norwood, NJ: Ablex, 1991); Rolling Stone, "This is War," (March 20, 2003); Richard Sobel, ed., *Public Opinion in U.S. Foreign Policy: The Controversy Over Contra Aid* (Lanham, MD: Rowman and Littlefield, 1993); Howard J. Wiarda, "The Media and Latin America: Why Coverage Goes Astray," *The Journalist* (fall 1985).

Mexican-American War (1846–1848) Westward expansion under **Manifest Destiny** and Mexico's inability to control its northern territory led to a war between the United States and Mexico, the only time war has been declared by the United States against a Latin American country. The war began on April 25, 1846, and ended on February 2, 1848, with the signing of the Treaty of **Guadalupe Hidalgo**. It was a humiliating, one-sided conflict caused by the Texas War of Independence (1835–1836) and U.S. annexation of Texas in 1845, President James

K. **Polk**'s desire to acquire California, at the time a province of Mexico, and racist stereotypes against the Mexican people and government. Once Mexico's breakaway province became an American state in 1845, the stage was set for a major clash between American and Mexican forces. President Polk provoked the war by insisting that Mexico accept the Rio Grande River as the southern Texas boundary instead of the Rio Nueces farther north. Mexico refused the offer, and Polk responded by sending U.S. forces into the disputed territory. A few days after U.S. and Mexican forces clashed in May 1846, Congress declared war on Mexico. Mexico was no match for the United States, since the country was deeply divided politically and its army was poorly trained and equipped. The superiority of U.S. forces made it possible to capture Mexican cities, defeat the Mexican military, and force Mexico to sign the onerous Treaty of Guadalupe-Hidalgo in February 1848. The humiliating defeat left Mexico embittered with its northern neighbor for years to come. According to Wilson and Dent (1998: 121), "Polk's imperialistic muscle-flexing confirmed the dogma of Manifest Destiny and established the Polk Corollary to the Monroe Doctrine, in effect restricting the transfer of territory from one foreign country to another in the Americas. By putting limits on the exercise of Latin American sovereignty, President Polk's interpretation was a precursor to the Big Stick policy of the United States fifty years later."

The Mexican-American War produced tensions in the United States, both within the U.S. Congress and the American public. Many Whig Party members, abolitionists, peace advocates, and other critics called the war with Mexico a crime and an outrage. President Polk was pilloried for his handling of the conflict and its impact on slavery, separatism, and the distrust of the United States in Mexico. The Whig Party claimed that the Mexican War was a clever ploy on the part of the slave states to acquire more slave territory. Representative Abraham Lincoln questioned Polk's assertions about the nature of the provocation. The intellectual elite in the United States who opposed the war—Ralph Waldo Emerson, James Russell Lowell, and Henry David Thoreau—helped lay the groundwork for future peace movements; however, their lectures and writings had little impact on the public mind during the war. The strongest arguments against the conflict focused on the death and destruction caused by the war with Mexico: on the U.S. side there were 15,000 deaths (1,733 were battle deaths; the others succumbed to tropical diseases or simply disappeared); the Mexican numbers are more difficult to obtain, but estimates range from 30,000 to 35,000 (4,000 were battle deaths and the rest died from diseases). The war cost the United States $100 million, including a payment of $15 million to Mexico and the responsibility to settle $3.5 million in claims against the Mexican government by U.S. citizens.

Despite the high cost of the war in lives and treasure, the Mexican War proved to be a pivotal event in U.S.–Latin American relations. First, the Mexican War sparked a drive for additional territory by private armies and **filibuster** expeditions into Latin America in the 1850s. Second, the interest in new territory led to a movement in the United States to bring the Caribbean under the control of southern slave owners. Third, the Mexican War was directly responsible for the U.S. Civil War because the thirst for more territory opened a national debate on the expansion of slavery, causing an irreparable rift between the forces in favor of slavery and those opposed to it. Last, the war created a distrust of the United States in Mexico that continues to affect the bilateral relationship. Unfortunately, many Americans have scant knowledge of this war; however, Mexicans remember it well because of the U.S. conduct of the war and the tremendous loss of territory due to the conflict. *See also* Anti-Americanism; Big Stick Diplomacy; Filibusters/Filibustering; Monroe Doctrine (1823); Taylor, Zachary; Trist, Nicholas Philip.

Suggested Reading

Jack K. Bauer, *The Mexican War, 1846–1848* (New York: Macmillan, 1974); Mark Crawford, David S. Heidler, and Jeanne T. Heidler, eds., *Encyclopedia of the Mexican-American War* (Santa Barbara, CA: ABC-CLIO, 1999); Donald S. Frazier, ed., *The United States and Mexico at War: Nineteenth-Century Expansionism and Conflict* (New York: Macmillan, 1998); James M. McCaffrey, *Army of Manifest Destiny: The American Soldier in the Mexican War, 1846–1848* (New York: New York University Press, 1992); John H. Schroeder, *Mr. Polk's War: American Opposition and Dissent, 1846–1848* (Madison: University of Wisconsin Press, 1973); Curtis Stokes, Theresa Meléndez, and Genice Rhodes-Reed, eds., *Race in Twenty-First–Century America* (East Lansing: Michigan State University Press, 2001); Larman C. Wilson and David W. Dent, *Historical Dictionary of Inter-American Organizations* (Lanham, MD: Scarecrow Press, 1998); Richard Bruce Winders, *Mr. Polk's Army: The American Military Experience in the Mexican War* (College Station: Texas A&M University Press, 1997).

Miranda, Carmen (1909–1955) Brazilian singer and actress whose films, songs and night club routines brought her to the attention of Hollywood in the 1930s and 1940s. She was hired during **World War II** to represent the spirit of the **Good Neighbor Policy**, and she quickly became a symbol of Brazil in the United States. Twentieth Century Fox recognized her singing and dancing skills, and she became a hit in musicals such as *Down Argentine Way* (1941), *Weekend in Havana* (1941), and *That Night in Rio* (1941). Her dress often resembled outfits worn by Bahian market women, including gaudy carnival costumes and headdresses adorned with tropical fruits. In a showgirl extravaganza directed by Busby Berkeley, *The Gangs All Here* (1943), she co-starred with Alice Faye and Cesar Romero and in one routine appeared holding gigantic bananas with other performers. During World War II, she was used to symbolize Pan American unity and **Franklin D. Roosevelt**'s Good Neighbor policy, another example of the use of music and dance for cultural diplomacy in Latin America. After a performance on the Jimmy Durante show in 1955, she died of heart failure, attributed to her depression, abuse of barbiturates, over work, a failed marriage, and her ostracism by members of Brazil's cultural elite. *See also* Cultural Imperialism; Pan Americanism.

Suggested Reading

Cynthia Enloe, *Bananas, Beaches and Bases: Making Feminist Sense of International Politics* (Berkeley: University of California Press, 1990); Martha Gil-Montero, *Brazilian Bombshell: The Biography of Carmen Miranda* (New York: D.I. Fine, 1989).

***Missing* (1982)** The feature-length film *Missing* is one of the classics of the **Cold War** era in which anti-communism played a major role in dealing with Latin American governments that were judged to be in opposition to the interests of the United States. With an award-winning performance by Jack Lemmon as Edmund Horman, *Missing* portrays the agony, frustration, and metamorphosis of Ed Horman in his search for Charles, his son who is missing in Chile after the U.S.–backed military coup that toppled Salvador **Allende**. In his search for his son, Ed Horman follows whatever leads he can find, meets repeatedly with U.S. diplomatic personnel, but finally realizes that the U.S. embassy is trying to conceal the fact that his son was tortured and killed shortly before his arrival in Santiago. The controversy surrounding the September 11, 1973, coup against Allende's socialist government became one of the defining moments of the Cold War, and a primary case of "**blowback**" from a misguided policy engineered by President Richard M. **Nixon** and his National Security Adviser, Henry A. **Kissinger** that would haunt the United States for years.

The two Americans—Charles Horman and Frank Teruggi—killed in the first days after the military coup, and **Central Intelligence Agency (CIA)** complicity in the overthrow of Allende sparked a congressional investigation by the U.S. Senate, and contributed to a sense of cynicism and distrust of **Washington policymakers** and American foreign policy during the 1970s and beyond. Once General Augusto **Pinochet** was in power, he went after his opposition through a South American joint intelligence network called **Operation Condor**. Special teams were trained in the techniques of torture and murder and instructed to travel anywhere in search of terrorists or supporters of terrorist organizations considered to be regime opponents. "Agents of Operation Condor," according to Chile scholar Brian Loveman, "hunted down, interrogated, tortured, and murdered leftists and other regime opponents throughout Latin America and elsewhere—sometimes with specialized collaboration from U.S. police and intelligence agencies, including surveillance and interrogation of subjects within the United States" (Loveman, 2001: 271–272). In 1976, Pinochet orchestrated the death of Allende's foreign minister, Orlando Letelier, and an American aide in a car bomb episode in Washington, D.C.'s Sheridan Circle (a memorial plaque is placed there with the names of deceased and wounded).

Missing dramatizes a series of events that transpired in Chile immediately before and after September 11, 1973. The death of two Americans under circumstances that stirred suspicions of CIA involvement and a possible coverup added to the controversy surrounding the film. In *Missing,* U.S. embassy officials treat Ed Horman as a naive father who is told that "Charlie was a bit of snoop" and when "you play with fire you can get burned." After the harrowing experience of searching for his son, Ed Horman finds out from a non-embassy source that Charles was abducted, tortured, and murdered by the Chilean government. At this point there is no doubt in Ed Horman's mind that the United States knew what had happened to his son from the very beginning. As he is being told about the shipment of his son's body to New York, he tells U.S. embassy personnel, "I'm going to sue you. Thank God we still live in a country where we can put people like you in jail."

Current efforts to apply **human rights** law universally for the deaths of foreigners in Chile, including Charles Horman and Frank Terrugi, carried out by General Augusto Pinochet led to Pinochet's arrest in London in 1999, but he was released after more than a year and allowed to return to Chile because of his age and poor health that the judges argued would inhibit him from testifying at trial. However, many of those who saw Pinochet after his arrival in Chile questioned the "poor health" evaluation since he appeared to many Chileans to be able to remember critical pieces of the past and make rational assessments of other situations. During the summer of 2001 Judge Juan Guzmán requested information from Henry **Kissinger** about the **assassination** of Charles Horman shortly after the 1973 coup. Judge Guzmán also prepared questions for Nathaniel Davis, the U.S. ambassador in Chile at the time. Kissinger is also the target of a lawsuit brought to American courts by the son of General René Schneider, the subject of a *60 Minutes* segment shown on September 9, 2001. Recently declassified documents clearly show that Kissinger was instrumental in the efforts to instigate a coup by getting rid of the coup-resistant General Schneider to prevent Allende from coming to power between Allende's election and inauguration in September 1970. General Schneider was killed in a botched kidnapping plot shortly after Allende's election. Although the consequences of the U.S.–backed coup against Allende are not treated in *Missing*, the "blowback" from U.S. covert action in Chile is remarkable and devastating, driven in part by the fact that the case against Pinochet is still underway and Henry Kissinger is now a target for his role in the crimes committed in Chile. The Pentagon and the CIA, the principal government agencies responsible for carrying out U.S. policy in Chile, have so far failed to declassify key records from the era. When asked in 2003 about the role of the United States in the 1973 military coup in Chile, Secretary of State Colin Powell admitted, "It is not a part of American history that we're proud of." *See also* Covert Operations.

Suggested Reading

Marc Cooper, *Pinochet and Me: A Chilean Anti-Memoir* (London: Verso, 2001); Brian Loveman, *Chile: The Legacy of Hispanic Capitalism*, 3rd ed. (New York: Oxford University Press, 2001); George Gedda, "Powell Regrets U.S. role in 1973 Chile Coup," www.salon.com (April 16, 2003); John J. Michalczyk, *Costa-Gavras, the Political Fiction Film* (Philadelphia, PA: Art Alliance Press, 1984).

Monroe, James (1758–1831) U.S. senator, diplomat, cabinet officer, and fifth president of the United States whose greatest achievements were in foreign policy. His message to Congress in 1823 that contained the **Monroe Doctrine** became the nation's first, and politically most significant, presidential **doctrine**, one that would give President Monroe a kind of political immortality that no other American president has acquired. Ironically, his message became acquainted with a policy toward

Latin America even though it was originally not a Latin American policy because it emphasized European relations and how the United States would deal with monarchies of the time. As president (1817–1825), Monroe faced the difficult task of dealing with the Latin American wars of independence against Spain, the problem of European encroachment in the Americas, and how to make the United States safe by putting more emphasis on the use of force rather than the complications and dangers of relying too heavily on diplomatic discourse.

Born in Virginia, Monroe served as an army officer in the American Revolution; afterward he devoted his life to politics and diplomacy. Although he supported democratic principles and national territorial expansion, Monroe was far more interested in Europe than in Latin America. He spoke no Spanish and had never traveled to any part of the former Spanish Empire. On a diplomatic mission to Spain in 1805, Monroe failed to acquire U.S. title to West Florida, claimed by the United States as a result of the Louisiana Purchase. A protégé of Thomas Jefferson and James Madison, James Monroe was aware acutely that the United States and Latin America shared a mutual interest in evicting Europe from the Western Hemisphere. At the same time that Monroe and John Quincy **Adams** worried about European intentions, they considered Latin Americans different in character from Anglo-Saxon Protestants. At the core of their beliefs was the notion that Latin Americans were unable or unwilling to defend themselves from European powers. Spain's remaining empire after Latin American independence, especially Cuba and Puerto Rico, were considered to be natural appendages of the United States. Over time they would naturally become part of U.S. territory. James Monroe was never considered an original thinker, but his foreign policy decisions were backed with careful deliberation and vision for what he hoped to accomplish in mapping out the contours of early U.S. foreign relations.

Suggested Reading

Harry Ammon, *James Monroe: The Quest for National Identity* (Charlottesville: University Press of Virginia, 1990); Samuel Flagg Bemis, *John Quincy Adams and the Foundations of American Foreign Policy* (Westport, CT: Greenwood Press, 1981); Noble E. Cunningham, Jr., *The Presidency of James Monroe* (Lawrence: University Press of Kansas, 1996); David W. Dent, *The Legacy of the Monroe Doctrine: A Reference Guide to U.S. Involvement in Latin America and the Caribbean* (Westport, CT: Greenwood Press, 1999); Ernest R. May, *The Making of the Monroe Doctrine* (Cambridge, MA: Belknap Press of Harvard University Press, 1975); Lars Schoultz, *Beneath the United States: A History of U.S. Policy Toward Latin America* (Cambridge, MA: Harvard University Press, 1998); Gaddis Smith, *The Last Years of the Monroe Doctrine: 1945–1993* (New York: Hill and Wang, 1994).

Monroe Doctrine (1823) In his annual message to Congress in 1823, President James **Monroe** set forth a number of principles that would become the basis of U.S. policy in the Americas until the end of the **Cold War**. President Monroe was concerned with Russia's encroachment along the northwest coast of the United States and the fear that European powers were planning to re-establish the Spanish colonial empire in the Americas. Monroe's message—written largely by John Quincy **Adams**—tried to balance two opposing currents of thought that were prevalent in Washington at the time: isolationism, and **intervention** and territorial expansion. The original Monroe Doctrine was an isolationist policy, opposed to extra-hemispheric intervention in the Americas and the involvement of the United States in European affairs. However, as the United States became more powerful toward the end of the nineteenth century, the Monroe Doctrine was amended through various corollaries and interpretations to allow the United States to engage in the unilateral use of force to handle a wide variety of situations in Latin America.

The Monroe Doctrine was based on three major principles, each designed to set forth a means of U.S. control over the Western Hemisphere. First, the principle of non-colonization stated that the hemisphere was closed to further colonization, particularly efforts by British and Russian moves to build new colonies on the northwest coast of North America. Second, the Monroe Doctrine set forth the doctrine of non-intervention, based on the fear that European powers might try to re-colonize Latin America for Spain. Third, the Monroe Doctrine stated a version of isolationism in which the United States pledged to stay out of European conflicts if Europe did the same in the Western Hemisphere. It was interpreted for years as a policy of "hands off" the Western Hemisphere and was taught to students as one of the founding myths of American foreign policy. The development of Monroeism—a combination of U.S. paternalism, interventionism, and **hegemony** in the Western Hemisphere—played a major part in Latin America's legal and political efforts to curb the imperialist tendencies of the United States throughout most of the twentieth century.

Despite the historical significance and longevity of the Monroe Doctrine and its symbolic value in justifying a wide variety of policies toward Latin America, there are numerous flaws in the original message and its corollaries. Some of the flaws in the Monroe Doctrine were directly related to the faulty assumptions inherent in the original message; other problems emerged over time as top officials in Washington used the doctrine to justify their actions and mollify the concerns of the American public about strategic matters in Latin America. While there are many problems with the Monroe Doctrine, the following criticisms have plagued the doctrine and its application in Latin America: (1) a unilateral pronouncement with no consultation with the newly independent states in the Americas; (2) the Monroe Doctrine was crafted by **Washington policymakers** with little knowledge of Latin America and its people; (3) Monroe's message contained no legal basis for conducting a hemispheric policy and the efforts by Latin American governments to change the doctrine into a binding inter-American commitment were rejected by the United States until the middle of the twentieth century; (4) the Monroe Doctrine became a destructive shibboleth for over a century and a half as Monroe's message was used by U.S. presidents, foreign investors, **filibusters**, and others who needed a slogan to legitimize their actions; and (5) the Monroe Doctrine served as a powerful rationalization for U.S. intervention and coercive diplomacy in dealing with Latin America.

The Monroe Doctrine played a major role in the evolution of the Latin American policy of the United States, often used at critical junctures to further the control and domination of the United States over Latin America. Beginning in the 1890s, the Monroe Doctrine was used to challenge the British in the first Venezuelan crisis and the effort to drive Spain out of the Caribbean during the **Spanish-Cuban-American War**. It became part of the **Big Stick diplomacy** of **Theodore Roosevelt** in dealing with debt-ridden and unstable countries like the Dominican Republic and Cuba. In the 1920s it was cited by those who opposed the **League of Nations**, in addition to those who supported the **United Nations (UN)** years later. The Monroe Doctrine was "rediscovered" by President Dwight **Eisenhower** and his advisers in the **Central Intelligence Agency (CIA)** plan to overthrow President Jacobo **Arbenz** in Guatemala in 1954 and by President John F. **Kennedy** as a justification for opposing the Cuban Revolution. In the 1980s, President Ronald **Reagan** used the Monroe Doctrine to support his policies in El Salvador and Nicaragua that he argued were necessary to make the Western Hemisphere safe from aggression from abroad. The Monroe Doctrine always contained an element of pre-emption in the way it was used by American presidents, particularly the motivations and requirements set forth in the **Roosevelt Corollary to the Monroe Doctrine**. Although it is no longer considered a guiding principle of American foreign policy, its spirit remains embodied in the legacies of U.S. involvement in the Americas and the essential prescriptions set forth by President **George W. Bush** and his top foreign policy advisers. The current war on **terrorism** has prompted some neo-conservatives to revive the Monroe Doctrine as a justification for fighting terrorism. In *An End to Evil: How to Win the War on Terror* (2003), David Frum and Richard Perle justify a future war against Iran by claiming "Iran defied the Monroe Doctrine and sponsored murder in our own hemisphere" because of an attack on a Jewish community center in Buenos Aires in the early 1990s that killed eighty-six people. Clearly, Monroe's ghosts still haunt the minds of neo-conservative intellectuals, and others, who command a great deal of influence over American foreign policy in Washington. The ideas set forth by John Quincy Adams almost two hundred years ago still influence the minds of America's foreign policy elite. *See also* Doctrines; Filibusters/Filibustering; Imperialism; Intervention and Non-Intervention.

Suggested Reading

Elliott Abrams, "The Spirit Behind the Monroe Doctrine," *Current Policy* 949 (Washington, DC: Department of State, 1987); Samuel F. Bemis, *John Quincy Adams and the Foundations of American Foreign Policy* (New York: Knopf, 1949); Hiram Bingham, *The Monroe Doctrine: An Obsolete Shibboleth* (New Haven: Yale University Press, 1913); Patrick J. Buchanan, "No End to War," *The American Conservative* (March 1, 2004); J. Ruben Clark, *Memorandum on the Monroe Doctrine* (Washington, DC: U.S. Government Printing Office, 1930); Donald M. Dozer, *The Monroe Doctrine: Its Modern Significance* (New York: Knopf, 1965); David Frum and Richard Perle, *An End to Evil: How to Win the War on Terror* (New York: Random House, 2003); Dana Lindaman and Kyle Ward, *History Lessons: How Textbooks from Around the World Portray U.S.*

History (New York: New Press, 2004); Ernest R. May, *The Making of the Monroe Doctrine* (Cambridge, MA: Belknap Press of Harvard University Press, 1975); John Bassett Moore, *The Monroe Doctrine: Its Origin and Meaning* (New York: The Evening Post Publishing Co., 1895); Kirby Page, *The Monroe Doctrine and World Peace* (Garden City, NY: Doubleday, Doran & Co., 1928); Dexter Perkins, *The Monroe Doctrine, 1823–1826* (Cambridge, MA: Harvard University Press, 1927); Gaddis Smith, *The Last Years of the Monroe Doctrine, 1945–1993* (New York: Hill and Wang, 1994).

Morrow, Dwight Whitney (1873–1931) Lawyer, politician, and U.S. ambassador to Mexico between 1927 and 1930 whose diplomatic skills helped improve U.S.–Mexican relations. Born in Huntington, West Virginia, in 1873, Morrow graduated from Amherst College (A.B., 1895) and the Columbia Law School in 1899. After settling in New Jersey, he practiced law from 1899 to 1914 before joining the Morgan banking empire where he remained until 1927. His one diplomatic tour to Mexico was a splendid success due to his respect and patience with Mexican President Plutarco E. Calles over divisive issues such as threats to American-held petroleum rights in Mexico, internal financial difficulties, and violence related to the post-revolutionary role of the Catholic church. Morrow's brilliant diplomacy helped pave the way for the implementation of the **Good Neighbor Policy**. His personal popularity among Mexicans was enhanced by arranging for his son-in-law, Charles A. Lindbergh, to fly to Mexico for a goodwill visit. After leaving Mexico, Morrow was elected to the U.S. Senate as a Republican representing New Jersey and was considered a potential candidate for the presidency of the United States before his sudden death in 1931.

Dwight Morrow was a confirmed capitalist with strong ties to Wall Street and corporate America; however, he represented a rare example of a diplomat who cared about U.S.–Latin American relations to the point that he was willing to sacrifice the interests of the U.S. petroleum industry, some of whom were clients of J.P. Morgan, to improve relations with Mexico and push a new brand of **Pan Americanism**. After his nomination and confirmation as U.S. ambassador to Mexico, Morrow spent two months studying **State Department** files to explain the prolonged impasse in U.S.–Mexican relations. What he found was such rigidity and recalcitrance in the diplomatic cables that he decided to hire his own private staff to sort out the diplomatic logjam concerning the constitutional basis of Mexico's petroleum law and U.S. economic interests. *See also* Ambassadors.

Suggested Reading

Lorenzo Meyer, *Mexico and the United States in the Oil Controversy, 1917–1942* (Austin: University of Texas Press, 1977); Harold Nicolson, *Dwight Morrow* (New York: Harcourt Brace, 1935); Robert Freeman Smith, *The United States and Revolutionary Nationalism in Mexico, 1916–1932* (Austin: University of Texas Press, 1995).

N

NAFTA. *See* North American Free Trade Agreement

National Endowment for Democracy (NED) Controversial Washington-based private organization, funded by the U.S. government, and dedicated to promoting **democracy** abroad. It currently funds programs in Eastern Europe, the former Soviet Union, Latin America, Asia, Africa, and the Middle East related to building democratic institutions and values. It grew out of the **Reagan** administration's interest in winning the "war of ideas" with the Soviet Union and the desire to privatize American foreign policy. The idea of having a government-funded private organization with a bipartisan structure to promote democracy and fight communism was popular because NED could intervene overtly on the government's behalf without suffering the consequences of other forms of government interventionism. A small group of Washington insiders promoted the idea and convinced the Reagan administration to establish the National Endowment for Democracy in 1983. The complex multipartisan structure of NED means that it can count on wide support in Congress and constant budgetary backing. It has four main grantees: the National Democratic Institute for International Affairs (NDI), the International Republican Institute (IRI), the Center for International Private Enterprise (CIPE), and the Free Trade Union Institute (FTUI). With political party, trade union, and business/commercial representation, there is specialization in the complex area of democracy promotion. NED's programs are designed to foster and strengthen democratic institutions and values, namely constitutional reform, legislative strengthening, free and fair elections, political party development, independent trade unions, **human rights** advocacy, and civic education. NED also funds interest groups and **think tanks** in the United States, including the Cuban American National Foundation, Freedom House, and the Center for Democracy.

The creation of the National Endowment for Democracy is one of the growth areas in U.S.–funded assistance programs oriented toward democracy promotion in the aftermath of the **Cold War**. At the twentieth anniversary of the founding of NED, President **George W. Bush** spoke of the positive achievements of NED in the administration's goals of bringing democracy and free markets to the rest of the world. Although NED is a little-known foreign aid program designed to promote democracy abroad, it has become a controversial institution in Washington. The current debate over the future of NED is not about democracy promotion and freedom enhancement as a part of American foreign policy; the NED controversy centers on the wisdom of giving a quasi-private organization the power to pursue what amounts to an independent foreign policy. With few political and administration controls, NED can operate much more freely than traditional democracy-building agencies such as the **Agency for International Development (AID)** and the U.S. Information Agency. There is also a difference between how NDI and IRI carry out their democracy-building abroad: NDI is known for its more non-partisan engagement in democratic politics while IRI typically favors only those groups that have conservative values typically espoused by the Republican Party. Other critics of NED claim that its Cold War rationale no longer is relevant, and it no longer has a national security purpose. NED is resented as foreign interference because it often attempts to deceive foreigners into viewing its programs as private assistance when in reality they are government-endorsed programs. In Latin America there are many instances of NED's meddling in national elections, something that would be illegal for foreign groups operating in the United States. Attempts to influence Latin American elections include the 1988 plebiscite to remove dictator Augusto **Pinochet** in Chile; channeling money to opposition candidate Violeta Chamorro in Nicaragua in the 1989 presidential campaign against Daniel Ortega; in Panama's 1984 presidential election, NED funded a military-backed candidate, Nicolás Ardito Barletta, in direct opposition to U.S. policy toward Panama that opposed military rule. Because Costa Rican president Oscar **Arias** opposed Reagan's Central American policy, NED funded the political opposition to Arias that had the backing of Panamanian dictator Manuel Antonio **Noriega**; and NED helped the Venezuelan opposition that sparked massive resistance to President Hugo Chávez that resulted in his temporary ouster in 2003. By having private organizations with public funding representing their agendas as American foreign policy, the United States may be actually harming fragile democracies in Latin America and elsewhere. It is obvious that the problem with NED is its blatant involvement in the internal political affairs of foreign nations and its lack of accountability when serious **scandals and blunders** occur. After IRI president George A. Folsom praised the (failed) coup against Venezuela's democratically elected president in 2003, it was later revealed that NED provided funds to those organizations that initiated the bloody revolt against Venezuela's leaders in the attempted coup. With strong support from the White House and the pork-barrel advantages to members of Congress, the National Endowment for Democracy is likely to remain an important tool for furthering U.S. foreign policy objectives. *See also* Cultural Imperialism; Democracy and Democracy Promotion; Propaganda.

Suggested Reading

Thomas Carothers, "The NED at 10," *Foreign Affairs* 95 (summer 1994); Carothers, *In the Name of Democracy: U.S. Policy Toward Latin America in the Reagan Years* (Berkeley: University of California Press, 1991); Barbara Conry, "Loose Cannon: The National Endowment for Democracy," *Cato Foreign Policy Briefing*, No. 27 (November 8, 1993); Robert A. Pastor, *Whirlpool: U.S. Foreign Policy Toward Latin America and the Caribbean* (Princeton, NJ: Princeton University Press, 1992).

National Security Council (NSC) The National Security Council (NSC) forms the apex of the presidential advisory system; its purpose is to help the president coordinate domestic, foreign, and military policies. The power of the NSC stems from its four statutory members—the president, vice-president, secretary of state, and secretary of defense—and two advisory members, the chairman of the Joint Chiefs of Staff and the director of the **Central Intelligence Agency (CIA)**. The major players in U.S.–Latin American policy are the NSC staff and the assistant to the president for national security affairs (the national security adviser). The president's national security adviser relies on the NSC's director of Latin American affairs for matters relating to Latin America and the Caribbean. Since the NSC is the most malleable component of the presidential advisory system, presidents can shape the agency's advisory role. For example, during the **Reagan** administration members of the NSC were given wide latitude in the implementation of Latin American policy. The secrecy and compartmentation of the NSC (and its staff) made it possible for a few insiders such as John Poindexter and Oliver **North** to take control of Latin American policy with little accountability and executive branch cover. Henry **Kissinger** was President Richard **Nixon**'s national security adviser during the time when the United States was involved in destabilizing Chile under President Salvador **Allende**. In *Years of Upheaval* (1982: 374), Kissinger claims that "our government had nothing to do with planning his overthrow and no involvement with the plotters. Allende was brought down by his own incompetence and inflexibility." This false and deceptive assessment is contradicted by recently declassified documents that show how deeply Kissinger was involved in clandestine efforts to prevent Allende from coming to power and then making sure Allende was brought down by a military coup. Oliver **North** worked for the National Security Council staff between 1984 and 1986 and was the key figure in the secret **Contra** supply network that eventually led to the **Iran-Contra scandal**. Those who were part of the NSC operation to resupply the Contras were well aware of the 1984 **Boland Amendment** prohibiting U.S. government assistance to the Contras but believed it did not specifically apply to the National Security Council because of the language contained in the amendment.

The director of Latin American affairs on the National Security Council staff is not the creator or implementor of inter-agency policy on Latin America, but a coordinator of U.S. policy toward the region. As part of the NSC staff, the director keeps abreast of significant events in the region, sets inter-agency agendas, and solicits input and develops consensus options for the national security adviser to present to the president of the United States. With these responsibilities, the director can influence the formulation of U.S.–Latin American relations in several ways. When the president of the United States decides to present a policy speech on Latin America, the director prepares an outline of the speech and presents it for approval at the senior level. The actual task of writing the speech often involves communication specialists in the **State Department**'s Bureau of Inter-American Affairs and the White House. Since the director of Latin American affairs on the National Security Council staff does not require Senate confirmation, appointees are frequently either senior-ranking diplomats or political appointees. Robert **Pastor** held the position during the Jimmy **Carter** presidency; President Reagan appointed five individuals—Roger Fontaine, Constantine Menges, Raymond Burghardt, José Sorzano, and Jacqueline Tilman—during his two terms in the 1980s. President **Clinton** appointed Richard E. Feinberg, formerly executive vice-president of the Overseas Development Council and president of the **Inter-American Dialogue**, to be his director; later, Arturo **Valenzuela**, Georgetown University political science professor, was appointed by Clinton to the post. Republican appointees are often "hardliners" with strong views and ideological axes to grind, particularly in defining the threat to national security and in formulating a tough response. According to Carothers, during the **Cold War**, "The hardliners espoused the East-West, crisis-oriented view of El Salvador . . . and were the force behind the high-profile policy of 'drawing the line' in El Salvador." President **George W. Bush** appointed hard-line opponents of Fidel **Castro**'s government to handle U.S.–Cuban relations. In most cases, hard-line appointees are not interested in building bipartisan coalitions, enlisting congressional support, or seeking out non-punitive solutions to a particular Latin American policy question. *See also* Washington Policymakers.

Suggested Reading

Thomas Carothers, *In the Name of Democracy: U.S. Policy Toward Latin America in the Reagan Years* (Berkeley: University of California Press, 1991); Roy Gutman, *Banana Diplomacy: The Making of American Policy in Nicaragua, 1981–1987* (New York: Simon and Schuster, 1988); Henry Kissinger, *Years of Upheaval* (Boston: Little, Brown, 1982); Gabriel Marcella, "The Presidential Advisory System," in David W. Dent, ed., *U.S.–Latin American Policymaking: A Reference Handbook* (Westport, CT: Greenwood Press, 1995); Constantine C. Menges, *Inside the National Security Council: The True Story of the Making and Unmaking of Reagan's Foreign Policy* (New York: Touchstone, 1988); Robert A. Pastor, *Condemned to Repetition: The United States and Nicaragua* (Princeton, NJ: Princeton University Press, 1987); Christopher Shoemaker, *The NSC Staff: Counseling the Council* (Boulder, CO: Westview Press, 1991); Howard J. Wiarda, *Foreign Policy Without Illusion: How Foreign Policy-Making Works and Fails to Work in the United States* (Glenview, Ill.: Scott, Foresman/Little Brown, 1990).

NED. *See* National Endowment for Democracy

Negroponte, John Dimitri (1939–) Controversial career foreign service officer whose diplomatic experience with the travails of the Vietnam War brought him several posts in Latin America. John Negroponte was born in London, but attended schools in the United States. After graduating from Phillips Exeter Academy in 1956 and Yale University in 1960, he served at eight different foreign service posts. While serving as a staff member on the **National Security Council (NSC)** (1970–1973), he advised Henry **Kissinger** on matters related to ending the Vietnam War. This experience contributed to foreign posts in Quito, Ecuador, and ambassador to Honduras during the first **Reagan** administration. While in Tegucigalpa, Negroponte oversaw the **Contra** war against Nicaragua, maintaining close ties with the Honduran military and often ignoring reported **human rights** abuses associated with the conflict. His power over Honduras reached a level in which many Hondurans believed that he was running the country, not the president of Honduras. He returned to Washington in 1985 where he served as assistant secretary of state for the international environment and scientific bureau. Revelations from the **Iran-Contra scandal** damaged Negroponte's career and his role as U.S. ambassador to Honduras; however, he managed to obtain Senate confirmation in 2001 for U.S. ambassador to the **United Nations (UN)** shortly after the terrorist attacks of **September 11, 2001**. His experience with large embassies and secretive foreign policy were factors in his nomination to be the first U.S. ambassador in post–Saddam Hussein Iraq in 2004. At his Senate hearings in 2004, his actions as a former ambassador in Central America were ignored, and some senators who were once critical of Negroponte for his pro-consul work applauded him for his diplomatic work. President **George W. Bush** named Negroponte to be national intelligence director in 2005, a nomination that revived criticisms of his activities as ambassador to Honduras in the 1980s. Despite his denials, recent documents from Negroponte's **State Department** file support his critics who argue he did little to protest human rights abuses by the Honduran military. *See also* Ambassadors; North, Oliver Lawrence.

Suggested Reading

Jack R. Binns, *The United States in Honduras, 1980–1981: An Ambassador's Memoir* (Jefferson, NC: McFarland, 2000); "Bush Picks Longtime Diplomat for New Top Intelligence Job," *New York Times* (February 18, 2005); Christopher Dickey, *With the Contras: A Reporter in the Wilds of Nicaragua* (New York: Simon and Schuster, 1985); Scott Shane, "Cables Show Central Negroponte Role in 80s Covert War Against Nicaragua," *New York Times* (April 13, 2005).

New Grenada, Treaty of. *See* Bidlack-Mallarino Treaty (1846)

Nixon, Richard Milhous (1913–1994) Lawyer and politician known for his interest in foreign affairs and **Cold War** views that attributed many of the problems confronting the United States in the Third World to Communist insurgencies. His

Latin American policy was rooted in benign neglect, an effort to lower the profile and reduce the presence of the United States in Latin America by shrinking U.S. aid programs and toning down U.S. rhetoric. As vice-president (1953–1961) and president (1969–1974) of the United States, Richard Nixon gained a national reputation as one of the leading anti-Communist politicians in the United States. During his tenure as vice-president under **Dwight D. Eisenhower**, Nixon made several trips to Latin America where he courted "**friendly dictators**" who opposed communism in the name of stability and offered unfailing support of the United States. Worried about the advances of communism in the Western Hemisphere, Nixon argued that the United States should have a new policy toward Latin America, one that offered "a formal handshake for dictators; an *embraso* [*sic*] for leaders in freedom." On a "good will" tour of Latin America in 1958, Nixon was attacked by unruly mobs for the support the United States provided to brutal dictators. On the advice of his brother, **Milton Eisenhower**, President Eisenhower developed new economic initiatives that served as a precursor to President John F. **Kennedy**'s **Alliance for Progress**. During the last two years in office, the Eisenhower administration committed approximately $850 million in economic assistance to Latin American countries. In most cases, the catalyst for such economic assistance was the fear of revolutionary nationalism and communism, not a commitment to progress and change in the region. Vice-President Nixon met with Fidel **Castro** for three hours in the Old Executive Office Building in April 1959 to discuss the Cuban Revolution and U.S. policy. Although Castro disclaimed any intention of creating a Communist regime in Cuba, Nixon wrote in *Six Crises* (1979) that Castro was either a Communist or under Communist influence. After Castro departed, Nixon wrote a memo to President Eisenhower recommending a plan to depose Castro; the memo became the genesis of the **Bay of Pigs** invasion that was carried out by President Kennedy two years later.

After losing the presidential election to John F. Kennedy in 1960, and the governor's race in California in 1962, Nixon began a slow process of building a foundation within the Republican Party to take another shot at the presidency in 1968. Once he was elected president in 1968, Nixon and his national security adviser, Henry **Kissinger**, focused U.S. attention on Vietnam and relations with China and the Soviet Union. Nixon and Kissinger devoted little time to Latin America, except when countries like Salvador **Allende**'s Chile presented a challenge to U.S. interests. According to Schmitz (1999: 295), "Allende would provide a base for anti-American attacks, support for Castro, and eventually an alliance with the Soviet Union." At first, the Nixon administration tried to prevent Salvador Allende's election. When this failed, Nixon used the **Central Intelligence Agency (CIA)** to destabilize Chile through U.S. economic warfare and covert activity. Before Allende could complete his constitutional term of office, Allende was overthrown by the Chilean military and committed suicide before the presidential palace was turned over to the coup-plotters on September 11, 1973. The Chilean coup brought General Augusto **Pinochet** to power, and President Nixon extended immediate support to Pinochet despite the brutality of his regime. In Nixon's mind, Pinochet deserved U.S. support because he would protect American economic interests, provide order, and combat communism.

After Nixon resigned over the Watergate Affair in August 1974, he retired to California and later moved to New Jersey where he gradually re-emerged as a foreign policy analyst and informal adviser. Most of his books on foreign policy were self-serving attempts to justify his handling of the war in Vietnam and Sino-Soviet relations. He said little in his memoirs about blunders associated with his advice on how to handle right-wing dictators, the Cuban Revolution, or the destruction of democracy in Chile. Like many of those who preceded him in office, Nixon believed that Latin Americans were immature, or mentally unstable, and best governed by tough leaders who are willing to forego freedom for the sake of order and stability. *See also* Democracy and Democracy Promotion; Dictatorships; Operation Condor; Scandals and Blunders; Washington Policymakers.

Suggested Reading

Seymour M. Hersh, *The Price of Power: Kissinger in the Nixon White House* (New York: Summit Books, 1983); Richard M. Nixon, *Six Crises* (New York: Warner Books, 1979); David F. Schmitz, *Thank God They're on Our Side: The United States and Right-Wing Dictatorships, 1921–1965* (Chapel Hill: University of North Carolina Press, 1999).

No-Transfer Resolution. *See* Bidlack-Mallarino Treaty (1846)

Non-Intervention. *See* Intervention and Non-Intervention

Non-Recognition. *See* Recognition and Non-Recognition

Noriega, Manuel Antonio (1940–) Panamanian dictator who, as chief of the National Guard from 1983 to 1989, played a key role in U.S.–Central American relations during the **Reagan** and **George H.W. Bush** administrations. Born to poor parents in Panama City, Manuel Noriega attended public school in Panama and a military academy in Peru. After graduating from the Peruvian Military Academy, which enabled him to become a National Guard officer, Noriega received additional training at the U.S. Army **School of the Americas (SOA)** in Panama. General Noriega built a career from his military training, friendship with fellow officer Omar Torrijos, and his ability to manipulate the United States during a time when the United States was involved in fighting leftist guerrillas in Central American and **drug traffickers** in South America. After the death of Torrijos in a plane crash in 1981, General Noriega established control over the National Guard, renamed it the Panamanian Defense Force (PDF), and proceeded to rule from behind the scenes through a series of puppet presidents. Despite his ruthless and anti-democratic methods of governing Panama, Noriega provided intelligence and logistical support for U.S. policies in the region. Often playing both sides of the fence, Noriega provided critical intelligence to the United States, Cuba, and Israel while at the same time helping the Medellín drug cartel smuggle drugs and launder money.

While on the **Central Intelligence Agency (CIA)** payroll, Noriega helped ship arms from Cuba to the **Sandinista** rebels in Nicaragua and later joined the United States in channeling weapons to the right-wing **Contras** during the Reagan administration. Noriega had face-to-face meetings with then–Vice-President George H.W. Bush and CIA Director William **Casey**, a sign of Noriega's value to the United States as a friendly dictator and source of intelligence. Noriega's complicated political life came to an end after annulling the 1989 presidential elections in Panama and his own drug trafficking led to his indictment by the U.S. Justice Department in 1988. By now Noriega was a troublemaker who could embarrass the United States if he remained in power. At first the United States tried to remove Noriega by pressuring the **Organization of American States (OAS)** to coordinate his removal, instituting trade sanctions, and assisting in several coup attempts to put an end to Noriega's rule. By December 1989 President George H.W. Bush decided that the only way to rid Panama of General Noriega was through a U.S. military invasion. On December 20, 1989, 12,000 U.S. troops invaded Panama to try to capture the Panamanian dictator. While the **United Nations (UN)** and the OAS condemned the intervention, Noriega spent two weeks in hiding. With the assistance of the Papal Nuncio in Panama City, Noriega finally gave himself up to U.S. agents and was quickly taken to Miami where he was convicted in court on a variety of narcotics charges and sentenced to a forty-year term in a federal prison. His prison time was reduced to thirty years in 1999 because the judge argued he deserved credit for helping the United States pursue its interests in Central America; however, all efforts to have a retrial have failed. The capture and imprisonment of Manuel Antonio Noriega helped to boost President Bush's ratings as legitimate leader, but it had virtually no impact on money laundering and drug trafficking in Latin America. The invasion eventually achieved its objective, but it cost the United States $163 million in military operations, the loss of twenty-four American lives with over 350 injured, and the wrath of the world community for its use of force. Over 1,000 Panamanians died in the invasion that resulted in the destruction of a whole neighborhood through gunfire, looting, and burning. General Noriega continues to blame the invasion on George H.W. Bush and others in the Reagan administration who betrayed him for actions carried out in the name of U.S. intelligence agencies. Noriega is eligible for mandatory release in 2007 if his prison behavior is good. *See also* Dictatorships; Friendly Dictators; Intervention and Non-Intervention; Operation Just Cause.

Suggested Reading

Kevin Buckley, *Panama: The Whole Story* (New York: Simon and Schuster, 1991); John Dinges, *Our Man in Panama: How General Noriega Used the United States, and Made Millions in Drugs and Arms*, rev. ed. (New York: Random House, 1991); Manuel Noriega and Peter Eisner, *The Memoirs of Manuel Noriega: America's Prisoner* (New York: Random House, 1997); William Scott Malone, "The Panama Debacle—Uncle Sam Wimp's Out," *Washington Post* (April 23, 1989).

North, Oliver Lawrence (1943–) A gung-ho U.S. Marine who became a central figure in the **Iran-Contra scandal** while a staff member of the **National Security Council (NSC)** (1981–1986). As one of the supporters of the **Reagan Doctrine**, North also helped carry out the U.S. policy in the **Falklands/Malvinas War** (1982), the 1983 invasion of **Grenada**, and several anti-**terrorism** initiatives. As an aide to **Central Intelligence Agency (CIA)** Director William **Casey**, Colonel North organized the secret scheme to funnel money earned from arms sales to Iran into Swiss bank accounts that could then be used to fund right-wing Nicaraguan guerrillas, contrary to U.S. law. After the scandal broke and North was fired by President Ronald **Reagan**, the U.S. Congress investigated the affair and found numerous high officials in the Reagan administration in violation of several laws. North was convicted of three felonies—aiding and abetting the obstruction of Congress; altering and destroying NSC documents; and receiving an illegal gratuity—but his convictions were subsequently overturned because of technicalities. Then in 1994, with the support of evangelical Christian conservatives, North made an unsuccessful bid for a Senate seat from Virginia.

While North impressed some of his superiors with his can-do attitude and sixteen-hour work days, others found the marine to be too much of a self-promoter, willing to stretch or overlook bureaucratic or constitutional obstacles when his actions served a higher goal. He worked with General Manuel **Noriega** in Panama and had a hand in **Contra**-related corruption tied to the drug trade. Since he failed in his bid for a Senate seat, North has been active with a company that sells bullet-proof vests and is popular among conservatives on the lecture circuit. He started a non-profit charity called The Freedom Alliance, a radio talk show, and a TV program, *War Stories*, on the Fox News Channel. He made an attempt to defend himself in *Under Fire: An American Story* (1992), an autobiography of his early years, war experience, and work as an NSC functionary. He maintains that his work to overthrow the Nicaraguan **Sandinista** government was both legal and necessary to halt the growing Cuban-Soviet influence in Central America and the Caribbean. In a meeting with Panamanian dictator General Noriega, North received an offer from Noriega in which Noriega said he would get rid of the top Sandinista leadership for the United States in exchange for improving his tarnished political image. North turned down the offer, telling General Noriega it would not be legal.

To commemorate the twentieth anniversary of the Grenada invasion in 2003, Oliver North organized a cruise that included many hawkish conservatives—Edwin Meese, Wayne LaPierre, Dana Rohrabacher, and Michael Reagan—that passengers could dine with in the main cabin. Those who joined North on the cruise were surprised to find that the Cubans that Reagan dispelled from the island are now back building hospitals and clinics in Grenada. Oliver North continues to maintain that the Reagan Doctrine as applied to Grenada helped change the world for the good by greasing the skids for the eventual collapse of the Soviet empire. *See also* Abrams, Elliott; Washington Policymakers.

Suggested Reading

Ben Bradlee, Jr., *Guts and Glory: The Rise and Fall of Oliver North* (New York: D.I. Fine, 1988); Theodore Draper, *A Very Thin Line: The Iran-Contra Affairs* (New York: Simon and Schuster, 1981); Oliver Lawrence North, *Under Fire: An American Story* (New York: Harper Collins, 1992).

North American Free Trade Agreement (NAFTA) A bold and comprehensive trade agreement between Canada, Mexico, and the United States signed in October 1992, ratified in November 1993, and entered into force on January 1, 1994. The accord known as NAFTA was contentious and controversial from the beginning; with little support among the American public, the White House (first under President **George H.W. Bush**, later under President Bill **Clinton**) engaged in an arm-twisting debate to bring NAFTA into effect. The main provisions of NAFTA include the almost total removal of trade and investment restrictions over a fifteen-year period and the use of intergovernmental consultation to settle trade disputes. Protectionist opposition in the United States required the passage of two "side agreements" dealing with safeguards for workers' rights and environmental protection measures. Those who supported NAFTA wanted it to serve as a first step toward a hemisphere-wide trade agreement. Once ratified, NAFTA brought under one roof three hugely different economies, but political leaders in all three countries promised the accord would create millions of good jobs, raise living standards, and curb illegal immigration to the United States. Those who spoke of the benefits of NAFTA claimed that free trade would benefit all and should serve as a first step toward free trade agreements with other countries in the hemisphere. After ten years, NAFTA is still a politically charged symbol of promises and perils of free trade as a solution to economic and political development in the hemisphere.

For many political analysts and economists who have attempted to measure the effects of NAFTA, the accord has stimulated trade and overall growth, but it has also brought painful dislocations, particularly among some sectors of the Mexican and U.S. economies. Those who point to positive economic gains from NAFTA highlight lower priced consumer goods and increased corporate earnings; those who emphasize the negatives of NAFTA point to the loss of manufacturing jobs in the United States and lower income, the widening gap between rich and poor in Mexico, the move of NAFTA-related jobs to low-wage China, the damage to Mexico's agricultural sector, and the dramatic increase of Mexicans moving to the United States in search of higher paying employment. The growing impact of globalization makes it difficult to sort out the effects of NAFTA on the three economies that comprise the trade agreement. Despite the mixed picture of NAFTA after more than a decade, the United States has signed free trade agreements with Chile and four Central American countries. As with the original NAFTA, ratification of these and future agreements will not be easy, despite the marginal benefits from the multination agreement.

The process of enforcing compliance with NAFTA rules has not been easy, either by relying on the Free Trade Commission as dispute-settlement mechanism, or the use of one's own legal system (Canada). In March 1996, Canada requested consultations with the United States over the extra-territorial claims of the **Helms-Burton** Act. Canada considered the legislation an improper extra-territorial extension of U.S. jurisdiction that violates principles of international law when dealing with claims for expropriated property in Cuba. The U.S. efforts to punish Cuba by passing laws that obstruct international trade and investment such as Helms-Burton, failed to convince Latin American countries and Canada of the merits of such policies. As the United States pushes forward with more free trade pacts, either in Latin America or elsewhere around the globe, interest in a hemispheric free trade agreement declines and Cuba struggles to improve its economy while being excluded from these "capitalist" pacts. It remains to be seen whether a post-Castro Cuba will be forced to compete with Mexico for *maquiladora* (assembly plants for exporting goods to the United States) jobs as foreign countries try to capitalize on cheap labor in Cuba. Canada's benefits from NAFTA stem from its well-educated middle class, close proximity to the U.S. border, and the existence of a social safety net—liberal unemployment benefits and universal health insurance—to ease the transformation to a more export-oriented economy.

Low-wage competitors from around the world will continue the painful effects of free trade ideology in a global economy. Critics of NAFTA maintain that what is needed is more emphasis on "fair trade" where those who export goods and services receive a living wage and agricultural pursuits are carried out to emphasize sustainable development. Unfortunately the vicissitudes of NAFTA are closely tied to the corporate search for places on the planet that offer low-wage advantages over those at home. *See also* Free Trade Area of the Americas (FTAA); Summit of the Americas; Washington Consensus.

Suggested Reading

M. Delal Baer and Sidney Weintraub, eds., *The NAFTA Debate: Grappling with Unconventional Trade Issues* (Boulder, CO: Lynne Rienner, 1994); Stephen Blank and Jerry Haar, *Making NAFTA Work: U.S. Firms and the New North American Business Environment* (Miami: North-South Center Press, 1999); Maxwell A. Cameron and Brian W. Tomlin, *The Making of NAFTA: How the Deal Was Done* (Ithaca, NY: Cornell University Press, 2001); Jorge G. Castañeda, *The Mexican Shock: Its Meaning for the United States* (New York: Norton, 1996); "Free Trade Accord at Age 10: The Growing Pains Are Clear," *New York Times* (December 27, 2003); George W. Grayson, *The North American Free Trade Agreement: Regional Community and the New World Order* (Lanham, MD: University Press of America, 1994); Gary Clyde Hufbauer and Jeffrey Schott, *NAFTA: An Assessment* (Washington, DC: Institute for International Economics, 1993); Ann E. Kingsolver, *NAFTA Stories: Fears and Hopes in Mexico and the United States* (Boulder, CO: Lynne Rienner, 2001); John J. Kirton and Virginia W. Maclaren, eds., *Linking Trade, Environment, and Social Cohesion: NAFTA Experiences, Global Challenges* (Burlington, VT: Ashgate, 2002); John R. MacArthur, *The Selling of "Free Trade": NAFTA, Washington, and the Subversion of American Democracy* (Berkeley: University of California Press, 2001); William A. Orme, Jr., *Understanding NAFTA: Mexico, Free Trade, and the New North America* (Austin: University of Texas Press, 1996); Manuel Pastor, Jr., "Mexican Trade Liberalization and

NAFTA," *Latin American Research Review* (summer 1994); Guy Poitras, *Inventing North America: Canada, Mexico, and the United States* (Boulder, CO: Lynne Rienner, 2001); Joseph E. Stiglitz, "The Broken Promise of NAFTA," *New York Times* (January 6, 2004); Hermann von Bertrab, *Negotiating NAFTA: A Mexican Envoy's Account* (Westport, CT: Greenwood Press, 1997).

NSC. *See* National Security Council

O

OAS. *See* Organization of American States

Office of the Coordinator of Inter-American Affairs (OCIAA). *See* Rockefeller, Nelson Aldrich (1908–1979)

Office of Public Safety (OPS). *See State of Siege* (1973)

Olney, Richard (1835–1917) Lawyer, politician, and secretary of state who played a major role in U.S.–Latin American relations between 1895 and 1897. When Secretary of State Walter Gresham died on May 28, 1895, President Grover **Cleveland** selected his attorney general, Richard Olney as his replacement. He soon confronted the British over the Venezuelan boundary dispute with a diplomatic note that declared the right of the United States to police the Western Hemisphere to keep out extra-hemispheric powers and the inherent right to hemispheric **hegemony**. It was a bold assertion that Olney based on the **Monroe Doctrine** and the physical strength of the United States. In what became known as the Olney Corollary to the Monroe Doctrine, Richard Olney declared in 1895 that the Monroe Doctrine justified the American position toward Europe and the Latin American states by stating that "no European power or combination of European powers [should] forcibly deprive an American state of the right and power of self-government and of shaping for itself its own political fortunes and destinies." Without any apparent concern for the arrogance and hypocrisy of his words, Olney then added: "Today the United States is practically sovereign on this continent, and its fiat is law upon the subjects to which it confines its interposition." The Olney note was not well received in Latin America, but it provided a hegemonic mind-set—Washington possessed the right to dictate the behavior for other states—that would continue over the next three decades, if not longer. Olney's handling of the Venezuelan boundary dispute forced Great Britain to accept the validity of the Monroe Doctrine, greatly enhancing the power of the doctrine as an acceptable guide to U.S.–Latin American policy. Prior to the **Spanish-Cuban-American War**, Olney attempted, with little success, to convince the Spanish that only by instituting serious political reforms could it expect to keep Cuba as a colony. The U.S. imperial offensive of the 1890s prompted a strong reaction by Latin American intellectuals at the time, led by José Enrique Rodó, a Uruguayan writer and philosopher whose book, *Ariel* (1900) provided the spark for a generation of anti-American sentiment found in polemics directed at the United States by other Latin American writers. Richard Olney returned to his Boston law practice after 1897, avoided the political arena, and died in 1917 at the age of eighty-two. *See also* Anti-Americanism; Imperialism.

Suggested Reading

Gerald G. Eggert, *Richard Olney: Evolution of a Statesman* (University Park: Pennsylvania State University Press, 1974); Federico G. Gil, *Latin American–United States Relations* (New York: Harcourt Brace Jovanovich, 1971).

Operation Blast Furnace Current U.S.–Bolivian relations have been influenced by corruption, **human rights** violations, competing economic development theories, the power of the Bolivian military and the frequency of military takeovers, and efforts to reduce drug production and **drug trafficking** in the Andes mountains. The election of Víctor Paz Estenssoro—his fourth term (1985–1989) as president of Bolivia—helped to improve relations with the United States because of Paz's willingness to comply with Washington's need to display resolve against narcotics trafficking. In July 1986, at the invitation of Bolivia's new president, hundreds of U.S. military personnel were sent into Bolivia as part of a joint counter-narcotics campaign called Operation Blast Furnace. The **intervention** to halt the processing and transportation of cocaine helped the **Reagan** administration publicize the seriousness of a problem that had become a major domestic and hemispheric issue. However, in Bolivia, Operation Blast Furnace stirred up anti–United States feelings with major newspaper headlines like "U.S. Invades Bolivia" that undermined the joint effort. Bolivia's major concern was the influence of the drug trade on Bolivian politics and its inability to obtain badly needed financial assistance from the United States without bilateral cooperation on drug matters. Although Bolivia remains one of the principal sites for U.S. anti-drug activities in the Andes, Operation Blast Furnace proved to be only a temporary solution to a far more serious problem in U.S.–Latin American relations. *See also* Anti-Americanism; Drug Trafficking; Intervention and Non-Intervention; Plan Colombia.

Suggested Reading

Bruce M. Bagley and William O. Walker III, eds., *Drug Trafficking in the Americas* (Boulder, CO: Lynne Rienner, 1994); Madeline Barbara Leons and Harry Sanabria, eds., *Coca, Cocaine, and the Bolivian Reality* (Albany: State University of New York Press, 1997); Sewall H. Menzel, *Fire in the Andes: U.S. Foreign Policy and Cocaine Politics in Bolivia and Peru* (Lanham, MD: University Press of America, 1996).

Operation Condor Shadowy Latin American anti-Communist alliance of military governments created in the 1970s that defied **international law** and traditions of political asylum to carry out a crusade against purported political enemies. As an organized system of state terror with a transnational reach, Operation Condor, according to a political scientist who has studied the system, "was an anticommunist international that went far beyond targeting 'communists,' and it signified an unprecedented level of coordinated repression by right-wing military regimes in Latin America" (McSherry, 2002: 39). Members of the network of state terror included Chile, Argentina, Uruguay, Bolivia, Paraguay, and Brazil. Operation Condor was later joined by Peru and Ecuador; the U.S. **State Department**, the Defense Department, and the **Central Intelligence Agency (CIA)** were all well informed of Operation Condor and secretly aided and facilitated Condor operations, including some that involved the murder of U.S. citizens. Operation Condor consisted of surveillance, abductions of dissidents, detentions, torture and **assassinations** by authoritarian regimes engaged in a highly sophisticated, clandestine network of systematic, transnational state-sponsored **terrorism** throughout the Southern Cone of South America. Condor commandos—military and paramilitary—hunted down thousands of leftist dissidents, union and peasant leaders, priests and nuns, intellectuals, students, teachers, former government officials, as well as suspected guerrillas. According to McSherry (2002: 40), recently declassified files indicate that "U.S. officials considered Condor a legitimate 'counter-terror' organization and that Condor was assisted and encouraged by U.S. military and intelligence forces." These ruthless operations against political opposition figures and organizations were part of the war against communism and the desire to thwart **Castro**-style **revolutions** in the Western Hemisphere. Any populist, nationalist, or socialist movement was considered a threat to Latin American oligarchies as well as U.S. political and economic interests in the region.

Operation Condor occurred within the context of the anti-Communist foreign policy of the United States and Latin America during the **Cold War**. There were many parallels between Condor and other U.S. military and intelligence programs in the 1960s, including the Phoenix Program (Vietnam) and the U.S. Army's Project X (Latin America). Condor operated on three levels of coordination and operation. The first involved mutual cooperation among military intelligence services. The second involved organized cross-border operations to capture and "disappear" political dissidents and so-called terrorists. The third was the most secret (Phase III) and involved the formation of special teams of assassins to travel anywhere in the world to eliminate "subversive" enemies. The victims of what Condor called

"Phase III" included the car-bombing deaths of Chilean Orlando Letelier and his American colleague Ronni Moffitt in Washington, D.C., in 1976; the 1973 abduction and murder of U.S. citizens Charles Horman and Frank Teruggi shortly after the overthrow of Salvador **Allende** in Chile; the assassinations of General Carlos Prats (Chilean), Juan José Torres (Bolivian ex-president), and two Uruguayan legislators known for their opposition to the military government. U.S. intelligence and military training manuals discovered at the U.S. Army Intelligence School at Fort Holabird in Maryland and at the **School of the Americas (SOA)** endorsed "counter-terror" methods that included torture, electroshock, drugs and hypnosis, and psychological warfare to create a climate of fear and eliminate perceived enemies of the military state. In recently released documentation by the CIA in 2000, the agency admitted that Chile's intelligence chief, Manuel Contreras (known as "Condor One"), was a CIA asset between 1974 and 1977 when severe repression was being carried out by General Augusto **Pinochet**. In the Horman and Teruggi cases immediately after the September 11, 1973, Chilean coup, documents released in a 1999 report include accusations by a Chilean intelligence officer that a CIA officer was present when a Chilean general made the decision to execute Horman because it was believed that he "knew too much." Other documents reveal that the CIA and its then-director, **George H.W. Bush**, was well aware of General Pinochet's cross-border assassination efforts to hunt down leftists, but refused to share the information with federal criminal authorities that might have shed light on the skullduggery of Operation Condor.

The new "bureaucratic-authoritarian" regimes (professionalized militaries in alliance with civilian technocrats) that came to power in the 1960s and 1970s were not content to simply re-establish an orderly status quo and return to the barracks as praetorian regimes had done in the past. Instead, they envisioned a long-term institutional rule and employed massive levels of repression to eradicate leftism, instill patriotism, restructure participation, and deepen (privatize) the economic development process. Many of these regimes pursued neo-liberal economic policies that benefited from the prevention of pluralist forces demanding greater benefits from economic growth. These new military officers viewed their *golpes* (military takeovers) and the installation of their *juntas* as only the first battle in an ideological war of national survival against Marxism. Although many of these military men were imbued with the same sort of "national security" doctrine that framed their strategies as logical responses to the threat of Communist subversion directed by Moscow and Havana, they were mostly fearful of new popular movements—not Communist guerrillas—demanding major socioeconomic and political change. Operation Condor was driven by the military's belief in an organic conception of society and a virulent nationalism that required unity and the containment of conflict through an authoritarian, centralized state. Under siege by forces opposed to traditional values and Christian beliefs, the military leaders became obsessed with the need to cleanse their societies of leftist subversion and civilian politicians who appealed to the chaotic and insubordinate masses. The military **dictatorships** that made up Operation Condor believed that the solution to social conflict was massive demobilization and "anti-politics," coupled with disciplined administrative solutions to under-development imposed by fiat from above. Argentina's Jorge Rafael Videla—a key member of the junta that held power in Argentina between 1976 and 1983—was the first former Latin American dictator to be indicted for Operation Condor in 2001. Judges in Argentina and Chile, following the arrest and detention of Chilean dictator Augusto Pinochet in 1998, have targeted other participants in Operation Condor, including President Richard **Nixon**'s national security adviser and secretary of state during the 1970s, Henry A. **Kissinger**. As a result of a lawsuit brought on behalf of victims of Operation Condor in 2004, Chile's Supreme Court stripped Pinochet of immunity from prosecution, paving the way for a possible trial of the former dictator on charges of **human rights** abuses. Pinochet was declared fit to stand trial and indicted on December 13, 2004, by Juan Guzmán, a Chilean judge, for human rights crimes committed between 1975 and 1977, allegedly as part of Operation Condor.

Out of the shadowy network of Operation Condor came the "dirty wars" that plagued Latin American societies during the Cold War. These internal wars quickly developed a penetrative, totalitarian cast in which security interests and anti-communism ranked higher than freedom, **democracy**, and human rights. The counter-terror doctrine and special-forces model promoted by the United States contributed to the Cold War repression in Latin America and the human rights crimes of Operation Condor. Although the documentary record is incomplete because many sources remain classified, new evidence sheds considerable light on the unfortunate legacies of state-sponsored terrorism and "**blowback**" from doctrines that rationalized human rights violations as a legitimate means to suspicious ends. Operation Condor has also become the testing ground for the universal application of international law to crimes against humanity. *See also* Democracy and Democracy Promotion; International Criminal Court (ICC); *Missing* (1982).

Suggested Reading

Pierre Abramovici, "Latin America: The 30 Years Dirty War," *Le Monde Diplomatique* (August 2001); John Dinges, "Pulling Back the Veil on Condor," *The Nation* (July 24–31, 2000); Thomas Hauser, *The Execution of Charles Horman* (New York: Harcourt Brace Jovanovich, 1978); Kermit D. Johnson, *Ethics and Counterrevolution: American Involvement in Internal Wars* (Lanham, MD: University Press of America, 1998); Lucy Komisar, "Into the Murky Depths of 'Operation Condor,' " *Los Angeles Times* (November 1, 1998); Michael McClintock, *Instruments of Statecraft: U.S. Guerrilla Warfare, Counterinsurgency, Counterterrorism, 1940–1990* (New York: Pantheon Books, 1992); J. Patrice McSherry, "Tracking the Origins of a State Terror Network: Operation Condor," *Latin American Perspectives*, Vol. 29, No. 1 (January 2002): 38–68; McSherry, "Operation Condor: Deciphering the U.S. Role," *Crimes of War* (July 2001); McSherry, "Operation Condor: Clandestine Interamerican System," *Social Justice*, Vol. 26, No. 4 (winter 1999): 144–174; Diana Jean Schemo, "U.S. victims of Chile's Coup: The Uncensored File," *New York Times* (February 13, 2000); Jeffrey A. Sluka, ed., *Death Squad: The Anthropology of State Terror* (Philadelphia: University of Pennsylvania Press, 2000); Michael Stohl and George Lopez, eds., *Terrible Beyond Endurance? The Foreign Policy of State Terrorism* (Westport, CT: Greenwood Press, 1988); Robert E. White, "Too many spies, too little intelligence," in Craig Eisendrath, ed., *National Insecurity: U.S. Intelligence After the Cold War* (Philadelphia: Temple University Press, 2000).

Operation Just Cause In December 1989, U.S. military forces—Army, Air Force and Navy—participated in Operation Just Cause: the invasion of Panama to remove General Manuel A. **Noriega** from power. The U.S. invasion of Panama was the first post–Cold War invasion of a Latin American country that was not justified (at least explicitly) on a global-ideological basis. The invasion was preceded by two years of diplomatic bungling by the **Reagan** and **George H.W. Bush** administrations, Noriega's increasing defiance of the United States, vilification of Noriega in the American press for his dictatorial rule and illegal **drug trafficking**, and the growing importance of drugs and drug trafficking as an issue in American politics. General Noriega's assistance with the task of removing the **Sandinistas** from power in Nicaragua and close ties to George H.W. Bush meant that Washington could not do much about the troublesome Panamanian until after the 1988 presidential election. At first the United States suspended millions of dollars in aid to Panama in hopes that **economic sanctions** would force Noriega from office. But Noriega only became more defiant, and relations deteriorated over a span of almost two years. President Ronald Reagan tried to pay off Noriega and find him a country for his exile, but to no avail.

Once George H.W. Bush took office in January 1989, pressure increased inside the White House to solve the Panama problem. Since it was no longer possible to justify the use of force on grounds that General Noriega was a Communist aligned with Cuba and the Soviet Union, the United States faced the dilemma of basing **regime change** on other threats such as drug trafficking and the mistreatment of Americans in the Canal Zone. After the media focused on the saliency of drugs as a political issue and depicted Noriega as a dangerous "drug thug," public support for an invasion mounted and Congress opened hearings on what should be done about Panama. Bush's conundrum was compounded by the fact that his image as a weak and indecisive leader had reached the point where he was being referred to as a wimp, lacking the essential machismo to confront a tin-horned dictator like Noriega.

As the **Cold War** came to a close with the collapse of the Soviet Union, President Bush began to ponder his options for dealing with the Panamanian dictator. The first option was to try to negotiate Noriega's removal from power. While this option seemed attractive from the standpoint of minimum negative fall out, Bush's domestic policy advisers cautioned that there could be partisan repercussions if a deal with Noriega was perceived as treating him too favorably. After all, Noriega had been on the **Central Intelligence Agency (CIA)** payroll for years and had collaborated with the **National Security Council (NSC)** to help the United States rid Nicaragua of the Sandinistas. With hard information that the United States had known about Noriega's drug involvement since 1972, including the years that Bush headed the CIA, Bush's top advisers concluded this was certainly possible but the political fallout at home might be too damaging to the Republican Party. The second option was collective intervention using the **Organization of American States (OAS)**. The OAS was willing to go along with economic sanctions against Noriega, but opposed the use of force to drive him from power. Only the Panamanians, with close ties to the Bush administration, were in favor of collective intervention. The third option was to wait out the economic blockade in hopes that with enough economic "pain" the Panamanian opposition would rise up and overthrow Noriega. The domestic political situation in the United States would not allow the Bush administration the luxury of waiting for the economic sanctions to deliver the final blow as people from within Bush's party were denouncing him for his spineless leadership. "We are being perceived as cowards, lacking the resolve to deal with a tin-horned dictator," yelled New York Senator Gus D'Amato. According to the *Washington Post*, "getting rid of Noriega became the test of U.S. manhood." The fourth option was to organize a coup d'état in which a Panamanian revolt would topple Noriega. With the blessings of President Bush, the Panamanian military struck on October 3, 1989. Noriega was captured for a short time, but poor coordination and planning failed to hold him, and he returned to power, more defiant than before against the United States. After meeting in the Situation Room on the evening of December 19 with members of the **State Department**, National Security Council, and the Pentagon, President Bush ordered over 20,000 U.S. forces to invade Panama to capture General Noriega. He was given talking papers and a speech to deliver on television the following morning to the American people. When President Bush spoke to the nation at 7:00 A.M., he delivered the following words (Bush, 1990: 194–195):

> Fellow citizens, last night I ordered U.S. military forces to Panama. For nearly two years the United States, nations of Latin America and the Caribbean have worked together to resolve the crisis in Panama. The goals of the United States have been to safeguard the lives of Americans, to defend democracy in Panama, to combat drug trafficking, and to protect the integrity of the Panama Canal Treaty. Many attempts have been made to resolve the crisis through diplomacy and negotiations. All were rejected by the dictator of Panama, General Manuel A. Noriega, an indicted drug trafficker.
>
> Last Friday Noriega declared his military dictatorship to be in a state of war with the United States and publicly threatened the lives of Americans in Panama. The very next day forces under his command shot and killed an unarmed American serviceman, wounded another, arrested and brutally beat a third American serviceman and then brutally interrogated his wife, threatening her with sexual abuse. That was enough.
>
> General Noriega's reckless threats and attacks upon Americans created an imminent danger to the thirty-five thousand American citizens in Panama. As President I have no higher obligation than to safeguard the lives of American citizens. And that is why I directed our armed

> forces to protect the lives of American citizens in Panama and to bring General Noriega to justice in the United States. . . .
>
> I took this action only after reaching the conclusion that every other avenue was closed and the lives of American citizens were in grave danger. . . .

The Bush administration claimed the right to use force in Panama was just and legal. The U.S. Department of State cited three legal bases for the military action. First, the United States had exercised its legitimate right of self-defense as defined in the charters of the **United Nations (UN)** and the Organization of American States. Article 51 of the UN Charter recognizes the right of self-defense if an armed attack occurs against a country and Article 21 of the OAS Charter prohibits the use of force against another country except in the case of self-defense. Second, the United States had the legal right to protect and defend the Panama Canal under the existing **Panama Canal Treaties**. Finally, the U.S. intervention took place with the consent of the legitimate government of Panama, and President Bush acted under his constitutional authority to conduct foreign relations and as commander in chief. In a statement before the Organization of American States on December 22, 1989, U.S. Ambassador Luigi R. Einaudi defended Operation Just Cause by criticizing the OAS for a failure of will to remove General Noriega. "By improperly invoking the legitimate principle of non-intervention," claimed Einaudi, "the OAS will find itself cast on the side of the dictators and the tyrants of this world who are en route to extinction. It will find itself, in objective terms, defending the indefensible. It will find itself on the side of Noriega." He continued his scolding of the OAS by saying that because the United States acted with military force, "Noriega got his due, the thugs are out of power, and Panama will at last be governed by representatives of the sovereign will of the Panamanian people."

Critics of Operation Just Cause questioned the legal basis cited by the Bush administration for the use of force; the implications of the violation of the non-intervention clauses in international organizations for U.S. foreign policy in Latin America; the heavy costs of the invasion in terms of lives lost, injuries, looting, and destruction of property; the falsehoods and omissions contained in Bush's rhetorical justification for the U.S. invasion; and the hidden domestic agenda surrounding the invasion. The December 1989 invasion of Panama was denounced by the Organization of American States in a resolution that condemned Washington for its violation of the non-intervention principle. After the invasion, and before the capture of Noriega, a *Newsweek* poll found that 80 percent of U.S. respondents felt that the U.S. should halt or delay the process of turning over the canal to the Panamanians at the end of 1999. Although six Latin American countries were not pleased by the long-standing violation of the policy of non-intervention, they insisted that the U.S. invasion of Panama was a special case due to close U.S. involvement in that country since 1903. While recognizing the failure of OAS diplomatic efforts, they also condemned Noriega for his corruption, involvement in drug trafficking, and disrespect for representative **democracy**. President Bush used Noriega's "declaration of war" against the United States as a basis for his decision to use force against the Panamanian leader. Bush's statement was a flagrant distortion of what Noriega said in his speech on December 15, 1989, stating the United States, "through constant psychological and military harassment," had declared war on Panama and urged the Panamanian people to unite to fight against the aggressor. The mainstream **media** was grossly inadequate in its coverage of the events leading up to the **intervention**, failing to report that Noriega's declaration of war was a "charade" that presented absolutely no threat to the security of the United States.

After more than a week of searching, Operation Just Cause achieved its objective—the capture and arrest of General Noriega—but it cost the United States $163 million in military operations expenditures, 24 American lives and over 350 injuries, and the enmity of its Latin American neighbors and others around the world who doubted Bush's "war" against Noriega. Nineteen U.S. military personnel were court-martialed for offenses committed during Operation Just Cause and of the nineteen, seventeen were convicted in courts-martial for alleged offenses. Panamanians bore the brunt of a costly invasion; hundreds lost their lives, thousands were injured and lost their homes, and little of the promised reconstruction funds arrived to put Panama back together again. Representative Charles B. Rangel (D-NY) was one of the most critical members of Congress, claiming after the invasion that the Bush administration came up with "Operation Just Cause" just because we could and Panama was such an easy target with 12,000 U.S. troops already in Panama, six military bases, and control of key communication links to carry out the operation. *See also* Dictatorships; Friendly Dictators; Intervention and Non-Intervention; North, Oliver Lawrence.

Suggested Readings

George Bush, "Panama—The Decision to Use Force," from *Vital Speeches of the Day*, Vol. 56 (January 15, 1990): 194–195; David W. Dent, *The Legacy of the Monroe Doctrine: A Reference Guide to U.S. Involvement in Latin America and the Caribbean* (Westport, CT: Greenwood Press, 1999); John Dinges, *Our Man in Panama: How General Noriega Used the United States, and Made Millions in Drugs and Arms* (New York: Random House, 1990); Luigi R. Einaudi, "Statement of Ambassador Luigi R. Einaudi, United States Permanent Representative to the Organization of American States, December 22, 1989" (typed speech); General Accounting Office, *Panama: Issues Relating to the Invasion* (Washington, DC: General Accounting Office, 1991).

Operation Mongoose A **Central Intelligence Agency (CIA)**-Mafia conspiracy to assassinate Fidel **Castro** and enable Las Vegas mobsters to resume their gambling activities in Cuba. The Central Intelligence Agency contacted the Mafia to do the **assassination** since it already had a network established among the Cuban underground, and Las Vegas mobsters would provide a secret cover for the "hit" on Fidel. The reasoning within the CIA was that if the assassins were caught that most people would believe that their action was a result of Castro's seizure of the Mafia's criminal enterprises. Attorney General Robert Kennedy launched Operation Mongoose in November 1961, hoping to cripple the Castro government by helping the people of Cuba to overthrow the Communist regime from within. Operation Mongoose continued until the end of the Cuban Missile crisis, although further assassination plots were concocted, but never carried out successfully. General Edward Lansdale was appointed commander of Operation Mongoose, but realized early on that the "indigenous resources" to topple Castro would ultimately require decisive U.S. military **intervention**.

Meyer **Lansky** realized that for the mob to resume its lucrative gambling enterprises after the success of Fidel Castro in toppling Fulgencio **Batista**, Castro would have to be killed. Howard Hughes was approached by one of Lansky's partners, who in turn encouraged Robert Maheu, his associate and former CIA agent, to prepare for the murder scheme. Three mob figures were recruited—John Roselli, Sam Giancana, and Santos Trafficante, Jr.—to do the job of assassinating Castro. The U.S. government offered $150,000 for the "hit" on Fidel Castro, but the mob figures proudly declared that as "patriotic" Americans they would do the job for free. The plot failed because of mistrust between the CIA and the three mobsters and Giancana's concern that if the mob destroyed Castro for the U.S. government, the U.S. government would gain unprecedented power over organized crime in the United States. If the plot was ever fully uncovered, it would have clearly led to a scandal in that **Washington policymakers** collaborated with criminals to engage in an illegal international political act. The plot to kill Castro was not discovered until the Church Committee investigated numerous plots to kill foreign leaders in the aftermath of Watergate. Each of the three mobsters contracted to kill Castro were murdered just before they were scheduled to testify before Senate committees after the nefarious affair. Those who worked for General Lansdale sent him numerous plans of action to provoke or harass the Cuban government. In one such plan—Operation Bingo—the military proposed the creation of an incident that would have the appearance of an attack on U.S. facilities at the **Guantánamo Bay** Naval Base that would provide a pretext for the U.S. military to overthrow Castro. Years later, one of the architects of the policy, Richard Bissell, admitted that it was unwise to join hands with mobsters for the conduct of American foreign policy for fear of blackmail. Looking back at these top secret plans, it is remarkable how many in the U.S. government thought it would be easy to remove Fidel Castro from office. *See also* Church Committee Report; Scandals and Blunders.

Suggested Reading

James Bamford, *Body of Secrets: Anatomy of the Ultra-Secret National Security Agency* (New York: Doubleday, 2001); Lawrence Freedman, *Kennedy's Wars: Berlin, Cuba, Laos, and Vietnam* (New York: Oxford University Press, 2002); Gus Russo, *Live by the Sword: The Secret War Against Castro and the Death of JFK* (Baltimore, MD: Bancroft Press, 1998); Mark J. White, ed., *The Kennedys and Cuba: The Declassified Documentary History* (Chicago: Ivan R. Dee, 1999).

Operation Northwoods After the **Central Intelligence Agency (CIA)**-backed failure to topple Fidel **Castro** at the **Bay of Pigs** in 1961, the highest U.S. military authorities decided it was their turn to remove Castro. Operation Northwoods was a plan by the Joint Chiefs of Staff to create a series of incidents involving the loss of American and Cuban exile lives through the actions of phony Cubans to convince the American people that a war against Cuba was just and necessary. The elaborate plan was promoted by General Lyman Lemnitzer, a veteran of **World War II** who participated in the exfiltration of Nazi **human rights** criminals to Latin America in the 1950s. He also served on the U.S. President's Commission on CIA Activities within the United States in 1975.

The military document detailing this plan was first published by Jon Elliston (1999). The story also appeared a few years later in James Bamford's *Body of Secrets* (2001). The plans contained in Operation Northwoods had the written approval of all of the members of the Joint Chiefs of Staff and were presented to President **Kennedy**'s defense secretary, Robert McNamara, in March 1962. The plan was presented to Secretary of Defense Robert McNamara by General William H. Craig and General Lemnitzer. McNamara met with Kennedy's military representative, General Maxwell Taylor, but little is known about what transpired at the meeting. Three days later President Kennedy said that there was no chance the United States would use military force against Cuba, dashing the plans drafted by the military. The controversial documents remained undisclosed for almost forty years. Many speculate that the reason they were held secret for so long was fear among members of the Joint Chiefs of Staff that they would embarrass the military and diminish the respect earned by General Lemnitzer over the span of his military career. *See also* Covert Operations.

Suggested Reading

James Bamford, *Body of Secrets: Anatomy of the Ultra-Secret National Security Agency* (New York: Doubleday, 2001); John Elliston, ed., *Psywar on Cuba: The Declassified History of the U.S. Anti-Castro Propaganda* (New York: Ocean Press, 1999); Gus Russo, *Live by the Sword: The Secret War Against Castro and the Death of JFK* (Baltimore, MD: Bancroft Press, 1998).

Operation Pan America A precursor program for the economic and social development of Latin America proposed by Juscelino Kubitschek, president of Brazil, in 1958. President Kubitschek (1956–1960) argued in a letter to President **Dwight Eisenhower** that Latin America's underdevelopment problems would have to be solved before the region could effectively resist leftist subversion and serve the interests of the United States in the **Cold War**. Kubitschek's proposal ran counter to the U.S. emphasis on private initiatives for Latin America, including $40 billion in economic assistance for development over a twenty-year period. Despite continuing promises from the Eisenhower administration, it was not until Richard **Nixon**'s trip to Latin America in 1958 and the January 1, 1959, triumph of Fidel **Castro** that a sense of urgency to go forth with a new economic program in the region swept Washington. Eventually Kubitschek's development plan was incorporated into the **Alliance for Progress** in 1961. In his Alliance for Progress speech at the White House in 1961, President Kennedy announced that he was offering those in the Americas a bold "approach consistent with the majestic concept of Operation Pan America," a cooperative approach to development that would satisfy the "basic needs of the American people for homes, work and land, health and schools—*techo, trabajo, y tierra, salud y escuela.*"

The election of President Kubitschek marked the beginning of a Brazilian foreign policy of greater independence from the United States. Unable to secure financial assistance for his economic development programs, Kubitschek proposed Operation Pan America (OPA), an opportunity to encourage a new U.S.–Latin American policy emphasizing a form of cooperative economic development along the lines of the Marshall Plan to reconstruct Europe after **World War II**. Operation Pan America was not a radical departure in Brazilian foreign policy because it embodied aspirations for greater hemispheric unity, Cold War anti-communism, and trade expansionism. By stressing the importance of economic development as a deterrent to Communist revolution in Latin America, Kubitschek's OPA also included the creation of the **Inter-American Development Bank**, social development loans, and more economic assistance with fewer strings attached. However, Brazil and the United States differed over economic development strategies. The United States preferred that Latin Americans rely on their own private initiatives, whereas Brazilians believed in a hemisphere-wide economic plan. Despite Kubitschek's efforts, disputes with the United States and the International Monetary Fund led to OPA's failure. However, in an effort to reverse the negative trends in U.S.–Latin American relations left over from the Eisenhower years, President John F. **Kennedy** decided it was time to try to mobilize hemispheric unity in the battle against poverty and communism with his own Alliance for Progress.

Suggested Reading

Federico G. Gil, *Latin American–United States Relations* (New York: Harcourt Brace Jovanovich, 1971); Jerome Levinson and Juan de Onís, *The Alliance That Lost its Way: A Critical Report on the Alliance for Progress* (Chicago: Quadrangle Books, 1970); Stephen G. Rabe, *Eisenhower and Latin America: The Foreign Policy of Anti-Communism* (Chapel Hill: University of North Carolina Press, 1988); Peter H. Smith, *Talons of the Eagle: Dynamics of U.S.–Latin American Relations*, 2nd ed. (New York: Oxford University Press, 2000).

Operation Success. *See* Arbenz Guzmán, Jacobo (1913–1971)

Operation Urgent Fury (1983) Codename of the U.S. military invasion of the Caribbean island of Grenada on October 25, 1983. The armed **intervention** followed years of tensions between the leaders of the Grenadian revolution (1979–1983) and the U.S. government over the radical foreign policy put into effect by Prime Minister Maurice Bishop. The **Carter** administration recognized the Bishop government despite its socialist orientation and economic and political ties with the Soviet Union, other Eastern bloc countries, and Fidel **Castro**'s Cuba. However, tensions increased after Ronald **Reagan** became president in 1981 due to the use of Cuban military advisers and Cuban construction crews called on to help build a longer runway at the international airport, as well as growing rhetorical hostility between the two governments. **Threat perceptions** based on repeated charges of communism by Reagan and his foreign policy advisers helped set the stage for the invasion of Grenada in 1983, the first time the United States used military force in an English-speaking Caribbean country and the first U.S. military intervention in the Caribbean since President's Lyndon **Johnson**'s massive invasion of the Dominican Republic in 1965. *See also* Grenada Invasion (1983); North, Oliver Lawrence; Revolutions.

Suggested Reading

Robert Beck, *The Grenada Invasion: Politics, Law, and Foreign Policy* (Boulder, CO: Westview Press, 1991); Reynold A. Burrowes, *Revolution and Rescue in Grenada* (Westport, CT: Greenwood Press, 1988); Peter M. Dunn and Bruce W. Watson, eds., *American Intervention in Grenada: The Implications of Operation Urgent Fury* (Boulder, CO: Westview Press, 1985); Kai Schoenhals and Richard Melanson, *Revolution and Intervention in Grenada* (Boulder, CO: Westview Press, 1985).

Operation Zapata. *See* Bay of Pigs (1961)

Organization of American States (OAS) Although the Organization of American States was created in 1948 to strengthen the peace and security of the Western Hemisphere, it has deep roots in the Pan American movement going back to the Panama Conference that Simón **Bolívar** organized in 1826. The present-day OAS is the direct descendent of the first International Conference of American States organized by U.S. Secretary of State James G. **Blaine** and held in Washington, D.C., from 1889 to 1890. At the Fourth International Conference in 1910 assembled in Buenos Aires, Argentina, the name of the organization, and its new building in Washington, D.C., was changed from "International Bureau of American Republics" to that of the "**Pan American Union**." Although the Pan American Union ceased to exist after the Charter of the Organization of American States was ratified, the building at 17th Street and Constitution Avenue retained the old name until 1970. From the onset the United States dominated the agenda of this regional organization and the head was always a citizen of the United States until the OAS was formed. The cornerstone of the OAS has always been non-intervention, a principle set forth with great clarity in Chapter III on the Fundamental Rights and Duties of States. The original number of OAS members was twenty-one: twenty Latin American countries (including Haiti) and the United States. With the gradual addition of numerous Central American states the OAS now has a membership of thirty-five, although Cuba's government was suspended from participation in 1962 and continues to operate outside of the OAS framework throughout the hemisphere. Canada joined the OAS in 1990, an additional vote in the organization that made U.S. domination more difficult.

After the U.S. **intervention** in the Dominican Republic in 1965, the OAS created a military mission to assist with the post-invasion reconstruction of the island nation. The OAS divided over U.S. intervention in Central America in the 1970s and 1980s and unanimously opposed the U.S. invasion of Grenada in 1983, a decision that was made without consulting the OAS. As the **Cold War** came to an end, the OAS played a constructive role in ending the wars in El Salvador and Nicaragua, showing that it could fulfil its role as a peacemaker in Latin America. Although there have been repeated efforts to bring Cuba back into the OAS as a participating member, the renewed interest in "representative democracy" as a prerequisite for membership has reduced the chances of Cuba's return.

The organs and structure of the OAS are fairly complicated, but the General Secretariat and the Permanent Council provide most of the administrative tasks. The General Assembly is a plenary body that meets once a year in different OAS countries where most of the resolutions are approved unanimously by the member states. The General Secretariat is headed by the secretary general and the assistant secretary general who both serve for five-year terms. The OAS has assumed an expanding number of functions over the past several decades, the most important being: collective security, conflict resolution, peaceful settlement of disputes, peacekeeping/making, protection of **human rights** and the promotion of democracy, economic development, integration and trade. In its recently approved Democratic Charter, the OAS has set up rules to help maintain democratic rule and forestall military takeovers. The OAS played a major role in Venezuela between 2002 and 2004 when opposition to President Hugo Chávez provoked strikes, an attempted coup, violence, and a constitutional recall referendum that ultimately failed. After the Costa Rican secretary general was forced to resign due to a corruption scandal in 2004, the OAS struggled to find a consensus candidate to replace him. *See also* Barrett, John; Democracy and Democracy Promotion; Intervention and Non-Intervention; Pan Americanism; United Nations (UN).

Suggested Reading

G. Pope Atkins, *Latin America in the International Political System*, 2nd ed. (Boulder, CO: Westview Press, 1989); Carolyn M. Shaw, *Cooperation, Conflict, and Consensus in the Organization of American States* (New York: Palgrave, 2004); Peter H. Smith, *Talons of the Eagle: Dynamics of U.S.–Latin American Relations*, 2nd ed. (New York: Oxford University Press, 2000); O. Carlos Stoetzer, *The Organization of American States*, 2nd ed. (New York: Praeger, 1993); Viron P. Vaky and Heraldo Muñoz, *The Future of the Organization of American States* (New York: Twentieth Century Fund, 1993); Larman C. Wilson and David W. Dent, "The United States and the OAS," in David W. Dent, ed., *U.S.–Latin American Policymaking: A Reference Handbook* (Westport, CT: Greenwood Press, 1995).

Ostend Manifesto (1854) The growing interest in Cuba prior to the U.S. Civil War led to a joint statement by three U.S. ministers—Pierre Soulé, James **Buchanan**, and John Y. Mason—in 1854 urging the United States to use force to take Cuba from Spain if Spain refused to sell the island to the United States. The search for a way to forcibly separate Cuba from Spain was motivated by **Manifest Destiny**, the desire for more slave territory, and rumors that Spain was going to free Cuban slaves as a concession to discontent on the island. The Ostend Manifesto failed to achieve its primary purpose because it upset many Whigs in Congress and only made Spain more defiant in its determination to hold on to Cuba at all costs. President Franklin **Pierce** rejected the manifesto, clearly concerned about the potential for negative consequences in the United States and abroad if such a proposal was put in motion. Had the Ostend Manifesto succeeded in wrestling Cuba from Spain, it would have altered radically the future development of Cuba and its relationship with the rest of Latin America and the world. *See also* Imperialism; Race and Racism.

Suggested Reading

Richard W. Van Alstyne, *The Rising American Empire* (New York: W.W. Norton, 1974); Albert K. Weinberg, *Manifest Destiny: A Study of Nationalist Expansionism in American History* (Baltimore, MD: Johns Hopkins University Press, 1935).

P

Panama Canal Treaties U.S.–Panamanian relations were greatly influenced by treaties designed to mix U.S. **hegemony** in the isthmus and Panama's independence and sovereignty. After President **Theodore Roosevelt** assisted in separating Panama from Colombia in 1903, U.S.–Panamanian relations were determined by the **Hay-Bunau-Varilla Treaty**, which gave the United States control "in perpetuity" over a ten-mile strip of land and the right to act as "if it were sovereign of the territory." It was a lopsided treaty highly favorable to the United States and formed the basis of future tension between the two countries. Although annual payments to Panama were steadily increased after the completion of the Panama Canal, Panamanians objected to their second-class status, the privileges of U.S. citizens in the Canal Zone, the use of Panama for numerous military bases, and the general feeling that Panama was receiving inadequate compensation for the canal. Riots and nationalist tensions plagued Panama and the United States from the 1950s until the presidency of Jimmy **Carter**. Carter was a strong supporter of two new treaties to redefine a new relationship between Panama and the United States. His opponent in the 1976 and 1980 presidential races, Ronald **Reagan**, opposed the treaties, calling them a "give-away" to a tin-horned dictator. In one of his most significant diplomatic achievements, Carter sought two new treaties that would revoke the Hay-Bunau-Varilla Treaty (1903), one would provide for the operation and defense of the canal, the other called for permanent neutrality. The Carter-Torrijos Treaties, named after the respective presidents of the two countries, set forth December 31, 1999 as the date in which Panama would take over complete management of the canal. Each country has a right to defend the security and neutrality of the canal, and in the event of a canal shutdown, the United States could use force to reopen or restore the canal's operation and during wartime, and U.S. ships would be allowed to move "to the head of the line" to cross through. After a long and rancorous debate in the U.S. Senate in 1978, the two treaties were adopted by a one-vote (a two-thirds majority was required for passage) majority of 68–32. After ratifications were exchanged in June of that year, the **Organization of American States (OAS)** formally endorsed the treaties. *See also* Bunker, Ellsworth; Operation Just Cause.

Suggested Reading

J. Michael Hogan, *The Panama Canal in American Politics* (Carbondale: Southern Illinois University Press, 1986); Robert H. Holden and Eric Zolov, eds., *Latin America and the United States: A Documentary History* (New York: Oxford University Press, 2000); William J. Jorden, *Panama Odyssey* (Austin: University of Texas Press, 1984); George D. Moffett III, *The Limits of Victory: The Ratification of the Panama Canal Treaties* (Ithaca, NY: Cornell University Press, 1985); Larman C. Wilson and David W. Dent, *Historical Dictionary of Inter-American Organizations* (Lanham, MD: Scarecrow Press, 1998).

Pan-Americanism A diplomatic and rhetorical concept of unity, cooperation, and common interests among the American republics that provided the basis for the inter-American conferences, wartime alliances, hemispheric trade pacts, and mutual security arrangements. The term was first employed in 1882 to reflect a common separation from the rest of the world and the belief in a common history. Those who believed in the Pan-American ideal were convinced that hemispheric unity would increase the power of all the member states against extra-hemispheric powers with claims on the Americas. Pan-Americanism emerged during the first Pan-American conference held in Washington, D.C., in 1889 at the behest of Secretary of State James G. **Blaine**. While Pan-Americanism often assumes a hemisphere of shared interests such as peace, mutual security, common commercial advantage, adoption of representative **democracy**, and an aversion to European **imperialism** in the Western Hemisphere, critics of the concept point to a growing divergence in interests and values. Efforts to promote the existence of a common heritage with geographical uniqueness often ignore the fact that there is no common language, culture, or religion in Latin America. With millions of people of African heritage or those who are indigenous to the Americas, it is difficult to argue the degree of similarities among the people of Latin America that the concept of Pan-Americanism implies.

Pan-Americanism declined dramatically during the period of U.S. **intervention** between 1895 and 1930, but was revived with the **Good Neighbor Policy** that took shape under Presidents Herbert **Hoover** and Franklin D. **Roosevelt**. Over time the Pan-American conferences coalesced into a much broader inter-American system with the **Organization of American States (OAS)** as its hub. The term Pan-Americanism is often used by the United States to improve a relationship that has gone sour or to promote a more positive image of Latin American people to the American public. According to Eldon Kenworthy (1995: 28), prior to **World War II** "the federal government promoted positive images, casting Latins as fellow 'Americans.' New York City's Sixth Avenue was renamed 'Avenue of the Americas'. 'Pan-Americana' was invented, fusing the Virgin Mary with the Statue of Liberty. Pressure was brought to bear on Hollywood to revise its stereotypes; Walt Disney obliged with a likeable parrot in a sombrero. The name of this movement, Pan-Americanism, says it all." The world has changed dramatically since Pan-Americanism became part of the inter-American dialogue in the nineteenth century. While the original reasons for the Pan-American movement were to provide hemispheric political security and mutual trade benefits, the growing divide between Latin American development priorities and U.S. security interests have undermined the spirit of Pan-Americanism. Nevertheless, Pan American Day is celebrated throughout the Americas every April 14, an annual reminder of the importance of multilateral diplomacy for dealing with the new realities of the times. *See also* Democracy and Democracy Promotion; Intervention and Non-Intervention; Pan American Union; Partisanship and Policy; Washington Consensus; Wilson, Woodrow.

Suggested Reading

Alonzo Aguilar, *Pan-Americanism from the Monroe Doctrine to the Present* (New York, Monthly Review Press, 1968); Mark T. Gilderhus, *Pan American Visions: Woodrow Wilson in the Western Hemisphere, 1913–1921* (Tucson: University of Arizona Press, 1986); John J. Johnson, *A Hemisphere Apart: The Foundations of United States Policy toward Latin America* (Baltimore, MD: Johns Hopkins University Press, 1990); Eldon Kenworthy, *America/Américas: Myth in the Making of U.S. Policy Toward Latin America* (University Park: Pennsylvania State University Press, 1995); James B. Lockey, *Pan-Americanism: Its Beginnings* (New York: Arno Press, 1970); J. Lloyd Mecham, *A Survey of United States–Latin American Relations* (1965); David Sheinin, ed., *Beyond the Ideal: Pan-Americanism in Inter-American Affairs* (Westport, CT: Greenwood Press, 2000).

Pan American Union One of the first hemispheric organizations established in 1910 to facilitate a variety of inter-American activities. Andrew **Carnegie** donated the headquarters building located at 17th and Constitution Avenue in Washington, D.C., today the **Organization of American States (OAS)**. The Pan American Union had its roots in the purely commercial Bureau of American Republics established in 1890 and until the founding of the OAS in 1948, the organization was dominated by the United States. Its first director-general, John **Barrett**, provided most of the leadership in the early years of the organization. The name "Organization of American States" did not replace that of the "Pan American Union" on the front of the building until the early 1970s. *See also* Pan-Americanism.

Suggested Reading

G. Pope Atkins, *Encyclopedia of the Inter-American System* (Westport, CT: Greenwood Press, 1997); Samuel F. Bemis, *The Latin American Policy of the United States* (1943; reprint, New York: W.W. Norton, 1967); J. Lloyd Mecham, *A Survey of United States–Latin American Relations* (Boston: Houghton Mifflin, 1965); Larman C. Wilson and David W. Dent, *Historical Dictionary of Inter-American Organizations* (Lanham, MD: Scarecrow Press, 1998).

Partisanship and Policy The U.S. government is motivated by a number of concerns when dealing with countries in Latin America and the Caribbean. While U.S. security and political stability have dominated the interests and values of **Washington policymakers**, other concerns—economic aid, financial investments, nation building, **human rights**, democratic governance, immigration, social reform, and **drug trafficking**—have also played a role in what U.S. presidents and members of Congress judge as most important to the United States. The alternation between political parties—Republican versus Democrat—tends to overstate political differences at the beginning of an administration to justify its mandate for change in policy. President Jimmy **Carter** was critical of the covert acts to destabilize Latin American governments and the support of right-wing **dictators** of his predecessors while President Ronald **Reagan** admonished Carter for advancing communism in Central America and the Caribbean in the name of human rights and economic justice.

What distinguishes Republicans from Democrats in constructing a policy toward Latin America and the Caribbean? Since **World War II**, Republicans have given a higher priority to security and stability and less to economic assistance, social reform, and human rights. This means that Republicans tend to be more interested in conservative principles of free trade and privatization, anti-communism, and anti-terrorism. To achieve these interests and values, Republicans give more emphasis to military aid, covert operations, support for **friendly dictators**, military maneuvers and **gunboat diplomacy**, private investment, and bilateral aid rather than providing capital to international organizations. Democrats tend to choose diplomacy and negotiations, economic aid, human rights, and the use of multilateral institutions. At the core of why partisanship results in the choice of different policies is the administration's perception of the nature and intensity of threat posed to the United States. As Robert A. **Pastor** (1987: 276) points out, "The more distant the threat the more likely an Administration will adhere to its initial principles; the more immediate the threat the more likely the Administration's policy will evolve." Thus, **threat perception** plays a major role in explaining the partisan differences between administrations. Both Presidents Reagan and Carter differed in their perceptions of the nature and intensity of the threat posed by what was happening in Nicaragua in the 1970s and 1980s. (See Appendix for an example of Reagan's speeches.) "To Reagan, the **Sandinistas** represented an immediate, grave, Soviet-inspired threat that was testing the will and jeopardizing the interests of the United States [in Central America]. . . . To Carter, the Sandinistas represented a Central American revolution; the United States should try to help it and contain it simultaneously" (Pastor, 1987: 277). Of course, when it comes to partisanship and

U.S. Latin American policy all Democrats and all Republicans are not the same and different administrations always contain divergent voices from within, particularly among foreign policy elites in the Pentagon, **State Department**, and the **Central Intelligence Agency (CIA)**. *See also* Threat Perception/Assessment.

Suggested Reading

Robert A. Pastor, *Condemned to Repetition: The United States and Nicaragua* (Princeton, NJ: Princeton University Press, 1987).

Pastor, Robert A. (1947–) Robert Pastor is a political scientist who has combined an academic career with public and private sector involvement in the study of U.S.–Latin American relations. He is one of a new class of foreign policy professionals who came to Washington in the early 1970s with personal ambition, knowledge of foreign policy issues, and a strong desire to work for presidents who would allow him to push a new (and improved) Latin American policy. Former **State Department** and **National Security Council (NSC)** official, Anthony Lake, calls Pastor an "inner/outer," someone with professional expertise both inside and outside government. Many like Pastor came to Washington with a more partisan and assertive policy agenda than those in the Foreign Service or the inners and outers of the 1950s. The path that Pastor followed to the National Security Council (NSC) in the **Carter** White House was based on his ability to parlay his academic studies with field experience, research, and writing on U.S. policy toward Latin America, and a chain of pivotal high-level contacts with foreign policy elites who boosted him up the ladder of power.

Born in Newark, New Jersey, Robert A. Pastor earned a B.A. at Lafayette College where he developed a fascination with Latin America and U.S.–Latin American relations. After graduating in 1969, Robert Pastor spent a summer at the Congressional Research Service where he prepared briefing papers for congressmen and senators on U.S. policy toward Latin America and on international organizations. He then served for two years as a Peace Corps Volunteer in Malaysia before beginning his graduate work at Harvard (1972–1976) where he earned his M.P.A. and Ph.D. in the Department of Government. While at Harvard, Pastor joined the staff of the Murphy Commission where he worked with a group of academics and policy practitioners studying the impact of government organization on the conduct of foreign affairs. Soon after he joined the Linowitz Commission that issued two reports on ways to improve the Latin American policy of the United States. Nearly all of the commission's recommendations were implemented between 1977 and 1979, particularly the signing of two new treaties relinquishing U.S. control over the Panama Canal and a policy of engagement with Fidel **Castro**'s Cuba.

Pastor's work on the Linowitz Commission caught the eye of Carter's future National Security Adviser, Zbigniew Brzezinski, then in search of volunteers to advise presidential hopeful Jimmy Carter on foreign policy issues. After the 1976 election of Jimmy Carter, Brzezinski asked Pastor to join him on the NSC as the

Director of the Office of Latin American and Caribbean Affairs. While working for Carter and Brzezinski at the White House, Pastor gained valuable first-hand policy experience on Latin American affairs in Washington and during his travels in Latin America. For the first two years, the task of negotiating two new treaties with Panama and moving them through the U.S. Senate consumed most of Pastor's energy and time. The final two years brought Pastor the grief of dealing with the State Department and domestic groups over the political turmoil and revolution in Nicaragua. While in the Carter While House, Pastor learned first-hand about the meaning of bureaucratic politics and press sniping, particularly the accusations that he was a dangerous academic with left-wing tendencies, or hearing from other critics who viewed him as a Brzezinski hard-line Cold Warrior. After Carter's defeat in the 1980 presidential election, Pastor returned to the world of **think tanks** and university teaching and research where he was able to apply some of his government experience and academic training to the challenge of improving the Latin American policy of the United States. From 1985 to 1998 Professor Pastor was a fellow and founding director of the **Carter Center**'s Latin American and Caribbean Program, the Democracy Program, and the China Election Project.

Robert Pastor was nominated by President **Clinton** to be U.S. ambassador to Panama in 1993, but after being approved by the Senate Foreign Relations Committee 16–3, his nomination was held up for years by Jesse **Helms** (R-NC), the new chairman of the Foreign Relations Committee who resented Pastor for his role in negotiating the new **Panama Canal Treaties**. Disgusted with the obstructionist maneuvers of Senator Helms, Pastor decided to withdraw his nomination in 1995 and continue his teaching and writing while at Emory University and the Carter Center. With an endowed chair—Goodrich C. White Professor of International Relations—in the political science department at Emory University (1996–2002), Robert Pastor pursued a broad range of activities related to U.S.–Latin American relations. In 2002 Pastor became vice-president of International Affairs and professor of International Relations at American University, a position from which he plans to create and direct two new centers—the Institute for Democracy and Election Management and the Center for North American Studies—to address themes of globalization and democratization.

Pastor's books have stressed the need for what he calls an "interactive approach" to the study of inter-American relations instead of the more pessimistic "dependency paradigm" with its emphasis on the asymmetries of power and the United States as a malevolent hegemon. He argues that to improve U.S.–Latin American relations, the United States needs to enlist the support of Latin American and the Caribbean governments in building a hemispheric market and forging a democratic community of nations. This means more emphasis on multilateralism and the inter-American system than was the case during the **Cold War**. Robert Pastor's research also reflects his deep interest in the creation of a more peaceful and harmonious hemisphere, particularly in the pursuit of better economic policies and the reinforcement of democracy and human rights south of the border. *See also* Democracy and Democracy Promotion; Washington Policymakers.

Suggested Reading

Sally Acharya, "New VP Robert Pastor Brings Adventurous Intellect to Job," *American Weekly* (August 27, 2002); Robert A. Pastor, *Not Condemned to Repetition: The United States and Nicaragua* (Boulder, CO: Westview Press, 2002); Pastor, *Exiting the Whirlpool: U.S. Foreign Policy toward Latin America and the Caribbean*, 2nd ed. (Boulder, CO: Westview Press, 2001); Pastor, *Integration with Mexico: Options for U.S. Policy* (New York: Twentieth Century Fund, 1993); Pastor and Jorge G. Castañeda, *Limits to Friendship: The United States and Mexico* (New York: Alfred A. Knopf, 1988); Pastor, *Congress and the Politics of U.S. Foreign Economic Policy* (Berkeley: University of California Press, 1980).

Pérez Jiménez, Marcos (1914–2001) General Marcos Pérez Jiménez ruled Venezuela with an iron fist between 1948 and 1958, the last military dictator before the creation of the two-party democratic government that ruled the country from 1958 until the election of Hugo Chávez in 1998. Although he was despised and feared inside Venezuela because of the corruption and brutality of his **dictatorship**, his virulent anti-communism and friendly attitude toward foreign oil companies gained him the admiration and friendship of Washington. In a gesture that contributed to his downfall and a rash of anti-American demonstrations, four years before his downfall he was awarded the Legion of Merit by the **Dwight Eisenhower** administration. After an attempted coup failed on January 1, 1958, massive street demonstrations, a general strike, and a successful naval revolt succeeded in toppling the military ruler and sending him into exile. His government was notorious for the theft of oil revenue, the brutal way he treated his political opponents, and lavish spending on costly and superfluous construction projects.

Pérez Jiménez was born in Táchira, a state near the border with Colombia; his choice of a military career brought him into the turbulent world of Venezuelan politics in the 1940s and 1950s. As a young army captain he participated in the military coup in 1945 that put the left-leaning Democratic Action Party (AD) in power for the first time. He and other officers became concerned with the accelerating changes taking place under the AD government and in 1948 staged another coup in which they installed themselves at the helm, voided the democratic Constitution, and outlawed the governing party. After the **assassination** of his main rival in the governing junta one year later, Pérez Jiménez took charge and quickly became the strongman leader of Venezuela.

During his decade-long dictatorship, Pérez Jiménez ruled by brutality and corruption. His "New National Ideal" masked the viciousness of his military dictatorship in which many opponents were sent to a concentration camp in the Orinoco jungle, prison torture was widespread, the national university was closed, independent labor unions were abolished, and the press was muzzled by fear and intimidation. The mainstay of his rule was the much feared National Security police force, operated by a notorious sadist and friend of General Marcos Pérez Jiménez, Pedro Estrada. In his book on the history of Latin America, **Hubert Herring** (1972) calls Estrada "as vicious a man-hunter as Hitler ever employed." During the "oil boom" of the 1950s, the dictatorship slashed spending on education and health and diverted oil profits to expensive and unnecessary construction projects (e.g., a new highway between Caracas and the Caribbean coast and a lavish mountaintop hotel with the world's most expensive officer's club with views of downtown Caracas). The rest of the oil profits were pocketed by the dictator and his small group of army colonels from his home state. Washington linked arms with the oil companies and instructed the main opposition parties to keep the Communists out of their organizations. However, the growing number of popular movements and an economic recession in 1957 led to a general strike in January 1958. After big business joined the strike, air force officers tried to lead an attempted coup, but it failed to remove the dictatorship. After Estrada's secret police killed more than 300 people and wounded 1,000 more, Pérez Jiménez put as much of the national treasury in his bags as possible and fled to the Dominican Republic and a military-civilian junta took power. Venezuelan's danced in the streets after hearing of the general's downfall, but resented Washington's backing of the ousted ruler. With another military-civilian junta in charge, the Eisenhower administration paid little attention to Venezuela until angry mobs stoned Vice-President Richard **Nixon**'s motorcade in Caracas a few months later. Those who advised the president on Latin American policy at the time believed that dictatorships provided the best route to **democracy**, a rather convoluted argument rooted in **race**, culture, and the danger of liberal or left-wing parties coming to power during a period of political instability and social chaos. The benefits of having a dictator such as Pérez Jiménez in power was rooted in the belief that Venezuelans were not ready for democracy. The American chargé in Caracas at the time, Franklin W. Wolf, justified the absence of democracy in Venezuela with the view that "the people of Venezuela are not yet ready nor adequately prepared for democracy" because of the lack of experience with it. If General Pérez Jiménez committed electoral fraud and engaged in repression of opposition forces, this was acceptable to Washington as long as the dictatorship helped to preserve hemispheric solidarity, maintain law and order, and eliminate communism.

After his friend and fellow dictator, Rafael Leónidas **Trujillo**, was assassinated in 1961, Pérez Jiménez moved to Spain where he lived comfortably on the estimated $250 million he stole from the state treasury during his time in power. Until murder charges were lifted in 1999, the aging dictator feared that he would either be killed or extradited back to Venezuela were he was loathed by millions who had not forgotten his brutal dictatorship. Although the election of President Hugo Chávez, a former army colonel and a bitter critic of the corrupt two-party system that succeeded the downfall of Pérez Jiménez, served to rehabilitate his battered image, he remained in Spain until his death in 2001 at the age of eighty-seven. *See also* Friendly Dictators; Human Rights; Scandals and Blunders.

Suggested Reading

Judith Ewell, *Venezuela and the United States: From Monroe's Hemisphere to Petroleum's Empire* (Athens: University of Georgia Press, 1996); Ewell, *Indictment of a Dictator: The Extradition of Marcos Pérez Jiménez* (College Station: Texas A&M Press, 1981); Hubert C. Herring, *A*

History of Latin America, 3rd ed. (New York: Alfred A. Knopf, 1972); Sheldon B. Liss, *Diplomacy and Dependency: Venezuela, the United States, and the Americas* (Salisbury, NC: Documentary Publications, 1978); Stephen G. Rabe, *Eisenhower and Latin America: The Foreign Policy of Anticommunism* (Chapel Hill: University of North Carolina Press, 1988); Larry Rohter, "Marcos Pérez Jiménez, 87, Venezuela Ruler," *New York Times* (September 22, 2001).

Perón, Eva. *See* Perón, Juan Domingo (1895–1974)

Perón, Juan Domingo (1895–1974) Highly nationalistic military figure and president of Argentina (1946–1955; 1973–1974) who clashed with the United States during **World War II** and intermittently during the **Truman** administration. During World War II Argentina was governed by a conservative military government that opposed the Soviet Union (a wartime ally of the United States) and expressed open admiration for Germany and Italy. Until March 1945, Argentina resisted U.S. efforts at hemispheric solidarity against the coalition of fascist states that lost World War II. Under pressure from Latin American and U.S. representatives at the **Chapultepec Conference** in Mexico City in 1945, Argentina's government accepted the invitation to rejoin the inter-American community, declared war against the Axis powers, and agreed to the provisions set forth in the Act of Chapultepec, a collective security system and precursor to the Rio Treaty. This made it possible for Argentina to be admitted to the San Francisco Conference in 1945 and thus a charter member of the **United Nations (UN)**. Cordial relations between the United States and Argentina were short-lived, since it was not long before diplomatic hostilities returned to the relationship.

Argentina's pro-Nazi stance and its opposition to American **imperialism** set the stage for a two-year feud between Washington diplomats and Juan Perón beginning with Perón's decision to run for president in the 1946 elections. In an attempt to prevent Perón from winning the presidency, Spruille **Braden**, outspoken U.S. ambassador to Argentina (1945–1946), circulated a **State Department** manuscript—"Blue Book on Argentina"—that denounced Perón for his links to the Nazis during World War II. Perón retaliated by calling Braden another agent of North American imperialism and accused the United States of intervening in Argentina's internal affairs. Braden's bluster and diplomatic blunder failed to prevent Perón's electoral victory and severely damaged Argentine-American relations and President **Franklin D. Roosevelt**'s **Good Neighbor Policy**. The "Blue Book" became a symbol of Yankee arrogance and throughout Latin America the United States was condemned for returning to the era of **Big Stick diplomacy** and interventionism. According to Yale historian Gaddis Smith (1994: 57), "By any definition of diplomatic protocol Braden was guilty of egregious intervention in Argentine internal affairs—not only egregious but counterproductive in that his attacks increased Perón's popularity."

Shortly after Perón's victory Braden returned to Washington as assistant secretary of state for Latin American affairs. However, the Argentine-American feud did not end until 1947 when General George C. Marshall replaced James F. Byrnes as secretary of state, and Braden resigned and retired from public life. President Perón sent members of Peronist Youth, along with other Latin American university students, to Bogotá, Colombia, in 1948 to demonstrate against the inter-American meetings that would create the **Organization of American States (OAS)**. Fidel **Castro**, along with other Cuban university students, participated in these demonstrations.

During his first term in office (1946–1952), Juan Perón welcomed Nazis who fled Germany after World War II and espoused a form of working-class populism based on an eclectic mix of political ideologies. In an effort to distance his government from the United States and the Soviet Union, Perón maintained a neutral "third position" in the **Cold War**. Stressing Argentine nationalism, Perón opposed both U.S. and British involvement in Latin American affairs. The Truman administration resented Perón's non-alignment in the Cold War and his economic nationalism angered foreign business interests. His populist and personalist dictatorship—tight control over the media, limited dissent, a single ruling party, state control of the economy, and a cult of personality—lasted until 1955 when he was ousted by the military and left for exile in Spain. Perón left a legacy of antagonism between the Argentine armed forces and Peronists (devoted followers of Perón's working-class, highly nationalistic, political movement) that would dominate the politics of Argentina for more than three decades after his departure. Until her death in 1952, Perón's charismatic wife, Eva Duarte de Perón ("Evita"), assisted her husband by mobilizing the urban underprivileged as a mainstay of Peronist rule. Peronism is a political doctrine based on social justice (*justicialismo*), personalism (*personalismo*), machismo, national socialism, industrialization, and the elimination of economic/financial dependence on foreign investors.

Although a few of the civilian rulers who ruled Argentina after 1955 supported Cold War–U.S. policy in Latin America, authoritarian rule and cyclical economic crises continued to plague Argentina. Military rulers tried to implement a development strategy emphasing economic self-reliance and reduced government spending; however, these economic development policies eventually spawned the turmoil that paved the way for Perón's return from exile and his electoral victory in 1973. With his third wife, Isabel ("Isabelita"), as vice-president, Perón (ill and close to eighty years of age) was never able to govern with any degree of success; after his death in 1974, Isabel assumed the presidency in a situation of increasing chaos. Until the military removed her from the presidency in 1976, the Peronist movement split into warring factions that spiraled into **terrorism** and anarchy. With inflation close to 400 percent in 1976, and terrorist violence increasing, a military junta seized power and began a process of national reorganization that soon became known abroad as the dirty war (*la guerra sucia*). In an effort to eradicate terrorism with the use of state terror, the military arrested, tortured, and murdered tens of thousands until democracy was restored in 1982. At first, **Washington policymakers** welcomed the return of the military and seemed willing to tacitly support Argentina's dirty war. However, as the extent of the brutality and **human rights** violations became known to the world, the United States stopped supporting repressive military regimes regardless of their anti-communism and elevated human rights as a vital interest of the United States in world affairs. After the Argentine military was descredited after the **Falklands/Malvinas War** in 1982, Peronism regained some of its earlier luster and Carlos Saúl Menem captured the popular vote in 1989 and a Peronist majority in the Senate. Menem's Peronism departed from Juan Perón's **anti-Americanism** and interventionist political economy while retaining some of Perón's ideas about balancing the various power contenders in Argentine politics, particularly the military, business elites, labor, and the United States. Relations with the United States improved under President Menem (1989–1999) by endorsing the **Washington Consensus**, signing the Treaty of **Tlatelolco**, supporting UN peace-keeping operations, and sending a naval force to the Persian Gulf in 1990. *See also* Dictatorships; Truman, Harry S.

Suggested Reading

Jerome R. Adams, *Latin American Heroes: Liberators and Patriots from 1500 to the Present* (New York: Ballentine Books, 1991); Leslie Bethell and Ian Roxborough, eds., *Latin America Between the Second World War and the Cold War, 1944–1948* (New York: Cambridge University Press, 1992); Gordon Connell-Smith, *The United States and Latin America: An Historical Analysis of Inter-American Relations* (New York: Wiley, 1974); David W. Dent, *The Legacy of the Monroe Doctrine: A Reference Guide to U.S. Involvement in Latin America and the Caribbean* (Westport, CT: Greenwood Press, 1999); Gaddis Smith, *The Last Years of the Monroe Doctrine, 1945–1993* (New York: Hill and Wang, 1994); Joseph Tulchin, *Argentina and the United States: Conflicted Relationship* (Boston: Twayne, 1990).

Peurifoy, John Emil (1907–1955) Controversial businessman and diplomat who was a central figure in the Guatemala crisis in 1954 that involved the **Central Intelligence Agency (CIA)** removal of President Jacobo **Arbenz**. John Peurifoy was born in Walterboro, South Carolina, attended West Point, George Washington University, and American University, but never graduated. From 1928 to 1934, Peurifoy worked in banking, insurance, and several federal positions before joining the **State Department** in 1938. A staunch anti-Communist, he was appointed ambassador to Guatemala in 1953 with the expectation that he would do something about the leftist Arbenz. He knew nothing about Latin America, but was convinced that the Guatemalan leader represented a threat to U.S. interests in Central America. Like many diplomats of his generation, Peurifoy believed in the **Monroe Doctrine** and removal of Latin American leaders who thwarted U.S. interests as a just cause. He was proud of his role in the sordid affair in defeating Soviet despotism in Guatemala, although the threat was greatly exaggerated for domestic political purposes. Following his diplomatic post in Guatemala, Peurifoy was named ambassador to Thailand in 1954. He remained there until he was killed in an automobile accident there the following year. *See also* Ambassadors; Bernays, Edward L.; Scandals and Blunders.

Suggested Readings

Piero Gleijeses, *Shattered Hope: The Guatemalan Revolution and the United States, 1944–1954* (Princeton, NJ: Princeton University Press, 1991); Richard Immerman, *The CIA in Guatemala: The Foreign Policy of Intervention* (Austin: University of Texas Press, 1982); Stephen Schlesinger and Stephen Kinzer, *Bitter Fruit: The Untold Story of the American Coup in Guatemala* (New York: Doubleday, 1983); Steven Schwartzberg, *Democracy and U.S. Policy in Latin America During the Truman Years* (Gainesville: University Press of Florida, 2003).

Pierce, Franklin (1804–1869) Lawyer, politician, and Democratic president (1853–1857) known for his aggressive and expansionist foreign policy prior to the U.S. Civil War. Pierce was a firm believer in **Manifest Destiny**, the **Monroe Doctrine**, and the acquisition of more slave territory during his administration. Born in New Hampshire to a father who had fought in the American Revolution and was twice New Hampshire governor, Pierce graduated from Bowdoin College in 1824, studied law, and was admitted to the bar in 1827. He entered the political arena shortly thereafter as a Jacksonian Democrat who rebuked the abolitionist movement in the North, opposed federal efforts to halt slavery in the territories, and joined hands with those who believed in Southern states rights. He volunteered to serve in the **Mexican-American War**, rose to the rank of brigadier general, and then returned to New Hampshire politics at war's end. He captured the Democratic presidential nomination in 1852, campaigned as a strong supporter of the Compromise of 1850, and defeated Whig candidate Winfield Scott.

Pierce's belief in Manifest Destiny contributed to his effort to extend sovereignty over the whole continent by acquiring land from Mexico as well as protest the British colonial presence in Central America. It also motivated him to acquire a naval base in the Dominican Republic and attempt to acquire Cuba from Spain as a slave territory. He supported private filibustering expeditions in the Caribbean and Central America until anti-slavery forces in Congress pressured him to end his administration's **recognition** of the pro-slavery American filibuster and self-appointed president of Nicaragua, William **Walker**. Under pressure from Southerners in search of slave territory, Pierce made an all-out diplomatic effort to purchase Cuba from Spain, asserting at one point that "Cuba is as necessary to the North American republic as any of its present members." Spain was not interested in the offer—known as the **Ostend Manifesto**—and Pierce was forced to abandon the audacious move after the Democratic Party suffered heavy losses after passage of the Kansas-Nebraska Act. This anti-slavery legislation helped deny Pierce renomination in 1856. Instead, the Democrats turned to James **Buchanan**, another Democrat who entered the White House in 1857 convinced "Cuba belonged to the United States" and over the next three years led the United States into a bloody civil war over slavery, expansionism, and annexation. Cuba became equally important to abolitionists, but the intensity of feelings about race and territory eventually destroyed any efforts to make Cuba part of the United States. The Ostend Manifesto was as close as the United States got to acquiring Cuba from Spain;

however, if it had not been for the intractable issue of slavery it is quite possible that Cuba would have been invaded, occupied, and made another state of the union in the 1850s. Nevertheless, by the end of the century Cuba would fall into the hands of the United States as a result of the **Spanish-Cuban-American War**, not as a state, but a newly minted protectorate designed by Elihu **Root** and other imperialists of the era. Franklin Pierce traveled to Europe after leaving the White House in 1857 and then returned to his law practice in New Hampshire. *See also* Filibusters/Filibustering; Intervention and Non-Intervention; Race and Racism.

Suggested Reading

Lars Schoultz, *Beneath the United States: A History of U.S. Policy Toward Latin America* (Cambridge, MA: Harvard University Press, 1998).

Pinochet Ugarte, Augusto (1915–) Supreme Chief of the Nation (and Army) when the military government took power in Chile, ousting the leftist democratically elected government of President Salvador **Allende** on September 11, 1973. To put an end to Allende's peaceful road to socialism, high-level military officials orchestrated a violent attack on the government as Chilean Air Force jets strafed and bombed the presidential palace (Moneda) with Allende resisting the illegal takeover from inside. Rather than submit to military rule, Allende committed suicide with a rifle given to him by Fidel **Castro** on Castro's prior visit to Chile. The military *junta*, consisting of the commanders of the various branches, seized power and declared a "Holy War" on the highly contagious "Marxist cancer" that was gradually destroying the nation. President Nixon and his national security advisers, including Henry **Kissinger**, viewed Salvador Allende as a threat to U.S. economic interests in Chile and a threat to U.S. security interests worldwide. General Pinochet remains a controversial figure in Chile despite the string of democratic governments that have tried to grapple with the general's legacy of **human rights** abuses.

The son of a customs official, Augusto Pinochet was born in the important coastal city of Valparaíso in 1915. He enrolled in the Military Academy at a young age, rose slowly through the ranks, and in 1972 was promoted to army chief of staff at a time of increasing political polarization between President Allende's radical programs and a hostile Congress. General Pinochet headed the governing junta in the aftermath of the coup, and in December 1974 he was designated president of the republic by the Junta Militar, a position he held until democracy returned in March 1990. Until the 1973 coup, Chile was one of Latin America's most durable democracies, consistently ranked in the top three by a panel of U.S. political scientists. Since 1833, with only two interruptions (civil war in 1891 and military rule between 1925 and 1932), Chile's stable democracy had followed institutionalized constitutional procedures, upheld the rule of law, promoted civil liberties, tolerated political dissent, and held regular elections. Under Pinochet's harsh authoritarian rule, Chileans lived in an atmosphere of fear based on: repression of political opposition, press censorship, summary executions, imprisonment, torture, disappearances, and exile. Under Pinochet's command, a secret police, the National Intelligence Directorate (DINA in the Spanish acronym) was put in place to ferret out real and potential enemies of the regime. While Pinochet was in power, nearly 3,000 opponents of the **dictatorship** were killed, and another 1,000 disappeared in the military's effort to save Chile from communism. Recently declassified documents reveal incontrovertible evidence of the depth and range of U.S. **covert operations** to prevent Allende from taking office in 1970 and after President Allende took office to promote a military coup in Chile.

Pinochet's dictatorship was different from the other "new" military authoritarian regimes in South America in that it was more clearly identified with a single person. Although a collegial government of the armed forces was initially planned, General Pinochet quickly consolidated and centralized personal power. Through purges and various power shifts, Pinochet adeptly eliminated his peers from the officer corps: a cohesive ruling elite that was subordinated to Pinochet in his combined roles as head of the army, commander in chief, and president of the republic. It is noteworthy that Pinochet was the only general of the "new militarisms" in southern South America to remain in power during the entire authoritarian project. Unlike the rather faceless generals in Argentina, Brazil, or Uruguay, Pinochet was not simply *primus inter pares* within a military junta, he was a personalist dictator who totally dominated the authoritarian apparatus. In this sense Pinochet's despotism more closely resembled the unusually long tyranny of General Alfredo Stroessner in Paraguay (1954–1989).

Pinochet's economic policies were driven by young technocrats and foreign economic advisers called the **Chicago Boys** (many had studied economics at the University of Chicago under the tutelage of Milton Friedman and Arnold Harberger) who pushed free-market economic policies, foreign investment and loans, and denationalization of major sectors of the economy, a reversal of President Allende's socialist economic solutions to Chile's development problems. After being repudiated in a plebiscite in 1988, Pinochet decided not to run for president the following year but managed to retain the post of army commander in chief following the return to democratic rule with the election of Patricio Aylwin in 1990. The long period of military dictatorship—and the provisions of the 1980 constitution that included the creation of a "protected democracy"—expanded the powers of the Chilean military over civilian politics, making the transition to democratic rule a difficult step for the elected governments that followed General Pinochet. Throughout most of the decade of the 1990s, Pinochet maintained a sort of shadow government made up of a military and civilian group determined to prevent Chile from lapsing into another Allende-style revolution. Furthermore, as political scientist Brian Loveman (2001: 311) points out, "Significant social support remained for the authoritarian neoliberal regime, impressive evidence that the military government from 1973 to 1990 neither existed in a vacuum nor imposed itself without deep roots in civil society." Unlike other cases in the aftermath of the **Cold War**, General Pinochet was awarded immunity and a role in future governments in exchange for ending his dictatorship, a form of blackmail and injustice that undermined the revival of Chilean democracy. Post-Pinochet presidents faced the difficult task of governing because of the great influence that the ex-dictator exerted over public life, especially in prosecuting the human rights abuses committed during Pinochet's seventeen-year dictatorship.

The arrest of General Pinochet on charges of human rights violations on October 17, 1998, while recovering from back surgery in a London hospital proved to be one of those defining moments for Chilean politics. It helped expose the crimes of other Latin American dictatorships that engaged in "dirty war" tactics, the sordid history of U.S.–Chilean relations, and the application of new standards of international law regarding such concepts as "sovereign immunity," and ways to punish those who carried out repressive measures to eliminate large segments of the population. In this case, a Spanish judge, Baltasar Garzón, requested that Pinochet be extradited to Spain to stand trial for human rights abuses committed in Chile during his rule. Pinochet's arrest stirred the same ideological fault lines that had polarized Chilean society prior to his 1973 *golpe*. Senator-for-Life Augusto Pinochet was revered as a national savior by a large minority of the population. For the Chilean right, Pinochet was someone whose overthrow of Allende proved to be a last-ditch act to halt the consolidation of a Communist regime. For the country's left and center, General Pinochet was evil incarnate in heading a military dictatorship that had destroyed Chilean democracy and murdered and tortured thousands. After he was allowed to return to Chile in March 1999, Pinochet ran into more legal actions by those—a majority of Chileans, according to opinion polls—who wanted him to stand trial in Chile for the disappearance of nineteen political prisoners after the 1973 coup. Since the end of the Pinochet era in 1990, Chilean socialists have disavowed the extremism of the Allende years; however, the armed forces have neither admitted nor apologized for the reign of terror they inflicted on unarmed opponents following the coup. Pinochet's unsettled legacy will continue to haunt Chile as long as he is alive and manages to stay out of the courts for his past deeds. In any case, his arrest and the release of a new report, "CIA Activities in Chile," in September 2000 makes the clearest case to date that the **Central Intelligence Agency (CIA)**, under orders from the **Nixon** administration, played a major role in bringing Pinochet to power and keeping him there for seventeen years. Although Chile's Supreme Court stopped a trial of Pinochet in 2001 on grounds that he was mentally unfit, after an interview with a Miami television station in 2003 in which the old dictator appeared alert and articulate, Chile's lawyers indicated they would resume efforts to try Pinochet for human rights crimes. Pinochet's shifting legal difficulties surfaced again in 2004 after an interview in which he defiantly declared that "everything I did, I would do again," and a report from the U.S. Senate that from 1994 to 2002 Augusto Pinochet maintained accounts at the Riggs Bank in Washington with deposits of $4 million to $8 million. In the meantime, Chilean courts continue to investigate the ex-dictator's activities while civilian governments struggle with the deep scars inflicted by the dark years of a brutal military regime. *See also* International Criminal Court (ICC); International Law; Operation Condor; Threat Perception/Assessment.

Suggested Reading

Edward Cleary, *The Struggle for Human Rights in Latin America* (Westport, CT: Praeger, 1997); Pamela Constable and Arturo Valenzuela, *Chile Under Pinochet, a Nation of Enemies* (New York: W.W. Norton, 1991); Marc Cooper, *Pinochet and Me* (London: Verso, 2001); Madeleine Davis, ed., *The Pinochet Case: Origins, Progress and Implications* (London: University of London, Institute of Latin American Studies, 2003); Mark Ensalaco, *Chile Under Pinochet: Recovering the Truth* (Philadelphia: University of Pennsylvania Press, 2000); Manuel Antonio Garretón, *The Chilean Political Process* (Boston: Unwin Hyman, 1989); Darren G. Hawkins, *International Human Rights and Authoritarian Rule in Chile* (Lincoln: University of Nebraska Press, 2002); Christopher Hitchens, *The Trials of Henry Kissinger* (London: Verso, 2001); Peter Kornbluh, *The Pinochet File: A Declassified Dossier on Atrocity and Accountability* (New York: The New Press, 2003); Brian Loveman, *Chile: The Legacy of Hispanic Capitalism*, 3rd ed. (New York: Oxford University Press, 2001); Robert Perry, "Bush and the Condor Mystery," *iF Magazine* (October 5, 1999); Larry Rohter, "Pinochet Continues to Haunt Chile's Civilian Government," *New York Times* (July 18, 2004); Paul Sigmund, *The United States and Democracy in Chile* (Baltimore, MD: Johns Hopkins University Press, 1993); Paul C. Sondrol, "The English Patient: General Augusto Pinochet and International Law," *Institute for the Study of Diplomacy* (Washington, DC: Georgetown University, 2000); Mary Helen Spooner, *Soldiers in a Narrow Land, The Pinochet Regime in Chile* (Berkeley: University of California Press, 1994); J. Samuel Valenzuela and Arturo Valenzuela, eds., *Military Rule in Chile: Dictatorship and Oppositions* (Baltimore, MD: Johns Hopkins University Press, 1986).

Plan Colombia One of many efforts by the United States and Colombia to fight the war on drugs in Latin America that emerged after a hotly debated policy discussion in the U.S. Congress in 2000. It provided $1.3 billion in funds to carry out a reinvigorated anti-drug initiative, but raised many concerns about the possibility of Colombia becoming a Vietnam-like quagmire. The brainchild of Colombian president Andrés Pastrana in 1998, it offered another way to save Colombia from its self-destruction and to do something to help end drug abuse in the United States. What Pastrana envisioned was an economic development program based on increasing Colombia's legal exports—primarily coffee, textiles, and cut flowers—to the United States. This would have required reducing the high tariffs and strict regulations on these legal products, something absent in the flow of cocaine and heroin flowing into the growing U.S. market. However, President Pastrana's plan was never realized as it ran into powerful political groups in Washington opposed to such a strategy. Eventually the Pentagon transformed Plan Colombia from a concept of human development into a military assistance program, one that would provide members of Congress with pork barrel projects for their home districts. Three-quarters of the assistance package was destined for military and police equipment and training.

The plan was reminiscent of the **Andean Initiative** put together by President **George H.W. Bush** in 1991, but this time the emphasis was on a militarized effort to stamp out narcotics using satellite imaging to locate coca fields, chemical defoliants sprayed by companies under contract with the **State Department**, and a warmed-over effort at crop substitution. With American technology and funds, the prevailing view seemed to be that the war on drugs could be finally won. Once the U.S. Congress was convinced of the merits of Plan Colombia, the State Department turned President Pastrana's plan from an "enlightened" aid program into a military program. Using U.S. contractors such as DynCorp, a Virginia consulting firm used by the **Central Intelligence Agency (CIA)** and the Pentagon, to oversee the fumigation campaign, and subcontractors like Eagle Aviation Services and Technology (EAST), a company that assisted the **Contras** during the **Iran-Contra scandal**, the United States managed the drug war without direct military involvement since EAST paid U.S. pilot crews in Colombia to fumigate coca plants. This process had a negative impact on legitimate crops and the farmers who tend them. After four years and a new Colombian president (Alvaro Uribe), Plan Colombia had produced few results, and little news of the predicament faced by Colombian farmers. As Allman (2002: 65) emphasizes, "These private subcontractors are harder to scrutinize than government agencies; if there are casualties or foul-ups, they make smaller headlines." The work of **private military contractors** in Colombia is perilous. For example, eleven contractors, Americans and other foreign nationals, have been killed between 1998 and 2004; others have been taken hostage and remain in guerrilla hands.

Aerial defoliation has not worked according to plan; Colombian coca cultivation has increased in volume since Plan Colombia was launched in 1998, but the United States claimed Colombia's coca crop was being reduced under Plan Colombia with the help of extra helicopters and crop dusting planes to defoliate with toxic herbicides. The "success" of the drug war as measured by the amount of land under coca cultivation tends to avoid the "balloon effect" in which production moves to other areas, drug-related corruption, distorted economies, wrecked forests, and the financial enrichment of armed guerrillas and paramilitary combatants.

Despite the spectacular failure of the militaristic counter-narcotics efforts in Colombia, the **George W. Bush** administration has allowed Colombia to use military equipment given to it by the United States to fight **terrorism**, not just narco-guerrillas. In the meantime, 90 percent of the cocaine that arrives in the United States is grown and manufactured in Colombia. Since the days of the Andean Initiative in the George H.W. Bush administration, the U.S. response to the drug problem has been to increase militarization, rather than a serious programmatic attempt to resolve social, economic, and political problems in the region. At home, the United States has tried to solve the costly drug war by filling prisons with people given mandatory sentences for non-violent drug offenses. Surveys in the United States continue to show dissatisfaction with the way the war on drugs is being waged, particularly the incarceration of non-violent offenders and the militarization of the anti-drug measures in Latin America. In a 2001 Pew Research Center poll, more than three-quarters of Americans—both Republicans and Democrats—believe the war on drugs is a failure. In the *Bad Neighbor Policy* (2003), Ted Galen Carpenter examines Washington's anti-drug effort and concludes that legalization—like tobacco and alcohol—is the most sensible policy, not what is currently in place. In 2004, the U.S. Congress approved doubling the number of U.S. troops in Colombia to 800 and increasing the number of private contractors in Colombia from 400 to 600, a clear sign that Colombia is becoming a serious military commitment by Washington. The optimistic words of General James Hill, commander of American military operations in Bogotá, that "we will stay the course and win the war" have a hollow ring to those on the front lines of the "war" on drugs. Plan Colombia has also included dramatic increases in the number of troop and police officers trained by the U.S. forces. *See also* Drug Trafficking.

Suggested Reading

T.D. Allman, "Blow Back," *Rolling Stone* (May 9, 2002); "The Balloon Goes Up," *Economist* (March 6, 2003); Ted Galen Carpenter, *Bad Neighbor Policy: Washington's Futile War on Drugs in Latin America* (New York: Palgrave Macmillan, 2003); Juan Forero, "Congress Approves Doubling of U.S. Troops in Colombia to 800," *New York Times* (October 11, 2004); Angel Rabasa and Peter Chalk, *Colombian Labyrinth: The Synergy of Drugs and Insurgency and its Implications for Regional Stability* (Santa Monica, CA: Rand Corporation, 2001); Giraldo Rivera, "Colombia's Enduring Drug War," on *Dateline NBC*, August 31, 2001; Winifred Tate, "Into the Andean Quagmire: Bush II Keeps Up March to Militarization," *NACLA Report on the Americas*, Vol. 35, No. 3 (November/December, 2001); Lally Weymouth, "Trouble Everywhere," *Newsweek* (February 10, 2003).

Platt Amendment (1902) Highly controversial amendment to the Cuban constitution that limited Cuba's sovereignty and granted the United States the right to intervene in Cuba to protect lives and property, protect Cuba's newly acquired independence from Spain, and acquire territory with which to protect U.S. security in the Caribbean region. It was written by Secretary of War Elihu **Root**, but named after Connecticut Senator Orville H. Platt. Platt was originally opposed to U.S. involvement in the **Spanish-Cuban-American War** but turned to expansionism after the successful war driving Spain from the Western Hemisphere. The Platt Amendment was approved by the U.S. Congress in 1901 and attached to the new Cuban Constitution in 1902. The audacity of the Platt Amendment set the stage for the creation of numerous U.S. protectorates throughout Central America and the Caribbean that would require military **intervention** and occupation. The specific language of the Platt Amendment reflected the basic principles of the **Monroe Doctrine** and its corollaries. Unfortunately, it provided grist for anti-American nationalism that spawned both the 1933 Revolution and the 1959 Revolution carried out by Fidel **Castro**. Even today, the term "platista" is a pejorative used by Cubans to refer to the historic U.S. involvement in Cuba's internal affairs. *See also* Anti-Americanism; Hegemony; Intervention and Non-Intervention; Revolutions; Root, Elihu.

Suggested Reading

Samuel Flagg Bemis, *The Latin American Policy of the United States: An Historical Interpretation* (1943; reprint, New York: W.W. Norton, 1971); Louis A. Pérez, *Cuba Under the Platt Amendment, 1902–1934* (Pittsburgh: University of Pittsburgh Press, 1986).

Poinsett, Joel Roberts (1779–1851) Politician, special agent, and diplomatic representative who played a major role in the internal affairs of several Latin American countries from 1806 until 1829 when he returned to his native South Carolina. Born in Charleston, South Carolina, Joel R. Poinsett attended private schools in the United States as well as a medical school and military academy in the United Kingdom. As a special agent in Argentina and Chile, Poinsett advised revolutionary leaders about the struggle for independence from Spain. After serving nine years as a state and national representative, Poinsett was named the first U.S. minister to Mexico, a wise appointment at the time because he had knowledge of Spanish and a knack for diplomatic persuasion. Despite these obvious skills, Poinsett became embroiled in a conflict with the British chargé d'affaires, angered the Mexicans because of his determination to spread **democracy**, and eventually left Mexico in 1829 at the request of the government in Mexico City. He returned to South Carolina, served as secretary of war under Martin Van Buren, and became a vocal opponent of the **Mexican-American War**. He is perhaps best known for introducing the poinsettia flower to the United States. *See also* Ambassadors; Intervention and Non-Intervention.

Suggested Reading

William Ray Maning, *Early Diplomatic Relations Between the U.S. and Mexico* (Baltimore, MD: Johns Hopkins University Press, 1916); J. Fred Rippy, *Joel R. Poinsett, Versatile American* (1935; reprint, Westport, CT: Greenwood Press, 1970).

Political Cartoons The craft of penning cartoons for major U.S. newspapers can be an instructive source for understanding U.S.–Latin American relations, at least from a North American perspective. Historian John J. Johnson found that editorial cartoons that he studied illuminated many things about how the United States views Latin America and how this affects their relationship. Cartoonists usually rely on a relatively small number of symbols and metaphors designed to elicit the most readily understandable responses from their readers. In Johnson's classic work, *Latin America in Caricature*, he analyzes four of the most popular human metaphors used by North American caricaturists during the first half of the twentieth century: adult women, infants and youth, stereotyped Southern blacks, and non-black makes (either *mestizo* or *criollo*). The popularity of this style of cartooning, according to Johnson (1980: 1), is based on the assumption that (1) artists "somehow feel qualified to humanize an abstraction such as a state or nation" and (2) that human metaphors have been employed to deny that the Latin American republics "can act responsibly in the international community or in their own interests and, most emphatically, to strip them of any status that might, however remotely, suggest a capability to challenge United States **hegemony** in this quarter of the planet." During the 1980s it was common for political cartoonists to warn of "another Vietnam" in their works, often referring to places like El Salvador and Nicaragua as foreign policy blunders (and quagmires) similar to what had happened previously in Vietnam.

Using a baseball metaphor, political cartoonist Jim Morin portrays the forty-year-old U.S. embargo of Cuba as a failed policy in this July 6, 2002, caricature. With Fidel Castro playing catcher, the overweight, and out-of-shape "U.S.–Cuba Policy" batter swings (and misses) his "Embargo" bat another time as the umpire yells "Strike Forty" after the baseball lands in Castro's mitt. Although the U.S. embargo of Cuba has failed to bring about regime change on the island, ten U.S. presidents have concluded that it deserves to be kept in place despite public opinion polls that show otherwise. Analysis of cartoon provided by Gregory J. Uehlinger. Reprinted courtesy Jim Morin, *The Miami Herald*, CWS.

Editorial cartoonists are a rare breed of artists whose talents are used by major newspapers to offer critical and biting views of foreign policies, political rhetoric, and the foibles of political leaders. Some of the best-known editorial cartoonists in the past fifty years include Tom Flannery, Bill Mauldin, Patrick Oliphant, Herbert Block (Herblock), Kevin Kelleher (KAL), and Tom Toles. These are talented individuals who draw for one newspaper, but are usually syndicated through other outlets. They rarely collaborate with the newspaper's editors and usually never seek the approval of the editorial board. Some see them as artistic "guns-for-hire" whose work is expected to generate responses from the readership of the newspapers. In dealing with subjects related to U.S.–Latin American relations and political news about Latin America, they often mirror the way in which political news about Latin America is reported. This means that both news stories and political cartoons often cast an unfavorable light on Latin Americans. In *Latin America in Caricature*, Johnson's main criticism of North American cartoonists' work is the overwhelming use of the negative image, reinforced with stereotypes and symbols that are relatively easy for the attentive public in the United States to understand. This use of uncomplicated themes and human metaphors are both the strength and weakness of editorial cartooning. That is, the artist must catch the reader's attention with satire based on a few lines and phrases intended to evoke an immediate response, and it is this aspect of the craft that can lead to the use of the negative image or metaphor. Ironically, North American editorial caricaturists, while directing their barbed attacks on American presidents (both Republicans and Democrats alike) and institutions, often end up portraying Latin Americans and their governments negatively. While it is also possible that this may accurately reflect the image of Latin America in the minds of **Washington policymakers**, it can also lead to a serious distortion in our understanding of our neighbors to the south, as well as misguided foreign policies.

The amount of White House and congressional attention devoted to Central America during the **Reagan** administration produced far more political cartoons criticizing the United States than during the time of any other American president. President Reagan devoted a great deal of his speeches and press conferences to his Central American policy, namely El Salvador and Nicaragua. This in turn provided a constant flow of materials for editorial cartoonists. However, for many political cartoonists, Reagan differed from his predecessors—**Carter**, **Ford**, and **Nixon**—because of his acting and radio announcing background and his avuncular manner of communicating with the American people. According to Herbert Block (1984: 17), *Washington Post* caricaturist until his death in 2001, Reagan was different "not simply because he had been an actor and an announcer but because to him there was apparently no distinction between delivering statements as president and delivering lines as an actor—*it didn't matter* whether the words were factual. It only mattered that they were presented well and that they sounded good to the audience. If an anecdote worked effectively in a speech, he would use it again, even if it turned out to have no basis in fact." Reagan's penchant for the well-delivered speech over factual reality became the hallmark of his rhetorical strategy for dealing with revolutionaries and reformers of all kinds in Latin America. Reagan's speeches to the nation were designed to both appease his conservative constituency and undermine those who questioned his "facts" by stressing the evils of communism, totalitarian dungeons, East-West battlegrounds, and the **domino theory** (see Appendix: President Ronald Reagan's Speech on Congressional Aid for the Contras).

The press—print and broadcast—had a significant impact on both the success and failure of Reagan's policies toward Latin America. Political cartoonists welcomed Reagan's approach to the presidency, but also found much to criticize in Reagan's Latin American policy and offered the public a steady diet of negative caricatures of President Reagan and his Latin American policy. For example, the press welcomed Reagan for his carefully orchestrated "sound bites" designed to evoke the maximum amount of emotional support from bedrock political symbols. Reagan was clearly a master of political symbolism and used television and radio to communicate his impassioned anti-communism to the American people. However, there were also frustrations for those journalists covering his Central American policy because of his interest in making the United States a hegemonic power through distortions, lies, and obfuscations designed to undermine opposition to his controversial policies. No other region of the world was more vexing for the Reagan administration than Central America where policy errors piled one on top of the other producing consistently negative ratings among the American people for his handling of both El Salvador and Nicaragua. The political cartoons of the Reagan era reveal time and again the negative portrayal of the president's policies along with negative stereotypes of the governments and people of Central America.

Since the Cuban Revolution in 1959 there has been a tendency of editorial cartoonists to portray Latin America in dichotomous terms—rich-or-poor, order-or-chaos, reform-or-revolution—rather than a large number of states with strong dissimilarities. These are durable symbols and metaphors that often reflect the nature of **threat perception** and the emphasis on security interests when it comes to dealing with Latin America. Two important themes stressed by editorial cartoonists in the 1980s was the "Vietnam syndrome" and the growing realization that interventionism and go-it-alone policies were often counter-productive in dealing with Latin America. The metaphor of another Vietnam was used by editorial cartoonists to both criticize and educate readers about U.S. policy in Central America. Congressional critics also voiced concern about getting militarily involved in a region with ill-defined policy goals and where the American people expressed little interest in the use of force to stop communism unless the quick-and-easy invasion of Grenada in 1983 could be duplicated with minimum costs.

Although political cartoons are always controversial, depending on the political ideology of the artist and the newspaper, they can serve as a useful medium for stirring public interest in U.S.–Latin American relations. Nevertheless, the satire and symbolism used to inform North American readers is often distorted by negative stereotypes passed from one generation to the next and the constraints associated with the craft of political cartooning. It may take a more enlightened view of Latin Americans and U.S.–Latin American relations before a more positive view takes hold in the American press. *See also* Media; Propaganda; Public Opinion; Race and Racism; Scandals and Blunders.

Suggested Reading

George Black, *The Good Neighbor: How the United States Wrote the History of Central America and the Caribbean* (New York: Pantheon Books, 1988); Herbert Block, *Herblock Through the Looking Glass* (New York: W.W. Norton, 1984); John J. Johnson, *Latin America in Caricature* (Austin: University of Texas Press, 1980).

Polk, James Knox (1795–1849) Lawyer, one-term president (1845–1849) and expansionist politician who became a strong believer in the **Monroe Doctrine**, **Manifest Destiny**, slavery, and war as a tool for acquiring territory. James K. Polk was born in North Carolina, raised in Tennessee, and educated at the University of North Carolina. After practicing law for a few years Polk moved from state politics to the U.S. House of Representatives where he became speaker of the House in 1835. He returned to Tennessee to serve a term as governor, failed to retain and recapture the office between 1840 and 1843, and in 1844 became a dark horse presidential candidate for the Democratic Party. In his 1844 campaign against Whig candidate, Henry **Clay**, Polk argued that it was essential that what John Quincy **Adams** had "unwisely ceded away" in 1819—Texas and Oregon—be reannexed, or reoccupied. This was a popular view among the American public, helped Polk win the presidency, and quickly led to diplomatic battles with Mexico and Britain.

The newly elected Polk wanted to acquire California, at the time a large province of Mexico, but Mexico rejected his offer to purchase the territory in late 1845. President Polk then increased the pressure on Mexico until a minor provocation near the U.S.–Mexican border gave him the necessary justification to declare war in 1846. After Polk ordered the U.S. Army to occupy the land between the Nueces River and the Rio Grande, Mexico countered on the grounds that its national territory had been violated. Claiming Mexico had "shed American blood upon the American soil," Polk asked Congress for a declaration of war on May 9, 1846. Mexico was no match for the United States, since the nation was divided politically with an army that was poorly equipped and with little training for war. Although there have been repeated instances of U.S. **intervention** in Latin America's internal affairs, the **Mexican-American War** marks the first time the United States declared war on a Latin American country.

The war with Mexico was brutal, unjust, racist, and detrimental to future U.S.–Mexican relations. According to Schoultz (1998: 33), "It involved much pain and suffering, and its long-term effect was to poison relations between the people of Mexico and the United States." President Polk faced a hostile Congress and an angry public divided over the conduct of the war with Mexico. The major critics of the war included members of the Whig Party, abolitionists, peace advocates, and others who called the war with Mexico a crime and demanded the withdrawal of all U.S. forces from Mexican territory. Although there was pressure on Polk to take all of Mexico, he resisted these demands in favor of settling for more limited gains from the war. The brutal and unjust nature of the war with Mexico contributed to the highest desertion rate (13 percent of the regular army and thousands of draftees) in U.S. military history.

American troops entered Mexico in 1846 and left in 1848 after Mexico had ratified the onerous treaty of **Guadalupe Hidalgo**, which ceded to the United States 55 percent of Mexican territory. In return, the United States agreed to pay Mexico $15 million and assumed responsibility for $3.5 million in claims against the Mexican government by U.S. citizens. The war cost the United States $100 million and 15,000 lives, although only 1,733 were battlefield deaths. Mexico lost more than territory and lives (more than 50,000); it also damaged Mexican pride and engendered bitter feelings toward the United States.

President Polk's **imperialism** confirmed the dogma of Manifest Destiny and established the Polk Corollary to the Monroe Doctrine, enlarging Monroe's message by restricting the transfer of territory from one foreign country to another. After annexation of Texas in 1845, Polk declared that "the people of this continent alone have the right to decide their own destiny." Furthermore, Latin American countries wishing to unite themselves with the United States will need to consult with the United States "without any foreign interposition." The transfer of Latin American territory to the United States was permissible, but unacceptable for a European nation to engage in such a transfer of territory. After more than 150 years, the trauma of the war started by President Polk in the 1840s is still very much alive in Mexico where the event is known as the American intervention. Polk's imperialism exacerbated the national crisis over slavery by raising the question of admission of several new states taken from Mexico as either slave state or free soil applicants. Polk retired after his single term in office and then returned to his home in Nashville where he died shortly thereafter. *See also* Intervention and Non-Intervention; Race and Racism; Taylor, Zachary.

Suggested Reading

Jack K. Bauer, Paul H. Bergeron, *The Presidency of James K. Polk* (Lawrence: University Press of Kansas, 1987); *The Mexican War, 1846–1848* (Lincoln: University of Nebraska Press, 1992); David W. Dent, *The Legacy of the Monroe Doctrine: A Reference Guide to U.S. Involvement in Latin America and the Caribbean* (Westport, CT: Greenwood Press, 1999); Lars Schoultz, *Beneath the United States: A History of U.S. Policy Toward Latin America* (Cambridge, MA: Harvard University Press, 1998); Charles G. Sellers, *James K. Polk, Continentalist, 1843–1856* (Princeton, NJ: Princeton University Press, 1966).

Private Military Contractors A controversial practice of the U.S. government to rely on civilian contractors to perform jobs once reserved for the military, including training of armed forces in foreign lands, providing security for foreign leaders, delivering mail, feeding soldiers, interrogating prisoners, and participation in counter-drug and counter-terror operations worldwide. The use of U.S. contractors overseas has brought more civilians into dangerous situations, raised questions of accountability and openness, generated repeated cases of conflict of interest between ex-government officials working for private companies, and clouded efforts to measure the effectiveness of turning over some military jobs to private contractors. As the U.S. military is called upon to perform more and more missions overseas, the number of private military contractors grows. This means that the more civilian employees of private contractors accompany troops abroad, the more they are likely to encounter life-threatening situations. The process of using private contractors expanded under the Reagan administration and contributed to the **Iran-Contra scandal**. As Marshall, Scott, and Hunter (1987: 8) argue, "Farming such covert operations outside even the CIA served to insulate the president and his advisors from scrutiny and responsibility." The **Reagan** White House relied on a host of covert operators and private individuals and organizations to carry out the war against Nicaragua. They included Cuban exile terrorist groups, former **Central Intelligence Agency (CIA)** contract pilots, former Pentagon special operations officers, the World Anti-Communist League, Sovereign Military Order of Malta and

CAUSA, one of the political arms of Sun Myung Moon's Unification Church. The strategy of contracting-out **covert operations** became an important part of foreign policy operations in the war with Iraq where there was one contractor for every ten soldiers during the height of the U.S. occupation in 2003–2005.

There are many civilian contractors, but the best known contemporary examples in Latin America are DynCorp, Northrop Grumman Corp., Steele Foundation, Blackwater USA, and Kellogg, Brown, and Root. DynCorp began as an air cargo shipper in the 1940s, but realized it could make more money by expanding into a service agency for the Pentagon and Department of State. The U.S. Congress estimated in 2004 that there are thousands of these companies making over $100 billion in government work. Former Green Berets, Army Rangers, and Navy Seals now serve as soldiers-for-hire, working for private firms to carry out services—counter-terrorism, urban warfare, dictator protection, and the operation of military prisons and detention facilities. Since many have high-level security clearances, finding a job with civilian contractors is fairly simple. As a cost-cutting measure, U.S. private military contractors began recruiting young men in Colombia, El Salvador, and Nicaragua to fight in Iraq in 2004.

The **State Department** has used DynCorp employees to train Colombian military personnel, conduct anti-drug missions, and repair infrastructure damaged by opposition forces. The number of Americans working in Colombia for private military contractors grew from a little over 200 in 2002 to 400 in 2004, the revised congressional limit. Congress increased the number of contractors to 600 in 2004, and in the same year changed the limit on U.S. military forces in Colombia to 800. By 2004 over two dozen American companies were working in Colombia, with contracts for anti-drug programs worth $178 million in 2003. Those who fly the dangerous missions in Colombia are usually paid $150,000 annually to spray coca fields, operate eavesdropping devices, repair airplanes, organize alternative development programs, assess intelligence, and advise the Colombian military. More than twenty private military contractors have been killed in Colombia since 1998. In the early 1990s, DynCorp guarded President Jean-Bertrand **Aristide** of Haiti. Much of the danger involved in this kind of work is that as long as private military contractors are seen as part of the U.S. military/security/intelligence apparatus, the more likely they are to be viewed as legitimate targets for kidnapping, ransom, and worse. In 2003, three Northrop employees were taken hostage in Colombia when their single-engine plane crashed in guerrilla territory and have yet to be rescued. Private military contractors are heavily involved in **Guantánamo Bay**, Cuba, where "enemy combatants" are being held as suspected terrorists by the **George W. Bush** administration. The pilots and technicians who work in Colombia as military contractors are overseen by the Southern Command, head of the Latin American military mission based in Miami, Florida. Since the State Department considers the FARC (Fuerzas Armadas Revoluciónarias de Colombia) a terrorist organization, **Washington policymakers** make little effort to talk to the Colombian guerrillas in hopes of the release of the American hostages.

Haiti's president Jean-Bertrand Aristide was forced from office in early 2004 when former U.S. Special Forces working for the Steele Foundation, a San Francisco-based company that specializes in executive security, abandoned him as armed rebels closed in on the national palace. After Aristide's American security detail refused his request to send reinforcements, purportedly after pressure from the U.S. embassy in Port-au-Prince, Aristide was forced out of office and taken by the United States to the Central African Republic, the second time in his political career his democratically elected terms of office has been interrupted. After President Aristide was removed from power, with the assistance of the United States, members of the U.S. Congress questioned whether U.S. government contacts with Steele helped drive him from office since he claims that he did not resign and fell victim to a coup d'état. The murky circumstances surrounding Aristide's slow-motion removal from office have left many in the policy-making community worried about what some critics call the "corporatization of the mercenary trade." With the growing number of former soldiers, law enforcement agents, and intelligence operatives engaged in work formerly done by U.S. military forces and intelligence agents, many analysts worry about the consequences of outsourcing American foreign policy in the name of budgetary savings. Private military contractors are supposed to be more cost effective than regular military employees, but their cost effectiveness has not been proved. Furthermore, congressional oversight is minimal because many members of Congress don't want to tackle such a thorny political issue. More important to the Pentagon is that by substituting contractors for soldiers helps to avoid the negative publicity of unpopular military forays. When U.S. National Guard and regular military forces are fighting side-by-side with private military contractors who are paid up to ten times what a U.S. soldier-employee is paid, serious morale problems occur and lead to problems in recruiting and retaining qualified military personnel. If Latin American **dictatorships** can hire U.S.–based private military contractors to maintain themselves in power, what leverage does the State Department or the Pentagon have over these leaders? The more important question is how to restrict the power of future presidents to avoid public accountability when it is obvious that this practice is often a major contributor to foreign policy **scandals and blunders**. *See also* Plan Colombia.

Suggested Reading

James Dao, " 'Outsourced' or 'Mercenary,' He's No Soldier," *New York Times* (April 25, 2004); Juan Forero, "Private U.S. Operatives on Risky Missions in Colombia," *New York Times* (February 14, 2004); General Accounting Office, report on private contracting personnel (June 2003); Chalmers Johnson, *Blowback: The Costs and Consequences of American Empire* (New York: Henry Holt, 2000); Jonathan Marshall, Peter Dale Scott, and Jane Hunter, *The Iran Contra Connection: Secret Teams and Covert Operations in the Reagan Era* (Boston: South End Press, 1987); Renae Merle, "U.S. Contractors Are Targets Overseas," *Washington Post* (October 16, 2003); Richard H. Shultz, *The Secret War Against Hanoi: Kennedy's and Johnson's use of Spies, Sabateurs, and Covert Warriors in North Vietnam* (New York: HarperCollins, 1999); Peter W. Singer, *Corporate Warriors: The Rise of the Privatized Military Industry* (Ithaca, NY: Cornell University Press, 2003); Barry Yeoman, "Need an Army? Just Pick Up the Phone," *New York Times* (April 2, 2004).

Propaganda The United States has used propaganda as an instrument of foreign policy reaching back to the nineteenth century, particularly during times of war and international crisis. The difficulty of defining propaganda has contributed to the use of a wide variety of terms to convey meaning to a deliberate technique and product for the purpose of obtaining foreign policy objectives. At times the United States has resorted to propaganda to "sell" its Latin American policy, both at home and inside Latin America. Propaganda is usually a deliberate distortion of information through the presentation of disinformation or half-truths by government agencies or leaders. Private non-governmental propaganda has also played a role in U.S.–Latin American relations.

Beginning with the **Spanish-Cuban-American War**, the U.S. government has used propaganda to achieve its foreign policy objectives. However, since propaganda carries a negative connotation as a deceitful and manipulative practice, many Americans have come to think of what the United States does as education, persuasion, and information. This tendency has also produced a number of euphemisms to soften the use of propaganda in the conduct of foreign policy. These would include such terms as public diplomacy, public information, war information, public communication, psychological operations, winning hearts and minds, and spin. The U.S. Army abandoned the use of the word propaganda in **World War I**, using instead psychological warfare (psyops).

Prior to the twentieth century, propaganda was used to arouse public sentiment in times of war. Public and private groups engaged in propaganda techniques to push their agendas, including support for the American Revolution, Union support for abolition, Confederate support for slavery, **Manifest Destiny**, the **Mexican-American War**, the Spanish-Cuban American War, and imperialist expansion. The "yellow journalism" that propelled the United States into the war with Spain in 1898 emphasized the noble and civilized intentions of the United States in contrast to the sensational reporting and fabrication of Spanish atrocities by the U.S. **media**. Political cartoonists liked to characterize Latin Americans as immature and inferior, often drawing them as blacks, children, or women in need of guidance and supervision. A great deal of this propaganda was private, not governmental, but it was often an accurate reflection of popular sentiment and official attitudes, if not actual policy at the time.

The use of government propaganda expanded and became widespread in the twentieth century as communication technology changed, and the United States realized that it could not compete with foreign adversaries without some form of opinion manipulation. The arrival of modern mass media—radio, television, and forms of instant communication—forced the U.S. government to place more emphasis on public information designed to meet the needs of the foreign policy elite. During **World War II**, Nelson **Rockefeller**'s Office of the Coordinator of Inter-American Affairs was given the task of countering Nazi influence in Latin America with U.S. propaganda. This included the use of all types of media, from magazines to shortwave broadcasts to motion pictures, some produced by Walt Disney Studios. The **Central Intelligence Agency (CIA)** was created in 1947 and took over the job of covert propaganda. The **Eisenhower** administration used the "Voice of Liberation" to overthrow Guatemalan President Jacobo **Arbenz**, broadcasting outrageous claims about the strength of the opposition against the regime in power. After the success of the Guatemalan operation in 1954, the CIA used Radio Swan to broadcast disinformation during the **Bay of Pigs** invasion, proclaiming the Cuban army had been routed and calling on the Cuban people to rise up in revolt against their leader. Under pressure from the **Cuba Lobby** and the **Reagan** administration, in 1985 the U.S. Congress established **Radio Martí**, and in 1991 added TV Martí, to broadcast anti-**Castro** propaganda to the island in hopes of toppling the regime. President Reagan created a public diplomacy office in the 1980s to build support for the **Contra** war at home and undermine the **Sandinistas** in Nicaragua. The U.S. military has censored the news media to create a favorable image of operations and minimize the fallout from negative reporting on invasions and special operations.

United States–sponsored clandestine radio stations have played a key role in **covert operations** designed to remove unwanted political leaders in Latin America. The U.S. Central Intelligence Agency created these radio stations and falsified broadcasts to undermine **revolutions**, labor unions, progressive leaders, and ideologies considered incompatible with American interests. In 1954, broadcasts from a station called "Voice of Liberation" demanded that democratically elected President Jacobo Arbenz resign because of his efforts to turn Guatemala into a Communist dictatorship (false) and that thousands of rebel soldiers were marching on the capital city (false). Unable to counter the falsified stories, Arbenz shortly resigned and fled to Mexico. Several years later Radio Swan was created to demand the same of Fidel Castro, referred to as a "Communist dictator." To rid Nicaragua of the Sandinista government during the 1980s the Reagan administration created Radio Quince de Septiembre, a secret radio station that operated on behalf of the contra guerrillas operating out of Honduras. Radio Quince de Septiembre was part of a strategy to arm anti-Communist rebels, label them "freedom fighters," and then proclaim their heroism in the battle against Soviet Communist expansion in the Western Hemisphere. The contra war was never very secret; however, it didn't matter to President Reagan—a former radio broadcaster and film actor—since he was a master of alarmist rhetoric and political symbolism. In each case where this type of political broadcasting took place, the assumption was always that the target governments—Guatemala, Cuba, Suriname, Nicaragua—were Soviet puppets rather than indigenous governments, opposing them would weaken the Soviet Union at minimal cost to the United States, and offered major domestic political benefits for American presidents (and their political party) who could easily portray themselves as tough on communism. As Soley points out in *Radio Warfare* (1989: 6), "The policy [of fighting Soviet expansion] was also very popular with immigrants who entered the United States from Cuba, Vietnam, Cambodia, and other countries where Communist governments had come to power. Because of the president's policies, they gave the Republican party substantial monetary and political support."

The global war on **terrorism** has placed a premium on psychological operations, war propaganda, and censorship as a strategy for winning the support of allies and countering negative views of the United States abroad, especially in the Middle East. Shortly after **September 11, 2001**, the **George W. Bush** administration created the office of undersecretary for public diplomacy and public affairs within the Department of State to promote American values in the Islamic world. Former advertising executives were hired, and films were made featuring Muslims in the United States who made claims that they have never encountered prejudice in American society. However, the videos were widely rejected in Islamic countries as unconvincing, patronizing, and ineffective. Despite the widespread opposition in Latin America to the war in Iraq and the Bush administration's doctrine of "**regime change**," Washington has done little to reverse the growing **anti-Americanism** through the use of similar propaganda efforts. *See also* Bernays, Edward L.; Miranda, Carmen; Scandals and Blunders; Terrorism; Threat Perception/Assessment.

Suggested Reading

James Bamford, *A Pretext for War: 9/11, Iraq, and the Abuse of America's Intelligence Agencies* (New York: Doubleday, 2004); Dennis L. Bark, ed., *The Red Orchestra* (Stanford, CA: Hoover Institution Press, 1986); Roger Cohen, "Democracy as a Brand: Wooing Hearts, European or Muslim," *New York Times* (October 16, 2004); Fred Fejes, *Imperialism, Media, and the Good Neighbor: New Deal Foreign Policy and United States Shortwave Broadcasting to Latin America* (Norwood, NJ: Ablex, 1986); Ron T. Robin, *The Making of the Cold War Enemy: Culture and Politics in the Military-Intellectual Complex* (Princeton, NJ: Princeton University Press, 2001); Lawrence C. Soley, *Radio Warfare: OSS and CIA Subversive Propaganda* (New York: Praeger, 1989); Philip M. Taylor, *War and the Media: Propaganda and Persuasion in the Gulf War* (New York: St. Martin's Press, 1992).

Public Opinion The ebb and flow of U.S.–Latin American policy over the past thirty years tends to reaffirm some of the better-known generalizations about the role of public opinion in the conduct of American foreign policy. First, the mass public is generally ill-informed and disinterested in Latin America and inter-American issues. Second, although public opinion tends to offer constraints on the direction of U.S.–Latin American policy, it almost never is the decisive factor with Congress and the president where it is quite common to have perceived national interests outweigh constituency interests. For example, two-thirds of the American public opposed the **Panama Canal treaties**, the war against the Nicaraguan Contras, and the **North American Free Trade Agreement (NAFTA)**, but this did not stop the president of the United States from pursuing these policies. Third, public opinion is most effective when it is organized into specific issue-oriented groups that contribute to political parties and candidates. Fourth, government efforts to manipulate public opinion through speeches and covert **propaganda** strategies may backfire, as President Ronald **Reagan** found out when he created the Office of Public Diplomacy within the **State Department** to distort the public debate in favor of the White House and when he claimed falsely that Pope John Paul II supported all his activities in Central America. Fifth, Americans generally place a higher value on security—anti-communism during the **Cold War**; anti-terrorism after the Cold War—than protecting **human rights** and promoting **democracy**. Sixth, there is a surprising convergence of opinion about the problems of the hemisphere throughout the Americas, including the United States. In polls that ask respondents about the role of the United States in Latin America, there is strong criticism—the United States only pursues its own interests and interferes too much in Latin America—on both sides of the border. Seventh, Latin America is not viewed as a region of economic opportunity, but rather as a region with severe problems such as drugs, violence, and political instability. When it comes to pursuing a regional free trade zone such as the **Free Trade Area of the Americas (FTAA)**, there is more enthusiasm in Latin America than in the United States. Eighth, the way the news from Latin America is covered by the *New York Times*, *Washington Post*, CBS, CNN, and Fox News can affect public opinion. The public's reaction to the harsh rhetoric used by the Reagan administration in Central America was largely negative, with the press reports frequently decrying the "Vietnam syndrome" as a major reason to avoid military action in the region.

What is the relationship between Latin American **dictatorships** and the attitudes of the American public about either supporting or opposing them as part of American foreign policy? Most Americans are ideologically opposed to dictators but resist the use of force to eliminate governments that display the distasteful characteristics of authoritarian rule: human rights violations, lack of dissent, etc. Robert **Pastor** argues that U.S. policymakers were uncomfortable with the **Somozas** in Nicaragua going back to the origins of the family dynasty in the 1930s. For example, in *Condemned to Repetition* (1987: 271), he writes that "what is most surprising in U.S. policy toward Nicaragua is not the moments when it has treated Somoza well but the historically longer-lasting periods of detachment from and distaste for the regime." If the American public believes that it is morally wrong to support Latin American dictators, then **Washington policymakers** would need a rationalization for supporting them when the perceived needs of American business and defense are threatened. In supporting some of the most brutal regimes in Latin America, the United States believed that strong dictators would provide political stability, generous support for American policies, and a favorable climate for American economic interests. In a lesser-of-two-evils foreign policy, the policy of supporting right-wing dictators generated critics who argued, "Dictatorships created political polarization, blocked any effective means for reforms, destroyed the center, and created a backlash of anti-American sentiment that opened the door to radical nationalist movements that brought to power the exact forms of governments the United States most opposed and originally sought to prevent" (Schmitz, 1999: 6).

It is sometimes easy for Washington policymakers to ignore public opinion and seek legitimacy for their actions by framing their policies in ways that counter the public's views and mask the reality of what is actually happening in U.S.–Latin American relations. Despite the fact that Washington policymakers pay little attention to public opinion, students of the American presidency have found that all presidents now use focus groups to devise strategies for crafting speeches on Latin America, campaign issues, and topics to avoid when addressing Latin American leaders. *See also* Anti-Americanism; Bernays, Edward L.; Media; Propaganda.

Suggested Reading

John Spicer Nichols, "The Media," in David W. Dent, ed., *U.S.–Latin American Policymaking: A Reference Handbook* (Wesport, CT: Greenwood Press, 1995); Robert A. Pastor, *Condemned to Repetition: The United States and Nicaragua* (Princeton, NJ: Princeton University Press, 1987); David I. Schmitz, *Thank God They're on Our Side: The United States and Right-Wing Dictatorships, 1921–1965* (Chapel Hill: University of North Carolina Press, 1999); Richard Sobel, ed., *Public Opinion in U.S. Foreign Policy: The Controversy over Contra Aid* (Lanham, MD: Rowman and Littlefield, 1993); Frederick C. Turner, "Public Opinion," in David W. Dent, ed., *U.S.–Latin American Policymaking: A Reference Handbook* (Westport, CT: Greenwood Press, 1995).

R

Race and Racism Racial thinking—the idea that observable characteristics such as skin color and related theories of racial superiority can explain individual differences and national capabilities—has been pervasive in U.S.–Latin American relations from the nineteenth century forward. Notions of Anglo-Saxon superiority came with English colonists in the eighteenth century and flourished with westward expansion. From the earliest days of U.S. independence, American foreign relations became intertwined with the subjugation of people of color. The **Monroe Doctrine** was based on strategic denial, a foreign policy aimed at keeping European powers out of the Western Hemisphere. John Quincy **Adams** put little faith in countries of Catholic religion and Latin temperaments, telling his friends, "It was one thing to tell Europe to keep its hands off the Western Hemisphere, but it was another to join hands with those weak Latin governments in the spirit of equality and fraternal affection." U.S. Minister to Mexico in the 1820s, Joel **Poinsett**, was the first in a long line of U.S. representatives in Latin America whose reports contained racist views of Mexicans. Poinsett's dispatches referred to Mexicans as "an ignorant and immoral race" and became so undiplomatic that the Mexican government requested his recall. As the United States became more involved in Latin America toward the end of the nineteenth century, negative stereotypes with distinct racist overtones became an essential ingredient of presidential rhetoric in dealing with Latin America. Although racial theories of Latin Americans diminished with the creation of the **Good Neighbor Policy** in the 1920s and 1930s, the residue of racism continued to influence inter-American relations.

Manifest Destiny and White Man's Burden helped to justify American **imperialism** after the independence of Latin American countries in the 1820s. The

Mexican-American War (1846–1848) was a racially motivated conflict; **filibusters** carried racist views with their exploits in the 1840s and 1850s; Cuba's delayed independence was caused by its large black population and the fear of a second Haiti; the **Spanish-Cuban-American War** brought some of the same views of racial superiority that the U.S. Army used against Apaches and Sioux at home; U.S. immigration laws were designed to favor some races over others while preserving a predominantly Anglo-Saxon population; during the **Cold War** in the United States the Civil Rights movement caused **Washington policymakers** to address the fact that racial bigotry was having a negative effect on American foreign policy. While racist views of Latin Americans still influence U.S.–Latin American relations, the more explicit racially motivated prejudice and the negative imagery found in **political cartoons** has subsided out of fear that blatant attitudes of racial inferiority run the risk of undermining American good will and influence in the Western Hemisphere.

It was not uncommon for those with backgrounds in parts of the American south to project racist views of Negro inferiority and backwardness on the "dark-skinned" people of Latin America. **Theodore Roosevelt** believed in racial inequality and in his later years concluded that there was a connection between race and **democracy**, arguing that the failure of democracy and the need for policing Latin America was due to racial inferiority. Only the "very highest of races are fit" for self-government, Roosevelt concluded in his later years. In a letter to President Theodore Roosevelt in 1900, Governor-General Leonard Wood explained the slow pace of Cuba's transition to independence by telling the president: "We are going ahead as fast as we can, but we are dealing with a race that has steadily been going down for a hundred years into which we have got to infuse new life, new principles and new methods of doing things. This is not the work of a day or of a year, but of a longer period" (quoted in Schoultz, 2002: 400).

The justification for supporting Latin American dictators was often rooted in the belief that non-white people can be maintained only by strong discipline. During the U.S. occupation of the Dominican Republic (1916–1924), the *Marine Corps Gazette* printed an article that spelled out how best to treat Dominicans (quoted in Roorda, 1998: 241): "The Dominican is himself indoctrinated with one thing—respect for FORCE. I do not mean to say that a brutal application of force is all that he understands or respects, but I do most emphatically say that to gain his respect one must have and exert the strong hand in dealing with him." Such reasoning suggests that those who made up the military occupation of Caribbean lands believed that respect was not the result of "hand-shaking politicians" and others who failed to recognize these essential traits. If "force" (**dictatorship**) is the best method of resolving conflicts and differences in opinion, then democracy is not very likely until their cultural orientation is altered to reflect greater tolerance of dissenting views.

U.S. Latin American policy continues to be undergirded with paternalistic racism and a serious lack of knowledge about Latin America and the Caribbean. President Harry **Truman** may have expressed fewer negative views of blacks after

World War II, but he believed that Latin Americans are like "Jews and the Irish, 'very emotional' and difficult to handle." **State Department** records during the Cold War are full of references to Latin Americans as "mentally deficient," "unreasonable," and "childlike." Guatemalan leaders were often considered like children: trying to reason with them was "rather like consulting with babies as to whether or not we should take candy away from them" (quoted in Schmitz, 1999: 149). After his April 1959 meeting with Fidel **Castro**, Vice-President Richard **Nixon** expressed his hope that he could lead the revolutionary leader "in the right direction" and said during the meeting that "I talked to him like a Dutch uncle." Undersecretary of State Christian Herter told President **Dwight Eisenhower** that Castro was "very much like a child" who often spoke Spanish in "wild" and "emotional" tones (Paterson, 1994: 257). Historian John J. Johnson found that political cartoons prior to the Good Neighbor Policy often depicted Latin Americans as children, too immature and unruly to govern themselves in a democratic fashion.

While it is true that the indicators of Latin American "underdevelopment" have changed over time, from corruption, poverty, authoritarianism, unreasonable radicalism, and other cultural defects, according to Lars Schoultz (1998: xv), "A belief in Latin American inferiority is the essential core of United States policy toward Latin America because it determines the precise steps the United States takes to protect its interests in the region." It is the nature of this persistent mindset that is shared by a broad spectrum of the U.S. public and its leaders. It is tempting to disregard these racial assertions and explanations as no longer applicable in how U.S. policy is formulated and implemented in Latin America; however, if this distinct mental orientation is at the core of U.S.–Latin American relations, then multilateral efforts to deal with serious hemispheric issues seems remote indeed. *See also* Bemis, Samuel Flagg; Friendly Dictators; Herring, Hubert Clinton.

Suggested Reading

Alexander DeConde, *Ethnicity, Race, and American Foreign Policy: A History* (Boston: Northeastern University Press, 1992); George M. Frederickson, *The Black Image in the White Mind: The Debate on Afro-American Character and Destiny, 1817–1914* (New York: Harper, 1971); Michael H. Hunt, *Ideology and American Foreign Policy* (New Haven: Yale University Press, 1987); John J. Johnson, *Latin America in Caricature* (Austin: University of Texas Press, 1980); Michael L. Krenn, ed., *Race and U.S. Foreign Policy in the Ages of Territorial and Market Expansion, 1840–1900* (New York: Garland, 1998); Michael LaRosa and Frank O. Mora, eds., *Neighborly Adversaries: Readings in U.S.–Latin American Relations* (Lanham, MD: Rowman and Littlefield, 1999); Phil Gordon Lauren, *Power and Prejudice: The Politics and Diplomacy of Racial Discrimination* (Boulder, CO: Westview Press, 1988); Thomas G. Paterson, *Contesting Castro: The United States and the Triumph of the Cuban Revolution* (New York: Oxford University Press, 1994), Frederick Pike, *The United States and Latin America: Myths and Stereotypes of Civilization and Nature* (Austin: University of Texas Press, 1992); Eric Paul Roorda, *The Dictator Next Door: The Good Neighbor Policy and the Trujillo Regime in the Dominican Republic, 1930–1945* (Durham, NC: Duke University Press, 1998); David F. Schmitz, *Thank God They're on Our Side: The United States and Right-Wing Dictatorships, 1921–1965* (Chapel

Hill: University of North Carolina Press, 1999); Lars Schoultz, "Blessings of Liberty: The United States and the Promotion of Democracy in Cuba," *Journal of Latin American Studies*, 34 (2002); Schoultz, *Beneath the United States: A History of U.S. Policy Toward Latin America* (Cambridge, MA: Harvard University Press, 1998); Steve Striffler and Mark Moberg, eds., *Banana Wars: Power, Production, and History in the Americas* (Durham: Duke University Press, 2003); Josiah Strong, *Our Country: Its Possible Future and Its Present Crisis* (New York: Baker and Taylor, 1885); Allen L. Woll, *The Latin Image in American Films* (Los Angeles: Latin American Center Publications, 1977).

Radio Martí Miami-based **propaganda** weapon created during the **Reagan** administration in 1985 to "promote the cause of freedom" in Cuba by providing an alternative to state-run **media**. Named after nineteenth-century revolutionist and principal architect of the war for independence, José **Martí**, the United States Information Agency established Radio Martí to broadcast regular anti-**Castro** messages/stories into Cuba from Florida in the hopes of fomenting **regime change** on the island. A television twin, TV Martí was started by the **George H.W. Bush** administration in 1989 and began operations in 1990. The two Martís were designed to be a special arm of the Voice of America, considered a successful tool of public diplomacy that contributed to the collapse of the Soviet Union. The Cuban American National Foundation played a major role in lobbying for each program and had a significant impact on the programming. Both broadcasting efforts are located in the heart of the exile community in Miami and operate with a generous $25 million annual budget.

There are critics of this form of communication warfare, but the value of being able to appease the majority of anti-Castro exiles to win Florida's valuable twenty-seven electoral votes is often too powerful a lever to obtain the votes in Congress to shut down the program. TV Martí is only seen by those who work in the U.S. Interests Section in Havana because of transmission complications and Castro's jamming efforts; Radio Martí draws a very small Cuban audience, particularly among younger Cubans. Those who believe the two Martís are not worth the cost and criticism argue the following: the move to Miami has weakened the Voice of America's standards of accuracy and objectivity and become shrill and propagandistic; the high cost of the programs, frequent transmission jamming, and dull programming are a waste of taxpayers' money; without objective news and programming, the current "bullet theory" of communication will have virtually no affect on bringing the "truth" to the Cuban people and assist the pro-**democracy** dissidents on the island; and as long as the **Cuba Lobby** in Washington allows the exile community in Florida to call the shots, any efforts to restore some degree of credibility will be futile. All of Cuba's radio stations are run by the government, but along the northwest coast you can tune in to radio stations from southern Florida. Those Cubans who listen surreptitiously to Radio Martí are more interested in the music than the right-wing, anti-Castro messages.

Even though few Cubans are interested in messages of freedom and solidarity, President **George W. Bush** uses Radio Martí to broadcast in Spanish to commemorate Cuban Independence Day (May 20) every year. The purpose of this White House propaganda is not to rally Cubans on the island to rise up and depose Fidel Castro, but to assuage the anger of Cuban Americans and hope that they will vote the Republican ticket in national elections. Periodic efforts by members of the U.S. Congress to shut down the two Martís have been futile. To keep the two Martís alive and well, the **Helms-Burton Law** indicates that a transition government in Cuba must make sure that the air waves are free of jamming, a common practice under Fidel Castro. The Bush administration's new measures to bring down the Castro regime, announced in 2004, call for military aircraft to transmit TV and Radio Martí signals onto the island, a costly endeavor that if carried out will violate international broadcasting regulations. *See also* Propaganda; Media; Public Opinion; Reich, Otto.

Suggested Reading

Ann Louise Bardach, *Cuba Confidential: Love and Vengeance in Miami and Havana* (New York: Random House, 2002); Marcela Sánchez, "U.S. Propaganda Sputters in Anti-Castro Crusade," *Washington Post* (May 23, 2003).

Reagan, Ronald W. (1911–2004) Governor of California (1966–1974) and president of the United States (1981–1989) whose career as a radio sportscaster and Hollywood actor helped him enter the political arena late and excel as a communicator of conservative values, such as anti-communism, free-market economics, patriotism, small government, and support for **friendly dictators**, in the aftermath of the Watergate scandal, Middle East **terrorism**, and the failures of the **Carter** administration. Born in Tampico, Illinois, Reagan moved frequently as his alcoholic father searched for work during the Depression. He graduated from Eureka College, a small Disciples of Christ school in his native Illinois; his first career was as a sportscaster in Iowa. He moved to Hollywood in 1937 and spent the next twenty-five years as a movie actor, appearing in over fifty films. During **World War II**, he served in the U.S. Army where he narrated **propaganda** films in Culver City, California, a job that allowed him to avoid combat and live off base. As head of the Screen Actors Guild in the early years of the **Cold War**, Reagan became active in union politics and spearheaded efforts to purge alleged Communists from the film industry. After his film career hit the skids in the late 1940s and 1950s, he divorced Jane Wyman and married Nancy Davis and in the process changed from a New Deal Democrat to a conservative Republican. Reagan made the shift to television, working as a corporate spokesman for General Electric before becoming governor of California in 1966. By 1970, Ronald Reagan had emerged as a prominent conservative political figure and started to lay the groundwork for a run for the Republican presidential nomination. He challenged President Gerald R. **Ford** in 1976, arguing that the United States lacked sufficient military strength to fight the Soviet Union and vigorously opposed any "give-away" of the Panama Canal. Reagan refined his political message after losing the nomination to Gerald Ford in 1976 and in 1980 defeated Jimmy Carter to begin a two-term presidency determined to restore U.S. power in the world.

Despite the standard line that Reagan won the Cold War, more critical assessments give far more credit to the long and steady policy of containment by previous administrations, Mikhail Gorbachev's non-violent response to Soviet-bloc uprisings, and Soviet military backwardness. Reagan's desire to bring freedom and **democracy** to Soviet-bloc nations was not matched by his concern for democracy and **human rights** in Latin America where his policies often proved to be counterproductive to American values. In Argentina, the Reagan administration aligned the United States with fascist (and anti-Semitic) military juntas; in El Salvador and Guatemala, Reagan backed military regimes that massacred hundreds of thousands of civilians. In Chile, Reagan endorsed the tyrant Augusto **Pinochet** by normalizing relations and praising the junta's economic policies. In an effort to defeat the **Sandinista** government in Nicaragua, Reagan pursued a quasi-secret war that violated **international law** and circumvented Congress to fund **Contra** rebels who engaged in documented human rights abuses and worked with suspected **drug traffickers**. Reagan was the first president to tackle the war on drugs as a component of foreign policy by pushing anti-drug measures through Congress, allocating additional funds for the policy, and merging military and civilian law enforcement authorities to fight the war on drugs.

The **Iran-Contra scandal** was the most damaging to the Reagan presidency and U.S.–Latin American relations because it undercut the president's anti-terrorism policy, revealed glaring violations of law, and tarnished Reagan's reputation and credibility and undermined his administration's effectiveness. Many people questioned Reagan's resolve on his drug war when evidence began to surface that cargo planes carrying weapons shipments to the Contras were returning to the United States with illicit drugs with no questions asked. When public pressure to investigate such allegations mounted, the U.S. Senate initiated hearings under the leadership of Senator John F. **Kerry**, a Democrat from Massachusetts. The Kerry Commission found evidence that the U.S. government had turned a blind eye to "freedom fighter" involvement in the drug trade and that **Central Intelligence Agency (CIA)**–sponsored **covert operations** were involved with drug smuggling. Nevertheless, Reagan managed to finish the last two years of his presidency without impeachment proceedings due in large part to the incriminating documents that were destroyed by **National Security Council (NSC)** aide Oliver **North**. The fact that most of the nation's elite either supported Reagan or, in the case of the opposition, were afraid to criticize him, allowed Reagan to leave office on a positive note. However, critics charged that by the time Reagan left office there was little to show for the drug war; tough drug penalties did not deter many Americans from the risk of jail, drug use and crime increased, and the U.S. prison population swelled to historic levels, making the United States the world's leader in terms of the proportion of its population in prison.

Known as the Teflon President, President Reagan led a charmed life in his relationship with the **media**; his foreign policy **scandals and blunders** never seemed to touch him directly and his advisers excelled in turning the media, especially television, into a national billboard for his policies. According to many journalists, politicians, and commentators, much of the positive coverage of President Reagan stemmed from his sunny personality, self-censorship by the press itself because ordinary Americans were tired of hearing critical assessments of the avuncular president, and the power of the public relations apparatus crafted by the White House that provided interesting stories and appealing visuals. Reagan's ability to get away with deceptions also rested to a great extent on his skillful use of the manipulative techniques of Hollywood. As Nathan Miller (1984: 68) points out, "Employing an array of acting and script writing clichés—the self-deprecating joke; the heartwarming anecdote; the boyish grin; the look of principled determination; even, on occasion, the catch in the voice and the hint of a tear in the eye—he has cast himself in the classic Hollywood role of the embattled Honest Politician, a role that was most memorably played by his friend Jimmy Stewart, in *Mr. Smith Goes to Washington*." After leaving office in 1989, Reagan retired to California to work on his memoirs, *An American Life* (1990). After being diagnosed with Alzheimer's disease in the early 1990s, Reagan spent the rest of his life confined to his home in southern California and out of the public eye. During this time, the Reagan family became outspoken supporters of stem-cell research as a way to alleviate the painful disease that inflict so many. *See also* Grenada Invasion (1983); Intervention and Non-Intervention; Political Cartoons; Reagan Doctrine.

Suggested Reading

William M. LeoGrande, *Our Own Backyard: The United States in Central America, 1977–1992* (Chapel Hill: University of North Carolina Press, 1998); James Nathan Miller, "Ronald Reagan and the Techniques of Deception," *Atlantic Monthly* (February 1984); Ronald Reagan, *An American Life* (New York: Simon and Schuster, 1990).

Reagan Doctrine A controversial foreign policy of President Ronald **Reagan** that called for aid to all anti-Communist insurgents fighting Soviet-backed Marxist regimes in Asia, Africa, and Latin America. Unlike other presidential **doctrines**, the Reagan Doctrine is not the result of a single definitive statement contained in a presidential speech. The doctrine emerged from Reagan's speeches during the 1980 presidential campaign in which he criticized President **Carter** for not backing anti-Communist **friendly dictators** and gained momentum with the creation and support of the Nicaraguan **Contras** and the U.S. invasion of Grenada in 1983. To gain domestic support for his controversial foreign policy, President Reagan referred to his anti-Communist guerrillas as a "democratic resistance" and "freedom fighters," the moral equivalent of those who fought in the American War of Independence. In Reagan's view, the Nicaraguan **Sandinistas** had betrayed their revolution, brutalized their own land, and were in the process of exporting their terror throughout Latin America. Political theorist Jeane **Kirkpatrick** supplied Reagan with the logic of supporting friendly authoritarians over other kinds of regimes: authoritarian regimes (civilian and military) deserve U.S. support because they could be influenced and pressured to change into more democratic regimes; totalitarian, or any leftist government, deserved U.S. opposition because they invariably resisted such "conversion." By supplying aid to indigenous resistance groups, whether in Afghanistan or Nicaragua, the United States could carry out a low-cost war against the Soviets.

The Reagan Doctrine was costly and failed to achieve its diplomatic objectives in Latin America. The doctrine relied on both covert (mining Nicaragua's harbors and organizing and funding the contras) and overt (supplying the contras in Honduras and providing billions of dollars in military and economic aid to El Salvador and other Central American countries) means of achieving U.S. foreign policy objectives. The methods attached to the Reagan Doctrine led to the **Iran-Contra scandal** and a negative ruling by the **International Court of Justice (ICJ)** in *Nicaragua v. The United States of America* for the **Central Intelligence Agency (CIA)** mining of Nicaragua's harbors. The Reagan Doctrine was premised on the belief that any Communist victory constituted an irreversible trend in hostile regimes. To carry out the goals of the Reagan Doctrine required the United States to be militarily involved throughout the world, and the exclusion of hostile forces from the Western Hemisphere was necessary to prevent the United States from being tied down in areas close to its southern border. Historian Gaddis Smith (1994) calls this the Reagan Corollary to the **Monroe Doctrine**. Reagan tried to justify his more offensive foreign policy by exaggerating the threat posed by indigenous forces with ties to the Soviet Union and Cuba. The Iran-Contra scandal, the electoral defeat of leftist president Daniel Ortega of Nicaragua, and the collapse of the Soviet Union served to repudiate the Reagan Doctrine as it was articulated during his administration. *See also* Cold War; Domino Theory; Regime Change.

Suggested Reading

Alexander Haig, Jr., *Caveat: Realism, Reagan and Foreign Policy* (New York: Macmillan, 1984); Charles Krauthammer, "Morality and the Reagan Doctrine: The Rights and Wrongs of Guerrilla Warfare," *The New Republic*, 17 (February 1986); Mark P. Lagon, *The Reagan Doctrine: Sources of American Conduct in the Cold War's Last Chapter* (Westport, CT: Praeger, 1994); Constantine C. Menges, *Inside the National Security Council: The True Story of the Making and the Unmaking of Reagan's Foreign Policy* (New York: Simon and Schuster, 1988); William Ratliff, "The Reagan Doctrine and the Contras," in Georges A. Fauriol, ed., *Security in the Americas* (Washington, DC: National Defense University Press, 1989); William Schneider, "Rambo and Reality: Having it Both Ways," in Kenneth A. Oye, Robert J. Lieber, and Donald Rothchild, eds., *Eagle Resurgent? The Reagan Era in American Foreign Policy* (Boston: Little, Brown, 1987); Gaddis Smith, *The Last Years of the Monroe Doctrine, 1945–1993* (New York: Hill and Wang, 1994).

Receiverships. *See* Dollar Diplomacy

Recognition and Non-Recognition U.S. presidents have the power of diplomatic recognition and non-recognition of governments and have used it many times when

Latin American governments change leadership. It is often a potent weapon for the president since recognition involves the formal exchange of ambassadorial credentials and the decision to supply economic and military assistance. The power of recognition and non-recognition determines the basis for exchanging diplomats, trading, borrowing money, and protecting one's citizens. Under **international law**, states have the right to recognize a newly independent state or a state's new government. At times the United States has regularly refused to recognize military governments that overthrew civilian elected ones, expressing a determined effort to curry favor with democracies over **dictatorships**. For much of the nineteenth century the United States recognized governments on the basis of Jefferson's view that it was unwise to deny any nation the right to govern itself according to whatever form it wished and at the same time had the will of the nation behind it. President Woodrow **Wilson** found this unworkable in dealing with Latin American governments and implemented a new principle that to be recognized, a government must have been established through constitutional means. Wilson used recognition as a weapon to dictate the behavior of Latin American governments, often with little impact on revolutionaries, corrupt governments, and predatory foreign powers such as Germany.

Working through the **Organization of American States (OAS)**, the United States has backed collective non-recognition of illegal transfers of power, particularly when a military junta removed a democratically elected leaders. President Rómulo **Betancourt** of Venezuela advocated such a policy, and a Mexican diplomat, Carlos Tobar of Mexico, became well known for his proposal to establish a policy of joint intervention to put an end to **revolutions** and refuse recognition of de facto governments that came to power through a revolution, or a coup d'état against constitutional regimes.

International law also recognizes the right of sovereign governments to grant belligerency status to anti-government insurgents (belligerents) who are fighting to overthrow an existing government, in effect giving non-governmental fighters legal status of being at war. When this happens, an armed struggle ceases being a domestic, internal matter, and allows outside states to aid openly the insurgents by selling them arms and sending them money. There are many examples of this form of recognition, including the popular **Sandinista**-led insurrection against the **Somoza** Debayle dictatorship in Nicaragua in 1979. After Somoza was overthrown in July 1979, the **Reagan** administration maintained diplomatic relations with Managua even while covertly attempting to overthrow the Sandinista government. The United States broke relations with Fidel **Castro**'s Cuba in 1961 and has refused to consider full diplomatic ties ever since. After almost two decades of not having an embassy in Havana, the **Carter** administration decided in 1979 to create an "interest section" run by a friendly third country (the Swiss embassy for the United States; the Czech Embassy for the Cubans) out of its own diplomatic facilities as a way to maintain contact after the diplomatic break years earlier. This device enabled the two countries' representatives to negotiate agreements without having official diplomatic relations. The United States refuses to give Cuba full recognition after almost forty-five years without a U.S. ambassador in Havana. *See also* Ambassadors; Tobar Doctrine.

Suggested Reading

U.S. Department of State, "U.S. Policy Toward Latin America: Recognition and Non-Recognition of Governments and Interruptions in Diplomatic Relations, 1933–1974," (Washington, DC: Bureau of Public Affairs, U.S. Department of State, June 1975); Larman C. Wilson and David W. Dent, *Historical Dictionary of Inter-American Organizations* (Lanham, MD: Scarecrow Press, 1998).

Regime Change A process of dislodging leaders of a foreign government based on a threat-based judgment requiring the use of force or **intervention**. The U.S. justification for changing regimes in Latin America has shifted over the years, from keeping out foreign powers and regime ideas (fascism, communism, monarchism) and threats (**drug trafficking**, **terrorism**, ethnic cleansing, petroleum wealth) to the promotion of **democracy** and **human rights**. During the **Cold War** a great deal of covert action was directed at regime change abroad. Although Washington has committed its own troops to achieve these tasks, it has also funded rebel insurgencies, hired Mafia assassins, organized military coups, and encouraged popular non-violent uprisings to get rid of troublesome regimes. Other non-violent methods of regime change include diplomatic pressure, **economic sanctions**, international boycotts, **propaganda**, trade embargoes, and support for political factions sympathetic to the United States. President **George W. Bush**'s strategy for the war on terrorism included a new doctrine of "pre-emptive strikes" to remove (and capture) recalcitrant leaders such as Saddam Hussein of Iraq in 2003. Roger Noriega, assistant secretary of state for Western Hemisphere affairs, told Congress in 2003 that "The President [George W. Bush] is determined to see the end of the **Castro** regime and the dismantling of the apparatus that has kept him in office for so long." During the Cold War the fight against Communist expansion (in what was often referred to as the U.S. "backyard") prompted Washington to remove left-leaning governments in Guatemala, Cuba, the Dominican Republic, Nicaragua, Guyana, Grenada, and Chile. With the end of the Cold War in 1989–1991, the United States has justified military intervention and regime change on the grounds of protecting human rights, disarmament, and promoting democracy. The rhetoric used to justify regime change and democracy promotion has helped to build the case for overt or covert intervention, but the U.S. record of installing democracy after getting rid of a brutal dictator is poor, according to experts who have studied the matter. While it is tempting to try to transform unfriendly and brutal regimes to pluralist democracies friendly to the United States, the reality is far more complex, costly, and time-consuming than the United States can implement with success. **Covert operations** that pervert democracy in the name of "saving democracy" do not help instill a democracy culture from which a compliant regime can form and grow. For example, the **Central Intelligence Agency (CIA)**–organized military coup that overthrew the democratically elected and progressive government of Jacobo **Arbenz** in 1954 was a disaster for Guatemala. The removal of Arbenz led to forty years of **death squads**, torture, disappearances, mass executions, and genocide, indisputably one of the most inhuman chapters in U.S.–Latin American relations. In many cases the justifications for regime change are false or grossly exaggerated, making the democratic reconstruction even more dubious. When Latin American democracies have been overthrown by the United States, as was the case in Brazil, Chile, and Guatemala, the prevailing view in Washington was that "saving the country from communism" made the whole effort worthwhile. When "**blowback**" results from these misguided efforts, there is a tendency to divert attention from the obvious connection to past policies. The Chilean opposition to a U.S.–led war against Iraq in 2003 was based largely on the events of September 11, 1973, when a military coup supported by Washington achieved "regime change" by overthrowing the democratically elected government of Salvador **Allende**. General Augusto **Pinochet** replaced Allende and conducted a brutal **dictatorship** in which thousands were murdered or disappeared. After seventeen years of military repression, Chile finally achieved its liberation—in spite of the United States, not because of the wisdom of American foreign policy. Restoring President Jean-Bertrand **Aristide** to Haiti during the **Clinton** years did not result in any meaningful movement toward democracy and pluralism. Some scholars argue that covert regime change that occurred during the Cold War era may be over because governments and leaders have learned to protect themselves against covert interventions. The United States backed failed coups attempts against General Manuel Antonio **Noriega**, Hugo Chávez, and Saddam Hussein. In a *New York Times*/CBS News Poll conducted in July 2004 among a sample of registered voters, only 25 percent of these voters indicated that the "United States should try to change a dictatorship to a democracy where it can." While the Bush Doctrine of "pre-emptive" intervention may resonate within some government agencies in Washington, and among a few allies, the level of support for such a doctrine would appear to be minimal. Nevertheless, with the collapse of the Soviet Union, the United States is more likely to resort to military force and pre-emptive strikes knowing that it does not have to contend with opposition from the Soviets and the risk of a wider, and costly, war with its major adversary. *See also* Backyard Metaphor; Threat Perception/Assessment.

Suggested Reading

Peter Ford, "Regime Change," *Christian Science Monitor* (January 27, 2003); David E. Rosenbaum and Janet Elder, "Delegates Lean Left and Oppose the War," *New York Times* (July 25, 2004); Wayne S. Smith, "Bush and Cuba: Still the Full Moon," *NACLA Report on the Americas* (September/October 2004); Martin Staniland, ed., *Falling Friends: The United States and Regime Change Abroad* (Boulder, CO: Westview Press, 1991).

Reich, Otto Juan (1945–) Conservative businessman and diplomat, with close ties to Republican Party leaders in Washington, members of the Cuban American community in Miami, Florida, and an adviser to multinational corporations involved in trade and economic development in Latin America. Born in Cuba in 1945, his father was an Austrian Jew who fled the Nazis in 1938 for safe haven in the Caribbean, then ruled mostly by fascist right-wing dictators. Reich's father saw similarities between the style and rhetoric of Hitler and Fidel **Castro** that prompted the family's move to the United States. Otto J. Reich was fifteen when he fled Cuba for the United States. He studied international relations at the University of North Carolina, received a master's degree in Latin American affairs at Georgetown University, and then took a job with the Florida Department of Commerce. Known for his ardent anti-Communist views, Otto Reich emerged in the early 1980s as the director of the **Council of the Americas (COA)** in Washington, D.C. He was picked by President Ronald **Reagan** to head the Office of Public Diplomacy in the **State Department** from 1983 to 1986, a secretive job in which he promoted the **Contra** guerrillas fighting the **Sandinistas** in Nicaragua. Reich became a master of deception with his pro-Contra **propaganda** in the United States, but once the **Iran-Contra scandal** was exposed Reich also got dragged into the affair for engaging in what the U.S. comptroller general called "prohibited, covert propaganda activities." Although he was not accused of breaking laws, his value to the anti-Castro cause was undermined by his work in the State Department. He left Washington to become U.S. ambassador to Venezuela in 1986. When he left this post he worked as a corporate lobbyist in the 1990s, helping to sell F-16 jets to Chile and representing Bacardi rum in a trademark dispute with Castro's Cuba. He is revered in some Latin American countries where he is portrayed as a key figure in Washington's dislike for leftist politicians, particularly Fidel Castro, Hugo Chávez, and Daniel Ortega, the former head of the Nicaraguan revolution.

The selection of **George W. Bush** in the 2000 election and the defeat of Al Gore opened the door for Reich's return to Washington with a post dealing with Latin American affairs. In 2001 President Bush nominated him to the position of assistant secretary of state for Western Hemisphere affairs, a position he had coveted for years. When the Senate refused to confirm him because of his strong political views, he received a "recess appointment" (a maneuver that allows the U.S. president to side-step the Senate confirmation process with a one-year temporary appointment) in 2002 that allowed him to take the position for one year. Although in office for less than a year, Reich was a key figure in the bungled U.S. support for the coup leaders who failed in an effort to topple Venezuelan President Hugo Chávez in April 2002 and in keeping the trade embargo against Cuba insulated from attacks by trade proponents in Congress. Once his temporary appointment expired, Reich remained in limbo, receiving less senior titles because a growing number of Democrats and Republicans announced that they would oppose his nomination. Senator Christopher Dodd (D-CT) called Reich an unreconstructed cold warrior addicted to a failing Cuba policy while Senator Richard Lugar and a growing chorus of Republicans opposed Reich because of his refusal to back a policy of lifting the trade embargo on Cuba. After President Bush named Roger Noriega, a Mexican American with diplomatic credentials to be assistant secretary of state for Western Hemisphere affairs, Reich was given a low-level advisory position in the **National Security Council (NSC)**. With his close ties to the Bush family dynasty, including Florida Governor Jeb Bush, and the **Cuba Lobby**, Reich was able to influence U.S.–Latin American relations that reflected his conservative, anti-leftist roots.

As special envoy for the Western Hemisphere, Reich managed to remain an adviser to President George W. Bush until his resignation in June 2004. He continued to exert power over U.S.–Latin American relations during the last months of his special envoy position. In the case of the 2004 presidential election in El Salvador, Otto Reich made sure that Antonio Saca, a conservative pro-American businessman, received the endorsement of the Bush White House while at the same time condemning the former Communist guerrilla, Schafik Handal, as an admirer of Fidel Castro and Hugo Chávez. "We could not have the same confidence," proclaimed Reich, "in an El Salvador led by a person who is obviously an admirer of Fidel Castro and of Hugo Chávez" (Weiner, 2004). It is this kind of interference in the democratic process that angers political party leaders in Latin America and contributes to anti-American sentiment. Reich cited "personal and financial reasons" for his resignation, but the declining importance of Latin America in the wake of the **September 11, 2001**, attacks gave him far less power in the area of inter-American affairs than he once had and enjoyed. *See also* Anti-Americanism; Washington Policymakers.

Suggested Reading

James Dao, "An American Diplomat Waits in Political Limbo," *New York Times* (December 15, 2002); Tim Weiner, "Bush Envoy Puts Latin Post, and a Stormy Past, Behind Him," *New York Times* (June 17, 2004).

Revolutions Revolutions are the result of individual or group violence directed against the state apparatus. Because of the scope of their ultimate goal—a relatively quick and fundamental transformation of the organizations of the state, distribution of values, and the class structure—revolutions are often bloody and difficult to achieve, particularly if they are opposed by the United States. In general, Latin American revolutionaries have employed four broad strategies of revolutionary change: **terrorism**, **guerrilla warfare**, revolution from above, and "democratic" revolutionary change. In some cases, various strategies become intertwined such as when bandits with pecuniary interests become politically motivated and engage in guerrilla warfare. The U.S. Marines labeled Nicaraguan rebel Augusto **Sandino** a "bandit" and invaded Nicaragua in the 1920s to capture him and his Defending Army of National Sovereignty, but after six years of searching in vain were unable to find and capture the popular anti-imperialist rebel.

Revolts and revolutions in Latin America were common during the twentieth century, often coinciding with heightened concerns about threats to U.S. security from extra-hemispheric enemies. There are only a few Latin American countries that have experienced a real social revolution, namely ones in which rapid change is social, economic, political, and cultural. It is noteworthy that most of Latin

America's revolutions occurred in countries located between the Panama Canal and the southern border of the United States. This would include the most dramatic and significant revolutions in Mexico (1910–1917), Guatemala (1944–1954) Cuba (1959–), and Nicaragua (1979–1989). In each case, economic, political, and international factors contributed to the uprising that deposed corrupt elites and deep-rooted elite alliances with the United States. Those who have studied Latin American revolutions indicate there is no single cause that explains all revolutions. In most cases, Latin American revolutions have been associated with states that have little political legitimacy, intra-elite conflict, and deep-rooted grievances that lead to popular uprisings. Economic and social inequality, often tied to patterns of landownership and political control, are major sparks to ignite revolutionary activity. Intellectual elites—journalists, lawyers, writers, and teachers—play an important pre-revolutionary role by their relentless attacks on the old regime. Cuba's Fidel **Castro** was only one of many Cuban intellectuals who criticized regime performance and encouraged popular revolt as a form of "cleansing" the rot from the existing regime. Revolutions gain strength from nationalist and anti-imperialist ideology that promises a new world when foreign capitalists and hegemonic bureaucrats are removed from native soil. U.S. responses to revolutionary change in Latin America often depends on the pace and degree of change being advanced by the revolutionary leadership. In his classic study of revolutionary movements in Latin America, Cole Blasier finds that Latin American revolutions tend to pass through three stages—rebellion, reformism, and revolutionary change—and hostile responses can often produce the exact opposite of what **Washington policymakers** intended. The United States was able to come to terms with the Mexican and Bolivian revolutionaries, but suppressed, or attempted to suppress, the revolutions in Guatemala, Cuba, and Nicaragua. Blasier (1976: 273) concludes his study by saying, "The United States has often brought on itself what it most seeks to avoid, the interference of rival Great Powers in the hemisphere. In this sense, the United States has long been its own worst enemy in Latin America. Latin American governments tend not to appeal to extra-hemispheric powers for assistance, especially military assistance, without good reason."

What have Latin American revolutions accomplished? There is no doubt that judging revolutions is a difficult and controversial process; however, we can ascribe the following changes to revolutions, regardless of their duration. On the positive side, revolutions have redistributed land and brought to an end oppressive systems of land tenure, eliminated dictators, many of whom were on friendly terms with the United States, removed the hereditary privileges of traditional aristocracies, decreased illiteracy, improved the lot of minorities and women, brought better education and health care, and a much stronger sense of national identity. There are clearly areas where Latin American revolutions have failed or been less successful: greater freedom, material well-being, equality for all. In some cases, revolutions have led to stronger **dictatorships** than the ones they replaced. Revolutions designed to improve the lot of the peasantry have faced difficulties in diverting resources to other priorities once the initial policies designed to benefit workers and peasants were carried out. The tendency of inequality to reassert itself after revolution has been evident in Cuba after the collapse of Soviet subsidies in the early 1990s. While it is true that revolutionary outcomes are unpredictable and costly, there will always be a search for enlightened leadership who can address the inequalities in society and the corruption in government that continue to plague Latin American nations. *See also* Friendly Dictators; German Threat; Guerrilla Warfare; Guevara, Ernesto "Che"; Threat Perception/Assessment; Tobar Doctrine; Wilson, Woodrow Thomas.

Suggested Reading

Cole Blasier, *The Hovering Giant: U.S. Response to Revolutionary Change in Latin America* (Pittsburgh: University of Pittsburgh Press, 1976); Michael D. Gambone, *Capturing the Revolution: The United States, Central America, and Nicaragua, 1961–1972* (Westport, CT: Praeger, 2001); Jack Goldstone, ed., *The Encyclopedia of Political Revolutions* (Washington, DC: Congressional Quarterly Press, 1998); Goldstone, ed., *Revolutions: Theoretical, Comparative, and Historical Studies* (San Diego: Harcourt, Brace Jovanovich, 1986); Brian Meeks, *Caribbean Revolutions and Revolutionary Theory: An Assessment of Cuba, Nicaragua, and Grenada* (London: Macmillan, 1993); James F. Rochlin, *Vanguard Revolutionaries in Latin America: Peru, Colombia, Mexico* (Boulder, CO: Lynne Rienner, 2003); Eric Selbin, *Modern Latin American Revolutions* (Boulder, CO: Westview Press, 1993); Timothy P. Wickham-Crowley, *Exploring Revolution: Essays on Latin American Insurgencies and Revolutionary Theory* (Armonk, NY: M.E. Sharpe, 1991).

Rio Treaty. *See* Inter-American Treaty of Reciprocal Assistance (1947)

Rockefeller, Nelson Aldrich (1908–1979) Nelson A. Rockefeller played a major role in U.S.–Latin American relations from the 1930s to the 1970s. He was involved in banking, international business, inter-American trade, philanthropy, art collecting, and the conduct of American foreign policy. In public office, he headed the war agency with responsibility for promoting inter-American trade and countering Nazi propaganda (1940–1944); he was also assistant secretary for American Republic Affairs (1944–1945), governor of New York (1958–1973), and vice-president of the United States (1974–1977). Born into the wealthy Rockefeller family of New York, Nelson Rockefeller believed in **Pan-Americanism** and the social responsibilities of private ownership, a doctrine he practiced as director of the Creole Petroleum Corporation in Venezuela from 1935 to 1940.

Born in Bar Harbor, Maine, in 1908, the son of John D. Rockefeller, Jr., and grandson of Standard Oil millionaire John D. Rockefeller, Nelson Rockefeller graduated from Dartmouth College in 1930 and after a year of travel worked for Chase National Bank. During the 1930s he developed an interest in Latin America that stimulated his interest in collecting Mexican pre-Columbian and contemporary art. He hired Mexican muralist Diego Rivera to paint a large mural for the lobby for the new Rockefeller Center in midtown Manhattan and became friends with Miguel Covarrubias, a writer and caricaturist for the *New Yorker*. A controversial likeness of Lenin sketched in the New York mural led to a bitter feud with Rivera, and Rockefeller had the partially completed mural destroyed rather than accept the Russian anti-capitalist in his building.

Alarmed over Germany's growing influence throughout Latin America, Rockefeller wrote a memo to President **Franklin D. Roosevelt** in 1938 urging him to launch a **propaganda** counter-offensive. Roosevelt hired Rockefeller as director of the Office of the Coordinator of Inter-American Affairs (OCIAA), where he improved economic ties in the hemisphere by securing U.S. markets for Latin American goods formerly sold to Europe. To counter Nazi influence in Latin America, Rockefeller used motion pictures, recorded radio programs, and magazine articles to counter the **German threat** and build support among Latin American countries for the war aims of the United States. Rockefeller's OCIAA used radio and filmmaking to bolster support for the war and goodwill throughout Latin America. Walt Disney was hired to make a goodwill tour of Latin America to see if he might be able to promote the war with entertainment propaganda. On his return, Disney made two musical films—*Saludos Amigos* (1943) and *The Three Caballeros* (1945) in which the people of Latin America were portrayed in a positive way, a first for Hollywood.

Although Rockefeller played a major role in wartime security and anti-Nazi propaganda, his major contribution was to create the first U.S. economic assistance program for Mexico and the rest of Latin America. President Harry S. **Truman** named him chairman of the International Development Advisory Board, a position he used to influence Latin American affairs by funding economic and social development projects. While assistant secretary of American Republic Affairs he signed the Act of Chapultepec for the United States in 1945. During the 1950s and 1960s he worked closely with the **Central Intelligence Agency (CIA)** and ultraconservative religious organizations to help spread American values and protect American interests. He was instrumental in launching the career of Henry A. **Kissinger** by introducing him to Richard **Nixon** in the 1960s.

In 1969, while governor of New York, Nelson Rockefeller was appointed by President Richard Nixon to head a fact-finding mission to Latin America, but his entourage was met by anti-American demonstrations and violence at each of his stops, and some of his recommendations for U.S.–Latin American policy paved the way for the rise in military **dictatorships**. After serving as vice-president of the United States (1974–1977) he left politics and devoted his life to his artistic interests. Nelson A. Rockefeller died in New York City on January 26, 1979. *See also* Anti-Americanism.

Suggested Reading

J. Lloyd Mecham, *The United States and Inter-American Security, 1889–1960* (Austin: University of Texas Press, 1961); Joseph E. Persico, *The Imperial Rockefeller: A Biography of Nelson A. Rockefeller* (New York: Simon and Schuster, 1981); Cary Reich, *The Life of Nelson A. Rockefeller: Worlds to Conquer, 1908–1958* (New York: Doubleday, 1996); Nelson A. Rockefeller, *Unity, Freedom & Peace* (New York: Random House, 1968); *New York Times* (January 27–28,

1979); Randall B. Woods, *The Roosevelt Foreign Policy Establishment and the "Good Neighbor": The United States and Argentina, 1941–1945* (Lawrence: Regents Press of Kansas, 1979).

Roosevelt, Franklin Delano (1882–1945) Lawyer, politician, and U.S. president (1933–1945) known for his efforts to improve U.S.–Latin American relations after decades of unilateral **intervention**, military occupation, and economic paternalism. The change in U.S. behavior toward Latin America, known as the **Good Neighbor Policy**, rejected the interventionist features of U.S. **imperialism** in favor of policy coordination, economic symbiosis, cultural appreciation, and a shared heritage. However, the pledge of non-intervention also resulted in having to tolerate dictators who often undermined U.S. interests by pursuing policy agendas that disrupted regional harmony or threatened U.S. **hegemony** in Latin America. Born in Hyde Park, New York, Roosevelt graduated from Harvard and attended Columbia Law School before being admitted to the bar. He then practiced law and served in the New York State Senate before being appointed assistant secretary of the Navy in 1913 by President Woodrow **Wilson**. Between his unsuccessful run for vice-president in 1920 and his presidential election in 1932, Roosevelt was stricken with polio, continued to practice law, and was elected governor of New York (1928–1932). As president, Roosevelt pursued a variety of progressive legislation to reform public policy in the wake of the great Depression, was re-elected three times and died in office on April 12, 1945.

The main features of the Good Neighbor Policy—non-intervention, trade reciprocity, multilateral consultation—were tentatively established during the administration of Herbert **Hoover** (1929–1933), which rejected the **Roosevelt Corollary to the Monroe Doctrine**, significantly reduced U.S. intervention in the Caribbean, and put more emphasis on **Pan-Americanism** and mutual understanding. Franklin D. Roosevelt (FDR) recognized the importance of a dramatic change in U.S.–Latin American relations and explicitly enunciated the policy and expanded on earlier Republican efforts. In his inaugural address on March 4, 1933, FDR vowed that "in the field of foreign policy I would dedicate this nation to the policy of the good neighbor." In a Pan American Day speech the following month, Roosevelt applied the Good Neighbor Policy to Latin America and emphasized the change in relationship with the following words: "The essential qualities of a true Pan Americanism must be the same as those which constitute a good neighbor, namely, mutual understanding, a sympathetic appreciation of the other's point of view. It is only in this manner that we can hope to build up a system of which confidence, friendship, and good will are the cornerstones."

Roosevelt's Good Neighbor Policy, as directed by Secretary of State Cordell **Hull** and by Sumner **Welles**, emphasized multilateral efforts to place non-intervention in the internal affairs of states as the cornerstone of inter-American relations. The United States accepted several treaties that spelled out the principle of non-intervention and proceeded to demonstrate its commitment to this principle by the abandonment of its five protectorates—Cuba, Haiti, the Dominican Republic, Nicaragua and Panama—including the abrogation or modification of the treaties on which they were based. Roosevelt appointed "Good Neighbor" ambassadors, refused to send troops when U.S. interests were obviously threatened, signed reciprocal trade agreements with nine Latin American states, and signed treaties of non-aggression with six Latin American states. He stuck to his non-intervention pledge after being pressured by American business to invade Mexico to reverse the expropriation of U.S. oil company interests. President Roosevelt engaged in personal diplomacy by traveling to Latin America and attending inter-American conferences.

President Roosevelt faced the problem of fascist activities in Latin America and the **German threat** by the creation of a cooperative hemispheric security system during **World War II**. His Good Neighbor Policy enabled him to gain the cooperation of most Latin American states during the war, even though this sometimes forced Roosevelt to accept military fascists in Latin America while fighting other forms of fascism abroad. Many of the military and economic assistance programs continued after World War II to the benefit of the United States in dealing with the threat posed by the Soviet Union. Although mostly judged a foreign policy success, the Good Neighbor Policy suffered when the **Cold War** policies of the United States reverted again to unilateral diplomacy, covert intervention, and efforts to coerce an anti-Communist bloc among the Latin American states. Some U.S. **ambassadors** in Latin America were criticized for placating the actions of dictators in the region such as Rafael L. **Trujillo** in the Dominican Republic, Brazil's Getúlio Vargas, and Anastasio **Somoza** Gracía in Nicaragua. However, **dictatorships** and military rule served American interests during the Roosevelt era by maintaining order, eliminating radical reform movements, and protecting American investments. As Schmitz (1999: 84) points out, "strong authoritarian regimes appeared necessary for the Good Neighbor Policy to succeed." In the end, Roosevelt's Good Neighbor Policy proved that the United States could alter its Latin American policy for the sake of hemispheric harmony and cooperation. *See also* Cultural Imperialism; Friendly Dictators; Intervention and Non-Intervention; Rockefeller, Nelson Aldrich.

Suggested Reading

Irwin F. Gellman, *Good Neighbor Diplomacy: United States Policies in Latin America, 1933–1945* (Baltimore, MD: Johns Hopkins University Press, 1979); Edward O. Guerrant, *Roosevelt's Good Neighbor Policy* (Albuquerque: University of New Mexico Press, 1950); Eric Paul Roorda, *The Dictator Next Door: The Good Neighbor Policy and the Trujillo Regime in the Dominican Republic, 1930–1945* (Durham, NC: Duke University Press, 1998); David F. Schmitz, *Thank God They're on Our Side: The United States and Right-Wing Dictatorships, 1921–1965* (Chapel Hill: University of North Carolina Press, 1999).

Roosevelt, Theodore (1858–1919) Republican politician, soldier, statesman, and president of the United States (1901–1909) who played a major role in defining U.S.–Latin American relations during the early twentieth century. He was a staunch advocate of U.S. expansion, a believer in the superiority of the Anglo-Saxon race, and the creator of a macho-based foreign policy that required the use of **Big Stick diplomacy** when dealing with Latin America. Roosevelt championed a war with Spain as early as 1896 and soon after the outbreak of war in 1898 he joined the Rough Riders, a volunteer cavalry unit commanded by Col. Leonard Wood. Roosevelt became a national hero for leading a charge of Rough Riders in the battle of San Juan hill in Eastern Cuba. He took credit for defeating the Spanish, and this feat helped him in his rapid ascent up the ladder of national politics. Roosevelt's reputation for bravado and bluster came from his policies in Latin America, particularly his outspoken views and bellicose rhetoric to establish U.S. **hegemony** in the Western Hemisphere.

Theodore Roosevelt was born in New York City in 1858 to wealthy parents who influenced his early life. He was a sickly child who suffered from asthma, often missed school, and consequently was tutored by a maternal aunt and others. He attended Harvard University in 1876, graduated in 1880, and then entered law school at Columbia University. After one year he dropped out to run for the New York State Assembly. After his election, Roosevelt joined the national guard, served in a number of government posts, ran unsuccessfully for mayor of New York, served as a member of the U.S. Civil Service Commission, and as president of the New York City Police Board. President William **McKinley** appointed Roosevelt assistant secretary of the navy in 1897, but he resigned to command the Rough Riders during the **Spanish-Cuban-American War** the following year. Returning as a hero, Roosevelt was elected governor of New York, became McKinley's running mate with the support of Henry Cabot **Lodge** of Massachusetts, assumed the presidency on September 14, 1901, after the assassination of McKinley while campaigning in Buffalo, New York. At the age of forty-two he became the youngest man to ever serve as president; his popularity led to an easy renomination in 1904 for a four-year term.

During his presidency Theodore Roosevelt played a key role in separating Panama from Colombia, securing a favorable treaty with Panama to complete the construction of the Panama Canal, expanding U.S. power in the Caribbean with the Big Stick and the **Roosevelt Corollary to the Monroe Doctrine**, and keeping predatory Germans out of the U.S. sphere of influence. Charges of corruption were made against President Roosevelt for his handling of the amount of money paid to buy land for the canal and the way the canal's route was decided. The **media** played up accusations that some of the $40 million paid to the French for their defunct project flowed into the hands of Americans with ties to Roosevelt. However, the Panama route was popular in the United States, and the allegations were difficult to prove. Nevertheless, Roosevelt started criminal libel charges in federal court against several newspapers, but his attempt failed.

Roosevelt was famous for his outspoken attitudes toward Latin Americans, views he learned from close friends and racist diplomats who conducted inter-American relations. It didn't matter whether he was dealing with Colombians, Panamanians, Nicaraguans, Venezuelans, Dominicans, or Cubans, Roosevelt rarely had anything favorable to say about these nations. His views were compounded by his lack of patience with people he considered racially inferior and his belief that only the United States has the power and wisdom to solve the hemisphere's problems. In a letter to Henry White about his frustrations with the newly independent Cuban republic, Roosevelt wrote (quoted in Schoultz, 1998: 198–199):

> I am so angry with that infernal little Cuban republic that I would like to wipe its people off the face of the earth. All we have wanted from them was that they would behave themselves and be prosperous and happy so that we would not have to interfere. And now, lo and behold, they have started an utterly unjustifiable and pointless revolution and may get things into such a snarl that we have no alternative save to intervene.

During his frustration with the recalcitrant Colombians over their northern province of Panama, Roosevelt called them "contemptible little creatures," "jack rabbits," and "foolish homicidal corruptionists." For Roosevelt Latin Americans were "children" who required adult supervision, severe punishment (spanking) for misconduct, and constant efforts to change their unruly behavior. Latin Americans were constantly disparaged with terms like "savages," "bandits," "Dagos," "restless and warlike," "spics," and references to the inherent inferior nature of Hispanic culture. Roosevelt was the most outspoken political leader in the United States to assert Anglo-Saxon superiority and the inferiority of people in the Third World. Despite these inherent limitations, Roosevelt dismissed political and cultural explanations and argued that it was the duty of the United States to make these nations fit for self-government and truly free societies; he also found it impossible to believe that Latin Americans would object to the rule and good intentions of the United States. Roosevelt ran on the Bull Moose ticket, a third-party effort that helped Woodrow **Wilson** win the presidency in 1912. He tried to convince Woodrow Wilson of early entry into **World War I** and later opposed Wilson's "peace without victors" strategy of dealing with Germany. *See also* German Threat; Imperialism; Monroe Doctrine (1823); Platt Amendment (1901); Propaganda; Race and Racism; Root, Elihu; Taft, William Howard.

Suggested Reading

Richard H. Collin, *Theodore Roosevelt's Caribbean: The Panama Canal, the Monroe Doctrine, and the Latin American Context* (Baton Rouge: Louisiana State University Press, 1990); Collin, *Theodore Roosevelt, Culture, Diplomacy, and Expansion: A New View of American Imperialism* (Baton Rouge: Louisiana State University Press, 1985); David W. Dent, *The Legacy of the Monroe Doctrine: A Reference Guide to U.S. Involvement in Latin America and the Caribbean* (Westport, CT: Greenwood Press, 1999); David Healy, *Drive to Hegemony: The United States in the Caribbean, 1889–1917* (Madison: University of Wisconsin Press, 1988); Frederick W. Marks III, *Velvet on Iron: The Diplomacy of Theodore Roosevelt* (Lincoln: University of Nebraska Press, 1979); Lars Schoultz, *Beneath the United States: A History of U.S. Policy Toward Latin America* (Cambridge, MA: Harvard University Press, 1998).

Roosevelt Corollary to the Monroe Doctrine In his annual message to Congress in December 1904, **Theodore Roosevelt** enunciated his corollary to the **Monroe Doctrine**, clearly his most comprehensive statement of policy toward Latin America and the Caribbean. Although it restated U.S. responsibility to stand against European **intervention** in the Americas, and promised corrected measures when Latin Americans reneged on international debts, it changed the original message of President James **Monroe** from a prohibition of European involvement in the Western Hemisphere to a policy of pre-emptive intervention as justification for U.S. intervention. Roosevelt's reputation for bravado and bluster was reaffirmed in the policy statement that came to carry his name, but his major intent was to maintain order in the Western Hemisphere by keeping out Europeans rather than expand the **hegemony** of the United States over Latin America. President Roosevelt was convinced that incompetent governments in the Caribbean region might provoke European **imperialism** in violation of the Monroe Doctrine. In a speech that completely changed the meaning of the Monroe Doctrine—in effect making the United States the international policeman and prime debt-collecting agency in the Western Hemisphere, Roosevelt stated the following (quoted in Dent, 1999: 139):

> If a nation shows that it knows how to act with reasonable efficiency and decency in social and political matters; if it keeps order and pays its obligations, it need fear no interference from the United States. Chronic wrongdoing, or an impotence which results in a general loosening of the ties of civilized society, may in America, as elsewhere, ultimately require intervention by some civilized nation, and in the Western Hemisphere the adherence of the United States to the Monroe Doctrine may force the United States, however reluctantly, in flagrant cases of such wrongdoing or impotence, to the exercise of an international police power. . . . It is a mere truism to say that every nation, whether in America or anywhere else, which desires to maintain its freedom, its independence, must ultimately realize that the right of such independence cannot be separated from the responsibility of making good use of it.

The significance of the Roosevelt Corollary to the Monroe Doctrine is that it put forth the belief among many **Washington policymakers** that viewed Latin Americans as people in need of supervision, that the United States had the right to use the Monroe Doctrine to maintain hegemony in the Western Hemisphere, by force if necessary, and Latin Americans would accept such presumptions. The Monroe Doctrine had now been transformed from its original negative and passive character into a more aggressive policy toward Latin America. It soon became the mainstay of **Big Stick diplomacy**, using threats and chronic intervention to produce the desired effect in Latin America. While some Latin American nations welcomed Monroe's message as a form of international protection, the Roosevelt Corollary soon gave way to resentment and hatred of the United States for what Washington actually did in the name of the Monroe Doctrine. The Roosevelt Corollary also carried the legal right of one state to use force against another to collect debts based on a case involving Venezuela that came before the Hague Permanent Court of Arbitration in 1904. At the time of Roosevelt's message to Congress he worried about the **German threat** of intervention in the Dominican Republic being more than a replay of the Venezuelan case. The Roosevelt Corollary to the Monroe Doctrine was followed by the imposition of U.S.–imposed customs collectors who would operate out of financially delinquent governments to ensure that foreign debts were paid on time. The Roosevelt Corollary lasted more than two decades (1904–1928), but it would leave a legacy of hegemony, militarism, paternalism, and racism that would linger into and beyond the period of the **Good Neighbor Policy**. *See also* Anti-Americanism; Doctrines; Intervention and Non-Intervention; Propaganda.

Suggested Reading

Richard H. Collin, *Theodore Roosevelt's Caribbean: The Panama Canal, the Monroe Doctrine, and the Latin American Context* (Baton Rouge: Louisiana State University Press, 1990); Gordon Connell-Smith, *The United States and Latin America: An Historical Analysis of Inter-American Relations* (New York: John Wiley and Sons, 1992); David W. Dent, *The Legacy of the Monroe Doctrine: A Reference Guide to U.S. Involvement in Latin America and the Caribbean* (Westport, CT: Greenwood Press, 1999); David Healy, *Drive to Hegemony: The United States in the Caribbean, 1889–1917* (Madison: University of Wisconsin Press, 1988); Lars Schoultz, *Beneath United States: A History of U.S. Policy Toward Latin America* (Cambridge, MA: Harvard University Press, 1998).

Root, Elihu (1845–1937) As secretary of war under Presidents William **McKinley** and **Theodore Roosevelt** (1899–1904), and secretary of state under Theodore Roosevelt (1905–1909), Elihu Root played a major role in the Latin American policy of the United States. Known as a Republican internationalist or globalist, Root was instrumental in devising the **Platt Amendment** to provide the United States with a protectorate over Cuba and helped President Roosevelt with the **Roosevelt Corollary to the Monroe Doctrine**. Like Roosevelt and many of his close advisers, Root believed in Anglo-Saxon superiority and the inferiority of others, particularly the former colonies of Spain in the aftermath of the **Spanish-Cuban-American War**. Both he and President Roosevelt considered the people of Latin America as children, incapable of self-government and in need of protection and guidance by the more civilized United States. Later, as the senior foreign policy spokesman of the Republican Party, Elihu Root provided the early rationale and logic of supporting right-wing **dictatorships**, believing they represented traditional authority and provided the firmness needed to prepare a country for democratic rule.

Elihu Root was born in Clinton, New York, in 1845, the son of a professor of mathematics at Hamilton College. Root was educated at Hamilton College (B.A., 1864), and the University of the City of New York (law degree, 1867). As a corporate lawyer in New York, Elihu Root had many clients who were leaders of New York society and finance. In 1881 Root met Theodore Roosevelt, a friendship formed based on their mutual conservatism, ties to Harvard, and Root's legal expertise. Before the war with Spain in 1898, Root displayed little interest in Latin American affairs; however, he agreed with Roosevelt and others that the Cuban struggle for freedom was just and that the United States had a right to intervene on humanitarian grounds. Through his friendship with Roosevelt, Root became acquainted with John **Hay**, William Howard **Taft**, and Henry Cabot **Lodge**, key figures who would play major roles in formulating the Latin American policy of the United States.

Although the Platt Amendment was named after Senator Orville H. Platt of Connecticut, five of the eight conditions embodied in the law were Root's. The two key provisions of the amendment gave the United States the right to intervene (point 3) and the right to lease land for naval bases (point 7). It was Root's view that the terms of the Platt Amendment be incorporated into the Cuban Constitution of 1901 and the U.S.–Cuban Treaty of 1903. The Cuban Convention rejected the terms of the Platt Amendment at first, arguing that it was an infringement of sovereignty. In the end, the Cubans were faced with either quasi-independence under the Platt Amendment or a continuation of military rule until the law was agreed to. The Cuban Convention reluctantly accepted Root's demands, and it passed by one vote. By 1903, with Root's diplomatic engineering, the United States possessed a Cuban protectorate and a prize piece of naval real estate at **Guantánamo Bay** on the southeastern end of the island. The genius of the Platt Amendment, according to Elihu Root, was that it avoided total U.S. annexation yet at the same time gave Cuba's its political independence. During his ten years as secretary of war and secretary of state, Root helped create a Latin American policy based on the combined use of U.S. power and **international law**. The Platt Amendment epitomized this mode of thinking since it was both part of Cuba's constitution and a treaty with the United States; by granting the United States the right of **intervention** in Cuba, Root believed that the **Monroe Doctrine** had been transformed from a mere doctrine of national policy to the form of an international treaty sanctioned by the law of nations.

As secretary of state (1905–1909), Elihu Root worked with President Roosevelt to use the Roosevelt Corollary to the Monroe Doctrine to promote hemispheric solidarity and assure stability in Latin America through the use of "international police power" to prevent further European encroachment in the Caribbean. When "chronic wrongdoing" and "impotence" erupted in the Dominican Republic in 1905, Root was forced to find some way to achieve order and financial stability by appointing an American collector of customs. Colombia's loss of Panama due to Roosevelt's role in the revolution of 1903 brought continuing demands for compensation for the loss of its province. Root also spent years working out a diplomatic solution that seemed to assuage the interests of Colombia, Panama, and the United States. However, a change of government in Bogotá rejected Root's terms and the issue of restitution was not settled until the 1920s.

While secretary of state, Elihu Root tried to be a "good neighbor" by promoting peace and goodwill throughout the hemisphere. He went out of his way to make friends with Latin American diplomats in Washington, led a delegation to the Third

Inter-American Conference in Rio de Janeiro in 1906, and tried to bring peace to Central America in 1907. Root's tour of the southern hemisphere was the first time a secretary of state had been outside of the country while in office, and he used the voyage to Brazil to circumnavigate the continent, visiting Uruguay, Argentina, Chile, Peru, Colombia, and Panama. Root's goodwill tour in 1906 was a public relations bonanza: many of the Latin Americans were flattered by Root's presence, and this helped to overcome some of the resentment lingering from the expansion of the Monroe Doctrine, the separation of Panama from Colombia, and the creation of protectorates in the Caribbean and Central America. Root was also a believer in **Pan-Americanism** and worked with his friend Andrew **Carnegie** to plan the construction of a **Pan American Union** building in Washington, D.C. In 1912 Elihu Root was awarded the Nobel Peace Prize for his efforts to establish peaceful relations with Latin America and Japan. Although Root recognized the power of armed force in dealing with the Latin American states, he believed that arbitration and international law could be more useful in enhancing America's place in the world. Root was critical of President Woodrow **Wilson**'s reluctance to enter **World War I**, and after the war was a proponent—with reservations opposed by President Wilson—of American membership in the **League of Nations**. During the inter-war years Root worked on the proposal to establish a Permanent Court of International Justice at the Hague. Root saw the World Court as a way to arbitrate international disputes in a peaceful manner, but he was unable to convince the U.S. Senate of this.

During his later career Root devoted his time to the arts and philanthropy, serving on boards and commissions in New York. He was instrumental in bringing the first major Mexican Art Exhibition to the United States. As a senior foreign policy spokesman for the Republican Party, Elihu Root left a legacy based on the expediency of having supportive allies in Latin America and the Caribbean, regardless of how brutal and corrupt they were in governing their peoples. By supporting right-wing dictatorships in places like Mexico and Nicaragua, Root believed that the United States could maintain political stability and economic growth in Latin America. After his death in 1937, Root's formula for stability and peace had a profound impact on U.S. policy toward Latin America during the **Cold War**. *See also* Teller Amendment or Resolution (1898).

Suggested Reading

David Healy, *U.S. Expansionism: The Imperialist Urge in the 1890s* (Madison: University of Wisconsin Press, 1970); Richard W. Leopold, *Elihu Root and the Conservative Tradition* (Boston: Little, Brown and Company, 1954); *New York Times* (February 8, 1937); David F. Schmitz, *Thank God They're on Our Side: The United States and Right-Wing Dictatorships, 1921–1965* (Chapel Hill: University of North Carolina Press, 1999); Charles W. Toth, "Elihu Root," in Norman A. Graebner, ed., *An Uncertain Tradition: American Secretaries of State in the Twentieth Century* (New York: Random House, 1961).

S

Sandinistas Members of a Nicaraguan guerrilla/revolutionary movement/government (*Frente Sandinista de Liberación Nacional—FSLN*) named after Augusto **Sandino**, a Nicaraguan rebel and popular symbol of resistance to U.S. **imperialism** in Central America. After a successful revolution that toppled the **Somoza** dynasty in 1979, the Sandinistas tried to carry out a socialist revolution with the help of Cuba, the Soviet Union, several European governments, and others throughout Latin America. However, the **Reagan** administration was opposed to the Sandinista revolution, mounted a counter-revolution against it, and ended up undermining democracy at home to force Nicaragua to its knees. The FSLN was forced to relinquish power in 1990 after being defeated by a broad coalition of opposition parties headed by Violeta Barrios de Chamorro. The war-weary electorate realized that a vote for the FSLN candidate, Daniel Ortega, meant more misery and suffering from the U.S.–backed **Contra** war that had contributed needlessly to the deaths of close to 30,000 Nicaraguans. Despite the fact that the FSLN remains the largest political party in Nicaragua, and Daniel Ortega is contemplating another presidential race, the long-term prospects for the party are unclear. *See also* Democracy and Democracy Promotion; Imperialism; Revolutions.

Suggested Reading

Glen Garvin, *Everybody Has His Own Gringo: The CIA and the Contras* (Washington, DC: Brassey's, 1992); Lynn Horton, *Peasants in Arms: War and Peace in the Mountains of Nicaragua, 1979–1994* (Athens: Ohio University Center for International Studies, 1998); David Ryan, *U.S.–Sandinista Diplomatic Relations: Voice of Intolerance* (New York: St. Martin's Press, 1996); Harry E. Vanden and Gary Prevost, *Democracy and Socialism in Sandinista Nicaragua* (Boulder, CO: Lynne Rienner, 1993); Thomas Walker, *Nicaragua in Revolution* (New York: Praeger, 1982); Thomas Walker, ed., *Reagan vs. the Sandinistas* (Boulder, CO: Westview Press, 1987).

Sandino, Augusto César (1895–1934) Nicaraguan freedom fighter and staunch nationalist who fought against the Nicaraguan government and its most important ally, the U.S. Marines who had occupied Nicaragua three times between 1909 and 1932. In an effort to bring the Nicaraguan civil war to an end, President Calvin Coolidge sent Henry L. Stimson to Managua in 1928 to work out an agreement between the two major factions. Stimson managed to bring the two factions together with the 1927 Peace of Tipitapa, offering U.S. supervision of the forthcoming presidential election and the establishment of a national guard. The outcome of the election did not satisfy Sandino, and he refused to accept the peace settlement and disband his forces. Charging the new regime with trampling on Nicaraguan sovereignty, Sandino took to the mountains of northern Nicaragua where he carried out **guerrilla warfare** against the U.S. Marines for the next four years. Despite more than 5,000 American troops in Nicaragua, Sandino managed to avoid capture, keep the spotlight on the objectionable aspects of U.S. **intervention**, and create the image of an anti-imperialist folk-hero struggling against Yankee **imperialism**. When Stimson, now secretary of state, observed the negative effects of U.S. intervention, he announced a date for the withdrawal of American forces after the 1932 elections. The inability to capture the "bandit" Sandino, and the clamor for withdrawal of U.S. forces in the United States prompted President Herbert **Hoover** to admit defeat and order the troops home. As soon as the last marine had departed, Sandino made peace with the winner of the election and agreed to lay down his arms. However, following a dinner party in February 1934, Sandino and some of his aides were murdered after being driven to a Managua airfield by members of the newly created national guard. The evidence of who killed Sandino is murky, but most Nicaraguans are certain the members of the guard were acting on the orders of Anastasio Somoza García, the American-trained leader of the national guard who would become dictator in 1936. The national guard officers who carried out the murder plan said later that they received their instructions from Somoza and that he made it clear that the U.S. ambassador was fully aware of the scheme.

Sandino remains a hero in Nicaragua and throughout Latin America for his nationalist defense of the homeland against U.S. aggression. The revolt that toppled the Somoza dynasty in 1979 was carried out against Somoza's son, Anastasio "Tachito" **Somoza** Debayle, by a group of guerrilla fighters calling themselves **Sandinistas**, after the hero of a previous era. Sandino's anti-imperialist struggle against the United States attracted worldwide attention from other rebels and the **media**, including American journalist Carleton **Beals** who described Sandino in the *Nation* magazine as "a man utterly without vices, with an unequivocal sense of justice, [and] a keen eye for the welfare of the humblest soldier." Beals' enthusiastic reporting on Sandino enhanced his own career as a foreign correspondent, but he was scorned by Washington and conservative Nicaraguans for interfering in the conflict. *See also* Anti-Americanism; Imperialism.

Suggested Reading

Jerome Adams, *Latin American Heroes: Liberators and Patriots From 1500 to the Present* (New York: Ballantine Books, 1991); Carleton Beals, "With Sandino in Nicaragua," *The Nation* (February 22, February 29, March 7, and March 14, 1928 issues); Samuel Flagg Bemis, *The Latin American Policy of the United States: An Historical Interpretation* (New York: Harcourt Brace Jovanovich, 1943); Thomas W. Walker, *Nicaragua, The Land of Sandino* (Boulder, CO: Westview Press, 1981); Bryce Wood, *The Making of the Good Neighbor Policy* (New York: Columbia University Press, 1961).

Scandals and Blunders Faulty decisions, or policies, that result in foreign policy disasters with negative or counter-productive outcomes. Scandals are considered policy actions that violate general values and more specific norms that serve as a guide to the process of implementing a policy; blunders suggest a lack of congruence with the stated policy preferences of key foreign policy elites. The frequency of scandals and blunders associated with U.S. policy in Latin America raises important questions about the role of **Washington policymakers** (particularly the intelligence community) in the conduct of hemispheric relations. Some of the classic cases of foreign policy scandals and blunders associated with U.S.–Latin American relations occurred during the **Cold War**, particularly in dealing with revolutionary governments with anti-American agendas. In its efforts to establish **hegemony** in the Western Hemisphere, the United States committed numerous blunders in Guatemala, Cuba, Chile, El Salvador, Nicaragua, Guyana, and Panama. President John F. **Kennedy** was humbled and frustrated by his policy failure at the **Bay of Pigs**, admitted that it was a colossal blunder, but this admission did not stop his administration from searching for other covert strategies to remove Cuba's leader Fidel **Castro**. The Joint Chiefs of Staff concocted **Operation Northwoods** to provide a pretext for a military invasion to get rid of Fidel Castro in 1962. President Bill **Clinton**, in a speech in Guatemala City in 1999, asserted: "It is important that I state clearly that support for military forces and intelligence units which engaged in violence and widespread repression was wrong, and the United States must not repeat that mistake. . . . The United States will no longer take part in campaigns of repression."

Although the failure at the Bay of Pigs contributed to other blunders in dealing with Castro's Cuba, including a showdown with the Soviets over missiles on the island, few lessons were learned and few paid much attention to the unintended consequences from such foreign policy disasters. As a result, some of the same mistakes were repeated when the time came to deal with the fall of Anastasio "Tachito" **Somoza** Debayle in Nicaragua and the **Sandinista** revolution between 1979 and 1989. The U.S. military intervention in Panama to remove General Manuel **Noriega** was judged a failure on the basis of the cost of "**regime change**" for the United States and Panama. Karin von Hippel (2000: 51) goes further, claiming the United States blundered by nurturing Noriega for decades while at the same time ignoring his illicit activities, the inadequate preparation of U.S. troops for "nation building," rhetorical justifications were interpreted as smoke-screens for a more personal dispute between President **George H.W. Bush** and Noriega, and the excuses used by the White House were not entirely legitimate according to **international law**.

The **Iran-Contra scandal** contained multiple scandals and blunders—the mining of Nicaraguan harbors, the publication of training manuals for U.S.–backed "freedom fighters" that offered instruction in **terrorism** and **assassination**, and the covert backing of **death squads**. The major participants in the Iran-Contra scandal had no background in Latin America, but were convinced that with enough committed, aggressive, take-charge people dealing with Nicaragua and El Salvador, the "Communist assault" on Central America could be reversed, regardless of the legality or morality of the whole enterprise. Surprisingly, those who participated in these activities suffered little in the aftermath of a failed policy. For mining of the harbors of Nicaragua, the United States was taken before the **International Court of Justice (ICJ)** in a suit filed by the Nicaraguan government. Although the World Court ruled in favor of the Nicaraguans against the United States, the **Reagan** administration ignored the ruling, arguing the court had no jurisdiction over what it maintained was a political dispute. One of the highest ranking officials of the **Central Intelligence Agency (CIA)**, who was fired for failing to inform Congress about the agency's ties to **human rights** abuses in Guatemala in 1995, was awarded the CIA's Distinguished Career Intelligence Medal, despite substantial evidence that he was aware of such abuses. Elliott **Abrams**, assistant secretary of state for inter-American affairs, after being convicted of lying to Congress and serving a two-year sentence, was pardoned by George H.W. Bush in 1992. In July 2001 Abrams was named senior director of the National Security Council's (NSC) office of democracy, human rights, and international operations by President **George W. Bush**. Is it possible to devise a constructive Latin American policy when presidential appointments consist of unrepentant policymakers linked to earlier scandals and blunders that violated the law and acceptable norms of American foreign policy?

Scholars who have studied foreign policy scandals and blunders are not clueless when it comes to understanding the reasons why Latin American policymaking often malfunctions. A number of theories have been put forth to better understand scandals and blunders, including symbolic discourse theory, institutionalism, group-think, and rational decision-making. Which seems to offer the most insights into flawed decision-making? According to Dent (2001: 18–19), "Symbolic discourse theory, with its emphasis on the meaning and interpretation of cultural values, seems to offer the most promise for understanding and explaining the persistence of misguided policymaking." With little knowledge of Latin American countries, leaders, and cultural values (and the sociopolitical structures that embody these values), policymakers often fail to comprehend the meaning of historical events that involved revolutionary socialism or nationalism. Faulty understanding contributes to the use of misplaced analogies and flawed metaphors in deciding what to do about foreign policy crisis situations. Many blunders occurred during the demise of "**friendly dictators**" such as Somoza in Nicaragua, **Batista** in Cuba, and **Trujillo** in the Dominican Republic.

Faulty analogic thinking among policymakers often leads to the procrustean tendency of forcing a political event in Latin America into some previous historical context. Cold War "threats" were often viewed through the prism of the rise of Adolf Hitler, **World War II**, and the Vietnam War. Blunders happened when policymakers tried to equate events in Europe and Asia with those in Latin America. Unable to understand fully the difference between nationalism and communism, policymakers used false analogies and political symbols as a form of discourse. Some of the more common include: falling dominoes, Vietnam syndrome, vital security interests, Munich and appeasement, Cuban-inspired Marxist guerrillas, a violation of the **Monroe Doctrine**, and the necessity of Communist containment. The attraction of revolutionary doctrines in Latin America baffled Washington policymakers who often expressed confusion about Soviet intentions, Fidel Castro's rhetoric and motivations, the problems of poverty and corruption in the Third World, and the inability of people in less developed countries to accept fully the advantages of free-market capitalism and pluralist **democracy**. One of the major misconceptions, according to Matthias (2001: 147), was the "tendency to regard all revolutionary agitation and ferment as Soviet-inspired and susceptible to Soviet exploitation."

The thinking and planning that dominated the presidential advisory system in the 1950s continued throughout the Cold War, leading to foreign policy blunders in Cuba, Nicaragua, El Salvador, Guatemala, Chile, Argentina, and Vietnam. Those who played a major role in the covert world of defining and protecting American interests included **Allen Dulles**, **John Foster Dulles**, George **Kennan**, Paul Nitze, Henry **Kissinger**, and others. **Think tanks** and organized groups such as the Committee on the Present Danger and the Santa Fe Committee contributed to the prevailing discourse. The real appeal of the Cuban Revolution was its nationalistic orientation (some would say hyper-nationalistic), something the CIA planners and the Kennedy administration never understood. Failing to recognize that the Cuban Revolution was a fundamentally nationalist movement, the Bay of Pigs invasion was a "gift of the gods" for Castro in his effort to consolidate power and pursue his radical reforms. At an inter-American conference held in Punta del Este, Uruguay, in 1962, Che **Guevara** went so far as to thank Kennedy aide Richard Goodwin for the invasion; it meant that as long as Fidel Castro remained in power, Cuban leaders would perceive the United States as opposed to Cuba's national interests. With no interest in dialogue, the United States continues to "punish" Fidel Castro through trade and travel restrictions, official lectures on the evils lurking on the island, and the security benefits of ostracizing Castro.

When the Central American crisis erupted in 1979 with an end of the Somoza **dictatorship** and guerrilla warfare in El Salvador, Washington policymakers relied on what had transpired in previous conflicts such as World War II and the Vietnam

War. President Reagan's top foreign policy team—George H.W. Bush, Alexander Haig, Robert McFarlane, George Shultz, Oliver **North**, Dewey Clarridge, John Poindexter, Allen Fiers, Elliott Abrams, and Casper Weinberger—were individuals whose reasoning stemmed from what happened (or failed to happen) in Europe or Asia prior to and during the Cold War. The heavy involvement in El Salvador in the 1980s was rooted more in the perceived opportunity to "win" a military victory in the wake of the U.S. defeat in Vietnam and the failure to prevent the Nicaraguan revolution, than an authentic need to protect the Central American region from Soviet or Cuban communism and growing human rights violations. Most of Reagan's top policymakers had little knowledge of Central America and the history of U.S. involvement in the region. According to Gaddis Smith (1994: 188), "None of those in the administration who made high policy toward Central America knew very much about the region, nor did they consider such knowledge relevant or necessary." Oliver North, who ran the operational side of the Iran-Contra fiasco, admitted in his autobiography that he knew nothing about **covert operations** and relied on Director of Central Intelligence (DCI) William **Casey** for expertise in supporting the **Contras**. The overwhelming power of the United States in dealing with small Central American countries can often lead top decision makers to ignore the connection between understanding a crisis and achieving U.S. strategic objectives. Why worry about a policy mistake or blunder that might arise out of covert operations when it is always possible to apply more power, including invasion and occupation?

Symbolic discourse theory is also tied to how policy is communicated within the Washington bureaucracy and to the general public. By offering simplistic and often distorted views of what is happening in Latin America, policymakers are able to provide a form of persuasive rhetoric to a public that knows and cares little about what is happening in Latin America and the Caribbean. The initial costs and negative long-term effects of the Bay of Pigs invasion and the Iran-Contra scandal should be enough to make the case that Washington needs to place greater emphasis on policy design and implementation, including the recruitment of individuals with an understanding and commitment to avoid repeating the ill-planned disasters of the past.

The frequent occurrence of policy scandals and blunders can be costly affairs, from the build up of reservoirs of resentment with lethal results against all Americans to the waste of resources on irrelevant defense and security policies. Scandals and blunders often produce what political scientist Chalmers Johnson calls "**blowback**," the unintended consequences of secretive (covert) policies: U.S.–sponsored campaigns of state **terrorism**, bombing raids and mining harbors, or the use of the CIA to remove foreign leaders. By shoring up repressive regimes and selling vast amounts of weapons worldwide, the United States often invites much of what it tries to avoid. During the Cold War covert policies that contributed to the military overthrow of Jacobo **Arbenz** in Guatemala (1953) and Salvador **Allende** in Chile (1973) produced deadly consequences for those who were tortured, killed, or disappeared in the name of anti-communism and national or hemispheric security. It is ironic that the United States spends so much on intelligence and then chooses to ignore or distort it. As long as there remains a distinct disconnect between policymakers and the intelligence community, scandals and blunders will continue to plague the decision-making process and result in policies that undermine U.S.–Latin American relations. *See also* Bissell, Richard; Noriega, Manuel Antonio; Regime Change.

Suggested Reading

James G. Blight and Peter Kornbluh, *Politics of Illusion: The Bay of Pigs Invasion Reexamined* (Boulder, CO: Lynne Rienner, 1998); Charles Philippe David, *Foreign Policy Failure in the White House: Reappraising the Fall of the Shah and the Iran-Contra Affair* (Lanham, MD: University Press of America, 2001); David W. Dent, "Scandals and Blunders: A Theoretical Guide to U.S.–Latin American Policymaking," paper presented at the 2001 meeting of the Latin American Studies Association (Washington, DC, September 6–8, 2001); Willard C. Matthias, *America's Strategic Blunders: Intelligence Analysis and National Security Policy, 1936–1991* (University Park: Pennsylvania State University Press, 2001); Gaddis Smith, *The Last Years of the Monroe Doctrine 1945–1993* (New York: Hill and Wang, 1994); Karin von Hippel, *Democracy By Force: U.S. Military Intervention in the Post–Cold War World* (New York: Cambridge University Press, 2000).

School of the Americas (SOA) Shortly after **World War II**, the U.S. Army began offering courses to Latin American military personnel in the Panama Canal Zone. Since its inception in 1946, the army training school has changed its name several times. It was renamed the U.S. Army School of the Americas in 1963 and has remained a controversial element in U.S.–Latin American relations due to its secrecy, training programs and manuals, and the substantial number of graduates who returned to their homeland to commit **human rights** violations, sometimes in conjunction with U.S. military and **Central Intelligence Agency (CIA)** personnel. Under the new **Panama Canal treaties** of 1977, the United States agreed to close the school in Panama, and it was moved to Fort Benning, Georgia in 1984. When declassified documents revealed that U.S. Army training manuals used by the school provided instruction on the detection and suppression of anti-government political and military activities, and opponents of the brutality of the school's graduates were publicized, the U.S. Congress headed calls to close the school for good. After a series of votes came close to putting the school out of business, the school again changed its name in 2001 to the Western Hemisphere Institute for Security Cooperation (WHINSEC). Despite the controversy over the school's mission and graduates, it remains open and now accepts a small number of civilians from Latin America for short-term programs. Nevertheless, anti-SOA organizations continue to mark the anniversary of the deaths of Salvadoran Jesuits and others in 1989 with protests at the school in hopes of convincing Congress and the American public to close the training school. By 2005, the SOA had trained more than 65,000 Latin American military and police personnel and continues to operate with a new emphasis on training both military and civilian personnel.

At the heart of the controversy over the School of the Americas is its mission, curriculum, and the lack of accountability for graduates of the school. The Fort Benning curriculum is focused mainly on counter-insurgency, military intelligence, interrogation techniques, sniper fire, commando tactics, psychological warfare, and jungle operations. A small amount of time is devoted to democratic values, civil-military relations, and human rights. All of the instruction (including reading materials) is in Spanish, the only military institution in the United States that offers instruction solely in this language. (At the Inter-American Defense College in Washington, D.C., all presentations, although not with classes, are translated into Portuguese, Spanish, and English.) With the **George W. Bush** administration now embroiled in a global war against **terrorism**, the SOA has gained valuable legitimacy because of the close fit between the school's activities and the need to wipe out terrorism and insurgency in the Western Hemisphere. Most of the current learning is being applied in Colombia against leftist guerrillas and in southern Mexico where the Zapatistas are opposed to the **North American Free Trade Agreement (NAFTA)** and the mistreatment of indigenous *campesinos* (peasant, or poor farmers).

For the past twenty-five years critics of the army training school have engaged in a variety of tactics designed to shut down the school, without success. At the center of the anti-SOA movement is Father Roy Bourgeois, a Vietnam veteran and Maryknoll priest who created SOA Watch, coordinated demonstrations at the base site, and served time in prison for his antics. With the argument that "you can't teach democracy through the barrel of a gun," opponents of the SOA struggle in their quest to remove the school from U.S. soil. Their case is made more difficult by the fact that few Americans are aware of the school and therefore have no idea what the U.S. military, and graduates of the SOA, actually do abroad. SOA Watch obtained through the Freedom of Information Act a comprehensive list of the school's graduates and found that the roster of alumni is a Who's Who of Latin America's most infamous dictators, mass murderers, and **death squad** directors. Nevertheless, anti-SOA protesters must take into account changes in public sentiment since **September 11, 2001**, including many Americans whose nationalistic sensibilities have been intensified by fear of terrorism.

There are also many defenders of the school, both within the military and on Capitol Hill. They argue that the positives outweigh the negatives, namely, the school serves a national purpose and furthermore you cannot close a training school because of a "few bad apples." The tradition of peaceful resistance is now an annual affair sponsored by various peace groups and SOA Watch at Fort Benning, protesting the policy of training military personnel for repressive Latin American regimes. The U.S. Department of Defense still maintains that the institute's new mission (and name) is to focus on twenty-first-century–challenges facing the United States. After being tarred with the label "School of Assassins," the new facility reformulated its course offerings to include more benign and acceptable titles such as "Democratic Sustainment," "Humanitarian De-Mining," and "Civil-Military Operations." It now has a mandatory human rights curriculum to erase the lingering image from its training manuals that advocated torture, beatings, and executions for detainees suspected of terrorism and insurgency. With the recent revelations of mistreatment—torture, death, and abuse—of suspected terrorists captured by the CIA and U.S. special forces in Afghanistan and Iraq, the relevance of the School of the Americas takes on added importance in understanding military and police training in the current global war on terrorism. Because of negative publicity and closer congressional scrutiny that anti-SOA activists have brought upon the school, the most sinister training practices have been relocated to other locations. With the passage of the USA Patriot Act in 2001, those who engage in peaceful democratic dissent now face a government that is less concerned about constitutional freedoms and privacy rights than was the case before September 11, 2001. The U.S. military continues to portray the non-violent protesters as a threat to public safety and praise the value of military instruction, political orientation, and career advantages that the school imparts. *See also* Anti-Americanism; *Father Roy: Inside the School of Assassins*; Noriega, Manuel Antonio.

Suggested Reading

Father Roy: Inside the School of Assassins (PBS documentary, 1997); Lesley Gill, *The School of the Americas: Military Training and Political Violence in the Americas* (Durham: Duke University Press, 2004); Gill, "Soldiering the Empire," *NACLA Report on the Americas* (September/October 2004); Peter Kornbluh, "Lessons in Cruelty," *Washington Post* (October 31, 2004).

September 11, 2001 The simultaneous terrorist attacks on New York City and Washington, D.C., by individuals associated with Osama bin Laden's Al-Qaeda network had important consequences for the United States and Latin America. The acts of terror by foreign nationals on U.S. soil were the most deadly since Francisco "Pancho" **Villa**'s attacks on New Mexican towns in 1916. Thirty of the thirty-four member states of the **Organization of American States (OAS)** lost citizens in the attacks, mostly Mexicans in the Twin Towers in New York. Immediately after the attacks there was an outpouring of sympathy for the United States from Latin American governments and the news **media**. Fidel **Castro** was the first foreign leader to offer condolences and sympathy on behalf of Cuba. However, in the months that followed the tragedy the positive sentiment toward American citizens slowly disappeared due in large part to the way in which the **George W. Bush** administration conducted its global war on **terrorism**. The terrorist attacks helped to forge a new foreign policy, as the Bush administration struggled to rethink **Cold War** ideas about national security, namely containment, deterrence and multilateralism. The policies that emerged from 9/11 had roots in long-standing neo-conservative theories about the need for a more assertive foreign policy in the world.

The pre-emptive war on Saddam Hussein was particularly troublesome to Latin Americans because it reminded them of similar strategies that were applied to Latin

America reaching back to the nineteenth century. The events of September 11, 2001, the global war on terrorism, and the Iraq war, influenced U.S.–Latin American relations in the following ways.

First, **Washington policymakers** reverted to the tendency to view Latin America through a fairly narrow ideological lens, in this case the "global war on terrorism." Previous frameworks—**Monroe Doctrine**, **Manifest Destiny**, Cold War, **human rights**, War on Drugs—provided Washington policymakers with a catchy slogan to approach the complex realities of the Western Hemisphere. As with previous frameworks for defining inter-American affairs, the global war on terrorism lens provided a new legitimacy for returning to a traditional military approach to the region's problems. The use of such a broad framework allowed the United States to define the Cuban Revolution, Venezuelan populism, **drug trafficking**, and the regional spread of the Colombian conflict as part of a terrorist threat to the entire Western Hemisphere. The U.S. Army has used the tragedy of September 11, 2001 to reaffirm the importance of the **School of the Americas (SOA)** at Ft. Benning, Georgia, as a vital component of joint military engagement to deal with terrorist threats in the Americas.

Second, the events of 9/11 reduced the importance of diplomacy, human rights, and democracy promotion in favor of a military approach to help fight terrorism. Immediately after the terrorist attacks, the Bush administration sent a bill to Congress that would have lifted all restrictions on military aid and arms transfers to Latin American countries for the next five years where necessary to help win the war on terrorism. By reducing the importance of human rights practices, the United States jeopardized its moral authority to criticize other governments' human rights practices. The prison-abuse scandals at Abu Ghraib and Camp Delta (**Guantánamo Bay**) by U.S. forces and the curtailment of civil liberties in the United States allowed many critics to argue that U.S. congressional concerns about torture and human rights abuses in Latin America are sheer hypocrisy. Despite evidence of widespread torture of prisoners in these camps, President Bush has denied all knowledge and blamed the abuses on a few bad apples, then insisted "freedom from torture is an inalienable human right." If it is alright to torture alleged suspects of terrorism in Iraq, Cuba, and elsewhere, why is it inappropriate for Latin American militaries to do the same in their own countries? September 11, 2001, altered the way the U.S. public views torture and human rights violations. As Gill points out, "The legitimacy of torture is now debated openly, and its definition is being rendered more elastic." Army instructors who teach courses on counterterrorism are now more willing to admit that torture is necessary, and useful, in handling suspected terrorists.

Third, the global war on terrorism that followed the events of 9/11 downplayed issues of importance to Latin American governments such as immigration reform (Mexico) and the destructive affects of globalization—poverty, unemployment, drug trafficking, and crime—throughout Latin America. In a post-election meeting with Mexican President Vicente **Fox**, Secretary of State Colin L. Powell said that President Bush would place a "high priority" on his plan to grant legal status to millions of undocumented aliens in the United States. Despite the renewed interest in achieving an agreement on immigration, many Mexicans remain skeptical that President Bush is serious about immigration reform given the strong opposition among Republican lawmakers on Capitol Hill. Immigration is now viewed mainly as a homeland security issue, rather than economic or cultural in nature.

Fourth, the September 11, 2001, attacks altered the prospects for two of President Bush's nominees for key diplomatic posts. For example, despite an unsavory record of supporting U.S.–backed **death squads** while ambassador to Honduras in the 1980s, the U.S. Senate approved John **Negroponte's** nomination—once in danger of rejection—on September 14, 2001, claiming the United States needed someone in the **United Nations (UN)** immediately to handle sensitive diplomatic matters. Latin Americans were angered by the Negroponte nomination since they considered him a "terrorist" for administering the **Contra** war against Nicaragua during his tenure as U.S. ambassador in Tegucigalpa. It is remarkable that Negroponte's past diplomatic activities did not hinder his nominations, and approvals, for U.S. ambassador in Iraq and director of national intelligence during the second George W. Bush administration. The events of 9/11 also helped Otto J. **Reich** receive a recess appointment to be assistant secretary of state for Western Hemisphere affairs after it was stalled for months because of his close ties to anti-Castro terrorist Orlando Bosch. Many in Latin America were appalled by the negative symbolism and hypocrisy of Reich's nomination despite his close ties to well-known Miami terrorists in light of President Bush's call for all-out cooperation in the global war on terrorism.

Fifth, the terrorist attacks of September 11, 2001, contributed to greater U.S.–Mexican cooperation on border-related issues. President Vicente Fox provided the Bush administration with intelligence information on suspected terrorists, tracking the flow of money alleged to be associated with terrorists and drug traffickers, and maintaining order along Mexico's long international boundary. The tightened security contributed to a dramatic decline in illegal border crossings for a few months and shelved the idea of a blanket amnesty for undocumented Mexicans in the United States until President Bush's re-election in November 2004. President George W. Bush met with Mexican president Vincente Fox in March 2005 to discuss immigration reform, but any serious change will confront both public opposition and a skeptical Congress.

Sixth, Latin Americans rejected the Bush administration's rationale that attempted to link the events of 9/11 with Saddam Hussein and opposed the decision to attack Iraq in March 2003. Almost all Latin American governments refused to support the U.S. demand for a second UN Security Council resolution prior to the war and criticized Washington for going to war for dubious reasons. Only four small Latin American countries—Honduras, El Salvador, Nicaragua, and the Dominican Republic—sent troops to Iraq as part of the "Coalition of the Willing." By early 2005, most of the small contingent of Latin American troops had left Iraq. The war confirmed the worst view of the United States in Latin America. The blatant disregard for the Geneva Conventions and other international standards regarding the treatment of prisoners was particularly disturbing to Latin Americans. In a six-country poll taken in 2003, only 12 percent of Latin American business, government, and other leaders rated President Bush's performance on Latin America as positive. The most critical responses in Latin America were in Argentina, Uruguay, and Brazil where President Bush was rated very low. From the Latin American viewpoint, the United States is resented because of the growing power of American multinational corporations and the arrogance of U.S. foreign policy. A healthy majority (58 percent) of Latin Americans believe that U.S. policies and actions—not the hatred of America's freedom—in the world were a major or minor cause of the September 11, 2001, attacks. Only 18 percent shared this view in the United States.

Seventh, many U.S. citizens fled to Mexico after September 11, 2001, buying coastal real estate, particularly on the Pacific coast of Baja California. As one American in San Felipe stated, many Americans went to Mexico to "get away from the regulations and rhetoric, and get out of the bull's eye" north of the border. Others found that with the slumping American economy and changes in Mexican law making it easier to own property, Mexico offered a higher standard of living and greater degree of freedom and safety than in the United States. This trend will no doubt continue as long as Americans remain fearful of terrorist attacks and find their disposable income shrinking.

Eighth, after 9/11 there was a dramatic increase in military aid to Latin America and in the numbers of Latin American soldiers trained. Between 2002 and 2003 the United States trained 22,821 Latin American soldiers, a 52 percent increase. Most of this increase is due to the expansion of the U.S. mission in Colombia where the number of U.S. troops permitted to operate have doubled in number. Most of the Latin American soldiers trained under the Counter-terrorism Terrorism Fellowship program were from Colombia and Peru, a sign of the conflation of the domestic drug war and domestic terrorism. Traditional aid programs for Latin American are not seen as a priority and are often vulnerable to budget cuts. The insurgent groups in Colombia have been labeled "terrorist," and this has allowed the United States to explain the rationale for U.S. support in Colombia as part of a more expansive conflict that combined drugs and terror. *See also* Abrams, Elliott; Ambassadors; Anti-Americanism; Threat Perception/Assessment.

Suggested Reading

David W. Dent, *Encyclopedia of Modern Mexico* (Lanham, MD: Scarecrow Press, 2002); John Feffer, *Power Trip: U.S. Unilateralism and Global Strategy After September 11* (New York: Seven Stories Books, 2003); Lesley Gill, "Soldiering the Empire," *NACLA Report on the Americas* (September/October 2004); Lisa Haugaard, et al., *September's Shadow: Post–9/11 U.S.–Latin American Relations* (Washington, DC: Latin American Working Group, September 2004); Eric Hershberg and Kevin W. Moore, eds., *Critical Views of September 11: Analyses from Around the World* (New York: New Press, 2002); Kevin Sullivan, "U.S. Relations Suddenly Change for Mexico," *Washington Post* (September 21, 2001).

Slidell, John (1793–1871) Lawyer, politician, and diplomat who played a role in the Texas-Mexico boundary dispute, the war with Mexico, efforts to annex Cuba, and the **filibustering** expeditions that plagued Latin America before the U.S. Civil War. Born in New York City, Slidell graduated from Columbia College. After a business venture failed, he moved to New Orleans where he became a lawyer, district attorney, and U.S. representative. U.S. efforts to annex Texas increased hostilities between Mexico and the United States. After James K. **Polk** was inaugurated as president, Mexico severed relations and began to prepare for war. After Mexico agreed to discuss the renewal of relations, President Polk sent John Slidell as a new minister with instructions to resolve the Texas boundary controversy and acquire Mexican territory. Although Slidell appeared to be an excellent choice for the mission—he was fluent in Spanish, possessed a gracious demeanor, and was given full diplomatic powers—his instructions included demands for more Mexican territory. After being notified of Slidell's mission, Mexicans became angry over the grounds for negotiations and refused to receive him after he arrived in Mexico. Those who represented the United States in Mexico portrayed Mexicans as incompetent, disorganized, and debauched, and these negative stereotypes became the basis for Polk's decision that a war with Mexico would be nothing short of a pushover. Each of Slidell's efforts to engage the Mexicans in negotiations were rejected, and he withdrew in frustration from Mexico in 1846. John Slidell's failure hastened the outbreak of the **Mexican-American War** by providing President Polk with the pretext to attack Mexico. While in the U.S. Senate (1853 to 1861), Slidell backed efforts to annex Cuba and supported filibustering expeditions by favoring legislation that would give limited power to the president to suspect U.S. neutrality laws. After the U.S. Civil War broke out, Slidell was selected to represent the Confederacy as its diplomatic agent in France, but he was captured en route to Europe. After being imprisoned by the Union, he gained his release and completed his voyage to Paris. He failed in his efforts to get the French to recognize the South, but remained in Europe following the war. Slidell never returned to the United States and died in London in 1871. *See also* Race and Racism.

Suggested Reading

William R. Manning, *Early Diplomatic Relations between the United States and Mexico* (Baltimore, MD: The Johns Hopkins Press, 1916); Lars Schoultz, *Beneath the United States: A History of U.S. Policy Toward Latin America* (Cambridge, MA: Harvard University Press, 1998); Graham H. Stuart and James L. Tigner, *Latin America and the United States*, 6th ed. (Englewood Cliffs, NJ: Prentice-Hall, 1975).

Smith, Earl E.T. (1903–1991) Businessman with solid Republican connections who became ambassador to Cuba from 1957 to 1959. Earl Smith was born in Newport, Rhode Island, in 1903, attended Yale University in the mid-1920s, and became a stockbroker in 1926. Smith was appointed as a member of the War Production Board in 1941, but left shortly after his appointment to serve in the U.S. Army and Air Force during **World War II**. His business success as a Wall Street investment broker enabled him to forge tight bonds with the **Eisenhower** administration. While ambassador to Cuba, Smith criticized both Fulgencio **Batista**

and Fidel **Castro**. He became deeply involved in **regime change** in Cuba, hoping that he could engineer a peaceful transfer of power to prevent Fidel Castro from assuming leadership of the island. Ambassador Smith fought with the **State Department** in an attempt to reverse the decision to cut off arms to Batista in 1958 and attempted to cooperate with him instead of siding with Castro. According to Domínguez (1978), "Ambassador Smith publicly and privately supported Batista at the same time that State Department policy undercut his legitimacy and weakened military morale." While Ambassador Smith was trying to prop up Batista, the U.S. government was working unsuccessfully to ease Batista out of office. Without informing Smith, the White House sent William D. Pawley, a Republican businessman long connected to Cuba, to Havana with instructions to offer Batista a safe haven for him and his family in Florida, provided Batista form a caretaker government that would prevent a Castro victory. Pawley insisted that the "new" government would have to be subservient to Washington, a last ditch effort that had no bearing on Batista's decision to remain in power. In the fever-pitched nationalism of the Cuban Revolution, Smith was excoriated for his meddling in Cuba's internal affairs, which only reinforced Fidel Castro's decision to make a complete break with the United States for his revolution to proceed.

After Castro's guerrilla struggle succeeded in toppling Batista in 1959, Smith blamed state department officials sympathetic to Castro for the bearded leader's success. In his memoirs, *The Fourth Floor*, Smith attacked the State Department and embassy officers with whom he had disagreed over the handling of Batista and Castro's insurgency. After leaving his post in Cuba, Ambassador Smith settled in Palm Beach, Florida, where he later served as mayor. President Ronald **Reagan** appointed Smith to the Presidential Commission on Broadcasting to Cuba, which helped establish the Voice of America's **Radio Martí** in 1985. Ambassador Earl E.T. Smith died in Palm Beach at the age of eighty-seven in 1991. *See also* Ambassadors; Revolutions.

Suggested Reading

Jorge I. Domínguez, *Cuba: Order and Revolution* (Cambridge, MA: Harvard University Press, 1978); Lester D. Langley, *The Cuban Policy of the United States: A Brief History* (New York: John Wiley, 1968); Earl E.T. Smith, *The Fourth Floor: An Account of the Castro Communist Revolution* (New York: Random House, 1962); Richard E. Welch, *Response to Revolution: The United States and the Cuban Revolution, 1959–1987* (Chapel Hill: University of North Carolina Press, 1985).

Soccer War (1969) A major military conflict between Honduras and El Salvador that erupted in July 1969 after several violence-plagued soccer matches throughout June of that year. The causes of the war were rooted in U.S. military doctrine, the expulsion of thousands of Salvadoran peasants living, and working, illegally in neighboring Honduras, many for generations without title to the land. Many of the early Salvadoran immigrants had come from densely populated El Salvador in search of work with the banana companies. Pressure over land and jobs had been building up for years, but when Honduran president Oswaldo López Arellano decided to distribute government-owned lands to Honduran peasants and force Salvadorans living in Honduras to return to El Salvador, tensions increased dramatically. The massive exodus of Salvadorans back to their homeland brought horrific tales of mistreatment while in Honduras and put pressure on Salvadoran president Fidel Sánchez Hernández from the military and conservative opponents of land reform. This led to the termination of diplomatic relations and Salvadoran troop movements and air force attacks on Honduran territory. By the time the conflict was over, the United States and the **Organization of American States (OAS)** became involved in the dispute.

Beginning in 1963, U.S. defense policy led to the creation of the Central American Defense Council (CONDECA) to formalize military cooperation among the high commands of El Salvador, Guatemala, Honduras, and Nicaragua. The Pentagon arranged, and participated in, CONDECA's joint military maneuvers that were aimed at preventing a potential invasion from the Caribbean, and threat from Communist insurgents and guerrillas. When two CONDECA members attacked each other, the promise of a regional security organization was undermined by the Soccer War in which U.S.–trained soldiers and officers from El Salvador and Honduras engaged in fighting each other, not defending their countries against Communist attacks. As a result, CONDECA sank into remission until it was revived during the Central American conflicts in the 1980s.

By the time of the Soccer War, the **Nixon** administration had adopted a "low-profile" approach to Central America as it focused on Vietnam, China, and the Soviet Union. President John F. **Kennedy**'s **Alliance for Progress** had all but disappeared as a mainstay of Latin American policy, economic assistance was cut drastically, and the growing number of military rulers were either ignored or hailed as necessary bulwarks against spreading Castroism. As El Salvador and Honduras prepared for war, the Pentagon kept the U.S. embassies in the dark while secretly assisting the Salvadorans in their war efforts. U.S. officials in Tegucigalpa had no awareness of the military mobilization and attack planning next door in San Salvador. The deceit and duplicity on behalf of U.S. military officials led to an intelligence failure for the United States that contributed to a bloody war when a diplomatic solution offered strong possibilities of success. Moreover, the U.S. military officers who secretly sided with El Salvador helped pave the way for the internal conflicts that would come ten years later.

The Organization of American States became involved early in the conflict, appointed a special committee to investigate the war, and passed resolutions calling for the suspension of hostilities and the withdrawal of troops, the creation of a vigilance system, the end to mass-**media propaganda** that was being used to inflame tensions, and **human rights** guarantees for non-nationals. These inter-American efforts to bring about peace did not prevent Honduras and El Salvador from blaming the United States for the conflict, although for different reasons. The Nixon administration was also criticized by some in Congress who blamed the United States for supplying the weapons that each country used to attach the other. Although the fighting lasted only four days, the Soccer War was brutal and costly for all of Central America. Estimates place the number of dead at 2,000 and twice that number wounded on both sides. More than 100,000 refugees were created in a war that cost both countries over $50 million. Although it took more than ten years for both sides to agree to a final peace arrangement, the brief war had a lasting impact on Central America and the two hostile neighbors. The Soccer War left a simmering border dispute that harmed relations, all but destroyed the Central American Common Market, and contributed to the social crisis that would erupt in El Salvador in the 1970s and lead to massive U.S. involvement in its civil war for a decade. The sad affair increased the militarization of each society, undermined the democratic process, and human rights violations during the 1980s led to the exodus of hundreds of thousands of Salvadorans to the United States. *See also* Scandals and Blunders; Washington Policymakers.

Suggested Reading

Raymond Bonner, *Weakness and Deceit: U.S. Policy and El Salvador* (New York: Times Books, 1984); David W. Dent, *The Legacy of the Monroe Doctrine: A Reference Guide to U.S. Involvement in Latin America and the Caribbean* (Westport, CT: Greenwood Press, 1999); Larman C. Wilson and David W. Dent, *Historical Dictionary of Inter-American Organizations* (Lanham, MD: Scarecrow Press, 1998).

Somoza Debayle, Anastasio "Tachito" (1925–1980) Nicaraguan military figure and dictator from 1967 to 1979 known for his corruption, greed, ruthless treatment of all political opposition, and close ties with the United States. Part of a powerful dynasty started by his father, Anastasio "Tacho" Somoza García, in 1936, Tachito followed the same path to power as his father and elder brother Luis, who succeeded his father following his **assassination** in 1955. The building blocks of power for the Somozas consisted of military training in the United States, including the U.S. Military Academy at West Point, followed by top positions in the Nicaraguan National Guard. All three members of the Somoza dynasty were fluent in English, conversant in the language of politics and American slang, and displayed a fawning obedience to the needs of American foreign policy.

Somoza's brutal **dictatorship** contributed to the formation of a liberation movement named after Augusto **Sandino** (*Frente Sandinista de Liberación Nacional—FSLN*) that waged a long war against Somoza that finally succeeded in his downfall in July 1979. As the FSLN gained strength inside Nicaragua and among sympathetic Latin American governments, Washington faced the unpleasant task of having to deal with a right-wing dictator who was about to be toppled by a broad-based revolutionary movement. At first the United States tried to disassociate itself from the Nicaraguan dictator. Washington then tried to find what political scientist Robert **Pastor** calls a "middle option" that would prevent the **Sandinistas** from coming to power. When this failed, the Jimmy **Carter** administration made a half-hearted attempt to support the revolution, but in the end was left with a confrontation that would consume U.S.–Latin American policy for the next ten years.

Washington's reluctance to overthrow Somoza Debayle in the midst of a succession crisis illustrates one of the key aspects of American foreign policy. As Pastor points out (1987: 274), the reluctance to overthrow a friendly right-wing dictator was consistent with previous policies: "Eisenhower and Kennedy in the Dominican Republic (1960–61), Kennedy (1961–63) and Reagan (1985–86) in Haiti, and Reagan (1985–86) in the Philippines." Only in Vietnam (Diem) did the United States push out a right-wing dictator and President **Kennedy** later expressed regret at having done so. After being overthrown by Sandinista-led forces in 1979, Somoza flew to Miami, Florida, but was denied exile in the United States. He then left for Paraguay, where he was given asylum by the dictator General Alfredo Stroessner until Somoza was assassinated by Argentine leftists in 1980. Before he was killed, Tachito Somoza criticized the United States for not supporting him in his final moment against the Sandinistas in Nicaragua in 1979. He called President Carter "Fidel Carter" and told the U.S. embassy in Managua before leaving that "I helped them [**Washington policymakers**] for thirty years to fight communism. I'd like the American people to pay back the help we gave in the **Cold War**. The U.S. can't afford to lose a good partner. I am transitory but the reds are not." Although the United States did not intervene to prevent the overthrow of Tachito Somoza, it did mount a counter-revolution that helped destroy the Sandinista revolution after ten years in power. Somoza's legacy still haunts Nicaragua as its lack of development and corrupt and greedy political class have contributed to its current status as the poorest Central American country and second poorest in Latin America after Haiti. *See also* Eisenhower, Dwight David; Friendly Dictators; Reagan, Ronald W.

Suggested Reading

Eduardo Crawley, *Dictators Never Die: A Portrait of Nicaragua and the Somozas* (New York: St. Martin's Press, 1979); Bernard Diederich, *Somoza and the Legacy of U.S. Involvement in Central America* (Maplewood, NJ: Waterfront Press, 1989); Roy Gutman, *Banana Diplomacy: The Making of American Policy in Nicaragua, 1981–1987* (New York: Simon and Schuster, 1988); Richard Millett, *Guardians of the Dynasty: A History of the U.S.–Created Guardia Nacional de Nicaragua and the Somoza Family* (Maryknoll, NY: Orbis Books, 1977); Robert A. Pastor, *Condemned to Repetition: The United States and Nicaragua* (Princeton, NJ: Princeton University Press, 1987); Anastasio Somoza, at told to Jack Cox, *Nicaragua Betrayed* (Boston: Western Islands, 1980); Thomas W. Walker, ed., *Revolution and Counter-Revolution in Nicaragua* (Boulder, CO: Westview Press, 1991).

Southern Command The U.S. Southern Command (SOUTHCOM) is one of several unified commands within the Defense Department with major responsibilities for conducting foreign policy and military activities in mainland Latin America from Guatemala to Chile. The Atlantic Command holds corresponding responsibilities for the Caribbean islands and sea. From the 1940s to the 1990s, SOUTHCOM was based in Quarry Heights, Panama. Before the transfer of full sovereignty to Panama in 1999, SOUTHCOM moved to Miami, Florida, in 1997. The Atlantic

Command is based in Norfolk, Virginia. The U.S. Southern Command has a wide operational role in Latin American policymaking with responsibility for anti-narcotics, counter-insurgency/**terrorism**, and civic action. Other executive branch agencies such as the Justice and **State Departments** often find that they must respond to SOUTHCOM proposals, and these civilian agencies in turn often influence SOUTHCOM's mission in Latin America. The commander in chief of SOUTHCOM often acts as a "soldier-diplomat" and plays an important role in U.S.–Latin American relations, giving public addresses and mobilizing support for policies related to anti-narcotics, counter-insurgency, and anti-terrorism efforts. The members of U.S. Military Groups (MilGroups) in each U.S. embassy in Latin America receive their orders from SOUTHCOM, but military advisers also must obey the authority of the U.S. **ambassador** of their country of assignment. This form of dual authority can lead to conflict between military and civilian personnel over different interpretations of the same policy.

When high-level decisions are made regarding the timing and strategy of U.S. military intervention in Latin America, the commander of SOUTHCOM plays a vital role. In the lead up to the U.S. invasion of Panama in 1989, SOUTHCOM commander General Fred Woerner was replaced by General Maxwell Thurman in preparation for the attack because he was not sufficiently "gung-ho" about the use of military force to remove General Manuel **Noriega** from Panama. Unlike most SOUTHCOM commanders, General Woerner was experienced and knowledgeable about Latin America and U.S.–Latin American relations; he spoke Spanish, was married to a Bolivian, and argued strongly against the White House plans to invade Panama to deal with Noriega and other matters. There have also been times when SOUTHCOM commanders have delivered stern messages to Latin American military officers planning coups: to do so would irreparably damage U.S. relations with that nation. In carrying out its missions in Latin America, SOUTHCOM relies on thousands of military personnel, civilian contractors, and forces from other Defense Department commands such as the Army Special Forces ("Green Berets") and the Navy SEALS. There are numerous U.S. military training programs where Latin American soldiers are trained for specific periods of time before returning to their home countries. The best known institution for this purpose is the Western Hemisphere Institute for Security Cooperation (formerly known as the U.S. Army **School of the Americas (SOA)**) located at Ft. Benning, Georgia. Within Latin America, Mobile Training Teams (MTTs) from all services conduct training programs ranging from a few days to several months. The Inter-American Affairs Office of the secretary of defense is the principal Pentagon office for policy toward the region. This office advises the secretary of defense on all matters related to Latin America and coordinates policy with the State Department, **Central Intelligence Agency (CIA)**, and the Drug Enforcement Administration. The current commander of SOUTHCOM is General Bantz Craddock. *See also Father Roy: Inside the School of Assassins* (1997); National Security Council (NSC); Washington Policymakers.

Suggested Reading

Jan Knippers Black, *Sentinels of Empire: The United States and Latin American Militaries* (Westport, CT: Greenwood Press, 1986); Charles T. Call, "The U.S. Military," in David W. Dent, ed., *U.S.–Latin American Policymaking: A Reference Handbook* (Westport, CT: Greenwood Press, 1995); Thomas Donnelly, Margaret Roth, and Caleb Baker, *Operation Just Cause: The Storming of Panama* (New York: Lexington Books, 1991); J. Samuel Fitch, "The Decline of U.S. Military Influence in Latin America," *Journal of Interamerican Studies and World Affairs*, Vol. 35, No. 2 (winter 1993); Frederick Kempe, *Divorcing the Dictator: America's Bungled Affair with Noriega* (New York: G.P. Putnam's Sons, 1990); Michael T. Klare and Peter Kornbluh, eds., *Low Intensity Warfare: Counterinsurgency, Proinsurgency, and Antiterrorism in the Eighties* (New York: Pantheon, 1987); Michael McClintock, *Instruments of Statecraft: U.S. Guerrilla Warfare, Counterinsurgency and Counterterrorism, 1940–1990* (New York: Pantheon, 1992); Bob Woodward, *The Commanders* (New York: Simon and Schuster, 1992).

Spanish-American War. *See* Spanish-Cuban-American War (1898)

Spanish-Cuban-American War (1898) Although the United States opposed Cuban independence in the early part of the nineteenth century, largely on the grounds that a free and independent Cuba might foment a slave revolt or that a hostile European power might decide to use the island as a base of operations against the United States, by the end of the century there was considerable support for a free Cuba (*Cuba libre*) among the American people, U.S. sugar and business interests, and government leaders imbued with expansionist fever and hegemonic desires. The second war of independence began in 1895 and dragged on for more than three years before the United States was drawn into the conflict by the horrors of the struggle and the newspaper battle between William Randolph Hearst and Joseph Pulitzer over who would be the first to reach one million subscribers. Although President William **McKinley** tried to avoid war with Spain, the dramatic press reports—based on lies and fabrications known as "yellow journalism"—on the turmoil and the sinking of the USS *Maine*, and imperialist elements within the Republican Party clamored for U.S. **intervention**, eventually drove him into a war against Spain to help liberate Cuba. Hearst blamed the Spanish for the sinking of the battleship *Maine* in Havana harbor and coined the phrase "Remember the *Maine*, the hell with Spain" to reinforce his jingoistic views. Congress declared war two months after the *Maine* disaster, but the first American battle against Spain was fought in the Philippines, resulting in the sinking of the Spanish fleet. By June 1898, U.S. troops landed and quickly defeated the poorly equipped and demoralized Spanish. Among the forces that landed in Cuba were the Rough Riders, a band of U.S. Army volunteers that included **Theodore Roosevelt**. Within a few months the Spanish navy was defeated, and Spain surrendered in August 1898. With the Treaty of Paris (signed in December 1898), Spain lost the remains of its empire in Latin America, and the United States acquired Guam, Puerto Rico, and the Philippines. Cuba would eventually become a protectorate of the United States that would last for close to sixty years.

The defeat of Spain was followed by four years of U.S. military occupation of Cuba, fumbled efforts to rebuild Cuba and placate those Cubans who had struggled for so long to achieve their independence from Spain. At first, the United States maintained it was only fighting to liberate Cuba and establish peace, not to exercise sovereignty, control, or jurisdiction over the island. This turned out to be a smokescreen to placate the Mambí, Cuban freedom fighters who were close to winning the war before U.S. forces landed. The U.S. military forces brought with them negative stereotypes and racist views of the Cubans that both undermined Cuban contributions to the military defeat of Spain and their capacity for self-government. The victory over the Spanish provided Washington with the will and justification for maintaining a protectorate over Cuba. The United States could have easily annexed Cuba, but chose to exercise control over the island through a strange provision attached to its first constitution called the **Platt Amendment**, which gave the United States the right to intervene to assure Cuban independence, maintain law and order among what some called "a collection of real tropical savages" and the right to acquire **Guantánamo Bay**, where it established a major naval base. The Platt Amendment lasted until 1934, but by the time it was abolished it had created a pseudo-republic subject to U.S. control and domination. The creation of the Platt Amendment, named after Senator Orville Platt, but the handiwork of Elihu **Root**, led to more protectorates in the Caribbean and the transformation of the United States into a hegemonic power in the Western Hemisphere. Theodore Roosevelt used his war experience, often distorted and inaccurate for public consumption, to advance his political career and influence over Latin America with his **"Big Stick" diplomacy**. The mistreatment of the Cubans during the time of the Platt Amendment contributed to the rise of anti-American nationalism and the creation of a revolutionary political culture. What began as a war of liberation with good intentions led to the creation of a sordid system based on graft, corruption, violence, and social injustice that would last six decades, until bearded rebels again descended from the mountains of Oriente to begin another renovation of the island. *See also* Hegemony; Media; Race and Racism; Teller Amendment or Resolution (1898).

Suggested Reading

David W. Dent, *The Legacy of the Monroe Doctrine: A Reference Guide to U.S. Involvement in Latin America and the Caribbean* (Westport, CT: Greenwood Press, 1999); Kenneth E. Hendrickson, Jr., *The Spanish-American War* (Westport, CT: Greenwood Press, 2003); John B. Judis, *The Folly of Empire: What George W. Bush Could Learn from Theodore Roosevelt and Woodrow Wilson* (New York: Scribner, 2004); Christopher Lasch, "Race and American Expansion in Cuba and Puerto Rico," in Michael L. Krenn, ed., *Race and U.S. Foreign Policy in the Ages of Territorial and Market Expansion, 1840 to 1900* (New York: Garland, 1998); Larman C. Wilson and David Dent, *Historical Dictionary of Inter-American Organizations* (Lanham, MD: Scarecrow Press, 1998).

State Department The U.S. State Department is a large bureaucracy that is a key part of the presidential advisory system. It shares this role with the **National Se-**

curity Council (NSC) and its staff, the **Central Intelligence Agency (CIA)**, and the Department of Defense (DOD). Other executive branch agencies also play a role in policy implementation such as Treasury, Commerce, U.S. **ambassadors**, and the Office of Trade Representative (OTR). The State Department is a large bureaucratic organization with close to 25,000 employees and over 250 diplomatic missions overseas. The secretary of state ranks first among the president's cabinet members and he or she plays a major role in the selection of the assistant secretary of state for inter-American affairs who has the major responsibility for Latin American and Caribbean affairs. However, since the creation of the National Security Council in 1947, some control over Latin American policy has moved to other executive agencies. Increasing multiagency involvement in Latin American policy has generated more conflict and coordination difficulties within the advisory system. The NSC staff and the Department of State must engage in a delicate balancing act to satisfy the wishes of the president. This tension stems in part from the NSC's control of the policy agenda and the Department of State's responsibility for implementation. Within the State Department is the Bureau of Inter-American Affairs, headed by the assistant secretary of state for inter-American affairs. When Congress wants someone from the executive branch to testify during a hearing on a Latin American policy issue, the assistant secretary of state for inter-American affairs will come to Capitol Hill for the gathering.

Whether political appointees or career diplomats, the assistant secretary of state for inter-American affairs is often caught in a tug-of-war that characterizes U.S.–Latin American policymaking. As Gabriel Marcella points out (1995: 287), "It is often a thankless job within the foreign policy bureaucracy, fraught with chronic symptoms of the Rodney Dangerfield syndrome: no policymaking respect." The **Carter** administration relied on career diplomats for the Latin American post while the **Reagan** and **George H.W. Bush** administrations preferred political appointees. President **Clinton** was more inclined to select career diplomats; **George W. Bush** picked political appointees, many of whom were Cuban American with strong ties to the exile community in Miami. When George W. Bush picked career diplomats such as John D. **Negroponte** for government posts, he expected to have someone under his command who understands the flow of power and acts as a loyal foot soldier. Whatever the background of the nominee, political ideology plays a major role in the confirmation process, far more than knowledge or experience in the region. *See also* Pastor, Robert A.; Washington Policymakers.

Suggested Reading

David W. Dent, ed., *U.S.–Latin American Policymaking: A Reference Handbook* (Westport, CT: Greenwood Press, 1995); Gabriel Marcella, "The Presidential Advisory System," in David W. Dent, ed., *U.S.–Latin American Policymaking: A Reference Handbook* (Westport, CT: Greenwood Press, 1995); Carla Anne Robbins, "A State Department Purge," *New York Times* (November 3, 1981); Jerel A. Rosati, *The Politics of United States Foreign Policy* (Ft. Worth, TX: Harcourt Brace Jovanovich, 1993); Barry Rubin, *Secrets of State: The State Department and the Struggle Over U.S. Foreign Policy* (New York: Oxford University Press, 1985); George P. Shultz,

Turmoil and Triumph: My Years as Secretary of State (New York: Maxwell Macmillan International, 1993); Howard J. Wiarda, *Foreign Policy Without Illusion: How Foreign Policy-Making Works and Fails to Work in the United States* (Glenview, IL: Scott, Foresman, 1990).

***State of Siege* (1973)** A highly charged political film by Greek filmmaker Constantin Costa-Gavras who used a true story to convey his contempt for fascism in all its forms. In this film, shot on location in Salvador **Allende**'s Chile (1970–1973), Uruguay is being slowly transformed from one of Latin America's most democratic and stable countries into a military-authoritarian regime. Uruguay was one of many South American countries in the 1970s that experienced revolutionary turmoil, government repression (torture, political **assassination**, censorship, and mass disappearances), and military rule. By the late 1960s, Uruguay was in the midst of severe economic decline and a democratic system on life support. Labor strikes, student demonstrations, and militant street violence became increasingly normal and part of day-to-day life in Uruguay.

Costa-Gavras' *State of Siege* reflects his interest in politics, U.S.–Latin American relations, and political ideologies, arguing that there is far more to fear from fascism than communism. Costa-Gavras' father, a Greek who emigrated from the USSR to Athens in the early 1930s, was a small bureaucrat suspected of Communist agitation and whose son (Constantin, born in 1933) suffered from the persecution of leftists in Greece. He studied literature at the Sorbonne in France and later attended the main French film school in Paris. There are circles of conflict, power, conscience, and moral ambiguity woven into this film that centers on an American (Philip M. Santori played by Yves Montand) working for the **Agency for International Development (AID)** who is kidnaped by left-wing urban revolutionaries in Montevideo in 1970. The real-life figure who is the subject of this film, Dan Mitrione, worked for AID's Office of Public Safety (OPS) as an adviser who helped "professionalize" torture and psychological techniques on political prisoners. The OPS was the major international police trainer for the **Central Intelligence Agency (CIA)** until it was abolished by the U.S. Congress in 1974 because of revelations about teaching the techniques of torture and repression. Once Congress outlawed the use of foreign assistance money for police training (except for drug enforcement programs), OPS agents like Dan Mitrione simply became Drug Enforcement Agency (DEA) agents using similar strategies and techniques. During the **Nixon** administration, at least twenty Uruguayan police officers attended an eight-week course at CIA/OPS schools in Washington, D.C., and Los Fresnos, Texas, where they learned about the design, manufacture, and employment of bombs and incendiary devises. The official rationale for this type of training was that policemen needed such training to handle bombs placed by suspected terrorists.

The well-organized and secretive guerrilla group in Uruguay called themselves Tupamaros (Movement of National Liberation—Tupamaros) and at first tried to avoid bloodshed whenever possible. William Blum, author of *Killing Hope* (1995), refers to them as, "Perhaps the cleverest, most resourceful and most sophisticated urban guerrillas the world has ever seen." With a Robin Hood philosophy, they were adept at capturing the public's sympathy and support. Their tactics focused on exposing corruption and deceit at the highest levels. Prominent figures who engaged in nefarious activities and skulduggery and escaped the wrath of the courts, legislature, and press, were kidnaped and then tried before a "People's Court." The resulting embarrassing and intriguing dialogues and interrogations were recorded and published (or broadcast) for public consumption. For top officials, these were outrageous actions that Uruguay's government could not tolerate. The success of the Tupamaros stemmed from the fact that their members and secret supporters held key positions in the government, banks, universities, military, police, and the world of art and other professions. As the conflict between the Tupamaros and the Uruguayan authorities escalated, the government resorted to more repressive and systematic methods of squashing the troublesome urban guerrillas. Many were arrested and tortured, often with the approval of the United States. After Santori is kidnaped, he and one of the Tupamaro leaders have the following exchange, reflecting vastly different views of the world:

> TUPAMARO GUERRILLA: You're not just another civil servant, Mr. Santori. You are neither a minor official nor the average specialist. You are a leader. You directed the police in Brazil, Santo Domingo [Dominican Republic], and our police. This you do yourself, and the men you send to Washington where they are taught to betray their own countries. You claim to defend freedom and democracy; your methods are war, torture, fascism. You agree don't you, Mr. Santori?
>
> SANTORI: You are subversives, you're communists, you work for the ruination of our society, the values that uphold civilization and Christianity, the free world's very way of life. You're an enemy to be fought and beaten, even in war. I'm curious about the type of civilization you want to build?
>
> TUPAMARO GUERRILLA: You're curious? That's a sign of weakness, Mr. Santori.

While Dan Mitrione did not introduce the practice of torturing dissidents in Uruguay, or elsewhere, his job was to teach scientific refinement of the unpleasant task of inflicting pain on prisoners to extract information that could be used to intimidate or capture more "subversives" and induce a fear of meddling in further subversive activities. Mitrione used a sound-proof room in the basement of his house in Montevideo to demonstrate torture techniques. He was an expert in the philosophy and art of modern torture; he explained that his interrogations always succeeded because he followed strict rules for treating the prisoner. After determining the prisoner's physical state, his degree of resistance (by means of medical examination), Mitrione explained, the chance of death is minimized. Mitrione developed a motto for his torture techniques: "The precise pain, in the precise place, in the precise amount, for the desired effect." Efforts to use **international law** to prevent the use of torture have not been successful in fully eliminating the practice worldwide, as documented by Amnesty International in its annual reports on **human rights** violations.

While in Tupamaro captivity, Dan Mitrione (Philip Michael Santori) was not tortured, but they demanded the release of some 150 prisoners in exchange for letting him go. When the Nixon administration sent over 100 FBI agents to search for Mitrione, and the Uruguayan government refused to meet the Tupamaro demands, Mitrione was killed on July 31, 1970, five days after his capture. By 1972 the military had taken over the government of Uruguay, Congress was dissolved, and most of the Tupamaros had been jailed, killed, or driven into exile. For the next eleven years, Uruguay remained under a state of siege (a situation where constitutional guarantees were suspended and the president was granted dictatorial powers to handle the domestic turmoil or external invasion) and became one of South America's most repressive **dictatorships** where torture was routine and automatic. At one point it had the highest number of political prisoners per capita in the world, including Cuba.

State of Siege opens without a title or any introduction, as if the story had already begun. It is a bit slow and without much dialogue at first, but the pace increases as the Uruguayan political system creaks under the growing pressure of domestic turmoil and resistance. It comes full circle at the end as Mitrione's flag-draped body is sent back to the United States and his replacement arrives on another Braniff flight with similar orders and responsibilities in Uruguay. The dark and somber tones in this film resonate with its message of the brutality of **Cold War** anti-Communism. *See also* Anti-Americanism; Guerrilla Warfare; Kissinger, Henry Alfred; School of the Americas (SOA); Terrorism.

Suggested Reading

William Blum, *Killing Hope: U.S. Military and CIA Interventions Since World War II* (Monroe, ME: Common Courage Press, 1995); Blum, *Rogue State: A Guide to the World's Only Superpower* (Monroe, ME: Common Courage Press, 2000); Arturo C. Porzecanski, *Uruguay's Tupamaros: The Urban Guerrilla* (New York: Praeger, 1973).

Summit of the Americas As of 2004, there have been three important meetings by the member states of the hemisphere in Miami, Florida (1994); Santiago, Chile (1998); and Ottawa, Canada (2001). A fourth Summit of the Americas is scheduled for November 2005 in Mar del Plata, Argentina. The first meeting was held in Miami, Florida, in December 1994 and attended by thirty-four democratically elected heads of state in the Americas. President Bill **Clinton** called for the meeting, the first of several to take place in the hemisphere over the next decade, and presided over its deliberations that eventually culminated in a new agenda for the members of the **Organization of American States (OAS)**. Fidel **Castro** was not invited to the meeting, which led to some criticism of U.S.–Cuba policy, particularly the punitive trade embargo. The Summit of the Americas reflected the growing importance of hemispheric issues after the **Cold War**, contained in the four major categories of attention by the member states: democracy, trade, poverty, and sustainable development. In a Plan of Action document, the OAS was assigned specific duties in addressing the problems of **democracy**, **drug trafficking**, **human rights**, **terrorism**, and security. The priorities reflected the need for collective and individual action and the recognition that the OAS was the multilateral institution to handle the pressing problems facing the hemisphere. In dealing with two areas—promoting trade and strengthening democracy—principal agencies of the OAS were given the task of implementing what the heads of states had agreed to pursue. At the end of the 1994 Miami Summit, plans were made to invite Chile to join the **North American Free Trade Agreement (NAFTA)**, an invitation that was stalled by conservative members of the U.S. Congress, and to plan the next Summit of the Americas for Santiago, Chile, in 1998. The United States and Chile signed a Free Trade Agreement (FTA) in 2003 that entered into force on January 1, 2004, but Chile remains outside of the NAFTA arrangement. A third Summit of the Americas was held in Ottawa, Canada in 2001 to be followed by a fourth in Argentina in 2005. The connection between the OAS and the three summit meetings was designed to facilitate the establishment of the **Free Trade Area of the Americas (FTAA)** by the year 2005, but it also remains in limbo because of major differences between the United States and key Latin American countries on trade matters. *See also* Bush, George W.

Suggested Reading

Feinberg, Richard, *Summitry in the Americas: A Progress Report* (Washington, DC: Institute for International Economics, 1997); Robin Rosenberg and Stephen Stein, eds., *Advancing the Miami Process: Civil Society and the Summit of the Americas* (Coral Gables, FL: North-South Center, 1995); Peter H. Smith, *Talons of the Eagle: Dynamics of U.S.–Latin American Relations*, 2nd ed. (New York: Oxford University Press, 2000).

Szulc, Tadeusz Witold (1926–2001) Tad Szulc was a foreign correspondent for the *New York Times* between 1953 and 1972, covering revolutions, military takeovers, and **Cold War** intrigue, mostly in Latin America. After retiring from the *Times* he developed a career as an author of books on foreign affairs and as a critical commentator on foreign policy. Szulc was known as a persistent and aggressive reporter, but he also had a charmed way of being in key areas of Latin America at the right time, covering the overthrow of Juan **Perón** in Argentina and Marcos **Pérez Jiménez** in Venezuela, and the early years of the Cuban Revolution. He is best known for uncovering the imminent assault on Cuba in April 1961 that later became known as the **Bay of Pigs** invasion. While on a stopover in Miami, Szulc picked up the news story that anti-**Castro** partisans, with **Central Intelligence Agency (CIA)** direction and financing, were planning an invasion of Cuba that later became a major foreign policy blunder and one of the defining events of the Cold War. His invasion of Cuba story that appeared on the front page of the *New York Times* on April 7, 1961, was partially censored—references to the timing of the attack and specific references to the Central Intelligence Agency were omitted—because of concerns about national security. The following day he wrote another story describing how legions of exiled Cubans were planning secret missions into Cuba with the goal of gaining a beachhead and establishing a "Government in Arms" that would then request diplomatic recognition by other governments. He was considered one of the key chroniclers of the Cuban Revolution, along with other correspondents such as Ruby Hart Phillips, Herbert **Matthews**, and Haynes Johnson.

Tad Szulc was born in Poland in 1926 and educated in Switzerland and Brazil. His parents moved to Brazil in the 1930s, but he was left behind at a Swiss boarding school until he had finished in 1941. He then joined his family and began his studies at the University of Brazil from 1943 to 1945. On finishing at the university he worked as a reporter for the Associated Press in Rio de Janeiro from 1945 until 1949 before taking a job with United Press International covering the **United Nations (UN)**. In 1953 he started work for the *New York Times* where he was known for his custom-made shirts, fancy tailored suits, and an appetite for gourmet food and classy restaurants.

Tad Szulc's reporting on the Bay of Pigs invasion and a co-authored book—*The Cuban Invasion: The Chronicle of a Disaster* (1962)—covering the magnitude of the foreign policy blunder angered the CIA, particularly since they were embarrassed and tried to coverup the fiasco. A CIA dossier on him later revealed that he was characterized as "anti-agency" and "under suspicion as a hostile foreign agent" yet the agency admitted they had no case against Mr. Szulc. In his Bay of Pigs reporting, he detailed the anti-Castro intrigue in Miami, including sabotage and gunrunning into Cuba, night flights to military training camps in Guatemala, and plans to set up a beachhead in Cuba with an exile government prepared to request diplomatic recognition from foreign governments. President **Kennedy**—publicly furious about disclosures of the pending invasion—told *New York Times* editor Turner Catledge that had he printed more about the **covert operation**, "you would have saved us from a colossal mistake." He also had the fortune of being in Argentina to cover the military coup that removed Juan Perón from power, and the insurrectionary movement in Cuba that removed dictator Fulgencio **Batista** in late 1958.

Szulc was a prolific writer who chronicled the dramatic changes in Latin America and U.S.–Latin American relations wrought by the Cuban Revolution and the collapse of the *caudillo* (a strong-man ruler, often connected to the military) tyrants, beginning with Getulio Vargas (Brazil, 1954) and continuing with the downfall of Juan D. Perón (Argentina, 1955), Gustavo Rojas Pinilla (Colombia, 1957), Manuel Odría (Peru, 1957), Marcos Pérez Jiménez (Venezuela, 1958), and Fulgencio Batista (Cuba, 1958). After leaving the *New York Times* in 1972 he wrote ten more books, including a critical assessment of Henry **Kissinger**'s role in the downfall of Salvador **Allende** (*Illusion of Peace: Foreign Policy of the Nixon Years,* 1978) and a critical biography of Fidel Castro (*Fidel: A Critical Portrait*, 1987). His treatment of Latin American **revolutions**, **Washington policymaking**, and Cold War intrigue earned him the respect of reporters who operated with far less knowledge and dedication to understanding U.S.–Latin American relations. Tad Szulc died of cancer at his home in Washington, D.C., in 2001. *See also* Media; Scandals and Blunders.

Suggested Reading

Daniel Lewis, "Tad Szulc, Times Correspondent Who Uncovered Bay of Pigs Imbroglio, Dies at 74," *New York Times* (May 22, 2001); Karl E. Meyer and Tad Szulc, *The Cuban Invasion: The Chronicle of a Disaster* (New York: Praeger, 1962); Tad Szulc, *The Illusion of Peace: Foreign Policy in the Nixon Years* (New York: Viking, 1978); Szulc, ed., *The United States and the Caribbean* (Englewood Cliffs, NJ: Prentice Hall, 1971); Szulc, *Latin America* (New York: Atheneum, 1970); Szulc, *Dominican Diary* (New York: Delacorte Press, 1965); Szulc, *Winds of Revolution; Latin America Today and Tomorrow* (New York: Praeger, 1963); Szulc, *New Trends in Latin America* (New York: Foreign Policy Association, 1960); Szulc, *Twilight of the Tyrants* (New York: Henry Holt, 1959).

T

Taft, William Howard (1857–1930) Lawyer, judge, politician, and president of the United States (1909–1913) known for **Dollar Diplomacy**, a policy devised to increase U.S. diplomatic influence in Latin America and the Far East. By promoting government-backed American commercial expansion, Taft hoped to overcome the negative consequences of **Theodore Roosevelt**'s **Big Stick diplomacy** and plant the seeds of development through benevolent American supervision and counsel. In Taft's view, Dollar Diplomacy meant diplomacy helping dollars rather than dollars helping diplomacy. In reality, there was a blurring of the two—public and private—as Dollar Diplomacy ultimately boiled down to controlling the finances of nations in Central America and the Caribbean as a means of protecting U.S. business interests. President Taft used Dollar Diplomacy to create a protectorate in Nicaragua.

William Howard Taft was born in Cincinnati, Ohio, graduated from Yale (1878) and the Cincinnati Law School (1880). His early career was devoted to the practice of law and several judgeships. Prior to running for president in 1908, Taft headed a commission devoted to ending American military rule in the Philippines by establishing a civil government controlled by the United States. As the first civil governor of the Philippines (1901–1904), Taft worked to improve public education and economic development projects. A Republican, Taft served as secretary of war during the Theodore Roosevelt administration (1901–1909) and played a major role in the construction of the Panama Canal. When Roosevelt intervened in Cuba in 1906 to bring order and protect American investments, Taft oversaw the creation of a provisional government on the island. He defeated Democratic candidate William Jennings **Bryan** to win the presidency in 1908, was re-nominated in 1912, but finished a distant third behind Woodrow **Wilson** and Theodore Roosevelt. He retired to Yale University where he became a professor of law. Between 1921 and 1930, he served as chief justice of the Supreme Court, but illness forced Taft's resignation from the court in early 1930 and he died shortly thereafter.

Taft's proconsular assignments provided him with some exposure to tropical lands, particularly their political problems and the relationship between culture and economic development. Although he despised the people and their governments in Latin America, he believed that benevolent supervision would help to bring peace and prosperity to these lands. Since Taft and his secretary of state, Philander C. **Knox**, had limited knowledge of Latin America, responsibility for U.S.–Latin American relations came to rest on the shoulders of assistant secretary Francis Mairs Huntington Wilson. Huntington's diplomatic skills were tactless and insensitive; he had nothing positive to say about his impressions of Hispanic culture. He blamed the plight of the Latin American countries on the racial mixture of African and Indian with the Spaniard and always emphasized violence, alcohol, and the violation of women as common traits. For Taft and his Republican friends, only the firm hand (force, meaning **dictatorship**) and intellectual guidance of the United States would bring civilization and progress to the people of Latin America. *See also* Race and Racism.

Suggested Reading

Dana G. Munro, *Intervention and Dollar Diplomacy in the Caribbean, 1900–1921* (Princeton, NJ: Princeton University Press, 1964); Scott Nearing and Joseph Freeman, *Dollar Diplomacy: A Study in American Imperialism* (New York: Huebesch and Vicking, 1925); Cyrus Vesser, *A World Safe for Capitalism: Dollar Diplomacy and America's Rise to Global Power* (New York: Columbia University Press, 2002).

Taylor, Zachary (1784–1850) Military hero and president of the United States (1849–1850) who fought in the **Mexican-American War**, opposed the annexation of Cuba, and contributed to the agreement with Great Britain to settle disputes in Central America with the **Clayton-Bulwer Treaty** of 1850. Born in Montebello, Virginia, Taylor devoted his life to military service before his Whig Party nomination for the presidency in 1848. Known as "Old Rough and Ready," Taylor's biggest battlefield achievement was his defense of Buena Vista against Mexican General Santa Anna that contributed to the U.S. victory over Mexico in the Mexican-American War. His military record—War of 1812, Black Hawk War, Seminole Wars, and the Mexican-American War—earned him the Whig Party nomination and election to the presidency in 1848. With little experience in foreign affairs, Taylor had little success in resolving the heated debate over the extension of slavery and Anglo-American relations. His military background was unsuitable for compromising with European countries, and his disregard for diplomatic protocol often resulted in crises with France, Portugal, and Spain. However, his desire for harmonious relations with Great Britain over Central America did produce the Clayton-Bulwer Treaty that established joint control and protection over any future isthmian canal. Had he not opposed the annexation of Cuba—a desire of southern slaveholders—and conceded British control over Central America, the events that would eventually create a protectorate over Cuba and a U.S.–built canal in Panama may have never occurred. He died in office in 1850. *See also* Filibusters/Filibustering.

Suggested Reading

Karl Jack Bauer, *Zachary Taylor: Soldier, Planter, Statesman of the Old Southwest* (Baton Rouge: Louisiana University Press, 1985); Elbert Smith, *The Presidencies of Zachary Taylor and Millard Fillmore* (Lawrence: University of Kansas Press, 1988).

Teller Amendment or Resolution (1898) Amendment added to the joint resolution for war with Spain in 1898 by Senator Henry M. Teller (R-Colo.) that disavowed any intentions of exercising sovereignty over Cuba (except for peacekeeping) and declared that American control would be withdrawn as soon as pacification was achieved. The amendment was accepted without debate, but some members of Congress feared that the **McKinley** administration might use war with Spain to annex the island. Although the resolution declared that the Cuban people "are, and of right ought to be free, and independent," the **Spanish-Cuban-American War** and the subsequent military occupation altered this thinking and Cuba sovereignty. American troops remained on the island from 1898 to 1902, long after the war was over. Washington officials used the phrase "except for the pacification thereof" to justify the long military occupation and the approval of the **Platt Amendment** four years later. The Teller Resolution embodies one of the constant themes in U.S.–Latin American relations: the urge to maintain **hegemony** over places like Cuba while at the same time asserting the right of Caribbean people to liberty, sovereignty, independence, and self-government. The wording of the Teller Amendment—particularly the disavowal of interest in exercising sovereignty over Cuba after it achieved independence from Spain—provided hope to many Cubans that they would finally take charge of their own destiny. When the United States reneged on this pledge and made Cuba a protectorate of Washington, Cubans felt a sense of betrayal and frustration with the true intentions of the United States. *See also* Batista, Fulgencio; Castro Ruz, Fidel.

Suggested Reading

Samuel Flagg Bemis, *The Latin American Policy of the United States* (New York: Harcourt Brace, 1943); Robert H. Holden and Eric Zolov, eds., *Latin America and the United States: A Documentary History* (New York: Oxford University Press, 2000).

Terrorism Latin American governments and societies have faced threats from rebel groups—foreign and domestic—going back to the nineteenth century; however, the level of U.S. interest in countering these groups is a recent phenomenon. The difficulties in fighting terrorism in Latin America have been compounded by the following factors: (1) the lack of a precise definition of what exactly constitutes terrorism; (2) the declining power of the state in Latin America at a time when the United States is most concerned with terrorism; (3) directing most of the war against terrorism at Colombia where U.S. military and intelligence agencies have been ordered to assist the Colombian military hunt down and wipe out terrorist groups; (4) Islamic terrorist groups are located far from the United States, mostly in the Triple Frontier area that connects Paraguay, Brazil, and Argentina; (5) few, if any, links have been found between Latin American terrorist/rebel groups and Osama bin Laden's Al-Qaeda network; and (6) the refusal to believe that some terrorists are the creation of American foreign policy. Currently, Colombia is the center of the U.S. war on terrorism in Latin America where the **George W. Bush** administration has widened the role of the U.S. military to shift from fighting the drug war to fighting the global war on terrorism.

The U.S. government has opted for a definition of terrorism that allows the intelligence community to confront the threat in the broadest possible manner. For example, the **Central Intelligence Agency (CIA)** is guided by Title 22 of the U.S. Code, Section 2656f(d), which defines "terrorism" as "a premeditated, politically motivated violence perpetrated against noncombatant targets by sub-national groups or clandestine agents, usually intended to influence an audience." The official definition places more emphasis on "international terrorism" than domestic terrorism, meaning activity that involves the territory or the citizens of more than one country. In the official view, terrorist groups are far more likely to engage in international terrorism than domestic groups, or subgroups, with no international affiliation.

In Washington, the **State Department**'s counter-terrorism coordinator works with the Pentagon, the Central Intelligence Agency, and the Office of Homeland Security to fight terrorism in Latin America. Parts of Latin America where drug trade and covert action have been the most pronounced are also where terrorism has thrived. In the wake of **September 11, 2001**, the George W. Bush administration has placed the Pentagon at the center of the war on terrorism. In what some considered a bizarre move, John Poindexter, working out of the Pentagon, concocted a plan that would allow speculators (including terrorists) to profit from anonymous bets on future attacks against U.S. personnel and interests. Poindexter, once convicted for lying to Congress about the **Iran-Contra scandal**, designed a program known as Total Information Awareness (later renamed to Terrorist Information Awareness) to identify potential terrorists by compiling a detailed electronic file on millions of Americans. His "Policy Analysis Market" was shut down in July 2003, and Poindexter resigned from his Pentagon post several weeks later. As of 2005, the U.S. Department of State continued to list opposition groups in Colombia (ELN, FARC, ANUC) and Peru (Sendero Luminoso, Tupac Amaru) as terrorist organizations. The United States began implementing new anti-terror regulations in 2004 that required citizens from twenty-seven nations to be fingerprinted and photographed when entering the United States. Brazil responded by requiring the same rules for Americans entering Brazil.

One of the ironies of terrorism is that its spread after the Vietnam War is largely attributable to American **Cold War** foreign policy. Once the United States decided to shift from a strategy of direct military **intervention** in the fight against global and regional communism to one of supporting low-level insurgency by private armed groups, it entered a new world of supporting terrorist and proto-terrorist movements in Latin America and elsewhere. The **Reagan Doctrine** was aimed at the creation of private militias capable of creating terror and spreading information about how to produce and spread violence after the Cold War ended. In an effort to defeat Cuban-inspired Marxist guerrillas in Central America, President Ronald **Reagan** and the head of the CIA, William **Casey**, spawned their own homegrown terrorist network that would last beyond the creation of proxy warriors. The United States was able to disarm the Nicaraguan **Contras** with the help of Central America, but members of the Afghan mujahdeen turned on the United States after the Soviets were defeated in Afghanistan. The best known of the CIA-trained terrorists was Osama bin Laden. While there are still competing theories of the roots of terrorism, there is mounting evidence that the era of proxy warfare that grew out of the late Cold War is more of a political phenomenon than a cultural or philosophical one. Clearly, the danger in creating a privatized and ideologically stateless resistance force is the potential for "**blowback**" from a "realist" foreign policy based on the perceived advantages of low-intensity warfare and ideologically motivated terrorist networks.

Since the United States declared war on terrorism in 2001 there have been ten times more government resources devoted to investigations of Cuban embargo violations than efforts to track Al-Qaeda and Saddam Hussein's money. The Treasury Department seems to be unable to adjust from the Cold War hostility toward Fidel **Castro**'s Cuba to the war on terrorism. In early 2004 the Office of Foreign Assets Control, the government agency responsible for punishing those who travel illegally to Cuba, had twenty-one full-time agents working on Cuba violations and just four full-time personnel hunting Osama bin Laden and Saddam's bounty of stolen riches. In what seems like an obvious bureaucratic distortion, the U.S. government needs to examine its priorities in dealing with threats from terrorism. The Pentagon is now advocating the expansion of Latin American armies to wage war on terrorists in Latin America, noting the threats from "traditional" terrorists (**drug traffickers**, urban crime syndicates, and paramilitary groups) and "emerging" terrorists (radical populists such as now exist in Venezuela and Bolivia). In addition to expanding military-to-military contacts, the U.S. military wants to remove legal barriers that ban the armed forces from cooperating with police and civilian intelligence agencies. This change in relationship worries those who fear expanding SOUTHCOM's role in Latin America will lead to **human rights** violations against anyone labeled a "terrorist." In the wake of the September 11, 2001, terrorist attacks on the United States, attitudes toward fighting terrorism have changed dramatically, including the acceptable use of torture to get information that will save society from terrorism. The documented abuse of suspected detainees in Afghanistan, Iraq, and **Guantánamo Bay**, Cuba, suggest that future **anti-Americanism** in Latin America may be rooted in the process of defining and handling threats to the United States. *See also* Southern Command; Threat Perception/Assessment.

Suggested Reading

William Blum, *Rogue State: A Guide to the World's Only Superpower* (Monroe, ME: Common Courage Press, 2000); Ari Chaplin, *Terror: The New Theater of War: Mao's Legacy: Selected Cases of Terrorism in the 20th and 21st Centuries* (Lanham, MD: University Press of America, 2003); Juan E. Corradi, Patricia Weiss Fagen, and Manuel A. Garretón, eds., *Fear at the Edge: State Terror and Resistance in Latin America* (Berkeley: University of California Press, 1992); Jack Epstein, "General Seeks Boost for Latin American Armies," *San Francisco Chronicle* (April 30, 2004); Robert H. Holden, *Armies Without Nations: Public Violence and State Formation in Central America, 1821–1960* (New York: Oxford University Press, 2004); Kees Kooning and Dirk Kruijt, *Societies of Fear: The Legacy of Civil War, Violence and Terror in Latin America* (London: Zed Books, 1999); *Latin America and the U.S. "War on Terror"* (London: Latin American Newsletters, 2003); Max G. Manwaring, *Latin America* (Carlisle Barracks, PA: Strategic Studies Institute; U.S. Army War College, 2003); Linda Robinson, "Warrior Class," *U.S. News and World Report* (February 10, 2003); Larry Rohter, "South America Region Under Watch for Signs of Terrorists," *New York Times* (December 15, 2002); John Solomon, "More Agents Track Castro than Bin Laden," *Associated Press* (April 29, 2004); "The War on Terrorism," www.cia.gov/terrorism/faqs; U.S. House of Representatives, Special Oversight Panel on Terrorism of the Committee on Armed Services, *Terrorism and Threats to U.S. in Latin America* (June 29, 2000).

Think Tanks Think tanks have become major factors in the formulation and execution of U.S.–Latin American policy. Their primary activity is research, not lobbying, the major focus of interest groups. Nevertheless, there is a fuzzy boundary between interest groups and think tanks when it comes to the policy-making process. Some think tanks do engage in lobbying and at times form coalitions with other non-governmental organizations to influence Latin American policy issues. As private, policy-oriented groups, think tanks have grown dramatically over the past twenty-five years and have become important components of the policy-making process. Most of the Latin America–focused think tanks are smaller and have less political clout than the larger, more established, think tanks in Washington. The smaller, specialized Latin American policy think tanks include the **Inter-American Dialogue**, the **Council on Hemispheric Affairs (COHA)**, and the Council on Hemispheric Security. According to Howard **Wiarda**, the rise of think tanks is related to significant changes in the American political landscape. First, the increasing need for experts has helped the boom in private non-governmental think tanks. Second, the increased bureaucratization of American politics have led policymakers to turn to private think tanks as way of cutting through layers of official bureaucracy. Third, the difficulty of getting new or innovative policy ideas accepted has helped to create the need for more think tanks. Think tanks can funnel ideas and recommendations to policymakers much faster than the tradition foreign policy bureaucracies in Washington. Fourth, think tank growth is part of a broader trend toward direct representation in the policy-making process, surpassing the more common political intermediaries such as political parties, periodic elections, or the U.S. Congress. Last, the growth of think tanks can be attributed to the trend in the privatization of government functions.

What is the source of think tank influence? Think tanks have developed a number of strategies for influencing **Washington policymakers**. First, think tanks have influence because they are perceived as having expertise and knowledge on a particular policy issue. Second, think tanks often host lunches, dinners, and seminars where members of Congress, **ambassadors**, aides, journalists, and executive branch personnel can mix in informal get-togethers. Third, think tank scholars appear frequently on television and are often quoted in the print **media**. In this way think tank representatives can influence the debate over a particular Latin American policy issue. Fourth, think tank representatives testify at congressional hearings. Fifth, think tanks have high-level advisory boards and councils that draw upon prominent diplomats, members of Congress, businesspeople, and foundation officials to assist in various projects. Sixth, think tanks publish materials of value for policy formulation and have public relations offices to target influential policymakers in Washington. Over time, successful think tanks develop a reputation for solid research, successful fund-raising, and for having a measurable impact on the policy-making process. Unfortunately, there is an ebb and flow of influence in Washington that is connected to the salience of the Latin American policy issue, the party in power in Washington, and the importance of Latin America to the president of the United States. In any case, one cannot understand the policy-making process, or the outcome, without considering the role of research organizations devoted to public policy analysis and influence. Political ideology is important for the success of think tanks as measured by media citations. For example, think tanks with a centrist or conservative political orientation receive at least ten times more coverage than those with a progressive political orientation (Table 2). *See also* American Enterprise Institute (AEI); Carter Center; Heritage Foundation.

Table 2
Media Citations of Major Think Tanks, 2003

Think Tank	Political Orientation	Year, 2003
Brookings Institution	Centrist	4,784
Council on Foreign Relations	Centrist	3,393
Heritage Foundation	Conservative	3,141
American Enterprise Institute	Conservative	2,645
Center for Strategic and International Studies	Conservative	2,386
Carter Center	Centrist	458
Institute for Policy Studies	Progressive	358

Source: Michael Dolny, "Think Tank Coverage," *Extra!* (June 2004), p. 28.

Suggested Reading

Howard J. Wiarda, "Think Tanks," in David W. Dent, ed., *U.S.–Latin American Policymaking: A Reference Handbook* (Westport, CT: Greenwood Press, 1995).

Thomson-Urrutia Treaty (1921) Treaty between the United States and Colombia that provided recompense for U.S. involvement in separating Panama from Colombia in 1903. The loss of Panama was a traumatic event for Colombia, one that resulted in **anti-Americanism** from the way the nation's leaders were treated by President **Theodore Roosevelt**. Roosevelt's exercise of **Big Stick diplomacy** also fanned resentment against U.S. **imperialism** throughout Latin America. In Colombia, bitter feelings increased after negotiations over compensation dragged on for more than a decade. President Woodrow **Wilson** tried to heal the inter-American rift caused by the loss of Panama by submitting a treaty to the U.S. Senate that attempted to mollify Colombia and improve relations with the rest of Latin America. In April 1914, Thaddeus A. Thomson, U.S. minister to Colombia, and Colombian Foreign Minister José Urrutia negotiated a treaty that expressed regret for the U.S. role in the 1903 Panamanian uprising and offered an indemnity of $25 million to Colombia. Wilson faced strong opposition from former President Roosevelt who called the proposed agreement "blackmail" and two Republican senators, Albert Fall and Henry Cabot **Lodge**, who objected to any apology and wanted to use the treaty to wrestle oil concessions from the Colombians. After the Colombians announced that their government would control all petroleum rights, the U.S. Senate remained stalwart and refused to act on the treaty for the remainder of Wilson's term. After a seven-year interval, the U.S. Congress revived the treaty, made several modifications, and the Senate finally approved the amended version. In the final version, the United States consented to pay Colombia $25 million as compensation for the Panama affair but refused to offer a formal apology. In the final agreement the United States was able to obtain oil concessions that previously had been denied to American companies. Colombia accepted the changes in the treaty and ratified the settlement in 1922, thereby recognizing Panama's independence for the first time. The Thomson-Urrutia treaty settled the matter of Panama, but the sordid affair left a bitter legacy that complicated future relations. Nevertheless, U.S.–Colombian relations gradually improved as the Colombian government came to realize that prudent statecraft should not challenge Washington, but bend to the wishes of its northern neighbor in matters of economic and security policy. *See also* Panama Canal Treaties.

Suggested Reading

David W. Dent, *The Legacy of the Monroe Doctrine: A Reference Guide to U.S. Involvement in Latin America and the Caribbean* (Westport, CT: Greenwood Press, 1999).

Threat Perception/Assessment The United States has been concerned since the War of 1812 that an extra-hemispheric adversary might seize territory in Latin America and use it as a base to attack the United States. This fear was founded on the belief that Latin Americans were inferior and immature and incapable of running their own affairs, thus inoculating themselves from foreign intruders capable of threatening the United States. With the exception of Francisco "Pancho" **Villa**'s raid on Columbus, New Mexico, in 1916, this fear has been unfounded; the United States has never been attacked militarily by a Latin American country, with or without foreign involvement. Despite the threats posed by **revolutions**, two world wars, the East-West conflict known as the **Cold War**, the **Cuban Missile Crisis**, and the war on **terrorism**, the basic security of the United States has never been really jeopardized from Latin American sources.

This has not stopped the United States—the only hemispheric power to possess nuclear weapons—from *perceiving or manufacturing* a wide variety of threats inside Latin America, many of which could damage the security of the United States. In some cases the threats were minimal, but exaggerated for domestic political purposes. President Ronald **Reagan**'s strategy for dealing with **Sandinista** Nicaragua was to pressure U.S. allies in Europe to prevent them from supplying arms to Managua once the **Contra** war was underway. This left the Nicaraguans with little choice but to seek weapons from the Soviet Union and Cuba to defend itself from U.S. aggression. Nicaragua was never a threat to the United States, but the arrival of Soviet weapons and Cuban advisers—a direct result of U.S. policy—provided the perfect justification for the **Reagan Doctrine** of supporting anti-Communist freedom fighters. In other cases the U.S. response to perceived threats actually increased the security threat to the United States. The United States is no longer threatened by **Castro**'s Cuba, but the **State Department** continues to define Cuba as a threat to punish Castro for his defiance and humiliation of the United States over such a long period of time.

Threat perception in Washington varies according to regime type in Latin America and the Caribbean. The United States has been much more tolerant of right-wing **dictatorships** and military regimes in Latin America than governments on the left. Since the time of the **Monroe Doctrine**, the Latin American policy of the United States has had little to do with Latin America as such, but a great deal to do with how U.S. power is projected around the globe and the fear of the projected power of adversaries in the Western Hemisphere. In cases where other governments were perceived as incapable of dealing with these threats and attacks, then the United States would be forced to back autocratic governments willing to carry out harsh measures of repression. Of the many instances of U.S. **intervention** in Latin America, most have been carried out to prevent, or pre-empt, perceived threats to the ability of the United States to project power in Latin America and beyond. **Washington policymakers** have learned that the use of extra-hemispheric threats can serve as powerful tools of public persuasion and forceful rationales for implementing policy initiatives. Furthermore, the **media** often fail to scrutinize skeptically the claims about whether foreign powers, terrorists, or Communists actually pose a threat to the security of the United States. The Monroe Doctrine was the perfect instrument to justify a U.S. response to almost any kind of enemy or threat in the Americas, from monarchism to terrorism. And the media often finds it irresistible to report the doomsayer arguments and the security threats verbatim.

In the early years of the Cold War scholars found that the Soviet threat was manipulated by reactionary southern members of Congress before the Cold War, not after. Beginning in 1945, House Un-American Activities Committee (HUAC) investigations targeted many on the left in Latin America as enemies of the state. This search for fifth-column threats did serious damage to the policy-making process by reinforcing the myth that there was a monolithic Communist movement directed from Moscow, promoted the idea that Communist movements lacked popular support and only came to power through deceitful fifth-column tactics, and only remained in power through the use of terror against their people. These false premises encouraged the use of anti-Communist radio broadcasting, the use of counter-revolutionary armies, **assassination** plots, and other forms of **propaganda** to bring about **regime change**. This meant that all Latin American leftists were Soviet agents and therefore a "threat" to the United States. President **Eisenhower**'s view of ideological threats was consistent with the HUAC and on this basis he created a psychological warfare committee to advise him on covert ways of removing suspect Latin American leaders. Because Jacobo **Arbenz** of Guatemala appointed a few Communists to cabinet posts, advanced a progressive land reform program, and issued a decree nationalizing the **United Fruit Company**, he became the target of a plan to oust him in 1954. The plan worked and Arbenz resigned, but the same tactics—radio broadcasts coordinated with a covert military operation—failed to remove Fidel Castro seven years later. The **Central Intelligence Agency (CIA)**–supported troops—mostly disgruntled military men or members of the old elite—had no interest in **democracy** because of its capacity to upset the status quo. In the aftermath of **World War II**, congressional opponents of the New Deal, racial integration, and democracy—Karl Mundt and John Rankin to name a few—helped foster the postwar anti-Communist hysteria that would prove to be so damaging to U.S.–Latin American relations during the Cold War.

The high-level meetings in Washington that planned the **Bay of Pigs** invasion blundered because much of the intelligence distorted the threat from Castro's Cuba and falsely claimed that a small invasion force made up of American-backed rebels, once established on the island, would face little resistance because the Cuban people would rise up against Castro and topple the revolutionary government. When Richard **Bissell**, architect of the Bay of Pigs intelligence, was quizzed about the logic of such a plan, he lied by claiming he possessed a classified National Intelligence Estimate to back his case. President John F. **Kennedy** went along with intelligence that led to the debacle based on Bissell's misconception, and enthusiasm, that Cuban exiles were correct in their assessment of Castro's weak hold on the island. At least Kennedy learned from the blunder that threat estimates by intelligence and military advisers had to be thoroughly challenged.

With the Dominican Republic in turmoil in 1965, President Lyndon B. **Johnson** invaded the island on the basis of a panicky telegram from W. Tapley Bennett, U.S. **ambassador** in Santo Domingo at the time. With Juan Bosch leading a revolt against the Dominican military that had replaced him after he was duly elected, President Johnson ordered 20,000 U.S. forces to the Dominican Republic to quell the threat because he was told by the ambassador and U.S. intelligence agencies that Communists had infiltrated, perhaps even dominated, the Bosch insurgency. In this case, there was not a single American injured in the revolt, the handful of "Communists" were non-existent, yet the president decided that the facts (and inherently the threat) required the introduction of heavy American firepower. Clearly, there were other options that could have been employed to handle the "fear of another Communist takeover in the Dominican Republic." In the view of scholar Jerome Slater, "the risk [of Castroite forces taking over] was not yet sufficiently great to justify the predictably enormous political and moral costs that the intervention entailed" (Slater, 1970: 194).

Chile became a classic case of how U.S. government intelligence estimates were either used selectively or completely ignored by three American presidents (Johnson, **Nixon**, and **Ford**) and their senior advisers (**Kissinger**, **Helms**, McCone) who all believed that Salvador **Allende** posed a serious national security threat to the United States and as such deserved the covert intervention he confronted from his election through his truncated presidency. As documented in the **Church Committee**'s investigation, *Covert Action in Chile*, a CIA Intelligence Memorandum, issued shortly after Allende's September 4, 1970, electoral victory, stated that an Allende regime would pose no threat to U.S. national security. "The Group [Interdepartmental Group for Inter-American Affairs], made up of officials representing CIA, State, Defense, and the White House, concluded that the United States had no vital interests within Chile, the world military balance of power would not be significantly altered by an Allende regime, and an Allende victory in Chile would not pose any likely threat to the peace of the region." This denial of a strategic threat by U.S. intelligence forces, and other estimates, did not stop Henry Kissinger and other members of the Nixon administration, from arguing that an Allende victory would constitute a serious threat to U.S. security. For example, in September 1970, Henry Kissinger reasoned that if Allende was allowed to take office he would not only create "some sort of communist government," and a second Cuba, but also present "massive problems" for the United States and "the whole Western Hemisphere." No one seemed to question whether the perceived threat of an Allende regime justified the magnitude of the U.S. response and the ensuing cost of having a brutal dictatorship so closely tied to the United States at a time of growing concern over the lack of democracy, disappearances, torture, and serious violations of **human rights** in Chile.

The logic of responding to external threats from the Monroe Doctrine forward is often tied to a strategic argument that great powers carry the burden of credibility and responsibility others do not possess. At the core of the **Kissinger Commission** report was the belief that if the United States cannot prevail in Central America, then it will lose the credibility of major allies and treaty commitments abroad, regardless of the logic of the response to change in the Central American region. In 1985, the U.S. Department of State published *The Soviet-Cuban Connection in Central America and the Caribbean* to demonstrate what the Reagan administration perceived as a major threat from Soviet-backed guerrilla movements in the region. In one of many of Reagan's televised speeches to the nation on May 9, 1984, he attempted to demonstrate the magnitude of the Communist threat in Central America:

> As the National Bipartisan Commission on Central America, chaired by Henry Kissinger, agreed, if we do nothing or if we continue to provide too little help, our choice will be a Communist Central America with additional Communist military bases on the mainland of this hemisphere, and Communist subversion spreading southward and northward. This Communist subversion poses the threat that 100 million people from Panama to the open border on our south could come under the control of pro-Soviet regimes.

President Reagan's apocalyptic vision of threat, and his persuasive speaking skills, gave him considerable power to define the nature of the threat and the appropriate response. In a long and alarming speech to the nation on March 16, 1986 (see Appendix), President Reagan delivered a threat-based argument for funding his Nicaraguan "freedom fighters." The frequent rhetoric that presidents use of protecting American lives is often false or exaggerated. Threats can be easily manufactured, as with the case of State Department White Papers, Pentagon intelligence reports, congressional testimony, **think tank** documents; or the hired work of lobbyist and public relations firms. The United Fruit Company's public relations counsel, Edward **Bernays**, had little trouble manufacturing a Communist threat in Guatemala that eventually convinced the Eisenhower administration to organize an elaborate covert intervention to remove the country's democratically elected president, Jacobo Arbenz. Cuba remains a "threat" to the United States because it is listed as one of six countries in the world that sponsor terrorism, despite the fact there is no evidence to back up this assertion. When conservative Republicans took charge of Latin American policy after the election of Ronald Reagan, many of the holdovers from the Carter years were purged from the Latin American bureau because they had not taken the threat of communism in Latin American seriously enough.

The Cuban American National Foundation (CANF) has spent years trying to demonstrate to Washington the security threat posed by Castro's Cuba. In *Cuba: Assessing the Threat to U.S. Security*, the Castro regime is linked to international terrorism; in addition, Cuba is accused of being a "hotbed for terrorists," possesses biochemical weapons, and engages in cyber-warfare against the United States. In the aftermath of **September 11, 2001**, and the pre-emptive war to remove Saddam Hussein in Iraq, hard-line Cuban Americans have gone to great lengths to establish the magnitude of Cuba's threat to the United States. Although the **George W. Bush** administration still insists that Castro's government remain on the list of six nations (Iran, Libya, North Korea, Sudan, and Syria) that "support terrorism," there is no evidence that the United States is planning another invasion of Cuba.

Presidents have tremendous power when it comes to oversimplifying security threats and framing a foreign crisis for maximum partisan benefit. The American public is susceptible to presidential manipulation of threats to the nation because of the public's lack of interest in news from Latin America, fragmentary or conflicting media reports devoid of depth or skepticism, and the capacity of Washington policymakers to sell just about any foreign conflict through obfuscation and distortion of the facts related to the perceived threat. It doesn't seem to bother the White House or the State Department that at the same time the president is condemning other nations for "sponsoring terrorism," anti-Castro Cuban exiles in Miami have committed hundreds of terrorist acts in the name of freedom and anti-communism. The basic flaw in the intelligence gathering and threat perception process, according to Richard Goodwin, is that "we are more likely to 'know' what we want to know than what we don't want to know" (Goodwin, 2004: 15). *See also* German Threat; Guatemala, U.S. Invasion of (1954); Scandals and Blunders.

Suggested Reading

Richard Goodwin, "Making the Facts Fit the Case for War," *New York Times* (February 8, 2004); Robert Kagan and William Kristol, eds., *Present Dangers: Crisis and Opportunity in American Foreign and Defense Policy* (San Francisco: Encounter Books, 2000); Adolfo Leyva de Varona, ed., *Cuba: Assessing the Threat to U.S. Security* (Miami: The Endowment for Cuban American Studies, 2001); David J. Myers, ed., *Regional Hegemons: Threat Perception and Strategic Responses* (Boulder, CO: Westview Press, 1991); Ronald Reagan, "Nicaragua: Aiding the Contras," speech delivered to the American people, Washington, DC, March 16, 1986 from *Vital Speeches of the Day* (April 15, 1986); Jerome Slater, *Intervention and Negotiation: The United States and the Dominican Revolution* (New York: Harper and Row, 1970); Wayne S. Smith, ed., *The Russians Aren't Coming: New Soviet Policy in Latin America* (Boulder, CO: Lynne Rienner, 1992); Laura Sullivan, "Government to Open Terror Threat Center," *Baltimore Sun* (May 1, 2003); U.S. Senate, Select Committee to Study Governmental Operations With Respect to Intelligence Activities, *Covert Action in Chile, 1963–1973* (Washington, DC: U.S. Government Printing Office, 1975).

Tlatelolco, Treaty of (1968) An international agreement, formally known as the Treaty for the Prohibition of Nuclear Weapons in Latin America, signed by fourteen states in 1967 (in effect in 1968) declaring the Latin American region a "nuclear-weapons-free zone." Alfonso García Robles, a Mexican diplomat working in the Ministry of Foreign Affairs, played a key role in bringing about the agreement, an effort that earned him the 1982 Nobel Peace Prize. As of 2005, all of the Latin American states except Cuba had ratified the treaty and appropriate protocols and all declared members of the nuclear "club" have agreed to the zone defined in the treaty. Rivals Argentina and Brazil refused to become parties for many years, each waiting for the other to move toward ratification. Argentina made the first move by ratifying it in January 1994 (Chile became a party at the same time), followed by Brazil in May of that year. Although it contains no sanctions against states that violate the treaty, it is considered a milestone in the prohibition of nuclear weapons and a beneficial complement to the Nuclear Non-proliferation Treaty signed in 1968. On a visit to India and Pakistan in 2000, President Bill **Clinton** praised Brazil and Argentina for ending their nuclear programs.

In early 2003, a senior Brazilian official in the left-wing government of Luiz Inácio da Silva, caused a furor throughout the hemisphere by arguing that Brazil should acquire the capacity to produce a nuclear weapon. Although President da Silva criticized the Nuclear Non-proliferation Treaty as unjustly favoring the United States and other nations during his 2002 campaign, he made a point to distance his administration from the remarks of newly appointed minister of science and technology, Roberto Amaral. Although the Brazilian Constitution (1988) forbids the development of nuclear weapons or their presence in Brazil, the United States found the remarks disturbing, coming at a time of nuclear crisis with North Korea and a pending war with Iraq over its weapons programs. While it is possible that the large South American countries such as Brazil and Argentina are interested mainly in solving deep-seated economic and social problems, their governments have also taken an interest in nuclear technology for peaceful purposes. A few conservative members of the U.S. Congress sent a letter to President **George W. Bush** complaining of da Silva's friendship with Fidel **Castro** and expressing grave concerns that Brazilian foreign policy appeared to be counter to U.S. interests in the region. *See also* Arms Trade; Threat Perception/Assessment.

Suggested Reading

Larry Rohter, "Brazil Needs A-Bomb Ability, Aide Says, Setting Off Furor," *New York Times* (January 9, 2003: A-5); Larman C. Wilson and David W. Dent, *Historical Dictionary of Inter-American Organizations* (Lanham, MD: Scarecrow Press, 1998).

Tobar Doctrine A formula developed by Ecuadorian diplomat Carlos R. Tobar in 1907 to put an end to **revolutions** in Latin America and later adopted by U.S. President Woodrow **Wilson** in his policy of non-recognition of revolutionary governments. Tobar reasoned that by denying the right of revolution, through collective **intervention** or the refusal to recognize *de facto* governments that came to power through revolutions against a constitutional regime, political stability could be achieved. At the Central American Peace Conference, held in Washington, D.C., in 1907, Tobar's proposal was adopted with a pledge that the signatories would refuse to recognize any Latin American government that came into existence by revolution until the country was constitutionally reorganized by the freely elected representatives of the people. President Wilson had to deviate from the Jeffersonian principle of recognizing any government that expressed the will of the people, regardless of its origin. In practice, President Wilson's attempt to apply Tobar-like principles to Latin American governments with his doctrine of "constitutionalism" was denounced by Latin Americans as another form of intervention. It served to compound the growing **anti-Americanism** aimed at the Colossus of the North for its **Big Stick diplomacy** reaching back to the administration of **Theodore Roosevelt**. *See also* Intervention and Non-Intervention; Recognition and Non-Recognition.

Suggested Reading

Federico G. Gil, *Latin American–United States Relations* (New York: Harcourt Brace Jovanovich, 1971).

Torture. *See* Human Rights; *Missing* (1982); Operation Condor; Regime Change; *State of Siege* (1973); Terrorism

Transcontinental Treaty. *See* Adams-Onís Treaty (1819)

Trist, Nicholas Philip (1800–1874) Lawyer and diplomat during the 1840s who played a key role in negotiating the terms of the settlement ending the **Mexican-American War** in 1848. Born in Charlottesville, Virginia, in 1800, Nicholas Trist attended West Point, married a granddaughter of Thomas Jefferson, and worked his way up the career ladder at the **State Department** before becoming consul in Cuba and peace commissioner to Mexico in 1847. Once in Mexico City, Trist befriended General Winfield Scott, a Whig and one of Democratic President James K. **Polk**'s political rivals, and made little progress with his negotiations with the Mexicans. Polk tried to recall Trist, but he remained in Mexico, violated his earlier instructions from the president, and successfully negotiated the onerous Treaty of **Guadalupe Hidalgo** in February 1848, which ceded to the United States approximately 55 percent of its national territory. Trist was not proud of his diplomatic achievements, later declaring that "could those Mexicans have seen into my heart at the moment, they would have known that my feeling of shame as an American was far stronger than theirs could be as Mexicans." Nevertheless, President Polk's imperialistic muscle-flexing confirmed the prevailing dogma of **Manifest Destiny** and the **Monroe Doctrine** and served as a precursor to the **Big Stick diplomacy** followed by the United States fifty years later. After the Mexican-American War, Trist returned to Virginia to practice law. In 1860, he opposed secession and voted for Abraham Lincoln as a solution to the issue of abolition.

Suggested Reading

David W. Dent, *Encyclopedia of Modern Mexico* (Lanham, MD: Scarecrow Press, 2002); David Pletcher, *The Diplomacy of Annexation: Texas, Oregon, and the Mexican War* (Columbia: University of Missouri Press, 1973).

Trujillo Molina, Rafael Leónidas (1891–1961) Dominican dictator known for his repressive and corrupt rule from 1930 until his **assassination** in 1961. Born into a lower class family, Trujillo used the military, and connections with members of the U.S. occupation from 1916 to 1924, to advance his career and power. By the time the U.S. Marines were ready to end the U.S. occupation, they had created and trained a police constabulary that would serve as a base for Trujillo's future **dictatorship**. He used his position as head of the National Armed Forces to manipulate the 1930 presidential election in his favor. For the next three decades, he and his family ruled the Dominican Republic like a fiefdom, growing ostentatiously wealthy over the years.

Rafael Trujillo received a basic education before joining the Dominican National Guard in 1919. The National Guard was set up by U.S. forces during the occupation of the Dominican Republic (1916–1924). With a solid position in the U.S.–supported guard, Trujillo was able to advance his political career. After intimidating his rivals, he managed to win the 1930 presidential election and begin the establishment of one of Latin America's most brutal and oppressive dictatorships. The thoroughness of his control was achieved by allowing only one political party and permitting only his supporters to serve in Congress. His ability to cultivate close diplomatic and political relations with the United States proved invaluable in his pursuit of unlimited power. According to Dent (1999: 142), "In return for his unwavering support of the United States, Trujillo's dictatorship was given money, weapons, and moral support. U.S. presidents accepted Trujillo because he provided political stability, was strongly anti-Communist, and served as a better alternative to revolution." Trujillo's friends in the U.S. Congress enjoyed gifts and lavish vacations in the Dominican Republic while the Dominican dictator gained credibility and international support because of his pro-Americanism, anti-communism, and government economic policies that were portrayed as progressive and of benefit to the small nation. According to Roorda (1998: 234–235),

> He [Trujillo] solicited, purchased, and sometimes coerced other sources of support having the power to influence relations with the United States, including the Marine Corps, the Dominican lobby, the American Colony, and various communications media. The "foreign policy" of the United States may have been debated and defined at the State Department, but the full spectrum of U.S. "relations" with the Trujillo regime frequently overlapped and contradicted the official line.

The fall of the Trujillo dictatorship coincided with the policy changes recommended by Vice-President Richard **Nixon** after his 1958 "good will" trip and the rise of Fidel **Castro**. Worried about the rise of a Dominican Fidel Castro, the United States tried to persuade Trujillo to leave his island peacefully. This effort failed so the United States developed a covert plan to arm conspirators to overthrow the aging autocrat. With weapons supplied by the **Central Intelligence Agency (CIA)**, Dominican conspirators ambushed and assassinated Trujillo in May 1961 as he was on his way to see his mistress on the outskirts of Santo Domingo. The death of Trujillo left a political vacuum that was not filled until after the eruption of a civil war in 1965 and the massive invasion of over 22,000 U.S. forces to stop the spread of communism and Castroism in the Caribbean. Trujillo's son and brothers struggled in vain to retain power after the tyrant's assassination, but were driven from power by the use of **gunboat diplomacy** by the United States. Despite recent efforts to bring about democratic reform, the Dominican Republic continues to suffer from the legacy of Trujillo's tyranny. *See also* Covert Operations; Friendly Dictators; Johnson, Lyndon Baines; State Department.

Suggested Reading

G. Pope Atkins and Larman C. Wilson, *The Dominican Republic and the United States: From Imperialism to Transnationalism* (Athens: University of Georgia Press, 1998); Atkins and Wilson, *The United States and the Trujillo Regime* (New Brunswick, NJ: Rutgers University Press, 1972); David W. Dent, *The Legacy of the Monroe Doctrine: A Reference Guide to U.S. Involvement in Latin America and the Caribbean* (Westport, CT: Greenwood Press, 1999); Frank Moya Pons, *The Dominican Republic: A National History* (New Rochelle, NY: Hispaniola Books, 1995); Eric Paul Roorda, *The Dictator Next Door: The Good Neighbor Policy and the Trujillo Regime in the Dominican Republic, 1930–1945* (Durham, NC: Duke University Press, 1998); Gaddis Smith, *The Last Years of the Monroe Doctrine: 1945–1993* (New York: Hill and Wang, 1994).

Truman, Harry S. (1884–1972) Businessman, Democratic politician (senator and vice president) and U.S. president (1945–1953) during the early years of the **Cold War**. Born in rural Missouri, Harry Truman was unable to attend college because of his family's economic difficulties. He joined the U.S. Army and served with distinction during **World War I**. After the war he started several businesses, none successful, before entering state politics in Missouri. After winning a U.S. Senate seat in 1934 he served for ten years (1935–1945) before he was chosen to serve as **Franklin D. Roosevelt**'s running mate in 1944. Truman had very little foreign policy experience when Roosevelt died of a massive cerebral hemorrhage, and he suddenly became president in April 1945. Although at first disposed to continue Roosevelt's policy of compromise and alliance with the Soviet Union, it did not take long before Truman decided to resist and contain Soviet power and influence.

President Truman was one of many **Washington policymakers** after **World War II** who laid the foundations of America's Cold War policies, both globally and in Latin America. He maintained an interventionist foreign policy designed to prevent the spread of communism and touted the Marshall Plan to supply the necessary economic resources to Western Europe in hopes that it would resist the appeal of communism. The Truman Doctrine (1947) put to rest the prewar isolationism and the notion that world peace could be preserved by building alliances through the **United Nations (UN)** and the **Organization of American States (OAS)**. Washington's negative perceptions of Soviet and Chinese global intentions forced Truman to reorganize American defense and intellgence agencies in order to assume responsibility for the defense of the non-Communist world. At the center of this bureaucratic transformation was the passage of the National Security Act of 1947, a massive reorganization that created the **National Security Council (NSC)**, the National Security Agency, the **Central Intelligence Agency (CIA)** and the consolidation of the armed forces into a single Department of Defense. Each of these would play a major role in the conduct of the Cold War in Latin America and the rest of the world. Like many U.S. presidents, Harry Truman started out his administration with little intention of becoming actively involved in settling international disputes; however, world events beyond his control forced him to embrace the principal arguments of his internationalist advisers who felt the United States needed to be more assertive and interventionist in its foreign policy. Despite Truman's anti-Communist rhetoric—often a response to Republican claims that he was "soft on communism"—he was reluctant to engage Soviet power with American weaponry. Instead, he preferred to use economic power until the outbreak of the Korean War in June 1950.

Truman's Latin American policy reflected his concern with international communism and his belief in maintaining a suitable climate for U.S. private investment in the hemisphere. To this end he worked to integrate the Latin American militaries into U.S. defense arrangements and backed measures to protect U.S. investments from arbitrary expropriations and just compensation for any expropriated properties. Truman announced his Point Four Programs in early 1949 in an effort to offer scientific and industrial expertise to underdeveloped countries. During the Truman years there was no effort to commit major resources for "planned" development programs in Latin America since the reconstruction of Europe took priority and **friendly dictators** provided the United States with insurance that communism would not advance in Latin America. Economic development—not Soviet expansionism or international communism—was the most presssing need in Latin America during the Truman years, but it would take the success of the Cuban Revolution to provide the motivation to implement the **Alliance for Progress**, a "Marshall Plan" for Latin America.

When the Truman administration did focus on Latin America, it was primarily to deal with collective security in the Western Hemisphere. President Truman and his Secretary of State George Marshall attended the conference in Rio de Janeiro that produced the **Inter-American Treaty of Reciprocal Assistance** in 1947. Known as the Rio Treaty, it was the first in a series of regional security arrangements entered into by the United States after World War II. The divergent views that produced the Rio Treaty became a part of U.S.–Latin American relations throughout the Cold War: the Latin Americans viewed the treaty as a means of improving a system of regional cooperation for development; for the United States the treaty was only part of a global policy to oppose communism. The next hemispheric meeting, held in Bogotá, Colombia, established the Organization of American States, a reinvigorated inter-American organization that established the principles that would guide inter-American relations with particular emphasis on non-intervention. The Truman years emphasized military alliances in Latin America and support for anti-Communist dictators such as Anastasio Somoza García (Nicaragua), Marcos **Pérez Jiménez** (Venezuela), and Fulgencio **Batista** (Cuba). In May 1947 Somoza deposed his hand-picked successor as president of Nicaragua. At first the Truman administration tried to employ non-recognition as a sanction, but in the absence of hemispheric support for collective action it decided to recognize the dictator and forget about trying to distinguish between democratic and dictatorial governments.

Throughout the Truman years the United States continued to stall on Latin American proposals to garner economic assistance from the United States. During the Korean War President Truman begin a program of military assistance to Latin America in 1951 to promote the defense of the Western Hemisphere through bilateral military agreements with twelve Latin American nations. The program was lop-sided in favor of the United States as the amount of all aid directed at Latin America was less than 1 percent of the entire military assistance program in 1951. Truman also had to deal with **revolutions** in Guatemala and Bolivia that contained elements of perceived harmful ideologies and nationalist policies that threatened the economic interests of the United States. The Truman administration provided some initial aid to the revolutionary government in Bolivia; however, Guatemala was a different story because of the powerful **United Fruit Company** and the appearance of Communists in the government of Jacobo **Arbenz**. Although the Truman administration resisted United Fruit pressure to reverse a new pro-labor policy that would have raised wages for banana workers, the **Eisenhower** administration sided with United Fruit in 1953–1954 and eventually conducted a covert campaign that ousted the Guatemalan government in 1954. Despite the positive assessments of the Truman presidency, his diplomacy lacked vision, and he often stuck with simplistic historical analogies and refused to accept views that were contrary to his. After leaving the presidency in January 1953, Truman retired to his home in Independence, Missouri, wrote his memoirs, and coordinated the construction of the Harry S. Truman Library where he worked until his health failed in the late 1960s. *See also* Intervention and Non-Intervention; Perón, Juan Domingo.

Suggested Reading

Bert Cochran, *Harry Truman and the Crisis Presidency* (New York: Funk and Wagnalls, 1973); Robert J. Donovan, *Tumultuous Years: The Presidency of Harry S. Truman, 1949–1953* (New York: Norton, 1982); Donald R. McCoy, *The Presidency of Harry S. Truman* (Lawrence: University Press of Kansas, 1984); David G. McCullough, *Truman* (New York: Simon and Schuster, 1992); Steven Schwartzberg, *Democracy and U.S. Policy in Latin America during the Truman Years* (Gainesville: University Press of Florida, 2003); Athan G. Theoharis, ed., *The Truman Presidency: The Origins of the Imperial Presidency and the National Security State* (Stanfordville, NY: E.M. Coleman Enterprises, 1979).

U

United Fruit Company The lack of effective political institutions and the scarcity of local capital contributed to the development of dependent economies in Central America and the Caribbean based on agricultural exports. Coffee and bananas came to dominate economic life and contributed to the politics and culture of the region. Once bananas were introduced to the United States, business groups with numerous subsidiaries were formed to ship bananas from Central America to the United States. The United Fruit Company was formed in 1899 by three banana entrepreneurs—Lorenzo Baker, Andrew Preston, and Minor C. Keith—who realized a business alliance would serve to offset the vicissitudes of weather, Central American politics, and crop diseases by spreading their production base to several producer countries in the region. Within a few years, the United Fruit Company, headquartered in Boston, Massachusetts, became the world's largest banana producer; it owned vast tracks of land in Cuba, Colombia, Guatemala, Honduras, and Costa Rica, as well as railroad track, a fleet of banana boats, and control of the almost 90 percent of all bananas shipped to the United States. In its formative years, the banana industry was linked to foreign capital and liberal concessions from a string of **friendly dictators** who ruled what were often called **banana republics**. Thomas P. McCann, a United Fruit employee who worked in Publicity and Advertising, explained that the United Fruit Company chose Guatemala because of its perfect investment climate. Not only did Guatemala contain prime banana land, its "government was the region's weakest, most corrupt and most pliable" (McCann, 1976: 45).

For over fifty years, United Fruit was the most important private enterprise in Central America. By the end of **World War II**, the United Fruit Company was the largest landowner and largest employer in Guatemala. Most of the property was acquired during the **dictatorship** of Jorge Ubico, a ruthless dictator who worked closely with the United States until he was ousted by the Guatemalan military in 1944. A decade of reform followed that threatened the holdings of United Fruit. After President Jacobo **Arbenz** moved to expropriate about 40 percent of United Fruit's land, the company asked Washington for help. The amount of corporate influence that United Fruit had on U.S. foreign policy was remarkable and, according to Lars Schoultz (1998: 337), "The list of overlapping interests [with the Eisenhower administration] is so long that it is difficult to identify anyone who made or directly influenced U.S. policy toward Guatemala in the early 1950s who did not have a direct tie to United Fruit." Once the specter of communism in the Arbenz government was raised as a threat to U.S. interests, Guatemala's reformist government was doomed. The **Eisenhower** administration ruled out armed **intervention** to root out Communist infiltration, but the nature of the threat defined by Washington eventually led to a **Central Intelligence Agency (CIA)**-backed covert intervention in 1954 that drove Arbenz from power, restored the lands that United Fruit once owned, and installed a puppet regime under the leadership of Colonel Carlos Castillo Armas. The Eisenhower administration had little evidence that communism was gaining ground in Guatemala, but it was clear that Arbenz's reforms were intended to alter the fundamental structure of privilege that was so corrosive to Guatemala's sad history. Castillo Armas was cast as a democratic leader and treated as a savior and conquering hero in the United States when he visited after the coup d'état.

After United Fruit merged with Cuyamel Fruit Company in 1929, Samuel **Zemurray** replaced Minor Keith as the prime mover of the company. Until his retirement as president of United Fruit in 1951, Zemmuray was the most powerful person in Central America, worth an estimated $30 million after more than fifty years of selling bananas. After a scandal was uncovered over United Fruit's bribing of officials in Honduras for tax breaks, Eli Black, president of United Brands (the new name of United Fruit), jumped to his death from his New York office window in early 1975. *See also* Bernays, Edward L.; Covert Operations; Dulles, John Foster.

Suggested Reading

Edward L. Bernays, *Biography of an Idea: Memoirs of Public Relations Counsel Edward L. Bernays* (New York: Simon and Schuster, 1965); Paul J. Dosal, *Doing Business with the Dictators: A Political History of United Fruit in Guatemala, 1899–1944* (Wilmington, DE: SR Books, 1993); Richard Allen LaBarge, *Impact of the United Fruit Company on the Economic Development of Guatemala, 1946–1954* (New Orleans: Middle American Research Institute, Tulane University, 1960); Thomas P. McCann, *An American Company: The Tragedy of United Fruit* (New York: Crown Publishers, 1976); Lars Schoultz, *Beneath the United States: A History of U.S. Policy Toward Latin America* (Cambridge, MA: Harvard University Press, 1998); Steve Striffler and Mark Moberg, eds., *Banana Wars: Power, Production, and History in the Americas* (Durham: Duke University Press, 2003).

United Nations (UN) The failure of the **League of Nations**, war in Europe in the 1930s, and the lingering Monroeist attitudes among **Washington policymakers** were critical factors in the formation of the United Nations. The genesis of the new world organization came from the U.S. **State Department** in late 1939 followed by President **Franklin D. Roosevelt**'s use of the term in 1941 to describe the countries fighting against the Axis powers. Several international conferences between 1943 and 1945 set the stage for the San Francisco Conference in 1945 (April 25–June 26, 1945) that drafted the United Nations Charter that established the composition, organization, and functions of the United Nations, a multipurpose international organization devoted to peace, collective security, cooperation, and the promotion of economic development. The member states agreed to locate the UN headquarters in New York and the General Assembly accepted the $8.5 million gift by John D. Rockefeller, Jr., to purchase a tract of land along the East River to construct the main buildings—the Secretariat, the General Assembly, and the Conference Building—that would serve the new international organization.

When the General Assembly first met in London on January 10, 1946, there were fifty-one members, composed largely of the Allies who fought in **World War II**. Although Latin America's contribution to the war effort was mainly economic, Washington policymakers accorded special attention to the Latin American nations because they formed a bloc of nearly two-fifths of the votes in the General Assembly and offered U.S. producers a significant export market and site for future direct investment. However, the United States and Latin America expressed differing views on what the United Nations would mean for both development and regional security. Washington envisioned a continuation of the **Good Neighbor Policy** and the right to place constraints on the foreign policy of Latin American countries. At the founding conference of the United Nations the United States endorsed Latin America's desire for a regional security organization that would provide protection for existing governments and place constraints on the historical tendency of the United States to assert **hegemony** over the Americas. Although Article 51 of the UN Charter provided the legal foundation for the Rio Treaty of 1947, the establishment of a mutual defense treaty elicited different interpretations of its implementation. Henry L. Stimson, secretary of war, claimed that Article 51 preserved the "unilateral character of the **Monroe Doctrine**" since it allowed Washington to avoid having to obtain the assent of the UN Security Council. Latin Americans rejected this view, believing that Article 51 would offer protection from **intervention** and offer greater hope that international legal principles could be used to further their interests. The Latin Americans tried to bolster their autonomy by insisting on the principle of non-intervention included in the charter of the **Organization of American States (OAS)** in 1948. The creation of the United Nations and the Organization of American States helped to extend the spirit of the Good Neighbor Policy until 1953; however, without a Marshall Plan for the Western Hemisphere and the apparent lack of Communist threats, Latin America was not considered an important region as long as client states and anti-Communist regimes were able to subdue nationalist, populist, and working-class movements. In practice this meant embracing **dictatorships** and ignoring the principles established in the United Nations and the Organization of American States.

The original vision of the United Nations as a body of "peace-loving" nations committed to preventing future aggression and advancing the humanitarian needs of the world was soon undermined by the frictions caused by the **Cold War** that in turn led to a dysfunctional Security Council, often crippled by veto power and other efforts to bypass the UN system. The United Nations has also faced the problem of a far more diverse membership of 191 in 2003, growing demands for dealing with numerous world crises, declining legitimacy as an international organization, severe financial pressures due to the refusal of a number of countries to pay for UN activities, and the tendency of the major powers to increasingly deal with each other outside the framework of the United Nations. Despite these obstacles, the United Nations has attempted to expand its activities in Latin America and other less-developed regions of the world. From an emphasis on preventing aggression and encouraging peaceful resolution of conflicts, the United Nations has expanded into the following areas: health; women, children and population; environment and ecology; economics, trade, and development; education, science, and culture; humanitarian aid and food security; **human rights**, justice and democracy; crime corruption and drugs; peacekeeping, disarmament, and security; and the elimination of poverty.

Those who wrote the UN Charter believed that they could replace the crude forms of intervention with a more legitimate form of collective intervention through the United Nations or the appropriate regional organization. The United Nations recognized the OAS as the appropriate organization to handle disputes in the Western Hemisphere, thus giving the OAS a dominant role in collective peace, security, and development matters since the 1950s. The Latin American states have tended to use the General Assembly of the United Nations as a forum for expressing opposition views to the major powers that dominate the Security Council, particularly the United States. Since its founding in 1946, the United Nations has been involved in the following events in Latin America: U.S. intervention in Guatemala; trade and economic development strategies; **Cuban Missile crisis**, **Falklands/Malvinas War**; Central American peacekeeping, human rights, and democracy promotion efforts, and election monitoring and various democracy restorations projects such as in Haiti. Given their preoccupation with non-intervention and economic development, the Latin American states have been strong supporters of **international law** and the powers of the **International Court of Justice (ICJ)** and the role of the International Monetary Fund and the World Bank.

Operating as a bloc, the Latin American and Caribbean states have used the United Nations as a counter-poise to the United States. Their growing influence in the United Nations comes from membership in the South/developing bloc in the General Assembly, the Economic and Social Council, and in the UN Educational, Scientific, and Cultural Organization. Considerable influence is also derived through membership in the International Court of Justice where the Latin American states have two seats, and in the Security Council, where they hold two non-permanent, rotating seats. The growing international power of Brazil and Mexico has added pressure on the United Nations to increase the size of the Security Council to reflect this international reality. Although there have been numerous efforts to stem the interventionist power of the United States, the Latin American states were most successful in the ICJ case against the United States in *Nicaragua v. United States of America*. The Nicaraguan's won the case against the **Reagan** administration for mining its harbors, but the United States ignored the ruling against it. For the past twenty years the Latin American states have voted unanimously for resolutions in the UN General Assembly condemning the United States for its decades-long embargo of Cuba. In its efforts to assist the **Clinton** administration to reinstate Father Jean-Bertrand **Aristide** in Haiti, the Security Council approved a resolution authorizing the United States "to use all necessary means to facilitate the departure from Haiti of the military leadership" and accept the ousted leader's return. The repeated use of U.S. force in Latin America and the increasing demands on UN peacekeepers in places like Haiti and elsewhere point to the absence of international rules of the game and the lack of concern for national sovereignty. The United Nations serves a valuable role in U.S.–Latin American relations, but the debate and resolutions that are produced in such international bodies have had little impact on restraining the hegemony of the United States in Latin America. In April 2004, the UN Development Program published a depressing report that after more than a dozen Latin American countries have moved to one degree or another into democratic rule, more than half of the people surveyed indicated they would support an authoritarian regime if it would improve their lives. The fact that Latin American and Caribbean nations are losing faith in **democracy** does not augur well for future U.S.–Latin American relations. *See also* Intervention and Non-Intervention.

Suggested Reading

G. Pope Atkins, *Encyclopedia of the Inter-American System* (Westport, CT: Greenwood Press, 1997); A. LeRoy Bennett, *Historical Dictionary of the United Nations* (Lanham, MD: Scarecrow Press, 1995); Edmund Jan Osmanczyk, ed., *Encyclopedia of the United Nations and International Agreements* (Philadelphia: Taylor and Francis, 1995); Giuseppe Schiavone, *International Organizations: A Dictionary and Directory*, 3rd ed. (New York: St. Martin's Press, 1993); Peter H. Smith, *Talons of the Eagle: Dynamics of U.S.–Latin American Relations*, 2nd ed. (New York: Oxford University Press, 2002).

USAID. *See* Agency for International Development

U.S. Southern Command. *See* Southern Command

V

Valenzuela, Arturo (1944–) Political scientist, professor of government, consultant to non-profit organizations and the Democratic Party, and foreign policy adviser during both **Clinton** administrations. Since 1987 he has been professor of government and director, Center for Latin American Studies, at the Edmund A. Walsh School of Foreign Service, Georgetown University in the nation's capital. A native of Chile, Arturo Valenzuela studied in the United States, earning degrees from Drew University (B.A., 1965) and Columbia University (M.A., 1967; Ph.D., 1971). While at Columbia, he studied with Juan Linz and developed an interest in **democracy** and authoritarianism. His interest in Latin American politics grew out of the rise and fall of Salvador **Allende** in Chile, the role of the United States in Allende's removal, and the subsequent support of General Augusto **Pinochet**. Arturo Valenzuela has pursued several careers that have brought together his interest in comparative Latin American politics (consolidation of democracy, civil-military relations, political parties, regime transitions and U.S.–Latin American relations) with policymaking inside the White House and the U.S. Department of State. He served as deputy assistant secretary for Inter-American Affairs in the **State Department** during the first Clinton administration with responsibilities for global issues (democracy, environment, **human rights**, migration, and refugees) for the Americas and the formulation and implementation of U.S. policy toward Mexico. During the second Clinton administration (1997–2001), Dr. Valenzuela served at the White House as special assistant to the president and senior director for Inter-American Affairs at the **National Security Council (NSC)**. While at the NSC he advised the Clinton administration on foreign, defense, intelligence, economic, and other policy issues concerning the Western Hemisphere. It was in this capacity that he managed the formulation and implementation of multilateral and bilateral foreign policy initiatives and as well as several regional crises (Haiti, Colombia, Paraguay, Panama, Peru, and Venezuela) in the Americas.

Professor Valenzuela's background and experience with the breakdown (and recovery) of democracy in Chile, military rule under General Pinochet, and the relative merits of presidential versus parliamentary government contributed to his scholarship on Latin American politics. He is the author or co-author of nine books and is one of the leading scholars on the consolidation of democracy and civil-military relations in Latin America. Valenzuela is one of the few "inner/outers" who has a background in political science and Latin American studies; most of the **ambassadors** and top-level advisers who become "inner/outers" have backgrounds in law, economics, and policy advocacy at major **think tanks**, which would include individuals such as Lincoln **Gordon**, Albert Fishlow, Sidney Weintraub, and Richard Feinberg. Each had real line authority and operated within the Latin American field. *See also* Washington Policymakers.

Suggested Reading

Pamela Constable and Arturo Valenzuela, *A Nation of Enemies: Chile Under Pinochet* (New York: W.W. Norton, 1991); Juan J. Linz and Arturo Valenzuela, *The Failure of Presidential Democracy* (Baltimore, MD: Johns Hopkins University Press, 1994); Arturo Valenzuela, *The Breakdown of Democratic Regimes, Chile* (Baltimore, MD: Johns Hopkins University Press, 1978); J. Samuel Valenzuela and Arturo Valenzuela, eds., *Military Rule in Chile: Dictatorships and Oppositions* (Baltimore, MD: Johns Hopkins University Press, 1986).

Vanderbilt, Cornelius (1794–1877) Millionaire shipping tycoon who played a major role in transporting passengers and cargo across Nicaragua to California in the 1850s and in the downfall of **filibusterer** William **Walker**. Vanderbilt developed an interest in shipping early in his life and took advantage of the demand for passenger travel to California during the gold rush days. He established a transit company that operated in Nicaragua to provide service to California that was two days faster than the Panama route. After William Walker captured control of the Nicaraguan government in 1855 and arbitrarily cancelled Vanderbilt's Accessory Transit Company, Vanderbilt conspired with other Central American forces to drive Walker out of power. Cornelius Vanderbilt later sold his Nicaragua line to the operators of the Panama route and returned to the United States where he prospered in the shipping and railroad business during and after the U.S. Civil War. At the time of his death in 1877 he had accumulated a fortune estimated at over $100 million.

Suggested Reading

Lars Schoultz, *Beneath the United States: A History of U.S. Policy Toward Latin America* (Cambridge, MA: Harvard University Press, 1998); William O. Scroggs, *Filibusters and Financiers: The Story of William Walker and His Associates* (1916; reprint, Russell and Russell, 1969).

Vaughn, Jack Hood (1920–) Latin Americanist, highly effective diplomat and government official from the 1950s to the 1970s who moved throughout Latin America in a variety of diplomatic and administrative posts. Vaughn was born in Columbus, Montana, and graduated from the University of Michigan with an M.A. in Latin American Studies. He worked with the United States Information Agency as director in La Paz, Bolivia, and San José, Costa Rica, between 1949 and 1952. President John F. **Kennedy** appointed him Latin American regional director of the Peace Corps in 1961, which brought him in contact with **Washington policy-makers** and key figures in Latin America. He left the Peace Corps in 1964 and began a tour as U.S. **ambassador** to Panama for one year. He arrived in Panama during a time of turmoil over the U.S. control of the canal and the politics of the Canal Zone. He traveled extensively throughout Panama, helping to heal the wounds over the Flag Riots and started negotiations on a new **Panama Canal treaty**. He returned to Washington in 1965 to become assistant secretary of state for Inter-American Affairs, where he helped to implement the **Alliance for Progress**, coordinate inter-American affairs, and made frequent "good will" trips to the region. He directed the Peace Corps from 1969 to 1970 followed by a short stint as U.S. ambassador to Colombia. With his background in Latin American Studies and fluency in Spanish and French, Vaughn was considered one of the most effective diplomats in Latin America, admired both in Washington and among Latin American leaders. He left diplomatic life in 1972 and assumed a variety of non–Latin American jobs, including president of the National Urban Coalition, Children's Television Workshop, and Planned Parenthood.

Venezuelan Boundary Dispute. *See* Olney, Richard (1835–1917)

Villa, Francisco "Pancho" (1878–1923) Guerrilla fighter and one of the great heroes of the Mexican Revolution who played a key role in driving General Victoriano Huerta from power in 1914. Born in Rio Grande, Durango, he gave up his birth name, Doroteo Arango, adopting Francisco "Pancho" Villa as his new name. A master of desert survival and **guerrilla warfare**, Villa fought on the side of the Constitutionalists in the revolutionary conflict. After being defeated in a series of battles in the north-central region of Mexico, Villa retreated to the deserts of Chihuahua where he continued to fight the Constitutionalist forces of Venustiano Carranza who had the backing of the United States. Once President Woodrow **Wilson** recognized Carranza as the de facto government of Mexico in 1915, and allowed Mexican troops to use U.S. territory to attack Villa's forces, Pancho Villa struck back, attacking a train in Santa Isabel and killing seventeen U.S. citizens and later struck Columbus, New Mexico, where he killed more U.S. citizens on American soil. After these brutal attacks, President Wilson sent a "punitive expedition" under the command of General John J. Pershing to capture the terrorist bandit Villa "dead or alive." General Villa was too smart for Pershing's military and an **assassination**

attempt by the U.S. **State Department**; the United States failed to capture the guerrilla leader or win a single battle in the Mexican desert. After Carranza was assassinated in 1920, Villa signed a peace treaty with the new president, Adolfo de la Huerta, and withdrew from political life and devoted his time to community development in Chihuahua. Villa was assassinated by government-backed **death squads** in 1923, but did not assume the rank of a revolutionary hero until decades later. Pancho Villa was a master of public relations and once managed to convince the United States of the justness of his cause, despite persistent negative stereotypes of the guerrilla leader and his followers in the American press. Villa remains a colorful figure among the pantheon of Mexican revolutionaries and is often mentioned in the *corridas* (a narrative ballad or story song) of contemporary Mexican ballad music. His raid on Columbus, New Mexico, marks the first, and only, time the United States was attacked from a Latin American country. *See also* Media; Revolutions.

Suggested Reading

Mark C. Anderson, *Pancho Villa's Revolution by Headlines* (Norman: Oklahoma University Press, 2000); Friedrich Katz, *The Life and Times of Pancho Villa* (Stanford, CA: Stanford University Press, 1998).

W

Walker, William (1824–1860) American **filibusterer** and staunch advocate of **Manifest Destiny** who led several private military expeditions to Latin America in the 1850s, undermining the meaning of the **Monroe Doctrine** and damaging U.S.–Latin American relations. His armed colonizing expeditions were aimed at acquiring more slave territory for the American South and carving out a tropical empire in Latin America that could be Americanized in the name of glory, fortune, and the Monroe Doctrine. Walker's greatest exploits took place in Nicaragua where he became embroiled in a revolution between warring factions located Grenada and León.

A native of Tennessee, William Walker graduated from the University of Nashville in 1838; five years later he received a medical degree from the University of Pennsylvania, although he never practiced medicine. He continued his medical studies in Europe, but returned to New Orleans where he studied law, was admitted to the Louisiana bar, and became a newspaper editor in the late 1840s. By the early 1850s, imbued with the spirit of Manifest Destiny, Walker moved to San Francisco where he turned his ambitions to filibustering. His first adventure southward was to conquer and occupy the Mexican province of Baja California. Although he succeeded in conquering Baja and proclaiming himself president of the independent republic, the Mexicans forced his retreat to the United States where he was captured and brought to trial for violating American neutrality laws. In a controversial trial in 1854, Walker was acquitted by a sympathetic jury and soon marched off to Nicaragua where he hoped to annex the land as a slave state and part of the Union.

With the support of financial backers from New Orleans who wanted more slave territory, Walker invaded Nicaragua in 1855 with fifty-seven other Americans and before long had captured Grenada and taken over the country. With the backing of officials in Washington, Walker had himself "elected" president of Nicaragua, the only time a U.S. citizen ruled as chief of state in Latin America. In his effort to build a Central American empire, Walker legalized slavery, decreed English as the national language, decreed an anti-vagrancy law to ensure forced peasant labor for landowners, and offered large land grants to attract more American troops to Nicaragua. In addition, Walker's grandiose schemes included an interoceanic canal that would facilitate world shipping through Nicaragua. President James **Buchanan** recognized the fraudulent government, but abolitionist forces in the North pressured President Franklin **Pierce** to revoke American recognition of Walker's Nicaraguan government.

To get rid of Walker, Central Americans—with the help of American commercial baron Cornelius **Vanderbilt**—united in a national war that resulted in expelling the "Yankee President" in 1857. Walker returned to the United States, but he regrouped and returned to Nicaragua three more times to pursue his dreams of wealth and empire, still claiming to be the lawful president of Nicaragua. He continued his forays into Central America until his capture in Honduras by British naval forces. They turned him over to Honduran authorities, he was condemned by a court-martial, and executed by firing squad in 1860.

The Walker episode left deep scars in U.S.–Nicaraguan relations. It discredited the United States throughout Central America and raised fears among many leaders in the region of losing sovereignty at the hands of Manifest Destiny or the Monroe Doctrine. When the U.S. Marines began to intervene and occupy Nicaragua during the first three decades of the twentieth century, Nicaraguans were reminded immediately of the exploits of William Walker sixty years earlier, now considered by Nicaraguans the first U.S. "Marine" to intervene in their country. The efforts of William Walker to use repeated military expeditions to achieve a pro-slavery tropical empire were of little benefit to those on the receiving end of his predatory forces. Walker's band of mercenaries did not bring prosperity to the region and closed the transit route across the isthmus. Walker and other filibusters hastened the U.S. Civil War by attempting to spread slavery into Central America and the Caribbean and their greed, arrogance, and racism seriously eroded support for the Monroe Doctrine as a strategic strategy against foreign interference in Latin America. President **Reagan**'s war against Nicaragua in the 1980s brought to light Walker's misguided efforts to dictate the fate of Nicaragua, and a Hollywood film (*Walker*) was made with Ed Harris starring as the daring American adventurer William Walker. *See also* Race and Racism.

Suggested Reading

David W. Dent, *The Legacy of the Monroe Doctrine: A Reference Guide to U.S. Involvement in Latin America and the Caribbean* (Westport, CT: Greenwood Press, 1999); William O. Scroggs, *Filibusters and Financiers: The Story of William Walker and His Associates* (1916; reprint, Russell and Russell, 1969); Albert Weinberg, *Manifest Destiny: A Study of Nationalist Expansionism in American History* (Baltimore, MD: Johns Hopkins University Press, 1935).

Walters, Vernon A. (1917–2002) Military officer, intelligence official, and diplomat who played a key role in an array of historic events in the post–**World War II** era. Vernon Anthony Walters was born in New York City in 1917, but moved to Europe at age six where he lived in Paris and attended school in England. He did not complete his secondary education in England and did not attend college since he went to work for his father at age sixteen. His career in the U.S. Army (1941–1976) and his fluency in more than six languages proved to be a valuable asset in work as a diplomat and as an intelligence officer. From 1955 to 1960 Walters was a staff assistant to President Dwight **Eisenhower**, acting as interpreter for the president, vice-president, and senior diplomats and military officials in Washington and abroad. He accompanied Vice-President Richard **Nixon** during his long good-will tour of Latin America in 1958 and was injured when an anti-American mob stoned the president's limousine in Caracas. A firm believer in the **Cold War** doctrine of anti-communism, Vernon Walters worked in the shadowy world of secrecy, codes, and diplomatic intrigue. While military attaché to Brazil in 1964, Walters was one of the key players in the U.S.–backed coup against President Goulart, along with U.S. **ambassador** Lincoln **Gordon**, and Assistant Secretary of State Thomas **Mann**. Most U.S. officials admitted privately that Goulart was not a Communist but that his foreign policy suggested the possibility of a Communist takeover in Brazil if things were not "corrected." Colonel Walters, who had served as liaison officer with the Brazilian Expeditionary Force in Italy during World War II, was on friendly terms with the military conspirators and was fully aware of the details surrounding the coup. Walters communicated what he knew about the coup to Ambassador Gordon, who in turn informed Thomas Mann of the military conspiracy.

During the Nixon and **Ford** eras Walters worked for the **Central Intelligence Agency (CIA)**, first as deputy director and then as acting director of the agency. During the **Reagan** and **George H.W. Bush** presidencies he worked as ambassador at large, ambassador to the **United Nations (UN)**, and ambassador to Germany until 1991. He often used his military background to further U.S. interests among the military **dictatorships** of Latin America. After Jeane **Kirkpatrick** resigned as UN ambassador in 1985, Vernon Walters was chosen to replace her. Walters proved to be less abrasive and confrontational than his predecessor, despite his involvement with the Iran-Iraq War and international **terrorism**. His uncanny ability to be present during some of the major events of the Cold War gained him the reputation as a quiet American and the U.S. version of James Bond, a label he dismissed as ludicrous. General Walters wrote two books about his service to his country, one that profiled the famous people with whom he worked and the other an autobiography. When asked by a reporter what kept him going after five decades of public service, General Walters replied, "My perception that the United States was the only real chance freedom had to survive in the world." He died in West Palm Beach, Florida, in February 2002. *See also* Covert Operations; Friendly Dictators.

Suggested Reading

Michael Massing, "America's Top Messenger Boy," *New Republic* (September 16–23, 1987); Vernon A. Walters, *The Mighty and the Meek: Dispatches from the Front Line of Diplomacy* (London: St. Ermin's Press, 2001); Walters, *Silent Missions* (Garden City, NY: Doubleday, 1978).

Washington Consensus A set of dogmatic ideas about international trade, finance, political economy, and strategies of growth and economic development. This gospel, also known as "free trade" or "market fundamentalism," is designed to apply the preferential wisdom of the U.S. Treasury Department, the World Bank, and the International Monetary Fund to solve Latin American development problems in the aftermath of the **Cold War**. The term was originally coined in 1989 by John Williamson, an economist at the Institute for International Economics, to describe the triumph of capitalist thinking among both members of the U.S. foreign policy elite and those who administer multilateral financial/lending agencies. The Washington Consensus claims to have found a "single sustainable model" for bringing **democracy**, development, free markets, equality, and free trade throughout the world. Those who believe in the core tenets of deregulation, privatization, lower taxes, unrestricted movement of capital, and receptiveness to foreign investment are convinced this prescription is the only way to develop economically, and every Latin American country would be wise to adopt such a strategy. William Finnegan calls this a belief system that constitutes "an economics of empire" and argues that it is currently under attack throughout Latin America (Finnegan, 2003: p. 42). For example, Bolivia's president was forced to resign from office in 2003 after month-long protests over an international agreement to ship natural gas through Chile to the United States.

Despite the heavy criticism of Washington's free trade doctrine in Latin America, the **George W. Bush** administration campaigned on the promise to create a hemisphere-wide free trade zone known as the **Free Trade Area of the Americas (FTAA)**. In a speech to the **Council of the Americas (COA)**, a U.S. business organization that supports the Washington Consensus, Secretary of State Colin Powell congratulated Latin American governments for sticking to democracy despite severe economic setbacks and asserted that globalism offers a better life, but it must deliver the goods or both democracy and the free-market system have no meaning. As of 2003, after more than fifteen years of neo-liberal reforms, the economic failures outnumber the successes in Latin America.

The results of the Washington Consensus on Latin American economies are not encouraging. Argentina followed the neo-liberal policy prescriptions—privatization, deregulation, trade liberalization, tax reform—throughout the 1990s only to suffer a catastrophic collapse in 2001. Bolivia—the poorest country in South America—was advised by Jeffrey Sachs, a free-market economist, that it had no choice but to endure a severe recession to stabilize prices and improve its relationship with foreign creditors, including the World Bank, the International Monetary Fund, and the United States. The pain caused by this kind of economic medicine has contributed to the growing lack of faith in democratic institutions and civilian leadership.

In 2003, Brazil and Argentina signed a formal agreement to resist U.S. trade policy in the Americas. The statement, signed by presidents Nestor Kirchner of Argentina and Luiz Inácio Lula da Silva of Brazil, emphasized jobs over profits and fair trade over free trade and came to be known as the Buenos Aires Consensus. As a rebuttal to the Washington Consensus, it reflected the growing gap between the United States and Latin America over the best path to growth and development in Latin America. At the core of the trade dispute is agricultural subsidies and the repeated refusal of the United States to include subsidies in such global talks. Brazil and Argentina are emerging as potential agricultural superpowers with less dependence on trade with the United States and Europe than in Asia and the Pacific Rim where there is high demand for food such as soybeans, wheat, and rice. After the collapse of the World Trade Organization Cancún summit, the United States blamed Brazil for the failure to reach an agreement, calling it the leader of the "won't do" countries in contrast to those more willing to strike deals with Washington. *See also* Summit of the Americas.

Suggested Reading

William Easterly, *The Elusive Quest for Growth: Economists' Adventures and Misadventures in the Tropics* (Cambridge, MA: MIT Press, 2001); William Finnegan, "The Economics of Empire: Notes on the Washington Consensus," *Harper's Magazine* (May 2003); Moíses Naím, "Fads and Fashions in Economic Reforms: Washington Consensus or Washington Confusion?" Working Draft of a Paper Prepared for the IMF Conference on Second Generation Reforms, Washington, DC (October 26, 1999); Tony Smith, "Argentina and Brazil Align to Fight U.S. Trade Policy," *New York Times* (October 21, 2003).

Washington Office on Latin America (WOLA) One of several major **human rights** interest groups concerned with U.S.–Latin American relations, WOLA was founded in 1974 to address the massive violations of human rights being carried out by military-authoritarian governments at the time. The rise of Latin American policy interest groups is the result of four factors: the growing interdependence of the world economy and technological advances in international communication; the activism created by the civil rights movement and covert action programs directed at Latin American governments by the United States; opposition to the U.S. war in Vietnam that gave rise to the formation of numerous ideological interest groups such as WOLA; and the anger that developed in church groups in the United States over the killing of priests, nuns, and others caught in acts of state-sponsored **terrorism**. Over the past twenty-five years WOLA has engaged in a wide variety of efforts to challenge existing U.S. policies in Latin America and to lobby for changes that would improve U.S.–Latin American relations. Working with a small staff in Washington, D.C., WOLA provides up-to-date information and analyses on human rights, democratization, and other matters concerning U.S. policy in Latin America. As a not-for-profit, non-partisan education group, WOLA receives its funding largely from four sources: related organizations, churches, non-governmental/non-corporate funding, and foundations such as the Ford Foundation. In its efforts to educate and promote a knowledgeable dialogue regarding U.S. policies in Latin America, WOLA conducts educational conferences, seminars, meetings with visitors from Latin America, and fact-finding trips to Latin America. Its publications—newsletters, books, and monographs—are designed to inform policymakers, academics, religious organizations, the press, and the public at large. The Washington Office on Latin America works closely with other non-governmental human rights organizations and uses coalition-building strategies to expand its influence over U.S.–Latin American policies. Because of organizations like WOLA, human rights must be considered in the process of formulating policy toward Latin America. WOLA was heavily involved in the policy debates over Central America in the 1980s and more recently with human rights consequences of **Plan Colombia**, greater freedom to travel to Cuba, and the breakdown of democracy throughout Latin America as a consequence of flaws in neo-liberal strategies of economic development. *See also* Democracy and Democracy Promotion; Think Tanks; Washington Consensus.

Suggested Reading

David W. Dent, ed., *U.S.–Latin American Policymaking: A Reference Handbook* (Westport, CT: Greenwood Press, 1995); Lars Schoultz, *Human Rights and United States Policy Toward Latin America* (Princeton, NJ: Princeton University Press, 1981).

Washington Policymakers U.S.–Latin American policymaking is a complex process that involves different stages, patterns, and interests among a wide array of governmental and non-governmental actors in Washington and Latin America. At the core of governmental decision-making toward Latin America is the office of the presidency and the presidential advisory system consisting of the **National Security Council (NSC)**, **State Department**, **Central Intelligence Agency (CIA)**, and the Defense Department. Although there are a plethora of issues that confront the United States in dealing with Latin America, most of the executive branch decisions fall into three categories: strategic or security, crisis, and intermestic where Congress and the White House struggle over hemispheric and domestic decisions that deal with immigration, **drug trafficking**, **terrorism**, border security, and trade matters. It is not uncommon for the presidential advisory system to work at cross-purposes in producing Latin American policy. This policy-making dilemma results in poor policy coordination and is often due to the lack of presidential attention to Latin American affairs and the intense competition among government actors in Washington.

There is a formal and informal advisory system that is at the core of U.S.–Latin American policymaking. The formal advisory system has a structure and staff in the executive office of the president that advises the president on U.S.–Latin American policy. The most significant government agencies include the National Security Council, Office of National Drug Control Policy, Office of the U.S. Trade Representative, and the National Economic Council. The key players outside this arena that are in charge of Latin American policy include the following Departments: State (mainly the Bureau of Inter-American Affairs), Defense (mainly the Joint Chiefs of Staff), Treasury, and Commerce. The U.S. Congress is also part of the process since it must debate the merits of policy, approve all related funding, and maintain oversight over expenditure and policy implementation and evaluation. The primary purposes of these executive departments, offices, and other bodies are to provide the president with accurate information, recommend policy options, and assist with the implementation of policy decisions having to do with the region. One of the paradoxes in U.S.–Latin American policymaking, given the wide range of issues of importance to the relationship between the United States and Latin America, is the small number of top policymakers within the executive branch who have direct responsibility for Latin America. Out of a total of approximately 550 positions, more than half are in the Defense Department—more than double the number that work in the Bureau of Inter-American Affairs within the State Department.

The apex of the formal advisory system for the president is the National Security Council and staff. The National Security Council—consisting of the president, vice-president, secretary of state, secretary of defense, director of the Central Intelligence Agency, chairman of the Joint Chiefs of Staff, and two advisory members. However, the key players in U.S.–Latin American policymaking are the NSC staff and the director of Latin American affairs on the National Security staff. The director of Latin American affairs coordinates domestic, foreign, and military policies that pertain to Latin America and the Caribbean. He or she is not the creator or implementor of interagency policy on Latin America. With numerous policy-related responsibilities, the director can influence U.S.–Latin American policy in numerous ways, particularly policy speeches on Latin America and strategic advice on the impact of a crisis in Latin America on U.S. domestic politics.

Within the U.S. Department of State, Latin American and Caribbean affairs are the responsibility of the Bureau of Inter-American Affairs, headed by the assistant secretary of state for inter-American affairs. The person who holds this position ranks higher (by protocol) in decision-making authority than the director of Latin American affairs on the NSC staff. The assistant secretary of state for inter-American affairs is subject to Senate confirmation while the director of Latin American affairs on the NSC staff is not. This means that the head Latin American position in the State Department is a more influential and controversial position. Many of those who have served the president, and the secretary of state, as assistant secretary of state for inter-American affairs have often found themselves embroiled in a political tug-of-war that characterizes U.S.–Latin American policymaking. Since assistant secretaries of state for inter-American affairs need Senate confirmation, and are frequently asked to testify on Capitol Hill, they often serve as lightning rods and whipping boys. There is a difference between Democratic and Republic presidents in terms of the people they choose for this controversial, and often politically weak, position. Presidents Jimmy **Carter** and Bill **Clinton** relied mostly on career diplomats for the Latin American post while Presidents Ronald **Reagan**, **George H.W. Bush**, and **George W. Bush** preferred political appointees that would serve as a form of party patronage or payback for their election victory among ethnic or religious groups. This means that those who are appointed to the Latin American position in the Department of State are more likely to have a legal career and a strong attachment to a particular ideology than diplomatic experience, knowledge of Latin America and the inter-American system, and no background in the inner working of American foreign policy. The most controversial—some approved by the Senate, others not—appointees over the past several decades would include Elliott **Abrams** (confirmed), Mario Baeza (unconfirmed), Robert **Pastor** (unconfirmed), and Otto **Reich** (recess appointment for one year only). The person in charge of U.S.–Latin American policy in the State Department has a daunting task within the foreign policy bureaucracy. It is often a delicate balancing act among the government and non-governmental players, in the complex and frustrating world of U.S.–Latin American relations. According to Gabriel Marcella (1995: 289), the job "requires the ability to conceptualize and articulate U.S.–Latin American policy, mobilize broad support within and outside the U.S. government for controversial policies, and frequently fight policy battles in which there are no clear-cut winners." Among the five regional bureaus that make up the Department of State organizational structure, the Inter-American affairs position can certainly be challenging, but may also damage those who have foreign policy career aspirations with the United States government. Table 3 offers a brief examination of the U.S. government officials who have had responsibility for Latin American and Caribbean affairs since 1945.

The informal advisory system is located outside the executive office of the president and can include any number of the following as a source of information for those in the formal advisory system: major media outlets (*New York Times*, *Washington Post*, *Wall Street Journal*, *Miami Herald*, *Los Angeles Times*, CNN, and Fox television); personal friends and contacts with compatible political and ideological outlooks; **think tanks**, prominent academics, particularly from Harvard, Stanford, and the University of Chicago, political party activists, state governors, Latin American leaders, and prominent members of the religious community. Although the president of the United States has access to a wide variety of information, this doesn't mean that presidents will either seek advice from relevant sources or listen to a variety of contending policy proposals. American presidents are far more likely to opt for loyal implementers of Latin American policy than to rely on independent minds who may have contrary views on the correct course of action on any given issue. There are times when U.S. presidents bond with Latin American leaders who in turn offer advice about the best approach to a Latin American problem. President John F. **Kennedy** sought advice from José Figueres (Costa Rica) and Rómulo Betancourt (Venezuela). President Jimmy Carter struck up a strong relationship with Carlos Andrés Pérez (Venezuela) and Omar Torrijos (Panama). President George H.W. Bush developed strong ties via reciprocal visits and telephone conversations with Carlos Menem (Argentina) and Carlos Salinas de Gortari (Mexico). President George W. Bush's close ties with Vicente **Fox** (Mexico) provided him with advice on border security, terrorism, and immigration reform. *See also* Valenzuela, Arturo; Washington Office on Latin America (WOLA).

Suggested Reading

David W. Dent, ed., *U.S.–Latin American Policymaking: A Reference Handbook* (Westport, CT: Greenwood Press, 1995); Gabriel Marcella, "The Presidential Advisory System," in David W. Dent, ed., *U.S.–Latin American Policymaking: A Reference Handbook* (Westport, CT: Greenwood Press, 1995); Howard J. Wiarda, ed., *Policy Passages: Career Choices for Policy Wonks* (Westport, CT: Praeger, 2002).

Welles, Benjamin Sumner (1892–1961) Controversial career diplomat and philanthropist who played a major role in U.S.–Latin American relations during the 1930s and 1940s. Welles was born in New York City in 1892, graduated from Harvard in 1914, and joined the U.S. Department of State in 1915. President **Franklin D. Roosevelt** named him assistant secretary of state in 1933, a position with major responsibility for implementing the **Good Neighbor Policy**. Although Welles was credited with originating the phrase "Good Neighbor Policy," he believed in **intervention** and **regime change** when it became apparent that U.S. interests were at stake. Roosevelt sent him to Cuba in 1933 to stabilize a violent situation and improve U.S.–Cuban trade relations. Ambassador Welles managed to engineer the downfall of Gerardo Machado, but Machado's replacement proved to be distinctly anti-American and incapable of governing. After the Sergeant's Revolt of September 5, 1933, Dr. Ramón Grau San Martín became president; however, Welles considered Dr. Grau a threat to U.S. business interests and a radical leftist and forced his departure after 1,000 days. Welles was eventually forced to leave Cuba, although he left Fulgencio **Batista** in charge, setting in motion Fidel **Castro**'s insurrection and the next generation of Cuban revolutionaries to take up the cause of challenging the **hegemony** of the United States. He continued to stay involved in hemispheric affairs and after 1937, as undersecretary of state, for inter-American security he was associated with the decisions that preceded U.S. involvement in **World War II**. He resigned in 1943 over disagreements with Secretary of State Cordell Hull concerning attitudes toward the Soviet Union and other controversies in the press. Welles often worked with Nelson **Rockefeller**'s Office of the Coordinator of Inter-American Affairs (OCIAA) to counter Nazi **propaganda** in Latin America. *See also* Ambassadors; German Threat; Revolutions.

Suggested Reading

Samuel Flagg Bemis, *The American Secretaries of State and Their Diplomacy*, Vol. 13 (New York: Cooper Square, 1963); C. Neale Ronning and Albert P. Vannucci, eds., *Ambassadors in Foreign Policy: The Influence of Individuals on U.S.–Latin American Policy* (New York: Praeger, 1987); Robert F. Smith, *The United States and Cuba: Business and Diplomacy, 1917–1960* (New

Table 3
U.S. Government Officials Responsible for Latin American-Caribbean Affairs

President	Secretary of State	Assistant Secretary for Inter-Am. Affairs	Amb. to the OAS	NSC Staff: Ass't to the Pres. for NS Affs (Sr Dir. for LA)
Truman[2,7] (1945–1953)	James Byrnes[5,7] George Marshall[6] Dean Acheson[5,4]	Nelson Rockefeller[2] *Spruille Braden* *Norman Armour** Edward Miller, Jr.[5,4]	*Wm Dawson* *Paul Daniels*	NSC est. in 1947 Sidney Souers[6] & James Lay,[6] Exec Sec'y (none)
Eisenhower[6] (1953–1961)	John Foster Dulles[5,4] Christian Herter*[4,8]	*John Cabot*, Henry Holland[5,4] *Roy* *Richard Rubottom, Jr.*	*John Dreier*	Position est. in 1953 Robert Cutler[5] Dillon Anderson[4] Wm Jackson[4] Gordon Gray[4] (none)
Kennedy[7] (1961–1963)	Dean Rusk[3,4]	*Thomas Mann, Robert* *Woodward, Edwin* *Martin*	deLesseps Morrison[5,4]	McGeorge Bundy[3] (*Robert Sayre*)
Johnson[7] (1963–1969)	Dean Rusk[3,4]	*Mann*, Jack Vaughn[4] Lincoln Gordon[3,4] Covey Oliver[3,4]	Ellsworth Bunker[2,4] Sol Linowitz[2,4]	Bundy, Walt Rostow[3,4] (Samuel Lewis)
Nixon[7] (1969–1974)	Wm P. Rogers[5,4] Kissinger	Charles Meyer[2] *Jack Kubisch*	*John Jova*	Henry Kissinger*[3] (*Viron Vaky*)
Ford[7] (1974–1977)	Kissinger	Wm D. Rogers[5,4] *Harry Shlaudeman*	Wm Maillard[7]	Brent Scowcroft[6] (*William Pryce*)
Carter[6,8] (1977–1981)	Cyrus Vance[5,4] Edmund Muskie[8,7]	*Terence Todman*[1] *Viron Vaky* *Wm Bowdler**	Gale McGee[3,7]	Zbigniew Brzezinski*[3] (Robert Pastor)[4,1]
Reagan[2,8] (1981–1989)	Alexander Haig[6] George Shultz[2,4]	*Thomas Enders* Langhorne Motley*[2,4] Elliott Abrams[5,4]	Wm Middendorf[2] Richard McCormack[4,1] John Poindexter[6,4]	Richard Allen[1,4] (Roger Fontaine[1]), Wm Clark[5,4] Robert McFarlane[6,4] (Constantine Menges*[4]) Frank Carlucci[4] and Colin Powell[6] (*Raymond Burghardt*)
Bush[7,2,4] (1989–1993)	James Baker[2,4] *Lawrence* *Eagleberger*	Bernard Aronson[1]	Luigi Einaudi[3]	Brent Scowcroft[6] (Richard Feinberg[1,4])
Clinton[8] (1993–2001)	Warren Christopher[5,4]	*Alexander Watson* *Jeffrey Davidow*	Harriet Babbit[5]	Anthony Lake[4,3] and Samuel Berger[1,4] (*William Pryce* and *James Dobbins*)
	Madeleine Albright*[4,3]	*Peter Romero*	Victor Marrero[5,4]	

Table 3 (continued)

President	Secretary of State	Assistant Secretary for Inter-Am. Affairs	Amb. to the OAS	NSC Staff: Ass't to the Pres. for NS Affs (Sr Dir. for LA)
Bush[2 8] (2001–2009)	Colin Powell*#[1 2] Condoleezza Rice#[3 4]	Otto Reich*[1 2] *Roger Noriega*[1]	Roger Noriega[1]	Condoleezza Rice#[3 4] (*John Maisto* and *Thomas Shannon*)
			John Maisto[4]	Stephen J. Hadley[1 4] (*Thomas Shannon*[4])

Key: * foreign born; # African-American; *italics* foreign service officer; numbers indicate prior career or positions—1 adviser, consultant or official of private organization (e.g., think tank) or for member of Congress or congressional committee; 2 businessman, in firm (e.g., film); 3 educator, professor or teacher; 4 U.S. executive branch service, in Washington, D.C., or abroad; 5 lawyer, in legal practice; 6 U.S. military officer, career or long service; 7 politician, member of U.S. Congress; and 8 politician, at state level (e.g., legislature or governor).

Source: Larman C. Wilson. From revised draft: "United States Decision-Making in Relations with Latin America and the Caribbean: Organization, Personnel and Politics," 1999.

York: Bookman, 1961); Benjamin Sumner Welles, *Seven Decisions that Shaped History* (New York: Harper, 1950); Welles, *Where are We Heading* (New York: Harper and Brothers, 1946); Welles, *The Time for Decision* (New York: Harper and Brothers, 1944); Randall B. Woods, *The Roosevelt Foreign Policy Establishment and the "Good Neighbor": The United States and Argentina, 1941–1945* (Lawrence: Regents Press of Kansas, 1979).

Western Hemisphere Institute for Security Cooperation (WHINSC). *See* School of the Americas (SOA)

Wiarda, Howard J. (1939–) Conservative political scientist, policy consultant, and prolific writer on U.S.–Latin American relations. He is currently Dean Rusk Professor of International Relations, and Head, Department of International Affairs at the University of Georgia. He was one of the Latin American experts at the **American Enterprise Institute (AEI)** during the years when AEI had considerable influence over U.S.–Central American policy. Born in Grosse Pointe, Michigan, Howard Wiarda grew up in Grand Rapids, Michigan, in a Dutch Calvinist community where his grandparents settled after immigrating to the United States in the 1880s and 1890s. He received his B.A. from the University of Michigan and Ph.D. from the University of Florida, Gainesville. Key figures in the Latin American studies program such as Lyle N. McAlister, Donald Worcester, W. Harry Hutchinson, T. Lynn Smith, and Harry Kantor influenced Wiarda's thinking on Latin America and U.S.–Latin American relations. It was at the University of Florida that he developed a life-long interest in corporatism, focusing some of his early research on the Dominican Republic and Paraguay. While he sometimes claims to have centrist opinions, his writings on U.S.–Latin American relations often dovetail with those of conservative analysts such as Jeane **Kirkpatrick**, Mark Falcoff, and

Lawrence Harrison. In much of his writings on U.S.–Latin American relations, Professor Wiarda relies on his conception of Latin American culture as the foundation for advice to **Washington policymakers**. Wiarda's time in Washington was spent at the American Enterprise Institute, the Center for Strategic and International Studies where he is still a senior associate, and as an instructor at the National Defense University. Until 2004, he was a political science professor at the University of Massachusetts in Amherst: he retains his position as a scholar at the Woodrow Wilson International Center for Scholars.

Howard Wiarda entered the world of **think tanks** through an appointment to be director of the Latin American program at the American Enterprise Institute in 1981. Jeane Kirkpatrick, after inviting him to join her at the **United Nations (UN)**, had to withdraw the position because of overstaffing, apologized and offered him the AEI position. He hired Mark Falcoff as his associate director, an ideological neo-conservative who would provide Wiarda "cover" from the right. In his memoir *Universities, Think Tanks & War Colleges* (1999), Wiarda describes the excitement of being in Washington and having a hand in the creation of Latin American policy during the **Reagan** years when the hot topics were El Salvador, Nicaragua, and the **Falklands/Malvinas War**. From his think tank experience at AEI, Wiarda concluded, "Washington policy-makers tend to think they already have all the answers: if you can lend arguments to their entrenched beliefs, fine; but don't think you can truly educate policy-makers." Wiarda claims that he was asked by the Reagan administration to attend conferences and make speeches to explain the government's position on Latin American policy issues. He traveled widely in this role in an attempt to offer a rational explanation of Reagan administration policies. After doing this for several years he concluded that "while Latin America had become an main focus of Administration policy, the level of knowledge both it and its vocal opposition often had about the area was exceedingly thin" (Wiarda, 1999: 227). After leaving AEI to return to teaching at the University of Massachusetts, Amherst, Wiarda continued to return to Washington for consulting and other activities. From 1991–1994, Wiarda returned to Washington again on a full-time basis, this time teaching at the National War College where he learned a great deal about security issues and the "military mind."

Howard Wiarda continues his work as a college professor and foreign policy analyst, blending his academic life with consulting and scholarly pursuits. His interest in corporatism and comparative politics has taken him beyond Latin America where he has devoted most of his interest and life work. His has published over forty books on comparative politics, U.S.–Latin American policy, think tanks, and a wide range of policy issues. Despite his work with the American Enterprise Institute and the National War College, Wiarda has never worked on Capitol Hill or in the executive branch of the U.S. government.

Suggested Reading

Howard J. Wiarda, ed., *Policy Passages: Career Choices for Policy Wonks* (Westport, CT: Praeger, 2002); Wiarda, *Universities, Think Tanks & War Colleges: The Main Institutions of*

American Educational Life—A Memoir (Brookeville, MD: Washington Center for International Politics, 1999).

Wilson, Thomas Woodrow (1856–1924) Democratic president of the United States (1913–1921) who in his first term of office attempted to shift U.S. policy concerning Latin America away from the military **intervention** and **Dollar Diplomacy** of his predecessors. He was the guiding force in trying to establish the **League of Nations**, the world's first permanent international security organization. In an effort to put a partisan stamp on his presidency after sixteen years of Republican dominance, Wilson offered lofty and humanitarian views designed to change Latin American government and society. His idealism focused on his determination to ensure that constitutional democracies would be established and protected in Latin America. In a famous address before the Southern Commercial Congress held at Mobile, Alabama, on October 27, 1913, Wilson expressed what became known as Wilsonian diplomacy, namely a faith in **democracy**, a belief in spiritual unity in the Americas, and the positive features of investment capital. In many ways his Mobile speech contained the seeds of **Franklin D. Roosevelt**'s **Good Neighbor Policy** in the 1930s and Jimmy **Carter**'s emphasis on **human rights** in the 1970s. In his efforts to convince an audience of businesspeople of the merits of his new Latin American policy, Wilson stated that the United States "must show ourselves friends by comprehending their interest whether or not it squares with our own interest or not. . . . Human rights, national integrity, and opportunity as against material interests . . . is the issue which we now face. I want to take this occasion to say that the United States will never again seek one additional foot of territory by conquest."

Wilson's rhetoric clashed with events—the Mexican Revolution, **World War I**, and Caribbean turmoil—that would contradict his words and return the United States to acts of intervention that the president thought he could avoid. Over the course of his eight-year administration Wilson sent U.S. troops to control unstable situations in Cuba, the Dominican Republic, Haiti, Nicaragua, and Mexico. Wilson's faith in democracy led him to propose a new policy of non-recognition of revolutionary governments to "teach the South Americans to elect good men" and foster a just government based upon law instead of violence and force. Wilson's approach to Latin America was opposed by those in the United States and Europe who believed that intervening on behalf of democratic principles was inappropriate and counter-productive to U.S. interests as well as opposed by Latin Americans who believed that the American president was more interested in expanding markets for U.S. goods than enhancing Latin American security. According to Schoultz (1998: 252), "Wilson implemented a policy that was largely indistinguishable from Dollar Diplomacy, adding only the high minded rhetoric of democracy, which at the time prompted greater intervention and encouraged a paternalistic attitude [toward the Latin American nations]." In each case where Wilson sent U.S. troops into a Latin American country, liberation and constitutionalism turned into occupation and resentment. In the end, Wilson's "civilizing interventions" did more to solidify **dictatorship** regimes in Latin American than encourage constitutional rule and good governance. Where Wilson intervened the most—Central America and the Caribbean—political dependence and subservience to Washington increased and U.S.–trained repressive military regimes thrived at the expense of the local population. Woodrow Wilson brought a strong-willed personality and new ideas to the presidency, but his reliance on intervention in the name of democracy failed to make a lasting commitment to democracy and political stability. Even when U.S. military occupiers temporarily raised living standards and improved the economic infrastructure, Latin American nationalists hated being occupied and governed by a foreign military. Wilson's Latin American policy was hampered by a close network of advisers who knew little about political conflict in Latin America, some having never set foot in the region, but nevertheless called the shots for the frustrated president.

There were times when Wilson thought he could act as his own secretary of state in handling matters in Mexico, Central America, and the Caribbean. Wilson came to detest **revolutions** and viewed democracy and elections as a cure-all for Latin America. When his policies failed, Wilson refused to admit that either he or his advisers were to blame. He often ignored expert authorities in favor of amateur diplomats and agents who were responsible to him or his secretary of state, William Jennings **Bryan**. Many of these diplomats and agents did not speak Spanish, knew little about the region, and often displayed negative stereotypes of Mexicans and others in their official rhetoric. After Wilson sent John Lind as special envoy to Mexico, Lind's reports about the situation contained frequent references to inferiority and immaturity of the Mexican people. In one report, he judged the Mexicans to be "more like children than men" and the people in the valley of Mexico are clearly of an inferior race, "debauched by pulque and vice and oppression" (quoted in Schoultz, 1998: 343).

Thomas Woodrow Wilson was born in Staunton, Virginia, the son of a prominent Presbyterian minister. As his father moved from church to church in the south—Georgia, South Carolina, and North Carolina—Wilson experienced the racial politics and attitudes of the middle decades of the nineteenth century. The first and only president to earn a Ph.D., Wilson was educated at Davidson College, Princeton University, University of Virginia Law School, and Johns Hopkins University (Ph.D. in history and political science, 1885). After graduation from Johns Hopkins, Wilson began an academic career of teaching and administration. He was elected president of Princeton University in 1902 where his strong-willed character brought him both success and failure in his campus pursuits. His difficulties with other administrators and faculty at Princeton led him to run for governor of New Jersey in 1910; the success he experienced as governor led to his Democratic presidential nomination in 1912. During his successful presidential campaign that year against William Howard **Taft** and **Theodore Roosevelt**, Wilson concentrated on domestic issues while also advocating the application of Christian moral principles to American foreign policy and the promotion of democracy abroad. Those who have studied the political life of Woodrow Wilson feel that the certitude of his religious convictions contributed to his belief that his foreign policies were virtuous and correct. He never doubted that he and his nation were the instruments of a divine plan to promote constitutionalism and democracy around the world. Wilson faced a number of health problems that grew progressively worse throughout his presidency. The victim of several strokes, Wilson finished his presidency in illness in March 1921 and died three years later at his residence in Washington, D.C. Scholars and policymakers debated **Wilsonianism** for decades after Wilson's death, some convinced that his idealism increased the threats to U.S. security while others wondered whether the European aggression that led to **World War II** could have been avoided if there had been more support for Wilson's ideas. Two prominent **Cold War** policy advisers—George F. **Kennan** and Henry A. **Kissinger**—criticized Wilsonian moralism while stressing a "realist" perspective based on national interest expressed in terms of power politics. Many twentieth-century historians considered Wilson a statesman ahead of his time. *See also* Ambassadors; German Threat; Race and Racism; Recognition and Non-Recognition; Roosevelt Corollary to the Monroe Doctrine; Tobar Doctrine; Villa, Francisco "Pancho."

Suggested Reading

Cole Blasier, *The Hovering Giant: U.S. Response to Revolutionary Change in Latin America* (Pittsburgh: University of Pittsburgh Press, 1976); Frederick S. Calhoun, *Power and Principle: Armed Intervention in Wilsonian Foreign Policy* (Kent, OH: Kent State University Press, 1986); Kendrick A. Clements, *The Presidency of Woodrow Wilson* (Lawrence: University Press of Kansas, 1992); John Milton Cooper, Jr., *Breaking the Heart of the World: Woodrow Wilson and the Fight for the League of Nations* (Cambridge, MA: Cambridge University Press, 2001); Cooper, *The Warrior and the Priest: Woodrow Wilson and Theodore Roosevelt* (Cambridge, MA: Belknap Press of Harvard University Press, 1983); Mark T. Gilderhus, *Pan American Visions: Woodrow Wilson in the Western Hemisphere, 1913–1921* (Tucson: University of Arizona Press, 1986); Michael H. Hunt, *Ideology and U.S. Foreign Policy* (New Haven: Yale University Press, 1987); Thomas J. Knock, *To End all Wars: Woodrow Wilson and the Quest for a New World Order* (Princeton, NJ: Princeton University Press, 1992); Arthur S. Link, ed., *Woodrow Wilson and a Revolutionary War, 1913–1921* (Chapel Hill: University of North Carolina Press, 1982); Hans Schmidt, *The United States Occupation of Haiti, 1915–1934* (New Brunswick, NJ: Rutgers University Press, 1971); Lars Schoultz, *Beneath the United States: A History of U.S. Policy Toward Latin America* (Cambridge, MA: Harvard University Press, 1998); Tony Smith, *America's Mission: The United States and the Worldwide Struggle for Democracy in the Twentieth Century* (Princeton, NJ: Princeton University Press, 1994).

Wilsonianism The set of foreign policies carried out by Woodrow **Wilson** (1913–1921) based on (1) the promotion of democratic government or "national self-determination" in Latin America and the world; (2) the use of multilateralism to create a more peaceful world; (3) a more open international economic system that would eliminate special privileges to enhance prosperity and trade; and (4) internationalism, that is, greater involvement in international affairs to promote peace through promoting **democracy**, protecting **human rights**, and establishing the foundation for American **hegemony**. President Wilson faced the conundrum of means and ends as his blueprint for liberal democracy in Latin America, which was difficult to construct after the old order was destroyed. The dim prospects for democracy in Latin America clouded Wilson's dream of constitutional rule and eventually led to **intervention**, occupation, and Yankeephobia. While Wilson's motives for pursuing a Latin American policy that would bring democracy and constitutionalism appear sincere, he also realized that interventionism and occupation were needed to carry out his missionary diplomacy. Democracy promotion as a mainstay of American foreign policy did not end with Wilson's presidency as subsequent presidents from Dwight D. **Eisenhower** to **George W. Bush** have advanced Wilsonian principles. *See also* Dictatorships; Friendly Dictators; League of Nations; Recognition and Non-Recognition.

Suggested Reading

Frederick S. Calhoun, *Uses of Force and Wilsonian Foreign Policy* (Kent, OH: Kent State University Press, 1993); David W. Dent, *The Legacy of the Monroe Doctrine: A Reference Guide to U.S. Involvement in Latin America and the Caribbean* (Westport, CT: Greenwood Press, 1999); Friedrich Katz, *The Secret War in Mexico: Europe, the United States, and the Mexican Revolution* (Chicago: University of Chicago Press, 1981).

WOLA. *See* Washington Office on Latin America

World War I Major international conflict between 1914 and 1918 that, despite its late entry into the war in April 1917, helped to elevate the United States to world power status. Although the war was fought mainly in Europe, the Latin American states faced the unwanted burden of having to take sides or remain neutral in the conflict. Germany's rise to world power status heightened the tension between the United States and the nations of Latin America. The war challenged the ability of rapidly industrializing states to manage the international system, particularly the rise of ethnic and nationalist tensions that produced serious threats to capitalism and aristocratic power. At first President Woodrow **Wilson** tried to avoid U.S. involvement in the war, declaring the United States neutral in the conflict. Later, Wilson realized that he would have to get the United States into the war on the Allied side. This was delayed when Francisco "Pancho" **Villa**'s forces raided Columbus, New Mexico, in 1916, leading Wilson to retaliate by sending the U.S. Army to search for Villa in the Mexican desert. By April 1917, the U.S. Congress voted to declare war on Germany, although there were a significant number of votes against the resolution. The **German threat** from U-boat maneuvers in the Western Hemisphere compelled the Latin American governments to decide whether it was in their interests to follow the U.S. lead. Although most Latin American governments applauded the U.S. entry into World War I, and those that backed the United States expected material rewards for doing so, the responses to the conflict were not uniform.

Despite the need for German investment, distrust of Great Britain, and resentment of recent U.S. expansion and **hegemony**, most of the Latin American nations followed the lead of the U.S. government. Brazil, Cuba, Costa Rica, Guatemala, Haiti, Honduras, Nicaragua, and Panama joined the United States in declaring war on Germany. Five Latin American countries—Bolivia, the Dominican Republic, Ecuador, Peru, and Uruguay—severed diplomatic relations with Germany. The Latin American states with substantial ties to Germany, conflicts with the United States, and animosity toward Great Britain—Argentina, Chile, and Mexico—remained fully neutral during World War I. Mexico was tempted to support the Germans due to the lingering resentment over the loss of large amounts of territory in the **Mexican-American War** in the 1840s, but resisted and opted for neutrality.

World War I increased Latin American economic and financial reliance on the United States by directing more trade northward; however, Latin America's international stature improved with its involvement with the **League of Nations** and the **International Court of Justice (IJC)**. World War I proved to be a watershed in U.S.–Latin American relations by giving the Latin American states—all ultimately became members of the League of Nations—the confidence to confront the United States on matters of mutual concern, including defense, trade, and chronic military **intervention** and occupation. The United States never joined the League of Nations. President Wilson's emphasis on the right of national self-determination clashed with the existing hegemonic practices of the United States in the Western Hemisphere. Latin Americans were quick to detect the discrepancies in Wilson's peace-making efforts in dealing with Europe and the self-proclaimed hemispheric police power by the United States in its relationship with Latin America. Clearly the **Monroe Doctrine**'s ability to serve as a justification for U.S. intervention worried the Latin American states when they were given limited powers to challenge such arrangements at the Paris Peace Conference in 1919. In the end, World War I proved that the United States was far more concerned about events in Europe than those in the Western Hemisphere. *See also* Threat Perception/Assessment.

Suggested Reading

Jenny McLeod and Pierre Purseigle, eds., *Uncovered Fields: Perspectives in First World War Studies* (Leiden; Boston: Brill, 2004); Emily S. Rosenberg, *World War I and the Growth of United States Predominance in Latin America* (New York: Garland, 1987); Larman C. Wilson and David W. Dent, *Historical Dictionary of Inter-American Organizations* (Lanham, MD: Scarecrow Press, 1998).

World War II Unlike the diverse reactions among the Latin American states to **World War I**, World War II elicited unprecedented diplomatic cooperation among the nations of the Western Hemisphere. The reasons for the greater sense of inter-American solidarity (with the exception of Argentina) were rooted in the series of inter-American conferences that preceded the war and produced a commitment to non-intervention and hemispheric solidarity against foreign involvement, particularly the concern over German military bases in the Western Hemisphere in violation of the **Monroe Doctrine**. Even without military bases, **Washington pol-**

icymakers worried about Nazi subversion and **propaganda** and the existence of over one million German residents living throughout Latin America. The German economic penetration of Latin America raised concerns about the continued access to raw materials by the United States.

Before 1940, Latin American governments were more interested in President **Franklin D. Roosevelt**'s **Good Neighbor Policy** than the threat from fascism in Europe. However, after the German invasion of Poland in 1939 and the fall of France in 1940, the Latin American states were convinced that it was in their interests to join in the anti-Axis war effort. The Declaration of Panama (1939) produced the first collective effort to confront the Axis powers, proclaiming a security zone of 300 to 1,000 miles around the Western Hemisphere. It was agreed at the conference that Latin American armies would not be raised to the status of a fighting ally and could act only to meet an attack until the arrival of U.S. military forces. This led to the installation of U.S. military missions in all the Latin American countries except Bolivia and would serve as foundation for future military alliances during the **Cold War**.

With the few exceptions—Chile (copper), Bolivia (tin), and Venezuela (oil)—the Latin American countries did not benefit from World War II. Latin American dependence on such agricultural products as coffee, sugar, and bananas were not seen as critical to the war effort. Brazil and Mexico received financial assistance from the United States to build steel mills, but these efforts proved to be highly inefficient means of pursuing industrialization programs. Both Brazil and Mexico sent troops to fight in World War II; Brazilian soldiers went to Italy and Mexican fighter pilots fought in the Philippines. Brazil's was by far the most ambitious contribution with the introduction of over 25,000 troops to fight in Italy against the Axis powers. The struggle against fascism in Europe helped to produce demands throughout Latin America for democratic reforms after the war was settled. It proved difficult for many Latin American governments to support propaganda against tyranny and brutal **dictatorships** when many existed in Latin America as well as in Europe. Nevertheless, World War II led to diplomatic efforts to strengthen inter-American security and contributed to Latin American participation and membership in the **United Nations (UN)**. The war also improved Soviet–Latin American relations with most governments recognizing the USSR for the first time. Despite Latin America's contribution to the outcome of World War II, there turned out to be no equivalent of a Marshall Plan to help in the post-war economic and political restoration efforts in the Western Hemisphere. This would not change until anti-American nationalism and the successful revolution in Cuba under Fidel **Castro** forced Washington to confront the forces of change in Latin America. *See also* Bryan, William Jennings; German Threat; Intervention and Non-Intervention; Villa, "Pancho"; Wilson, Thomas Woodrow; Wilsonianism.

Suggested Reading

Samuel Flagg Bemis, *The Latin American Policy of the United States* (1943; reprint, New York: W.W. Norton, 1967); Robert A. Devine, *Roosevelt and World War II* (Baltimore, MD: Johns Hopkins University Press, 1969); Irwin F. Gellman, *Secret Affairs: Franklin Roosevelt, Cordell Hull, and Sumner Welles* (Baltimore, MD: Johns Hopkins University Press, 1995); Gellman, *Good Neighbor Diplomacy: United States Policies in Latin America, 1933–1945* (Baltimore, MD: Johns Hopkins University Press, 1979); Stanley E. Hilton, *Hitler's Secret War in South America, 1939–1945: German Military Espionage and Allied Counterespionage in Brazil* (Baton Rouge: Louisana State University Press, 1981); R.A. Humphreys, *Latin America and the Second World War*, 2 vols. (London: University of London Athlone Press, 1982).

Y

Yankee *Fidelistas* Mostly young people and older liberals in the United States who developed a fascination with the Cuban Revolution from the end of 1956 through the triumph of the insurrection on January 1, 1959. In a term developed by Gossse (1993: 61), the Yankee *Fidelistas* admired Fidel **Castro** for his "noble revolution" and felt he was worthy of North American admiration and support. Some went beyond fascination and empathy for Castro's 26th of July Movement (M–26–7) and joined the fight against dictator Fulgencio **Batista** directly. Although only a few entered the world of revolutionary conspiracy and guerrilla combat, North American solidarity with the Cuban Revolution was spurred by the journalistic accounts of what the Cuban rebels were fighting for, including reports by Herbert **Matthews**, Robert Taber, Neill Macaulay, Don Soldini, William Morgan, Frank Fiorini, and others drawn by the romanticism, idealism, and passion of a revolt in the tropics. There were a few U.S. troops from **Guantánamo Bay** who deserted and joined the rebels in the nearby Sierra Maestra mountains. According to Gosse (1993: 86–87), "After the revolutionary victory, Macaulay was made an officer and commanded a heavy-weapons platoon that functioned as an execution squad for the numerous *batistianos* [followers of dictator Batista] found guilty of war crimes." Many of the Yankee *fidelistas* like Macaulay were motivated by the long history of Washington supporting odious **dictatorships** in Latin America and the Caribbean and felt compelled to give a hand in putting an end to this process. The different radical currents that emerged in response to the Cuban rebels' fight for freedom and justice in the mountains of Cuba paved the way for the Fairplay for Cuba Movement in 1960, the anti-war and anti-imperialist movement in the 1960s and 1970s, and the solidarity movement with El Salvador and Nicaragua (as well as South Africa) in the 1980s. It should be noted that North Americans with a rightist ideology have participated in cross-border activities in support of Latin American right-wing dictators and counter-revolutionary movements with support from the U.S. government. Readers of *Soldier of Fortune* magazine and members of the World Anti-Communist League (WACL) joined hands with the Nicaraguan **Contras** against the **Sandinista** government in the 1980s, often with the same degree of passion and enthusiasm among the Yankee *Fidelistas*. *See also* Friendly Dictators; Media; Revolutions.

Suggested Reading

Van Gosse, *Where the Boys Are: Cuba, Cold War America and the Making of the New Left* (London: Verso, 1993); Neil Macaulay, *A Rebel in Cuba* (New York: Quadrangle Books, 1970); Robert Taber, *M-26-7: Biography of a Revolution* (New York: Lyle Stuart, 1961).

Yankeephobia. *See* Anti-Americanism

Yard Metaphor. *See* Backyard Metaphor

Z

Zemurray, Samuel (1877–1961) Wealthy banana exporter and philanthropist who played a major role in Central American politics and development from the 1890s to 1950s. Born in Bessarabia, Samuel Zemurray came to the United States in 1892 and settled in New Orleans. He founded a steamship company to transport bananas from Honduras to the port of New Orleans. After 1899 his company became a subsidiary, and competitor, of the newly formed **United Fruit Company**. With his tremendous wealth and political power, Zemurray found a network of **friendly dictators** to bribe to further his banana business. Known in Central America as "Sam the Banana Man," Zemurray supported successful **revolutions** against governments he could not manipulate to his favor. He also made friends in Washington who helped bring the interests of his banana business in line with American interests.

After selling Cuyamel Fruit Company to United Fruit in 1930, Zemurray emerged as United's largest stockholder, improved the company's profit margin, and rose to the presidency of the fruit company in 1938. He remained in this position until 1951 when he retired and devoted the rest of life to philanthropy. With access to large amounts of investment capital, close ties to Central American dictators, friends in Washington, and keen entrepreneurial skills, Zemurray played a major role in the political development of Honduras and Guatemala. After his retirement and more than fifty years in the banana business, Samuel Zemurray was worth an estimated $30 million. For many years he was the most powerful man in Central America, able to dictate the fate of small **banana republics**, run by corrupt and venal dictators who granted him concessions to solve the plethora of deep-seated development problems. When the United Fruit Company was threatened by reformist—land reform, labor rights, higher taxes on the wealthy—governments in the 1940s and 1950s, Sam Zemurray did not hesitate to ask the **Truman** and **Dwight D. Eisenhower** administrations for help in opposing these reforms. *See also* Bernays, Edward L.

Suggested Reading

Thomas McCann, *An American Company: The Tragedy of United Fruit* (New York: Crown, 1976); Dana G. Munro, *Intervention and Dollar Diplomacy in the Caribbean, 1900–1921* (Princeton, NJ: Princeton University Press, 1964); Stephen Schlesinger and Stephen Kinzer, *Bitter Fruit: The Story of the American Coup in Guatemala*, expanded Ed. (Cambridge, MA: Harvard University Press, 1999).

Zimmermann Telegram (1917) After U.S. troops abandoned their unsuccessful effort to capture Mexican revolutionary Francisco "Pancho" **Villa** in January 1917, Germany offered Mexico a plan for a secret military alliance where in return for joining Germany's war effort it could expect to reconquer its lost territory in Texas, New Mexico, and Arizona. Alfred Zimmermann, Germany's foreign secretary, sent an encrypted note on January 16, 1917, to Count Johann von Bernstorff, the German **ambassador** to Washington, who in turn forwarded it to Heinrich von Eckhardt, the German minister in Mexico. A month later Eckhardt proposed the deal to the Mexico government, but Great Britain had broken the code and passed a copy of the telegram to top officials in Washington. Once the note was in President Woodrow **Wilson**'s hands he leaked it to the press in hopes of gaining support for a declaration of war against Germany. Although Mexican President Venustiano Carranza demonstrated little interest in the German proposal, the telegram from Zimmermann was instrumental in bringing the United States into **World War I**. Instead of forming an alliance with Mexico and keeping the United States out of the war, the German plan backfired. Mexico, along with Chile and Argentina (all with significant German populations), remained neutral during the war and the United States shed its neutrality and soon joined the Allied war effort to defeat Germany. Yet, some historians believe that the telegram was a hoax carried out by the British to convince the United States to join the war on their side. *See also* German Threat.

Suggested Reading

Robert H. Holden and Eric Zolov, eds., *Latin America and the United States: A Documentary History* (New York: Oxford University Press, 2000); Barbara Tuchman, *The Zimmermann Telegram* (New York: Macmillan, 1966); Z.A.B. Zeman, *The Gentlemen Negotiators* (New York: Macmillan, 1971).

Epilogue: Lessons from the Past: Toward a More Enlightened Relationship

The entries in the *Historical Dictionary of U.S.–Latin American Relations* reveal many flaws in the way the United States has defined and carried out its Latin American policy. Of course, this is not the whole story because there have been individuals and episodes that demonstrate a cooperative and productive relationship between the United States and Latin America. Until the 1970s, U.S. policies toward Latin America were guided largely by what Abraham F. Lowenthal calls "a pervasive hegemonic presumption," the belief in Washington that it was perfectly acceptable for the United States to dictate the general course of events in Latin America and the Caribbean. In his history of U.S. policy toward Latin America, Lars Schoultz (1998) finds that the tendency of Washington policymakers to view Latin Americans as "a fundamentally inferior neighbor" has become a set of core beliefs that have changed little over the past two centuries. While there is some evidence that U.S. hegemony in Latin America is on the decline, the nature of the new relationship is not at all clear or consistent. However, there seems to be a consensus throughout the hemisphere that representative democracy and free trade are now permanent features of the new relationship. Nevertheless, there is plenty of evidence that the United States and Latin America have gone their separate ways since President George W. Bush declared his global war on terrorism. Opinion polling in Latin America reveals a growing trend toward anti-Americanism, directed both at the way the Bush administration has conducted itself around the world and the general neglect of serious hemispheric issues that have been sidelined since September 11, 2001.

If the United States can mount an attack and occupation of Iraq at a cost of over $300 billion with over 1,750 U.S. casualties and Iraqi deaths in the tens of thousands, then Washington can surely work to remove the obstacles to a more wise and productive relationship with Latin America. The following suggestions, derived from the *Historical Dictionary*, are aimed at a number of serious policy modifications that could form the basis for greater harmony between the United States and Latin America at a time when relations are at one of the lowest levels in recent memory. Instead of trying to get Latin Americans to change their ways of dealing with political life and social change, the time may have come to consider changing how the United States formulates and executes policy toward Latin America.

1. Given the importance of Latin America, Washington needs to give the region a higher priority than it has in the past. Latin America matters to the United States, not because it is in what some call "our backyard," but because the United States has one of the largest Spanish-speaking populations in the world. Also, U.S. trade flows with Latin America far exceed those with other regions, and increasing immigration to *el norte* (the United States) highlights the growing dependence on Latin American workers in the United States. There are simply far too many issues—trade, terrorism, border security, immigration, drug trafficking, environmental decay, and good governance—that require cooperation and commitment at the highest levels of government. The U.S. government is organized to define and coordinate policy toward the region; however, this is not enough to improve relations without presidential and congressional leadership. In September 2003, Secretary of State Colin Powell claimed "there is no region on earth that is more important to the American people than the Western Hemisphere." It is obvious from the paltry size of the current foreign aid budget for Latin America and the Caribbean and the lack of media attention to the region that there is a large gap between the secretary's rhetoric and the degree of interest in the Latin America and Caribbean region.

2. The United States needs to focus on ambassadorial and other appointments that are based on individuals who have the necessary qualifications to implement and evaluate Latin American policy. Those who have other political and ideological agendas should not be rewarded with jobs representing the United States in Latin America. The pattern of rewarding people on the basis of campaign contributions and a particular political ideology has not served the United States well in establishing a cooperative and productive relationship with Latin America. The American voter does not expect the president to be an expert on Latin American affairs, or to have the language skills to communicate in Spanish or Portuguese south of the border, but there is a reasonable expectation that the president will appoint competent people to conduct business with Latin America. The United States spends millions of dollars every year to train people for the Foreign Service. There is no reason that Foreign Service officers with regional expertise should be ignored in the appointment process. The appointment by the George W. Bush administration of hard-line Cuban exiles and former Reagan administration appointees—Elliott Abrams, Otto Reich, and John Negroponte—to run Latin American policy was

particularly disturbing to Latin Americans and detrimental to conducting a coherent and productive Latin American policy.

3. The United States should put an end to the current, narrowly defined, Latin American policy that is based largely on oil, cocaine, and terrorism. Colombia is a case in point where the United States is pumping hundreds of millions into supporting the government in a fight against "narco-guerrillas" without asking the Colombians to address some of the country's major social and economic problems, which are at the core of the rural insurgency. The so-called "war on drugs" is a losing cause and should not be part of the solution to illicit drug trafficking in the Americas. If the "war on terrorism" is the new lens to frame policy toward Latin America, it is unlikely that U.S. policymakers will come close to understanding the complex realities of Latin America. It is counter-productive to label poor farmers who plant coca, marijuana, or heroin poppies as "narco-terrorists" when this has no bearing on solving deep-seated economic and political problems.

4. U.S. military and police assistance should be reduced drastically and in some cases eliminated totally. The United States needs to disassociate itself from autocrats, death squads, torturers, and human rights violators, and from the long history of close ties with military fascists such as Somoza, Trujillo, Noriega, Pinochet, and others who have ruled Latin America with U.S. backing. From the early twentieth century establishment of police-military constabularies to the current military training missions, the United States has not made Latin America a better place to live, or more democratic, through the establishment and support of internal security systems. In most cases, the United States has made Latin American governments more efficient at repression and control, not in expanding freedom and liberty. The United States needs to put a stop to the international commercial trade in torture equipment that involves more than eighty U.S. manufacturers and suppliers of electro-shock weapons and restraints.

5. The United States supplies more arms to Latin American governments than any other country. To improve U.S.–Latin American relations, the United States needs to put an end to the hemispheric arms trade that contributes more to violence and conflict, expands the power of the military as a political player, and drains scarce resources from poor countries. Latin America's scarce resources should be devoted to fixing the problems of globalization rather than expanding arsenals that have technically advanced features to fight with neighbors.

6. The U.S. Army School of the Americas (SOA), now called the Western Hemisphere Institute for Security Training and located at Ft. Benning, Georgia, should be closed for good. In operation for almost sixty years, it is mainly a product of the Cold War and has failed to train people who believe in the protection of human rights and the promotion of democracy. The Venezuelan generals who engineered the failed coup against President Hugo Chávez in 2002 were graduates of the army school at Ft. Benning. Many others have been associated with torture, assassination, village massacres, disappearances, and other forms of repression.

7. U.S. foreign policy needs more multilateralism—based on international law, organizations, and diplomacy—rather than relying on the old habits of unilateral-

ism. By ignoring international treaties and international law, the United States makes it more difficult to deal legitimately with Latin American countries. Our unilateral sanctions against Cuba, in effect for more than forty years, have not only failed to bring about regime change on the island, but have alienated allies and made it more difficult to address pressing issues that plague the hemisphere. It is important to recognize that when the United States ignores international laws and norms, it destroys the moral authority to criticize Latin American governments that do exactly the same thing. If the United States wants others to adhere to human rights norms, then the United States must also support these well-established legal procedures. When President George W. Bush's legal counselor claims the fight against terrorism has rendered the Geneva Conventions "obsolete" when it comes to safeguarding the way people suspected of terrorism are interrogated, it sends a clear signal to Latin American governments that opponents of the regime can now be treated in the same manner.

8. Plan Colombia is not working, is doomed to failure, and should be replaced with a more comprehensive plan that stresses a major overhaul of Colombia's highly fragmented and unequal society. Until this is done, the "war" on drugs is not winnable, and Colombia's fragile democracy may ultimately collapse as a result of the current effort to eliminate drugs at the source rather than where drugs are consumed.

9. Morality has to play a greater role in the formulation and execution of U.S. policy toward Latin America. The historical pattern in which the United States has resorted to force and intervention in small, weak Latin American countries because they threaten our national security is absurd and counter-productive. The recommendations, and lessons learned, found in the National Commission on Terrorist Attacks upon the United States' *The 9/11 Commission Report* (2004: 376) suggest that "We [United States] should offer an example of moral leadership in the world, committed to treat people humanely, abide by the rule of law, and be generous and caring to our neighbors." After reviewing more than 2.5 million pages of documents and interviewing 1,200 individuals in ten countries, this recommendation carries a considerable amount of weight and should be considered seriously.

10. The blowback from supporting "friendly dictators" in Latin America and elsewhere undermines Washington's avowed commitment to liberalism and democracy internationally. If the United States continues to back repressive governments that humiliate their populations, it will face greater amounts of instability, terrorism, and the heavy cost of maintaining hegemony over large portions of the world. President George W. Bush recognized this flaw in American foreign policy in a speech after September 11, 2001; he should stick to his word on the need to change this unsavory policy. According to *The 9/11 Commission Report* (2004: 377), "One of the lessons of the long Cold War was that short-term gains in cooperating with the most repressive and brutal governments were too often outweighed by long-term setbacks for America's stature and interests." A policy change of this magnitude would go a long way toward improving U.S.–Latin American relations.

The history of U.S.–Latin American relations should not be disappearing, allowing those in positions of power to censor and cover up what has happened between the United States and Latin America. Chileans have not forgotten the thousands of deaths that resulted from the U.S.–backed military coup on September 11, 1973, that removed democratically elected Salvador Allende from power; very few in the United States remember this event, or offered sympathies to the Chileans who were forced into exile or "disappeared" at the hands of the Chilean military back in 1973.

11. The United States needs to do a better job of educating its population about Latin American societies and the history of U.S.–Latin American relations. Public opinion polls that reveal a glaring ignorance of Latin America serve to perpetuate negative stereotypes of the Latin American people. With anti-Americanism on the rise, this is a crucial area for investing in cultural diplomacy. The media need to pay more attention to the connection between Main Street and what is happening in Latin America and rely less on people who are worried about re-election or selling a political ideology than serious regional experts who are knowledgeable about Latin America. Moreover, public ignorance of Latin America means that presidents and Washington policymakers are less accountable and more likely to explain policies that have no bearing on the facts on the ground.

12. The U.S. government needs to create a "truth commission" to investigate the scandals and blunders that are part of the U.S.–Latin American relationship. It is time to declassify government documents that have been hidden from the American public because of unwarranted secrecy and the overused term "national security" as a justification for often misguided policies. The Church Committee managed to do this on a bipartisan basis after the overthrow of Allende in Chile; there is no reason this important congressional oversight could not be repeated. The work carried out by the National Security Archive in Washington, D.C., over the past twenty years demonstrates the need for more declassification of government documents and investigations of past historical misdeeds and coverups.

13. A firm commitment to improve U.S.–Latin American relations requires more economic assistance to Latin American governments than has been the case over the past several decades. The amount of U.S. aid to Latin America as a percentage of total foreign aid declined from roughly 25 percent in 1965 to approximately 5 percent in 2000. Colombia is now the third largest foreign aid recipient of the United States, behind Israel and Egypt; however, the rest of Latin America receives very little. This lopsided allocation of resources cannot help improve U.S.–Latin American relations. As a global strategy, *The 9/11 Commission Report* (2004: 379) recommends "economic policies that encourage development, more open societies, and opportunities for people to improve the lives of their families and to enhance prospects for their children's future."

14. The United States needs a forward-looking policy toward Cuba that sheds the confrontation and hostility of the past in favor of a dialogue that moves Cuba toward an economic and political system that is more compatible with the community of nations that constitutes the Western Hemisphere. What has the United

States gained from its delapated Cuba policy? Fidel Castro has outlived ten U.S. presidents since he came to power in 1959, the Cuban Revolution has not disappeared, the Cuban people continue to suffer from U.S. economic warfare against the island, and American businesses lose billions every year because of the current misguided policy. In a recent poll, 70 percent of the American people favor ending the embargo. Americans should have the freedom to travel to Cuba without being harassed and fined by their own government. According to the International Trade Commission, the United States has suffered a financial loss of $35 billion due to the U.S. trade embargo against Cuba reaching back to the Eisenhower administration.

15. The United States needs to develop a better way of defining, and responding to, perceived threats to national security. It cannot be denied that the United States acts with considerable coherence when Washington policymakers decide to respond to a threat from a foreign enemy in Latin America. However, threat perceptions are often distorted or exaggerated for domestic political reasons. This often leads to military intervention and unnecessary tensions in the relationship. A greater respect for national sovereignty south of the border would serve as a better guide to threat assessment than what the long history of U.S.–Latin American relations demonstrates.

There is a consensus throughout the Americas that a rethinking of U.S. policy is desperately needed and long overdue. However, if the past history of U.S.–Latin American relations is an indicator of a future pattern, it is hard to be sanguine about a more enlightened policy toward the region anytime soon.

Appendix: President Ronald Reagan's Speech on Congressional Aid for the Contras

President Ronald Reagan gave more than twenty speeches on the importance of Contra aid during his presidency. Although he was considered a master of political symbolism and persuasive delivery, Reagan's threat-laden speeches had little effect on Congress or public opinion. In this March 16, 1986, speech, Reagan used virtually every rhetorical tool at his disposal to convince the American people, and Congress, of the security threat to the Americas emanating from Nicaragua. In the entire history of the presidency, no speech assessing the magnitude of a security threat from Latin America can match President Reagan's for its tone, hyperbole, and deceitfulness.

> My fellow Americans, I must speak to you tonight about a mounting danger in Central America that threatens the security of the United States. This danger will not go away; it will grow worse, much worse, if we fail to take action now.
>
> I am speaking of Nicaragua, a Soviet ally on the American mainland only two hours' flying time from our own borders. With over a billion dollars in Soviet-bloc aid, the Communist Government of Nicaragua has launched a campaign to subvert and topple its democratic neighbors.
>
> Using Nicaragua as a base, the Soviets and Cubans can become the dominant power in the crucial corridor between North and South America. Established there, they will be in a position to threaten the Panama Canal, interdict our vital Caribbean sea lanes and, ultimately, move against Mexico. Should that happen, desperate Latin peoples by the mil-

lions would begin fleeing north into the cities of the southern United States, or to wherever some hope of freedom remained.

The United States Congress has before it a proposal to help stop this threat. The legislation is an aid package of $100 million for more than 20,000 freedom fighters struggling to bring democracy to their country and eliminate this Communist menace at its source. . . . We are asking only to be permitted to switch a small part of our present defense budget—to the defense of our own southern frontier.

Gathered in Nicaragua already are thousands of Cuban military advisers, contingents of Soviet and East Germans and all the elements of international terror—from the PLO to Italy's Red Brigades. Why are they there? Because, as Colonel Qaddafi has publicly exalted: "Nicaragua means a great thing, it means fighting America near its borders. Fighting America at its doorstep."

For our own security the United States must deny the Soviet Union a beachhead in North America. But let me make one thing plain, I am not talking about American troops. They are not needed; they have not been requested. The democratic resistance fighting in Nicaragua is only asking America for the supplies and support to save their own country from Communism.

The question the Congress of the United States will now answer is a simple one: "Will we give the Nicaraguan's democratic resistance the means to recapture their betrayed revolution, or will we turn our backs and ignore the malignancy in Managua until it spreads and becomes a mortal threat to the entire New World.

Will we permit the Soviet Union to put a second Cuba, a second Libya, right on the doorsteps of the United States?

How can such a small country pose such a great threat? It is not Nicaragua alone that threatens us, but those using Nicaragua as a privileged sanctuary for their struggle against the United States."

Their first target is Nicaragua's neighbors. With an army and militia of 120,000 men, backed by more than 3,000 Cuban military advisers, Nicaragua's armed forces are the largest Central America has ever seen. The Nicaraguan military machine is more powerful than all its neighbors combined.

This map [indicating] represents much of the Western Hemisphere. Now let me show you the countries in Central America where weapons supplied by Nicaraguan Communists have been found: Honduras, Costa Rica, El Salvador, Guatemala. Radicals from Panama—to the south—have been trained in Nicaragua. But the Sandinista revolutionary reach extends well beyond their immediate neighbors, in South America and the Caribbean, the Nicaraguan Communists have provided support in the form of military training, safe haven, communications, false documents, safe transit and sometimes weapons to radicals from the following countries: Colombia, Ecuador, Brazil, Chile, Argentina, Uruguay and the Dominican Republic. Even that is not all, for there was an old Communist slogan that the Sandinistas have made clear they will honor: the road to victory goes through Mexico. . . .

So, we are clear on the intentions of the Sandinistas and those who back them. Let us be equally clear about the nature of their regime. To begin with, the Sandinistas have revoked the civil liberties of the Nicaraguan people, depriving them of any legal right to speak, to publish, to assemble or to worship freely. Independent newspapers have been shut down. There is no longer any independent labor movement in Nicaragua nor any right to strike. . . .

I could go on about this nightmare—the blacklist, the secret prisons, the Sandinista-directed mob violence. But, as if all this brutality at home were not enough, the Sandinistas are transforming their nation into a safe house, a command post for international terror.

The Sandinistas not only sponsor terror in El Salvador, Costa Rica, Guatemala and Honduras—terror that led last summer to the murder of four U.S. marines in a café in Salvador—they provide a sanctuary for terror. Italy has charged Nicaragua with harboring their worst terrorists, the Red Brigades.

The Sandinistas have been involved themselves in the international drug trade. I know every American parent concerned about the drug problem will be outraged to learn that top Nicaraguan Government officials are deeply involved in drug trafficking. This picture [indicating], secretly taken at a military airfield outside Managua, show[s] Federico Vaughn, a top aide to one of the nine commandantes [*sic*] who rule Nicaragua, loading an aircraft with illegal narcotics, bound for the United States.

No, there seems to be no crime to which the Sandinistas will not stoop—this is an outlaw regime.

If we return for a moment to our map [indicating], it becomes clear why having this regime in Central America imperils our vital security interests.

Through this crucial part of the Western Hemisphere passes almost half our foreign trade, more than half our imports of crude oil and a significant portion of the military supplies we would have to send to the NATO alliance in the event of a crisis. These are the choke points where the sea lanes could be closed. . . .

Today, Warsaw Pact engineers are building a deep-water port on Nicaragua's Caribbean coast, similar to the naval base in Cuba for Soviet-built submarines. They are also constructing, outside Managua, the largest military airfield in Central America—similar to those in Cuba, from which Russian Bear Bombers patrol the U.S. East Coast from Maine to Florida.

How did this menace to the peace and security of our Latin neighbors—and ultimately ourselves—suddenly emerge? Let me give you a brief history.

In 1979, the people of Nicaragua rose up and overthrew a corrupt dictatorship. At first the revolutionary leaders promised free elections and respect for human rights. But among them was an organization called the Sandinistas. Theirs was a Communist organization, and their support of the revolutionary goals was sheer deceit. Quickly and ruthlessly, they took complete control.

Two months after the revolution, the Sandinista leadership met in secret, and, in what came to be known as the "72-hour document," described themselves as the "vanguard of a revolution that would sweep Central America, Latin America, and finally the world." Their true enemy, they declared: the United States.

Rather than make this document public, they followed the advice of Fidel Castro, who told them to put on a facade of democracy. While Castro viewed the democratic elements in Nicaragua with contempt, he urged his Nicaraguan friends to keep some of them in their coalition—in minor posts—as window dressing to deceive the West. That way, Castro said, you can have your revolution, and the Americans will pay for it. . . .

But there was another factor the Communists never counted on, a factor that now promises to give freedom a second chance—the freedom fighters of Nicaragua.

You see, when the Sandinistas betrayed the revolution, many who had fought the old Somoza dictatorship literally took to the hills, and like the French Resistance that fought the Nazis, began fighting the Soviet bloc Communists and the Nicaraguan collaborators. These few have now been joined by thousands.

With their blood and courage, the freedom fighters of Nicaragua have pinned down the Sandinista Army and bought the people of Central America precious time. . . .

Since its inception in 1982, the democratic resistance has grown democratically in strength. Today it numbers more than 20,000 volunteers and more come every day. But now the freedom fighters' supplies are running short, and they are virtually defenseless against the helicopter gunships Moscow has sent to Managua.

Now comes the crucial test for the Congress of the United States. Will they provide the assistance the freedom fighters need to deal with Russian tanks and gunships—or will they abandon the democratic resistance to its Communist enemy?

Clearly, the Soviet Union and the Warsaw Pact have grasped the great stakes involved, the strategic importance of Nicaragua. The Soviets have made their decision—to support the Communists. Fidel Castro has made his decision—to support the Communists. Arafat, Qaddafi, and the Ayatollah have made their decision[s]—to support the Communists. Now, we must make our decision. With Congress' help, we can prevent an outcome deeply injurious to the national security of the United States.

If we fail, there will be no evading responsibility, history will hold us accountable.

This is not some partisan issue; it is a national security issue, an issue on which we must act not as Republicans, not as Democrats, but as Americans. . . . My fellow Americans, you know where I stand. The Soviets and the Sandinistas must not be permitted to crush freedom in Central America and threaten our own security on our own doorstep. . . .

So tonight I ask you to do what you have done so often in the past. Get in touch with your representatives and senators and urge them to vote yes; tell them to help the freedom fighters—help us prevent a Communist takeover of Central America. I have only three years left to serve my country, three years to carry out the responsibilities you have entrusted to me, three years to work for peace. Could there be any greater tragedy than for us to sit back and permit this cancer to spread, leaving my successor to face far more agonizing decisions in the years ahead? . . .

We still have time to do what must be done so history will say of us, We had the vision, the courage and good sense to come together and act—Republicans and Democrats—when the price was not high and the risks were not great. We left America safe, we left America secure, we left America free, still a beacon of hope to mankind, still a light onto the nations.

Thank you and God bless you.

List of Online Resources

Amnesty International: http://www.amnesty.org/

CANF: www.canfnet.org

Center for International Policy: http://www.ciponline.org

Center for Strategic and International Studies: http://www.csis.org/

Central Intelligence Agency (CIA) World Factbook: http://www.cia.gov/cia/publications/factbook/index.html

Council of the Americas: http://www.americas-society.org/

Council on Hemispheric Affairs: http://www.coha.org

Cuba Policy Foundation: www.cubafoundation.org

Department of State: The United States and Cuba: www.state.gov/www/regions/wha/cuba/

Handbook of Latin American Studies, HLAS Online: http://lcweb2.loc.gov/hlas/

Havana Home Page: www.usembassy.state.gov/posts/cu1/wwwhmain.html

Human Rights Watch: http://www.igc.org/

Institute for Policy Studies: http://www.ips-dc.org

Inter-American Development Bank: http://www.iadb/

Inter-American Dialogue: http://www.iadialog.org/

International Monetary Fund: http://www.imf.org/

Latin American Data Base (LADB): http://www.ladb.unm.edu/

Latin American Network Information Center (LANIC): http://www.lanic.utexas.edu/

Latin American Newsletters (commercial): http://latinnews.com/

Latin American Working Group (LAWG): http://lawg.org/

National Security Archive: http://www.gwu.edu

New York Times, Americas Directory: http://www.nytimes.com/library/world/americas/

Organization of American States (OAS): http://www.oas.org

Political Database of the Americas: http://www.georgetown.edu.pdba/

Public Broadcasting System Online News Service: www.pbs.org/newshow/bb/latin_america/Cuba

United Nations–Economic Commission for Latin America and the Caribbean (ECLAC): http://www.eclac.org/

United States–Cuba Relations: www.rose-hulman.edu/m/dellacova/U.S.-Cuba.html

United States–Cuba Trade and Economic Council: www.cubatrade.org/

U.S. Agency for International Development (USAID): http://www.info.usaid.gov/countries/

U.S. Interventions in Latin America: http://www.smplanet.com/imperialism/teddy.html/

U.S.–Latin American Relations: http://www.fas.harvard.edu

Washington Office on Latin America: http://www.wola.org/

Washington Post, Americas Regional Coverage: http://www.washingtonpost.com/dyn/world/americas/

World Bank: http://www.worldbank.org/

Select Bibliography

Aguilar, Alonso. *Pan-Americanism from Monroe to the Present: A View from the Other Side*. New York: Monthly Review Press, 1968.

Atkins, G. Pope. *Handbook of Research on the International Relations of Latin America and the Caribbean*. Boulder, CO: Westview Press, 2001.

———. *Latin America and the Caribbean in the International System*. 4th ed. Boulder, CO: Westview Press, 1999.

———. *The United States and Latin America: Redefining U.S. Purposes in the Post–Cold War Era*. Austin: Lyndon B. Johnson School of Public Affairs, University of Texas, 1992.

Beisner, Robert L. *Twelve Against Empire: The Anti-Imperialists, 1898–1900*. 1968. Reprint, with a new preface, Chicago: University of Chicago Press, 1985.

Belnap, Jeffrey, and Raúl Fernández, eds. *José Martí's "Our America": From National to Hemispheric Cultural Studies*. Durham, NC: Duke University Press, 1998.

Bemis, Samuel Flagg. *The Latin American Policy of the United States: An Historical Interpretation*. 1943. Reprint, New York: W.W. Norton, 1967, 1971.

Berger, Mark T. *Under Northern Eyes: Latin American Studies and U.S. Hegemony in the Americas, 1898–1990*. Bloomington: Indiana University Press, 1995.

Biles, Robert, ed. *Inter-American Relations: The Latin American Perspective*. Boulder, CO: Lynne Rienner, 1988.

Bingham, Hiram. *The Monroe Doctrine: An Obsolete Shibboleth*. New Haven: Yale University Press, 1913.

Black, George. *The Good Neighbor: How the United States Wrote the History of Central America and the Caribbean*. New York: Pantheon Books, 1988.

Blasier, Cole. *The Hovering Giant: U.S. Response to Revolutionary Change in Latin America*. 1976. Rev. ed., Pittsburgh: University of Pittsburgh Press, 1985.

Bouvier, Virginia Marie, ed. *Whose America? The War of 1898 and the Battles to Define the Nation*. Westport, CT: Praeger, 2001.

Brands, H. W., Jr. *Cold Warriors: Eisenhower's Generation and American Foreign Policy.* New York: Columbia University Press, 1988.

Bulmer-Thomas, Victor. *The Economic History of Latin American Since Independence.* New York: Cambridge University Press, 1994.

Bulmer-Thomas, Victor, and James Dunkerley, eds. *The United States and Latin America: The New Agenda.* London: Institute of Latin American Studies, University of London, and David Rockefeller Center for Latin American Studies, Harvard University, 1999.

Calhoun, Frederick S. *Uses of Force and Wilsonian Foreign Policy.* Kent, OH: Kent State University Press, 1993.

Callcott, Wilfrid Hardy. *The Western Hemisphere: Its Influence on the United States to the End of World War II.* Austin: University of Texas Press, 1968.

———. *The Caribbean Policy of the United States, 1890–1920.* Baltimore, MD: Johns Hopkins University Press, 1942.

Carothers, Thomas. *In the Name of Democracy: U.S. Policy Toward Latin America in the Reagan Years.* Berkeley: University of California Press, 1991.

Castañeda, Jorge G. "The Forgotten Relationship." *Foreign Affairs* (May/June 2003).

Clark, Paul Coe, Jr. *The United States and Somoza, 1933–1956: A Revisionist Look.* Westport, CT: Praeger, 1992.

Coatsworth, John H. *Central America and the United States: The Clients and the Colossus.* New York: Twayne, 1994.

Coerver, Don M., and Linda B. Hall. *Tangled Destinies: Latin America and the United States.* Albuquerque: University of New Mexico Press, 1999.

Collin, Richard H. *Theodore Roosevelt's Caribbean: The Panama Canal, the Monroe Doctrine, and the Latin American Context.* Baton Rouge: Louisiana State University Press, 1990.

Connell-Smith, Gordon. *The United States and Latin America: An Historical Analysis of Inter-American Relations.* New York: Wiley, 1974.

Cotler, Julio, and Richard Fagen, eds. *Latin America and the United States.* Stanford, CA: Stanford University Press, 1974.

DeConde, Alexander. *Herbert Hoover's Latin-American Policy.* Stanford, CA: Stanford University Press, 1951.

Dent, David W. *The Legacy of the Monroe Doctrine: A Reference Guide to U.S. Involvement in Latin America and the Caribbean.* Westport, CT: Greenwood Press, 1999.

Dent, David W., ed. *U.S.–Latin American Policymaking: A Reference Handbook.* Westport, CT: Greenwood Press, 1995.

Domínguez, Jorge I., ed. *The Future of Inter-American Relations.* New York: Routledge, 2000.

———. *International Security and Democracy: Latin America and the Caribbean in the Post–Cold War Era.* Pittsburgh: University of Pittsburgh Press, 1998.

Dosal, Paul J. *Doing Business with the Dictators: A Political History of United Fruit in Guatemala, 1899–1994.* Wilmington, DE: Scholarly Resources, 1993.

Dozer, Donald. *Are We Good Neighbors? Three Decades of Inter-American Relations, 1930–1960.* Gainesville: University of Florida Press, 1959.

Eisenhower, Milton S. *The Wine Is Bitter: The United States and Latin America.* Garden City, NY: Doubleday, 1963.

Farer, Tom. *The United States and the Inter-American Security System.* St. Paul, MN: West, 1974.

Field, James A. "American Imperialism: The Worst Chapter in Almost Any Book." *American Historical Review* 83 (June 1978).

Friedman, Max Paul. *Nazis and Good Neighbors: The United States Campaign Against the Germans of Latin America in World War II*. New York: Cambridge University Press, 2003.

Gellman, Irwin F. *Good Neighbor Diplomacy: United States Policies in Latin America, 1933–1945*. Baltimore, MD: Johns Hopkins University Press, 1979.

Gil, Federico G. *Latin American–United States Relations*. New York: Harcourt Brace Jovanovich, 1971.

Gilderhus, Mark T. *The Second Century: U.S.–Latin American Relations Since 1889*. Wilmington, DE: Scholarly Resources, 2000.

———. *Pan American Visions: Woodrow Wilson in the Western Hemisphere, 1913–1921*. Tucson: University of Arizona Press, 1986.

Gleijeses, Piero. *Shattered Hope: The Guatemalan Revolution and the United States, 1944–1954*. Princeton, NJ: Princeton University Press, 1991.

Green, David. *The Containment of Latin America: A History of the Myths and Realities of the Good Neighbor Policy*. Chicago: Quadrangle Books, 1971.

Grieb, Kenneth. *The Latin American Policy of Warren G. Harding*. Fort Worth: Texas Christian University Press, 1976.

Gutman, Roy. *Banana Diplomacy: The Making of American Policy in Nicaragua, 1981–1987*. New York: Simon and Schuster, 1988.

Harrison, Lawrence. *The Pan American Dream: Do Latin America's Cultural Values Discourage True Partnership with the United States and Canada?* New York: Basic Books, 1997.

Hartlyn, Jonathan, Lars Schoultz, and Augusto Varas, eds. *The United States and Latin America in the 1990s: Beyond the Cold War*. Chapel Hill: University of North Carolina Press, 1992.

Healy, David. *U.S. Expansionism: The Imperialist Urge in the 1890s*. Madison: University of Wisconsin Press, 1970.

Holden, Robert H., and Eric Zolov, eds. *Latin America and the United States: A Documentary History*. New York: Oxford University Press, 2000.

Huggins, Martha K. *Political Policing: The United States and Latin America*. Durham, NC: Duke University Press, 1998.

Immerman, Richard. *The CIA in Guatemala: The Foreign Policy of Intervention*. Austin: University of Texas Press, 1982.

Johnson, John J. *A Hemisphere Apart: The Foundations of United States Policy toward Latin America*. Baltimore, MD: Johns Hopkins University Press, 1990.

———. *Latin America in Caricature*. Austin: University of Texas Press, 1980.

Kenworthy, Eldon. *America/Américas: Myth in the Making of U.S. Policy Toward Latin America*. University Park: Pennsylvania State University Press, 1995.

Krenn, Michael L. *The Chains of Interdependence: U.S. Policy toward Central America, 1945–1954*. New York: M.E. Sharpe, 1996.

Kryzanek, Michael J. *U.S.–Latin American Relations*. 3rd ed. Westport, CT: Praeger, 1996.

LaFeber, Walter. *Inevitable Revolutions: The United States in Central America*. New York: W.W. Norton, 1983.

Langley, Lester. *America and the Americas: The United States in the Western Hemisphere*. Athens: University of Georgia Press, 1989.

LeoGrande, William M. *Our Own Back Yard: The United States in Central America, 1977–1992*. Chapel Hill: University of North Carolina Press, 1998.

Leonard, Thomas M. *Central America and the United States: The Search for Stability*. Athens: University of Georgia Press, 1991.

Leonard, Thomas M., ed. *United States–Latin American Relations, 1850–1903: Establishing a Relationship*. Tuscaloosa: University of Alabama Press, 1999.

Lieuwen, Edwin. *U.S. Policy in Latin America*. New York: Praeger, 1965.

Lowenthal, Abraham F. *Partners in Conflict: The United States and Latin America*. 1987. Rev. ed., Baltimore, MD: Johns Hopkins University Press, 1990.

———. "United States Policy Toward Latin America: 'Liberal,' 'Radical,' and 'Bureaucratic' Perspectives." *Latin American Research Review* 8 (fall 1973).

Lowenthal, Abraham F., ed. *Exporting Democracy: The United States and Latin America*. Vol. 1, *Themes and Issues*; Vol. 2, *Case Studies*. Baltimore, MD: Johns Hopkins University Press, 1991.

Martz, John, and Lars Schoultz, eds. *Latin America, the United States and the Inter-American System*. Boulder, CO: Westview Press, 1981.

McPherson, Alan L. *Yankee No! Anti-Americanism in U.S.–Latin American Relations*. Cambridge, MA: Harvard University Press, 2003.

Mecham, J. Lloyd. *A Survey of United States–Latin American Relations*. Boston: Allen and Unwin, 1965.

———. *The United States and Inter-American Security, 1889–1960*. Austin: University of Texas Press, 1961.

Merk, Frederick. *Manifest Destiny and Mission in American History: A Reinterpretation*. New York: Alfred A. Knopf, 1963.

Mitchell, Nancy. *The Danger of Dreams: German and American Imperialism in Latin America*. Chapel Hill: University of North Carolina Press, 1999.

Molineu, Harold. *U.S. Policy Toward Latin America: From Regionalism to Globalism*. Boulder, CO: Westview Press, 1986.

Montgomery, Tommie Sue, ed. *Peacemaking and Democratization in the Western Hemisphere*. Boulder, CO: Lynne Rienner, 2000.

Munro, Dana G. *Intervention and Dollar Diplomacy in the Caribbean, 1900–1921*. Princeton, NJ: Princeton University Press, 1964.

National Commission on Terrorist Attacks upon the United States. *The 9/11 Commission Report*. New York: W.W. Norton, 2004.

Niess, Frank. *A Hemisphere to Itself: A History of U.S.–Latin American Relations*. Translated by Harry Drost. London: Zed Books, 1990.

O'Brien, Thomas. *The Century of U.S. Capitalism in Latin America*. Albuquerque: University of New Mexico Press, 1999.

Pastor, Robert A. *Exiting the Whirlpool: U.S. Foreign Policy toward Latin America and the Caribbean*. 2nd ed. Boulder, CO: Westview Press, 2001.

———. *Condemned to Repetition: The United States and Nicaragua*. Rev. ed. Princeton, NJ: Princeton University Press, 1988.

Paterson, Thomas G. *Contesting Castro: The United States and the Triumph of the Cuban Revolution*. New York: Oxford University Press, 1994.

Perkins, Dexter. *The United States and Latin America*. Baton Rouge: Louisiana State University Press, 1961.

Pike, Frederick. *The United States and Latin America: Myths and Stereotypes of Civilization and Nature*. Austin: University of Texas Press, 1992.

Poitras, Guy. *The Ordeal of Hegemony: The United States and Latin America*. Boulder, CO: Westview, 1990.

Rabe, Stephen G. *The Most Dangerous Area in the World: John F. Kennedy Confronts Communist Revolution in Latin America*. Chapel Hill: University of North Carolina Press, 1999.

Raymont, Henry. *Troubled Neighbors: The Story of U.S.–Latin American Relations from FDR to the Present*. Boulder, CO: Westview Press, 2005.

Ronning, C. Neale, and Albert P. Vannucci, eds. *Ambassadors in Foreign Policy: The Influence of Individuals on U.S.–Latin American Policy.* New York: Praeger, 1987.

Roorda, Eric Paul. *The Dictator Next Door: The Good Neighbor Policy and the Trujillo Regime in the Dominican Republic, 1930–1945*. Durham, NC: Duke University Press, 1998.

Schmitz, David F. *Thank God They're on Our Side: The United States and Right-Wing Dictatorships, 1921–1965*. Chapel Hill: University of North Carolina Press, 1999.

Schoultz, Lars. *Beneath the United States: A History of U.S. Policy Toward Latin America*. Cambridge, MA: Harvard University Press, 1998.

———. *National Security and United States Policy toward Latin America*. Princeton, NJ: Princeton University Press, 1987.

———. *Human Rights and United States Policy Toward Latin America*. Princeton, NJ: Princeton University Press, 1981.

Schulz, Donald E. *The United States and Latin America: Shaping An Elusive Future*. Carlisle Barracks, PA: U.S. Army War College, 2000.

Seidel, Robert. *Progressive Pan Americanism: Development and United States Policy toward South America*. Ithaca, NY: Cornell University Press, 1973.

Shavit, David. *The United States in Latin America: A Historical Dictionary*. Westport, CT: Greenwood Press, 1992.

Sheinin, David, ed. *Beyond the Ideal: Pan Americanism in Inter-American Affairs*. Westport, CT: Greenwood Press, 2000.

Slater, Jerome. *The OAS and United States Foreign Policy*. Columbus: Ohio State University Press, 1967.

Smith, Gaddis. *The Last Years of the Monroe Doctrine: 1945–1993*. New York: Hill and Wang, 1994.

Smith, Peter H. *Talons of the Eagle: Dynamics of U.S.–Latin American Relations*. 2nd ed. New York: Oxford University Press, 2000.

Smith, Tony. *America's Mission: The United States and the Worldwide Struggle for Democracy in the Twentieth Century*. Princeton, NJ: Princeton University Press, 1994.

Stark, Jeffrey, ed. *The Challenge of Change in Latin America and the Caribbean*. Coral Gables, FL: University of Miami Press, 2001.

Thompson, John A. "Exaggeration of American Vulnerability: The Anatomy of a Tradition." *Diplomatic History* 16 (winter 1992).

Trask, Roger R. "The Impact of the Cold War on United States–Latin American Relations, 1945–1949." *Diplomatic History* 1 (summer 1977).

Tulchin, Joseph S., and Ralph H. Espach, eds. *Latin America in the New International System*. Boulder, CO: Lynne Rienner, 2001.

Whitaker, Arthur. *The Western Hemisphere Idea: Its Rise and Decline*. Ithaca, NY: Cornell University Press, 1954.

Wiarda, Howard J. *Finding Our Way: Maturity in U.S.–Latin American Relations*. Washington, DC: University Press of America, 1987.

Williams, Edward J. *The Political Themes of Inter-American Relations*. Belmont, CA: Duxbury Press, 1971.

Williams, Virginia S. *Radical Journalists, Generalist Intellectuals, and U.S.–Latin American Relations*. Lewiston, NY: Edwin Mellen Press, 2001.

Wilson, Larman C., and David W. Dent. *Historical Dictionary of Inter-American Organizations*. Lanham, MD: Scarecrow Press, 1998.

Wood, Bryce. *The United States and Latin American Wars, 1932–1942*. New York: Columbia University Press, 1966.

———. *The Making of the Good Neighbor Policy*. New York: Columbia University Press, 1961.

Woodward, Bob. *VEIL: The Secret Wars of the CIA, 1981–1987*. New York: Simon and Schuster, 1987.

Index

Note: **Boldface** page references denote main entries.

About the Author

DAVID W. DENT is professor emeritus of political science at Towson University in Baltimore, MD. He the author of *Encyclopedia of Modern Mexico* (2002), *The Legacy of the Monroe Doctrine: A Reference Guide to U.S. Involvement in Latin America and the Caribbean* (Greenwood, 1999), the co-author of *Historical Dictionary of Inter-American Organizations* (1998), and the editor of *U.S.–Latin American Policymaking: A Reference Handbook* (1995) and *Handbook of Political Science Research on Latin America: Trends from the 1960s to the 1990s* (1990). Dent is the author of over 100 articles, essays, and chapters on Latin American and U.S.–Latin American relations. For the past thirty years he has been a contributing editor for the *Handbook of Latin American Studies*, a biannual reference book published by the Hispanic Division of the Library of Congress in Washington, D.C.